Evidence-Based Addiction Treatment

Evidence-Based Addiction Treatment

Edited by

Peter M. Miller

AMSTERDAM • BOSTON • HEIDELBERG • LONDON • NEW YORK • OXFORD
PARIS • SAN DIEGO • SAN FRANCISCO • SINGAPORE • SYDNEY • TOKYO
Academic Press is an imprint of Elsevier

ELSEVIER

Academic Press is an imprint of Elsevier
30 Corporate Drive, Suite 400, Burlington, MA 01803, USA
525 B Street, Suite 1900, San Diego, CA 92101-4495, USA
32 Jamestown Road, London, NW1 7BY, UK
360 Park Avenue South, New York, NY 10010-1710, USA

First edition 2009

Library of Congress Cataloging-in-Publication Data
Miller, Peter M. (Peter Michael), 1942-
Evidence-based addiction treatment/Peter M. Miller.
p. cm.
ISBN 978-0-12-374348-0
1. Substance abuse—Treatment. 2. Drug abuse—Treatment. I. Title.
RC564.M5396 2009
616.86′06—dc22

2008053914

British Library Cataloguing in Publication Data
A catalogue record for this book is available from the British Library

ISBN: 978-0-12-374348-0

For information on all Academic Press publications
visit our website at www.elsevierdirect.com

Typeset by Macmillan Publishing Solutions
www.macmillansolutions.com

Printed and bound in the United States of America

09 10 11 12 13 9 8 7 6 5 4 3 2 1

Contents

Preface

The addictions treatment field is undergoing a period of increased scrutiny, upheaval, and change (McLellan, Carise, & Kleber, 2003). The growing emphasis on treatment accountability and cost-effectiveness is leading to major changes in standards of care. Inconsistent practices based on clinical experience and intuition rather than hard scientific evidence of treatment efficacy are rapidly becoming unacceptable. Consumers, administrators, and legislators are increasingly unwilling to support treatments for which there is little or no empirical support.

Evidence-based treatments are interventions that show consistent scientific evidence for positive therapeutic outcomes. It seems self-evident that, as is true in medical practice, interventions that have demonstrated their effectiveness through rigorous scientific investigation would be the treatments of choice by practitioners. Unfortunately, in the field of substance abuse treatment, this has not been the case. Substance abuse clinicians are only recently beginning to be exposed to efforts aimed at the translation of addictions science into practice (Miller & Kavanagh, 2007).

Translating science-based treatments into clinical settings is an important priority in the addictions field and has been the subject of an influential Institute of Medicine report (Lamb, Greenlick, & McCarty, 1998). The report estimated that, historically, it has taken approximately 17 years for science-based therapeutic interventions to be implemented in substance abuse treatment programs. This disquieting fact prompted substantial responses from several federal agencies. Such programs as the Center for Substance Abuse Treatment's Addiction Technology Transfer Centers and its Practice Research Collaboratives, the National Institute on Alcohol Abuse and Alcoholism's Research-to-Practice Forums and its Researcher-in-Residence Program, and the National Institute on Drug Abuse's (NIDA) Clinical Trials Network were established to address this problem.

To further expedite this process, treatment programs in the United States are being mandated to provide evidence-based therapies, with funding and insurance reimbursement being contingent on their doing so. In addition, in 2001, NIDA, in collaboration with the Addiction Technology Transfer Center of the Substance Abuse and Mental Health Services Administration (Center for Substance Abuse Treatment), launched the Blending Initiative, designed to improve the development, effectiveness, and utility of evidence-based practices (Condon, Miner, Balmer, & Pintello, 2008). It is hoped that these noteworthy efforts will speed up the process of adoption and implementation.

In the meantime, the push is on for future and current clinicians to learn science-based treatments and begin the process of putting them into routine clinical practice. To that end, this textbook provides a state-of-the-art compilation of evidence-based assessment and treatment practices in the treatment of addictions. While research on treatment effectiveness is still ongoing, a substantial body of evidence is available to provide students, academics, and clinicians with specific science-based practices that work.

APPROACH

This book is written at a level appropriate for graduate students, upper-level undergraduate students, and students enrolled in courses preparing them for licensure or certification in alcohol and drug counseling. In addition, the book also provides practicing counselors with a much-needed, up-to-date resource on evidence-based assessment and treatment methods. While research studies are discussed in the chapters, a highly sophisticated knowledge of research methodology is not required.

The chapters provide a timely resource for evidence-based practice just when such methods are being required and monitored in addiction treatment centers. While the theoretical basis of treatment methods will be addressed, this coverage will be relatively brief, with emphasis on descriptions of methods (along with case examples) and evidence of efficacy and effectiveness (with emphasis on controlled clinical trials and meta-analyses).

Chapters are authored by well-recognized authorities in the field of substance abuse treatment. Authors demonstrate the rare quality of being top behavioral scientists that conduct and publish treatment research as well as being dedicated, experienced, and caring clinicians.

TEXT ORGANIZATION

The book's 23 chapters are divided into six major sections. In Section 1, two chapters provide an introduction to an evidence-based approach to treatment and an overview of nonspecific factors influencing the therapeutic process with addicted individuals. Section 2 includes chapters focusing on clinical assessment of alcohol and substance use patterns (both currently and historically), diagnosis and dependence, psychiatric comorbidities frequently associated with addiction, and cognitive, behavioral, and lifestyle problems that are closely related to chemical dependency. In addition, these assessment methods are equally useful in objectively monitoring treatment progress and outcome.

Section 3 consists of chapters describing current major evidence-based treatments for addictive behaviors, including cognitive–behavioral therapy, motivational interviewing, brief intervention, relapse prevention, behavioral couples' therapy, contingency management and the community reinforcement approach, self-change, and adjunctive pharmacotherapy. In Section 4, chapters address special populations and special applications of evidence-based approaches, including ethnic and minority populations, clients with psychiatric comorbidities, adolescents, college students, and Internet-based treatments. The chapters in Section 5 discuss evidence-based treatment in action both with the individual client and on a clinical organizational level. Finally, Section 6 consists of a chapter on challenges posed by evidence-based treatments and their implementation in clinical practice.

A FINAL WORD

This volume is designed to provide both the student and the practicing clinician with a basic knowledge and understanding of current major evidence-based assessment and treatment methods. While the goal is to educate students and health professionals in the latest practice methodologies, the eventual aim is to improve the quality of care for addicted individuals and improve their lives.

REFERENCES

Condon, T. P., Miner, L. L., Balmer, C. W., & Pintello, D. (2008). Blending addiction research and practice: Strategies for technology transfer. *Journal of Substance Abuse Treatment*, *35*, 156–160.

Lamb, S., Greenlick, M., & McCarty, D. (Eds.). (1998). *Bridging the gap: Forging new partnerships in community-based drug abuse treatment*. Washington, DC: National Academy Press.

McLellan, A. T., Carise, D., & Kleber, H. D. (2003). Can the national addiction treatment infrastructure support the public's demand for quality care? *Journal of Substance Abuse Treatment*, *25*, 117–121.

Miller, P. M., & Kavanagh, D. J. (Eds.). (2007). *Translation of addictions science into practice*. Amsterdam, The Netherlands: Elsevier.

Contributors

Danielle Barry
Department of Psychiatry, University of Connecticut Health Center, Farmington, CT, USA

Sarah W. Bowen
Department of Psychology, University of Washington, Addictive Behaviors Research Center, Seattle, WA, USA

Arthur W. Blume
Department of Psychology, University of North Carolina at Charlotte, Charlotte, NC, USA

Jennifer M. Connolly
Institute of Health & Biomedical Innovation and School of Psychology & Counselling, Queensland University of Technology, Brisbane, Qld, Australia

Ned L. Cooney
VA Connecticut Healthcare System, Yale University School of Medicine, Newington, CT, USA

John A. Cunningham
Centre for Addiction and Mental Health, Toronto, Ont, Canada

Patrick M. Flynn
Institute of Behavioral Research, Texas Christian University, Fort Worth, TX, USA

Lisa H. Glynn
University of New Mexico, Albuquerque, NM, USA

Josephine M. Hawke
Department of Psychiatry, University of Connecticut Health Center, Farmington, CT, USA

Nick Heather
Division of Psychology Northumbria University, New Castle upon Tyne, UK

Morten Hesse
Centre for Alcohol and Drug Research, Copenhagen Division, Aarhus University, Copenhagen C, Denmark

Jennifer E. Hettema
Department of Psychiatry, San Francisco General Hospital, San Francisco, CA, USA

Stephen T. Higgins
Department of Psychiatry, Human Behavioral Pharmacology Laboratory, University of Vermont, Burlington, VT, USA

Laura J. Holt
VA Connecticut Healthcare System, Yale University School of Medicine, Newington, CT, USA

Yifrah Kaminer
Department of Psychiatry, University of Connecticut Health Center, Farmington, CT, USA

Anthony V. Kantin
Department of Psychology, University of North Carolina at Charlotte, Charlotte, NC, USA

Eileen Kaner
Institute of Health and Society, The Medical School, Newcastle University, United Kingdom

David J. Kavanagh
Institute of Health & Biomedical Innovation, Queensland University of Technology, Brisbane, Qld, Australia

Adrian B. Kelly
School of Social Science, The University of Queensland, St Lucia, Qld, Australia

Harald Klingemann
Unit of Substance Use Disorders, University of Zürich, University Clinic, Vufflens-le-Château, Switzerland

Justyna Klingemann
Department of Alcohol and Drug Dependence, Institute of Psychiatry and Neurology, Warsaw, Poland

Linda S. Kranitz
VA Connecticut Healthcare System, Yale University School of Medicine, Newington, CT, USA

Marketa Krenek
Department of Psychology, Syracuse University, Center for Health and Behavior, Syracuse, NY, USA

Mary E. Larimer
Department of Psychiatry and Behavioral Sciences, University of Washington, Center for the Study of Health and Risk Behaviors, Seattle, WA, USA

Sandra Larios
Department of Psychiatry, San Francisco General Hospital, San Francisco, CA, USA

Lorenzo Leggio
Center for Alcohol and Addiction Studies, Brown University Medical School, Providence, RI, USA

Stephen A. Maisto
Department of Psychology, Syracuse University, Center for Health and Behavior, Syracuse, NY, USA

G. Alan Marlatt
Department of Psychology, University of Washington, Addictive Behaviors Research Center, Seattle, WA, USA

Peter M. Miller
Center for Drug and Alcohol Programs, Medical University of South Carolina, Charleston, SC, USA

Theresa B. Moyers
Department of Psychology, University of New Mexico, CASAA, Albuquerque, NM, USA

Clayton Neighbors
Department of Psychiatry and Behavioral Sciences, University of Washington, Center for the Study of Health and Risk Behaviors, Seattle, WA, USA

Dorothy Newbury-Birch
Institute of Health and Society, New Castle University, Newcastle upon Tyne, UK

Nora E. Noel
Social & Behavioral Sciences Building, University of North Carolina Wilmington, Department of Psychology, Wilmington, NC, USA

Eric R. Pedersen
Department of Psychiatry and Behavioral Sciences, University of Washington, Center for the Study of Health and Risk Behaviors, Seattle, WA, USA

Nancy M. Petry
Department of Psychiatry, University of Connecticut Health Center, Farmington, CT, USA

Michelle R. Resor
Department of Psychology, University of North Carolina at Charlotte, Charlotte, NC, USA

Randall E. Rogers
Department of Psychiatry, Human Behavioral Pharmacology Laboratory, University of Vermont, Burlington, VT, USA

D. Dwayne Simpson
Institute of Behavioral Research, Texas Christian University, Fort Worth, TX, USA

James L. Sorensen
Department of Psychiatry, San Francisco General Hospital, San Francisco, CA, USA

Scott H. Stewart
Medical University of South Carolina, Center for Drug and Alcohol Programs, Charleston, SC, USA

Robert Swift
Center for Alcohol and Addiction Studies, Brown University Medical School, Providence, RI, USA

T. Cameron Wild
School of Public Health, University of Alberta, Edmonton, AB, Canada

Katie Witkiewitz
Alcohol and Drug Abuse Institute, University of Washington, Seattle, WA, USA

Jody Wolfe
School of Public Health, University of Alberta, Edmonton, AB, Canada

PART | ONE

Introduction to Evidence-Based Practices

Chapter | one

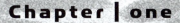

What Is Evidence-Based Treatment?

James L. Sorensen, Jennifer E. Hettema, and Sandra Larios
University of California, San Francisco

I am a firm believer in the people. If given the truth, they can be dependent upon to meet any national crisis. The great point is to bring them the real facts.

Abraham Lincoln

SUMMARY POINTS

- "Evidence based" has been defined in many ways; however, most definitions include components that emphasize the importance of the scientific method and the cumulative evidence base derived from research. This chapter defines *evidence-based treatment* as a treatment that has been scientifically tested and subjected to clinical judgment and determined to be appropriate for the treatment of a given individual, population, or problem area.
- Methodological issues may arise when evaluating evidence. Several factors important to consider when evaluating methodological quality include group allocation (were subjects randomly assigned to conditions), inclusion of collaterals, objective verification, treatment completion rates, generalizability, and the fidelity of the intervention.
- Examples of evidence-based treatment interventions have been divided into different types and include randomized clinical trials, effectiveness trials, reviews, and National Registration of Effective Programs and Practices.

Evidence-Based Addiction Treatment

- Specific interventions include cognitive behavioral therapy, motivational interviewing, brief interventions, relapse prevention, behavioral marital therapy, community reinforcement and contingency management, and adjunctive pharmacotherapy.

Imagine that you are approached by a close friend or family member who has developed an addiction to alcohol or another substance and wants to pursue treatment. This person asks you to visit a few treatment programs to help evaluate which offers the best treatment. What sort of questions would you want to ask the treatment program? What kind of answers would you find compelling? Would you be likely to choose a treatment option because the person explaining it to you had a salient and emotional story about how that treatment had helped a specific individual, perhaps even him or her, or would you want to know other things, such as how many people had been through the treatment program and what percentage have shown improvement? Perhaps you might even question how similar these people are to your loved one or how information on improvement rates was gathered and measured. This latter approach represents an evidence-based approach to treatment, and many of the questions that you may ask in this area are the same questions that scientists, policy makers, and treatment providers are beginning to ask regarding substance abuse interventions.

The substance abuse field is experiencing a transition from reliance on personal evidence and subjective testimony to a more objective, evidence-based approach. While testimony before public commissions about substance abuse treatment and policy has tended to use storytelling about the success or failure of a specific individual more than scientific evidence (Sorensen, Masson, Clark, & Morin, 1998), recent years have witnessed a growing emphasis on substance abuse treatments that have a strong scientific base. For example, the state of Oregon has implemented a policy requiring that 75% of state funds for substance abuse treatment go to support evidence-based practices by the 2009–2011 budget period (Oregon Department of Human Services, 2008). Across the country, there is increasing pressure for programs to justify their outcomes against competing approaches so that they can collect insurance reimbursement. Increasingly, treatment programs need hard scientific evidence to maintain their existence.

The emphasis on research is somewhat new to the field of substance abuse treatment. For a large part of the 20th century, treatment of addiction was conducted separately from mainstream medical or scientific establishments. Because of this, treatment grew from a movement of dedicated nonprofessionals, whose personal experience led to their involvement in the field (Lamb, Greenlick, & McCarty, 1998). These compassionate peers built a system of care that was relatively independent of the medical and scientific communities. For these treatment staff, personal experiences were regarded as much more valuable evidence than the findings of science. Although substance abuse treatment is becoming increasingly integrated into scientific and medical communities, there is still an emphasis on personal experience and distrust of scientific evidence among many treatment providers. Yet there is increasing scrutiny of substance abuse treatment programs, which need data to justify their place in financially strapped health care systems. Fortunately, a set of treatments is emerging that is "evidence based."

This chapter focuses on evidence-based interventions in the treatment of addiction. Several definitions of the term "evidence based" will be provided, and the readers will learn about the different types of evidence that are available when making treatment decisions. The chapter also focuses on the skills necessary to critically evaluate and weigh information regarding the effectiveness of a given intervention. Several key studies that have dramatically informed the field of substance abuse are highlighted. Finally, a list of widely accepted evidence-based practices is introduced, and the future of evidence-based practice is explored.

WHAT DOES "EVIDENCE BASED" MEAN?

While on the surface we may all agree about the importance of using evidence-based practice, defining the term "evidence based" is not a simple task. In fact, many different definitions have been put forward. Some definitions focus solely on the status of the intervention within the available scientific literature base. For example, Drake et al. define evidence-based practices as "interventions for which there is consistent scientific evidence showing that they improve client outcomes" (Drake et al., 2001, p. 180). Other definitions emphasize the important role the individual clinician plays in searching for, evaluating, and applying knowledge derived from the scientific evidence base. For example, the Center for Evidence Based Medicine points out that the literature base itself requires interpretation, which highlights the importance of clinical expertise when interpreting the findings of research (Sackett, Rosenberg, Gray, Haynes, & Richardson, 1996). Finally, other definitions focus on the importance of patient values in determining what constitutes evidence-based practice. For example, the Institute of Medicine (2001, p. 147) calls attention to the importance of scientific evidence, clinical judgment, and "the unique preferences, concerns, and values that each patient brings to a clinical encounter." Even more clinical judgment is necessary to apply the literature base to a specific treatment-seeking individual with a unique background and characteristics. For the purposes of this chapter, all of these important factors are taken into consideration, and **evidence-based treatment** is defined as *a treatment that has been scientifically tested and subjected to clinical judgment and determined to be appropriate for the treatment of a given individual, population, or problem area*.

Future sections of the chapter emphasize the importance of the scientific method and cumulative evidence base, but also highlight that the interpretation of evidence is rarely a straightforward task and typically requires subjective decision-making. This chapter describes several methods for identifying and evaluating the evidence base, describes several landmark studies that have informed the field, and identifies treatments that are widely considered to be evidence based.

EVALUATING THE EVIDENCE

A clinician interested in providing evidence-based treatment may turn to the literature in search of research articles that focus on the disorder, population, or intervention of interest. Some types of evidence, however, are more prone to bias than others, and several systems have been developed to help researchers and clinicians organize their thinking about types of research. Several important terms used when evaluating evidence-based treatments can be found in Table 1.1.

Evaluating evidence through clinical trials

In behavioral research, randomized controlled trials, or efficacy trials, have historically been the gold standards against which to evaluate interventions. As the name suggests, randomized controlled trials randomly allocate participants to treatment condition and control for extraneous factors that could confound interpretations of causality. However, recent critics have begun to question whether the findings achieved under such tightly controlled studies will translate into routine clinical practice. Instead, many researchers are suggesting effectiveness trials, which test interventions in real-world settings, with the patients and therapists likely to be using the intervention. This design choice consequently limits intervention studies to those that can be realistically administered given staff preferences, time, and resources (Hunsley & Lee, 2007).

In pharmacological research, clinical trials also vary in their applicability to real-world settings. The National Institute of Health identifies four types of research, each with their own methodological advantages and drawbacks (http://clinicalresearch.nih.gov/how.html). This type of research is typically conducted in phases and usually occurs only after

Table 1.1 Key terms for evaluating evidence

Term	Explanation
Internal validity	Internal validity is the degree to which research results are likely to be correct and free of bias. Bias can result from publication bias (file drawer problem), not having proper randomization, placebo effects, and many other factors.
External validity	External validity refers to the ability to generalize the results of one study to other settings and/or populations beyond those included in the study. This is also called generalizability, relevance, or transferability.
Efficacy	Efficacy is concerned with the question: Can a treatment work under ideal circumstances? Studies that focus on efficacy do everything possible to maximize the chances of showing an effect in an even-handed experimental design. Efficacy research is more concerned with internal validity.
Effectiveness	Effectiveness relates to whether a treatment works in practice. Effectiveness issues center on external validity.
Fidelity	Fidelity refers to the degree to which an intervention was administered as intended.

a particular intervention shows preclinical promise in laboratory or animal studies. Within this system, phase I research involves testing a novel drug with a small sample of the population. Due to the small number of participants, this type of research is not necessarily generalizable to the overall population, but can gather important preliminary information about the safety and/or side effects of an intervention. Phase II trials test the intervention with a larger sample of people and further monitor safety. In phase III, the drug is tested with an even larger population and is compared to another treatment or placebo control condition to determine its comparative efficacy. These first three phases of research are often conducted in research settings that maintain tight control over the type of participants allowed into the study and the way in which the treatment is administered. These methods help ensure that inferences about the causal effects of the treatment are accurate (internal validity), but decrease the applicability of the study findings to the general population (external validity). In phase IV research, a drug that is already being routinely administered is evaluated for effectiveness and safety in real-world settings and the long-term effects of the drug are determined. Here, less control over the administration of the intervention and those receiving it are possible, increasing the chance that confounding variables will bias research. However, the findings of such research may have more significance as they evaluate interventions as they are likely to be administered in the real world.

Evaluating evidence through scientific reviews

Early on in substance abuse treatment, groups of studies were reviewed and synthesized by interested researchers who read the available studies on a particular topic and made inferences regarding overall effectiveness using a narrative style. While such reviews could be helpful in seeing the big picture for a particular treatment, they often lacked scientific rigor and were highly prone to the biases and preconceptions of the people conducting them. Soon, methodologically driven reviews were conducted that provided more objective summaries of the literature base. One such strategy uses a "box tally" methodology in which the numbers of positive and negative findings for a particular intervention are tallied, producing a cumulative evidence score for an intervention of interest. This method can be further enhanced by differentially weighting studies based on important factors, such as their methodological quality or relevance to a population of interest.

Meta-analysis is another approach to synthesizing multiple studies, in which the different outcome variables of a group of studies are statistically combined to produce standard measures of effect. These effect sizes can allow researchers to make comparisons of different treatments, can be weighted by methodological quality, and are less influenced by the bias that can result from having an insufficient number of participants in significance testing. Meta-analysis can help summarize a research base by streamlining information and providing a common metric (i.e., effect size), that can be used as a standard to compare different interventions.

Meta-analysis, however, is also prone to some difficulties. For one, outcome studies in substance abuse research use a variety of outcome variables, including abstinence, quantity of use, frequency of use, and problems associated with use. Statistically combining these discrepant measures can be misleading. In addition, there is a bias in science, known as the "file drawer problem," to publish only positive findings (leaving negative studies in the file drawer), resulting in misrepresentative pictures of the total evidence base. Nonetheless, meta-analyses are important tools that can be used for evaluating treatment effectiveness. Using meta-analysis and other methodologies, an international network of researchers known as the Cochrane Collaboration (www.cochrane.org) conducts reviews of substance use behavioral and pharmacological treatments and disseminates their findings on their Web site.

Evaluating evidence—Special considerations

Although a great deal of research has been conducted on substance abuse intervention, clear-cut evaluation of the quality and relevance of such research is not easy. There are many factors to consider when deciding how much weight to give a particular piece of evidence.

First, some providers assert that the scientific method may not be the best way to evaluate interventions. This idea has been somewhat popular in psychodynamic or Freudian psychology, with some interventionists claiming that, despite the fact that psychodynamic theory makes causal claims, it should not be evaluated using experimental testing. The argument is that subjective experience should be the basis for evaluating interventions. In substance abuse, this sentiment is also popular among treatment providers outside of the psychodynamic movement. In fact, many substance abuse counselors report learning about interventions and evaluating their effectiveness based on personal experiences rather than from educational programs (Miller, Sorensen, Selzer, & Brigham, 2006).

If one does accept that substance abuse interventions should be evaluated using scientific standards, interpretation of the evidence is still not a simple task and requires an evaluation of several important constructs. For one, the methodological quality of studies varies highly and consumers of research typically place more weight on studies conducted with high methodological quality. Consider two studies that have been conducted on treatment A. One study found favorable results and the other study found unfavorable results for the treatment. This is not an unusual situation and, when making decisions about whether to use the intervention, many people look to the methodological quality of the respective studies. Imagine that the first study only measured outcome at treatment completion, was only able to locate half of participants for follow-up assessment, and had follow-up assessors who knew which participants were in the intervention versus controlled conditions. All of these issues could bias the findings of the first study, and this poor methodological quality may lead clinicians and researchers to give less weight to the findings. The second study, however, may have assessed patients for a year following treatment completion, demonstrated a high follow-up rate, and kept assessors blind to treatment conditions. In this case, one places much more importance on the findings of the second study. In addition to follow-up length, follow-up rates, and the blinding of assessors, other factors important to consider when evaluating methodological quality include group allocation (were subjects randomly assigned to conditions), inclusion of collaterals (were significant others interviewed to confirm participants' self-report), objective verification (were biological specimen, records, or other objective means used to confirm participants' self-report), and treatment completion rates (how many participants actually received the intervention of interest and how were those who did not statistically analyzed).

Another factor important to consider when evaluating evidence is the fidelity of the tested intervention. Fidelity refers to the degree to which an intervention was administered as intended. Borrelli et al. (2005) identified multiple fidelity factors that are important to consider when evaluating substance abuse research, including dose and content of treatment, characteristics and training of the interventionists, and procedures for monitoring adherence to the treatment model.

In addition, it is important to consider the generalizability of the research findings. Inclusion/exclusion criteria, severity of substance use, and demographic factors of the samples vary widely across studies, and some study samples may be more applicable to a given problem or question of interest than others. Some groups, including women, ethnic minorities, and those with comorbid disorders, have been historically underresearched in substance abuse research, often making generalizability of research findings to these populations difficult. Part IV of this book (Special Populations and Applications) describes treatment approaches for these populations in greater detail.

Finally, research should be evaluated in terms of its practicality or suitability for real-world adoptions. Some research methods designed to increase the internal validity of studies may interfere with the applicability of research findings to real-world settings. While aspects of methodological quality are important, they can also limit the generalizability of findings. When reflecting on the firewalls put in place to prevent bias and increase the ability to make causal attributions in a particular study, clinicians should also consider whether the intervention could be replicated in community-based treatment programs.

Evaluating evidence—The dodo bird effect

One common finding of many comparative clinical trials, reviews, and meta-analyses conducted in substance abuse research is that the evaluated treatments perform equally well. Some have drawn an analogy between treatment outcome research and the dodo bird's race in *Alice in Wonderland*, in which he enthusiastically declares that "everyone's won and all must have prizes" (Wampold, Mondin, Moody, Stich, Benson, & Ahn, 1997). Although some treatments, such as confrontational counseling, have been found to be ineffective in addiction treatment, most theoretically based or manualized behavioral treatments perform equally well when tested in the field. This is especially surprising considering that most treatments have very different assumptions about the change and recovery process.

EXAMPLES OF KEY STUDIES AND FINDINGS

Randomized clinical trials

Now we will turn our attention to several key studies in the substance abuse treatment research field. First, several large, multisite, randomized clinical trials (RCTs) have revealed an abundance of treatment efficacy in the addictions field. These studies are typically of a high methodological quality and, consequently, demonstrate excellent internal validity. However, addiction specialists have suggested that this methodological rigor, combined with extensive inclusion/exclusion criteria, limits generalizability to real-world clinical settings. Several multisite clinical trials have been particularly informative to the field of substance use and dependence, including Project MATCH (Matching Alcoholism Treatments to Client Heterogeneity), the COMBINE study (Combining Medications and Behavioral Interventions), and the Cannabis Youth Treatment study. These interventions are described in more detail.

PROJECT MATCH

Project MATCH was a multisite, collaborative project supported by the National Institute on Alcohol Abuse and Alcoholism. The study was designed to test matching hypotheses, which predicted that clients with certain characteristics would fare better in one treatment versus another. Clients were assigned randomly to one of three treatments (cognitive behavioral treatment [CBT], motivational enhancement therapy [MET], or 12-step facilitation [TSF]) and their outcomes were compared based on 10 client variables, including psychiatric severity and level of motivation (Project MATCH Research Group, 1993). At a 12-month follow-up, participants from all three treatments had more days abstinent and drank fewer drinks per episode when compared with baseline assessments. However, few of the matching hypotheses were supported. Findings indicated that CBT, MET, and TSF were equally effective in improving alcohol outcomes and that specific patient characteristics do not differentially influence the effectiveness of these interventions.

COMBINE

The COMBINE study expanded on the findings of Project MATCH to determine whether combining medications for alcohol dependence (naltrexone, acamprosate) could improve the effectiveness of behavioral interventions. In COMBINE, a combined behavioral intervention was created that incorporated aspects of all three treatments from Project MATCH. In addition, COMBINE tested a medication management (MM) intervention, a less involved treatment focusing on providing support and medication compliance. To explore which medication and behavioral treatment combination led to better outcomes, participants in the study were randomly assigned to one of nine treatment combinations. Results from the COMBINE study showed that adding a brief intervention (MM) to naltrexone can be a cost-effective way of treating alcohol dependence and that a combination of medication and behavioral treatment was more effective than medications alone (Anton et al., 2006). The implication of these results is that, via the use of a variation of MM (i.e., more focused and fewer sessions) combined with naltrexone, it may be possible to treat alcohol dependence in primary care settings.

CANNABIS YOUTH TREATMENT STUDY

The Cannabis Youth Treatment study was designed to compare the effectiveness and cost-effectiveness of five treatment modalities in real-world settings (Dennis et al., 2002). Adolescents (ages 12–18) enrolled in the study were randomly assigned to one of five group therapies (Motivational Enhancement Therapy/Cognitive Behavioral Treatment [MET/CBT] 5 sessions, MET/CBT 12 sessions, the Adolescent Community Reinforcement Approach [ACRA], Multi-dimensional Family Therapy, and Family Support Network). Results showed that participants in all five treatments showed significant improvements but the most cost-effective approaches included MET/CBT5, MET/CBT12, and ACRA (Dennis et al., 2004).

Effectiveness trials

While multisite RCTs can be conducted with high internal validity, they are often low in external validity. Tight restrictions in participant inclusion criteria and administration of interventions by highly trained therapists (following standardized treatment protocols) improve our ability to make causal attributions, but decrease the generalizability of findings to community treatment centers in which clients often have multiple and more severe problems and are dissimilar to RCT participants. Recognizing this limitation, the National Institute on Drug Abuse established the Clinical Trials Network (CTN). The CTN provides a setting in which treatment providers and researchers exchange information and develop research protocols together. Research protocols are then tested in front-line clinics, making results more generalizable to community-based treatment centers. Since its inception, CTN has funded nearly 30 large clinical trials to determine the most effective treatments for drug dependence through a variety of methods (behavioral treatments, medications, telephone support) and in different languages (e.g., Spanish). The dissemination of effective treatments is a principal goal, and the CTN dissemination library serves as a forum from which dissemination can occur. The library contains journal articles, presentations, reports, brochures, bibliographies, and descriptions of studies being conducted within the network. Researchers and clinicians can access this information at http://ctndisseminationlibrary.org/. To facilitate dissemination, the CTN developed the Blending Initiative, which is designed to blend resources, information, and expertise in order to encourage the use of current evidence-based treatment interventions in the drug abuse treatment field.

Reviews

MESA GRANDE

The Mesa Grande project (Miller & Wilbourne, 2002) is an influential review of 361 clinical trials of treatments for alcohol use disorders. Results showed that brief interventions, social skills training, community reinforcement approach, behavior contracting, behavioral marital therapy, and case management were all equally effective in treating alcohol use. Medications were also among the supported approaches, including opiate antagonists (naltrexone, nalmefene) and acamprosate. Ineffective interventions included confrontational counseling and mandated Alcoholics Anonymous.

MARIJUANA DEPENDENCE

In a review of marijuana-focused clinical trials, McRae, Budney, and Brady (2003) found that cognitive behavioral therapy/relapse prevention, motivational enhancement, and contingency management therapies were efficacious in the treatment of marijuana dependence and associated problems. The influence of treatment dose was also explored, and although few differences were found between brief interventions and more intensive CBT interventions, the most recent and largest controlled trial (the Marijuana Treatment Project) found an extended CBT intervention to be more effective than brief motivational therapy (Litt, Kadden, Stephens, & Marijuana Treatment Project Research Group, 2005). This review illustrated that the development of an evidence base for the treatment of marijuana dependence is still in its infancy. It should be noted that therapies for alcohol abuse/dependence and other drugs also proved to be efficacious for the treatment of marijuana dependence, but more research in treatment effectiveness (in real-world settings) is needed.

NATIONAL REGISTRY OF EVIDENCE-BASED PROGRAMS AND PRACTICES (NREPP)

Based on the evidence available in the treatment of substance abuse, the Substance Abuse and Mental Health Services Administration has created the National Registration of Effective Programs and Practices. NREPP contains a searchable database of interventions for the prevention and treatment of mental and substance abuse disorders. The NREPP system reviews interventions systematically and categorizes approaches as promising, effective, or model programs according to the quality of research evidence about their effectiveness, as well as their readiness for dissemination, based on what materials and training are available. The NREPP system lists over a dozen categories of interventions, including alcohol and drug prevention and treatment.

EXAMPLES OF EVIDENCE-BASED TREATMENTS

So far, this chapter has introduced the concept of evidence-based treatment and discussed important considerations in evaluating research. Now, specific treatment methods are described briefly. Table 1.2 summarizes each of these treatment approaches, all of which have received strong consistent support in the literature and are described in greater detail in upcoming chapters of the book.

Cognitive behavioral therapy

Cognitive behavioral approaches are based on the theory that learning processes play a formative role in the development and maintenance of addictive behaviors. These treatments are among the most widely studied. Considering the extensive research that has been conducted in establishing cognitive behavioral therapy as an empirically supported treatment and that few differences are found when comparing cognitive behavioral treatments (see the Mesa Grande study described earlier), researchers have suggested that effective elements across cognitive behavioral approaches be combined (Kadden, 2001). For more information on cognitive behavioral therapy as a treatment method, see Chapter 8.

Relapse prevention

Preventing a person from returning to substance use, or relapse prevention, has emerged as an important and effective treatment by taking into consideration the cognitive and behavioral components within the process of the relapse phenomenon. Paramount features of these interventions include the identification of high-risk situations and the provision of coping skills to manage them more effectively (Marlatt &

Table 1.2 Examples of empirically supported treatments

Treatment	Explanation
Cognitive behavioral therapy	Cognitive behavioral approaches are based on the theory that learning processes play a formative role in the development and maintenance of addictive behaviors.
Motivational interviewing	Motivational interviewing is a brief, client-centered, directive intervention that helps people explore and resolve ambivalence about change.
Brief intervention	Brief interventions with high levels of effectiveness tend to have certain characteristics, remembered by the acronym FRAMES: objective **F**eedback on personal risk, an emphasis on the **R**esponsibility of the patient for changing his or her own behavior, **A**dvice, providing a **M**enu of options, **E**xpressing empathy through reflective listening techniques, and supporting **S**elf-efficacy.
Relapse prevention	Interventions based on this model describe the identification of high-risk situations to reduce the risk of relapse and help people identify the types of coping skills that one can employ in these situations.
Behavioral marital therapy	Behavioral marital therapy can be used to rebuild trust, improve communication, reduce intimate partner violence, and help the substance-using partner sustain abstinence.
Community reinforcement and contingency management	Drug-free urine samples are used to monitor patient's abstinence and are reinforced by providing contingent vouchers that patients can exchange for retail goods.
Adjunctive pharmacotherapy	In treating alcohol abuse/dependence, disulfiram, naltrexone (an opiate receptor antagonist), and acamprosate have all been shown to be effective. For opioid dependence, methadone and buprenorphine have been deemed effective treatments.

Gordon, 1985). Effective use of new coping skills can help ward off relapse and increase self-efficacy, thereby making future relapse less likely. Relapse prevention has been shown to be effective in improving clinical outcomes for alcohol use, smoking, cocaine, and polysubstance use (Irvin, Bowers, Dunn, & Wang, 1999). Recent developments in the relapse prevention approach, including one that integrates meditation as a cognitive coping skill (Mindfulness-Based Relapse Prevention), are discussed in greater detail in Chapter 11.

Motivational interviewing

Motivational interviewing (MI) is a brief, client-centered, directive intervention that enables clients to explore and resolve ambivalence about change (Rollnick & Miller, 1995). In MI, therapists are encouraged to take a nonjudgmental stance and guide patients through the process of exploring their substance use in the context of personal goals and values. This intervention has been widely studied and shows moderate levels of efficacy in the treatment of alcohol and drug disorders, as well as in engaging people in other forms of addiction treatment (Hettema, Steele, & Miller, 2005). MI techniques are discussed further in Chapter 9.

Brief interventions

In addition to MI, other brief interventions have shown promise in the treatment of substance use disorders. Despite the common adage that "more is better," the literature has shown that brief interventions can have dramatic and prolonged effects and that increasing the intensity of an intervention does not consistently result in improved effectiveness (Miller, 2000). Effective brief interventions share common characteristics (often referenced by the acronym, FRAMES), including objective **F**eedback on personal risk, an emphasis on the **R**esponsibility of the patient for changing his or her own behavior, **A**dvice, providing a **M**enu of options, **E**xpressing empathy through reflective listening techniques, and supporting **S**elf-efficacy (Miller & Sanchez, 1993). Brief interventions are promising because they are inexpensive to administer, allow more addicted individuals to receive treatment, and can be administered in medical settings, where providers have limited time and resources to commit to behavioral issues. Chapter 10 describes brief interventions in greater detail.

Behavioral marital therapy

The goal of behavioral marital therapy is to improve marital behaviors that may affect the substance use of one or both partners. Substance use can damage the trust and communication necessary for a fulfilling relationship. Behavioral marital therapy is used to rebuild trust, improve communication, reduce intimate partner violence, and help the substance-using partner sustain abstinence. This intervention has a long history of effectiveness (Hahlweg & Markman, 1988). Therapists typically work with couples both in tandem and individually in outpatient settings. Chapter 12 in this volume describes behavioral marital therapy in more detail.

Community reinforcement approach and contingency management

This intervention has been applied primarily with cocaine use and to reduce alcohol consumption in clients whose drinking is associated with drug use (Higgins et al., 1994). Therapists typically provide about

6 months of outpatient therapy in individual counseling sessions, refer alcohol-abusing patients for disulfiram (antabuse) therapy, monitor patients for continuing drug use through the collection of regular urine samples, and reinforce their abstinence by providing contingent vouchers that patients can exchange for retail goods that are consistent with a drug-free life style. In this volume, Chapter 13 describes the community reinforcement and contingency management in more detail.

Pharmacological treatments

Pharmacological treatments are also available for the treatment of substance use disorders. Disulfiram, or antabuse, has been used in the treatment of alcohol disorders for several decades. One drawback of disulfiram is that it is effective only if taken daily and consistently. Because of this, meta-analyses have shown small effects from its use (Garbutt, West, Carey, Lohr, & Crews, 1999). Newer medications, including naltrexone, an opiate receptor antagonist, have been found to reduce the pleasurable effects of alcohol and, consequently, reduce alcohol cravings (Work Group on Substance Use Disorder, 2006). Finally, acamprosate has been shown to help maintain abstinence after detoxification from alcohol by normalizing metabolic processes that occur when heavy drinking is discontinued (Tempesta et al., 2000).

Several medications have also been developed to treat opioid dependence. Methadone is an opioid agonist that blocks the pleasurable effects of opiates, such as heroin, in the brain. This drug, which typically requires visiting a clinic for daily dosing, has been found to be effective and safe, particularly at higher doses (Gardner & Kosten, 2007). Buprenorphine has also been used in the treatment of opiate addiction. This drug is a partial opioid agonist that suppresses withdrawal, produces effects similar to other opiates at low doses, and blocks the effects of other opiates. Buprenorphine has shown promise in clinical trials (Johnson, Jaffe, & Fudala, 1992) and has had Food and Drug Administration approval for the treatment of opiate addiction since 2002. Unlike methadone, buprenorphine does not have to be dispensed in a specialized clinic, as physicians can prescribe buprenorphine directly. Further information on pharmacological treatments can be found in Chapter 15.

CONCLUSIONS AND FUTURE DIRECTIONS

This chapter focused on defining "evidence-based" interventions in the treatment of addiction. Evidence based refers to treatments that have been scientifically tested and subjected to clinical judgment and determined to be appropriate for the treatment of a given individual, population, or problem area.

It is important to acknowledge that diverse types of evidence must be considered when evaluating substance abuse treatments; interpreting available data is not always a clear-cut process. Clinical trials, reviews, and meta-analyses are all useful sources but should be evaluated in terms of internal validity, external validity, and applicability to the patient populations and the clinical expertise of clinicians.

Several interventions that have a strong evidence base were introduced and described briefly in this chapter. In addition, resources were provided to help in the process of exploring and identifying evidence-based practices, such as the NREPP site (Substance Abuse and Mental Health Services Administration, 2008). Specific interventions are explained in more detail in later chapters of this volume. If readers are looking for immediate implications of this work, the resources provided in this chapter and in this volume should provide skills, information, and other resources helpful in identifying evidence-based treatments that work best for the population of interest. In addition, the evidence base for existing as well as newly developed treatments is developing rapidly.

Finally, when looking to the future of evidence-based practice, it is clear that the emphasis on objective, testable outcome trials will continue. It is hoped that the field will also increase its use of effectiveness trials conducted in real-world settings so that findings of research can be more generalizable to treatment populations. In addition, increased emphasis should be placed on the dissemination of research so that research findings can reach practitioners who must ultimately adopt them. There are certainly obstacles to adopting an evidence-based mentality, but choosing treatment modalities based exclusively on personal testimony and subjective criteria is no longer a viable option. Echoing the sentiment in the quotation that began this chapter, the point is to bring facts to people and then let them decide.

REFERENCES

Anton, R. F., O'Malley, S. S., Ciraulo, D. A., Cisler, R. A., Couper, D., Donovan, D. M., et al., COMBINE Study Research Group. (2006). Combined pharmacotherapies and behavioral interventions for alcohol dependence: The COMBINE study: A randomized controlled trial. *Journal of the American Medical Association*, *295*(17), 2003–2017.

Borrelli, B., Sepinwall, D., Ernst, D., Bellg, A. J., Czajkowski, S., Breger, R., et al. (2005). A new tool to assess treatment fidelity and evaluation of treatment fidelity across 10 years of health behavior research. *Journal of Consulting and Clinical Psychology*, *73*(5), 852–860.

Dennis, M., Godley, S. H., Diamond, G., Tims, F. M., Babor, T., Donaldson, J., et al. (2004). The cannabis youth treatment (CYT) study: Main findings from two randomized trials. *Journal of Substance Abuse Treatment*, *27*(3), 197–213.

Dennis, M., Titus, J. C., Diamond, G., Donaldson, J., Godley, S. H., Tims, F. M., et al., C. Y. T. Steering Committee. (2002). The cannabis youth treatment

(CYT) experiment: Rationale, study design and analysis plans. *Addiction, 97*(Suppl. 1), 16–34.

Drake, R. E., Goldman, H. H., Leef, S., Lehman, A. F., Dixon, L., Mueser, K. T., et al. (2001). Implementing evidenced-based practices in routine mental health service settings. *Psychiatric Service, 52*, 179–182.

Garbutt, J. C., West, S. L., Carey, T. S., Lohr, K. N., & Crews, F. T. (1999). Pharmacological treatment of alcohol dependence: A review of the evidence. *Journal of the American Medical Association, 281*(14), 1318–1325.

Gardner, T. J., & Kosten, T. R. (2007). Therapeutic options and challenges for substances of abuse. *Dialogues in Clinical Neuroscience, 9*(4), 431–445.

Hahlweg, K., & Markman, H. J. (1988). Effectiveness of behavioral marital therapy: Empirical status of behavioral techniques in preventing and alleviating marital distress. *Journal of Consulting and Clinical Psychology, 56*(3), 440–447.

Hettema, J. E., Steele, J. M., & Miller, W. R. (2005). Motivational interviewing. *Annual Review of Clinical Psychology, 1*, 91–111.

Higgins, S. T., Budney, A. J., Bickel, W. K., Foerg, F. E., Donham, R., & Badger, G. J. (1994). Incentives improve outcome in outpatient behavioral treatment of cocaine dependence. *Archives of General Psychiatry, 51*, 568–576.

Hunsley, J., & Lee, C. M. (2007). Research-informed benchmarks for psychological treatments: Efficacy studies, efficacy studies, and beyond. *Professional Psychology Research and Practice, 38*, 21–33.

Institute of Medicine. (2001). *Crossing the quality chasm: A new health system for the 21st century*. Washington, DC: National Academy Press.

Irvin, J. E., Bowers, C. A., Dunn, M. E., & Wang, M. C. (1999). Efficacy of relapse prevention: A meta-analytic review. *Journal of Consulting and Clinical Psychology, 67*(4), 563–570.

Johnson, R. E., Jaffe, J. H., & Fudala, P. J. (1992). A controlled trial of buprenorphine treatment for opioid dependence. *Journal of the American Medical Association, 267*(20), 2750–2755.

Kadden, R. M. (2001). Behavioral and cognitive-behavioral treatments for alcoholism research opportunities. *Addictive Behaviors, 26*, 498–507.

Lamb, S. J., Greenlick, M. R., & McCarty, D. (1998). *Bridging the gap between practice and research: Forging partnerships with community-based drug and alcohol treatment*. Washington, DC: National Academy Press.

Litt, M. D., Kadden, R. M., & Stephens, R. S., Marijuana Treatment Project Research Group. (2005). Coping and self-efficacy in marijuana treatment: Results from the Marijuana Treatment Project. *Journal of Consulting and Clinical Psychology, 76*, 1015–1025.

Marlatt, G. A., & Gordon, J. R. (Eds.). (1985). *Relapse prevention: Maintenance strategies in the treatment of addictive behaviors*. New York: Guilford.

McRae, A. L., Budney, A. J., & Brady, K. T. (2003). Treatment of marijuana dependence: A review of the literature. *Journal of Substance Abuse Treatment, 24*, 369–376.

Miller, W. R. (2000). Rediscovering fire: Small interventions, large effects. *Psychology of Addictive Behaviors: Journal of the Society of Psychologists in Addictive Behaviors, 14*(1), 6–18.

Miller, W. R., & Sanchez, V. C. (1993). Motivating young adults for treatment and lifestyle change 55–81. In G. Howard (Ed.), *Issues in alcohol use and misuse in young adults*. Notre Dame, IN: University of Notre Dame Press.

Miller, W. R., Sorensen, J. L., Selzer, J. A., & Brigham, G. S. (2006). Disseminating evidence-based practices in substance abuse treatment: A review with suggestions. *Journal of Substance Abuse Treatment, 31*(1), 25–39.

Miller, W. R., & Wilbourne, P. L. (2002). Mesa grande: A methodological analysis of clinical trials of treatments for alcohol use disorders. *Addiction*, *97*(3), 265–277.

Oregon Department of Human Services. (2008, February). *Implementation of evidence-based practices (EBP) in Oregon*. Retrieved March 2008, from http://www.oregon.gov/DHS/mentalhealth/ebp//main.shtml.

Project MATCH Research Group. (1993). Project MATCH: Rationale and methods for a multisite clinical trial matching alcoholism patients to treatment. *Alcoholism: Clinical and Experimental Research*, *17*, 1130–1145.

Rollnick, S., & Miller, W. R. (1995). What is motivational interviewing? *Behavioural and Cognitive Psychotherapy*, *23*, 325–334.

Sackett, D. L., Rosenberg, W. M., Gray, J. A., Haynes, R. B., & Richardson, W. S. (1996). Evidence based medicine: What it is and what it isn't. *British Medical Journal*, *312*, 71–72.

Sorensen, J. L., Masson, C. L., Clark, W. W., & Morin, S. F. (1998). Providing public testimony: A guide for psychologists. *Professional Psychology Research and Practice*, *29*, 588–593.

Substance Abuse and Mental Health Services Administration. (2008, March). *National Registration of Effective Programs and Practices (NREPP)*. Retrieved April 2008, from http://nrepp.samhsa.gov/.

Tempesta, E., Janiri, L., Bignamini, A., Chabac, S., & Potgieter, A. (2000). Acamprosate and relapse prevention in the treatment of alcohol dependence: A placebo-controlled study. *Alcohol and Alcoholism*, *35*(2), 202–209.

Wampold, B. E., Mondin, G. W., Moody, M., Stich, F., Benson, K., & Ahn, H. (1997). A metanalysis of outcome studies comparing bona fide psychotherapies: Empirically, "all must have prizes." *Psychological Bulletin*, *122*, 203–215.

Work Group on Substance Use Disorder. (2006). *Treatment of patients with substance use disorder* (2nd ed.). Arlington, VA.

Chapter | two

The Clinical Course of Addiction Treatment: The Role of Nonspecific Therapeutic Factors

T. Cameron Wild and Jody Wolfe
University of Alberta

SUMMARY POINTS

- A thorough understanding of nonspecific factors is critical to understanding the clinical course of treatment from an evidence-based perspective. Nonspecific factors are elements of the treatment process that are common to all treatment modalities and contexts.
- Motivational factors play a key role in access to treatment programs, in-treatment engagement, and outcomes.
- A variety of predisposing, need, personal enabling, and service system enabling variables, as well as internal and external barriers, have been investigated as possible determinants of treatment access.
- Social control tactics have been shown to increase access to treatment, but do not necessarily correlate with treatment motivation or engagement.
- Client perceptions, counselor attitudes, and behavior and program characteristics all work to influence treatment engagement, retention, and post-treatment outcomes.

Evidence-Based Addiction Treatment

INTRODUCTION

The clinical course of addiction treatment can be understood from the perspective of either *nonspecific* or *specific* factors as determinants of treatment processes and outcomes. Nonspecific factors refer to *common* aspects of *all* addiction treatment contexts, for example, patient motivation for treatment and quality of patient–counselor therapeutic alliance. In contrast, *specific* factors refer to discrete intervention activities underlying *different* treatment approaches, for example, whether cognitive behavioral or motivational enhancement intervention activities are provided. Two arguments underlie our view that an understanding of nonspecific factors is critical for characterizing the clinical course of addiction treatment. First, evidence suggests that outcomes of addiction treatment may be influenced more by nonspecific factors than the relative efficacy or effectiveness of specific intervention activities or approaches per se. Second, performance measurement and continuous quality improvement increasingly require documentation of nonspecific factors in the provision of addiction treatment rather than assessment of specific activities tied to distinct types of interventions.

Nonspecific effects in addiction treatment

In recent years, several large, methodologically strong controlled trials of psychological and pharmacological interventions for alcohol problems have been conducted. Project Matching Alcohol Treatments to Client Heterogeneity (Project MATCH) tested 16 a priori "matching hypotheses," that is, predictions that one or more pretreatment client attributes would interact with treatment assignment (cognitive behavioral [CBT], motivation enhancement [MET], or 12-step facilitation [TSF]) in the prediction of post-treatment response. Over 1700 clients in nine treatment sites across the United States were studied, and all three treatments were equally effective in reducing alcohol use. Only one of the matching hypotheses was supported (Project MATCH Research Group, 1997a,b; but compare Witkiewitz van der Maas, Hufford, & Marlatt, 2007). Similarly, the United Kingdom Alcohol Treatment Trial (UKATT) compared the relative efficacy of a social and network therapy intervention to motivational enhancement therapy in a sample of over 700 clients seeking help for alcohol problems in the United Kingdom. Like Project MATCH, the UKATT showed that both interventions were equally successful in reducing alcohol use during the study period (UKATT Research Team, 2005).

Another large trial, the Combining Medications and Behavioral Interventions (COMBINE) study for alcohol dependence, assigned about 1400 patients to nine different combinations of pharmacological and behavioral interventions. COMBINE investigated whether treatment outcomes for alcohol dependence could be improved by combining pharmacotherapy and behavioral interventions. Consistent with results from Project MATCH and the UKATT, all nine combinations of treatment interventions were associated with reductions in alcohol use, including patients who had received a placebo, with no particular combination demonstrating superior treatment response (Anton et al., 2005; COMBINE Study Research Group, 2003).

Together, these results suggest that many different types of treatments for alcohol problems and dependence have equivalent effects, despite theoretical differences among them with respect to *who* might benefit from using an intervention approach or the hypothesized *mechanisms* of change initiated by exposure to the intervention. This phenomenon has long been observed, meta-analyzed, and debated in studies of psychotherapy (Kazdin, 1979; Messer & Wampold, 2002; Wampold et al., 1997), but has not received equivalent attention in the addiction treatment area. Nonetheless, commentators have argued that these results all point to the role of general features of addiction treatment not tied to particular treatment approaches or interventions as important variables influencing the clinical course of addiction treatment (Bergmark, 2008; Orford, 2008). For example, Buhringer and Pfieffer-Gerschel (2008) suggest that patient change processes in treatment of alcohol disorders are influenced by nonspecific factors, including pretreatment variables (e.g., social pressure to seek treatment; commitment for behavior change), setting variables during treatment (e.g., site characteristics, therapist behavior), and social environment (e.g., social supports and risk factors for relapse). Others have proposed taxonomies of such nonspecific variables. Simpson (2004) characterized pretreatment patient and treatment program variables, within-treatment engagement and recovery variables, and post-treatment outcome variables. Most recently, Longabaugh (2007) proposed a typology of potential mediators of treatment effects emphasizing three types of nonspecific factors: therapist/client contact, client behaviors outside treatment, and environment. The utility of this emphasis on nonspecific elements of addiction treatment is supported by research demonstrating their impact *across* different types of treatment intervention programs and modalities (e.g., Broome, Simpson, & Joe, 1999; Joe, Broome, Rowan-Szal, & Simpson, 2002).

Performance measurement in treatment programs and services

There is a growing trend toward the use of quality or performance indicators to document the nature and content of addiction treatment (McClellan, Chalk, & Bartlett, 2007). This trend is, in part, related to a perceived need to enhance accountability in both public and privately funded addiction treatment programs and services. In response, addiction treatment researchers, providers, and policy makers alike have begun to articulate generic treatment models, applicable to all types of programs and services, regardless of intervention approach or treatment modality. This has been accompanied by sets of indicators describing nonspecific service features over the clinical course of addiction treatment (Garnick et al., 2002; McCarty, 2007; McCorry, Garnick, Bartlett, Cotter, & Chalk, 2000). For example, the Washington Circle group (Garnick et al., 2002) proposed three performance measures in providing alcohol and other drug treatment services in managed care environments, including *identification*, that is, percentage of enrollees in a health plan diagnosed with an alcohol or other drug use (AOD) disorder, *initiation*, that is, the percentage of patients in a health plan admitted for addiction treatment who return for additional services following identification, and *engagement*, that is, the percentage of patients who initiated AOD treatment who receive more than one visit within 30 days of initiation of care. Finally, as Stout (2007) notes, recent technological and statistical advances have provided more opportunities to broaden the scope and enhance the sophistication of research into intermediating treatment processes.

Chapter overview

The role of nonspecific factors is critical for understanding the clinical course of addiction treatment, but is often overlooked in discussions of evidence-based practice, which are typically oriented to documenting the relative efficacy and effectiveness for specific, labeled, treatment interventions or to bolstering the evidentiary basis of a particular theoretical approach to treatment. This chapter reviews select classic and contemporary evidence on the role of nonspecific factors in addiction treatment. To organize this material, we emphasize nonspecific factors that fall under the umbrella of treatment motivation, broadly defined. Despite problems associated with conceptualizing and measuring treatment motivation (Dreischner, Lammers, & van der Staak, 2004), motivational factors are increasingly implicated in two important treatment phenomena, common to all types of programs and services: (1) only a small proportion of people exhibiting addictive behaviors and disorders actually seek out specialized addiction treatment (Cunningham & Breslin, 2004) and (2) drop out from treatment programs is very common when people actually do attend (Stark, 1992). The following sections summarize key evidence related to motivational issues across two phases common to all addiction treatment programs and services: *treatment access* and *treatment engagement and outcomes*.

ACCESSING TREATMENT

Treatment access is a nonspecific construct linking research on pathways to treatment to barriers and facilitators to treatment entry. Evidence consistently indicates that there is a sizable discrepancy between the number of people who might benefit from addiction treatment and those who eventually participate in formal treatment programs, either as in- or outpatients (Cartwright & Solano, 2005; Cunningham & Breslin, 2004; Perkonigg et al., 2006; Popova, Rehm, & Fischer, 2006). Some people who never seek treatment may naturally resolve their dependence or problems with alcohol and other drugs (Cunningham, 1999, 2000; Sobell, Cunningham, & Sobell, 1996), whereas others may make use of self-help programs or informal resources to facilitate behavior change (Perkonigg et al., 2006) or prefer not to enter formal treatment at all, usually because of stigma or embarrassment (Cunningham, Sobell, Sobell, Agrawal, & Toneatto, 1993; Grant, 1997). Still others are underserved in that they have a need and desire for treatment but are unable to attain it for one reason or another (Digiusto & Treloar, 2007). Identification of alcohol and other drug problems in primary health care is one systemic block to access. For example, Garnick, Horgan, Merrick, and Hoyt (2007) documented the relatively poor rate of identification of alcohol and other drug problems in routine health care, arguing that efforts to reduce the harm associated with substance misuse should be directed in part at increasing the overall number of people who access substance abuse treatment and greater fairness in accessibility of treatment.

Andersen (1995) proposed that access to treatment is related to *predisposing variables* (e.g., age, sex, ethnicity, or criminal history), *need variables* (i.e., the nature and severity of the problem precipitating treatment), and *enabling variables* (i.e., service system and personal resources necessary to obtain treatment). Others (Allen & Dixon, 1994) have identified *external* (e.g., characteristics of the health system, program structure, or sociocultural–environmental conditions) and *internal* (e.g., beliefs or perceptions held by the individual) barriers to treatment. These two approaches provide a way to organize the diverse literature on access to treatment. The following sections review representative findings in this area, with a special emphasis on motivation-related variables.

Predisposing and need variables

People who initiate treatment for substance abuse are more likely to be male (Greenfield et al., 2007; Weisner, Mertens, Tam, & Moore, 2001), employed (Weisner et al., 2001), older (Jackson, Booth, McGuire, & Salmon, 2006; Weisner, Matzger, Tam, & Schmidt, 2002), and to have no disability (Krahn, Deck, Gabriel, & Farrell, 2007). Having children, particularly when there are child custody issues, has been shown to undermine motivation for treatment among women (Wilke, Kamata, & Cash, 2005), perhaps because of emotional and practical difficulties of being away from one's children or because of legal implications of admitting to substance abuse problems. It is important to note, however, that some studies have found conflicting results regarding demographic predictors of treatment entry (Xu, Wang, Rapp, & Carlson, 2007), and there are likely complex interactions among these predisposing factors that require further research to untangle.

With regard to need for treatment, treatment seekers are more likely than those who do not enter treatment to exhibit greater impairment and/or greater severity of dependence (Breda & Heflinger, 2007; Carpenter, Miele, & Hasin; Weisner et al., 2002), to be using illicit drugs rather than licit substances (Weisner et al., 2002), to have a previous history of treatment utilization (Cunningham, 2004; Freyer et al., 2007), and to have some form of legal involvement (Epstein, Hourani, & Heller, 2004). A higher perceived need for treatment and motivation to quit has also been found to predict treatment entry (Neff & Zule, 2002). Also, higher levels of drug use prior to treatment and more supplemental service needs predict treatment reentry among those who were previously exposed to substance abuse treatment (Grella, Hser, & Hsieh, 2003). Digiusto and Treloar (2007) compared two groups of individuals with a history of illicit opioid or psychostimulant use: (1) those who had never received treatment and (2) those who had received treatment previously or who were currently in treatment. Participants were assessed on three predisposing variables (age, sex, and education), seven need variables, and nine enabling variables. Although none of the predisposing variables was related to receipt of treatment, a more frequent use of drug of choice and more drug-related health problems (including hepatitis or HIV) were associated with an increased chance of receiving treatment. This suggests that need factors may be more important determinants of treatment entry than predisposing factors.

Internal barriers and personal enabling variables

A wide variety of internal barriers have been identified by researchers as predictors of treatment entry. In a study of drug-dependent pregnant women, Jessop, Humphreys, Brindis, and Lee (2003) found that privacy concerns (e.g., "I hate being asked personal questions") and fear of treatment (e.g., "I am afraid of what might happen in treatment") hindered treatment entry. In addition, problem recognition, treatment readiness, desire for help, and desire for change (De Weert-Van Oene, Schippers,

De Jong, & Schrijvers, 2002; Rapp et al., 2007; Simpson & Joe, 1993) have also been identified as barriers among pretreatment individuals. Rapp and colleagues (2006) examined relationships among internal barriers and found that problem recognition predicted a desire for change, which, in turn, predicted treatment readiness. Perceived absence of a problem was associated with less desire for change and lower treatment readiness. Interestingly, these authors were able to differentiate between wanting one's behavior to improve versus endorsing treatment as the means to that end (see also Freyer et al., 2005). Treatment reluctance and treatment readiness may be distinct constructs that contribute uniquely to the prediction of treatment barriers and enabling factors.

External barriers and service system enabling variables

Among the features of treatment service systems that influence treatment entry, wait time (i.e., time required to obtain an assessment or time elapsed between assessment and treatment entry) is one of the most common (Appel, Ellison, Jansky, & Oldak, 2004) and is closely tied to the availability of treatment spaces in treatment programs (Wenger & Rosenbaum, 1994). There is fairly consistent evidence that longer wait times decrease the likelihood of entering treatment (Chawdhary et al., 2007; Claus & Kindleberger, 2002; Jackson et al., 2006; Redko, Rapp, & Carlson, 2006). However, it is unclear whether waiting time is related inversely to treatment motivation (Best et al., 2002). Sex differences may moderate influences of wait times. Downey, Rosengren, and Donovan (2003) reported that women waited longer before leaving a wait list to enter treatment or to withdraw from the process than men and were less likely to enter treatment after referral.

Perceptions of treatment services and treatment staff, including beliefs that appropriate treatment is not available, not being able to obtain desired treatment in the past, negative expectations about treatment staff (Digiusto & Treloar 2007), and fear of punitive actions by staff (Jessop et al., 2003), can all be barriers to accessing treatment, even if people have no direct experience with addiction treatment. Beyond relations with treatment staff, broader social relationships may serve as either a barrier or an enabling factor for treatment seeking. While having friends or family who engage in drug use (Kersetz et al., 2006) or who are discouraging may decrease the likelihood of seeking treatment (Rapp et al., 2006), significant others can also play a role in encouraging processes that help develop users' willingness to seek help, such as dealing with inner conflict and building hope for the benefits of treatment (Jakobsson, Hensing, & Spak, 2005). When the relative perceptions of patients and other stakeholders are compared in samples of injection drug users, street outreach, treatment staff, and government agency representatives, individual client factors were cited by the majority of treatment clients, while accessibility was the most predominant barrier identified by outreach workers and government representatives (Appel & Oldak, 2007).

Social control and coercion in treatment access

Addiction treatment programs and services have traditionally adopted an acute care perspective on the assumption that alcohol- and drug-dependent clients are sufficiently impaired and concerned by their problems to seek help voluntarily. However, the case mix of addiction treatment programs has evolved because of changes in substance use patterns and engagement of new sectors in treatment. This has broadened the pathways bringing clients into treatment. Specifically, a *social control pathway*—where people are forced to enter addiction treatment programs—is becoming increasingly entrenched, despite a limited evidence base on its use (Wild, 2006). A variety of social control tactics are used to facilitate addiction treatment. *Legal* social controls include court-ordered treatment and diversion to treatment, either as adjuncts or alternatives to criminal sanctions for offenders who also abuse alcohol and other drugs (Belenko, 2001; Gostin, 1991; Leukefeld & Tims, 1988; Wells-Parker, 1995; Wild, 1999). *Formal* social controls refer to institutionalized strategies to facilitate treatment outside of the criminal justice system, including mandatory treatment referrals by employers, children's aid, and/or social assistance programs (Lawental, McLellan, Grissom, Brill, & O'Brien, 1996; Trice & Sonnenstuhl, 1991; Watkins & Podus, 2000). *Informal* social controls refer to controlling interpersonal tactics (e.g., threats and ultimatums) issued by friends and family members to convince people who abuse alcohol and other drugs to enter treatment (Hasin, 1994; Johnson, 1986; Logan, 1983; Room, Greenfield, & Weisner, 1991).

Social control tactics are used frequently in addiction treatment around the world (Deschenes, Peters, Goldkamp, & Belenko, 2003; Fischer, Roberts, & Kirst, 2002; Stevens et al., 2005). Some 25–75% of admissions to U.S. and Canadian addiction treatment programs are associated with legal, formal, and informal social control (Gerdner & Holmberg, 2000; Gregoire & Burke, 2004; Joe, Simpson, & Broome, 1999; Polcin & Weisner, 1999; Rush & Wild, 2003). A systematic review indicated that the use of social control tactics is associated with an increased likelihood of treatment entry (Wild, Roberts, & Cooper, 2002). However, when patients are asked directly, legal pressures are not as influential as other factors in prompting help-seeking, such as concerns about health and social functioning (Anglin, Brecht, &

Maddahian, 1989; Marlowe et al., 1996, 2001). From a motivational perspective, there appears to be no one-to-one correspondence between objective administration of social control tactics and client perceptions that they have been coerced to enter treatment (Wild, Newton-Taylor, & Alletto, 1998), perceived concerns about legal problems (Vickers-Lahti et al., 1995), or perceived fairness of the treatment decision (Sallmen, Berglund, & Bokander, 1998). When policies shift from treating those with severe alcohol or drug dependence (i.e., those who have "hit bottom" and recognize a need for treatment) to treating drinkers and drug users who may not believe that their substance use contributes to their health and social problems, programs must accommodate a new client base who may resist imposed treatment and be ambivalent about changing their behavior. Indeed, people who are referred to addiction treatment by legal and formal routes tend to be younger, less severely dependent on alcohol and other drugs, and less likely to have previous treatment experience than others seeking treatment (Brecht, Anglin, & Dylan, 2005; Kelly, Finney, & Moos, 2005; Leukefeld & Tims, 1988; Marshall & Hser, 2002; Polcin & Beattie, 2007; Polcin & Weisner, 1999; Rush & Wild, 2003).

In general, most studies of treatment access compare those individuals who completed an intake or assessment but did not return to treatment with those who were retained. This means that little is known about those who never initiate treatment intake at all. Research attempting to capture those individuals who have no contact with treatment or referral services will provide a better understanding of the characteristics of this elusive portion of the alcohol- and other drug- dependent population and the reasons for their underrepresentation in treatment.

TREATMENT ENGAGEMENT AND OUTCOMES

Treatment engagement is a nonspecific construct linking research on service utilization, duration and quality of participation in treatment programs, and compliance with program demands. Despite research showing that the longer people stay in addiction treatment, the more likely they are to exhibit positive health and social outcomes (Hubbard, Craddock, & Anderson, 2003; Siqueland et al., 2002), about 50% of clients seeking help for alcohol and other drug problems drop out early in the treatment process (Stark, 1992). Consequently, addiction treatment researchers have begun to investigate the role of early treatment engagement in retention and postprogram outcomes (Simpson, 2001, 2004) and to identify processes that might mediate or moderate treatment effectiveness, regardless of the type of treatment received. Motivational concepts have played an important role in this work. For example, robust associations have been documented between treatment motivation and treatment engagement (see Dansereau, Dees, Greener, & Simpson, 1995; Joe, Dansereau, & Simpson, 1994; Simpson & Joe, 2004; Simpson, Joe, & Rowan-Szal, 1997a; Simpson, Joe, Rowan-Szal, & Greener, 1995, 1997b). Specifically, diverse measures of motivation (e.g., client attentiveness during treatment, counselor ratings of rapport with patients, motivation for behavior change, self-confidence, patient ratings of perceived counselor respect, perceived therapeutic progress, and perceived client milieu) relate consistently and positively to a variety of measures of engagement in substance abuse treatment, whether assessed objectively (via attendance and urine screens) or subjectively (through client ratings of treatment-related behavior and attitudes). These findings are consistent with those of De Leon, Melnick, and Kressel (1997) that the strongest predictors of both short- and long-term retention in opiate treatment programs are dynamic motivational factors reflecting circumstances, readiness, reasons, and suitability of treatment.

Other research confirms the importance of perceptions and characteristics of the treatment programs in retaining clients. For example, Condelli and De Leon (1993) reported that treatment retention is related positively to a perceived ease of access to programs and perceived quality of services provided. A large study of almost 2000 clients from 36 outpatient and inpatient substance abuse treatment programs revealed that higher levels of service intensity and client satisfaction predicted retention, which in turn predicted abstinence at a 9-month follow-up (Hser, Evans, Huang, & Anglin, 2004). Moderating effects have been studied relatively infrequently; however, a few studies illustrate the impact of nonspecific client and treatment characteristics on treatment engagement. For example, Melnick, Wexler, Chaple, and Banks (2006) studied 595 staff members and 3732 clients of 80 different substance abuse treatment programs. Program staff and clients each provided ratings of the perceived presence of treatment elements related to therapeutic communities, cognitive–behavior therapy, and 12-step treatment. Degree of agreement among staff members of a treatment venue (consensus) and between staff and clients (concordance) predicted self-ratings of client engagement, rapport with one's counselor, and confidence in treatment (Melnick et al., 2006).

Grella, Anglin, Wugalter, Rawson, and Hasson (1994) found that encouraging patient participation in setting methadone dose, transportation assistance, and assertive follow-up all enhanced the likelihood of avoiding program noncompliance and no-shows. In addition, De Weert-Van Oene, Schippers, De Jong, and Schrijvers (2001) reported that a "helping alliance" variable accounted for a significant proportion of variance with regard to short-term retention in an inpatient substance abuse treatment program. Early therapeutic alliance has been shown to be a consistent predictor of retention and engagement across a variety of studies of substance abuse treatment (Martin, Garske, & Davis, 2000; Meier, Barrowclough, & Donmall, 2005). Finally, White, Ryan, and Ali (1996) found that introducing medication management (MM) programs less restrictive in nature (i.e., no requirements for urine screens or abstinence) resulted in a 27% reduction in dropout rates in an Australian MM program. Together, these findings suggest that programs that facilitate patient perceptions of control over or involvement in treatment decisions can lead to more effective engagement in treatment, at least as assessed by retention rates.

Social control, coercion, and treatment engagement

Concern has been raised that the use of coercive social control tactics might hinder treatment engagement. However, results to date are mixed with regard to whether the presence of social controls is related to treatment motivation, engagement, or outcomes (Gregoire & Burke, 2004; Hiller, Knight, Leukefeld, & Simpson, 2002; Joe et al., 1999a; Joe, Simpson, Greener, & Rowan-Szal, 1999b; Marlowe, Merikle, Kirby, Festinger, & McLellean 2001; Rapp, Li, Siegel, & DeLiberty, 2003; Stevens et al., 2005; Wells-Parker, Kenne, Spratke, & Williams, 2000).

Wild, Cunningham, and Ryan (2006) investigated both referral source and perceptions of social pressure to enter treatment using a measure of self-determined motivation. Results showed that referral source (i.e., mandated treatment status) was unrelated to in-program measures of engagement. However, external motivation (i.e., feeling coerced to attend treatment) was positively associated with having a legal referral or social network pressures to obtain treatment and was negatively related to problem severity. In contrast, a stronger personal commitment and sense of personal choice about entering treatment (i.e., identified motivation) was positively associated with self-referral, problem severity, and several measures of early engagement in treatment. Longshore and Teruya (2006) reported that mandatory referral to substance abuse treatment was associated with poorer outcomes only when accompanied by resistance at the time of treatment entry (e.g., scepticism regarding treatment benefits). Further, in a study of outpatient addiction treatment, patients who entered treatment as a result of legal coercion evidenced greater readiness to change and were more likely to have engaged in recovery behavior just prior to treatment, even after controlling for addiction severity, gender, and previous treatment history (Gregoire & Burke, 2004). Taken together, findings from these three studies suggest that patient perceptions modify the impact of social control tactics on treatment engagement.

Incentive systems

Incentive systems, or contingency management approaches, provide tangible rewards for desired behavior as a means to increase treatment motivation or engagement. Considerable research has examined the effectiveness of these techniques in a variety of treatment contexts, with generally positive results with respect to attendance (Kidorf, Stitzer, Brooner, & Goldberg, 1994; Stitzer, Iguchi, & Felch, 1992; Svikis, Lee, Haug, & Stitzer, 1997), retention, and drug use abstinence (Higgins, Alessi, & Dantona, 2002; Prendergast, Podus, Finney, Greenwell, & Roll, 2006). For example, Petry and colleagues (2005) randomly assigned cocaine or methamphetamine users seeking treatment from a community-based outpatient program to a standard care or standard care plus abstinence incentive condition. Incentives consisted of opportunities to win prizes contingent upon clean urine screens, and incentives were increased with increased length of abstinence. Relative to those receiving standard care alone, those in the incentive condition were retained in the program longer and were more likely to achieve 4, 8, and 12 weeks of consecutive abstinence (Petry et al., 2005). Similarly, Brooner and colleagues (2004) compared a stepped care treatment model with and without behavioral contingencies intended to increase session attendance. They found that the contingency procedure was associated with a higher session attendance and a decreased rate of poor response to treatment (Brooner et al., 2004).

Although these findings clearly show the positive impact of incentive systems on treatment engagement, it is useful to consider the limitations of such programs. Specifically, Pani, Pirastu, Ricci, and Gessa (1996) reported that when injection drug users (IDUs) are aware that take-home privileges are to be discontinued (via program policy changes), dropout rates increase. Moreover, Silverman and colleagues (1996) documented that voucher systems providing escalating pay for sustained abstinence in treatment are successful in decreasing urine positives, but this effect disappears when incentives are removed and patients experience baseline (no incentive) conditions. Thus, behavioral contingency systems may impact treatment-related behavior but likely do not increase motivation in the process (Ledgerwood & Petry, 2006).

Impact of drug screening procedures

Drug monitoring procedures are often used as part of addiction treatment programs on the implicit assumption that monitoring is a deterrent to drug use or is a motivating factor to avoid drug use. However, there is little evidence to support this assumption. Baker, Rounds, and Carson (1995) compared the effects of preannounced versus unannounced urine testing on detected drug use in methadone maintenance patients and examined patients' attitudes toward and preferences regarding approaches to urine testing as a drug monitoring procedure. They found no difference in drug detection rates between preannounced versus unannounced testing. This finding suggests that there may be no particular advantage to initiating unannounced urine screens in MM programs. This is consistent with data reported by Saxon, Wells, Fleming, Jackson, and Calsyn (1996), who observed greater MM program retention when no sanctions (i.e., decreasing MM dose) occur for urine positive screens and when no expectations for abstinence are present. Over half of the patients in Baker and colleagues' (1995) study reported that urine testing was "not helpful at all" in avoiding illicit drug use during treatment. As to client preference for the approach to urine testing for drug monitoring, 77% of respondents in the Baker and colleagues (1995) study preferred preannounced testing (whether escorted or unescorted). The authors speculated that preannouncement may give patients a greater sense of control over treatment and recommended exploring further psychosocial interventions that increase self-control over drug use to compare their effectiveness and cost-effectiveness to monitoring techniques alone. Further research examining the impact of incentive systems and drug screening procedures on a wider array of motivational and engagement measures is warranted.

Gainey, Catalano, Haggerty, and Hoppe (1995) criticized an implicit assumption of many of the studies in this area, namely, that simple attendance rate measures are appropriate measures of treatment engagement and that attendance is the best predictor of responses to therapeutic outcomes. A broader view of treatment engagement was proposed, including judgments of the percentage of sessions attended in which clients (a) paid close attention, (b) participated in an active way (e.g., through role plays, involvement of family members), and (c) completed assigned homework (Gainey et al., 1995). Results from this study indicated that there was a large variation in levels of participation even among patients who attended the majority of treatment sessions and that the indicators of program participation were highly intercorrelated. Clearly, future research should not continue to use attendance rates as a proxy for "treatment engagement," either as an intermediate variable or as an outcome in its own right.

Several researchers have also pointed out that research has largely ignored structural characteristics of the treatment program (Craig, Rogalski, & Veltri, 1982; Gainey et al., 1995). This is an important omission given the wide variety of treatment practices represented within the "same" treatment programs (D'Aunno & Vaughn, 1992; Meier et al., 2005). Caplehorn, Lumley, and Irwig (1998) reported intriguing data relevant to this issue. Dropout rates were assessed among MM clients in relation to staff attitudes toward abstinence; results showed that clients' risk of discharge from treatment increased three times for every unit increase on the clinic staffs' median abstinence orientation score. These findings suggest that a productive line of research would be to systematically examine program policies and staff attitudes in relation to a broad array of treatment engagement variables, including retention rates.

In an important paper, McLellan, McKay, Forman, Cacciola, and Kemp (2005) argued that reliance on traditional outcome measures derived from an acute-care perspective (e.g., 6 and 12 month post-treatment outcomes) may be inappropriate for conceptualizing the course of addiction treatment. This is because an acute care perspective fails to acknowledge that addictions are chronic, recurring conditions and as such require outcome assessment strategies that emphasize outcomes over the course of exposure to treatment rather than 6 to 12 months following discontinuation of treatment activities. This "concurrent recovery monitoring" perspective is a useful way to conceptualize the literature on nonspecific effects on treatment engagement.

Post-treatment outcomes

Gossop, Green, Phillips, and Bradley (1990) examined predictors of 6-month follow-up outcomes among opiate users who had successfully withdrawn and found that two types of motivational factors most consistently predicted decreased drug use at follow-up: (1) situational factors, including persons, activities, and social structures rated by patients at admission to be supportive of abstinence, and (2) patients' ratings of confidence that they would not be using opiates. Similarly, Murphy and Bentall (1992) reported that both lifestyle factors (i.e., number of nonopiate drugs used 3 months prior to admission) and motivational factors (perceived negative impacts of heroin use) predicted discharge outcome. Tiet, Ilgen, Byrnes, Harris, and Finney (2007) found that those with more severe drug addiction (as measured by the Addiction Severity Index) at the time of treatment entry showed greater improvement post-treatment when they had participated in an intensive residential program as opposed to an outpatient program, while the opposite was true for those with less severe drug addiction at entry into treatment (who benefited more from outpatient programs).

Therapeutic alliance predicts client outcomes, particularly when rated by clients, as opposed to counselors (Barber et al., 1999; Diamond et al., 2006). For example, Ilgen and Moos (2005) reported that therapeutic alliance and more treatment sessions predicted better outcomes in terms of proportion of days abstinent 3 months post-treatment.

However, a few studies have provided contradictory results, suggesting that the relationship between therapeutic alliance and other nonspecific factors may be more complex. For example, while general evidence shows that the effect of counselor characteristics on client outcomes is lessened with greater adherence to a treatment model, another study reported that adherence was irrelevant with regard to client outcomes when there was a strong client–therapist alliance. When therapeutic alliance was low, a moderate level of adherence predicted optimal client outcomes (Barber et al., 2006).

A wide variety of other therapist qualities have been investigated as potential predictors of client outcomes (Najavits, Crits-Christoph, & Dierberger, 2000). Kasarabada, Hser, Boles, and Huang (2002) examined 12 such factors related to counselor characteristics (attractiveness, expertise, and trust), counselor attitudes and behaviors (directiveness, empathy, nurturance, genuineness, acceptance, confrontation, and self-disclosure), and counseling process (concreteness and immediacy), as well as two measures of client attitudes and behaviors (openness and responsibility). Six of these 14 characteristics were significant predictors of length of stay in both outpatient and residential subsamples. However, none of the characteristics predicted reductions in drug addiction severity at follow-up, and only immediacy and openness predicted improved alcohol addiction severity at follow-up.

Indirect relationships between motivational variables and outcomes have also been reported. For example, Dearing, Barrick, Derman, and Walitzer (2005) highlighted the role of treatment satisfaction as a mediator between client engagement (i.e., client expectations, therapeutic alliance, session attendance) and drug use post-treatment among alcohol outpatient treatment clients. Other studies have highlighted retention as a mediating process. In MM treatment, motivational variables, including desire for help at admission and counselor ratings of motivation (i.e., patients being perceived by counselors as dependable, organized, and cooperative), predicted the length of stay over a 12-month period. In turn, clients retained in MM treatment for 12 months or more were five times more likely than others to exhibit favorable outcomes at a 12-month follow up, including reduced substance use and criminal involvement (Simpson et al., 1997b). A study of individuals involved in a prison-based therapeutic community found that motivation and participation while in treatment predicted entry into an aftercare program, which in turn led to a decreased chance of drug use relapse at 12 months post-treatment (Melnick, De Leon, Thomas, Kressel, & Wexler, 2001). These studies indicate that motivational variables may help facilitate increased exposure to treatment, which promotes improved outcomes.

CONCLUSIONS

People who seek addiction treatment, their friends, and family members, along with professionals who provide treatment services and those who pay for programs and services, all expect that exposure to treatment will reduce alcohol and other drug misuse, reduce the devastating health and social problems that typically accompany addictions, and improve alcohol and drug misusers' quality of life. Every one of these stakeholders can and should demand that the kinds of treatment offered in addiction programs and services be supported by a robust evidence base on their efficacy and effectiveness and that ongoing efforts should be made to monitor and improve service delivery and outcomes facilitated by treatment providers (McLellan et al., 2007).

By illuminating the active ingredients that transcend treatment modalities, researchers have an opportunity to substantially improve all substance abuse treatment approaches. Further, although rarely the explicit focus of attention in research designed to demonstrate the relative superiority of a particular therapeutic approach, there is nevertheless a large body of research demonstrating that nonspecific factors play a key role in accessing treatment, as well as engagement and treatment outcomes. This chapter reviewed select literature on this phenomenon, with an eye toward highlighting the importance of motivational factors. Being aware that these motivational factors are influential and that they play important mediating and moderating roles in affecting treatment outcomes (Finney, 2007; Longabaugh, 2007) will, we believe, make it possible to more effectively implement different types of treatment interventions in novel contexts and to improve the delivery of treatment, regardless of the theoretical approach of the treatment.

REFERENCES

Allen, K., & Dixon, M. (1994). Psychometric assessment of the Allen Barriers to Treatment Instrument. *International Journal of Addictions*, *29*, 545–563.

Andersen, R. M. (1995). Revisiting the behavioural model and access to medical care: Does it matter? *Journal of Health and Social Behavior*, *36*, 1–10.

Anglin, M. D., Brecht, M. L., & Maddahian, E. (1989). Pre-treatment characteristics and treatment performance of legally coerced versus voluntary methadone maintenance admissions. *Criminology*, *27*, 537–557.

Anton, R., O'Malley, S., Ciraulo, D., Cisler, R., Couper, D., Donnovan, D., et al. (2006). Combined pharmacotherapies and behavioral interventions for alcohol dependence. The COMBINE study: A randomized controlled trial. *Journal of the American Medical Association*, *295*, 2003–2017.

Appel, P. W., Ellison, A. A., Jansky, H. K., & Oldak, R. (2004). Barriers to enrolment in drug abuse treatment and suggestions for reducing them: Client and other system stakeholders. *American Journal of Drug and Alcohol Abuse*, *30*, 129–153.

Appel, P. W., & Oldak, R. (2007). A preliminary comparison of major kinds of obstacles to enrolling in substance abuse treatment (AOD) reported by injecting street outreach clients and other stakeholders. *American Journal of Drug and Alcohol Abuse*, *33*, 699–705.

Baker, J. G., Rounds, J. B., & Carson, C. A. (1995). Monitoring in methadone maintenance treatment. *International Journal of the Addictions*, *30*, 1177–1185.

Barber, J. P., Gallop, R., Crits-Christoph, P., Frank, A., Thase, M. E., Weiss, R. D., & Gibbons, M. B. C. (2006). The role of therapist adherence, therapist competence, and alliance in predicting outcome of individual drug counseling: Results from the National Institute Drug Abuse Collaborative Cocaine Treatment Study. *Psychotherapy Research*, *16*, 229–240.

Barber, J. P., Luborsky, L., Crits-Christoph, P., Thase, M. E., Weiss, R., & Frank, A. (1999). Therapeutic alliance as a predictor of outcome in treatment of cocaine dependence. *Psychotherapy Research*, *9*, 54–73.

Belenko, S. (2001). *Research on drug courts: A critical review. 2001 update*. New York: National Centre on Addiction and Substance Abuse.

Bergmark, A. (2008). On treatment mechanisms: What can we learn from Project COMBINE? *Addiction*, *103*, 703–705.

Best, D., Noble, A., Ridge, G., Gossop, M., Farrell, M., & Strang, J. (2002). The relative impact of waiting time and treatment entry on drug and alcohol use. *Addiction Biology*, *7*, 67–74.

Brecht, M. L., Anglin, M. D., & Dylan, M. (2005). Coerced treatment for methamphetamine abuse: Differential patient characteristics and outcomes. *American Journal of Drug and Alcohol Abuse*, *31*, 337–356.

Breda, C. S., & Heflinger, C. A. (2007). The impact of motivation to change on substance use among adolescents in treatment. *Journal of Child and Adolescent Abuse*, *16*, 109–124.

Broome, K. M., Simpson, D. D., & Joe, G. W. (1999). Patient and program attributes related to treatment process indicators in DATOS. *Drug and Alcohol Dependence*, *57*, 113–125.

Brooner, R. K., Kidorf, M. S., King, V. L., Stoller, K. B., Peirce, J. M., Bigelow, G. E., et al. (2004). Behavioral contingencies improve counseling attendance in an adaptive treatment model. *Journal of Substance Abuse Treatment*, *27*, 223–232.

Buhringer, G., & Pfieffer-Gerschel, T. (2008). COMBINE and MATCH: The final blow for large scale black-box clinical trials. *Addiction*, *103*, 708–709.

Caplehorn, J. R. M., Lumley, T. S., & Irwig, L. (1998). Staff attitudes and retention of patients in methadone maintenance programs. *Drug & Alcohol Dependence*, *52*, 57–61.

Carpenter, K. M., Miele, G. M., & Hasin, D. S. (2002). Does motivation to change mediate the effect of DSM-IV substance use disorders on treatment utilization and substance use? *Addictive Behaviors*, *27*, 207–225.

Cartwright, W. S., & Solano, P. L. (2005). The economics of public health: Financing drug abuse treatment services. *Health Policy*, *66*, 247–260.

Chawdhary, A., Sayre, S. L., Green, C., Schmitz, J. M., Grabowski, J., & Mooney, M. E. (2007). Moderators of delay tolerance in treatment-seeking cocaine users. *Addictive Behaviors*, *32*, 370–376.

Claus, R. E., & Kindleberger, L. R. (2002). Engaging substance abusers after centralized assessment: Predictors of treatment entry and dropout. *Journal of Psychoactive Drugs*, *34*, 25–31.

COMBINE Study Research Group. (2003). Testing combined pharmacotherapies and behavioral interventions in alcohol dependence: Rationale and methods. *Alcoholism: Clinical and Experimental Research*, *27*, 1022–1107.

Condelli, W. S., & De Leon, G. (1993). Fixed and dynamic predictors of client retention in therapeutic communities. *Journal of Substance Abuse Treatment*, *19*, 11–16.

Craig, R. J., Rogalski, C., & Veltri, D. (1982). Predicting treatment dropouts from a drug abuse rehabilitation program. *The International Journal of the Addictions*, *17*, 641–653.

Cunningham, J. A. (1999). Resolving alcohol-related problems with and without treatment: The effects of different problem criteria. *Journal of Studies on Alcohol*, *60*, 463–466.

Cunningham, J. A. (2000). Remissions from drug dependence: Is treatment a prerequisite? *Drug and Alcohol Dependence*, *59*, 211–213.

Cunningham, J. A. (2004). Stopping illicit drug use without treatment: Any relation to frequency of drug use? *American Journal on Addictions*, *13*, 292–294.

Cunningham, J. A., & Breslin, F. C. (2004). Only one in three people with alcohol abuse or dependence ever seek treatment. *Addictive Behaviors*, *29*, 221–223.

Cunningham, J. A., Sobell, L. C., Sobell, M. B., Agrawal, S., & Toneatto, T. (1993). Barriers to treatment: Why alcohol and drug abusers delay or never seek treatment. *Addictive Behaviors*, *18*, 347–353.

Dansereau, D. F., Dees, S. M., Greener, J., & Simpson, D. D. (1995). Node-link mapping and the evaluation of drug abuse counseling sessions. *Psychology of Addictive Behaviors*, *9*, 195–203.

D'Aunno, T., & Vaughn, T. E. (1992). Variations in methadone treatment practices. *Journal of the American Medical Association*, *267*, 253–258.

Dearing, R. L., Barrick, C., Derman, K. H., & Walitzer, K. S. (2005). Indicators of client engagement: Influences on alcohol treatment satisfaction and outcomes. *Psychology of Addictive Behaviors*, *19*, 71–78.

De Leon, G., Melnick, G., & Kressel, D. (1997). Motivation and readiness for therapeutic community treatment among cocaine and other drug abusers. *American Journal of Drug & Alcohol Abuse*, *23*, 169–189.

Deschenes, E., Peters, R., Goldkamp, J., & Belenko, S. (2003). Drug courts. In J. Zweben (Ed.), *Research to practice, practice to research: Promoting scientific-clinical interchange in drug abuse treatment* (pp. 85–102). Washington, DC: U.S. Department of Justice, Office of Justice Programs.

De Weert-Van Oene, G., Schippers, G. M., De Jong, C. A. J., & Schrijvers, G. J. P. (2001). Retention in substance dependence treatment: The relevance of in-treatment factors. *Journal of Substance Abuse Treatment*, *20*, 253–261.

De Weert-Van Oene, G., Schippers, G. M., De Jong, C. A. J., & Schrijvers, G. J. P. (2002). Motivation for treatment in substance-dependent patients: Psychometric evaluation of the TCU motivation for treatment scales. *European Addiction Research*, *8*, 2–9.

Diamond, G. S., Liddle, H. A., Wintersteen, M. B., Dennis, M. L., Godley, S. H., & Tims, F. (2006). Early therapeutic alliance as a predictor of treatment outcome for adolescent cannabis users in outpatient treatment. *American Journal on Addictions*, *15*, 26–33.

Digiusto, E., & Treloar, C. (2007). Equity of access to treatment, and barriers to treatment for illicit drug use in Australia. *Addiction*, *102*, 958–969.

Downey, L., Rosengren, D., & Donovan, D. (2003). Gender, waitlists, and outcomes for public-sector drug treatment. *Journal of Substance Abuse Treatment, 25*, 19–28.

Dreischner, K. H., Lammers, S. M. M., & van der Staak, C. P. F. (2004). Treatment motivation: An attempt for clarification of an ambiguous concept. *Clinical Psychology Review, 23*, 1115–1137.

Epstein, J., Hourani, L., & Heller, D. (2004). Predictors of treatment receipt among adults with a drug use disorder. *American Journal of Drug and Alcohol Abuse, 30*, 841–869.

Finney, J. W. (2007). Treatment processes and mediators of substance use disorders treatment effects: The benefits of side road excursions. *Alcoholism: Clinical and Experimental Research, 31*, 80S–83S.

Fischer, B., Roberts, J. V., & Kirst, M. (2002). Compulsory treatment: What do we know and where should we go? *European Addiction Research, 8*, 52–53.

Freyer, J., Coder, B., Bischof, G., Baumeister, S. E., Rumpf, H. J., John, U., et al. (2007). Intention to utilize formal help in a sample with alcohol problems: A prospective study. *Drug and Alcohol Dependence, 87*, 210–216.

Freyer, J., Tonigan, J. S., Keller, S., Rumpf, H. J., John, U., & Hapke, U. (2005). Readiness for change and readiness for help-seeking: A composite assessment of client motivation. *Alcohol and Alcoholism, 40*, 540–544.

Gainey, R. R., Catalano, R. F., Haggerty, K. P., & Hoppe, M. J. (1995). Participation in a parent training program for methadone clients. *Addictive Behaviors, 20*, 117–125.

Garnick, D. W., Horgan, C. M., Merrick, E. L., & Hoyt, A. (2007). Identification and treatment of mental and substance use conditions. *Medical Care, 45*, 1060–1067.

Garnick, D. W., Lee, M. T., Chalk, M., Gastfriend, D., Horgan, C. M., McCorry, F., et al. (2002). Establishing the feasibility of performance measures for alcohol and other drugs. *Journal of Substance Abuse Treatment, 23*, 375–385.

Gerdner, A., & Holmberg, A. (2000). Factors affecting motivation to treatment in severely dependent alcoholics. *Journal of Studies on Alcohol, 61*, 548–560.

Gossop, M., Green, L., Phillips, G., & Bradley, B. (1990). Factors predicting outcome among opiate addicts after treatment. *British Journal of Clinical Psychology, 29*, 209–216.

Gostin, L. O. (1991). Compulsory treatment for drug-dependent persons: Justifications for a public health approach to drug dependency. *The Milbank Quarterly, 69*, 561–593.

Grant, B. F. (1997). Barriers to alcoholism treatment: Reasons for not seeking treatment in a general population sample. *Journal of Studies on Alcohol, 58*, 365–371.

Greenfield, S. F., Brooks, A. J., Gordon, S. M., Green, C. A., Kropp, F., McHugh, R. K., et al. (2007). Substance abuse treatment entry, retention, and outcome in women: A review of the literature. *Drug and Alcohol Dependence, 86*, 1–21.

Gregoire, T. K., & Burke, A. C. (2004). The relationship of legal coercion to readiness to change among adults with alcohol and other drug problems. *Journal of Substance Abuse Treatment, 26*, 337–343.

Grella, C. E., Anglin, M. D., Wugalter, S. E., Rawson, R. A., & Hasson, A. (1994). Reasons for discharge from methadone maintenance for addicts at high risk of HIV infection or transmission. *Journal of Psychoactive Drugs, 26*, 223–232.

Grella, C. E., Hser, Y. I., & Hsieh, S. C. (2003). Predictors of drug treatment re-entry following relapse to cocaine use in DATOS. *Journal of Substance Abuse Treatment*, *25*, 145–154.

Hasin, D. S. (1994). Treatment/self-help for alcohol-related problems: Relationship to social pressure and alcohol dependence. *Journal of Studies on Alcohol*, *55*, 660–666.

Hiller, M. L., Knight, K., Leukefeld, C., & Simpson, D. D. (2002). Motivation as a predictor of therapeutic engagement in mandated residential substance abuse treatment. *Criminal Justice and Behavior*, *29*, 56–75.

Higgins, S. T., Alessi, S. M., & Dantona, R. L. (2002). Voucher-based incentives: A substance abuse treatment innovation. *Addictive Behaviors*, *27*, 887–910.

Hser, Y. I., Evans, E., Huang, D., & Anglin, D. M. (2004). Relationship between drug treatment services, retention, and outcomes. *Psychiatric Services*, *55*, 767–774.

Hubbard, R. L., Craddock, S. G., & Anderson, J. (2003). Overview of 5-year follow-up outcomes in the drug abuse treatment outcome studies (DATOS). *Journal of Substance Abuse Treatment*, *25*, 125–134.

Ilgen, M., & Moos, R. (2005). Deterioration following alcohol-use disorder treatment in Project MATCH. *Journal of Studies on Alcohol*, *66*, 517–525.

Jackson, K. R., Booth, P. G., McGuire, J., & Salmon, P. (2006). Predictors of starting and remaining in treatment at a specialist alcohol clinic. *Journal of Substance Use*, *11*, 89–100.

Jakobsson, A., Hensing, G., & Spak, F. (2005). Developing a willingness to change: Treatment-seeking processes for people with alcohol problems. *Alcohol and Alcoholism*, *40*, 118–123.

Jessop, M. A., Humphreys, J. C., Brindis, C. D., & Lee, K. A. (2003). Extrinsic barriers to substance abuse treatment among pregnant women. *Journal of Drug Issues*, *33*, 285–304.

Joe, G., Simpson, D., & Broome, K. (1999a). Retention and patient engagement models of different treatment modalities in DATOS. *Drug and Alcohol Dependence*, *57*, 113–125.

Joe, G. W., Broome, K. M., Rowan-Szal, G. A., & Simpson, D. D. (2002). Measuring patient attributes and engagement in treatment. *Journal of Substance Abuse Treatment*, *22*, 183–196.

Joe, G. W., Dansereau, D. F., & Simpson, D. D. (1994). Node-link mapping for counseling cocaine users in methadone treatment. *Journal of Substance Abuse*, *6*, 393–406.

Joe, G. W., Simpson, D. D., Greener, J. M., & Rowan-Szal, G. A. (1999b). Integrative modeling of client engagement and outcomes during the first 6 months of methadone treatment. *Addictive Behaviors*, *24*, 649–659.

Johnson, V. (1986). *Intervention: How to help someone who doesn't want help*. Minneapolis, MN: Johnson Institute Books.

Kasarabada, N. D., Hser, Y. I., Boles, S. M., & Huang, Y. C. (2002). Do patients' perceptions of their counsellors influence outcomes of drug treatment?. *Journal of Substance Abuse Treatment*, *23*, 327–334.

Kazdin, A. E. (1979). Nonspecific treatment factors in psychotherapy outcome research. *Journal of Consulting and Clinical Psychology*, *57*, 698–704.

Kelly, J. F., Finney, J. W., & Moos, R. H. (2005). Substance use disorder patients who are mandated to treatment: Characteristics, treatment process, and 1- and 5-year outcomes. *Journal of Substance Abuse Treatment*, *28*, 213–223.

Kersetz, S. G., Larson, M. J., Cheng, D. M., Tucker, J. A., Winter, M., Mullins, A., et al. (2006). Need and non-need factors associated with addiction treatment utilization in a cohort of homeless and housed urban poor. *Medical Care*, *44*, 225–233.

Kidorf, M., Stitzer, M. L., Brooner, R. K., & Goldberg, J. (1994). Contingent methadone take-home doses reinforce adjunct therapy attendance of methadone maintenance patients. *Drug & Alcohol Dependence*, *36*, 221–226.

Krahn, G., Deck, D., Gabriel, R., & Farrell, N. (2007). A population-based study on substance abuse treatment for adults with disabilities: Access, utilization, and treatment outcomes. *American Journal of Drug and Alcohol Abuse*, *33*, 791–798.

Lawental, E., McLellan, A. T., Grissom, G. R., Brill, P., & O'Brien, C. (1996). Coerced treatment for substance abuse problems detected through workplace urine surveillance: Is it effective? *Journal of Substance Abuse*, *8*, 115–128.

Ledgerwood, D. M., & Petry, N. M. (2006). Does contingency management affect motivation to change substance use? *Drug and Alcohol Dependence*, *83*, 65–72.

Leukefeld, C. G., & Tims, F. M. (1988). Compulsory treatment of drug abuse: Research and clinical practice. *NIDA Research Monograph 86*. Rockville, MD: U.S. Department of Health and Human Services.

Logan, D. G. (1983). Getting alcoholics to treatment by social network intervention. *Hospital and Community Psychiatry*, *34*, 360–361.

Longabaugh, R. (2007). The search for mechanisms of change in behavioral treatments for alcohol use disorders: A commentary. *Alcoholism: Clinical and Experimental Research*, *31*(S3), 21S–32S.

Longshore, D., & Teruya, C. (2006). Treatment motivation in drug users: A theory-based analysis. *Drug and Alcohol Dependence*, *81*, 179–188.

Marlowe, D. B., Kirby, K. C., Bonieskie, L. M., Glass, D. J., Dodds, L. D., Husbands, S., et al. (1996). Assessment of coercive and noncoercive pressures to enter drug abuse treatment. *Drug and Alcohol Dependence*, *42*, 77–84.

Marlowe, D. B., Merikle, E. P., Kirby, K. C., Festinger, D. S., & McLellean, A. T. (2001). Multidimensional assessment of perceived treatment-entry pressures among substance abusers. *Psychology of Addictive Behavior*, *15*, 97–108.

Marshall, G. N., & Hser, Y. I. (2002). Characteristics of criminal justice and non-criminal justice clients receiving treatment for substance abuse. *Addictive Behaviors*, *27*, 179–192.

Martin, D. J., Garske, J. P., & Davis, M. K. (2000). Relation of the therapeutic alliance with outcome and other variables: A meta-analytic review. *Journal of Consulting and Clinical Psychology*, *68*, 438–450.

McCarty, D. (2007). Performance measurement systems for treating alcohol and drug use disorders. *Journal of Substance Abuse Treatment*, *33*, 353–354.

McCorry, F., Garnick, D. W., Bartlett, J., Cotter, F., & Chalk, M. (2000). Developing performance measures for alcohol and other drug services in managed care plans. *Journal on Quality Improvement*, *20*, 633–643.

McLellan, A. T., Chalk, M., & Bartlett, J. (2007). Outcomes, performance, and quality: What's the difference? *Journal of Substance Abuse Treatment*, *32*, 331–340.

McLellan, A. T., McKay, J. R., Forman, R., Cacciola, J., & Kemp, J. (2005). Reconsidering the evaluation of addiction treatment: From retrospective follow-up to concurrent recovery monitoring. *Addiction*, *100*, 447–458.

Meier, P. S., Barrowclough, C., & Donmall, M. C. (2005). The role of therapeutic alliance in the treatment of substance misuses: A critical review of the literature. *Addiction, 100*, 304–316.

Melnick, G., De Leon, G., Thomas, G., Kressel, D., & Wexler, H. K. (2001). Treatment process in prison therapeutic communities: Motivation, participation, and outcome. *American Journal of Drug and Alcohol Abuse, 27*, 633–650.

Melnick, G., Wexler, H. K., Chaple, M., & Banks, S. (2006). The contribution of consensus within staff and client groups as well as concordance between staff and clients to treatment engagement. *Journal of Substance Abuse Treatment, 31*, 277–285.

Messer, S. B., & Wampold, B. E. (2002). Let's face facts: Common factors are more potent than specific therapy ingredients. *Clinical Psychology: Science, Research and Practice, 9*, 21–25.

Murphy, P. N., & Bentall, R. P. (1992). Motivation to withdraw from heroin: A factor-analytic study. *British Journal of Addiction, 87*, 245–250.

Najavits, L. M., Crits-Christoph, P., & Dierberger, A. (2000). Clinicians' impact on the quality of substance use disorder treatment. *Substance Use and Misuse, 35*, 2161–2190.

Neff, J. A., & Zule, W. A. (2002). Predictive validity of a measure of treatment readiness for out-of-treatment drug users: Enhancing prediction beyond demographic and drug history variables. *American Journal of Drug and Alcohol Abuse, 28*, 147–169.

Orford, J. (2008). Asking the right questions in the right way: The need for a shift in research on psychological treatments for addiction. *Addiction, 103*, 875–885.

Pani, P. P., Pirastu, R., Ricci, A., & Gessa, G. L. (1996). Prohibition of take-home dosages: Negative consequences on methadone maintenance treatment. *Drug & Alcohol Dependence, 41*, 81–84.

Perkonigg, A., Settele, A., Pfister, H., Höfler, M., Fröhlich, C., Zimmermann, P., et al. (2006). Where have they been? Service use of regular substance users with and without abuse and dependence. *Social Psychiatry and Psychiatric Epidemiololgy, 41*, 470–479.

Petry, N. M., Peirce, J. M., Stitzer, M. L., Blaine, J., Roll, J. M., Cohen, A., et al. (2005). Effect of prize-based incentives on outcomes in stimulant abusers in outpatient psychosocial treatment programs: A national drug abuse treatment clinical trials network study. *Archives of General Psychiatry, 62*, 1148–1156.

Polcin, D. L., & Beattie, M. (2007). Relationship and institutional pressure to enter treatment: Differences by demographics, problem severity, and motivation. *Journal of Studies on Alcohol and Drugs, 68*, 428–436.

Polcin, D. L., & Weisner, C. (1999). Factors associated with coercion in entering treatment for alcohol problems. *Drug and Alcohol Dependence, 54*, 63–68.

Popova, S., Rehm, J., & Fischer, B. (2006). An overview of illegal opioid use and health service utilization in Canada. *Public Health, 120*, 320–328.

Prendergast, M., Podus, D., Finney, J., Greenwell, L., & Roll, J. (2006). Contingency management for treatment of substance use disorders: A meta-analysis. *Addiction, 101*, 1546–1560.

Project MATCH Research Group. (1997a). Matching alcoholism treatments to client heterogeneity: Project MATCH posttreatment drinking outcomes. *Journal of Studies on Alcohol, 58*, 7–29.

Project MATCH Research Group. (1997b). Project MATCH secondary a priori hypotheses. *Addiction, 92*, 1671–1698.

Rapp, R. C., Li, L., Siegal, H. A., & DeLiberty, R. N. (2003). Demographic and clinical correlates of client motivation among substance abusers. *Health and Social Work*, *28*, 107–115.

Rapp, R. C., Xu, J., Carr, C. A., Lane, T., Redko, C., Wang, J., et al. (2007). Understanding treatment readiness in recently assessed, pre-treatment substance abusers. *Substance Abuse*, *28*, 11–23.

Rapp, R. C., Xu, J., Carr, C. A., Lane, D. T., Wang, J., & Carlson, R. (2006). Treatment barriers identified by substance abusers assessed at a centralized intake unit. *Journal of Substance Abuse Treatment*, *30*, 327–335.

Redko, C., Rapp, R. C., & Carlson, R. G. (2006). Waiting time as a barrier to treatment entry: Perceptions of substance users. *Journal of Drug Issues*, *36*, 831–852.

Room, R., Greenfield, T. K., & Weisner, C. (1991). "People who might have liked you to drink less": Changing responses to drinking by U.S. family members and friends, 1979–1990. *Contemporary Drug Problems*, *18*, 573–595.

Rush, B. R., & Wild, T. C. (2003). Substance abuse treatment and pressures from the criminal justice system: Data from a provincial client monitoring system. *Addiction*, *98*, 1119–1128.

Sallmen, B., Berglund, M., & Bokander, B. (1998). Perceived coercion related to psychiatric comorbidity and locus of control in institutionalized alcoholics. *Medicine and Law*, *17*, 381–391.

Saxon, A. J., Wells, E. A., Fleming, C., Jackson, T. R., & Calsyn, D. A. (1996). Pre-treatment characteristics, program philosophy and level of ancillary services as predictors of methadone maintenance treatment outcome. *Addiction*, *91*, 1197–1209.

Silverman, K., Wong, C. J., Higgins, S. T., Brooner, R. K., Montoya, I. D., Contoreggi, C., et al. (1996). Increasing opiate abstinence through voucher-based reinforcement therapy. *Drug & Alcohol Dependence*, *41*, 157–165.

Simpson, D. D. (2001). Modeling treatment process and outcomes. *Addiction*, *96*, 207–211.

Simpson, D. D. (2004). A conceptual framework for drug treatment process and outcomes. *Journal of Substance Abuse Treatment*, *27*, 99–121.

Simpson, D. D., & Joe, G. W. (1993). Motivation as a predictor of early drop-out from drug abuse treatment. *Psychotherapy: Theory, Research, Practice, Training*, *30*, 357–368.

Simpson, D. D., & Joe, G. W. (2004). A longitudinal evaluation of treatment engagement and recovery stages. *Journal of Substance Abuse Treatment*, *27*, 89–97.

Simpson, D. D., Joe, G. W., & Rowan-Szal, G. A. (1997a). Drug abuse treatment retention and process effects on follow-up outcomes. *Drug & Alcohol Dependence*, *47*, 227–235.

Simpson, D. D., Joe, G. W., Rowan-Szal, G., & Greener, J. (1995). Client engagement and change during drug abuse treatment. *Journal of Substance Abuse*, *7*, 117–134.

Simpson, D. D., Joe, G. W., Rowan-Szal, G. A., & Greener, J. M. (1997b). Drug abuse treatment process components that improve retention. *Journal of Substance Abuse Treatment*, *14*, 565–572.

Siqueland, L., Crits-Cristoph, P., Gallop, R., Barber, J. P., Griffin, M. L., Thase, M. E., et al. (2002). Retention in psychosocial treatment of cocaine dependence: Predictors and impact on outcome. *American Journal on Addiction*, *11*, 24–40.

Sobell, L. C., Cunningham, J. A., & Sobell, M. B. (1996). Recovery from alcohol problem with and without treatment: Prevalence in two population surveys. *American Journal of Public Health*, *86*, 966–972.

Stark, M. (1992). Dropping out of substance abuse treatment: A clinically oriented review. *Clinical Psychology Review*, *12*, 93–116.

Stevens, A., Berto, D., Heckmann, W., Kerschl, V., Oeuvray, K., van Ooyen, M., et al. (2005). Quasi-compulsory treatment of drug dependent offenders: An international literature review. *Substance Use and Misuse*, *40*, 269–283.

Stitzer, M. L., Iguchi, M. Y., & Felch, L. J. (1992). Contingent take-home incentive: Effects on drug use of methadone maintenance patients. *Journal of Consulting & Clinical Psychology*, *60*, 927–934.

Stout, R. L. (2007). Advancing the analysis of treatment process. *Addiction*, *102*, 1539–1545.

Svikis, D. S., Lee, J. H., Haug, N. A., & Stitzer, M. L. (1997). Attendance incentives for outpatient treatment: Effects in methadone- and nonmethadone-maintained pregnant drug dependent women. *Drug & Alcohol Dependence*, *48*, 33–41.

Tiet, Q. Q., Ilgen, M. A., Byrnes, H. F., Harris, A. H. S., & Finney, J. W. (2007). Treatment setting and baseline substance use severity interact to predict patients' outcomes. *Addiction*, *102*, 432–440.

Trice, H. M., & Sonnenstuhl, W. J. (1991). Job behaviors and the denial syndrome. In D. J. Pittman & H. R. White (Eds.), *Society, culture, and drinking patterns reexamined*. New Brunswick, NJ: Rutgers Center of Alcohol Studies.

UKATT Research Team. (2005). Effectiveness of treatment for alcohol problems: Findings of the randomised UK alcohol treatment trial (UKATT). *British Medical Journal*, *331*, 541–544.

Vickers-Lahti, M., Garfield, F., McCusker, J., Hindin, R., Bigelow, C., Love, C., et al. (1995). The relationship between legal factors and attrition from residential drug abuse treatment programs. *Journal of Psychoactive Drugs*, *27*, 17–25.

Wampold, B. E., Mondin, G. W., Moody, M., Stich, F., Benson, K., & Ahn, H. (1997). A meta-analysis of outcome studies comparing bona fide psychotherapies: Empirically: "all must have prizes." *Psychological Bulletin*, *122*, 203–215.

Watkins, K. E., & Podus, D. (2000). The impact of terminating disability benefits for substance abusers on substance use and treatment participation. *Psychiatric Services*, *51*, 1371–1381.

Weisner, C., Matzger, H., Tam, T., & Schmidt, L. (2002). Who goes to alcohol and drug treatment? Understanding utilization within the context of insurance. *Journal of Studies on Alcohol*, *63*, 673–682.

Weisner, C., Mertens, J., Tam, T., & Moore, C. (2001). Factors affecting the initiation of substance abuse treatment in managed care. *Addiction*, *96*, 705–716.

Wells-Parker, E. (1995). Mandated treatment: Lessons from research with drinking and driving offenders. *Alcohol Health and Research World*, *18*, 302–306.

Wells-Parker, E., Kenne, D. R., Spratke, K. L., & Williams, M. T. (2000). Self-efficacy and motivation for controlling drinking and drinking/driving: An investigation of changes across a driving under the influence (DUI) intervention program and of recidivism prediction. *Addictive Behaviors*, *2*, 229–238.

Wenger, L. D., & Rosenbaum, M. (1994). Drug treatment on demand—not. *Journal of Psychoactive Drugs*, *26*, 1–11.

White, J. M., Ryan, C. F., & Ali, R. L. (1996). Improvements in retention rates and changes in client group with methadone maintenance streaming. *Drug & Alcohol Review*, *15*, 83–88.

Wild, T. C. (1999). Compulsory substance-user treatment and harm reduction: A critical analysis. *Substance Use and Misuse*, *34*, 83–102.

Wild, T. C. (2006). Social control and coercion in addiction treatment: Toward evidence-based policy and practice. *Addiction*, *101*, 40–49.

Wild, T. C., Cunningham, J. A., & Ryan, R. M. (2006). Social pressure, coercion, and client engagement at treatment entry: A self-determination theory perspective. *Addictive Behaviors*, *31*, 1858–1872.

Wild, T. C., Newton-Taylor, B., & Alletto, R. (1998). Perceived coercion among clients entering substance abuse treatment: Structural and psychological determinants. *Addictive Behaviors*, *23*, 81–95.

Wild, T. C., Roberts, A. R., & Cooper, E. L. (2002). Compulsory substance abuse treatment: An overview of recent findings and issues. *European Addiction Research*, *8*, 84–93.

Wilke, D. J., Kamata, A., & Cash, S. J. (2005). Modeling treatment motivation in substance-abusing women with children. *Child Abuse*, *29*, 1313–1323.

Witkiewitz, K., van der Maas, H., Hufford, M. R., & Marlatt, G. A. (2007). Nonnormality and divergence in posttreatment alcohol use: Reexamining the Project MATCH data another way. *Journal of Abnormal Psychology*, *116*, 378–394.

Xu, J., Wang, J., Rapp, R. C., & Carlson, R. G. (2007). The multidimensional structure on internal barriers to substance abuse treatment and its invariance across gender, ethnicity, and age. *Journal of Drug Issues*, *37*, 321–340.

PART | TWO

Clinical Assessment and Treatment Monitoring

Chapter | three

History and Current Substance Use

Stephen A. Maisto and Marketa Krenek
Department of Psychology, Center for Health and Behavior, Syracuse University

SUMMARY POINTS

Introduction

- The biopsychosocial model combines biological, psychological, and social dimensions when treating a patient.
- Empirically supported measures of substance use aid in planning individualized treatment of substance use-related problems and its evaluation.

Self-report/interview methods of alcohol and other drug consumption

- Consumption measures assess history of and current use by averaging across substance use occasions or at the event level.
- Screening measures typically assess consumption and substance use-related problems.
- Measures should be supported empirically and meet assessment goals.

Biomarker measures of alcohol and illicit drug consumption

- Biomarkers of illicit drug use measure the presence of drugs/metabolites in body fluids and tissues to estimate drug consumption. Urine is used most commonly.
- Biomarkers of heavy alcohol use each provide slightly different information and possess different psychometric properties. γ-Glutamyltransferase is used most commonly.
- Combined use of self-report/interview methods and biomarker measures increases reliability and accuracy of consumption assessment data.

Reliability and accuracy

- Conditions that maximize reliability and accuracy of self-report data are listed.
- Multiple methods of measurement of alcohol and other drug consumption increase confidence in data accuracy.

This chapter is the first of five in this book devoted to assessment, which, in the context of addiction treatment, refers to the acquisition of information about individuals to determine whether they have a substance use disorder or are at risk for developing one. While a variety of information may be collected in clinical settings for these purposes, this chapter describes the process of collecting data on the history of and current alcohol and other drug use.

The two most frequently used psychiatric diagnostic systems, the *Diagnostic and Statistical Manual of Mental Disorders*, Fourth Edition (DSM-IV) (American Psychiatric Association, 2000), and the *Tenth Revision of the International Classification of Diseases* (ICD) (World Health Organization, 1992), specify criteria for the formal diagnosis of two substance use disorders—substance dependence and substance abuse. Given the content of this chapter, it is interesting that the criteria constituting these diagnoses, which then are applied to specific drugs or drug classes, emphasize (in both systems) the biopsychosocial (BPS) effects of alcohol and other drugs and the behavioral patterns that may be involved in drug procurement. However, the criteria do not include a threshold of the history or current quantity or frequency of substance use. This raises the question of why there has been such an investment in developing, as shown later in the chapter, the large number of self-report and biological markers of substance use. The rationale for this may be rooted in conceptualizations of substance use and related problems and their implications for treatment of individuals with those problems.

Through the first three-quarters of the 20th century, models and theories about the development and maintenance of the substance use disorders that emphasized biological, psychological, or social factors frequently outpaced data available to evaluate them. More recently, the quality of research in each of these three domains has improved considerably, and each of these "single-factor" theories has been found to have some merit. Nevertheless, each set of factors alone, biological, psychological, or social, is lacking in its attempt to provide a satisfactory explanation of substance use disorders.

Empirical evidence and a newer way of conceptualizing health and illness merged in the latter 20th century to lead to the generation and broad influence of a "biopsychosocial" model of substance use disorders. Engel (1977, 1980) presented the BPS model first to psychiatry and then the rest of medicine and argued its superiority to the prevailing "biomedical" model in the treatment of patients presenting with medical or psychiatric disorders. Engel argued that viewing a medical or psychiatric disorder as one dimensional (whether it be purely biological, psychological, or social) likely results in missing significant aspects of a patient's problems and, subsequently, their amelioration. Engel maintained further that health, and thus illness, is best viewed as the outcome of nonrecursive (bidirectional causality, such that change in "A" causes change in "B," which in turn causes change in "A") interactions among the hierarchical components of biological, individual, family, and community systems, and of components within those systems. Moreover, "lower order" components (biological) are subsumed by "higher order" (e.g., community) systems. Engel argued that this level of complexity is essential to understanding illness and its manifestations. It is fair to say that the BPS approach is "state of the science" in substance use disorder clinical practice today (Donovan, 2005).

The BPS model is so wide ranging that it may be difficult to see what its specific implications are for understanding the substance use disorders and improving clinical practice. In fact, the BPS has a number of research and clinical implications; for our purposes, the most important pertain to assessment and treatment. In this regard, the BPS implies that individualized assessment and treatment planning are requisites to good clinical outcomes, based on the BPS model assumption that no two cases of substance use disorders can be presumed to be alike in manifestation, etiology, or course.

Three major reasons underlie the clinical importance of reliable and accurate (empirically supported) measures of past and current substance use. First, the primary behavior of interest to clinicians, clinical researchers, and the patients/clients and their significant others is substance use per se. Although individuals seeking treatment for substance use disorders may present with a host of physical, psychological, or social problems, often the root of such problems and/or their exacerbation is substance use. The second reason is related to the first: The primary outcome variable(s) in evaluations of the efficacy or effectiveness of the treatment of substance use disorders is alcohol and other drug use. Outcomes in other areas of functioning, such as physical and psychological health, may be and often are measured, but to present these alone in an analysis of substance use disorder treatment outcome would render it incomplete. This reason also suggests the importance of using measures that are reliable, accurate, and sensitive to change over time in order to obtain an accurate picture of whether a given treatment is working or was effective after a period of time. The third reason for measuring substance use as part of the assessment process derives from the BPS model and its implication about the importance of individualized assessment and treatment planning. Central to this task is obtaining an understanding of an individual's patterns of substance use and their antecedents (factors that precede a given pattern of substance use) and consequences as the core of treatment planning (e.g., Donovan, 2003). In the behavioral and cognitive behavioral approaches to treatment, this assessment task is referred to as a "functional analysis" (Haynes & O'Brien, 2000). Functional analysis remains central to treatment planning because current interventions, whether they are "pharmacological" or "psychosocial," still depend heavily on an analysis of individual substance use patterns and their determinants. Therefore, formal DSM or ICD diagnostic labels are only a part of treatment planning, often utilized in the earlier phases of the assessment process (Donovan, 2003). In addition, in recent years, there has been a rapid expansion of treatment into "nonspecialty" settings such as primary care clinics or emergency departments of hospitals. These interventions target alcohol and drug use that is labeled "at risk" (for incurring problems) because it often has not yet led to behavior that meets formal substance use disorder diagnostic criteria. In such cases, diagnosis is not relevant to interventions (typically brief), and the intervention focuses on reducing substance use quantity and frequency and the risks that such use incurs for the individual.

SELF-REPORT/INTERVIEW METHODS OF ALCOHOL AND OTHER DRUG CONSUMPTION

With the preceding background information we are ready to review measures of alcohol and other drug consumption that have empirical support. We begin with self-report/interview measures of consumption, which are summarized in Tables 3.1 and 3.2. In selecting information included in Tables 3.1 and 3.2, it should be noted that we drew considerably from the excellent review of Sobell and Sobell (2003). The information in Tables 3.1 and 3.2 has been organized around issues of clinical practicality, including categories describing materials involved in administering the measure, administration time, and training requirements (i.e., type and duration). Also included is essential information about substances being assessed, time frame of substance use, and populations for which the measure is appropriate and accurate.

Measures in Tables 3.1 and 3.2 also are divided into two general categories, namely, "consumption measures" and "screens." Consumption measures are used to assess current consumption and history of consumption and are typically of interest to clinicians and clinical researchers. These measures have a "retrospective" (time in the past) time frame that ranges from "lifetime" (e.g., lifetime drinking history) to "current" (e.g., last 30 days, such as in many quantity–frequency [QF] measures) to concurrent (self-monitoring log). Another critical distinction among these measures is whether they are concerned with measuring consumption averaged across alcohol or other drug use occasions or whether they seek to measure consumption on the event level or for each occasion. A number of empirically supported measures are available for both event-level and measurement across events assessment of both alcohol and other drugs in adults and adolescents. In addition, an "omnibus" (inclusive) measure of substance use and its consequences, the Addiction Severity Index and its adolescent counterpart, the Teen Addiction Severity Index, are included in the tables because these measures are staples of treatment settings in the United States. One of their advantages is that they include an alcohol and other drug consumption (last 30 days) component.

The considerable number of empirically supported measures that have been developed to assess history and current consumption of alcohol and other drugs raises the question of how clinicians select a particular measure. In this regard, there are several considerations. Foremost and fundamental among these are psychometric properties, that is, reliability and accuracy of the measure. Because this text focuses on evidence-based assessment and treatment issues, only measures with evidence of empirical support have been included in the tables and discussion. A second consideration in choosing an appropriate assessment instrument is the purpose or the goal of assessment. For example, what is the content and level of analysis that is needed? Often, both for clinical and for research purposes, an assessment of average patterns over a period of time is adequate to meet assessment goals. However, for

Table 3.1 Alcohol and drug use measures for adults and adolescents

Consumption measure	Reference	Reliability	Validity	Populations	Other languages
Timeline Follow back (TLFB)	Sobell, L. C., Maisto, S. A., Sobell, M. B., & Cooper, A. M. (1979). Reliability of alcohol abusers' self-reports of drinking behavior. *Behavior Research and Therapy, 17,* 157–160.	Test–retest (for alcohol)	Content, criterion, construct (for alcohol)	Adults Adolescents	Belgian Dutch Belgian French French German Japanese Polish Spanish Swedish
Form 90	Tonigan, J. S., Miller, W. R., & Brown, J. M. (1997). The reliability of Form 90: An instrument for assessing alcohol treatment outcome. *Journal of Studies on Alcohol, 58,* 358–364.	Test–retest, internal consistency	Criterion (predictive, concurrent, postdictive), construct	Adults Adolescents	None
Drinking self-monitoring log (DSLM)	Sobell, L. C., & Sobell, M. B. (1973). A self-feedback technique to monitor drinking behavior in alcoholics. *Behavior Research and Therapy, 11,* 237–238.	N/A	Content, construct	Adults Adolescents	None
Lifetime drinking history (LDH)	Skinner, H. A., & Sheu, W. J. (1982). Reliability of alcohol use indices: The Lifetime Drinking History and the MAST. *Journal of Studies on Alcohol, 43,* 1157–1170.	Test–retest	Content, construct	Adults Adolescents	None
QF measures	Room, R. (2000). Measuring drinking patterns: The experience of the last half century. *Journal of Substance Abuse, 12,* 23–31.	Test–retest	Content, criterion (predictive, concurrent), construct	Adults Adolescents	Spanish

Addiction Severity Index (ASI)	McLellan, A. T., Kushner, H., & Metzger, D. (1992). The fifth edition of the Addiction Severity Index. *Journal of Substance Abuse Treatment, 9,* 199–213.	Test–retest, split half, internal consistency	Criterion (predictive, concurrent, postdictive), construct	Adults	None
Teen Addiction Severity Index (T-ASI)	Kaminer, Y., Bukstein, O. G., & Tarter, R. E. (1991). The Teen Addiction Severity Index: Rationale and reliability. *The International Journal of the Addictions, 26,* 219–226.	Test–retest, interrater	Content, construct	Adolescents	Spanish
Customary Drinking and Drug Use Record (CDDR)	Brown et al. (1998). Psychometric evaluation of the Customary Drinking and Drug Use Record (CDDR): A measure of adolescent alcohol and drug involvement. *Journal of Studies on Alcohol, 59,* 427–438.	Test–retest, split half, internal consistency, interrater	Criterion (predictive, concurrent, postdictive), construct, convergent, discriminant	Adolescents	None
Screens	**Reference**	**Reliability**	**Validity**	**Populations**	**Other Languages**
Alcohol Use Disorder Identification Test (AUDIT)	Saunders, J. B., Aasland, O. G., Babor, T. F., de la Fuente, J. R., & Grant, M. (1993). Development of the Alcohol Use Disorders Screening Test (AUDIT): WHO collaborative project on early detection of persons with harmful alcohol consumption. II. *Addiction, 88,* 791–804.	Test–retest, internal consistency	Criterion (predictive, concurrent, postdictive), construct	Adults	Catalonian French Japanese Norwegian Romanian Spanish Slavic Swahili
Brief Alcohol Screening Instrument for Medical Care (BASIC)	Bischof et al. (2007). Development and evaluation of a screening instrument for alcohol-use disorders and at-risk drinking: The Brief Alcohol Screening Instrument for Medical Care (BASIC). *Journal of Studies on Alcohol and Drugs, 68,* 607–614.	Internal consistency	High sensitivity and specificity	Adults	None

Continued

Table 3.1 (Continued)

Consumption measure	References	Reliability	Validity	Populations	Other languages
Alcohol Use Disorder Identification Test–Consumption questions (AUDIT-C)	Bush, K., Kivlavan, D. R., McConell, M. B., Fihn, S. D., & Bradley, K. A. (1998). The AUDIT alcohol consumption questions (AUDIT-C): An effective brief screening test for problem drinking. *Archives of Internal Medicine, 158,* 1789–1795.	Test–retest, responsiveness to change	Criterion, discriminant	Adults	Catalonian French Japanese Norwegian Romanian Spanish Slavic Swahili
The Alcohol, Smoking and Substance Involvement Screening Test (ASSIST)	World Health Organization ASSIST Working Group. (2002). The Alcohol, Smoking and Substance Involvement Screening Test (ASSIST): Development, reliability and feasibility. *Addiction, 97*, 1183–1194.	Test–retest	Across gender and culture (7 countries)	Adults	Reliability studies done in the following countries: Australia, Brazil, India, Ireland, Israel, United Kingdom, Zimbabwe, Palestinian Territories, Puerto Rico

Cannabis Use Disorder Identification Test (CUDIT)	Adamson, S. J., & Sellman, J. D. (2003). A prototype screening instrument for cannabis use disorder: The Cannabis Use Disorders Identification Test (CUDIT) in an alcohol-dependent clinical sample. *Drug and Alcohol Review, 22,* 309–315.	Internal consistency	Predictive, sensitivity	Adults	None
Current Opioid Misuse Measure (COMM)	Butler et al. (2007). Development and validation of the current opioid misuse measure. *Pain, 130,* 144–156.	Test–retest, internal consistency	Concurrent	Adults	None
Adolescent Alcohol Involvement Scale (AAIS)	Mayer, J., & Filstead, W. J. (1979). The Adolescent Alcohol Involvement Scale: An instrument for measuring adolescents' use and misuse of alcohol. *Journal of Studies on Alcohol, 40,* 291–300.	Test-retest, Internal consistency	Criterion (predictive, concurrent, postdictive)	Adolescents	None
Adolescent Drug Involvement Scale (ADIS)	Moberg, D. P., & Hahn, L. (1991). The adolescent drug involvement scale. *Journal of Adolescent Chemical Dependency, 2,* 75–88.	Internal consistency	Concurrent	Adolescents	None
Problem Oriented Screening Instrument for Teenagers (POSIT)	Knight, J. R., Goodman, E., Pulerwitz, T., & DuRant, R. H. (2001). Reliability of the Problem Oriented Screening Instrument for Teenagers (POSIT) in adolescent medical practice. *Journal of Adolescent Health, 29,* 125–30.	Test–retest, Internal consistency	Content, criterion (predictive, concurrent)	Adolescents	Spanish

Table 3.2 Summary of alcohol and drug use measures for adults and adolescents

Consumption measures	Target substance(s)	Time frame	Administration					
			Format	Materials needed	Data presentation	Training required?	Time to administer	Scoring
Timeline Followback (TLFB)	Alcohol, drugs	30–360 days prior to assessment	Paper–pencil Interview Computer	–Calendar covering time frame of interest. Includes important dates to help anchor drinking –Standard drink cards Materials and instructions available online: www.nova.edu/~gsc	Amount consumed is collected for each day in the time frame of interest, resulting in event-level use data.	Yes, for interview. Training video available.	Varies for different time frames (about 30 minutes for 12 months)	5 minutes to score, either by hand or with a computer program. Variables of interest can be computed (e.g., percentage of abstinent days, number of heavy drinking days).
Form 90	Alcohol, drugs	90 days prior to assessment	Structured interview	–Calendar covering time frame of interest. Includes important dates to help anchor drinking –Standard drink cards –Form 90 grid (form; intake and follow-up versions available) –Drug cards Forms available online: casaaunm.edu/inst.html	Amount consumed is collected for each day in the time frame of interest, resulting in event-level use data. In addition, data are collected on medical/psych treatments, medications, criminal activity, work, school involvement, grids that detail patterns of use.	Yes	40–60 minutes	Scoring is done by computer. There are no norms available for this measure. Variables of interest can be computed (e.g., percentage of abstinent days, number of heavy drinking days).
Drinking Self-monitoring Log (DSLM)	Alcohol	Various, concurrent use	Individual keeps track of drinks consumed on a daily basis	–A log for recording consumption, can be anything from a slip of paper, to pocket-sized cards, to booklets –Standard drink conversion	Event-level use data obtained for a given time frame. Recorded information in logs can include number of drinks consumed in one day, type of beverage, and time use began.	N/A	N/A	Time to score depends on length of the time frame and the number of recorded variables.

Lifetime Drinking History (LDH)	Alcohol	Lifetime, beginning with the first year of regular drinking	Structured interview	–Measure (answer sheet)	Patterns of alcohol use are obtained: typical and maximum amount consumed during periods of person's life.	Yes	20–30 minutes	5–10 minutes to score. Scoring instructions are available.
QF measures	Alcohol	Various. 30 days to lifetime QF measures available	Paper–pencil	–Measure	Average use pattern (quantity and frequency), usually for each beverage type (beer, wine, spirits).	Yes, minimal	4–60 min, depending on QF measure	5 min to score by hand. Multiply average amount of drinks/drinking day (Q) and average number of days used (F). For some QF measures, a category is assigned. Scoring instructions are available.
Addiction Severity Index (ASI)	Alcohol, drugs	Lifetime, past 30 days	Paper–pencil Interview Computer	–Measure	7 domains (200 items): Medical status, legal status, employment, drug/alcohol use, family and social relationships, psychiatric status. In addition, assessors provide severity ratings.	Yes	50–60 min	5 minutes to compute assessors' severity ratings by hand. A computer program is available to compute composite scores for each domain. These composite scores range from 0 to 1, where 1 indicates very severe.
Teen Addiction Severity Index (T-ASI)	Alcohol, drugs	Lifetime, past month	Semi-structured Interview	–Measure	7 domains (154 items): chemical use, school status, employment, family relationships, peer relationships, legal status, psychiatric status. In addition, assessors provide comments and confidence ratings.	Yes	20–45 min	5 min to score by hand, 1 min on computer. Problem severity ratings are obtained for each of the 7 domains.

Continued

Table 3.2 (Continued)

Consumption measures	Target sustance(s)	Time frame	Administration					
			Format	Materials needed	Data presentation	Training required?	Scoring	
Customary Drinking and Drug Use Record (CDDR)	Alcohol, cannabis,cocaine, amphetamines, barbiturates, hallucinogens, inhalants, opiates, others	Lifetime and past 3 months	Structured interview	–Measure –Scoring key	Lifetime and past 3 months: frequency of use for 3 alcohol types and drug types. Age of first use and regular use. Quantity of alcohol and drug use in past 3 months. Plus, 12 items on psychological and behavioral dependence, withdrawal symptoms, 5 negative consequences of alcohol use and 3 most frequently used drugs in the past 3 months.	Yes	20–30 min	10 minutes to score. 4 domains: Level of involvement, withdrawal characteristics, psych/behavioral dependence symptoms, negative consequences. A scoring key is available.

Screens	Target Substance(s)	Time frame	Administration					
			Format	Materials Needed	Data Presentation	Training Required?	Time to Administer	Scoring
Alcohol Use Disorder Identification Test (AUDIT)	Alcohol	Past year	Paper–pencil Interview Computer	–Measure	10 items: 3 items—amount, frequency, and heavy episodic drinking. 3 items—alcohol dependence. 4 items—problems related to alcohol use. Used to identify those with alcohol use disorders.	Yes, for interview. Training video available	2 min	1 minute to score by hand. Each item has a certain number of points assigned to it. The total score is computed (possible = 40), cut-off score = 8. Norms are available for heavy drinkers and alcoholics. An easy-to-use brochure is available to help with scoring.

Brief Alcohol Screening Instrument for Medical Care (BASIC)	Alcohol	Past year	Paper–pencil	–Measure	6 items: first 3 items—amount, frequency, and heavy episodic drinking (same as AUDIT items 1–3). Last 3 items—emotional or interpersonal issues, used to identify at-risk drinkers and those with alcohol use disorders.	No	Less than 2 min	1 min to score by hand. Each item has a certain number of points assigned to it. The total score is computed, cutoff score = 2.
AUDIT-C	Alcohol	Past year	Paper–pencil Interview Computer	–Measure	3 items: same as the first 3 items on the AUDIT (amount, frequency, and heavy episodic drinking). Used to identify hazardous drinkers.	Yes, for interview. Training video available	1 min	Less than 1 min to score by hand. The total score is computed (possible = 12), cut-off score for men = 4, for women = 3.
The Alcohol, Smoking and Substance Involvement Screening Test (ASSIST)	Tobacco, alcohol, cannabis, cocaine, amphetamine-type stimulants, sedatives, hallucinogens, inhalants, opioids, others	Lifetime and past 3 months	Clinician-administered interview	–Measure –Response card for patients (specific drug for different countries) –The ASSIST Feedback Report Card (feedback for patients)	8 items: lifetime use of substances, frequency of use, dependence, and related problems in prior 3 months (0, never; 1, once or twice; 2, monthly; 3, weekly; 4, daily or almost daily); presence of dependence, related problems, and injection risk (0, never; 1, yes, but not in last 3 months; 2, yes, in last 3 months).	Yes, by a trained professional	Less than 5 min	Specific substance involvement: sum of items 2–7 within each drug class. Total substance involvement: Sum of all 8 items for all drugs. Cutoffs for Specific Substance Involvement score: Alcohol: 0–10, low risk; 11–26, moderate; 27+, high risk. All other substances: 0–3, low risk; 4–26, moderate risk; 27+, high risk.

Continued

Table 3.2 (Continued)

Screens	Target sustance(s)	Time frame	Administration					
			Format	Materials needed	Data presentation	Training required?	Scoring	
Cannabis Use Disorder Identification Test (CUDIT)	Cannabis	Past 6 months, current	Paper–pencil	–Measure	10 items: first 2 items—current use. Last 8 items—use in past 6 months. Each item scored using a 5-point Likert-type scale. Used to identify those with cannabis abuse or dependence.	No	2 min	1 min to score by hand. The total score is computed (possible = 40), cutoff score = 8.
Current Opioid Misuse Measure (COMM)	Prescription drugs (opioids)	Past 30 days	Paper–pencil	–Measure	17 items: frequency of their thoughts and behaviors related to their use of opiate medication. Each item scored using a 4-point Likert-type scale (0, never; 4, very often). Used to identify patients who might be misusing their medication.	No	Less than 10 min	Less than 5 min by hand. The total score is computed, cutoff score = 9. False positives are likely due to this low cutoff score.
Adolescent Drug Involvement Scale (ADIS)	Drugs	Current	Paper–pencil	–Measure	13 items: measures drug use on a continuum from no use to severe dependence. Used to identify heavy users from those less involved in drug use.	No	4–5 min	2–3 min to score. Each item has a certain number weight assigned to it. Weights from items 1 to 12 are summed for total score. Item 13 provides an index of multiple drug use.

Adolescent Alcohol Involvement Scale (AAIS)	Alcohol	Lifetime, current	Paper–pencil	–Measure		14 items: psychosocial and quantitative aspects of alcohol use across psychological functioning, social relations, and family living. Identifies adolescents with drinking problems.	No	5 min	10 min to score by hand. Norms are available for this measure.
Problem Oriented Screening Instrument for Teenagers (POSIT)	Alcohol, Drugs	Current	Paper–pencil	–Measure		139 yes/no items: Substance use, physical and mental health, family and peer relations, social skills, educational status, vocational skills, leisure, and aggressive behavior. Used to identify problem areas.	No	20–30 minutes	2–5 minutes to score using scoring templates, 2 seconds using computer. The total score is computed for each problem area. Cut-off scores indicate low, medium, and high risk.

other assessment contexts, it is preferable to obtain event-level data that typically take more time to collect but provide information that is not provided by assessments that measure averaged consumption over time. Event-level data are invaluable when specific pattern data are desired or, for the sake of treatment planning, when it is necessary to obtain information on the antecedents and consequences of particular consumption occasions (e.g., when conducting a functional analysis). A major example of an event-level measure is Timeline Followback (refer to Table 3.1). This measure has substantial empirical support for the assessment of alcohol or other drug use on an event level for various periods of time. Additional considerations in selecting a consumption measure include the financial resources available, staff assessment skills and training needs, and time available for assessment. We next present two hypothetical case examples that warrant collection of QF-type and event-level data, respectively.

Mr. X is a 48-year-old married white male who presented at a community outpatient substance abuse treatment program because of mounting financial, employment, and marital problems that were linked directly or indirectly to his use of alcohol and marijuana. At the program's general initial intake interview, Mr. X reported that he had had a problem with substance use for "at least" 15 years and had had two previous substance abuse treatment experiences, both of which included attendance at Alcoholics Anonymous meetings. Mr. X said that in the last 6 months he had been drinking just about every day, at least four to five drinks each time, and that he smokes marijuana cigarettes as well on about a third of those days. Mr. X reported that he believed that the only approach in treatment that could work for him was one that stressed complete abstinence from alcohol and other drugs, which was the goal that he wanted to pursue in this treatment.

In the case of Mr. X, additional formal assessment of alcohol and marijuana use beyond the use of an established QF measure, as well as possible use of biomarker data (described later), would seem unnecessary. In this regard, it is clear that Mr. X has recently been using substances at a level beyond what is agreed to be "at risk" levels, and that indeed his consumption of substances is causing him considerable life problems. Moreover, Mr. X desires a treatment outcome goal of abstinence from alcohol and other drugs, so that for purposes of evaluation, the basic question initially is whether there is any use or not. If the QF measure reveals that, at some point, there is use, then more precise data collection may be desirable, but initially it would seem that a good QF measure with the use of biomarker data would satisfy the need to establish a reliable and accurate consumption baseline and, with their repeated administration over the course of treatment and possibly afterward, a sensitive way to monitor progress on Mr. X's consumption goals. In contrast, the next scenario describes a case in which event-level data would be valuable for treatment planning and monitoring.

Ms. Y is a 24-year-old single African American female who self-presented at an outpatient substance abuse treatment program because several friends had commented recently on how much she drinks sometimes, especially on weekends. Ms. Y was concerned that they were seeing something that she was not and that maybe she was damaging her health. At the initial intake interview, Ms. Y reported using alcohol but no other drugs three to four times a week in the last 6 months, usually one to two drinks at a time on weekdays, but often six drinks or more per occasion during weekends and social events. Ms. Y agreed that this might represent a heavy drinking pattern, but also that she liked to drink on social occasions and did not want to give up drinking entirely. Ms. Y said that she'd heard about programs that teach people to "control" their drinking and was hoping that this program could help her moderate her drinking to levels that were not a threat to her health.

The use of event-level measurement of Ms. Y's drinking, such as timeline follow back, and self-monitoring data seem indicated in treatment planning and monitoring. Assuming that health considerations and other factors support it, if a moderation goal is to be pursued, it is essential to have as precise a picture as possible of the individual's pattern of alcohol use, which event-level data allow. In addition, those data may be combined with information about the situation and other factors (e.g., emotions) that tend to precede specific levels of consumption to form the bases of a drinking moderation intervention. In essence, these are the baseline functional analysis data needed for treatment planning and they need to be collected as well during the course of treatment to monitor progress and to inform possible adjustments in the intervention. It is clear that a QF measure of alcohol consumption could not meet these needs.

Screening measures

The second group of assessment tools included in Tables 3.1 and 3.2 are screening measures. These measures differ in major ways from consumption measures because they take very little time to administer and have, as their primary purpose, case identification. Case identification is often needed in "nonspecialty" settings (e.g., mental health clinics, primary care, hospital emergency departments) in which individuals present for care for reasons other than substance use. In such contexts, screening for alcohol or other drug use and its risk level are essential, as substance use is often associated with certain psychiatric (e.g., depression, social anxiety) and medical (e.g., hypertension, gastrointestinal disorders) conditions.

Screening measures included in Tables 3.1 and 3.2 require clinicians and researchers to collect information from respondents either by self-report (paper and pencil or computer based) or by personal interview. In addition, these screening measures by no means exhaust the list of empirically supported screening measures that are available, but are the most frequently used assessment tools. Third, these instruments are also designed to measure substance use-related problems or consequences ("symptoms" of abuse) or symptoms of substance dependence, as defined by DSM or ICD criteria. Fourth, because they are quick and easy to administer and score, minimal time and resources are needed for their application in clinical settings. Finally, empirically supported screening measures are available for use with both adolescents and adults. We next present a hypothetical case in which a standardized self-report screen was used to identify "at risk" (for alcohol use disorder) drinking.

Mr. Z is a 58-year-old divorced white male who presented at a primary care clinic at a U.S. Department of Veterans Affairs Medical Center. Mr. Z initially went to the clinic because of general fatigue and complaints of stomach distress. As part of the initial medical assessment, laboratory tests revealed high cholesterol, and Mr. Z also was identified as having moderately severe hypertension. Mr. Z's primary care provider asked Mr. Z if he drank alcohol because of its possible connection to both the hypertension and the gastric distress. Because Mr. Z reported that he currently does consume alcohol "a couple" of days a week, the primary care provider administered Mr. Z the AUDIT, which yields a score to formally determine if Mr. Z was "at risk" for alcohol use disorder and, if so, to conduct further assessment of such use and its possible connection to Mr. Z's physical complaints and problems.

Summary

Many excellent, empirically supported instruments have been developed to measure history of and current alcohol and other drug use. The characteristics of these instruments are varied enough to provide clinicians and researchers with reliable tools to meet any assessment need. This advanced level of development of self-report/interview methods of measuring alcohol and other drug consumption is a product of past and current emphasis on the use of empirically supported self-report or interview methods of data collection in both clinical and research contexts.

BIOMARKER MEASURES OF ALCOHOL AND ILLICIT DRUG CONSUMPTION

Biomarker measures of alcohol and other drug consumption include laboratory assays of blood and urine (and, sometimes, hair) samples to measure current or past consumption. Measuring substance use by biomarkers is not as well developed as the self-report/interview area, but the trend toward using biomarkers to corroborate self-reports is accelerating.

This section begins with biomarkers of the consumption of illicit (in the United States) drug use, although biomarkers are available for the detection of nicotine and alcohol consumption as well. Biomarkers relevant to alcohol use follow the discussion of illicit drug use detection. This overview reflects information presented in two excellent articles on the topic by Harrison, Martin, Enev, and Harrington (2007) and by Wolff and colleagues (1999).

Drug consumption may be estimated by the presence of a target drug or its metabolites in bodily fluid or tissue. Which specific biomarker selected for use depends on pharmacokinetics (its absorption into the blood, distribution through the body, and its metabolism and excretion) of a drug as well as the ease of laboratory analysis of the sample (Wolff et al., 1999). Wolff et al.'s summary of these factors includes (1) biological sample collection procedures and handling by the laboratory, (2) testing procedures that the laboratory uses and the screening and confirmation tests applied, (3) the determination of cut points, or the criterion that is used to define a drug as "present" (both the United States and the United Kingdom have national standards published for this purpose), and (4) detection times for different drugs in the biological medium sampled. There is considerable variability by drug on this final factor; for example, the times for detection of psychoactive drugs in urine range from 6–8 hours for cocaine, to 12 hours for nicotine, to 2–3 days for a metabolite of cocaine, and up to 36 days for chronic, heavy use of marijuana.

Urine is the biological fluid that is used most commonly for drug testing, as the sample collection procedure is minimally invasive and the sample preparation for laboratory analysis is relatively straightforward. In addition, the use of urinalysis for drug screening has a long history (beginning in the 1960s) and has been used on a large scale for many years. As a result, laboratory procedures for this method are more well developed than those using other biological samples. Other biological fluids or tissues used commonly include blood, saliva, and hair, and there is increasing research on the use of sweat and breath. Each method has its own advantages and disadvantages for testing specific drugs, and each provides somewhat different information (Harrison et al., 2007). In this regard, blood samples are best for the detection of acute use and quantification of use, relative to amounts known to be toxic or fatal, and hair analysis is best suited to detection of use in the more distant past. This suggests that tests using different samples, for example, urine and blood, may be the best way to achieve the overall goals of a particular drug testing effort.

Clinical and research use of drug biomarkers

A major question for this chapter is what biomarkers offer clinicians and clinical researchers in their need to estimate drug consumption. Biomarkers can be used to provide a measure (estimate) of whether a drug has been used during a particular time period, but cannot quantify the details of consumption (e.g., amount of drug used, frequency of use, or pattern of use) in the way that self-report or interview measures do. However, there are a number of situations in which detection of use is sufficient for assessment purposes, such as monitoring the effects of an abstinence-oriented intervention program or in the use of drug testing for "clean urines" in contingency contracting programs for drug abstinence. However, drug biomarkers do not provide diagnostic data and must be used in conjunction with self-report/interview or behavioral methods of data gathering for that purpose.

Biomarkers also can be valuable in contexts in which a more quantifiable estimate of drug consumption is desired. For example, biomarkers provide a complement to self-report/interview methods of obtaining consumption data in situations in which there may be an incentive for the client/patient, or the research participant, to underreport his or her consumption. In such contexts, which occur often in the alcohol and drug treatment field, biomarkers and self-report methods may be viewed from a methodological perspective as two different ways to estimate the same variable (actual consumption over a specified time), a point elaborated upon later in this chapter. This may translate into a clinical benefit: when biomarkers suggest that drug use has occurred but the patient or client reports no use. In that situation, the individual may be presented with the conflicting data. Presentation of the biomarker results could provide the basis of discussion and of obtaining a more accurate and clinically useful self-report of consumption for that occasion as well as in future assessments. In addition, when confronted with objective biomarker data, patients/clients often admit to substance use that they had denied previously. It is important to emphasize that biomarkers do not provide the final answer to the question of whether an individual has consumed a given drug during some time period. Because they are based on apparently objective, biological procedures, not subject to the frailty of self-report (i.e., intentional or unintentional [due to memory failings] inaccurate recall), biomarkers often are ascribed the status of the "goal standard" in a given assessment context. However, although this section has been necessarily brief, it is apparent from its contents that a number of factors (i.e., the chemical composition of the drug in question, its pharmacokinetics, the biological sample used, and the laboratory procedures followed in handling and analyzing a sample) may affect the validity or accuracy of a drug test. It is important that clinicians recognize these factors and how they may affect the interpretation of biomarker findings, as well as the need to follow up initial positive drug tests with a confirmatory test. Thus, drug biomarkers are one method of measurement with known strengths and weaknesses and are best used and interpreted in conjunction with self-reports and overall clinical judgment.

Biomarkers of heavy alcohol consumption

Much of the consideration regarding analysis and interpretation regarding biomarkers of illicit drug consumption applies equally well to biomarkers of alcohol consumption. Methods used to test for recent alcohol consumption by blood or breath analysis have been available for decades and are highly accurate. However, their clinical application is restricted (e.g., breath testing patients every time they present for outpatient assessment or treatment sessions) because a dose of alcohol and its metabolites clear the body very rapidly so that the assessment is essentially limited to episodes of acute intoxication. Although there is a place for using breath analysis because it is noninvasive, inexpensive, and highly accurate and precise, research and clinical activity in the last 20 years have begun to focus on biomarkers of chronic, heavy alcohol consumption.

In a comprehensive review, Allen, Sillanaukee, Strid, and Litten (2003) describe five alcohol biomarkers that have the most established clinical and research utility. These include γ-glutamyl-transferase (GGT), carbohydrate-deficient transferring (CDT), aspartate aminotransferase (AST), alanine aminotransferase (ALT), and mean corpuscular volume (MCV). As with biomarkers for illicit drug use, alcohol biomarkers have different characteristics from one another, with each providing somewhat different information about heavy alcohol consumption. In addition, each biomarker has different strengths and weaknesses in terms of stability and accuracy of results. GGT is the best known and most commonly used alcohol biomarker, although it is not without shortcomings. Elevations in this blood protein (e.g., $\geq$54 units/liter) are caused by consuming four or more drinks daily for 4 to 8 weeks. However, high levels of GGT can also be caused by nonalcoholic liver disease, biliary disease, obesity, and some medications, increasing the possibility of obtaining false-positive results. CDT, or %CDT, is a measure of the percentage of carbohydrate-lacking transferrin, a glycoprotein that transports iron, in the body. Consuming more than five standard drinks (>60 g) of alcohol per day for at least 2 weeks elevates CDT. False positives are less common because only end liver disease, biliary cirrhosis, and a rare genetic variability also increase CDT levels. Both GGT and CDT are highly sensitive, although CDT has superior specificity, making it a good indicator of relapse. Elevations in AST and ALT, enzymes that help metabolize amino acids, are caused by chronic alcohol use, although increased levels are often more indicative of liver disease. MCV, the volume of red blood cells in the body, increases with heavy chronic drinking. However, MCV has low sensitivity because levels remain elevated even after several months of abstinence. Specificity is also low because other conditions also increase MCV. Current research is focusing on developing and testing new biomarker sources (sweat is one notable case) and their applications and on using biomarkers in combination with self-report data in order to arrive at the most accurate clinical picture. Multiple estimates of alcohol consumption are needed, as alcohol biomarkers vary in their psychometric properties based on characteristics of the individual being tested (e.g., age, sex, ethnicity, health status). Allen and colleagues (2003) also note that alcohol biomarkers are better at discriminating between extreme groups (as defined by chronic patterns of alcohol consumption) rather than discriminating among individuals with heterogeneous drinking patterns.

Clinical use of biomarkers of heavy alcohol consumption

Alcohol biomarkers have been used primarily to screen for alcohol problems in nonspecialty treatment settings, such as primary care or hospital emergency rooms. There are, of course, self-report screens that are useful in these settings (as reviewed earlier), but biomarkers can also play an important role in instances in which self-reports are suspect or a patient is unable to provide self-reports (e.g., an unconscious patient in a trauma center). Overall, alcohol biomarkers should be viewed as one method of measuring alcohol consumption that has specific strengths and weaknesses and are best used in conjunction with other methods of measuring long-term alcohol consumption that have their own imperfections and strengths.

Reliability and accuracy of self-reports of alcohol and other drug use

It remains the case that clinicians and clinical researchers rely most heavily on self-reports to obtain information on alcohol and substance use. That is, individuals are asked to recall various aspects (such as quantity and frequency) of their use of alcohol and other drugs over varying periods of time in the past (lifetime, the last year, the last month, yesterday, hours ago), and clinicians and researchers use the information obtained under the assumption that it is accurate. Despite advances in the creation and evaluation of biomarkers in the last several decades, research and clinical practice in substance use disorders still depend on self-reports for assessment and/or treatment evaluation. Problems with the frailty of memory aside, is it reasonable to use retrospective self-reports about substance use with clinical populations? In past years, it was assumed by some clinicians that individuals with substance use disorders are unreliable in their self-reports because they are in denial about their central problem. However, beginning in the 1970s, a series of studies were conducted on the issue of validity of these self-reports.

Several reviews of studies on the reliability and accuracy of retrospective self-reports of alcohol and other drug use by individuals with substance use disorders have been published (Maisto, McKay, & Connors, 1990; O'Farrell & Maisto, 1987). This research is useful in that it identifies the conditions under which reliable and accurate self-reports are most likely to be obtained. That is, empirical investigations have changed the question from whether self-reports about substance use are reliable and accurate to the more heuristically useful question of under what conditions in a clinical setting are reliable and accurate self-reports most likely to occur. The major conditions that increase accuracy are as follow.

- When the patient or research participant is alcohol or drug free
- When the individual is stable and not showing major psychiatric or substance-related symptoms (e.g., acute withdrawal)
- When the individual is assessed with structured or standardized methods
- When the individual is aware that there is the possibility that the assessor will attempt to corroborate his/her self-report by the use of biomarkers or reports by significant others
- When the individual has a good rapport with the assessor
- When the individual is in compliance with other aspects of treatment
- When the individual is not motivated or does not have an incentive to distort

- When the individual is assured of and trusts that his/her self-report will remain confidential within boundaries specified at the outset of the assessment
- When the individual does not perceive that the assessor is judging him/her based on the behavior that is reported

Therefore, as with any attempt to measure behavior, the measurement of alcohol and other drug consumption in clinical settings should create the context that is needed to obtain the best (most accurate) data possible at a given time in a given context.

Convergent validity

When measuring past alcohol or other drug use, clinicians and researchers have been challenged by the basic problem that technology has not yet produced a "gold standard," that is, a referent measure that provides an exact standard of accuracy for the comparison of a measure of past substance consumption. In this context, it is necessary to rely on the "convergence" or agreement of different modes (self-report, biomarker, behavioral) of measuring the same variable or construct. This approach to assessment is known as establishing the "convergent validity" of data (e.g., Sobell & Sobell, 2003). In the case of self-reports of alcohol and other drug consumption data, applying the concept of convergent validity would mean obtaining the individual's self-report of consumption as well as at least one other indicator, such as a biomarker if applicable, or a report about the respondent's drinking from a significant individual in the respondent's life, such as a spouse or close friend (often called a "collateral"). To the degree that the different methods of measurement of the respondent's drinking agree or converge, there is increased confidence in the accuracy of the respondent's self-reports. Moreover, if there is considerable disagreement among the methods of measuring consumption, then it often is possible to return to the source(s) of measurement in an effort to resolve the discrepancy and obtain as accurate a picture as possible. For example, if the respondent and his/her spouse disagree considerably in their reports, the clinician may discuss the discrepancy with both parties in an effort to obtain a resolution. In this regard, it may be that the discrepancy was due to either person's memory lapse or to not having observed the drinking event(s) in question directly.

GENERAL SUMMARY AND CONCLUSIONS

This chapter provided an overview of empirically supported measures of alcohol and other drug consumption that can be applied in clinical and clinical research contexts. It is evident that a number of interview/

self-report measures are available for use with adolescents or adults that vary sufficiently in content and resources needed for their application to meet virtually all clinical and clinical research needs. The field is rapidly advancing in the technology of biomarkers, each providing different types of information. For both self-report/interview and biomarker measures, there is no one gold standard of perfect accuracy, so the strategy most likely to yield the most accurate representation of an individual's substance use is one utilizing a convergent validity approach.

REFERENCES

Adamson, S. J., & Sellman, J. D. (2003). A prototype screening instrument for cannabis use disorder: The Cannabis Use Disorders Identification Test (CUDIT) in an alcohol-dependent clinical sample. *Drug and Alcohol Review, 22*, 309–315.

Allen, J. P., Sillanaukee, P., Strid, N., & Litten, R. Z. (2003). Biomarkers of heavy drinking. In J. P. Allen & V. B. Wilson (Eds.), *Assessing alcohol problems: A guide for clinicians and researchers* (2nd ed., pp. 37–53). Bethesda, MD: National Institutes of Health.

American Psychiatric Association. (2000). *Diagnostic and statistical manual of mental disorders* (4th ed., text rev.). Washington, DC: Author.

Bischof, G., Reinhardt, S., Grothues, J., Meyer, C., John, U., & Rumpf, H. J. (2007). Development and evaluation of a screening instrument for alcohol-use disorders and at-risk drinking: The Brief Alcohol Screening Instrument for Medical Care (BASIC). *Journal of Studies on Alcohol and Drugs, 68*, 607–614.

Brown, S. A., Myers, M. G., Lippke, L., Tapert, S. F., Stewart, D. G., & Vik, P. W. (1998). Psychometric evaluation of the Customary Drinking and Drug Use Record (CDDR): A measure of adolescent alcohol and drug involvement. *Journal of Studies on Alcohol, 59*, 427–438.

Bush, K., Kivlavan, D. R., McConell, M. B., Fihn, S. D., & Bradley, K. A. (1998). The AUDIT alcohol consumption questions (AUDIT-C): An effective brief screening test for problem drinking. *Archives of Internal Medicine, 158*, 1789–1795.

Butler, S. F., Budman, S. H., Fernandez, K. C., Houle, B., Benoit, C., Katz, N., et al. (2007). Development and validation of the current opioid misuse measure. *Pain, 130*, 144–156.

Donovan, D. M. (2003). Assessment to aid in the treatment planning process. In J. P. Allen & V. B. Wilson (Eds.), *Assessing alcohol problems: A guide for clinicians and researchers* (2nd ed., pp. 125–188). Bethesda, MD: National Institutes of Health.

Donovan, D. M. (2005). Assessment of addictive behaviors for relapse prevention. In D. M. Donovan & G. A. Marlatt (Eds.), *Assessment of addictive behaviors* (2nd ed., pp. 1–48). New York, NY: Guilford Press.

Engel, G. L. (1977). The need for a new medical model: A challenge for biomedicine. *Science, 196*, 129–136.

Engel, G. L. (1980). The clinical application of the biosychosocial model. *American Journal of Psychiatry, 137*, 535–544.

Harrison, L. D., Martin, S. S., Enev, T., & Harrington, D. (2007). *Comparing drug testing and self-report of drug use among youths and young adults in the general population* (DHHS Publication No. SMA 07-4249, Methodology Series M-7). Rockville, MD: Substance Abuse and Mental Health Services Administration, Office of Applied Studies.

Haynes, S. N., & O'Brien, W. H. (2000). *Principles and practices of behavioral assessment*. Dordrecht, The Netherlands: Kluwer Academic Publishers.

Kaminer, Y., Bukstein, O. G., & Tarter, R. E. (1991). The Teen Addiction Severity Index: Rationale and reliability. *The International Journal of the Addictions, 26*, 219–226.

Knight, J. R., Goodman, E., Pulerwitz, T., & DuRant, R. H. (2001). Reliability of the Problem Oriented Screening Instrument for Teenagers (POSIT) in adolescent medical practice. *Journal of Adolescent Health, 29*, 125–130.

Maisto, S. A., McKay, J. R., & Connors, G. J. (1990). Self-report issues in substance abuse: State of the art and future directions. *Behavioral Assessment, 12*, 117–134.

Mayer, J., & Filstead, W. J. (1979). The Adolescent Alcohol Involvement Scale: An instrument for measuring adolescents' use and misuse of alcohol. *Journal of Studies on Alcohol, 40*, 291–300.

McLellan, A. T., Kushner, H., & Metzger, D. (1992). The fifth edition of the Addiction Severity Index. *Journal of Substance Abuse Treatment, 9*, 199–213.

Moberg, D. P., & Hahn, L. (1991). The adolescent drug involvement scale. *Journal of Adolescent Chemical Dependency, 2*, 75–88.

O'Farrell, T. J., & Maisto, S. A. (1987). The utility of self-report and biological measures of alcohol consumption in alcoholism treatment outcome studies. *Advances in Behaviour Research & Therapy, 9*, 91–125.

Room, R. (2000). Measuring drinking patterns: The experience of the last half century. *Journal of Substance Abuse, 12*, 23–31.

Saunders, J. B., Aasland, O. G., Babor, T. F., de la Fuente, J. R., & Grant, M. (1993). Development of the Alcohol Use Disorders Screening Test (AUDIT). WHO collaborative project on early detection of persons with harmful alcohol consumption: II. *Addiction, 88*, 791–804.

Skinner, H. A., & Sheu, W. J. (1982). Reliability of alcohol use indices: The Lifetime Drinking History and the MAST. *Journal of Studies on Alcohol, 43*, 1157–1170.

Sobell, L. C., Maisto, S. A., Sobell, M. B., & Cooper, A. M. (1979). Reliability of alcohol abusers' self-reports of drinking behavior. *Behavior Research and Therapy, 17*, 157–160.

Sobell, L. C., & Sobell, M. B. (1973). A self-feedback technique to monitor drinking behavior in alcoholics. *Behavior Research and Therapy, 11*, 237–238.

Sobell, L. C., & Sobell, M. B. (2003). Alcohol consumption measures. In J. P. Allen & V. B. Wilson (Eds.), *Assessing alcohol problems: A guide for clinicians and researchers* (2nd ed., pp. 75–99). Bethesda, MD: National Institutes of Health.

Tonigan, J. S., Miller, W. R., & Brown, J. M. (1997). The reliability of Form 90: An instrument for assessing alcohol treatment outcome. *Journal of Studies on Alcohol, 58*, 358–364.

Wolff, K., Farrell, M., Marsden, J., Monteiro, M. G., Ali, R., Welch, S., & Strang, J. (1999). A review of biological indicators of illicit drug use, practical considerations, and clinical usefulness. *Addiction, 94*, 1279–1298.

World Health Organization. (1992). *International statistical classification of diseases and related health problems, tenth revision (ICD-10)*. Geneva, Switzerland: Author.

World Health Organization ASSIST Working Group. (2002). The Alcohol, Smoking and Substance Involvement Screening Test (ASSIST): Development, reliability and feasibility. *Addiction*, *97*, 1183–1194.

Chapter | four

Dependence and Diagnosis

Scott H. Stewart
Center for Drug and Alcohol Programs, Department of Psychiatry and Behavioral Science and Division of General Internal Medicine, Department of Medicine
Medical University of South Carolina

SUMMARY POINTS

- Substance dependence implies that the use of a substance or thoughts about that substance have assumed excessive importance in an individual's life to the overall detriment of other important activities.
- Substance use disorders are common in the general population.
- The *Diagnostic and Statistical Manual* (DSM) and *International Classification of Diseases* (ICD) provide the diagnostic criteria for determining the presence of substance use disorders.
- Regardless of how individuals with potential substance use disorders are identified, the diagnosis should be confirmed using a valid diagnostic interview that assesses DSM or ICD criteria.
- Assessment of other factors linked to substance use disorders (e.g., physical and mental health comorbidities, legal trouble, employment issues, and family problems) should follow the diagnosis and is an important component of treatment planning.

Evidence-Based Addiction Treatment

INTRODUCTION

Substance dependence and abuse are common. In the United States, for example, about 8.5% of adults have current alcohol use disorders (Hasin, Stinson, Ogburn, & Grant, 2007) and 2% have other drug use disorders (Compton, Thomas, Stinson, & Grant, 2007). Given this high prevalence, the costs these disorders exact on individuals and the public and on treatment effectiveness, identification, and treatment are a critical issue for society. This chapter reviews the concept of substance dependence and abuse, how the diagnoses are made including initial detection and subsequent confirmation, and finally estimation of the severity of dependence. In essence, this chapter describes the necessary characteristics of people who are eligible for evidence-based addiction treatments. Other chapters in this book review associated characteristics and conditions (e.g., mental health comorbidities) and specific evidence-based treatment modalities.

DEFINING SUBSTANCE USE DISORDERS

Dependence

Substance dependence is defined similarly regardless of the specific substance(s) involved. In general, dependence is the use of a substance or excessive thoughts about a substance assuming great importance to the detriment of other activities that had previously had greater importance (World Health Organization, 1981). Thus, the critical distinction that must be made in order to classify an individual as having substance dependence is an overall negative impact of drug involvement on that individual's functioning. To allow for reliable identification of individuals with dependence, two main diagnostic systems have arisen. These include the *Diagnostic and Statistical Manual* (DSM) from the American Psychiatric Association (1994) and the *International Classification of Diseases* (ICD) from the World Health Organization (1993). Both systems are updated infrequently. At the time of this writing, the revised 4th edition is in use for the DSM (i.e., DSM-IV-R), and the 10th edition of the ICD (i.e., ICD-10). The criteria for dependence are nearly identical in DSM-IV-R and ICD-10, which are described in Table 4.1.

In addition to criteria in Table 1, the ICD-10 includes compulsive use, which is defined as a strong and persistent desire to use a substance.

An individual meeting at least three dependence criteria during the prior 12 months is considered to have current dependence. Some substances do not have a well-characterized withdrawal syndrome, in which case the requirements for a dependence diagnosis remain the

Table 4.1 Diagnostic criteria for substance dependence

Criterion	Definition
Tolerance	Need for higher doses to achieve the same effect or less effect with the same dose
Withdrawal	Characteristic withdrawal syndrome for a specific substance or use to prevent withdrawal
Impaired control	Persistent desire to use substance, unsuccessful attempts at controlling use, or using for longer period than intended
Neglecting activities	Alternative activities are neglected or abandoned due to substance use
Time spent using substance	Much time is devoted to obtaining, using, or recovering from the effects of substance use
Substance use despite resulting problems	Continued use despite knowledge or clear evidence of adverse consequences

same (i.e., meeting at least three of the remaining criteria). An individual who previously met at least three criteria during a 12-month period, but no longer meets at least three criteria, is considered to have a lifetime history of dependence. Individuals with tolerance or withdrawal have "physiologic dependence" (which often exists without meeting dependence criteria), and those with dependence but no evidence of tolerance or withdrawal are considered to have "dependence without physiologic dependence."

The DSM also includes several additional specifications to the diagnosis. Persons diagnosed previously with dependence but who have not met any dependence criteria for 1 to 12 months are considered to be in "early full remission." "Early partial remission" indicates that some criteria are satisfied but would not have been sufficient for an initial dependence diagnosis for 1 to 12 months. "Sustained full" and "sustained partial" are similarly defined for a period exceeding 12 months. "On agonist therapy" describes a dependent individual on replacement therapy (e.g., enrolled in a methadone maintenance program for opioid addiction) who has not met any criteria for at least 1 month. "In a controlled environment" describes individuals whose access to alcohol or drugs is eliminated and who have not met any dependence criteria for at least 1 month.

As the qualifier "with physiological dependence" implies, criteria in Table 4.1 can be categorized. The first two criteria listed in Table 4.1 reflect defined physiologic effects of a substance. These are expected, given regular use or regular heavy use of some drugs. The latter three criteria deal with effects that are clearly behavioral and more difficult to define physiologically. Moreover, the final three criteria can be driven by impaired control, which largely captures the concept of "addiction." Impaired control ultimately arises from the positive and negative reinforcing properties of abused substances and is related to adaptations in anatomically defined brain regions (Kalivas & Volkow, 2005; NIDA, 2007). Early substance use can be reinforced by effects that the user interprets as positive or pleasurable. In some individuals, this can progress to repeated substance use despite frequent severe consequences. This latter activity has been placed in the context of a nearly irresistible (i.e., compulsive), learned, motivated behavior, which can be triggered by a variety of environmental stimuli associated with the use of the drug. Such changes in the brain provide an explanation for the relapsing nature of addictive disorders. While much has been learned about the neural adaptations mediating such behavior, full characterization is an area of intense research.

The fact that only three criteria must be satisfied to diagnose dependence implies that individuals with dependence on any given substance are heterogeneous. Furthermore, there is no single criterion that is essential for the diagnosis, which makes it particularly difficult to develop a theoretical framework for the development of this disorder (Hughes, 2007). However, this limitation is not a unique characteristic of dependence, as other complex chronic disorders have similar classification systems and resulting heterogeneity among individuals with the disorder. For example, 4 of 11 criteria must be met to provide the diagnosis of systemic lupus erythematosus (a condition characterized by chronic inflammation of body tissues caused by autoimmune disease) (Gill, Quisel, Rocca, & Walters, 2003). However, in contrast to traditional medical diagnoses, substance dependence, on average, clearly has more behavioral than overtly physical effects, although the latter can certainly dominate in specific individuals (i.e., alcoholic cirrhosis, cocaine-induced stroke). The importance of behavioral manifestations is expected given the current characterization of addiction as a "brain disease" (Leshner, 1997).

Abuse (DSM) or harmful use (ICD)

Individuals may have severe involvement with a substance even if dependence criteria are not satisfied. Substance "abuse" (DSM) and "harmful use" (ICD) are categorical diagnoses reflecting such problematic use. These diagnoses require that an individual meets certain broad definitions for problem use, but does not merit the diagnosis of dependence. Relative to dependence, there is less overlap in DSM and

ICD diagnostic criteria for abuse/harmful use, which are included in Table 4.2.

The inclusion of terms such as "recurrent" and "pattern" indicates that a single occurrence of a substance-related problem does not allow for a diagnosis of abuse or harmful use. While abuse/harmful use has been categorically distinct from dependence since their inclusion in the diagnostic systems in the 1980s, controversy exists as to whether this is truly a unique condition, as opposed to substance use disorders existing on a continuum of dependence severity (Li, Hewitt, & Grant, 2007).

Potentially problematic use not meeting diagnostic criteria

Certain levels or patterns of substance use that have not resulted in the diagnosis of abuse/harmful use or dependence still have the potential to cause problems in the future. The DSM and ICD diagnostic systems describe intoxication, but do not include measures for broadly classifying potentially problematic substance use. This is largely related to conceptual problems on what constitutes problematic use across individuals and cultures. The term "hazardous use" has been developed to indicate substance use that has the potential to cause adverse consequences (Babor, Campbell, Room, & Saunders, 1994). This broad category may include, for example, a single episode of driving while impaired, drinking in excess of established guidelines for moderate consumption, or illicit use of any drug that has the potential to cause acute complications. The term "hazardous use" was developed based on the recognition that many substance-induced problems occur in the absence of dependence or abuse (Institute of Medicine, 1990) and has

Table 4.2 Diagnostic criteria for abuse and harmful use

Diagnostic category	Diagnostic criteria
Abuse (DSM)	Maladaptive pattern of substance use leading to clinically significant impairment or distress as manifested by one or more of the following: – Failure to fulfill major role obligations – Recurrent use in physically hazardous situations – Recurrent substance-related legal problems – Continued use despite recurrent substance-related social or interpersonal problems
Harmful use (ICD)	A pattern of use that is causing physical or mental health problems

largely been applied as a preventive tool for heavy alcohol use in primary care populations (Reid, Fiellin, & O'Connor, 1999).

A word on terminology: The debate between "dependence" and "addiction"

There is an ongoing controversy concerning the most appropriate terminology to include in pending revisions to the DSM. It has been suggested that "addiction" replace "dependence," as the presence of "physiologic dependence" (i.e., tolerance and withdrawal as normal pharmacologic responses to repeated administration of certain drugs) may be confused with the syndrome of "substance dependence" (i.e., the compulsive use of a substance or thoughts about a substance assuming great importance to the detriment of other activities). This may lead, for example, to a physician underprescribing opiate medication for a chronic pain patient due to his/her misinterpretation of "physical dependence" as "addiction" (O'Brien, Volkow, & Li, 2006). O'Brien et al. (2006) suggest that the term "addiction" will enhance focus on compulsive substance use and is distinguished more easily from "physical dependence." Others have argued that a change from "dependence" to "addiction" will (1) not solve this problem, (2) compromise past research on substance dependence, (3) substitute a less scientific and more pejorative term for dependence, and (4) represent a scientific step backward (Babor, 2008; Erickson, 2008; Miller, 2008).

The term "substance abuse" has also been criticized, as substances, unlike people or animals, do not themselves suffer from abuse. Also, many women with substance use disorders may be offended by the term, as they themselves are victims of physical and sexual abuse. Alternate terms, such as substance "misuse" (Erickson, 2008) or substance "problems" (Miller, 2008), have been suggested. Regardless of how the nomenclature debate ends for forthcoming editions of the DSM and ICD, the diagnostic criteria themselves will likely remain largely unchanged.

SCREENING METHODS

Most individuals with substance use disorders do not receive formal treatment. Those who do are initially identified in several ways, including self-referral or treatment mandated by the judicial system or an employer due to recognized or suspected substance-related problems, or identification of a substance-related medical condition (Saitz et al., 2003). Others are initially detected using a variety of brief screening instruments, which tend to vary based on the setting in which screening is conducted. While a comprehensive review of individual screening instruments is beyond the scope of this chapter, a brief discussion of the interpretation of screening results is germane. Most are interpreted as either positive (i.e., suggesting the disorder is present) or negative (i.e., suggesting the disorder is not present). "Positive" and "negative" screening results could be correct or incorrect, leading to four possible categorizations, as depicted in Table 4.3.

Sensitivity and specificity are estimated by comparing the results of a screening test with a reference standard for diagnosis. The reference standard itself is considered to perfectly identify all those with and without the disorder, but is typically too risky, lengthy, or costly for routine use. High sensitivity indicates that a test is good at ruling out a disorder, whereas high specificity indicates that a test is good at ruling in a disorder. However, regardless of the screening instrument used, it is important to bear in mind that none is perfectly sufficient for ruling in or ruling out a substance use disorder (i.e., there is always some misclassification relative to the reference standard). Persons referred due to a positive screen must undergo a diagnostic assessment, as discussed subsequently in this chapter. Several important characteristics of screening tests and their relevance are included in Table 4.4. These apply to any type of screening test, including self-report surveys, laboratory tests, or other means of early detection.

The sensitivity and specificity of a screening instrument will vary with the screened population (e.g., an instrument might have a sensitivity of 90% in rural adolescents and a sensitivity of 70% in urban adolescents). Moreover, the ability of a screening instrument to detect or rule out a substance disorder is not only a function of sensitivity and specificity, but is strongly related to the prevalence of the targeted disorder in the screened population. With higher prevalence, a positive result is more likely to be a true positive, whereas a negative result is more likely to be a false negative. With a low prevalence disorder the opposite is true.

An important point to bear in mind is that a screening instrument should have been validated in a population very similar to the one in which it is being applied. If so, then a positive screen indicates the need

Table 4.3 Possible results from a screening test[a]

	Disorder present	Disorder absent
Screen positive	True positive (TP)	False positive (FP)
Screen negative	False negative (FN)	True negative (TN)

[a]*Definitions: prevalence = proportion of population with the disorder = TP+FN; sensitivity = probability of a positive test in those with the disorder = TP fraction = TP/(TP+FN); and specificity = probability of a negative test in those without the disorder = TN fraction = TN/(TN+FP).*

Table 4.4 Factors pertinent to screening test interpretation

Characteristic	Relevance
Targeted disorder	This seems obvious but can be subtle (e.g., has the screen been validated for dependence alone or for dependence, abuse, and hazardous use?).
Populations studied	Screening test performance can vary substantially in different populations (e.g., females vs males, younger age vs older age). The screening test should be validated for a population similar to the one in which it is being applied.
Positive predictive value	Indicates the probability that a person with a positive screen has the target disorder. It is equal to the TP fraction divided by the sum of the TP and FP fractions.
Negative predictive value	Indicates the probability that a person with a negative screen does not have the target disorder. It is equal to the TN fraction divided by the sum of the TN and FN fractions.
Cutoff score	Generally, higher screening test cutoff scores increase specificity but decrease sensitivity (i.e., those with a positive test become more likely to have the disorder, but a negative test becomes less useful for ruling out the disorder).

for a thorough diagnostic assessment. Such assessments are typically not conducted by the person or organization administering the screen, but rather involve referral to an addiction specialist.

DIAGNOSTIC ASSESSMENT

Establishing the presence of dependence or abuse/harmful use

Regardless of the initial source of suspicion for a substance use disorder (i.e., a screening program, self-referral), additional assessment is needed for confirming or ruling out the diagnosis. In practice, perhaps the most common way of making the diagnosis of substance dependence is by reviewing the dependence criteria (see Table 4.1) with the individual suspected of having the diagnosis. This would typically be supplemented with other information (e.g., referral due to driving under the influence, a positive urine drug screen, or alcohol-related disease). This is an informal approach that may be acceptable in clinical settings. However, like a screening program, it is susceptible to misclassification, dependent on the skills of the provider, and is less reliable and transparent than a formal diagnostic process using validated assessment instruments. Several

Table 4.5 Selection of diagnostic interviews for substance use disorders

Diagnostic interview	Administration time for substance use modules	Structure
Diagnostic Interview Schedule (DIS) (Helzer, 1992)	15–25	Structured
Composite International Diagnostic Interview (CIDI) (Robins et al., 1988)	20–30	Structured
Structured Clinical Interview for DSM-IV (SCID) (Spitzer et al., 1992)	20–30	Semistructured
Substance Dependence Severity Scale (SDSS) (Miele et al., 2000)	30–45	Semistructured
Diagnostic and Statistical Manual-IV checklist (Hudziak et al., 1993)	10–15	Semistructured

comprehensive diagnostic interviews have been developed that specifically assess each domain of dependence per the framework of the DSM or ICD criteria. These interviews can be structured (no variation in administration) or semistructured (allowing the interviewer flexibility in administration). Structured interviews are preferable for administration by trained laypersons, whereas semistructured interviews are often preferred by skilled clinicians. Several diagnostic interviews with widespread use in clinical and research settings are listed in Table 4.5.

The instruments in Table 4.4 were included based on a study that compared their use in academic and community treatment programs (Forman, Svikis, Montoya, & Blaine, 2004). The Structured Clinical Interview for DSM-IV (SCID) (followed by the Composite International Diagnostic Interview [CIDI]) was rated most highly by clinicians, but the CIDI was chosen for use in the National Drug Abuse Treatment Clinical Trials Network (see www.nida.nih.gov/ctn for more information) due to the greater training and experience required for SCID administration (i.e., the SCID is semistructured) and the validity of the CIDI for both DSM and ICD diagnoses.

Additional assessment following a substance use disorder diagnosis

In addition to diagnostic categorization, certain interviews also include estimates of the severity of dependence (e.g., the SDSS and SCID). The CIDI does not do so, but does provide measures of past-month symptoms (which are likely to be perceived as most pertinent by individuals with substance use disorders), the quantity and frequency of substance use, and modules for diagnosing psychiatric conditions that are comorbid with a substance use disorder. These represent important additional assessments for individuals with a substance use disorder and are discussed in other chapters in this book. Such information may predict treatment needs and is useful for describing individuals and groups in communications between providers or researchers (Maisto & Saitz, 2003). The severity of each dependence criterion could vary between individuals or within individuals over time, and scales have been developed to capture such variation. For example, the Clinical Institute for Withdrawal Assessment for Alcohol (CIWA) and several variations of the original CIWA have been used extensively to measure the severity of alcohol withdrawal and estimate the need for medical detoxification (Sullivan, Sykora, Schneiderman, Naranjo, & Sellers, 1989). The Addiction Severity Index (ASI) is germane to all substance use diagnoses (McClellan et al., 1992). The ASI includes 200 items that assess multiple problem domains associated with substance use disorders, including alcohol and other drug use, medical and psychiatric problems, employment, legal problems, and family problems. Severity scores are generated for each of these domains corresponding to the examiner's rating of treatment needs in that area. Assessment time is about 1 hour. Results are used to highlight particular problems being experienced by an individual, allowing for the development of a unique treatment program that is attentive to that individual's needs. Thus the ASI (or other instruments designed to assess specific problem domains) serves an important adjunctive role after the diagnosis of a substance use disorder is established with a validated interview such as the CIDI.

SUMMARY

This chapter provided an overview on the nature of substance use disorders, the common diagnostic systems used to determine their presence, mechanisms leading to suspicion for the presence of a substance use disorder and referral to an addiction specialist, and diagnostic assessment. Once the diagnosis is established and the severity of substance involvement and its consequences defined, evidence-based treatments as described in subsequent chapters can lead to substantial improvement and long-term remission.

REFERENCES

American Psychiatric Association. (1994). *Diagnostic and Statistical Manual of Mental Disorders* (4th ed.). Washington, DC: American Psychiatric Association.

Babor, T. F. (2008). Terminology: Impossible dream or tilting at windmills? *Alcoholism: Clinical and Experimental Research*, *32*(1), 5.

Babor, T., Campbell, R., Room, R., & Saunders, J. (1994). *Lexicon of Alcohol and Drug Terms*. Geneva: World Health Organization.

Compton, W. M., Thomas, Y. F., Stinson, F. S., & Grant, B. F. (2007). Prevalence, correlates, disability, and comorbidity of DSM-IV drug abuse and dependence in the United States: Results from the National Epidemiologic Survey on Alcohol and Related Conditions. *Archives of General Psychiatry*, *64*(5), 566–576.

Erickson, C. K. (2008). In defense of "dependence." *Alcoholism: Clinical and Experimental Research*, *32*(1), 1–3.

Forman, R. F., Svikis, D., Montoya, I. D., & Blaine, J. (2004). Selection of a substance use disorder diagnostic instrument by the National Drug Abuse Treatment Clinical Trials Network. *Journal of Substance Abuse Treatment*, *27*(1), 1–8.

Gill, J. M., Quisel, A. M., Rocca, P. V., & Walters, D. T. (2003). Diagnosis of systemic lupus erythematosus. *American Family Physician*, *68*(11), 2179–2186.

Grant, B. F., Dawson, D. A., Stinson, F. S., Chou, S. P., Dufour, M. C., & Pickering, R. P. (2004). The 12-month prevalence and trends in DSM-IV alcohol abuse and dependence: United States, 1991-1992 and 2001-2002. *Drug and Alcohol Dependence*, *74*(3), 223–234.

Hasin, D. S., Stinson, F. S., Ogburn, E., & Grant, B. F. (2007). Prevalence, correlates, disability, and comorbidity of DSM-IV alcohol abuse and dependence in the United States: Results from the National Epidemiologic Survey on Alcohol and Related Conditions. *Archives of General Psychiatry*, *64*(7), 830–842.

Helzer, J. E. (1992). Development of the diagnostic interview schedule. In J. E. Helzer & G. L. Canino (Eds.), *Alcoholism in North America, Europe, and Asia*. New York: Oxford University Press.

Hudziak, J. J., Helzer, J. E., Wetzel, W. W., Kessel, K. B., McGee, B., Janca, A., & Przybeck, T. (1993). The use of the DSM-III-R checklist for initial diagnostic assessment. *Comprehensive Psychiatry*, *34*(6), 375–383.

Hughes, J. R. (2007). Defining dependence: Describing symptom clusters versus central constructs. *Addiction*, *102*(10), 1531–1532.

Institute of Medicine. (1990). *Broadening the base of treatment for alcohol problems*. Washington, DC: National Academy Press.

Kalivas, P. W., & Volkow, N. D. (2005). The neural basis of addiction: A pathology of motivation and choice. *American Journal of Psychiatry*, *162*(8), 1403–1413.

Leshner, A. I. (1997). Addiction is a brain disease, and it matters. *Science*, *278*, 45–47.

Li, T. K., Hewitt, B. G., & Grant, B. F. (2007). The alcohol dependence syndrome, 30 years later: A commentary. *Addiction*, *102*, 1522–1530.

Maisto, S. A., & Saitz, R. (2003). Alcohol use disorders: Screening and diagnosis. *American Journal on Addictions*, *12*(Suppl 1), 12–25.

McClellan, A. T., Kushner, H., Metzger, D., Peters, R., Smith, I., Grissom, G., Pettinati, H., & Argeriou, M. (1992). The fifth edition of the Addiction Severity Index. *Journal of Substance Abuse Treatment*, *9*(3), 199–213.

Miele, G. M., Carpenter, K. M., Cockerham, M. S., Trautman, K. D., Blaine, J., & Hasin, D. S. (2000). Substance Dependence Severity Scale (SDSS): Reliability and validity of a clinician-administered interview for DSM-IV substance use disorders. *Drug and Alcohol Dependence*, *59*, 63–75.

Miller, W. R. (2008). Dependence: Fear not. *Alcoholism: Clinical and Experimental Research*, *32*(1), 4.

National Institute on Drug Abuse. (2007). *Drugs, brain and behavior: The science of addiction*. NIH Pub No. 07-5605. Available at http://www.nida.nih.gov/scienceofaddiction/sciofaddiction.pdf.

O'Brien, C. P., Volkow, N., & Li, T. K. (2006). What's in a word? Addiction versus dependence in DSM-V. *American Journal of Psychiatry*, *163*(5), 764–765.

Reid, M. C., Fiellin, D. A., & O'Connor, P. G. (1999). Hazardous and harmful alcohol consumption in primary care. *Archives of Internal Medicine*, *159*(15), 1681–1689.

Robins, L. N., Wing, J., Wittchen, H. U., Helzer, J. E., Babor, T. F., Burke, J., et al. (1988). The composite international diagnostic interview: An epidemiologic instrument suitable for use in conjunction with different diagnostic systems and in different cultures. *Archives of General Psychiatry*, *45*, 1069–1077.

Saitz, R., Friedman, H. S., Haber, P. S., et al. (2003). Medical disorders and complications of addiction. In A. W. Graham, T. K. Schultz, M. F. Mayo-Smith, R. K. Ries, & B. B. Wilford (Eds.), *Principles of addiction medicine* (3rd ed.). Chevy Chase, MD: American Society of Addiction Medicine.

Spitzer, R. L., Williams, J. B. W., Gibbon, M., & First, M. B. (1992). The Structured Clinical Interview for DSM-III-R (SCID). *Archives of General Psychiatry*, *49*, 624–636.

Steinbauer, J. R., Cantor, S. B., Holzer, C. E., & Volk, R. J. (1998). Ethnic and sex bias in primary care screening tests for alcohol use disorders. *Annals of Internal Medicine*, *129*(5), 353–362.

Sullivan, J. T., Sykora, K., Schneiderman, J., Naranjo, C. A., & Sellers, E. M. (1989). Assessment of alcohol withdrawal: The revised Clinical Institute Withdrawal Assessment for Alcohol scale (CIWA-AR). *British Journal of Addictions*, *84*, 1353–1357.

World Health Organization. (1981). Nomenclature and classification of drugs and alcohol-related problems: A WHO memorandum. *Bulletin of the World Health Organization*, *59*, 225–242.

World Health Organization. (1993). *The ICD-10 classification of mental and behavioral disorders: Diagnostic criteria for research*. Geneva: World Health Organization.

Chapter | five

Assessment of Co-occurring Addictive and Other Mental Disorders

David J. Kavanagh and Jennifer M. Connolly
Institute of Health and Biomedical Innovation and School of Psychology and Counseling, Queensland University of Technology

SUMMARY POINTS

- Co-occurring addictive and other mental disorders (AMDs) are common, especially in treatment services, so screening for substance use and mental health symptoms should be routine.
- Low levels of substance use or psychological problems can have a substantial impact if a companion disorder is severe or if functioning is poor. Screening should not exclusively focus on severe disorder.
- AMDs are often more than dual, involving multiple substances and mental disorders, and complex life problems. Comprehensive management requires a wide-ranging assessment.
- Symptoms of disorders often overlap, and a confident diagnosis often requires repeated or retrospective assessments.
- AMDs sometimes occur in primary–secondary relationships, but often are mutually interacting, and their relationships may change over time. Treatment planning requires consideration of current and future relationships between problems.
- Several screening instruments have demonstrated utility in detecting AMDs. Detection of substance use can sometimes be increased by

Evidence-Based Addiction Treatment

the use of biomedical assays or collateral reports, but more accurate self-reports can often be obtained in AMD populations, provided that trust is developed.

- The range and extent of problems in these populations often appear daunting. A review of strengths is important to maintaining the motivation and confidence of both clients and practitioners.

DEFINITIONS

Presentations of addictive and other mental disorders often show some features of the other, which does not necessarily mean that there are two co-occurring disorders. As discussed later, features often overlap, symptoms can be secondary, and subsyndromal conditions may be present. This chapter focuses on separate disorders that co-occur at a particular point in time, while acknowledging the potential for interactions between them. This focus allows us to draw on definitions within the standard classification schemes (e.g., as summarized in Table 5.1), which assist in excluding secondary conditions. However, as is argued later, this is a field where isolated symptoms or subsyndromal conditions are often important, especially if the person's cognitive or functional status has been severely compromised by an existing disorder. In practice, a wider view that encompasses less clear-cut conditions is often required.

FEATURES OF CO-OCCURRING DISORDERS THAT INFORM ASSESSMENT

Co-occurring addictive and other mental disorders (AMDs) are common

Large-scale community surveys have shown consistently that the risk of other mental disorders is increased significantly if people have an alcohol or other addictive disorder and that rates of AMDs are very high (Table 5.2). Rates vary slightly across different surveys, but internationally 30–40% of people with alcohol disorders also have other mental disorders, as do around 40–50% of those misusing other substances (Kessler et al., 1996; Regier et al., 1990; Teesson, Hall, Lynskey, & Degenhardt, 2000). As shown in Table 5.2, the risk varies across disorders. In the Epidemiological Catchment Area study (Regier et al., 1990), the highest increase in relative odds occurred with antisocial personality disorder, where across people with any alcohol and other drug disorder, the odds ratio (OR) was 29.6, followed by bipolar I disorder (OR = 7.9) and schizophrenia (OR = 4.6). With the exception

Table 5.1 Examples of mental health disorders in DSM-IV (American Psychiatric Association, 1994)

Diagnostic groups	Examples[a]
Axis I: Clinical disorders	
Psychotic disorders	Schizophrenia
	Schizophreniform disorder
	Schizoaffective disorder
Mood disorders	Major depressive disorder (single episode or recurrent)
	Dysthymic disorder
	Bipolar I disorder (i.e., without depressive episodes)
	Bipolar II disorder (recurrent major depression with hypomanic episodes)
	Cyclothymic disorder
	Substance-induced mood disorder
Anxiety disorders	Panic disorder (with or without agoraphobia)
	Agoraphobia without a history of panic disorder
	Specific phobia
	Social phobia
	Obsessive-compulsive disorder
	Post-traumatic stress disorder
	Acute stress disorder
	Generalized anxiety disorder
	Substance-induced anxiety disorder
Axis II: Personality disorders (PDs) and mental retardation	
Cluster A	Paranoid PD
	Schizoid PD
	Schizotypal PD
Cluster B	Antisocial PD
	Borderline PD
	Histrionic PD
	Narcissistic PD
Cluster C	Avoidant PD
	Dependent PD
	Obsessive-compulsive PD

[a]*Neither category groups nor examples are exhaustive. Some examples omit qualifiers and may not correspond to the exact title. For a comprehensive list of disorders and features, refer to the DSM-IV manual (American Psychiatric Association, 1994).*

Table 5.2 Lifetime prevalence and odds ratios of mental disorders in people with substance use disorders: Data from the Epidemiological Catchment Area study[a]

Comorbid mental disorder	Alcohol use disorder		Other substance use disorder	
	%	Odds ratio	%	Odds ratio
Affective	13	1.9	26	4.7
Anxiety	19	1.5	28	2.5
Schizophrenia	4	3.3	7	6.2
Antisocial personality disorder	14	21.0	18	13.4
Any	37	2.3	53	4.5

[a]*Data drawn from Regier et al. (1990).*

of post-traumatic stress disorder and panic disorder (Burns & Teesson, 2002), the increased risk in anxiety disorders (OR = 1.7) and unipolar depression tends to be a little lower (OR = 1.9) (Regier et al., 1990), even though the percentages of affected people are high. This is because anxiety and depression are the most common types of mental disorders in the general population (Teesson et al., 2000).

The increased risk of co-occurrence also means that substance use disorders are high in people with mental disorders. For example, 40–50% of people with schizophrenia also have a substance use disorder other than nicotine dependence (Kavanagh et al., 2004; Regier et al., 1990). Substances most commonly misused are those that are most common in the general population—tobacco (74% in Australian schizophrenia sufferers (Kavanagh et al., 2004, caffeine (44% drinking more than 4 cups per day), alcohol (27%), and cannabis (27%). These percentages vary internationally and over time, as do the illegal drugs that are most available or popular: the general rule is that subpopulations with comorbidity share these trends with the rest of the community.

As common as AMDs are in the general population, they are even more common in treatment services. While the rate of mood disorders in the general population is about 13%, the rate of depression in treatment seekers with alcohol dependence can be 40% or more (Brown & Schuckit, 1988). The proportion of treatment seekers for substance misuse with a concurrent mental disorder can be as high as 80% (Ross, Glaser, & Germanson, 1988). This is partly because people with more than one disorder are more likely to seek and obtain treatment for at least one of them (Berkson, 1949) and partly because of the greater symptomatic and functional impact of multiple disorders. An implication of this high frequency within services is that screening for

AMDs should be routine. Without screening, many instances are missed (Ananth et al., 1989).

Legal drugs are most commonly involved

Practitioners are often particularly concerned about the impact of illegal substance use—and rightly so, since those substances are implicated in symptom exacerbations and their illegal status has significant potential impact on the user. However, these are not the substances that most commonly produce functional or other problems for people with mental disorders, except in settings where illegal drug use is particularly common. The high frequency of tobacco and alcohol use across the community, and the negative effects these substances can have on people with mental disorders, means that they most commonly emerge as problematic.

The high rate of alcohol use and its potential impact on psychotic symptoms, dysphoria, cognition, and social functioning are well known (Drake et al., 1990). However, it is not the only legal drug to cause problems. In recent research in Australia, people with schizophrenia were 3.2 times more likely to smoke than the general population (Kavanagh et al., 2004a), and people with depression were 2.7 times more likely (Wilhelm, Mitchell, Slade, Brownhill, & Andrews, 2003). Tobacco constitutes a significant contributor to morbidity and early death in people with mental disorder (Osborn et al., 2007), and there appears to be an increased risk of lung cancer in smokers with depression (OR = 19.67 vs nonsmokers) than in the general population of smokers (OR = 3.38; Knekt et al., 1996). While there may be a slight decrease in the risk of cancer in smokers with schizophrenia compared with other smokers (Catts et al., 2008), their high rate of smoking and the risk of other disorders mean that smoking remains a major cause of disease and early death in people with psychosis (Catts et al., 2008). Smoking can improve concentration and reduce akathisia (unpleasant sensations of "inner" restlessness that manifests itself with an inability to sit still or remain motionless) in people on antipsychotic medication (Barnes et al., 2006), but smokers require a higher dose of antipsychotic medication to impact on symptoms (Ziedonis et al., 1994).

Caffeine is also used more often by people with mental health problems (Kendler et al., 2006; Whalen et al., 2008), and heavier consumption is seen in caffeine users with schizophrenia (Gurpegui et al., 2006). Caffeine increases arousal and anxiety in an unselected population (Peeling, Dawson, Peeling, & Dawson, 2007), and unsurprisingly, panic attacks can be induced by a dose of caffeine in a sample with panic disorder (Nardi et al., 2007). In people with schizophrenia, caffeine and nicotine use are associated with each other (Gurpegui et al., 2006). The substances interact with each other (Hughes et al., 1998), and both can affect the metabolism of clozapine (Dratcu et al., 2007).

Despite their high frequency and potential impact, legal drugs have often been missed in assessments by mental health services in the past (Drake et al., 1990). During screening and assessment, clinicians need to pay attention to all substance use and its impact.

Addictive and other mental disorders have substantial impact, especially if one disorder is severe

Functional effects of each type of disorder are magnified by co-occurrence of the other (Mueser, Kavanagh, & Brunette, 2007). When one problem is severe, it may take only a minor concurrent problem to produce significant impairment. For example, someone on a very low income because of a severe and chronic mental disorder may have to miss meals or be at risk of losing their accommodations if they smoke cigarettes or use even small amounts of other drugs. Even mild intoxication with a stimulant can have catastrophic effects in someone with a tendency to paranoia. An implication is that screening tools designed to detect high levels of substance dependence may miss many people with addiction-related issues who are in treatment for a severe mental disorder. Conversely, within a service for people with severe levels of addictive disorders, most of the people with mental health problems will not have severe mental disorders and many may be subsyndromal. A screening instrument that focuses on detection of severe mental disorders will miss the majority of affected individuals. In both cases, the functional impact of co-occurring problems may still be substantial.

Detection of AMDs also has importance for the prevention of illness or injury during treatment. Not only is there potential for interaction with prescribed medication and a need to treat overdose and withdrawal, other issues include an increased risk of self-harm and suicide in depressed patients (D'Eramo, Prinstein, Freeman, Grapentine, & Spirito, 2004) and an increased risk of aggression or violence in psychiatric patients who are using stimulants (Miles, 2003).

Comorbidities are often more than dual

Addictive and other mental disorders are sometimes referred to as dual diagnoses (Minkoff & Drake, 1991; Mueser, Drake, & Wallach, 1998). However, it is important to recognize that many people have more than just two problems. Multiple substance use is common (Kavanagh et al., 2004), as are symptoms of more than one mental disorder (Andrews, Hall, Teesson, & Henderson, 1999; Castel, Rush, Urbanoski, & Toneatto,

2006; Potvin, Sepehry, & Stip, 2007), including a combination of DSM-IV axes I and II (Mueser et al., 2006). These people often also have physical disorders, some of which may be secondary, some unrelated. Some physical illnesses may mimic psychiatric symptoms or features of intoxication and withdrawal, and, if untreated, some may be life-threatening. People with AMDs are also likely to be facing multiple and complex life problems. Assessments should be comprehensive to detect this range of problems and design appropriate treatments.

Case Study A: More than dual diagnosis—Ben

Ben, 42, had self-referred for treatment of depression and alcohol problems. An assessment session confirmed that he met criteria for both a major depressive episode and alcohol dependence. However, Ben withdrew prior to commencing treatment, stating that attending sessions would be "too much for him." A review of Ben's assessments revealed that he also experienced significant anxiety about attending treatment. Had this been detected earlier and his depressive and anxiety cognitions about treatment been addressed satisfactorily, his outcome may have been more positive.

Causal relationships can take several forms

Several hypotheses have been advanced for the high frequency of AMDs (Figure 5.1; Mueser et al., 1998). Each has plausibility, and each may have implications for assessment and treatment. While these options for causal relationships are phrased in terms of substance use and mental disorder, they may also be applied to other issues of high co-occurrence in this population (e.g., physical, social, housing, financial, or legal).

Substance use triggering psychological symptoms

Such an influence may occur directly (e.g., via the effects of intoxication or withdrawal) or indirectly (e.g., because of effects of substance misuse on social relationships, finances, police actions, employment, housing, or health).

Psychological symptoms triggering substance use

One version of this hypothesis is that people with psychological symptoms may use substances as a coping strategy ("self-medication," or alleviation of dysphoria; Mueser et al., 2007). While that motivation is similar to mood enhancement in recreational use (with the person

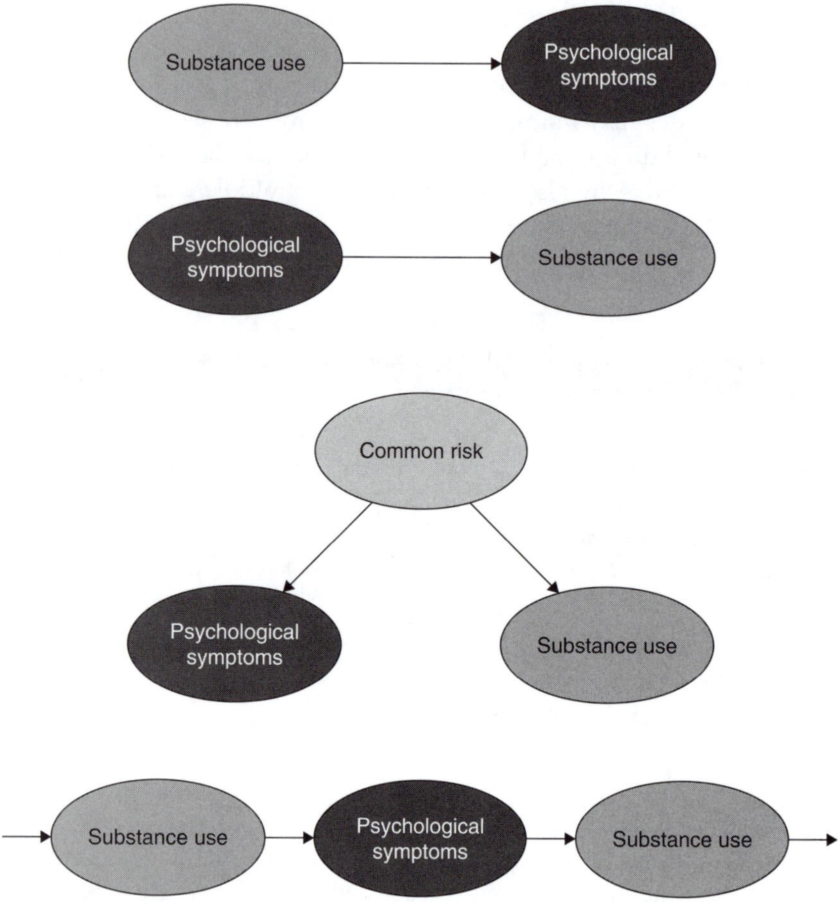

FIGURE 5.1 *Potential causal relationships between addictive and other mental disorders.*

starting at a lower point on a negative/positive mood continuum), tension reduction and mood enhancement are more pressing if the person is distressed (Green, Kavanagh, & Young, 2004). There may also be greater euphoric effects of alcohol in schizophrenia (D'Souza et al., 2006). Other versions of this hypothesis include substance use resulting from difficulties with assertion or impulsivity.

Common factor(s)

A third possibility is that one or more common factors (genetic, interpersonal, or contextual) increase the risk of both substance misuse and other mental disorder. An example is unemployment, which increases the likelihood of both dysphoria (an unpleasant or uncomfortable mood) and substance use (Khlat, Sermet, & Pape, 2004).

Mutual influence

In this model, psychological symptoms and substance use are locked in a relationship of mutual influence through time, with greater substance use triggering increased psychological symptoms, and vice versa. Evidence for this type of causal relationship is strongest in people with psychosis and substance misuse (Hides, Dawe, Kavanagh, & Young, 2006). As with unidirectional models, some of these relationships may be direct, whereas others are indirect.

It is likely that different causal chains are operating in different people. This idea, together with the related hypothesis that treatment of the determinants may be sufficient to treat the consequent problem, has led to attempts to identify "primary" and "secondary" disorders. The proposal gains traction from the fact that improvements in depression are often seen after treatment for alcohol (Brown & Schuckit, 1988) or opiate dependence (Nunes, Sullivan, & Levin, 1994), although there are other explanations for these observations (e.g., a halo effect of addressing a subset of problems). A primary/secondary distinction is mainly relevant to the first two models: if disorders were caused by another factor or mutually influenced each other, it would not make sense to look for the "primary" problem.

A strong version of the primary–secondary idea is that the disorders are not truly independent at all. Strictly speaking, that may indicate that the person does not really have co-occurring disorders—the symptoms of one are really due to the other. Independence of disorders is sometimes assessed by looking for episodes that have occurred in the absence of the companion disorder (Schuckit et al., 1997). A review of past episodes using a timeline (Figure 5.2) can help disentangle patterns of influence and provide evidence of independence. In the same way as a timeline follow back uses recent events to assist recall of substance use (Sobell & Sobell, 1992), major events in a person's life (e.g., graduation, marriage, birth of a child) are used to help in the generation of this timeline.

However, a lack of independent episodes does not preclude the presence of independent disorders, for example, exacerbations in a common factor may cause simultaneous episodes or they may coincide by chance. Furthermore, the fact that one disorder has triggered a second one does not preclude the second exacerbating the first in a mutually interacting manner (e.g., the resultant dysphoria leading to even more substance use, which in turn may exacerbate the dysphoria).

The timing of disorder onset carries particular risks for inference of causality. For example, the modal age for starting cannabis use tends to be in the midteens at present (Australian Institute of Health and Welfare, 2005), whereas the modal age for onset of schizophrenia is in

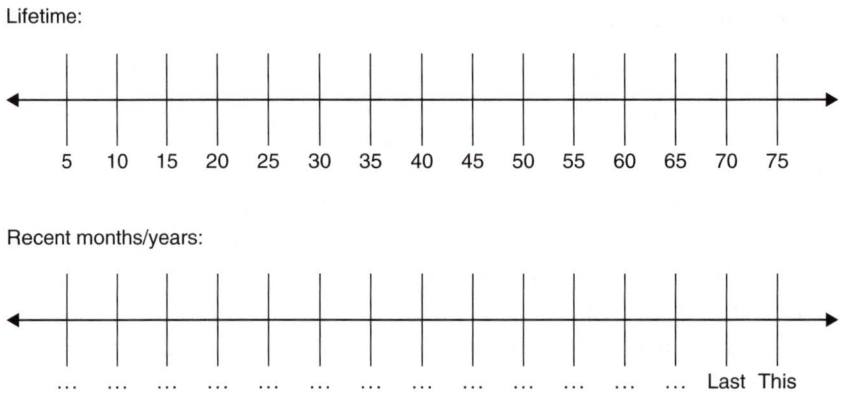

FIGURE 5.2 *History of substance use and psychological issues. Mark memorable* life events *(e.g., moved house, illness, started/ended job or relationship, arrest) and* psychological events *above the line (e.g., episodes, treatment). Mark* substance use issues *below the line (first use, problem use, abstinence/reduction, treatment).*

the 20s (Barnes, Mutsatsa, Hutton, Watt, & Joyce, 2006). Even if there were no relationship between the two, initiation of cannabis use would usually precede schizophrenia.

Conclusions based on past episodes assume that the same causal factors are operating through time. However, determinants of substance use often change over time, for example, it may often start through peer influence or curiosity, but later be increasingly driven by relief of withdrawal. The same is often true of AMDs (Hodgkins, el-Guebaly, Armstrong, & Dufour, 1999)—at some points, disorders may show one type of causal relationship, and at others, a different one. For example, even if a person's past depressive episodes have typically been associated with substance misuse and their depression is relieved temporarily by addiction treatment, they may still be at risk of relapse to substance misuse if they experience dysphoria that is triggered by another causal factor in the future.

An interview that has been specifically designed to clarify the relationships between symptoms and obtaining DSM-IV diagnoses is the Psychiatric Research Interview for Substance and Mental Disorders (PRISM; Hasin et al., 1996, 2006). This interview provides high 5- to 7-day test–retest reliabilities for substance dependence and for most psychiatric disorders, although reliabilities for some anxiety disorders and for substance abuse are somewhat lower. Consistent with DSM-IV, a substance-induced diagnosis is obtained in cases where the current episode of a mental disorder did extend outside a period of heavy substance use. While the PRISM is very useful for identifying independent disorders, it is important to appreciate that the substance-induced diagnosis does not necessarily mean that the substance use *caused* the mental disorder—only that the episode of mental disorder was not known to be independent. Nor does the diagnosis exclude the possibility that the onset of psychological symptoms exacerbated the substance use. Further questioning is needed to elucidate this possibility. An additional consideration is that an episode can be deemed substance induced on the PRISM, even if a previous episode is verified as not being substance induced. This decision rule contrasts with DSM-IV, which allows evidence of a previous independent episode to exclude a current substance-induced diagnosis and provides an opportunity to reflect differing associations between psychological symptoms and substance use that are evidenced over time. However, the usual DSM-IV rule needs to be borne in mind when recording lifetime diagnoses.

There is a further possible relationship between the problems

The foregoing are potential explanations for increased risk. When considering the cause of co-occurring disorders in an individual, it is important to remember that for some, *co-occurring problems may occur by chance* and have no relationship at all.

Case Study B: Causal relationships may change over time—Jill

On assessment, Jill, 46, was diagnosed with a major depressive episode and alcohol dependence, consuming an average 41 drinks (10 g ethanol) per week. She had recurrent episodes of depression from childhood, but did not develop hazardous alcohol use until her late 30s. The onset of problematic alcohol use coincided with an acute depressive episode, suggesting that depression may have triggered the alcohol problem. However, Jill went on to continue this pattern of heavy alcohol use after her depressive episode had resolved. The relationship between the two disorders evolved over time into one of mutual influence, such that her alcohol use was exacerbated by her dysphoria, but her alcohol use and its related problems contributed to her ongoing depression.

Common symptoms may occur across types of disorders

As noted in the previous section, symptoms or even whole disorder profiles can be secondary to other mental or physical disorders, and symptoms from a range of disorders may co-occur, making diagnosis difficult (Castel et al., 2006). Anxiety and other dysphoria are common during withdrawal from alcohol, as are paranoia and visual hallucinations during intoxication with amphetamine-like drugs, and so on. While symptom features may increase suspicion of their potential sources (e.g., visual and tactile hallucinations of crawling insects often occur in severe alcohol withdrawal), longitudinal assessment (and/or patients' retrospective reports) may often be needed for clinicians to be confident in their assessment. For example, amphetamine-induced psychosis usually clears within a week of ceasing use, even without treatment for the symptoms (Schuckit, 2000).

Case Study C

Jason had his first psychiatric admission to a public psychiatric ward, displaying delusions and hallucinations, accompanied with moderately disorganized speech. He was approached on day 2 of his admission, and several minutes were spent developing a rapport and determining his capacity for assessment. Once he was sufficiently stable to tolerate a brief assessment, he was asked about his substance use. A brief frequency and quantity screen for substance use in the previous 6 months was given, along with a DrugCheck Problem List, AUDIT, and SDS. The screen took 15 min and revealed daily amphetamine use of up to 1g, along with monthly cannabis use. The problem screeners indicated a strong likelihood of substance dependence (PL = 16, SDS = 3). Information from file notes and results of a urine drug screen corroborated these reports, and a diagnosis of amphetamine dependence was later confirmed on a structured interview (the CIDI). Jason's symptoms resolved substantially over the course of the next few days. Given the absence of a previous history of substance-independent psychosis, he received a discharge diagnosis of amphetamine-induced psychotic disorder.

SCREENING FOR AMDS

Steps to maximize the accuracy of self-reports

As in other populations, people with AMDs may deny or underreport substance use unless they are reassured that this acknowledgment will not have negative consequences. This issue is especially important in AMDs, as paranoia or other psychological symptoms and contextual factors (e.g., involuntary treatment) can make it difficult to generate trust. Then, we begin routinely by asking about caffeine, smoking, alcohol, and medication use before asking about cannabis and other illegal drugs. Reports of past use (ever used, used in the last number of months) are obtained before any reports of more recent use are requested. Reports of problems can be derived in a motivational interviewing style, within an attitude of curiosity about experiences (both positive and less so), and avoiding implications of labels (e.g., alcoholism) that may trigger denial.

Assessment of people with acute and severe mental disorders should take account of the significant cognitive deficits, including problems with sustained attention and working memory, which are shown by this group (Barbee, Clark, Crapazano, Heintz, & Kehoe, 1989). Complex questions should be avoided, and sentences kept simple. Requirements to keep material in memory (e.g., rating scales) while attending to questions should be avoided. Interviews should be kept brief (>15 min without a rest is sometimes very difficult for this group), and several sessions may be needed to gather extensive information.

Standard procedures to maximize accuracy of consumption reports are used. A timeline follow back (Sobell & Sobell, 1992), using salient recent activities or events to cue recall of consumption, can be applied in most people with AMDs (Sacks, Drake, Williams, Banks, & Herrell, 2003). Self-recording of daily substance use is often precluded in severe mental disorders, but daily telephone contact can obtain the same information if required. As in other substance use, collateral information is not necessarily more accurate than self-report (Carey & Simons, 2000)—both substance use and symptoms can be hidden from others, and collateral reports can be subject to either negative or positive bias. Collection of self-report data in the context of collateral information or biochemical assays can boost the accuracy of self-report (a "bogus pipeline" effect; Weiss et al., 1998), but care needs to be taken that this does not impair the therapeutic alliance (e.g., present it as a standard procedure rather than a reflection on honesty).

Screening instruments

Selected instruments, together with data from sample studies on detection of AMDs, are displayed in Tables 5.3 and 5.4. Unsurprisingly, screening instruments that assess lifetime disorders (e.g., MAST, CAGE) tend to overdiagnose current disorders (i.e., have lower specificity) than ones focusing on recent behavior. Because most people with serious mental disorders and substance use problems do not have high levels of dependence (Drake et al., 1990), measures that focus on substance dependence (e.g., CAGE) tend to have lower sensitivity than ones that include heavy use or abuse (e.g., AUDIT). While a study on MMPI-A-derived scales is included in Table 5.3 (Micucci, 2002), the MMPI MacAndrews Alcoholism Scale (MacAndrew, 1965) does not appear to perform as well in most studies conducted within psychiatric settings

Table 5.3 Examples of screening instruments for substance use disorders and of their performance in samples with psychiatric disorders[a]

Measure	Description	Sample study	Participants	Criterion[b]	Cutoff	Sensitivity[c]	Specificity[c]	PPV[c]	NPV[c]	AUC[c]
Addiction Severity Index (ASI; McLellan et al., 1980)	Structured interview	Appleby, Dyson, Altman, & Luchins (1997)	100 mixed inpatient psychiatric, predominantly psychotic	SCID-P (Spitzer, Williams, Gibbon, & First, 1990) recent alcohol/drug abuse	≥1	.93	.55–.59			
Alcohol Use Disorders Identification Test (AUDIT; Saunders, Aasland, Babor, De La Fuente, & Grant, 1993)	10-item, self-report	Maisto, Carey, Carey, Gordon, & Gleason (2000)	162 outpatients with severe persistent mental illness (psychosis, depression, bipolar)	SCID current alcohol use disorder	≥8	.90	.70	.32	.98	
		Cassidy, Schmitz, & Malla (2008)	79 inpatients/outpatients with first-episode psychosis	SCID current alcohol use disorder	≥10	.85	.91	.65	.97	.86
AUDIT-C	Three consumption items of the AUDIT	Dawson, Grant, & Stinson (2005)	Respondents to a community survey with mood (2818), anxiety (4755), or personality disorder (6295) in last year	AUDADIS-IV (Grant, Hasin, & Harford, 1988) 12-month alcohol use disorder	≥4 Mood Anxiety Personality	 .81 .83 .84	 .76 .77 .74			 .86 .88 .87

CAGE (*cut down, annoyed, guilty, eye-opener*, Mayfield, McLeod, & Hall, 1974)	4-item, self-report	Wolford et al. (1999)	320 inpatients with severe persistent mental illness (psychosis, depression, bipolar)	SCID + Clinician Rating Scale (CRS; Drake et al., 1990) 6-month alcohol use disorder	>1	.61	.70	.57	.73	.72
CAGE		Dervaux et al. (2006)	114 inpatients/outpatients with schizophrenia	CIDI (Robins et al., 1988) lifetime alcohol use disorder	≥2	.82	.94	.85		
Drug Abuse Screening Test (DAST; Skinner, 1982)	28-item, self-report	Wolford et al. (1999)	320 inpatients with severe persistent mental illness	SCID + CRS 6-month drug use disorder	≥6	.72	.77	.46	.91	.77
		Cassidy et al. (2008)	84 inpatients/outpatients with first-episode psychosis	SCID current alcohol use	≥3	.85	.73	.74	.84	.83
DAST-20	20-item, self-report	Cocco & Carey (1998)	97 outpatient psychiatric–mixed diagnoses	SCID 12-month drug use disorder	≥4	.84	.79			

Continued

Table 5.3 (Continued)

Measure	Description	Sample study	Participants	Criterion[b]	Cutoff	Sensitivity[c]	Specificity[c]	PPV[c]	NPV[c]	AUC[c]
DAST-10	10-item, self-report	Maisto et al. (2000)	162 outpatients with severe persistent mental illness (psychosis, depression, bipolar)	SCID current drug use disorder	≥2	.85	.78	.35	.97	
Dartmouth Assessment of Lifestyle Instrument (DALI) Alcohol screen (Rosenberg et al., 1998)	18-item, interview administered	Rosenberg et al. (1998)	73 psychiatric inpatients with severe and persistent mental illness	SCID+CRS 6-month alcohol use disorder	≥2	.8	.85	.78	.86	.84
DALI—Other drug screen	18-item, interview administered	Rosenberg et al. (1998)	73 psychiatric inpatients with severe and persistent mental illness	SCID+CRS 6-month drug use disorder	>−1	1.0	.80	.56	1.0	.93
DrugCheck Problem List	13-item, self-report	Kavanagh et al. (in submission)	50 early episode and 51 forensic inpatients	CIDI substance use disorders	>4	.91	.84	.91	.84	.92
Michigan Alcoholism Screening Test (MAST; Selzer, 1971)	25-item, self-report	Teitelbaum & Carey (2000)	Meta-analysis on 1171 with mixed psychiatric diagnoses from mixed settings	Presence of alcohol use disorder, assessed by various means	≥5	.88	.68			
MMPI-A scales MAC-R, ACK, PRO (Weed, Butcher, & Williams, 1994)	Self-report	Micucci (2002)	79 adolescent psychiatric inpatients	Chart diagnosis	MAC-R, ACK, or PRO ≥ 60	.83	.47	.41	.87	

NET (*normal*, *eye-opener*, *tolerance*; Bottoms, Martier, & Sokol, 1998)	3-item, self-report	Wolford et al. (1999)	320 inpatients with severe persistent mental illness	SCID+CRS 6-month alcohol use disorder	>1	.48	.84	.67	.71	.73
T-ACE (*tolerance*, *annoyed*, *cut down*, *eye-opener*; Sokol, Martier, & Ager, 1989)	4-item, self-report	Wolford et al. (1999)	As above	As above	>3	.47	.87	.71	.71	.76
TWEAK (*tolerance*, *expressed worry by friends/relatives*, *amnesia*, *eye-opener*; Russell et al., 1994)	5-item, self-report	Wolford et al. (1999)	As above	As above	>3	.58	.85	.72	.75	.78
Reasons for Drug Use Screening Test (RDU; Grant et al., 1988)	31-item, self-report	Wolford et al. (1999)	As above	SCID+CRS 6-month drug use disorder	>16	.73	.74	.44	.91	.81
Severity of Dependence Scale (SDS; Gossop, Darke, Griffiths, & Hando, 1995)	5-item, self-report	Hides, Dawe, Young, & Kavanagh (2007)	153 inpatients with psychotic disorder	CIDI 12-month cannabis use disorder	≥2	.86	.83	.86	.83	.90

[a]*Studies were selected on the basis of reporting a meta-analysis or on recency and sample size. Only selected results from studies are reported.*
[b]*Unless otherwise specified, current diagnoses are used.*
[c]*The sensitivity of a test is the proportion of individuals with the disorder who are identified correctly. Its specificity is the number without the disorder who are identified correctly. The positive predictive value (PPV) is the proportion of those screening positive who have the disorder, and the negative predictive value (NPV) is the proportion of those screening negative who do not have the disorder. The receiver operating characteristics (ROC) curve plots sensitivity against 1-specificity. The chance value of the area under the curve (AUC) is .50.*

Table 5.4 Examples of screening instruments for mental disorders and of their performance in samples with substance use disorders[a]

Measure	Description	Sample study	Participants	Criterion[b]	Cutoff	Sensitivity[c]	Specificity[c]	PPV[c]	NPV[c]	AUC[c]
Beck Depression Inventory II (BDI II; Beck et al., 1996)	21-item, self-report	Seignourel et al. (2008)	582 in substance abuse studies	SCID-IV (First, Spitzer, Gibbon, & Williams, 1996)	25	.73	.75	.45	.91	
		Lykke, Hesse, Austin, & Oestrich (2008)	144 psychiatric inpatients	ICD-10 Mood diagnosis on psychiatric interview	—					.65
BDI-Fast Screen (Beck et al., 2000)	7-item, self-report	Rissmiller, Biever, Mishra, & Steer (2006)	100 detoxifying inpatients with substance use disorder	DSM-IV-TR diagnosis made by experienced clinical psychiatrist	9	.9[illegible]	.77	.30	.99	.84
Brief Psychiatric Rating Scale (BPRS; Overall & Gorham, 1988)		Lykke et al. (2008)	144 psychiatric inpatients	ICD-10 schizophrenia spectrum diagnosis on psychiatric interview	—					.66
CAMH Concurrent Disorders Screener (CAMH-CDS) (Negrete et al., 2004)	Computerized self-report	Negrete et al. (2004)	171, 656, and 301 clients of an addiction service	Standard psychiatric diagnostic interview	DSM-IV criteria fulfilled	.92[d] .86[d]	.74[d] .39[d]	.91[d] .88[d]	.77[d] .37[d]	

General Health Questionnaire (GHQ-60; Goldberg, 1978)	60-item, self-report for nonpsychotic disorders	Ross & Glaser (1989)	511 (weighted sample) outpatients of an addictions research foundation	DIS (Robins et al., 1981)	>23	.69	.75	.77	.66	.78
Kessler 6 (K6; Andrews & Slade, 2001)	6-item, self-report	Swartz & Lurigio (2006)	10,069 on a general population screen, meeting substance disorder criteria within past year	CIDI-SF (Kessler et al., 2003)	13					
				MDD[f]		.86	.78			.86
				PD[g]		.81	.78			.77
				Nonaffect. Psychosis		.77	.75			.77
				Bipolar		.79	.74			.78
				Any		**.76**	**.81**			**.82**
Mood Module (MM), Primary Care Evaluation of Mental Disorders (PRIME-MD; Spitzer et al., 1995)	9-item, interviewing guide	Rissmiller et al. (2006)	100 detoxifying inpatients with substance use disorder	DSM-IV-TR diagnosis made by experienced clinical psychiatrist	≥7	.90	.72	.26	.98	.86

Continued

Table 5.4 (Continued)

Measure	Description	Sample study	Participants	Criterion[b]	Cutoff	Sensitivity[c]	Specificity[c]	PPV[c]	NPV[c]	AUC[c]
Psychiatric Diagnostic Screening Questionnaire (PDSQ; Zimmerman & Mattia, 2001)	Self-report	Zimmerman, Sheeran, Chelminski, & Young (2004)	133 psychiatric outpatients with substance use disorders	SCID	Varied across disorders	.92[e]	.63[e]	.35[e]	.97[e]	.86[e]
		Magruder, Sonne, Brady, Quello, & Martin (2005)	120 patients with substance use disorders	SCID						
				MDD	9	.87	.85	.57	.96	.90
				PD[g]	4	.59	.81	.33	.92	.78
				Psychosis	1	1.00	.67	.16	1.00	.94
				Average						.84[e]
Symptom Checklist-90R (SCL-90R; Derogatis, 1994)	Self-report	Benjamin et al. (2006)	171 active or retired military personnel in substance abuse program	SCID	25 (several cutoffs reported)	.86	.28			.88

[a]*Studies were selected on the basis of reporting a meta-analysis or on recency and sample size. Only selected results from studies are reported.*
[b]*Unless otherwise specified, current diagnoses are used.*
[c]*The sensitivity of a test is the proportion of individuals with the disorder who are identified correctly. Its specificity is the number without the disorder who are identified correctly. The positive predictive value (PPV) is the proportion of those screening positive who have the disorder, and the negative predictive value (NPV) is the proportion of those screening negative who do not have the disorder. The receiver operating characteristics (ROC) curve plots sensitivity against 1-specificity. The chance value of the area under the curve (AUC) is .50.*
[d]*Includes a match to a diagnostic interview result on another psychiatric disorder.*
[e]*Mean values across disorders.*
[f]*Major depressive disorder.*
[g]*Panic disorder.*

than in other contexts (Craig, 2005). Similarly, the Addiction Severity Index (McLellan, Luborsky, Woody, & O'Brien, 1980) shows mixed reliability and validity at best in people with severe mental disorders (Carey, Cocco, & Correia, 1997). Since even low levels of substance use can impact on psychological symptoms and community functioning, measures that assess changes in these areas may be especially useful.

Several standard screens for psychiatric symptoms are also applicable in AMDs (Table 5.4), although their performance is not always as good as in nonaddicted samples. Detailed psychometric data on the BDI-II (Beck, Steer, & Brown, 1996) in a sample of 416 inpatients with addictive disorders were published by Buckley, Parker, and Heggie (2001). The population had a mean of 22.1 (SD = 11.5), and the distribution approximated normality. Internal consistency was high (.91), and a three-factor model (cognitive, affective, somatic) best accounted for data. Other studies show that the BDI has acceptable sensitivity but variable specificity relative to diagnostic measures in samples with addictive disorders (Seignourel, Green, & Schmitz, 2008). Among other measures in Table 5.4, the seven-item BDI Fast Screen (Beck, Steer, & Brown, 2000) and Kessler-6 (Andrews & Slade, 2001) may be particularly useful for identification of major depression in addiction settings, given their brevity.

In both Tables 5.3 and 5.4, different cutoffs are sometimes required than in populations without AMDs. Optimal cutoffs in a particular setting may also vary from these figures, depending on the relative costs of missed or falsely identified cases. Positive and negative predictive values are also relative to the base rate of the disorder (cf. Benjamin, Mossman, Graves, & Sanders, 2006), as is the overall utility of the instrument (e.g., if a disorder is extremely common in a particular treatment setting, it is difficult for any instrument to do better than an assumption that all have the problem). In evaluating screening instruments, it is important to bear in mind that an interview-based criterion measure sometimes has limited reliability in people with AMDs (Ross, Swinson, Doumani, & Larkin, 1995), depending on the ability and willingness of the person to acknowledge problems to an interviewer.

A five-level clinician rating scale of substance use problems (none/mild/moderate/severe/extremely severe) that has detailed descriptors of each level and is based on all available data (self-report, interview, observation, biochemical, collateral) has demonstrated high sensitivity and specificity in detecting the presence of substance use disorders in psychiatric settings (Carey, Cocco, & Simons, 1996; Drake et al., 1990). While the scale has high potential utility for services, this apparently simple assessment gains accuracy only if based on substantial, sound information.

Biochemical assays for substance use

As in other groups with substance use problems, people with AMDs sometimes deny substance use. Urine, saliva, or blood screens can sometimes detect this substance use in psychiatric patients (Galletley, Field, & Prior, 1993), and as in other populations, a test that is given within about 48 h of substance use can detect most substances (Kavanagh, McGrath, Saunders, Dore, & Clark, 2001). In the case of marijuana, a urine test may detect substance use 2–6 weeks later, depending on the detection level that is used. While nicotine is metabolized rapidly into cotinine, the latter has a half-life of about 15 h in serum and saliva, and salivary thiocyanate has a half-life of 9.5 days (Kavanagh et al., 2001).

Breath analysis (for CO or alcohol) can also detect acute ingestion (e.g., over about 6 h for CO). However, reports by patients, in the context of high levels of trust and rapport, can give more accurate results than a urine screen or breath analysis, especially concerning substance use some weeks before. Hair samples have the advantage of detection of substance use over several weeks and are well tolerated in people with schizophrenia (McPhillips et al., 1997). However, as for other laboratory-based screens, the delay in receiving test results substantially reduces the utility of these tests in clinical practice.

Functional analyses

This step of the assessment process is the most complex and demanding in AMDs. For a comprehensive, prioritized management strategy to be put in place, an assessment of the nature of each disorder or problem and its impacts needs to be made, together with its triggers, maintaining conditions and existing coping strategies or compensatory environmental supports. Then, an analysis needs to be made of conditions under which each problem may influence each of the others. A diagram of these relationships can help, both to increase insight and to guide the negotiation of treatment plans. In cases in which the person already has effective coping skills, just the feedback of the relationships between disorders may be enough to initiate significant behavior change. However, in most cases, it is just the beginning of a long treatment process.

It is easy for both the client and the practitioner to be confused and demoralized by the number and complexity of the problems. In this situation, it is difficult to generate motivation to change, as the self-efficacy of both parties is low. It is particularly important to undertake as thorough an examination of strengths as would be done for deficits or problems. For example:

- Are there examples of more effective coping in the past or present? What other skills are they confident they can do?

- Are there times when their problems seem a little less severe? Is there anything about those times that could be used in other situations?
- What activities still bring them pleasure or give them hope to keep going? Are there aspects of their lives that are still unaffected by the problems or show less impact?
- Who can still be relied on to give practical assistance, advice, or emotional support?

The context of a hospital or treatment service and the ubiquitous presence of dysphoria can conspire with the clinician's focus on problems to cause important strengths to go unnoticed. Discussion of other things in the person's life—how they spend their time, with whom they spend time, when things have been different from the present—is often needed to elicit strengths, which may have potential application or may help build hope and self-efficacy.

REFERENCES

American Psychiatric Association. (1994). *Diagnostic and statistical manual of mental disorders (DSM-IV)*. Washington, DC: American Psychiatric Association.

Ananth, J., Vandewater, S., Kamal, M., Broksky, A., Gamal, R., & Miller, M. (1989). Missed diagnosis of substance abuse in psychiatric patients. *Hospital and Community Psychiatry*, *4*, 297–299.

Andrews, G., Hall, W., Teesson, M., & Henderson, S. (1999). *The mental health of Australians*. Canberra: Department of Health and Aged Care.

Andrews, G., & Slade, T. (2001). Interpreting scores on the Kessler psychological distress scale (K10). *Australian and New Zealand Journal of Public Health*, *25*, 494–497.

Appleby, L., Dyson, V., Altman, E., & Luchins, D. J. (1997). Assessing substance use in multiproblem patients: Reliability and validity of the Addiction Severity Index in a mental hospital population. *Journal of Nervous and Mental Disease*, *185*, 159–165.

Australian Institute of Health and Welfare. (2005). *2004 National Drug Strategy Household Survey: First results*. Canberra: AIHW.

Barbee, J. G., Clark, P. D., Crapazano, M. S., Heintz, G. C., & Kehoe, C. E. (1989). Alcohol and substance abuse among schizophrenic patients presenting to an emergency psychiatric service. *Journal of Nervous and Mental Disease*, *177*, 400–407.

Barnes, M., Lawford, B. R., Burton, S. C., Heslop, K. R., Noble, E. P., Hausdorf, K., et al. (2006). Smoking and schizophrenia: Is symptom profile related to smoking and which antipsychotic medication is of benefit in reducing cigarette use? *Australian and New Zealand Journal of Psychiatry*, *40*, 575–580.

Barnes, T. R., Mutsatsa, S. H., Hutton, S. B., Watt, H. C., & Joyce, E. M. (2006). Comorbid substance use and age at onset of schizophrenia. *British Journal of Psychiatry*, *188*, 237–242.

Beck, A. T., Steer, R. A., & Brown, G. K. (1996). *Manual for the Beck Depression Inventory-II* (2nd ed.). San Antonio, TX: Psychological Corporation.

Beck, A. T., Steer, R. A., & Brown, G. K. (2000). *Manual for the Beck depression inventory-fast screen for medical patients*. San Antonio, TX: Psychological Corporation.

Benjamin, A. B., Mossman, D., Graves, N. S., & Sanders, R. D. (2006). Tests of a symptom checklist to screen for comorbid psychiatric disorders in alcoholism. *Comprehensive Psychiatry*, *47*, 227–233.

Berkson, J. (1949). Limitations of the application of four-fold tables to hospital data. *Biological Bulletin*, *2*, 47–53.

Bottoms, S. F., Martier, S. S., & Sokol, F. J. (1998). Refinements in screening for risk drinking in reproductive aged women: The NET results. *Alcoholism*, *13*, 339.

Brown, S. A., & Schuckit, M. A. (1988). Changes in depression among abstinent alcoholics. *Journal of Studies on Alcohol*, *49*, 412–417.

Buckley, T. C., Parker, J. D., & Heggie, J. (2001). A psychometric evaluation of the BDI-II in treatment-seeking substance abusers. *Journal of Substance Abuse Treatment*, *20*, 197–204.

Burns, L. M., & Teesson, M. (2002). Alcohol use disorders comorbid with anxiety, depression and drug use disorders: Findings from the Australian National Survey of Mental Health and Well Being. *Drug and Alcohol Dependence*, *68*, 299–307.

Carey, K. B., Cocco, K. M., & Correia, C. J. (1997). Reliability and validity of the Addiction Severity Index among outpatients with severe mental illness. *Psychological Assessment*, *9*, 422–428.

Carey, K. B., Cocco, K. M., & Simons, J. S. (1996). Concurrent validity of clinicians' ratings of substance absue among psychiatric outpatients. *Psychiatric Services*, *47*, 842–847.

Carey, K. B., & Simons, J. (2000). Utility of collateral information in assessing substance use among psychiatric outpatients. *Journal of Substance Abuse*, *11*, 139–147.

Cassidy, C. M., Schmitz, N., & Malla, A. (2008). Validation of the Alcohol Use Disorders Identification Test and the Drug Abuse Screening Test in first episode psychosis. *Canadian Journal of Psychiatry*, *53*, 26–33.

Castel, S., Rush, B., Urbanoski, K., & Toneatto, T. (2006). Overlap of clusters of psychiatric symptoms among clients of a comprehensive addiction treatment service. *Psychology of Addictive Behaviors*, *20*, 28–35.

Catts, V. S., Catts, S. V., O'Toole, B. I., & Frost, A. D. (2008). Cancer incidence in patients with schizophrenia and their first-degree relatives: A meta-analysis. *Acta Psychiatrica Scandinavica*, *117*, 323–336.

Cocco, K. M., & Carey, K. B. (1998). Psychometric properties of the Drug Abuse Screening Test in psychiatric outpatients. *Psychological Assessment*, *10*, 408–414.

Craig, R. J. (2005). Assessing contemporary substance abusers with the MMPI Mac Andrews Alcoholism Scale: A review. *Substance Use and Abuse*, *40*, 427–450.

Dawson, D. A., Grant, B. F., & Stinson, F. S. (2005). The AUDIT-C: Screening for alcohol use disorders and risk drinking in the presence of other psychiatric disorders. *Comprehensive Psychiatry*, *46*, 405–416.

D'Eramo, K. S., Prinstein, M. J., Freeman, J., Grapentine, W. L., & Spirito, A. (2004). Psychiatric diagnoses and comorbidity in relation to suicidal behavior among psychiatrically hospitalized adolescents. *Child Psychiatry and Human Development*, *35*, 21–35.

Derogatis, L. R. (1994). *The Symptom Checklist 90-R: Administration, scoring and procedures manual*. Minneapolis, MN: National Computer Systems.

Dervaux, A., Bayle, F. J., Laqueille, X., Bourdel, M. C., Leborgne, M., Olie, J. P., et al. (2006). Validity of the CAGE questionnaire in schizophrenic patients with alcohol abuse and dependence. *Schizophrenia Research*, *81*, 151–155.

Drake, R. E., Osher, F. C., Noordsy, D. L., Hurlbut, S. C., Teague, G. B., & Beaudett, M. S. (1990). Diagnosis of alcohol use disorders in schizophrenia. *Schizophrenia Bulletin*, *16*, 57–67.

Dratcu, L., Grandison, A., McKay, G., Bamidele, A., & Vasudevan, V. (2007). Clozapine-resistant psychosis, smoking, and caffeine: Managing the neglected effects of substances that our patients consume every day. *American Journal of Therapeutics*, *14*, 314–318.

D'Souza, D. C., Gil, R. B., Madonick, S., Perry, E. B., Forselius-Bielen, K., Braley, G., et al. (2006). Enhanced sensitivity to the euphoric effects of alcohol in schizophrenia. *Neuropsychopharmacology*, *31*, 2767–2775.

First, M. B., Spitzer, R. L., Gibbon, M., & Williams, J. B. W. (1996). *Structured clinical interview for Axis I DSM-IV disorders research version: Psychotic screen*. New York: New York State Psychiatric Institute, Biometrics Research Department.

Galletley, C. A., Field, C. D., & Prior, M. (1993). Urine drug screening of patients admitted to a state psychiatric hospital. *Hospital and Community Psychiatry*, *44*, 587–589.

Goldberg, D. P. (1978). *Manual of the general health questionnaire*. Windsor, Ontario: NFER Publishing Co.

Gossop, M., Darke, S., Griffiths, P., & Hando, J. (1995). The Severity of Dependence Scale (SDS): Psychometrics properties of the SDS in English and Australian samples of heroin, cocaine and amphetamine users. *Addiction*, *90*, 607–614.

Grant, B., Hasin, D. S., & Harford, T. C. (1988). Screening for current drug use disorders in alcoholics: An application of receiver operating characteristic analysis. *Drug and Alcohol Dependence*, *21*, 113–125.

Green, B., Kavanagh, D. J., & Young, R. M. (2004). Reasons for cannabis use in men with and without psychosis. *Drug and Alcohol Review*, *23*, 445–453.

Gurpegui, M., Aguilar, M. C., Martinez-Ortega, J. M., Jurado, D., Diaz, F. J., Quintana, H. M., et al. (2006). Fewer but heavier caffeine consumers in schizophrenia: A case-control study. *Schizophrenia Research*, *86*, 276–283.

Hasin, D., Samet, S., Nunes, E., Meydan, J., Matseoane, K., Waxman, R., et al. (2006). Diagnosis of comorbid psychiatric disorders in substance users assessed with the Psychiatric Research Interview for Substance and Mental Disorders for DSM-IV. *American Journal of Psychiatry*, *163*, 689–696.

Hasin, D. S., Trautman, K. D., Miele, G. M., Samet, S., Smith, M., Endicott, J., et al. (1996). Psychiatric Research Interview for Substance and Mental Disorders (PRISM): Reliability for substance abusers. *American Journal of Psychiatry*, *153*, 1195–1201.

Hides, L., Dawe, S., Kavanagh, D. J., & Young, R. M. (2006). A prospective study of psychotic symptom and cannabis relapse in recent onset psychosis. *British Journal of Psychiatry*, *189*, 137–143.

Hides, L., Dawe, S., Young, R. M., & Kavanagh, D. J. (2007). The reliability and validity of the Severity of Dependence Scale for detecting cannabis dependence in psychosis. *Addiction*, *102*, 35–40.

Hodgkins, D. C., el-Guebaly, N., Armstrong, S., & Dufour, M. (1999). Implications of depression on outcome from alcohol dependence: A three-year prospective follow-up. *Alcoholism: Clinical and Experimental Research*, *23*, 151–157.

Hughes, J. R., McHugh, P., Holtzman, S., & Hughes. (1998). Caffeine and schizophrenia. *Psychiatric Services*, *49*, 1415–1417.

Kavanagh, D. J., McGrath, J., Saunders, J. B., Dore, G., & Clark, D. (2001). Substance abuse in patients with schizophrenia: Epidemiology and management. *Drugs*, *62*, 743–755.

Kavanagh, D. J., Trembath, M., Shockley, N., Connolly, J., White, A., Isailovic, A., Young, R. McD., Saunders, J. B., & Byrne, G. (in submission). The predictive validity of the DrugCheck Problem List as a screen for co-occurring substance use disorders in people with psychosis.

Kavanagh, D. J., Waghorn, G., Jenner, L., Chant, D. C., Carr, V., Evans, M., et al. (2004). Demographic and clinical correlates of comorbid substance use disorders in psychosis: Multivariate analyses from an epidemiological sample. *Schizophrenia Research*, *66*, 115–124.

Kendler, K. S., Myers, J., & Gardner, C. O. (2006). Caffeine intake, toxicity and dependence and lifetime risk for psychiatric and substance use disorders: An epidemiologic and co-twin control analysis. *Psychological Medicine*, *36*, 1717–1725.

Kessler, R. C., Barker, P. R., Colpe, L. J., Epstein, J. F., Gfroerer, J. C., Hiripi, E., et al. (2003). Screening for serious mental illness in the general population. *Archives of General Psychiatry*, *60*, 184–189.

Kessler, R. C., Nelson, C. B., McGonagle, K. A., Edlund, M. J., Frank, R. G., & Leaf, P. J. (1996). The epidemiology of co-occurring addictive and mental disorders: Implications for prevention and service utilization. *American Journal of Orthopsychiatry*, *66*, 17–31.

Khlat, M., Sermet, C., & Pape, A. L. (2004). Increased prevalence of depression, smoking, heavy drinking and use of psycho-active drugs among unemployed men in France. *European Journal of Epidemiology*, *19*, 445–451.

Knekt, P., Raitasalo, R., Heliovaara, M., Lehtinen, V., Pukkala, E., Teppo, L., et al. (1996). Elevated lung cancer risk among persons with depressed mood. *American Journal of Epidemiology*, *144*, 1096–1103.

Lykke, J., Hesse, M., Austin, S. F., & Oestrich, I. (2008). Validity of the BPRS, the BDI and the BAI in dual diagnosis patients. *Addictive Behaviors*, *33*, 292–300.

MacAndrew, C. (1965). The differentiation of male alcoholic outpatients from nonalcoholic psychaitric outpatients by means of the MMPI. *Quarterly Journal of Studies on Alcohol*, *26*, 238–246.

Magruder, K. M., Sonne, S. C., Brady, K. T., Quello, S., & Martin, R. H. (2005). Screening for co-occuring mental disorders in drug treatment populations. *Journal of Drug Issues*, *35*, 593–605.

Maisto, S. A., Carey, M. P., Carey, K. B., Gordon, C. M., & Gleason, J. R. (2000). Use of the AUDIT and the DAST-10 to identify alcohol and drug use disorders among adults with a severe and persistent mental illness. *Psychological Assessment*, *12*, 186–192.

Mayfield, D., McLeod, G., & Hall, P. (1974). The CAGE questionnaire: Validation of a new alcoholism screening instrument. *American Journal of Psychiatry*, *131*, 1121–1123.

McLellan, A. T., Luborsky, L., Woody, G. E., & O'Brien, C. P. (1980). An improved diagnostic evaluation instrument for substance abuse patients: The Addiction Severity Index. *Journal of Nervous and Mental Disease*, *168*, 26–33.

McPhillips, M. A., Kelly, F. J., Barnes, T. R., Duke, P. J., Gene-Cos, N., & Clark, K. (1997). Detecting comorbid substance misuse among people with schizophrenia in the community: A study comparing the results of questionnaires with analysis of hair and urine. *Schizophrenia Research*, *25*, 141–148.

Micucci, J. A. (2002). Accuracy of MMPI-A scales ACK, MAC-R, and PRO in detecting comorbid substance abuse among psychiatric inpatients. *Assessment*, *9*, 111–122.

Miles, H., Johnson, S., Amponsah-Afuwape, S., Finch, E., Leese, M., & Thornicroft, G. (2003). Characteristics of subgroups of individuals with psychotic illness and a comorbid substance use disorder. *Psychiatric Services*, *54*, 554–581.

Minkoff, K., & Drake, R. E. (Eds.) (1991). *Dual diagnosis of major mental illness and substance disorder:* Vol. 50. San Francisco: Jossey-Bass.

Mueser, K. T., Crocker, A. G., Frisman, L. B., Drake, R. E., Covell, N. H., & Essock, S. M. (2006). Conduct disorder and antisocial personality disorder in persons with severe psychiatric and substance use disorders. *Schizophrenia Bulletin*, *32*, 626–636.

Mueser, K. T., Drake, R., & Wallach, M. (1998). Dual diagnosis: A review of etiological theories. *Addictive Behaviors*, *23*, 717–734.

Mueser, K. T., Kavanagh, D. J., & Brunette, M. (2007). Implications of research on comorbidity for the nature and management of substance misuse. In P. M. Miller & D. J. Kavanagh (Eds.), *Translation of addictions science into practice: Update and future directions* (pp. 277–320). Oxford: Elsevier.

Nardi, A. E., Lopes, F. L., Valenca, A. M., Freire, R. C., Veras, A. B., de-Melo-Neto, V. L., et al. (2007). Caffeine challenge test in panic disorder and depression with panic attacks. *Comprehensive Psychiatry*, *48*, 257–263.

Negrete, J. C., Collins, J., Turner, N. E., & Skinner, W. (2004). The Centre for Addiction and Mental Health Concurrent Disorders Screener. *Canadian Journal of Psychiatry—Revue Canadienne de Psychiatrie*, *49*, 843–850.

Nunes, E. V., Sullivan, M. A., & Levin, F. R. (1994). Treatment of depression in patients with opiate dependence. *Biological Psychiatry*, *56*, 793–802.

Osborn, D. P. J., Levy, G., Nazareth, I., Petersen, I., Islam, A., & King, M. B. (2007). Relative risk of cardiovascular and cancer mortality in people with severe mental illness from the United Kingdom's general practice research database. *Archives of General Psychiatry*, *64*, 242–249.

Overall, J. E., & Gorham, D. R. (1988). The Brief Psychiatric Rating Scale: Recent developments in acertainment and scaling. *Psychopharmacological Bulletin*, *24*, 97–99.

Peeling, P., & Dawson, B. (2007). Influence of caffeine ingestion on perceived mood states, concentration, and arousal levels during a 75-min university lecture. *Advances in Physiology Education*, *31*, 332–335.

Potvin, S., Sepehry, A. A., & Stip, E. (2007). Meta-analysis of depressive symptoms in dual-diagnosis schizophrenia. *Australian and New Zealand Journal of Psychiatry*, *41*, 792–799.

Regier, D. A., Farmer, M. E., Rae, D. S., Locke, B. Z., Keith, S. J., Judd, L. L., et al. (1990). Comorbidity of mental disorders with alcohol and other drug abuse: Results from the epidemiologic catchment area (ECA) study. *Journal of the American Medical Association*, *264*, 2511–2518.

Rissmiller, D. J., Biever, M., Mishra, D., & Steer, R. A. (2006). Screening detoxifying inpatients with substance-related disorders for a major depressive disorder. *Journal of Clinical Psychology in Medical Settings*, *13*, 315–321.

Robins, L. N., Helzer, J. E., Croughan, J., & Ratcliff, K. S. (1981). National Institute of Mental Health Diagnostic Interview Schedule: History, characteristics and validity. *Archives of General Psychiatry*, *38*, 381–389.

Robins, L. N., Wing, J., Wittchen, H.-U., Helzer, J. E., Babor, T. F., Burke, J. D., et al. (1988). The Composite International Diagnostic Interview: An epidemiologic instrument suitable for use in conjunction with different diagnostic systems and in different cultures. *Archives of General Psychiatry*, *45*, 1069–1077.

Rosenberg, S. D., Drake, R. E., Wolford, G. L., Mueser, K. T., Oxman, T. E., Vidaver, R. M., et al. (1998). Dartmouth Assessment of Lifestyle Instrument (DALI): A substance use disorder screen for people with severe mental illness. *American Journal of Psychiatry*, *155*, 232–238.

Ross, H. E., & Glaser, F. B. (1989). Psychiatric screening of alcohol and drug patients: The validity of the GHQ-60 (General Health Questionnaire). *American Journal of Drug and Alcohol Abuse*, *15*, 429–437.

Ross, H. E., Glaser, F. B., & Germanson, T. (1988). The prevalence of psychiatric disorders in patients with alcohol or other drug problems. *Archives of General Psychiatry*, *45*, 1023–1031.

Ross, H. E., Swinson, R., Doumani, S., & Larkin, E. J. (1995). Diagnosing comorbidity in substance abusers: A comparison of the test-retest reliability of two interviews. *American Journal of Drug and Alcohol Abuse*, *21*, 167–185.

Russell, M., Martier, S. S., Sokol, R. J., Mudar, P., Bottoms, S. F., Jacobson, S., et al. (1994). Screening for pregnancy risk—Drinking. *Alcoholism: Clinical and Experimental Research*, *18*, 1156–1161.

Sacks, J. A., Drake, R. E., Williams, V. F., Banks, S. M., & Herrell, J. M. (2003). Utility of the Time-Line Follow-Back to assess substance use among homeless adults. *Journal of Nervous and Mental Disease*, *191*, 145–153.

Saunders, J. B., Aasland, O. G., Babor, T. F., De La Fuente, J. R., & Grant, M. (1993). Development of the Alcohol Use Disorders Identification Test (AUDIT): WHO collaborative project on early detection of persons with harmful alcohol consumption II. *Addiction*, *88*, 791–804.

Schuckit, M. A. (2000). *Drug and alcohol abuse: A clinical guide to diagnosis and treatment*. New York: Kluwer Academic/Plenum.

Schuckit, M. A., Tipp, J. E., Bergman, M., Reich, W., Hesselbrock, V. M., & Smith, T. L. (1997). Comparison of induced and independent major depressive disorders in 2945 alcoholics. *American Journal of Psychiatry*, 154, 948–957.

Seignourel, P. J., Green, C., & Schmitz, J. M. (2008). Factor structure and diagnositc efficiency of the BDI-II in treatment-seeking substance users. *Drug and Alcohol Dependence*, *93*, 271–278.

Selzer, M. (1971). The Michigan Alcoholism Screening Test: The quest for a new diagnostic instrument. *American Journal of Psychiatry*, *127*, 1653–1658.

Skinner, H. (1982). The Drug Abuse Screening Test. *Addictive Behaviors*, *7*, 363–371.

Sobell, L., & Sobell, M. (1992). Timeline followback: A technique for assessing self-reported alcohol consumption. In R. Litten & J. P. Allen (Eds.), *Measuring alcohol consumption: Psychosocial and biochemical methods* (pp. 41–72). Clifton, NJ: Humana Press.

Sokol, R. J., Martier, S. S., & Ager, J. W. (1989). The T-ACE questions: Practical prenatal detection of risk drinking. *American Journal of Obstetrics and Gynecology*, *160*, 863–870.

Spitzer, R. L., Williams, J. B. W., Gibbon, M., & First, M. B. (1990). *Structured Clinical Interview for DSM-III-R—Patient Version 1.0 (SCID-P)*. Washington, DC: American Psychiatric Press.

Spitzer, R. L., Williams, J. B. W., Kroenke, K., Linzer, M., deGruy, F. V. I., Hahn, S. R., et al. (1995). *Prime-MD instruction manual updated for DSM-IV*. New York: Biometrics Research Department, New York State Psychiatric Institute.

Swartz, J. A., & Lurigio, A. J. (2006). Screening for serious mental illness in populations with co-occuring substance use disorders: Performance of the K6 scale. *Journal of Substance Abuse Treatment*, *31*, 287–296.

Teesson, M., Hall, W., Lynskey, M., & Degenhardt, L. (2000). Alcohol- and drug-use disorders in Australia: Implications of the National Survey of Mental Health and Well being. *Australian and New Zealand Journal of Psychiatry*, *34*, 206–213.

Teitelbaum, L. M., & Carey, K. B. (2000). Temporal stability of alcohol screening measures in a psychiatric setting. *Psychology of Addictive Behaviors*, *14*, 401–404.

Weed, N. C., Butcher, H. N., & Williams, V. L. (1994). Development of MMPI-A alcohol/drug problem scales. *Journal of Studies on Alcohol*, 55, 296–302.

Weiss, R. D., Najavits, L. M., Greenfield, S. F., Soto, J. A., Shaw, S. R., & Wyner, D. (1998). Validity of substance use self-reports in dually diagnosed outpatients. *American Journal of Psychiatry*, *155*, 127–128.

Whalen, D. J., Silk, J. S., Semel, M., Forbes, E. E., Ryan, N. D., Axelson, D. A., et al. (2008). Caffeine consumption, sleep, and affect in the natural environments of depressed youth and healthy controls. *Journal of Pediatric Psychology*, *33*, 358–367.

Wilhelm, K., Mitchell, P., Slade, T., Brownhill, S., & Andrews, G. (2003). Prevalence and correlates of DSM-IV major depression in an Australian national survey. *Journal of Affective Disorders*, *75*, 155–162.

Wolford, G. L., Rosenberg, S. D., Drake, R. E., Mueser, K. T., Oxman, T. E., Hoffman, D., et al. (1999). Evaluation of methods for detecting substance use disorder in persons with severe mental illness. *Psychology of Addictive Behaviors*, *13*, 313–326.

Ziedonis, D. M., Kosten, T. R., Glazer, W. M., Frances, R. J., Ziedonis, D. M., Kosten, T. R., et al. (1994). Nicotine dependence and schizophrenia. *Hospital and Community Psychiatry*, *45*, 204–206.

Zimmerman, M., & Mattia, J. L. (2001). The Psychiatric Diagnostic Screening Questionnaire: Development, reliability and validity. *Comprehensive Psychiatry*, *42*, 175–189.

Zimmerman, M., Sheeran, T., Chelminski, I., & Young, D. (2004). Screening for psychiatric disorders in outpatients with DSM-IV substance use disorders. *Journal of Substance Abuse Treatment*, *26*, 181–188.

Chapter | six

Individualized Problem Assessment

I. Assessing Cognitive and Behavioral Factors

Laura J. Holt*, Linda S. Kranitz, and Ned L. Cooney
VA Connecticut Healthcare System and Yale University School of Medicine
*Trinity College, Hartford, Connecticut

SUMMARY POINTS

- Individualized assessment provides information that is crucial to the development and monitoring of a treatment plan. Numerous online repositories and print resources are available to assist clinicians with the selection and acquisition of assessment instruments.
- Several important dimensions rooted in the cognitive behavioral model should be assessed, including antecedents and expectations for substance use, self-efficacy for abstinence, motivation to change substance use, and craving for substances.
- Learning about a client's antecedents for substance use can inform the clinician about the thoughts, feelings, and circumstances that trigger a client's use; similarly, self-efficacy measures can assess a client's level of confidence in dealing with these triggers. This information can also provide a profile of high-risk situations that should be addressed in treatment.

Evidence-Based Addiction Treatment

- An assessment of substance use outcome expectancies can provide a clinician with an understanding of the positive and negative effects expected and desired by the client.
- Motivation to change behavior and motivation for treatment are dynamic processes that may fluctuate in response to a variety of internal and external factors.
- To assist with treatment planning and evaluation, motivation may be assessed from both the perspective of readiness to change and the degree to which internal or external factors are driving a client's motivation to change or to enter treatment for substance use.
- Craving for a substance can be considered to have multiple dimensions. The intensity of craving can fluctuate widely after exposure to substance-related cues, and it can be important to understand how clients experience craving.

In order to provide effective, individually tailored substance abuse treatment, a clinician should have a clear understanding of a number of unique factors associated with a client's addiction. In this chapter and the next, we discuss a range of assessment tools designed to measure addiction-related factors that vary across clients. The information gathered from these assessments is instrumental in the development and monitoring of a treatment plan that addresses the full range of a client's needs and circumstances. We describe the characteristics of these assessments tools, specify the populations with which they may be most useful, and provide a limited review of research related to their use.

Specifically, this chapter describes several assessments derived from a cognitive behavioral model, including antecedents and expectations for substance use, self-efficacy, motivation to change substance use, and craving. The next chapter addresses factors that are more broadly associated with addiction and recovery, including coping skills, treatment-related needs and preferences, personal and social consequences of substance use, social support, spirituality and religiosity, and involvement in 12-step groups. We also briefly review multidimensional assessment tools. Readers are encouraged to consult Chapter 4 on diagnosis/dependence and Chapter 5 on comorbidities given that assessment of these domains also is essential to treatment planning but beyond the scope of these chapters.

Our choice of assessments was guided by the relapse prevention model of addiction (Marlatt & Gordon, 2005) (see Chapter 11 for more details). This model contends that substance use and relapse result from the *interaction* of numerous factors both within (e.g., self-efficacy, coping, motivation, genetic predisposition) and outside (e.g., exposure to substance-related cues, availability of substance, quality of social support) the client. We strongly suggest that a clinician share the relapse prevention model with clients before conducting assessment, as it provides a client with a rationale for the clinician's use of these assessments.

Our list of assessments within each domain is by no means exhaustive. We considered several factors in our selection of measures, including how often a measure has been reported in the literature; its availability, cost, and ease of administration; and the applicability of the measure to multiple age groups and patient populations. Unless otherwise noted, the psychometric properties of each measure have been reported in published research. Since the majority of the measures described in this chapter are specific to alcohol, a clinician may find it helpful to substitute "drug use" or "drugs" for "drinking" or "alcohol" if necessary; however, research has not yet determined whether this substitution affects the instruments' validity and reliability.

Readers are encouraged to consult several online and print comprehensive reviews and instrument catalogs for more in-depth information about existing assessment tools. The National Institute of Alcohol Abuse and Alcoholism's *Assessing Alcohol Problems* (http://pubs.niaaa.nih.gov/publications/Assesing%20Alcohol/index.htm; Allen & Wilson, 2003), the University of Washington's *Alcohol and Drug Abuse Institute Library* (http://lib.adai.washington.edu/), the University of New Mexico's *Center on Alcoholism, Substance Abuse, and Addictions* instrument library (http://casaa.unm.edu/inst.html), the *Guided Self-Change Program* through Nova Southeastern University (http://www.nova.edu/gsc/online_files.html), and Donovan and Marlatt's (2005) *Assessment of Addictive Behaviors* are excellent resources.

ANTECEDENTS TO SUBSTANCE USE AND/OR RELAPSE

Clients with substance use disorders often identify similar triggers or cues for their substance use (e.g., stress, boredom) and report similar reasons for their use (e.g., to escape negative feelings; social pressure). Nonetheless, it is important to identify the unique triggers that place a client at risk for substance use so that he or she can anticipate and learn specific coping skills to deal with these situations. This section reviews assessments designed to assess the thoughts, feelings, and circumstances that may lead an individual to use drugs or alcohol and/or to relapse after a period of abstinence (Table 6.1). These assessments assist both the clinician and the client in determining which situations pose the greatest risk for substance use or substance relapse. A clinician may also assess a client's antecedents more informally at each

Table 6.1 Measures of antecedents to substance use/relapse

Instrument and number of items	Administration (time in minutes if known and method)	Availability	Target population(s)
Inventory of Drinking Situations (100/42 items)	15–20 min; computer[a]; paper and pencil	Fee for use[b]	Adolescents, college students, adults in alcohol treatment
Reasons for Drinking Questionnaire (16 items)	5 min; computer[a]; paper and pencil	Online[c] and Zywiak et al. (1996)	Adults in alcohol treatment
Drinking Motives Questionnaire (28/20/15 items)	Paper and pencil	Cooper et al. (1992), Cooper (1994), Grant et al. (2007)	Nontreatment-seeking adults, adolescents, college students
Inventory of Drug-Taking Situations (50 items)	10 min; computer; paper and pencil	Fee for use[b]	Adults seeking substance abuse treatment
Marijuana Motives Questionnaire (25 items)	Paper and pencil	Simons et al. (1998)	College students
Stimulant Relapse Risk Scale (30 items)	Paper and pencil	Ogai et al. (2007)	Adults in recovery for stimulant abuse

[a] *Computer access and scoring may be purchased at http://adai.washington.edu/sounddatasource/.*
[b] *Can be purchased from the Centre for Addiction and Mental Health: www.camh.net/publications/.*
[c] *http://casaa.unm.edu/inst.html.*

session by inquiring about the triggers that led to an urge or craving and/or to substance use.

The *Inventory of Drinking Situations* (IDS; Annis, Graham, & Davis, 1987) is an assessment of drinking triggers and has been used with adults, college students (Carey, 1993), and adolescents (Parra, Martin, & Clark, 2005). This 100-item measure is based on Marlatt's relapse taxonomy and contains questions about whether an individual drank heavily across eight situations, including unpleasant emotions, physical discomfort, pleasant emotions, testing personal control, urges and temptations, conflict with others, social pressure to drink, and pleasant times with others (Marlatt, 1996). Problem scores for each of these categories can be calculated to determine which situations pose the greatest risk for relapse. There are shorter 42-item versions of the IDS (Annis et al., 1987; Isenhart, 1993).

The *Reasons for Drinking Questionnaire* (RFDQ; Zywiak, Connors, Maisto, & Westerberg, 1996) is a briefer scale that asks clients to rate the importance of 16 reasons for using alcohol (e.g., "I felt anxious or tense"). Like the *Inventory of Drinking Situations*, the RFDQ is based on Marlatt's relapse taxonomy. The items on the RFDQ assess three main domains: negative emotions; social pressure/positive emotions; and a combination of withdrawal/testing control/urges/cues to drink. Research on the RFDQ has shown that drinking to cope with negative emotions was associated with greater dependence on alcohol, poorer treatment outcomes, and relapse (Zywiak et al., 1996). The *Drinking Motives Questionnaire* (DMQ) is similar to the RFDQ in that it assesses how often an individual drinks (i.e., *almost never/never* to *almost always/always*) across a range of situations and feelings. A 15-item DMQ with three subscales (i.e., social, coping, and enhancement) was developed for use with adults (Cooper, Russell, Skinner, & Windle, 1992). A 20-item DMQ (Cooper, 1994) was developed for use with adolescents and includes an additional "conformity" scale. The coping and enhancement motives subscales were associated with alcohol consumption, heavy drinking, and drinking problems (Cooper, 1994). Finally, Grant, Stewart, O'Connor, Blackwell, and Conrod (2007) examined a 28-item version of the DMQ (i.e., *Modified DMQ-Revised*) relevant to college students and suggested that this measure may be useful as a screening tool to identify young adults at risk for problematic drinking.

Some inventories focus on substances other than (or in addition to) alcohol. For example, the *Marijuana Motives Measure* (MMM; Simons, Correia, Carey, & Borsari, 1998) was developed based on the *Drinking Motives Questionnaire*; the 25 items on the MMM inquire about a client's motives to use marijuana related to enhancement, coping, socializing, conformity, and expansion (e.g., "to understand things differently"). Simons et al. (1998) reported that social motives showed the strongest association with marijuana-related problems.

Another measure, the *Inventory of Drug-Taking Situations* (IDTS; Annis, Turner, & Sklar, 1997), contains 50 items inquiring about the extent to which a client used a drug or drank across the eight situational categories from Marlatt's relapse taxonomy (e.g., unpleasant emotions, social pressure). Like the *Inventory of Drinking Situations*, information from the IDTS can be used for treatment planning purposes, as the IDTS generates a profile of the situations in which a client is most likely to use drugs or alcohol. In addition, if a client is abusing more than one substance, she or he may report on multiple drugs of abuse.

A newer measure designed to assess drug relapse risk is the 30-item *Stimulant Relapse Risk Scale* (SRRS; Ogai et al., 2007), which is based on the *Marijuana Craving Questionnaire* (Heishman, Singleton, & Liguori, 2001).

The SRRS was correlated with relapse and other measures of addiction severity in Japanese clients; however, it has not been studied with other populations.

SELF-EFFICACY

Self-efficacy refers to the belief that one can carry out the actions necessary to achieve a goal or outcome (Bandura, 1977). Applying this principle to addiction, some clients may feel overconfident in their ability to remain abstinent, whereas others may lack any confidence that they can abstain (DiClemente, Carbonari, Montgomery, & Hughes, 1994). Further, clients may have confidence in their ability to abstain in one situation (e.g., while socializing), but not in another (e.g., when feeling lonely). The relationship between self-efficacy and addiction has been researched widely, and findings generally show that a higher self-efficacy to abstain is associated with better long-term treatment outcomes (for a review, see Marlatt & Gordon, 2005).

Measures of self-efficacy are similar to measures of drinking/drug antecedents in that they ask about a wide range of situations that often pose a risk for relapse (e.g., positive and negative emotions, availability of a substance, social situations); however, they differ in the sense that they inquire about a client's *perceived ability* to abstain from substance use in these trigger situations. By learning the situations in which the individual feels least confident, the clinician can target these situations in treatment and assist the client in developing his/her confidence and coping skills where necessary. These measures, which are summarized in Table 6.2, also may be used throughout treatment to monitor changes in self-efficacy.

The *Alcohol Abstinence Self-Efficacy Scale* (AASE; DiClemente et al., 1994) assesses both confidence that one would *not drink* and temptation *to drink* on a scale of 0–4 (ranging from *not at all* to *extremely*) across 20 situations that often serve as triggers. The AASE comprises four subscales, including negative affect, social/positive, physical or other concerns, and withdrawal and urges. A lower self-efficacy to resist drinking in the context of a negative affect and withdrawal/urges were most closely associated with problematic drinking (DiClemente et al., 1994). Because the AASE assesses both confidence to resist drinking and temptation to drink, it can provide clinicians with valuable information about which situations may be most risky for clients (i.e., high temptation and low confidence); however, given that measures of confidence and temptation were related significantly to drinking and correlated inversely with one another (DiClemente et al., 1994), a clinician may use only one of the two scales if faced with time constraints.

Table 6.2 Self-efficacy measures

Instrument and number of items	Administration (time in minutes if known and method)	Availability	Target population(s)
Alcohol Abstinence Self-Efficacy Scale (40 items)	10 min; computer[a]; paper and pencil	Online[b] and DiClemente et al., 1994	Adults in alcohol treatment
Drinking Refusal Self-Efficacy Questionnaire (19 items)	10 min; computer[a]; paper and pencil	Online[c] and Oei et al. (2005), Young et al. (2007)	Adults in alcohol treatment, adult community drinkers, college students, and adolescents
Drug-Taking Confidence Questionnaire (50/8 items)	10 min; computer; paper and pencil	50-item: fee for use[d] 8-item: Sklar & Turner (1999)	Adults in substance abuse treatment
Situational Confidence Questionnaire (39/8 items)	8–10 min; computer[a,d]; paper and pencil	Online[e] (8 item)	Adults in substance abuse treatment
Situational Confidence Questionnaire–Heroin (22 items)	Paper and pencil	Online[b] and Barber et al. (1991)	Adults in substance abuse treatment

[a] *Computer access and scoring may be purchased at http://adai.washington.edu/sounddatasource/.*
[b] *http://lib.adai.washington.edu/instruments/.*
[c] *http://pubs.niaaa.nih.gov/publications/drseq.pdf.*
[d] *www.camh.net/publications/.*
[e] *http://www.nova.edu/gsc/online_files.html.*

The *Drinking Refusal Self-Efficacy Questionnaire-Revised* (DRSEQ-R; Oei, Hasking, & Young, 2005) contains 19 items that inquire about a client's ability to resist drinking in three main situations: social pressure, need for emotional relief, and opportunistic situations (e.g., "when you are by yourself"). The DRSEQ-R is versatile in that it has been used with social drinkers, problem drinkers, college students, and adolescents. An adolescent version, which has been modified to include situations that are more applicable to adolescents, also is available (DRSEQ-RA; Young, Hasking, Oei, & Loveday, 2007).

The *Situational Confidence Questionnaire* (SCQ-39; Annis & Graham, 1988) instructs clients to rate their level of confidence on a six-point scale based on an estimate of their ability to resist drinking *heavily* in 39 situations. If the client's treatment goal is abstinence, the

AASE or DRSEQ may be preferable because these instruments inquire about a client's confidence to resist any drinking (DiClemente et al., 1994; Donovan, 2003). The SCQ-39 covers the same eight domains as the *Inventory of Drinking Situations* (e.g., unpleasant emotions). A briefer, eight-item version is available (BSCQ; Sobell and Sobell, 2003) and its items correspond to the eight domains on the SCQ-39.

If a client is abusing drugs rather than alcohol, the *Drug Taking Confidence Questionnaire* (DTCQ; Annis, Sklar, & Turner, 1997) comprises 50 items that assess clients' confidence in their ability to abstain from substance use. Like the IDS and SCQ, the DTCQ items were developed from the eight categories associated with Marlatt's relapse taxonomy; however, research has shown that the items cluster into three categories: negative, positive, and tempting situations (Sklar, Annis, & Turner, 1997). A briefer eight-item version (DTCQ-8; Sklar & Turner, 1999) may be preferable if time and cost constraints are a factor.

Finally, the *Situational Confidence Questionnaire-Heroin* (SCQ-H; Barber, Cooper, & Heather, 1991) is similar to the SCQ-39, but contains only 22 items and is specific to heroin. There are three subscales: coping with or enhancing arousal states, casual or occasional usage, and coping with negative emotions (Barber et al., 1991).

EXPECTANCIES

Expectancies refer to an individual's beliefs or expectations about the various ways in which alcohol or drugs will affect them physically, emotionally, and behaviorally. For example, some clients might anticipate that using substances will help them feel calmer, improve their mood, or make it easier for them to socialize (Marlatt & Gordon, 2005). Understanding a client's expectations for using substances may not only help clinicians understand why a client uses, but also can help clients identify discrepancies between what they expect from their use (e.g., socializing) and what actually occurs (e.g., isolation) (Marlatt & Gordon, 2005). Numerous expectancy measures are available; most assess a combination of positive (e.g., enhanced mood, sociability, sexuality, relaxation) and negative (e.g., impairment, aggression) expectations. Research largely has shown that the more positive expectancies an individual holds, the more likely she or he is to use substances and have a poorer treatment outcome; conversely, individuals who hold more negative expectancies have a lower likelihood of initiating use (Aarons, Brown, Stice, & Coe, 2001; Schafer & Brown, 1991), endorse less substance use, and fare better in treatment (for a review, see Jones, Corbin, & Fromme, 2001).

Perhaps the most commonly used expectancy measure is the *Alcohol Expectancy Questionnaire* (AEQ; Brown, Christiansen, & Goldman, 1987), which contains 120 items (90 are scored) that assess six domains, including positive global changes in experience, sexual enhancement, social and physical pleasure, assertiveness, relaxation/tension reduction, and arousal/interpersonal power. The AEQ is easily accessed, widely used, and can be administered on a computer; however, it contains a large number of items, includes positive expectations only, and clients must choose whether they "agree" or "disagree" with an expected effect (Donovan, 2003). There is a 90-item adolescent version, the *Alcohol Expectancy Questionnaire-Adolescent* (Brown et al., 1987; Christiansen, Goldman, & Inn, 1982), and a briefer 7-item version available (Stein et al., 2006).

Several other expectancy measures include broader response scales and negative expectancies. For example, the 43-item *Drinking Expectancy Questionnaire* (Young, Oei, & Crook, 1991) includes domains that are similar to the AEQ (e.g., tension reduction) in addition to a domain that assesses a client's dependence on alcohol (e.g., "I cannot always control my drinking"), and clients rate their expectancies on a five-point scale. Finally, the 60-item *Negative Alcohol Expectancy Questionnaire* (Jones & McMahon, 1994a) may be particularly useful because it assesses the extent to which clients expect negative consequences over different time frames (same day, next day, or long term from continued drinking) if they were to "drink now." Given that negative expectancies for the *next day* (Jones & McMahon, 1994a) and for *continued drinking* (Jones & McMahon, 1994b) were significantly related to relapse, it may be useful to explore more distal negative expectancies with clients and investigate the ways in which these expectancies could motivate them to abstain.

Several measurement instruments assess drug-related expectancies, although these have been used less widely than the alcohol-related measures. The 48-item *Marijuana Effect Expectancy Questionnaire* (Schafer & Brown, 1991) and the 46-item *Stimulant Effect Expectancy Questionnaire* (Aarons et al., 2001) have been tested with both adults and adolescents and may be useful tools for ascertaining the drug-specific effects a client seeks. Table 6.3 summarizes the expectancy measures discussed in this section.

MOTIVATION

Measurement of a client's current level of motivation to change alcohol or drug use may prove valuable in treatment planning. In particular, both the degree to which the person feels ready to change and the relative influence of internal and external motivating factors in the individual's decision-making process may predict treatment outcome. The measurement of motivation, however, should be undertaken with

Table 6.3 Expectancy measures

Instrument and number of items	Administration (time in minutes if known and method)	Availability	Target population(s)
Alcohol Expectancy Questionnaire (90/7 items)	10–15 min; computer[a]; paper and pencil	Online[b] and Stein et al. (2006)	Adults in alcohol treatment, adult community drinkers, adolescents
Drinking Expectancy Questionnaire (43 items)	15 min; paper and pencil	Online[c]	Adult community drinkers, adults in alcohol treatment, college students
Marijuana Effect Expectancy Questionnaire (48 items)	Paper and pencil	Sandra A. Brown sanbrown@ucsd.edu	College students, adolescents
Negative Alcohol Expectancy Questionnaire (60/22 items)	15–20 min; computer[a]; interview; paper and pencil	Jones & McMahon (1994a)	Adults in alcohol treatment, DUI offenders
Stimulant Effect Expectancy Questionnaire (46 items)	Paper and pencil	Sandra A. Brown sanbrown@ucsd.edu	Adolescents

[a]*Computer access and scoring may be purchased at: http://adai.washington.edu/sounddatasource/.*
[b]*http://pubs.niaaa.nih.gov/publications/aeq.pdf (adult); http://pubs.niaaa.nih.gov/publications/aeqa.pdf (adolescent).*
[c]*http://pubs.niaaa.nih.gov/publications/insdeq.htm.*

the recognition that motivation is dynamic rather than static and may be influenced by external factors, such as interpersonal relationships, as well as internal factors, including mood, self-efficacy, and expectancies (Miller, 1985; Yahne & Miller, 1999). Numerous measures of motivation have been developed; this section highlights some of the more commonly used measures (see Table 6.4).

The transtheoretical model of behavior change (see, e.g., DiClemente, Schlundt, & Gemmell, 2004) suggests that as people change their behavior, they move among several phases of readiness and commitment to the change. The stage a client is in at any particular time reflects the level of motivation he or she is experiencing at that moment. The stages in the model are precontemplation (no current intention to change), contemplation (considering making a change in the foreseeable future), preparation (taking steps to prepare for the change), action (change in

Table 6.4 Motivation measures

Instrument and number of items	Administration (time in minutes if known and method)	Availability	Target population(s)
University of Rhode Island Change Assessment (32 items)	5–10 min; paper and pencil; interview	Online[a]	Adults
Stage of Change Readiness and Treatment Eagerness Scale (19 items)	3 min; paper and pencil	Online[b]	Adults
Readiness to Change Questionnaire–Treatment Version (15 items)	2–3 min; paper and pencil	Online[c]	Adults, adolescents seeking treatment
Readiness to Change Ruler (1 item)	Paper and pencil	LaBrie et al. (2005)	Adults
Cartoon Stage of Change Measure	Interview	Unknown	Adults
Reasons for Quitting Questionnaire (20 items)	5 min; paper and pencil	Downey et al. (2001)	Adults
Treatment Motivation Questionnaire (26 items)	5 min	Online[d]	Adults seeking treatment
Perceived Coercion Questionnaire (30 items)	Paper and pencil	Klag et al. (2006)	Adults, offenders

[a] *http://adai.washington.edu/instruments/pdf/University_of_Rhode_Island_Change_Assessment_258.pdf.*
[b] *http://casaa.unm.edu/inst.html.*
[c] *http://www.ncbi.nlm.nih.gov/books/bv.fcgi?rid=hstat5.table.62295.*
[d] *http://www.psych.rochester.edu/SDT/index.html.*

progress), and maintenance (solidifying the change and avoiding relapse) (DiClemente & Prochaska, 1998). By assessing the stage(s) a person is in at a particular time, the clinician can tailor treatment to move the client toward the action and maintenance stages.

Several questionnaires use this model to measure readiness to change. A commonly used assessment is the *University of Rhode Island Change Assessment* (URICA; McConnaughy, Prochaska, & Velicer, 1983), a 32-item questionnaire with subscales reflecting the precontemplation, contemplation, action, and maintenance stages. The URICA can be administered via self-report or interview and can be scored to provide a composite measure of readiness to change. One possible downside to the URICA, however, is that it is not specific to drug or alcohol use; rather, it asks about an individual's "problem" in general terms.

Two shorter questionnaires examine readiness to change drinking or drug use specifically. The *Stage of Change Readiness and Treatment Eagerness Scales–Version 8* (SOCRATES; Miller & Tonigan, 1996) contain 19 items shown to reflect three factors: recognition, ambivalence, and taking steps. The SOCRATES is available in two versions, one specific to alcohol and the other to drugs. Another readiness to change measure is the *Readiness to Change Questionnaire–Treatment Version* (RCQ-TV; Heather, Luce, Peck, Dunbar, & James, 1999). This scale comprises 15 questions that assess three stages of Prochaska and DiClemente's model (precontemplation, contemplation, and action) among treatment seekers.

Readiness to change also may be measured using other methods. One such tool is a ruler anchored with 0 ("Never think about my drinking") and 10 ("My drinking has changed; I now drink less than before") and various intermediate descriptions (LaBrie, Quinlan, Schiffman, & Earleywine, 2005). For populations that have difficulty with reading, the *Cartoon Stage of Change Measure* (C-SOC; Kinnaman, Bellack, Brown, & Yang, 2007) may be particularly useful. An interviewer presents a series of cartoons showing various attitudes and behaviors relating to drug use or abstinence, asks whether or not each picture is like the client now, and then asks the client to choose the picture most like him/her from the full array. By this method, a stage of change composite score can be calculated.

Readiness to change is not the only option for measuring motivation. The degree to which motivation is motivated intrinsically or extrinsically may also be important. Although research indicates that treatment can be successful even if it is initiated by external pressure or coercion (Miller & Flaherty, 2000), the likelihood of a successful and lasting change may be increased if intrinsic motivation is developed at some point (Downey, Rosengren, & Donovan, 2001; Ryan, Plant, & O'Malley, 1995).

Intrinsic and extrinsic motivation to change behavior can be measured via self-report. The Reasons for Quitting Questionnaire (RQQ; Curry, Wagner, & Grothaus, 1990; Downey et al., 2001) is a 20-item self-report questionnaire that asks clients to rate, on a five-point Likert scale, to what extent particular reasons for quitting substance use are relevant to them. The RQQ has been used with both alcohol and drug users (Downey et al., 2001). The *Treatment Motivation Questionnaire* (TMQ; Ryan et al., 1995) is similar to the RQQ in that it measures extrinsic and intrinsic motivation, but in the context of reasons for entering treatment rather than for changing behavior. Both measures may be useful because recent research indicates that motivation to change and motivation to enter treatment are not interchangeable constructs (Kranitz, 2007). The TMQ's 26 items map onto internal and external subscales (Ryan et al., 1995). The TMQ is based on self-determination theory (Deci & Ryan, 1980, 1985) and has been found to predict treatment retention among those in treatment for alcohol problems (Ryan et al., 1995). Finally, a measure that specifically assesses perceived coercion into treatment is the *Perceived Coercion Questionnaire* (PCQ; Klag, Creed, & O'Callaghan, 2006). The PCQ assesses coercion from a broad perspective, across six domains (work, legal, family, health, finances, and self), via a self-administered questionnaire.

ASSESSMENT OF CRAVING

In its most simplistic form, craving can be understood as a desire to use a drug. However, this definition masks some complex issues underlying the concept of craving and its assessment. There are several conceptualizations of craving. One model suggests that stimuli associated with drug or alcohol use become conditioned through repeated pairing with the substance, and, in turn, these stimuli elicit a conditioned craving response (Drummond, 2001). The cognitive processing model of craving postulates that alcohol or drug use becomes an automatic habit over time, requiring little conscious attention. Individuals then experience craving when they make an effort to block this automatic behavior (Tiffany, 1990). Craving is usually viewed as a subjective experience that is assessed with self-report measures. However, physiological, cognitive, and behavioral measures also tap the craving construct. For example, salivation in the presence of alcoholic beverages (Pomerleau, Fertig, Baker, & Cooney, 1983), reaction time (Sayette et al., 1994), and prepulse inhibition of the startle reflex (Monti, Rohsenow, & Hutchison, 2000) have been used as indicators of alcohol craving.

Craving has been studied in the laboratory by exposing people to alcohol and drug cues and measuring their reactivity to these cues. In a meta-analysis of 41 cue reactivity experiments conducted with smokers, alcoholics, opiate addicts, and cocaine addicts, Carter and Tiffany (1999) found that cue reactivity generally was associated with autonomic reactivity, including increased heart rate and sweat gland activity and decreased peripheral temperature. Interestingly, self-reports of craving were generally higher than autonomic measures of craving in response to cues. While cue reactivity methods have been criticized due to the artificial nature of the laboratory environment, they provide researchers with the ability to observe immediate psychological and physiological responses to substance cues. Ecological Momentary

Assessment (EMA; Stone & Shiffman, 1994) is another method used for assessing craving: it uses technology such as palm top computers or cellular telephones to assess self-reported craving in real time and in the natural environment.

Tiffany, Carter, and Singleton (2000) have criticized much of the cue reactivity literature for its use of single-item measures of craving. Although such measures take virtually no time to complete, this type of measure may have a lower level of reliability and validity than a multi-item craving questionnaire. Several multi-item craving scales are summarized in Table 6.5. These include the *Penn Alcohol Craving Scale* (PACS; Flannery et al., 1999), a five-item scale that assesses the intensity, frequency, and duration of craving; the ability to resist alcohol; and the average level of craving in the past week. The 14-item *Obsessive-Compulsive Drinking Scale* (OCDS; Anton, Moak, & Latham, 1995) consists of *Obsessive* and *Compulsive* subscales and refers to craving experienced over a 1- to 2-week period. The eight-item *Alcohol Urge Questionnaire* (AUQ; Bohn, Krahn, & Staehler, 1995) measures a client's current craving state. The PACS, OCDS, and AUQ were compared to determine their utility in predicting drinking during the course of alcohol treatment. The PACS and the six-item obsessive subscale of the ODS were better predictors of drinking during the subsequent week

Table 6.5 Craving measures

Instrument and number of items	Administration (time in minutes if known and method)	Availability	Target population(s)
Penn Alcohol Craving Scale (5 items)	1–2 min; paper and pencil	Flannery et al. (1999)	Adults in alcohol treatment
Obsessive Compulsive Drinking Scale (14/6 items)	5–10 min; paper and pencil	Online[a] and Raymond Anton	Adults in alcohol treatment
Alcohol Urge Questionnaire (8 items)	1–2 min; paper and pencil	Online[a] and Michael Bohn	Adults
Cocaine Craving Questionnaire (45/10 items)	15 min; paper and pencil	Heinz et al. (2006)	Adults in substance abuse treatment
Heroin Craving Questionnaire (45/14 items)	15 min; paper and pencil	Heinz et al. (2006)	Adults in substance abuse treatment

[a]*http://ncadi.samhsa.gov/govpubs/bkd268/28l.aspx.*

than was clients' drinking during the prior week (Flannery et al., 2001). The AUQ, with its emphasis on current craving, did not predict drinking as accurately as the PACS and OCDS.

Tiffany and colleagues have developed a family of multifaceted self-report craving scales. This group of measures includes a 45-item *Cocaine Craving Questionnaire* (CCQ; Tiffany, Singleton, Haertzen, & Henningfield, 1993) along with the CCQ-Now, which asks about current craving, the CCQ-Gen which asks about average craving over the preceding week, and the 10-item CCQ-Brief (Sussner et al., 2006). Heroin craving may be assessed with the 45-item *Heroin Craving Questionnaire* (HCQ-45; Heinz et al., 2006) or with the briefer 14-item HCQ-14. The AUQ, introduced in the previous paragraph, is also based on Tiffany's assessment model. These scales were based on a craving conceptualization consisting of desire to use, intention to use, anticipation of positive outcome from drug use, anticipation of relief from withdrawal or relief from negative mood, and lack of control over use.

SUMMARY

Clients with substance use disorders may share a common diagnosis, but they have unique profiles of antecedents for substance use, self-efficacy to abstain, expectations for use, motivation to enter treatment and remain abstinent, and the nature and intensity of craving. Accordingly, this chapter reviewed numerous assessments, each with unique strengths and potential drawbacks. When used at the beginning of treatment, information from these assessments can serve both as a benchmark for clients' functioning when they enter substance abuse treatment and as a guide for which area(s) they need assistance. When used throughout treatment, these assessments may indicate the extent to which a client has changed and which circumstances might pose the greatest risk for relapse. Given the large number of instruments, clinicians are encouraged to consider their client's unique circumstances and presentation, their own time constraints, availability, and cost in deciding which assessment tools can maximally inform case conceptualization and treatment planning.

REFERENCES

Aarons, G. A., Brown, S. A., Stice, E., & Coe, M. T. (2001). Psychometric evaluation of the marijuana and stimulant effect expectancy questionnaires for adolescents. *Addictive Behaviors*, *26*, 219–236.

Allen, J. P., & Wilson, V. B. (2003). *Assessing alcohol problems: A guide for clinicians and researchers* [NIH Publication No. 03–3745: Electronic version] (2nd ed.). Rockville, MD: U.S. Department of Health and Human Services, National Institute on Alcohol Abuse and Alcoholism.

Annis, H. M., & Graham, J. M. (1988). *Situational Confidence Questionnaire (SCQ-39) User's guide*. Toronto: Alcoholism and Drug Addiction Research Foundation.

Annis, H. M., Graham, J. M., & Davis, C. S. (1987). *Inventory of Drinking Situations (IDS): User's guide*. Toronto: Addiction Research Foundation.

Annis, H. M., Sklar, S. M., & Turner, N. E. (1997). *The Drug-Taking Confidence Questionnaire (DTCQ): User's guide*. Toronto: Addiction Research Foundation, Centre for Addiction and Mental Health.

Annis, H. M., Turner, N. E., & Sklar, S. M. (1997). *Inventory of Drug-Taking Situations: User's guide*. Toronto: Addiction Research Foundation.

Anton, R. F., Moak, D. H., & Latham, P. K. (1995). The Obsessive Compulsive Drinking Scale: A self-rated instrument for the quantification of thoughts about alcohol and drinking behavior. *Alcoholism: Clinical and Experimental Research*, *19*, 92–99.

Bandura, A. (1977). Self-efficacy: Toward a unifying theory of behavioral change. *Psychological Review*, *84*, 191–215.

Barber, J. G., Cooper, B. K., & Heather, N. (1991). The Situational Confidence Questionnaire (Heroin). *The International Journal of the Addictions*, *26*, 565–575.

Bohn, M. J., Krahn, D. D., & Staehler, R. A. (1995). Development and initial validation of a measure of drinking urges in abstinent alcoholics. *Alcoholism: Clinical and Experimental Research*, *19*, 600–606.

Brown, S. A., Christiansen, B. A., & Goldman, M. S. (1987). The Alcohol Expectancy Questionnaire: An instrument for the assessment of adolescent and adult alcohol expectancies. *Journal of Studies on Alcohol*, *48*, 483–491.

Carey, K. B. (1993). Situational determinants of heavy drinking among college students. *Journal of Counseling Psychology*, *40*, 217–220.

Carter, B. L., & Tiffany, S. T. (1999). Meta-analytical review of cue reactivity measures. *Addiction*, *94*, 327–340.

Christiansen, B. A., Goldman, M. S., & Inn, A. (1982). The development of alcohol-related expectancies in adolescents: Separating pharmacological from social learning influences. *Journal of Consulting and Clinical Psychology*, *50*, 336–344.

Cooper, M. L. (1994). Motivations for alcohol use among adolescents: Development and validation of a four-factor model. *Psychological Assessment*, *6*, 117–128.

Cooper, M. L., Russell, M., Skinner, J. B., & Windle, M. (1992). Development and validation of a three-dimensional measure of drinking motives. *Psychological Assessment*, *4*, 123–132.

Curry, S., Wagner, E. H., & Grothaus, L. C. (1990). Intrinsic and extrinsic motivation for smoking cessation. *Journal of Consulting and Clinical Psychology*, *58*, 310–316.

Deci, E. L., & Ryan, R. M. (1980). Self-determination theory: When mind mediates behavior. *Journal of Mind and Behavior*, *1*, 33–43.

Deci, E. L., & Ryan, R. M. (1985). *Intrinsic motivation and self-determination in human behavior*. New York: Plenum Press.

DiClemente, C. C., Carbonari, J. P., Montgomery, R. P. G., & Hughes, S. O. (1994). The Alcohol Abstinence Self-Efficacy Scale. *Journal of Studies on Alcohol*, *55*, 141–148.

DiClemente, C. C., & Prochaska, J. O. (1998). Toward a comprehensive, transtheoretical model of change: Stages of change and addictive behavior. In W. R. Miller & N. Heather(Eds.), *Treating addictive behaviors* (2nd ed., pp. 3–24). New York: Plenum.

DiClemente, C. C., Schlundt, D., & Gemmell, L. (2004). Readiness and stages of change in addiction treatment. *American Journal on Addictions, 13,* 103–119.

Donovan, D. M. (2003). Assessment to aid in the treatment planning process[NIH Publication No. 03-3745: Electronic version]. In J. P. Allen & V. B. Wilson(Eds.), *Assessing alcohol problems: A guide for clinicians and researchers* (2nd ed., pp. 125–188). Rockville, MD: U.S. Department of Health and Human Services, National Institute on Alcohol Abuse and Alcoholism.

Donovan, D. M., & Marlatt, G. A. (2005). *Assessment of addictive behaviors* (2nd ed.). New York: Guilford Press.

Downey, L., Rosengren, D. B., & Donovan, D. M. (2001). Sources of motivation for abstinence: A replication analysis of the Reasons for Quitting Questionnaire. *Addictive Behaviors, 26,* 79–89.

Drummond, D. C. (2001). Theories of drug craving, ancient and modern. *Addiction, 96,* 33–46.

Flannery, B. A., Roberts, A. J., Cooney, N., Swift, R. M., Anton, R. F., & Rohsenow, D. J. (2001). The role of craving in alcohol use, dependence, and treatment. *Alcoholism: Clinical and Experimental Research, 25,* 299–308.

Flannery, B. A., Volpicelli, J. R., & Pettinati, H. M. (1999). Psychometric properties of the Penn Alcohol Craving Scale. *Alcoholism: Clinical and Experimental Research, 25,* 1289–1295.

Grant, V. V., Stewart, S. H., O'Connor, R. M., Blackwell, E., & Conrod, P. J. (2007). Psychometric evaluation of the five-factor Modified Drinking Motives Questionnaire: Revised in undergraduates. *Addictive Behaviors, 32,* 2611–2632.

Heather, N., Luce, A., Peck, D., Dunbar, B., & James, I. (1999). The development of a treatment version of the Readiness to Change Questionnaire. *Addiction Research, 7,* 63–68.

Heinz, A. J., Epstein, D. H., Schroeder, J. R., Singleton, E. G., Heishman, S. J., & Preston, K. L. (2006). Heroin and cocaine craving and use during treatment: Measurement validation and potential relationships. *Journal of Substance Abuse Treatment, 31,* 355–364.

Heishman, S. J., Singleton, E. G., & Liguori, A. (2001). Marijuana Craving Questionnaire: Development and initial validation of a self-report instrument. *Addiction, 96,* 1023–1034.

Isenhart, C. E. (1993). Psychometric evaluation of a short form of the Inventory of Drinking Situations. *Journal of Studies on Alcohol, 54,* 345–349.

Jones, B. T., Corbin, W., & Fromme, K. (2001). A review of expectancy theory and alcohol consumption. *Addiction, 96,* 57–72.

Jones, B. T., & McMahon, J. (1994a). Negative alcohol expectancy predicts post-treatment abstinence survivorship: The whether, when and why of relapse to a first drink. *Addiction, 89,* 1653–1665.

Jones, B. T., & McMahon, J. (1994b). Negative and positive alcohol expectancies as predictors of abstinente alter discharge from a residencial treatment program: A one-month and three-month follow-up study in men. *Journal of Studies on Alcohol, 55,* 543–548.

Kinnaman, J. E. S., Bellack, A. S., Brown, C. H., & Yang, Y. (2007). Assessment of motivation to change substance use in dually-diagnosed schizophrenia patients. *Addictive Behaviors, 32,* 1798–1813.

Klag, S., Creed, P., & O'Callaghan, F. (2006). Development and initial validation of an instrument to measure perceived coercion to enter treatment for substance abuse. *Psychology of Addictive Behaviors, 20,* 463–470.

Kranitz, L. S. (2007). *Reasons for not drinking among veterans seeking treatment for alcohol dependence in a partial day hospital*. Unpublished doctoral dissertation, Rutgers University, New Brunswick, NJ.

LaBrie, J. W., Quinlan, T., Schiffman, J. E., & Earleywine, M. E. (2005). Performance of alcohol and safer sex change rulers compared with readiness to change questionnaires. *Psychology of Addictive Behaviors*, *19*, 112–115.

Marlatt, G. A. (1996). Taxonomy of high-risk situations for alcohol relapse: Evolution and development of a cognitive-behavioral model. *Addiction*, *91* (Suppl.), S37–S49.

Marlatt, G. A., & Gordon, J. R. (Eds.). (2005). *Relapse prevention: Maintenance strategies in the treatment of addictive behaviors*. New York: Guilford Press.

McConnaughy, E. A., Prochaska, J. O., & Velicer, W. F. (1983). Stages of change in psychotherapy: Measurement and sample profiles. *Psychotherapy: Theory, Research & Practice*, *20*, 368–375.

Miller, N. S., & Flaherty, J. A. (2000). Effectiveness of coerced addiction treatment (alternative consequences): A review of the clinical research. *Journal of Substance Abuse Treatment*, *18*, 9–16.

Miller, W. R. (1985). Motivation for treatment: A review with special emphasis on alcoholism. *Psychological Bulletin*, *98*, 84–107.

Miller, W. R., & Tonigan, J. S. (1996). Assessing drinkers' motivation for change: The Stages of Change Readiness and Treatment Eagerness Scale (SOCRATES). *Psychology of Addictive Behaviors*, *10*, 81–89.

Monti, P. M., Rohsenow, D. J., & Hutchison, K. E. (2000). Toward bridging the gap between biological, psychobiological and psychosocial models of alcohol craving. *Addiction*, *95*(Suppl. 2), S229–S236.

Oei, T. P. S., Hasking, P. A., & Young, R. M. (2005). Drinking refusal self-efficacy questionnaire–revised (DRSEQ-R): A new factor structure with confirmatory factor analysis. *Drug and Alcohol Dependence*, *78*, 297–307.

Ogai, Y., Haraguichi, A., Kondo, A., Ishibashi, Y., Umeno, M., Kikumoto, H., et al. (2007). Development and validation of the Stimulant Relapse Risk Scale for drug users in Japan. *Drug and Alcohol Dependence*, *88*, 174–181.

Parra, G. R., Martin, C. S., & Clark, D. B. (2005). The drinking situations of adolescents treated for alcohol use disorders: A psychometric and alcohol-related outcomes investigation. *Addictive Behaviors*, *30*, 1725–1736.

Pomerleau, O. F., Fertig, J., Baker, L., & Cooney, N. L. (1983). Reactivity to alcohol cues in alcoholics and non-alcoholics: Implications for a stimulus control analysis of drinking. *Addictive Behaviors*, *8*, 1–10.

Ryan, R. M., Plant, R. W., & O'Malley, S. (1995). Initial motivations for alcohol treatment: Relations with patient characteristics, treatment involvement, and dropout. *Addictive Behaviors*, *20*, 279–297.

Sayette, M. A., Monti, P. M., Rohsenow, D. J., Gulliver, S. B., Colby, S. M., Sirota, A. D., Niaura, R., & Abrams, D. B. (1994). The effects of cue exposure on reaction time in male alcoholics. *Journal of Studies on Alcohol*, *55*, 629–633.

Schafer, J., & Brown, S. A. (1991). Marijuana and cocaine effect expectancies and drug use patterns. *Journal of Consulting and Clinical Psychology*, *59*, 558–565.

Simons, J., Correia, C. J., Carey, K. B., & Borsari, B. E. (1998). Validating a five-factor marijuana motives measure: Relations with use, problems, and alcohol motives. *Journal of Counseling Psychology*, *45*, 265–273.

Sklar, S. M., Annis, H. M., & Turner, N. E. (1997). Development and validation of the Drug-Taking Confidence Questionnaire: A measure of coping self-efficacy. *Addictive Behaviors, 22*, 655–670.

Sklar, S. M., & Turner, N. E. (1999). A brief measure for the assessment of coping self-efficacy among alcohol and other drug users. *Addiction, 94*, 723–729.

Sobell, M. B., and Sobell, L. C. (2003). *The Brief Situational Confidence Questionnaire (BSCQ).* Retrieved March 14, 2008 from Healthy Lifestyles Guided Self-Change Program, Center for Psychological Studies, Nova Southeastern University Web site: http://www.nova.edu/gsc/forms/BSCQalcoholdrugform.pdf.

Stein, L. A. R., Katz, B., Colby, S. M., Barnett, N. P., Golembeske, C., Lebeau-Craven, R., & Monti, P. M. (2006). Validity and reliability of the Alcohol Expectancy Questionnaire–Adolescent, Brief. *Journal of Child and Adolescent Substance Abuse, 16*, 115–127.

Stone, A. A., & Shiffman, S. (1994). Ecological momentary assessment (EMA) in behavioral medicine. *Annals of Behavioral Medicine, 16*, 199–202.

Sussner, B. D., Smelson, D. A., Rodrigues, S., Kline, A., Losonczy, M., & Ziedonis, D. (2006). The validity and reliability of a brief measure of cocaine craving. *Drug and Alcohol Dependence, 83*, 233–237.

Tiffany, S. T. (1990). A cognitive model of drug urges and drug-use behavior: Role of automatic and nonautomatic processes. *Psychological Review, 97*, 147–168.

Tiffany, S. T., Carter, B. L., & Singleton, E. G. (2000). Challenges in the manipulation, assessment and interpretation of craving relevant variables. *Addiction, 95*(Suppl. 2), S177–S187.

Tiffany, S. T., Singleton, E., Haertzen, C. A., & Henningfield, J. E. (1993). The development and initial validation of a cocaine craving questionnaire. *Drug and Alcohol Dependence, 34*, 19–28.

Yahne, C. E., & Miller, W. R. (1999). Enhancing motivation for treatment and change. In B. S. McCrady & E. E. Epstein(Eds.), *Addictions: A comprehensive guidebook* (pp. 235–249). New York: Oxford University Press.

Young, R. M., Hasking, P. A., Oei, T. P., & Loveday, W. (2007). Validation of the Drinking Refusal Self-Efficacy Questionnaire-Revised in an adolescent sample (DRSEQ-RA). *Addictive Behaviors, 32*, 862–868.

Young, R. M., Oei, T. P. S., & Crook, C. M. (1991). Development of a drinking self-efficacy questionnaire. *Journal of Psychopathology and Behavioral Assessment, 13*, 1–15.

Zywiak, W. H., Connors, G. J., Maisto, S. A., & Westerberg, V. S. (1996). Relapse research and the Reasons for Drinking Questionnaire: A factor analysis of Marlatt's relapse taxonomy. *Addiction, 91*, S121–S130.

Chapter | seven

Individualized Problem Assessment

II. Assessing Clients from a Broader Perspective

Linda S. Kranitz, Laura J. Holt*, and Ned L. Cooney

VA Connecticut Healthcare System, Yale University School of Medicine

*Trinity College, Hartford, Connecticut

SUMMARY POINTS

- Successful addiction treatment and recovery must address a variety of intra- and interpersonal factors, including coping skills, consequences of substance use, clients' practical needs, social support, spiritual beliefs, and engagement in mutual self-help organizations. A number of measures are available to assist clinicians in evaluating these factors.
- Given that a primary goal of substance abuse treatment is to improve coping skills, coping skills measures can be used to identify targets for intervention and to assess progress in treatment.
- Assessing a client's experience of positive and negative consequences of substance use may help clinicians evaluate severity, enhance motivation, and plan treatment. In addition, understanding perceived consequences may help identify and overcome barriers to treatment and/or change.
- Social support measures have been developed that focus on the role of family, friends, and coworkers and their support for substance use or abstinence.

Evidence-Based Addiction Treatment

- Clients with addictions often present with multiple needs directly or distally related to their substance use. Several measures exist to assess their range of needs, their expectations for treatment, and their experiences in treatment.
- Involvement with Alcoholics Anonymous can be helpful in treatment planning, as it may provide clients with support for long-term sobriety. Brief measures of readiness for AA participation, as well as measures of degree of involvement or affiliation with AA, are available.
- Spirituality and religiosity are important factors to consider in treatment in 12-step and other treatment approaches.
- Multidimensional measures allow clinicians to obtain a broad understanding of multiple life domains that may be relevant to a client's substance use problems.

The previous chapter focused on assessments derived from the cognitive–behavioral model of addiction. We also refer the reader to the previous chapter for a listing of addiction assessment resources in print and online. This chapter focuses on the assessment of other issues commonly encountered in addiction treatment, such as skills for coping with high-risk situations; consequences of drug and alcohol use; and clients' practical needs, spiritual beliefs, and engagement in 12-step or mutual help groups. Regardless of a clinician's theoretical orientation, these measures are useful because they assess processes common to a variety of treatment methods, which have been linked to successful treatment outcomes (Finney, Noyes, Coutts, & Moos, 1998; Litt, Kadden, Cooney, & Kabela, 2003).

COPING SKILLS

One of the tenets of addiction treatment is that deficits in coping skills constitute a major determinant of substance use and relapse. An important goal of treatment, therefore, is to help the client acquire cognitive, affective, and behavioral skills for coping with potential relapse situations. Although studies have not demonstrated clearly that acquisition of coping skills is linked to successful cognitive–behavioral treatment outcome (Longabaugh, Donovan, Karno, McCrady, Morgenstern, & Tonigan, 2005; Morgenstern & Longabaugh, 2000), an assessment of these skills is useful to identify targets for intervention or to measure progress in treatment. A more detailed review of coping skills measures is available elsewhere (Finney, 2003). Coping skills measures selected for this review are summarized in Table 7.1.

Table 7.1 Coping skills measures

Instrument and number of items	Administration (time in minutes if known and method)	Availability	Target population(s)
Alcohol-Specific Role Play Test	20 min; audiotape	Peter Monti and online[a]	Adults
Coping Responses Inventory–Adult (48/24 items)	10–15 min; paper and pencil	Psychological Assessment Resources, Inc.	Adults
Processes of Change Questionnaire (40/15 items)	10–15 min; paper and pencil	Prochaska et al. (1988)	Adults
Coping Behaviours Inventory (36 items)	10 min; paper and pencil	Litman et al. (1983)	Adults in alcohol treatment
Adolescent Relapse Coping Questionnaire (34 items)	15 min; paper and pencil	Mark Myers and online[a]	Adolescents

[a] *http://lib.adai.washington.edu/instruments/.*

The role-play test is one method used to assess coping skills. The client is presented with a potential relapse scenario and acts out a response, which is rated for skill level. The *Alcohol Specific Role-Play Test* (Monti et al., 1993) is an example of this method. Role-play measures likely have better ecological validity than paper and pencil measures of coping skills. One often observes a discrepancy between how a person describes his or her skills and how those skills are actually performed. However, these measures are costly to administer and score and may be impractical for use in a typical clinic setting. One option is to use informal role-play methods with subjective scoring to assess coping skills as part of routine clinical practice.

Paper and pencil assessments of coping skills provide a convenient and inexpensive alternative to role-play tests. The *Coping Responses Inventory* (Moos, 1993) asks the client to select a recent stressor and rate his or her reliance on each of 48 strategies for coping with that stressor. To increase this measure's relevance to addiction treatment, the client could be asked to identify a drinking or drug trigger situation as the stressor. The Coping Responses Inventory yields eight subscales reflecting approach vs avoidance orientations and cognitive vs behavioral coping strategies. A briefer 24-item version of this scale has been described by Finney, Noyes, Coutts, and Moos (1998).

The *Processes of Change Questionnaire* originally was developed to assess change processes in smoking cessation (Prochaska, Velicer, DiClemente, & Fava, 1988), but has been adapted to assess substance use coping (Finney et al., 1998; Litt et al., 2003; Snow, Prochaska, & Rossi, 1994). Although the full Processes of Change scale consists of 40 items, Finney and colleagues developed a 15-item version with five subscales: *self-liberation* ("I tell myself I can choose to drink/use or not"), *stimulus control* ("I remove things from my home that remind me of drinking or using"), *counterconditioning* ("Instead of drinking or using, I engage in some physical activity"), *self-reevaluation* ("I remind myself that my dependence on drug or alcohol makes me feel disappointed with myself"), and *reinforcement management* ("I reward myself when I don't drink or use").

The *Coping Behaviours Inventory* (Litman, Stapleton, Oppenheim, & Peleg, 1983) is a 36-item measure comprising four factors: positive thinking, negative thinking, avoidance/distraction, and seeking social support. The *Adolescent Relapse Coping Questionnaire* (Myers, Brown, & Mott, 1993) describes a hypothetical high-risk relapse situation and then presents 34 items reflecting coping strategies. These items reflect three main factors: cognitive/behavioral problem-solving, self-critical thinking, and abstinence focus.

CONSEQUENCES

Substance use consequences are important to assess for several reasons. First, the consequences that a person has experienced from substance use may help a clinician understand the severity of the client's problem. Second, an individual's perception of the relative importance of such consequences also may assist with treatment planning and motivation enhancement. Third, an understanding of the perceived consequences—positive and negative—of treatment and/or of abstinence may allow the treatment provider to assist the client in identifying and overcoming barriers to treatment. Fourth, a reduction in negative consequences is a common treatment goal, and structured assessment of consequences can provide a measure of the efficacy of treatment. A number of assessment tools are available to assess the positive and negative consequences of alcohol and drug use or abstinence. These are discussed in turn and summarized in Table 7.2.

The *Drinker Inventory of Consequences* (DrInC; Miller, Tonigan, & Longabaugh, 1995) is a 50-item self-report questionnaire that measures lifetime and recent (past 3 months) negative consequences of alcohol use in five domains: interpersonal, physical, social, impulsive, and intrapersonal. A number of questionnaires based on the DrInC are available

Table 7.2 Measures of consequences of substance use

Instrument and number of items	Administration (time in minutes if known and method)	Availability	Target population(s)
Drinker Inventory of Consequences/Inventory of Drug Use Consequences/ Short Inventory of Problems (50/50/15)	Paper and pencil	Online[a]	Adults
Adverse Consequences of Substance Use Scale (8 items)	Paper and pencil	Mann et al. (2006)	Drinking drivers
Alcohol Use Disorders Identification Test (10 items)	2–3 min; paper and pencil	Online[b]	Adults
Rutgers Alcohol Problem Index (18 items)	10 min; paper and pencil; interview	Online[c]	Adolescents
Brief Young Adult Consequences Questionnaire (24 items)	Paper and pencil	Kahler et al. (2005)	College students
College Alcohol Problems Scale (8 items)	2–3 min; paper and pencil; interview	NIAAA	College students
Drinking Problems Index (17 items)	3–5 min; paper and pencil	Online[d]	Adults (age 55 and older)
Positive Drinking Consequences Questionnaire (14 items)	Paper and pencil	Corbin et al. (2008)	Adolescents
Perceived Benefit of Drinking Scale (5 items)	2–3 min; paper and pencil	Online[e]	Adolescents
Alcohol and Drug Consequences Questionnaire (28 items)	5–10 min; paper and pencil	Online[f]	Adults

[a] *http://pubs.niaaa.nih.gov/publications/drinc.pdf.*
[b] *http://whqlibdoc.who.int/hq/2001/WHO_MSD_MSB_01.6a.pdf.*
[c] *http://adai.washington.edu/instruments/pdf/Rutgers_Alcohol_Problem_Index_210.pdf.*
[d] *http://www.chce.research.va.gov/docs/pdfs/measures/DRINKINGPROBLEMSINDEX.pdf.*
[e] *http://adai.washington.edu/instruments/PDF/Perceived_Benefit_of_Drinking_Scale_172.pdf.*
[f] *http://www.ncbi.nlm.nih.gov/books/bv.fcgi?rid=hstat5.table.62219.*

and may be more appropriate in particular circumstances. These include the 50-item *Inventory of Drug Use Consequences* (Tonigan & Miller, 2002), which is parallel in structure to the DrInC but assesses polydrug use rather than just alcohol; the 15-item *Short Inventory of Problems*

(Forcehimes, Tonigan, Miller, Kenna, & Baer, 2007), which allows for a briefer assessment of problems related to drinking; and the *Modified Short Inventory of Problems* (Bender, Griffin, Gallop, & Weiss, 2007), with 15 questions about substance use consequences and 15 parallel questions relating to bipolar disorder consequences, which permits clients to attribute symptoms to one disorder or the other.

If a clinician is seeking an even briefer assessment, several options are available. The *Adverse Consequences of Substance Use Scale* (Mann, Rootman, Shuggi, & Adlaf, 2006) is an 8-item self-report questionnaire that asks respondents to rate on a scale from 0 (not experienced) to 3 (very severe) the recent or lifetime consequences of substance use they may have experienced in eight domains. The *Alcohol Use Disorders Identification Test* (AUDIT; Saunders, Aasland, Babor, de la Fuente, & Grant, 1993) is a 10-item screening questionnaire designed to identify individuals whose drinking patterns are hazardous or harmful. The AUDIT also is useful for measuring negative consequences of alcohol use. Developed by the World Health Organization (WHO), it has been used extensively in research and clinical settings (Allen, Litten, Fertig, & Babor, 1997). Related measures focus on the identification of various drug use disorders (e.g., *Cannabis Use Disorders Identification Test*, Adamson & Sellman, 2003; *Drug Use Disorders Identification Test*, Berman, Bergman, Palmstierna, & Schlyter, 2005).

A number of measures assess consequences in specific populations such as adolescents, young adults, or older adults. Age-targeted measures are particularly useful for assessing consequences because the most relevant adverse consequences of drinking may change with age. For example, problems with school and grades are more relevant for adolescents, whereas falls and neglect of self-care are more relevant among the elderly. The *Rutgers Alcohol Problem Index* (RAPI; White & Labouvie, 1989) is an 18-item self-report measure designed to assess adolescent drinking problems. In addition to assessing negative consequences of use, the RAPI can help clinicians evaluate the severity of an adolescent's problem. Two measures, both the 24-item *Brief Young Adult Consequences Questionnaire* (Kahler, Strong, & Read, 2005) and the 8-item *College Alcohol Problems Scale–revised* (Maddock, Laforge, Rossi, & O'Hare, 2001), are designed to assess alcohol problems in college students. Finally, for older adults, the *Drinking Problems Index* assesses consequences relevant to people ages 55 and older (Finney, Moos, & Brennan, 1991).

In addition to assessing adverse consequences of substance use, several scales focus on the client's perception of the benefits of use. Research indicates that perceived positive consequences and expectancies are distinct constructs (Corbin, Morean, & Benedict, 2008). The *Positive*

Drinking Consequences Questionnaire (Corbin et al., 2008) and the *Perceived Benefit of Drinking Scale* (Petchers & Singer, 1987) are brief self-report measures that assess experiences of specific positive consequences of drinking among adults and adolescents, respectively.

Finally, the perceived consequences of stopping or cutting down on drinking or drug use may influence treatment outcome. The *Alcohol and Drug Consequences Questionnaire* (Cunningham, Sobell, Gavin, Sobell, & Breslin, 1997) is a 28-item questionnaire that measures the expected costs and benefits of reducing or quitting substance use. Respondents are asked how important, on a six-point Likert scale, specific experiences would be if they cut down or quit substance use. Items all begin with the phrase "If I stop or cut down..."; sample completion phrases include "I will feel better physically" (benefits), "I will have fewer problems with my family" (benefits), "I will feel frustrated and anxious" (costs), and "I will miss the feeling of being high" (costs).

SOCIAL SUPPORT

Clients' social circles and work environment may serve as two significant influences on their substance use and course of treatment. Therefore, it is useful to examine the extent to which family, friends, and coworkers assist the client in recovery or hinder treatment progress. If a client has little or no support network or if members of her or his support network are actively drinking or using drugs, the treatment plan should address these circumstances and the therapist should assist the individual in developing relationships that support abstinence. Measures designed to assess these issues are discussed later and summarized in Table 7.3. If the use of formal assessment measures is impractical, a clinician may find it helpful to assess social support in an unstructured way by drawing a large circle and asking the client to write the names of individuals in the circle in a way that indicates the client's relative closeness to them (i.e., close to the center indicates that the individual is more significant to the client). The clinician and client can then discuss the substance use patterns of these individuals and how they may influence the client's engagement in treatment.

The *Important People and Activities Instrument* (IPA; Longabaugh, Wirtz, Zweben, & Stout, 1998) assesses a client's social network and its impact on treatment. The IPA is a structured interview with 11 indices that catalogs a client's associates (e.g., family, friends, coworkers, self-help group members), the importance of these relationships to the client, the drinking behavior of individuals in the client's social circle, their reactions to the client's drinking, and whether they support the client's efforts to engage in treatment. If a client indicates that much of his or

Table 7.3 Measures of social support

Instrument and number of items	Administration (time in minutes if known and method)	Availability	Target population(s)
Important People and Activities Instrument (19 items)	20–30 min; structured interview, some training required	Online[a,b]	Adults and young adults in alcohol treatment
Your Workplace (13 items)	5 min; paper and pencil	Online[c] and Beattie et al. (1992)	Adults in alcohol treatment
Significant-Other Behavior Questionnaire (24 items)	Paper and pencil	Love et al. (1993)	Adults in substance abuse treatment and their significant others

[a] *http://lib.adai.washington.edu/instruments/.*
[b] *http://casaa.unm.edu/inst.html (see* Important People Initial Interview*).*
[c] *http://pubs.niaaa.nih.gov/publications/ywp.pdf.*

her social circle encourages or facilitates drinking, research suggests that the client should be encouraged to become engaged in Alcoholics Anonymous (AA), which facilitates association with people who are seeking to remain sober (Longabaugh et al., 1998). A short form of the IPA, the *Brief Important People* interview, is available if time does not permit the administration of the full IPA. This measure assesses information pertaining to 3 of the 11 IPA indices: size of daily network, percentage of abstainers and recovering alcoholics, and network drinking frequency (Zywiak, Longabaugh, & Wirtz, 2002).

For clients who are married or in a committed relationship, it may be useful to examine how the significant other responds to the client's substance use, as well as how the client perceives support from the significant other. The Significant-Other Behavior Questionnaire (SBQ; Love, Longabaugh, Clifford, Beattie, & Peaslee, 1993) contains 24 items that assess a significant other's responses to a client's drinking. Four subscales include supporting drinking, withdrawing from the client when the client is drinking, punishing drinking, and supporting sobriety. The client *and* the significant other fill out parallel forms independently. Although the client's SBQ reports are not associated with drinking outcomes (and significant other reports are only mildly associated), the SBQ may be used to determine the client's perceptions of support and to examine potential changes in a significant other's support during treatment (Love et al., 1993).

Clients may find it especially difficult to remain abstinent if they work in an environment in which drinking or drug use is overlooked, condoned, or is a regular part of the workday and/or after work activities (Beattie, Longabaugh, & Fava, 1992). A very brief 13-item scale, *Your Workplace* (Beattie et al., 1992), contains three subscales that assess adverse effects of drinking on work performance, support for consumption, and support for abstinence. Support for abstinence may be particularly important, as research has shown that it is related inversely to the level of drinking on drinking days at both the 6- and the 12-month follow-up in a treatment sample (Beattie et al., 1992).

TREATMENT-RELATED NEEDS AND PREFERENCES

Clients presenting for substance abuse treatment often have needs and challenges related to their general functioning, psychiatric symptoms, health status, and other addictive behaviors that they wish to address during the course of treatment. To this end, two assessments may be useful in assessing a client's unique needs. Miller and Brown (1994) developed the *What I Want from Treatment*, a 69-item assessment, which allows clients to indicate the extent to which they are seeking help for various needs on a 0–3 scale. The three sections of this instrument inquire about specific help desired for (1) addictive behaviors (e.g., "I want to receive detoxification, to ease my withdrawal from alcohol or other drugs; I want to stop using tobacco"), (2) other concerns (e.g., "I need to fulfill a requirement of the courts; I want help with depression or moodiness; I could use help finding a job"), and (3) specific treatment preferences (e.g., "I would like to see a male counselor; I want to receive medication"). A 69-item companion instrument, *What I Got from Treatment*, permits assessment of treatment outcome.

The *Practical Needs Assessment* inquires about clients' problems or requests pertaining to housing, employment, finances, education, health care, legal issues, child care, and transportation (PNA; National Institute on Drug Abuse, 1998). The PNA was part of an assessment battery for a nationally funded cocaine treatment study; the information gained from this assessment can inform the clinician as to whether the client's basic needs are being met, as well as what resources a client needs to engage in treatment (see Table 7.4).

ALCOHOLICS ANONYMOUS INVOLVEMENT

In addition to formal treatment, individuals with alcohol or other drug problems may benefit from participation in 12-step groups such as Alcoholics Anonymous. In fact, many formal treatment programs rely at least in part on 12-step principles. Moreover, many people who do not seek formal treatment for alcohol or drug problems attend AA

Table 7.4 Measures of treatment-related needs and preferences

Instrument and number of items	Administration (time in minutes if known and method)	Availability	Target population(s)
What I Want from Treatment (69 items)	Paper and pencil	Online[a]	Adults in substance abuse treatment
What I Got from Treatment (69 Items)	Paper and pencil	Online[b]	Adults in substance abuse treatment
Practical Needs Assessment	Paper and pencil	Online[c]	Adults in substance abuse treatment

[a] *http://www.motivationalinterview.org/library/whatiwant.pdf.*
[b] *http://casaa.unm.edu/inst/What%20I%20Got%20From%20Treatment.pdf.*
[c] *http://www.nida.nih.gov/TXManuals/CRA/CRAX6.html.*

or other 12-step programs, perhaps because of their wide availability (see, e.g., Kingree et al., 2006; Tonigan, Connors, & Miller, 1996). Therefore, evaluation of an individual's degree of AA involvement and/or current readiness for involvement with AA can be helpful in treatment planning as it may provide clients with additional support for long-term sobriety.

Three measures assess constructs relevant to AA participation. The *Survey of Readiness for Alcoholics Anonymous Participation* (SYRAAP; Klingree et al., 2006) is based on the Health Belief Model (HBM)(Strecher & Rosenstock, 1997), which contends that six constructs (perceived severity of the problem, perceived susceptibility to relapse, perceived benefits and perceived barriers to participation, self-efficacy, and environmental cues to action) predict the degree of participation in AA. The SYRAAP is a 30-item measure that assesses three of the six HBM constructs (perceived severity, perceived benefits, and perceived barriers). A shorter, 15-item composite version also is available. Research indicates that the SYRAAP is correlated with recent AA attendance (Klingree et al., 2006).

The *Alcoholics Anonymous Involvement Scal*e (AAI; Tonigan, Connors, & Miller, 1996) and the *Alcoholics Anonymous Affiliation Scale* (AAF; Humphreys, Kaskutas, & Weisner, 1998) are two self-report measures that assess the degree to which a person reports attendance and involvement with AA. Both are brief (AAI: 13 items; AAF: 9 items) and both are specific to AA rather than inclusive of other 12-step programs (see Table 7.5).

Table 7.5 Measures of Alcoholics Anonymous involvement

Instrument and number of items	Administration (time in minutes if known and method)	Availability	Target population(s)
Survey of Readiness for Alcoholics Anonymous Participation (30/15 items)	Paper and pencil	J. B. Kingree kingree@clemson.edu	Adults
Alcoholics Anonymous Involvement Scale (13 items)	Paper and pencil	Tonigan et al. (1996)	Adults
Alcoholics Anonymous Affiliation Scale (9 items)	Paper and pencil	Humphreys et al. (1998)	Adults

SPIRITUALITY AND RELIGIOSITY

A large body of literature demonstrates that spiritual or religious involvement may be protective against substance use and abuse (Connors, Tonigan, & Miller, 1996; Miller, 1998) and that positive changes in spirituality and religiosity are critical for recovery in some clients (Robinson, Cranford, Webb, & Brower, 2007). Understanding the nature and strength of a client's spirituality or religiosity may inform treatment planning in several ways. Because 12-step programs regard spirituality as both the fundamental deficit leading to the development and maintenance of addiction and the cornerstone of recovery, clients who describe themselves as spiritual or religious may be more willing to engage in 12-step groups as an adjunct to other treatment (Connors et al., 1996). Spiritual and religious practices (e.g., meditation, prayer) also may enhance a client's ability to cope with difficult circumstances or emotions that previously would have prompted her or him to use substances. Clinicians can assess this domain informally by inquiring about clients' spiritual or religious practices and beliefs and about how their substance use and recovery are influenced by these beliefs and activities. The instruments described here may provide a clinician with an even deeper understanding of a client's beliefs, which may provide useful information for treatment planning purposes (see Table 7.6).

The *Religious Background and Behaviors* questionnaire (RBB; Connors et al., 1996) inquires about a client's religious orientation (e.g., atheist, spiritual); it includes six questions each about current and past spiritual and religious practices (e.g., prayer, reading scripture). The authors of the measure note that current *or* past items (in addition to the first item) may be used if time constraints are a factor (Connors

Table 7.6 Measures of spirituality and religiosity

Instrument and number of items	Administration (time in minutes if known and method)	Availability	Target population(s)
Religious Background and Behaviors (13 items)	Paper and pencil	Online[a] and Connors et al. (1996)	Adults in substance abuse treatment
Purpose in Life (20 items)	Paper and pencil	Marsh et al. (2003)	Adults in substance abuse treatment, college students

[a]*http://casaa.unm.edu/inst.html (see Religious Practices and Beliefs).*

et al., 1996). Higher scores on the RBB are associated with greater AA involvement; thus, this measure may be useful in assessing a client's suitability for and interest in 12-step groups (Connors et al., 1996).

The *Purpose in Life* test (PIL; Crumbaugh & Maholick, 1964) contains 20 items that assess existential beliefs about the meaning of life and related activities, life goals, and feelings of fulfillment. Research on the PIL suggests that clients entering substance abuse treatment have a low sense of purpose, but that purpose in life increases during treatment and ultimately is associated with less substance use (Robinson et al., 2007). Even among social drinkers, higher PIL scores are associated with lower scores of alcohol dependence and impaired control over drinking (Marsh, Smith, Piek, & Saunders, 2003).

MULTIDIMENSIONAL MEASURES

In addition to the numerous specialized instruments already described in this chapter, a number of measures assess multiple areas relevant to an individual's substance abuse, thus providing a more comprehensive picture of the individual and the problem. These measures are listed in Table 7.7. The *Addiction Severity Index* (ASI; McLellan, Luborsky, O'Brien, & Woody, 1980; McLellan et al., 1992) is the most widely used of these; it is well-studied and has several alternate versions, including a slightly shorter version (ASI-Lite; Cacciola, Alterman, McLellan, Lin, & Lynch, 2007; McLellan et al., 1980) and versions targeting adolescent populations such as the *Comprehensive Adolescent Severity Inventory* (Meyers, McLellan, Jaeger, & Pettinati, 1995) and the *Teen Addiction Severity Index* (Kaminer, Bukstein, & Tarter, 1991). Other multidimensional measures include the *Chemical Dependency Assessment Profile* (Harrell, Honaker, & Davis, 1991) and the *Comprehensive Drinker Profile* (Miller & Marlatt, 1984).

Table 7.7 Multidimensional measures

Instrument and number of items	Administration (time in minutes if known and method)	Availability	Domains assessed	Target population(s)
Addiction Severity Index, 5th ed. (200 items)	1 h; paper and pencil; computer; clinical interview	Online[a]	Demographics; medical history; drug and alcohol use history; treatment history	Adults seeking substance abuse treatment; other versions available for adolescents
Chemical Dependency Assessment Profile (224 items)	Paper and pencil	Fee for use[b]	Demographics; alcohol and drug use history and patterns; treatment history; beliefs and expectancies; symptoms; self-concept; personal relationships	Adults and adolescents seeking alcohol or drug treatment
Comprehensive Drinker Profile (88 items)	Clinical interview	Online[c]	Demographics; drinking history and pattern; alcohol-related life problems; drinking and drug use situations; medical history; motivation; goals	Adults seeking alcohol treatment

[a] *In the public domain: http://www.tresearch.org/asi.htm.*
[b] *Can be purchased from Multi-Health Systems, Inc.: http://www.mhs.com.*
[c] *In the public domain: http://casaa.unm.edu/inst.html.*

SUMMARY

The likelihood of long-term recovery from substance use disorders may be enhanced by the consideration of clients' life situations from a broader perspective. The instruments discussed in this chapter can provide clinicians with useful information about a wide range of potentially important obstacles to clients' treatment and recovery, as well as skills and supports that may enhance clients' chances of success as they attempt to recover from their addictions. Clinicians should consider whether a multidimensional assessment will provide the information needed for effective treatment planning or whether a client's unique circumstances warrant choosing instruments in one or more specific domains. Readers are encouraged to consult Chapters 4, 5, and 6 for information about instruments available to assess other important issues in substance abuse treatment.

REFERENCES

Adamson, S. J., & Sellman, J. (2003). A prototype screening instrument for cannabis use disorder: The cannabis use disorders identification test (CUDIT) in an alcohol-dependent clinical sample. *Drug and Alcohol Review*, *22*, 309–315.

Allen, J. P., Litten, R. Z., Fertig, J. B., & Babor, T. (1997). A review of research on the alcohol use disorders identification test (AUDIT). *Alcoholism: Clinical and Experimental Research*, *21*, 613–619.

Beattie, M. C., Longabaugh, R., & Fava, J. (1992). Assessment of alcohol-related workplace activities: Development and testing of "Your Workplace." *Journal of Studies on Alcohol*, *53*, 469–475.

Bender, R. E., Griffin, M. L., Gallop, R. J., & Weiss, R. D. (2007). Assessing negative consequences in patients with substance use and bipolar disorders: Psychometric properties of the short inventory of problems (SIP). *American Journal on Addictions*, *16*, 503–509.

Berman, A. H., Bergman, H., Palmstierna, T., & Schlyter, F. (2005). Evaluation of the drug use disorders identification test (DUDIT) in criminal justice and detoxification settings and in a Swedish population sample. *European Addiction Research*, *11*, 22–31.

Cacciola, J. S., Alterman, A. I., McLellan, A. T., Lin, Y. T., & Lynch, K. G. (2007). Initial evidence for the reliability and validity of a "Lite" version of the addiction severity index. *Drug and Alcohol Dependence*, *87*, 297–302.

Connors, G. J., Tonigan, J. S., & Miller, W. R. (1996). Measure of religious background and behavior for use in behavior change research. *Psychology of Addictive Behaviors*, *10*, 90–96.

Corbin, W. R., Morean, M. E., & Benedict, D. (2008). The positive drinking consequences questionnaire (PDCQ): Validation of a new assessment tool. *Addictive Behaviors*, *33*, 54–68.

Crumbaugh, J. C., & Maholick, L. T. (1964). An experimental study in existentialism: The psychometric approach to Frankl's concept of noogenic neurosis. *Journal of Clinical Psychology*, *20*, 589–596.

Cunningham, J. A., Sobell, L. C., Gavin, D. R., Sobell, M. B., & Breslin, F. (1997). Assessing motivation for change: Preliminary development and evaluation of a scale measuring the costs and benefits of changing alcohol or drug use. *Psychology of Addictive Behaviors*, *11*, 107–114.

Finney, J. W. (2003). Assessing treatment and treatment process. In J. P. Allen & V. Wilson(Eds.), *Assessing alcohol problems: A guide for clinicians and researchers* (2nd ed.). Bethesda, MD: U.S. Department of Health and Human Services, National Institute on Alcohol Abuse and Alcoholism (NIH Publication No. 03-3745).

Finney, J. W., Moos, R. H., & Brennan, P. L. (1991). The drinking problems index: A measure to assess alcohol-related problems among older adults. *Journal of Substance Abuse*, *3*, 395–404.

Finney, J. W., Noyes, C. A., Coutts, A. I., & Moos, R. H. (1998). Evaluating substance abuse treatment process models. I. Changes on proximal outcome variables during 12-step and cognitive-behavioral treatment. *Journal of Studies on Alcohol, 59*, 371–380.

Forcehimes, A. A., Tonigan, J. S., Miller, W. R., Kenna, G. A., & Baer, J. S. (2007). Psychometrics of the drinker inventory of consequences (DrInC). *Addictive Behaviors, 32*, 1699–1704.

Harrell, T. H., Honaker, L. M., & Davis, E. (1991). Cognitive and behavioral dimensions of dysfunction in alcohol and polydrug abusers. *Journal of Substance Abuse, 3*, 415–426.

Humphreys, K., Kaskutas, L. A., & Weisner, C. (1998). The alcoholics anonymous affiliation scale: Development, reliability, and norms for diverse treated and untreated populations. *Alcoholism: Clinical and Experimental Research, 22*, 974–978.

Kahler, C. W., Strong, D. R., & Read, J. P. (2005). Toward efficient and comprehensive measurement of the alcohol problems continuum in college students: The brief young adult alcohol consequences questionnaire. *Alcoholism: Clinical and Experimental Research, 29*, 1180–1189.

Kaminer, Y., Bukstein, O., & Tarter, R. E. (1991). The teen-addiction severity index: Rationale and reliability. *The International Journal of Addictions, 26*, 219–226.

Kingree, J. B., Simpson, A., Thompson, M., McCrady, B., Tonigan, J. S., & Lautenschlager, G. (2006). The development and initial evaluation of the survey of readiness for alcoholics anonymous participation. *Psychology of Addictive Behaviors, 20*, 453–462.

Litman, G. K, Stapleton, J., Oppenheim, A. N., & Peleg, M. (1983). An instrument for measuring coping behaviours in hospitalized alcoholics: Implications for relapse prevention treatment. *British Journal of Addictions, 78*, 269–276.

Litt, M. D., Kadden, R. M., Cooney, N. L., & Kabela, E. (2003). Coping skills and treatment outcomes in cognitive-behavioral and interactional group therapy for alcoholism. *Journal of Consulting and Clinical Psychology, 71*, 118–128.

Longabaugh, R., Donovan, D. M., Karno, M. P., McCrady, B. S., Morganstern, J., & Tonigan, J. S. (2005). Active ingredients: How and why evidence-based alcohol behavioral treatment interventions work. *Alcoholism: Clinical and Experimental Research, 29*, 235–247.

Longabaugh, R., Wirtz, P. W., Zweben, A., & Stout, R. L. (1998). Network support for drinking, alcoholics anonymous and long-term matching effects. *Addiction, 93*, 1313–1333.

Love, C. T., Longabaugh, R., Clifford, P. R., Beattie, M., & Peaslee, C. F. (1993). The significant-other behavior questionnaire (SBQ): An instrument for measuring the behavior of significant others towards a person's drinking and abstinence. *Addiction, 88*, 1267–1279.

Maddock, J. E., Laforge, R. G., Rossi, J. S., & O'Hare, T. (2001). The college alcohol problems scale. *Addictive Behaviors, 26*, 385–398.

Mann, R. E., Rootman, D. B., Shuggi, R., & Adlaf, E. (2006). Assessing consequences of alcohol and drug abuse in a drinking driving population. *Drugs: Education, Prevention & Policy, 13*, 313–326.

Marsh, A., Smith, L., Piek, J., & Saunders, B. (2003). The purpose in life scale: Psychometric properties for social drinkers and drinkers in alcohol treatment. *Educational and Psychological Measurement, 63*, 859–871.

McLellan, A. T., Kushner, H., Metzger, D., Peters, R., Smith, I., Grissom, G., et al. (1992). The fifth edition of the addiction severity index. *Journal of Substance Abuse Treatment*, *9*, 199–213.

McLellan, A. T., Luborsky, L., O'Brien, C. P., & Woody, G. E. (1980). An improved diagnostic instrument for substance abuse patients: The addiction severity index. *Journal of Nervous and Mental Disease*, *168*, 26–33.

Meyers, K., McLellan, A. T., Jaeger, J. L., & Pettinati, H. M. (1995). The development of the comprehensive addiction severity index for adolescents (CASI-A): An interview for assessing the multiple problems of adolescents. *Journal of Substance Abuse Treatment*, *12*, 181–193.

Miller, W. R. (1998). Researching the spiritual dimensions of alcohol and other drug problems. *Addiction*, *93*, 979–990.

Miller, W. R., & Brown, J. M. (1994). *What I want from treatment questionnaire 2.0*. CASAA Research Division. Retrieved February 28, 2008 from http://www.motivationalinterview.org/library/whatiwant.pdf.

Miller, W. R., Tonigan, J. S., & Longabaugh, R. (1995). *The drinker inventory of consequences (DrInC): An instrument for assessing adverse consequences of alcohol use. Test manual*. Rockville, MD: National Institute on Alcohol Abuse and Alcoholism.

Miller, W. R., & Marlatt, G. A. (1984). *Manual for the comprehensive drinker profile*. Odessa, FL: Psychological Assessment Resources.

Monti, P. M., Rohsenow, D. J., Abrams, D. B., Zwick, W. R., Binkoff, J. A., Munroe, S. M., et al. (1993). Development of a behavior analytically derived alcohol-specific role-play assessment instrument. *Journal of Studies on Alcohol*, *54*, 710–721.

Moos, R. H. (1993). *Coping response inventory professional manual*. Odessa, FL: Psychological Assessment Resources.

Morgenstern, J., & Longabaugh, R. (2000). Cognitive-behavioral treatment for alcohol dependence: A review of evidence for its hypothesized mechanism of action. *Addiction*, *95*, 1475–1490.

Myers, M. G., Brown, S. A., & Mott, M. A. (1993). Coping as a predictor of adolescent substance abuse treatment outcome. *Journal of Substance Abuse*, *5*, 15–29.

National Institute on Drug Abuse. (1998). *A Community Reinforcement Approach: Treating Cocaine Addiction*. NIH Publication Number 98-4309. Retrieved February 27, 2008, from http://www.nida.nih.gov/TXManuals/CRA/CRAX6.html.

Petchers, M. K., & Singer, M. I. (1987). Perceived-benefit-of-drinking scale: Approach to screening for adolescent alcohol abuse. *Journal of Pediatrics*, *110*, 977–981.

Prochaska, J. O., Velicer, W. F., DiClemente, C. C., & Fava, J. (1988). Measuring processes of change: Applications to the cessation of smoking. *Journal of Consulting and Clinical Psychology*, *56*, 520–528.

Robinson, E. A. R., Cranford, J. A., Webb, J. R., & Brower, K. J. (2007). Six-month changes in spirituality, religiousness, and heavy drinking in a treatment-seeking sample. *Journal of Studies on Alcohol and Drugs*, *68*, 282–290.

Saunders, J. B., Aasland, O. G., Babor, T. F., de la Fuente, J. R., & Grant, M. (1993). Development of the alcohol use disorders identification test (AUDIT): WHO collaborative project on early detection of persons with harmful alcohol consumption: II. *Addiction*, *88*, 791–804.

Snow, M. G., Prochaska, J. O., & Rossi, J. (1994). Processes of change in alcoholics anonymous: Maintenance factors in long-term sobriety. *Journal of Studies on Alcohol*, *55*, 362–371.

Strecher, V., & Rosenstock, I. (1997). The health belief model. In K. Glanz, F. Lewis, & B. Rimer(Eds.), *Health behavior and health education* (pp. 41–50). San Francisco: Jossey-Bass.

Tonigan, J. S., Connors, G. J., & Miller, W. R. (1996). Alcoholics anonymous involvement (AAI) scale: Reliability and norms. *Psychology of Addictive Behaviors*, *10*, 75–80.

Tonigan, J., & Miller, W. R. (2002). The inventory of drug use consequences (InDUC): Test-retest stability and sensitivity to detect change. *Psychology of Addictive Behaviors*, *16*, 165–168.

White, H. R., & Labouvie, E. W. (1989). Towards the assessment of adolescent problem drinking. *Journal of Studies on Alcohol*, *50*, 30–37.

Zywiak, W. H., Longabaugh, R., & Wirtz, P. W. (2002). Decomposing the relationships between pretreatment social network characteristics and alcohol treatment outcome. *Journal of Studies on Alcohol*, *63*, 114–121.

PART | THREE

Treatment Methods

Chapter | eight

Cognitive Behavioral Treatments for Substance Use Disorders

Danielle Barry and Nancy M. Petry
University of Connecticut Health Center

SUMMARY POINTS

Introduction

Review of behavioral therapy and cognitive therapy

- Cognitive–behavioral therapy (CBT) is based on behavioral and cognitive therapies.
- Behavior, including substance use, is learned through classical conditioning, operant conditioning, and modeling.
- CBT is based on the ABC (antecedents/beliefs/consequences) model of emotions and behaviors.

Cognitive behavioral therapy for substance use disorders

- There are several specific CBT interventions for substance use disorders (relapse prevention, cognitive behavioral coping skills training for alcohol dependence, cognitive behavioral therapy for cocaine addiction).

Evidence-Based Addiction Treatment

General format of CBT for substance use disorders

- Individual or group formats can be used.
- Functional analysis is obtained in Session 1.
- Sessions are highly structured (20/20/20 model).
  - First 20 min: Understanding current concerns, reviewing substance use in past week.
  - Second 20 min: Learning new skills.
  - Last 20 min: Planning practice for new skills, anticipating problems.
  - Sample Session 1 demonstrates the 20/20/20 model.

Evidence for efficacy of CBT for substance use disorders

- CBT interventions based on relapse prevention are effective in short and longer term.
- CBT interventions focusing on problem-solving skills training and social skills training are effective in reducing alcohol use.
- CBT for cocaine use disorders is comparable to or better than other therapies in the short term and more effective in producing long-term change and helping clients with more severe cocaine dependence.

SUMMARY

Cognitive behavioral therapy (CBT) represents a synthesis of two earlier therapeutic traditions: behavior therapy and cognitive therapy. This chapter first describes these therapeutic approaches and then how they are combined for CBT. We then point out specific issues that relate to the use of CBT in treating substance use disorders and outline the format for a CBT session. We then describe other topics or skills that are taught in CBT and detail empirical evidence of the efficacy of CBT in the treatment of substance use disorders.

REVIEW OF BEHAVIORAL THERAPY AND COGNITIVE THERAPY

Behavior therapy employs interventions based on classical and operant conditioning. An early example is Wolpe's (1954) systematic desensitization in which patients are taught progressive relaxation techniques and then are systematically exposed to stimuli that elicit fear while in a relaxed state. Because the relaxation response is incompatible with anxiety, it weakens the learned association between a stimulus and an anxiety response. Cognitive therapy views psychological distress as the result of an information processing problem that leads to a negative cognitive bias (Beck, 1963). The cognitive bias is learned and can be broken down into a number of specific cognitive distortions that perpetuate maladaptive feelings and behaviors (Beck, 1964). Cognitive therapy consists of identifying these cognitive distortions and helping clients learn to view the world more objectively, thus reducing psychological distress. Like behavior therapy, cognitive therapy is based on a learning model (Beck & Weishaar, 1989), although it focuses on changing underlying beliefs and thoughts, whereas behavior therapy addresses overt behaviors.

Cognitive behavioral therapy combines behavior therapy and cognitive therapy by applying learning theory to both observable behavior and to thoughts and emotions as well. CBT is based on social learning theory (Bandura, 1969) and the assumption that behavior, including maladaptive behavior such as substance abuse, is learned through a combination of classical conditioning, operant conditioning, and modeling (Carroll, 1998). When applied to substance use disorders, the CBT approach suggests that individuals first learn to use drugs or alcohol by observing other people using them. If their observations convince them to try a substance, then operant conditioning can occur as the individual experiences pleasurable effects and uses the substance repeatedly in order to recreate those effects. Anticipation of substance use can create a strong desire, or craving, and, consequently, elimination of craving by using the substance is strongly reinforcing. Classical conditioning contributes to dependence when substance use is paired repeatedly with environmental cues, such as certain people, locations, objects, times, situations, and moods (Marlatt, 1985). Over time, these cues can trigger craving for the substance. CBT models view addictive behaviors as acquired habits that are shaped by learning, and these models further maintain that habits can be changed through the development of behavioral skills and cognitive strategies (Marlatt, 1985).

Similar to behavior therapy, CBT uses techniques based on classical and operant conditioning. Because classical conditioning results in certain stimuli (e.g., particular people, places, or situations, sight or smell of substances, drug use equipment) being associated with substance use, clients experience cravings when exposed to those stimuli. To reduce risks of cravings, clients are taught to recognize and avoid conditioned triggers. When using operant techniques, clinicians instruct clients to reward themselves for meeting goals (e.g., engaging in an enjoyable activity or purchasing a desired item after a sustained period of abstinence).

As with cognitive therapy, a major tenet of CBT is that behaviors and feelings are caused by thoughts about other people, events, and situations (Beck, 1963, 1964; Ellis, 1957). The theory and practice of CBT are based on an ABC model of human emotions and behavior. People, events, and situations are considered determinants or antecedents (A) that may or may not lead to particular feelings or behaviors (consequences or C) depending on the intervening beliefs (B) (Thompson & Hollon, 2000). Ways of thinking about the world are learned, and maladaptive behavior and feelings can be changed if one learns to think in a different way. Antecedents for substance use can be negative events such as job loss, interpersonal conflicts, or financial problems. Although these events tend to be associated with stress and a range of negative emotions, the particular association depends on an individual's beliefs about the situation. One individual might believe, "This is difficult, but I can deal with it," while another believes, "This is terrible, and I can't cope with it unless I have a drink." Consequences are likely to be different for each of these individuals. The first will feel somewhat anxious but is likely to contact prospective employers, consider how to patch up relationships, or decide whether to take out a loan; the second will feel overwhelmed and may become intoxicated.

COGNITIVE BEHAVIORAL THERAPY FOR SUBSTANCE USE DISORDERS

An early CBT approach to addictions is relapse prevention (RP; Marlatt, 1985). Because relapse is the most common outcome of treatment for addictions, it must be addressed, anticipated, and prepared for during treatment. The RP model views relapse not as a failure, but as part of the recovery process and an opportunity for learning. Marlatt (1985) describes an abstinence violation effect (AVE) that leads people to respond to any return to drug or alcohol use after a period of abstinence with despair and a sense of failure. By undermining confidence, these negative thoughts and feelings increase the likelihood that an isolated "lapse" will lead to a full-blown relapse. If, however, individuals view lapses as temporary setbacks or errors in the process of learning a new skill, they can renew their efforts to remain abstinent. Lapses provide an opportunity for learning (Marlatt, 1985).

Two publications, *Cognitive Behavioral Coping Skills Training for Alcohol Dependence* (Kadden et al., 1994; Monti, Kadden, Rohsenow, Cooney, & Abrams, 2002) and *Cognitive Behavioral Therapy for Cocaine Addiction* (Carroll, 1998), are based on the RP model and techniques. Although specific CBT interventions may focus more or less on particular techniques or skills, the primary goal of CBT for addictions is to

Table 8.1 Sample monitoring form for use in cognitive behavioral therapy for substance use disorders[a]

Day/ time	Situation	Thoughts/ feelings	Substance use? What and how much?	Positive consequences	Negative consequences
Mon pm	Bad grade	Angry!	Alcohol 9–10 beers	Forgot about exam	Hung over next day. Missed classes.
Tues pm	Came back to room. Everyone drinking.	Want to drink with them.	Alcohol 6–7 beers	Hung out with friends	Wasn't really fun. Spent more money on alcohol this week than planned.

[a]*Adapted from Caroll (1998), Marlatt (1985), and Monti et al. (2002).*

assist clients in mastering skills that will allow them to become and remain abstinent from alcohol and/or drugs (Kadden et al., 1994). CBT treatments are usually guided by a manual, are relatively short term (12 to 16 weeks) in duration, and focus on the present and future. Clients are expected to monitor substance use (see Table 8.1) and complete homework exercises between sessions.

GENERAL FORMAT OF CBT FOR SUBSTANCE USE DISORDERS

Cognitive behavioral therapy can be delivered individually or in a group format. Although individual CBT can be tailored more specifically to the individual needs of each client, group CBT allows for greater sharing of ideas and strategies and immediate practice of new skills (Finney, Wilbourne, & Moos, 2007).

Cognitive behavioral therapy sessions are highly structured. Carroll (1998) describes a 20/20/20 format for a 60-min session. The first 20 min are devoted to understanding the client's current issues and level of functioning since the previous session and to reviewing episodes of substance use or cravings for substances in the prior week. New skills are introduced during the second 20 min, and the final 20 min are spent planning a between-session exercise to practice new skills and anticipating potential obstacles to successful practice (Carroll, 1998).

Cognitive behavioral therapy for addictive behaviors starts with a functional analysis to determine the unique set of contributors to substance use for a particular client (Carroll, 1998). The next section depicts a typical individual therapy session, introducing the concept of a functional analysis and use of the 20/20/20 format. In this case example, the patient is a 21-year-old college student who has been cited for intoxication in his dormitory three times and is at risk of being suspended from school.

Sample CBT session

THERAPIST: "Hi, John. It's nice to meet you. Why don't you tell me a bit about why you're here."

PATIENT: "Well, I'm only here because I have to be. I got written up for 'public intoxication' last weekend. They told me I had to come here, or else I'd get kicked out of school."

THERAPIST: "I see. How much would you say you were drinking when this happened?"

PATIENT: "Oh, I don't know. No more than usual. We all just got together and had a few beers. It was no big deal."

THERAPIST: "You had a few beers, and then what happened? How did the citation occur?"

PATIENT: "Some loser down the hall complained about the music. The RA came into our suite and saw all the beers. That guy has it in for me. It was just an excuse to get me. I wasn't even drinking that much."

THERAPIST: "What did the RA say to you?"

PATIENT: "He told us all to break it up. He started dumping our beers down the sink. That made me angry, because I'm 21 so I *can* drink."

THERAPIST: "So you got angry with him. What did you say?"

PATIENT: "I told him it was none of his business what we did in our own rooms. We were all 21, and we have a right to drink. He can't tell us what to do."

THERAPIST: "My guess is that he didn't respond very well to that. What happened next?"

PATIENT: "The little weasel left and called the campus cops. We all left the dorm, but they came while we were still in the courtyard area. We all got written up, but I had to come here because this is my third violation. It sucks. If I get one more, they won't let me graduate this year."

THERAPIST: "That sounds pretty serious then. And, you seem like you really do want to stay in school and graduate."

PATIENT: "Yeah. I mean, I've come this far, and I only have one semester to go. It would really suck if I had to drop out, and come back again next year after all my friends are finished."

THERAPIST: "You have a really good reason for wanting to make sure this doesn't happen again. What do you think you need to do so you can stay in school and graduate?"

PATIENT: "I just have to make sure I don't get caught drunk again."

THERAPIST: "How do you think you can ensure that?"

PATIENT: "If I don't drink at all, I can't get caught."

THERAPIST: "That's true. It is the safest option to ensure that you graduate on time. Do you think you can manage to not drink any more between now and May?"

PATIENT: "I'm not saying I'm not going to drink at all. But I can try to not drink when I'm on campus."

THERAPIST: "That would be a good start—to make sure you don't drink on campus, but it might also be difficult to arrange your drinking and nondrinking life like that. Have you ever tried to reduce how much you drink before?"

PATIENT: "Some days I just don't feel like drinking so I don't."

THERAPIST: "That is good that you can decide not to drink when you don't want to. Can you tell me a little more about those days? Why on some days do you not want to drink?"

PATIENT: "Oh, I don't know. I never really thought about it before. I just know sometimes I don't want to drink—that I shouldn't be drinking every day. So, some days I don't drink anything."

THERAPIST: "It seems as though you might be a little worried about your drinking, and you consciously decide not to drink some days."

PATIENT: "Yeah."

THERAPIST: "What is it that concerns you about your drinking?"

PATIENT: "I don't want to become a drunk. I don't want to *have* to drink. I only want to drink when I feel like drinking."

THERAPIST: "You know about alcoholism and the hold it can have on people. You're trying to avoid that."

PATIENT: "Yes. I know some guys who are, really, you know, like alcoholics. I'm not like that."

THERAPIST: "What worries you most about those people?"

PATIENT: "They're a mess. They drink all time. Don't care about anything. They drop out of school, or never really get a job. That would be awful. I mean, why even bother going to college at all if you're not going to finish and don't get a good job when you're done."

THERAPIST: "I think you're right about that. It certainly isn't where you want to end up."

PATIENT: "No way."

THERAPIST: "So, what are you going to do about making sure that you don't get another violation and end up where you don't want to be?"

PATIENT: "I don't know. I guess that's why I'm supposed to come here."

THERAPIST: "Yes, I think I can work with you on that. But it is going to take a lot of effort on your part. You're really going to have to change your lifestyle to make sure that drinking is no longer a part of it. Are you willing to try that?"

PATIENT: "I guess I have to. I don't really have a choice."

THERAPIST: "Actually, I'd disagree with you on that. I think you do have a choice. You have a choice to keep drinking the way you have been, knowing that is likely to result in your getting expelled from school, or you can choose to stop drinking, finish school, and get a good job, just like you've always wanted."

PATIENT: "Yes, I think you're right. I think those are my choices. I don't really like them, but I guess that's what I have to do."

THERAPIST: "What I'd like to talk with you about for the rest of the session is a type of treatment that we use here. It's called cognitive behavioral therapy, which means it involves better understanding the cognitions or thoughts you have around drinking, and your behaviors. The treatment lasts for 8 weeks, and each week we'll discuss some aspect of your drinking. Between each session, there will be exercises that I'll want you to do every day between the sessions. They won't take you long to complete, but they will help remind you to think about what we discuss. Each one will be just a page or so long, so you can keep them in your desk or backpack. It's best if you pick a time of the day to do these exercises so that they become part of your routine. Like right before bed, first thing when you get up each morning, or right before dinner. Do you think you can manage that?"

PATIENT: "Yeah. I can do that."

THERAPIST: "Good, because I want you to bring them in each week so that we can discuss them."

PATIENT: "Okay. But I don't have to write a lot, do I? I already have enough homework."

THERAPIST: "No, you don't need to write a lot, but I do want you to think a lot about what you do write. The point is not just to have the blanks filled in, but for it to be meaningful to you so that you can stop drinking and graduate on time."

PATIENT: "Okay. What do they look like?"

THERAPIST: "Here's the form I want to go over with you today. Basically, alcohol can change the way you think, the way you feel, and the way you act. For example, you probably wouldn't have gotten really angry if a neighbor complained about your stereo, and you were just listening to it—not drinking."

PATIENT: "I don't know about that. I might not have mouthed off to the RA, or at least not about the alcohol part. But I still would have been pissed."

THERAPIST: "You might be upset if someone complained, but I doubt the RA would have ended up calling the campus police."

PATIENT: "You're probably right about that."

THERAPIST: "Alcohol does lower our inhibitions, so you probably said things to the RA you wouldn't have had said if you were sober. And, you clearly wouldn't have gone out to the courtyard, making a loud scene if you weren't drinking."

PATIENT: "No, we wouldn't have done that. Plus, the cops wouldn't have given us violations just for being in the courtyard if we weren't drinking."

THERAPIST: "Right. So, alcohol affects how you feel—it can make you feel uninhibited. Can it also make you feel more sociable?"

PATIENT: "Yeah."

THERAPIST: "Because drinking changes the way you think, act and feel, we need to better understand what types of situations you are most likely to drink in. These are called 'high-risk situations.' What we want to figure out is the kinds of things that are triggering or maintaining your drinking so that we can develop other ways you can handle high-risk situations without drinking. What kind of situations do you drink in?"

PATIENT: "When I'm with my buddies."

THERAPIST: "You drink most often with friends. Do you drink at a particular time of day, with a specific group of friends, or on certain days?"

PATIENT: "All my friends drink. I mean, at least the ones I hang out with. We usually don't start drinking until evening. Like 8–9 o'clock. Sometimes earlier on the weekends."

THERAPIST: "What do you think about before you start drinking? Do you *plan* to start drinking or does it just seem to happen?"

PATIENT: "We do have a fridge full of beer. I might come back after a class or an exam and think, 'I'm wiped. I really need a beer.' If other people are around, they might be already drinking, and they'll give me one, or else I'll grab one for myself."

THERAPIST: "Do you think you tend to drink more when you're tired or stressed, or when you want to have a good time with your friends?"

PATIENT: "Both, I guess. I like to drink if everyone else is. But, yeah, I guess I also want to drink as soon as I get home if I've had a bad day."

THERAPIST: "Those are two good examples of high-risk situations. One, when you've had a bad day and you want to drink to relieve stress, and the second, when you see other people drinking and you want to be a part of it."

PATIENT: "So that's what you want me to write on this sheet?"

THERAPIST: "Yes, you can write those two examples down. Let's take that first example. Think back to the last time you had a bad day and tell me about what happened."

PATIENT: "Well, 4 days ago, I got back a bad grade on an exam I thought I had done really well on. It really irritated me."

THERAPIST: "And what happened after you got that exam back."

PATIENT: "I was pissed. I went back to the dorm and grabbed a beer. I thought I deserved it because I did study hard for that test."

THERAPIST: "You used drinking as a way to make it up to yourself that you got a grade you didn't deserve."

PATIENT: "Yeah, I guess so."

THERAPIST: "And what happened next? How much did you drink that day?"

PATIENT: "I had already had three to four beers by the time my suite-mates came back. They had a couple more with me. I guess I got pretty smashed that night."

THERAPIST: "What were the positive effects of your drinking in that situation?"

PATIENT: "The positive effects?"

THERAPIST: "Yes, what good things happened because of drinking that night? You wouldn't drink if drinking didn't have some positive consequences for you."

PATIENT: "It made me forget about the exam."

THERAPIST: "Alcohol can do that. Now, what about the bad things? What were the negative consequences of drinking so much that evening?"

PATIENT: "The next day, I was totally hung over. I couldn't even make it to class."

THERAPIST: "I see. The negative consequences of drinking were a bit delayed, they didn't occur until the following day. It also appears that the negative effects of missing class may lead to more triggers for drinking. You missed class the next day, which may have even longer term consequences, like missing out on important information for your next exam. And, doing poorly on exams is a trigger for your drinking. That is how drinking can lead to a vicious cycle. You drink for the positive effects, which are generally short-lived, but the negative effects are delayed and are often similar to the triggers themselves."

PATIENT: "I guess I see what you're saying."

THERAPIST: "Let's finish that example on the worksheet."

PATIENT: "Is that right?"

THERAPIST: "Yes. Now, let's go back to your other example—when you see your friends drinking, how does that make you think or feel?"

PATIENT: "Like I need a drink!"

THERAPIST: "Would you say it makes you crave a drink or more that you want to be social with your friends?"

PATIENT: "Both, I guess."

THERAPIST: "Then let's put both those down."

PATIENT: "And for the behavior column, that's where I write 'I drink.'"

THERAPIST: "That's right. Think back to the last time you came back to your suite and your friends were drinking. How much did you have that night to drink?"

PATIENT: "I don't know. Nine or 10 beers, I guess."

THERAPIST: "Write that down and then list the positive consequences of drinking that evening."

PATIENT: "I don't know that there were any. It wasn't like a really fun night or anything."

THERAPIST: "Then why did you keep drinking rather than just stop?"

PATIENT: "Because everyone else was. Because I didn't want to be a loser and say I had to go study or something."

THERAPIST: "So it sounds like the positive consequences were being with friends rather than alone."

PATIENT: "Yeah, I guess."

THERAPIST: "How about the negative consequences from that evening. Did you later regret how much you drank?"

PATIENT: "I don't know that I regretted it, but it was kind of stupid. I ended up spending more money on alcohol than I wanted that week. I ended up going to bed early anyway. It wasn't all that fun."

THERAPIST: "So, for the negative consequences, you might want to list spending too much money and not having a good time."

PATIENT: "And, not having a good time is sort of why I drink in the first place, because I'm bored or don't want to just hang out alone in my room."

THERAPIST: "That's right. Those negative consequences often lead right back to the triggers for drinking, just like you said. So, what we need to do now is start thinking about some other things you can do when you encounter triggers for drinking, like feeling bored, having a stressful day, or watching others drink. That way, when those things happen, you can start to behave differently than what you've been doing, which is drinking."

PATIENT: "I see. So, like I should go do something else fun that doesn't involve drinking if I have a bad day. Or, I should not start drinking just because my friends are, and maybe go to a movie or to the basketball court instead?"

THERAPIST: "Those are all excellent ideas! I think you get what this exercise is all about. How difficult do you think it will be to actually leave your room if you see everyone else drinking?"

PATIENT: "Oh, I can do that. It's not a big deal. I do stuff like that all the time—if I really need to study or if I feel like I need to exercise. I don't have to drink just because they are."

THERAPIST: "I'm glad you feel confident in your abilities to not drink. What I'd like you to do each day between now and when we meet next week is to write down at least one trigger for drinking you encounter each day. Indicate how it made you feel and whether you were able to refrain from drinking in response to it. If you don't drink, which is the goal, then you can indicate the positive consequence of not drinking that day. Hopefully, there will be no negative consequences to not drinking, but if there are, write them down in the last column. You can also indicate what the negative consequence of drinking may have been, had you drunk in that situation. If you do drink, write down the positive and negative consequences. Is that clear?"

PATIENT: "Yeah, I get it."

THERAPIST: "Good. Then, I'll see you next week. Please remember to bring in your form, and we can review it together. I think you've made great progress here today. I also know that you can make it to graduation if you work hard on this and stay committed to your goals."

As noted in the example just given, determinants of use (e.g., triggers, subjective experience, patterns of use), obstacles to recovery (e.g., problem recognition, relapse history), and strengths and skills (e.g., education, social support, motivation, employment) are assessed and used to determine appropriate goals (Carroll, 1998).

In the second CBT session, the therapist would start off with a review of self-monitoring forms for the previous week. Was the exercise difficult? How well did it work? Were there any unanticipated problems with completing the exercise? Most importantly, what did the client learn? A sample of this review appears here.

THERAPIST: "So you didn't drink throughout much of last week, which was really good for you—a big reduction from your usual drinking pattern. That is great!"

PATIENT: "Yeah. I did exactly what I said I would last week. I didn't drink when I was alone in my room, and if my roommates were drinking, I said I had to go to the library or the gym."

THERAPIST: "That is wonderful that you found other ways to handle your high-risk situations that worked so well for you."

PATIENT: "It wasn't hard. I knew I could do it."

THERAPIST: "I'm really proud of you. Not everyone stays so committed to remaining abstinent when triggers actually arise."

After reviewing self-monitoring, client and therapist would move on to the skills training component. Skills covered in CBT for substance use disorders include coping with craving, identifying and avoiding triggers, drink or drug refusal skills, assertiveness training, problem solving to deal with stressful life events, and anger management. As outlined in the initial session, skills training begins with a rationale for learning the skill (Monti et al., 2002). Next, specific skill guidelines are provided and explained and then the therapist models performance of the skill. When appropriate, the client will engage in role play of the skill with the therapist or another client if in group therapy (Monti et al., 2002). During the skills training component, the therapist may be highly directive, but it is important that the client collaborate with the process to ensure understanding.

EVIDENCE FOR EFFICACY OF CBT FOR SUBSTANCE USE DISORDERS

Studies show that CBT interventions based on RP can be effective in reducing the frequency and intensity of relapse episodes and in lowering drinking rates and the number of drinking-associated problems among alcohol dependent patients who relapse (Larimer, Palmer, & Marlatt, 1999). RP interventions for substance dependence are particularly effective when outcomes are evaluated immediately following the end of treatment (Irvin, Bowers, Dunn, & Wang, 1999), but the beneficial effects of CBT often emerge after treatment is complete, supporting the notion that the efficacy of RP is related to the skills training provided.

Because skills are likely to improve with practice over time, the benefits could be expected to strengthen over time (Larimer et al., 1999).

When a CBT treatment focusing on problem-solving skills was compared to a discussion group that did not provide skills training, individuals assigned to the skills training group drank to intoxication on fewer days, drank fewer drinks overall, and drank for shorter periods of time when drinking in the year following treatment (Chaney, O'Leary, & Marlatt, 1978). A similar intervention that used CBT techniques but focused primarily on social skills training was compared to a discussion group (Eriksen, Bjornstad, & Gotestam, 1986). Alcohol-dependent clients receiving social skills training consumed less alcohol and reported more sober days over the year following treatment than the control condition.

Cognitive–behavioral therapy is also effective for other substance use disorders. Urban crack cocaine abusers receiving CBT were more likely to achieve 4 or more consecutive weeks of cocaine abstinence compared to counterparts receiving another therapy based on the 12-step model (Maude-Griffin et al., 1998). In a randomized controlled trial comparing CBT for cocaine addiction to interpersonal therapy (IPT), patients assigned to CBT were slightly more likely to complete treatment, achieve 3 or more weeks of continuous abstinence during treatment, and maintain 4 or more weeks of continuous abstinence after leaving treatment, but results were not statistically significant (Carroll, Rounsaville, & Gawin, 1991). The difference between CBT and IPT was significant among patients with more severe cocaine abuse, however. When CBT was compared to a nonspecific therapy (clinical management), no significant overall differences emerged, but patients with more severe cocaine abuse again had better outcomes in CBT, suggesting that the structure of CBT is beneficial to those with severe cocaine use disorders (Carroll et al., 1994a). Furthermore, despite the comparability of CBT and clinical management at the conclusion of treatment, relative benefits of CBT emerged in the year following treatment among the entire sample. Patients receiving CBT reported decreased or stable cocaine use between completion of treatment and a 1-year follow-up compared to clinical management patients, whose use had returned to pretreatment levels (Carroll et al., 1994b).

A brief cognitive behavioral treatment (coping skills therapy [CST]; Monti, Rohsenow, Michalec, Martin, & Abrams, 1997) that focused on identifying and coping with triggers for cocaine use was evaluated as an addition to a comprehensive treatment program. Although patients who received CST were no more likely than patients receiving meditation and relaxation control therapy to be abstinent from cocaine 3 months after treatment, they used cocaine on fewer days and their longest binges were shorter (Monti et al., 1997). CBT, therefore, appears to have some potential benefits for patients with relatively severe cocaine dependence, and some of its effects may persist or even emerge after treatment is completed.

SUMMARY

Cognitive behavioral therapy helps individuals with addictions reduce their substance use by helping them identify environmental cues, thoughts, and feelings that work together to trigger substance use behaviors. CBT has demonstrated efficacy in reducing the use of alcohol and cocaine, particularly over the long term and for clients with severe cocaine dependence.

REFERENCES

Beck, A. T. (1963). Thinking and depression. I. Idiosyncratic content and cognitive distortions. *Archives of General Psychiatry*, *9*, 324–333.

Beck, A. T. (1964). Thinking and depression. II. Theory and therapy. *Archives of General Psychiatry*, *10*, 561–571.

Beck, A. T., & Weishaar, M. (1989). Cognitive therapy. In A. Freeman, K. M. Simon, L. E. Beutler, & H. Arkowitz (Eds.), *Comprehensive handbook of cognitive therapy* (pp. 21–36). New York: Plenum Press.

Carroll, K. M. (1998). *A cognitive-behavioral approach: Treating cocaine addiction*. Rockville, MD: National Institute on Drug Abuse.

Carroll, K. M., Rounsaville, B. J., & Gawin, F. H. (1991). A comparative trial of psychotherapies for ambulatory cocaine abusers: Relapse prevention and interpersonal psychotherapy. *American Journal of Drug and Alcohol Abuse*, *17*, 229–247.

Carroll, K. M., Rounsaville, B. J., Gordon, L. T., Nich, C., Jatlow, P., & Bisighini, R. M. (1994a). Psychotherapy and pharmacotherapy for ambulatory cocaine abusers. *Archives of General Psychiatry*, *51*, 177–187.

Carroll, K. M., Rounsaville, B. J., Nich, C., Gordon, L. T., Wirtz, P. W., & Gawin, F. (1994b). One-year follow-up of psychotherapy and pharmacotherapy for cocaine dependence. Delayed emergence of psychotherapy effects. *Archives of General Psychiatry*, *51*, 989–997.

Chaney, E. F., O'Leary, M. R., & Marlatt, G. A. (1978). Skill training with alcoholics. *Journal of Consulting and Clinical Psychology*, *46*, 1092–1104.

Ellis, A. (1957). Outcome of employing three techniques of psychotherapy. *Journal of Clinical Psychology*, *13*, 344–350.

Eriksen, L., Bjornstad, S., & Gotestam, K. G. (1986). Social skills training in groups for alcoholics: One-year treatment outcome for groups and individuals. *Addictive Behaviors*, *11*, 309–329.

Finney, J. W., Wilbourne, P. L., & Moos, R. H. (2007). Psychosocial treatments for substance use disorders. In P. E. Nathan & J. M. Gorman (Eds.), *A guide to treatments that work* (pp. 179–202). New York: Oxford University Press.

Irvin, J. E., Bowers, C. A., Dunn, M. E., & Wang, M. C. (1999). Efficacy of relapse prevention: A meta-analytic review. *Journal of Consulting and Clinical Psychology*, *67*, 563–570.

Kadden, R., Carroll, K. M., Donovan, D., Cooney, N., Monti, P., Abrams, D., et al. (1994). *Cognitive-behavioral coping skills therapy manual*. Rockville, MD: National Institutes of Health.

Larimer, M. E., Palmer, R. S., & Marlatt, G. A. (1999). Relapse prevention: An overview of Marlatt's cognitive-behavioral model. *Alcohol Research & Health*, *23*, 151–160.

Marlatt, G. A. (1985). Part I. Relapse prevention: General overview. In G. A. Marlatt & J. R. Gordon (Eds.), *Relapse prevention: Maintenance strategies in the treatment of addictive behaviors* (pp. 1–348). New York: The Guilford Press.

Maude-Griffin, P. M., Hohenstein, J. M., Humfleet, G. L., Reilly, P. M., Tusel, D. J., & Hall, S. M. (1998). Superior efficacy of cognitive-behavioral therapy for urban crack cocaine abusers: Main and matching effects. *Journal of Consulting and Clinical Psychology*, *66*, 832–837.

Monti, P. M., Kadden, R. M., Rohsenow, D. J., Cooney, N. L., & Abrams, D. B. (2002). *Treating alcohol dependence: A coping skills training guide*. New York: The Guilford Press.

Monti, P. M., Rohsenow, D. J., Michalec, E., Martin, R. A., & Abrams, D. B. (1997). Brief coping skills treatment for cocaine abuse: Substance use outcomes at three months. *Addiction*, *92*, 1717–1728.

Thompson, T., & Hollon, S. D. (2000). Behavioral and cognitive-behavioral interventions. In M. D. Ebert, P. T. Loosen, & B. Nurcombe (Eds.), *Current diagnosis and treatment in psychology* (pp. 18–28). New York: Lange Medical Books/McGraw Hill.

Wolpe, J. (1954). Reciprocal inhibition as the main basis of psychotherapeutic effects. *AMA Archives of Neurology and Psychiatry*, *72*, 205–226.

Chapter | nine

Motivational Interviewing for Addictions

Lisa H. Glynn and Theresa B. Moyers
University of New Mexico

SUMMARY POINTS

- Motivational interviewing is client-centered and directive, with a focus upon helping clients to resolve ambivalence.
- Motivational interviewing has received empirical support for treating addictions and other health behaviors.
- Motivational interviewing can be used by itself or in combination with other treatment styles.
- Motivational interviewing uses both common ingredients of treatment, such as expressing empathy and supporting self-efficacy, as well as unique elements, such as evoking change talk.

INTRODUCTION: THE COUNSELOR'S DILEMMA

COUNSELOR: Welcome to our facility. What brings you into treatment?

CLIENT: I got pulled over on a fluke and ended up with a DWI.

COUNSELOR: Was this your first time for drunk driving?

Evidence-Based Addiction Treatment

CLIENT: No, I wouldn't say "drunk." I was just out with some friends. We had a nice dinner, stuck around for a few beers afterward, and then it started getting late so I decided to get home. I would never drive drunk—it's irresponsible.

COUNSELOR: Okay, but it says on this report that your BAC was .17 when they arrested you. That's not DUI—it's *aggravated* DUI.

CLIENT: Like I said, I'd had a few beers, but I certainly wasn't *drunk*.

COUNSELOR: Well, at least I'm glad you ended up here today, where you can get some help.

CLIENT: I don't need "help"—I was in the wrong place at the wrong time, and now they're treating me like I'm some kind of alcoholic.

Perhaps you have overheard an interaction like this in your treatment setting. Although the session has just begun, it already has taken a negative turn. Clearly, the counselor and the client are approaching the interaction with reasonable viewpoints and intentions, but because they have discrepant goals the session is becoming an unproductive argument and an exercise in dominance, not change.

What would you do in this situation? What outcomes would you expect? Working with clients who seem unwilling to change harmful behavior can be frustrating. Well-meaning counselors sense danger for the client and are tempted to share their own solutions to problems—often by offering advice, lecturing, shaming, or warning—which is known as the "righting reflex." However, clients often hold their own solutions to substance abuse problems. What they may lack is the motivation to implement them. When the righting reflex is active, the counselor argues for change, and the client is naturally more likely to argue against it, which elicits arguments against change and does not bode well for changes in substance use.

WHAT IS MOTIVATIONAL INTERVIEWING?

Motivational interviewing (MI) is described by its founders as a "client-centered, directive method for enhancing intrinsic motivation to change by exploring and resolving ambivalence" (Miller & Rollnick, 2002, p. 25). The MI style originated in the addictions field, borrowing from Rogerian therapy, Prochaska and DiClemente's transtheoretical model of change, and behavioral methods.

FOUR PRINCIPLES OF MOTIVATIONAL INTERVIEWING: "COMMON INGREDIENTS"

Four principles form the foundation of MI: expressing empathy, developing discrepancy, rolling with resistance, and supporting self-efficacy.

These elements are not unique to MI, although they are combined and emphasized in a novel fashion.

- Expressing empathy: Attempting to understand and accept the client's viewpoint without judgment or hostility.
- Developing discrepancy: Leading the client to recognize differences between behaviors and deeply held values.
- Rolling with resistance: Avoiding arguments, instead offering support and expressing empathy for the client's situation. Resistance is viewed as a sign of incongruence between client and therapist goals.
- Supporting self-efficacy: Avoiding playing the expert, instead conveying that any decisions about change or maintenance of behaviors belong to the client alone.

Therapists are responsible for utilizing these principles throughout treatment in order to meet clients where they are and to create an environment that maximizes the likelihood of change.

Like other addictions-treatment styles, the goal of MI treatment is to help clients make important and lasting changes in their substance use in particular and in their lives in general. Unlike many addictions treatments, which conceptualize change as the product of gaining insight about a substance use problem or breaking through "denial," the MI style approaches ambivalence as a normal and expected precursor to change. Thus, the role of the counselor in MI is to facilitate clients' explorations of ambivalence, moving them gently toward behavioral change through empathy, MI "spirit," and selective reinforcement of statements in favor of change.

One aspect of the therapeutic relationship, counselor empathy, is particularly emphasized within MI. A key element of Rogerian and other therapies, *empathy* refers to the counselor's ability to understand the client's problem as the client sees it; this differs from both sympathy and having actually experienced what the client has experienced. Although not unique to MI, empathy is considered an important precursor to a strong client–counselor relationship, which belongs to this group of "common ingredients" believed to make treatment effective.

CLIENT LANGUAGE: A UNIQUE INGREDIENT IN MI

The client's language receives special attention within motivational interviewing. A client's self-motivating statements in favor of change are known as *change talk*. Conversely, *counterchange talk*, or *sustain talk*, refers to client statements against change or toward maintenance of the status quo. Change talk is believed to predict actual behavioral change in clients up to a year postsession, whereas counterchange talk can increase resistance and predict negative client outcomes (Miller, Benefield, & Tonigan, 1993; Moyers & Martin, 2006; Moyers, Miller, & Hendrickson, 2005; Patterson & Forgatch, 1985). For this reason, client language in favor of change is greatly preferred and therapists are encouraged to use specific methods to increase the chances that it will occur. Rather than simply respond to clients empathically as they speak, as might happen in straightforward client-centered psychotherapy, therapists are encouraged to actively attempt to evoke change talk. One way of doing this is to ask specific questions that will provoke change talk, and another is to selectively reinforce what clients say so that they are rewarded by offering change talk.

Some evidence shows that therapists can indeed influence clients' expressions of this change talk, which may lead to better client outcomes. Several studies (e.g., Amrhein, Miller, Yahne, Palmer, & Fulcher, 2003; Moyers et al., 2007) have demonstrated the power of the therapist in guiding client outcomes: Change talk tends to predict meaningful and long-lasting changes in client behavior, whereas sustain talk predicts poorer treatment outcomes and a reduced likelihood of making positive changes. What clients say about the changes they are considering during treatment sessions may be more powerful than we think.

THE SPIRIT OF MOTIVATIONAL INTERVIEWING

Behavioral treatments for substance abuse tend to rely on specific techniques for their success. In MI, a much greater emphasis is placed on having the right approach to clients, or having the right spirit. The idea here is that when therapists can adopt the right attitude toward change, the use of technique will be much less important in determining outcomes. MI spirit comprises three components: *collaboration*—working together with the client as a partner or helper rather than as an expert, *evocation*—"drawing out" discussion of change from the client, and *autonomy*—recognizing that any decision to change or not change lies only with the client. MI spirit has been compared to music: Without it, the words just don't create a song no matter how good they are.

REVISITING THE INITIAL CONSULTATION

In the client–counselor interaction at the beginning of this chapter, how might adopting an empathic and MI-consistent spirit have led to a different outcome? Consider this alternate scenario:

COUNSELOR: Welcome to our facility. What brings you into treatment?

CLIENT: I got pulled over on a fluke and ended up with a DWI.

COUNSELOR: You were in the wrong place at the wrong time.

CLIENT: Definitely. I've never driven after more than just a few beers, but because of one overzealous cop, now they're sending me to rehab and treating me like I'm some kind of alcoholic.

COUNSELOR: That label doesn't really fit who you really are.

CLIENT: Right. I mean, I wouldn't say that I've never done anything stupid while I was drinking, but I'm not an alcoholic and I've never driven drunk—that's just irresponsible.

COUNSELOR: On one hand, you feel like they're really blowing this out of proportion, and on the other hand, you're seeing that this hasn't been the first time something negative has happened after drinking and you're wondering what that means for you.

CLIENT: I guess so. I don't think that I have to worry about alcohol, but I also need to make sure that I don't get arrested again.

Although the differences were subtle, the outcome was very different. In the first interaction, the client reacted to the therapist's confrontational approach and, because of this, resistance actually increased over the course of the dialogue. In the second, the counselor sided with the client, showing empathy, reducing resistance, and improving the client–counselor relationship. When clients feel respected and listened to, the possibility of change can be explored more easily.

THE TRANSTHEORETICAL MODEL OF CHANGE

Motivational interviewing is not the same as the transtheoretical model (TTM) of change (e.g., Prochaska, DiClemente, & Norcross, 1992). In the TTM, the path to change is viewed not as a singular event, but instead as a five-step and potentially cyclical process. *Precontemplative* individuals are not considering change, either because they are unaware of dangers that might result from their current behavior or because they view making a change as too difficult. Those in the *contemplative* stage are considering change, but lack a sense of importance or confidence (or both) about completing the change; these individuals often are called "ambivalent" because they "feel two ways" about their behavior. People in the *preparation* stage plan to make a change soon and are setting up their environments to facilitate change, but have not yet implemented changes. Those in the *action* stage are actively and currently making a change. Finally, individuals who have completed the behavior change and need only to avoid relapse into their previous behavior are considered to be in the *maintenance* stage. The TTM is a way of understanding the larger process of changing a difficult behavior, whereas MI is one treatment that fits within a specific part of this process.

Specifically, MI is most useful for clients who are precontemplative or contemplative about their drinking or drug use. The MI style is less appropriate for clients in the action stage (i.e., who are already willing and prepared to make a change); these clients likely will benefit more from a little planning and support, but already have overcome the major barriers to change. Once the ambivalence has been resolved, discussing the merits of changing or sustaining behavior becomes less relevant (Miller & Rollnick, 2002). An effective alternative can be to initiate the therapeutic process by using MI to develop rapport, introduce the problem, and work through ambivalence and then transitioning into another therapeutic style or technique.

Motivational interviewing techniques may be used as a stand-alone style (e.g., brief intervention), as a precursor to another method (e.g., cognitive–behavioral therapy), or as an adjunct to another treatment (e.g., medication, token economy). Clients can benefit from just a single MI session (e.g., Miller, Benefield, & Tonigan, 1993), but sometimes MI is used instead as a way to build motivation to engage in treatment (e.g., Carroll et al., 2006; Hettema, Steele, & Miller, 2005). For example, MI may be used to encourage attendance at group therapy sessions or to promote adherence to treatment-related medications. The MI style also can be incorporated throughout a lengthy treatment whenever client–counselor resistance is present.

COMMON MISCONCEPTIONS ABOUT MOTIVATIONAL INTERVIEWING

Motivational interviewing is sometimes confused with other treatments and some of the elements of MI are easy to misunderstand. The following are some common myths about MI.

- *Motivational interviewing is just "being nice" to a client.* Although empathy is an important component of MI, it is considered an insufficient condition for change. Other therapist factors, such as direction and evocation of change talk, are also likely play a role in treatment outcomes.
- *Motivational interviewing should be used with every substance abuse client.* As mentioned earlier, MI is useful for very specific (and common) problems in substance abuse treatment. When clients are ambivalent about changing, research tells us that MI is likely to be helpful. Other approaches, including cognitive–behavioral treatments, are often needed as well.
- *Clients who have not recognized their addiction cannot benefit from therapy.* Individuals who are precontemplative actually can

benefit greatly from MI therapy. The therapist's job is to raise importance by educating the client about the risks of current behavior (only after asking permission) and then soliciting the client's take on that information. Offering "what if" scenarios can be helpful here.

- *Motivational interviewing can be used to treat nearly any condition*. Although MI has empirical support for a number of addictions and other health behaviors, it should not be considered a cure for every condition. Nonetheless, reflective listening and the MI "way of being" can be useful in many interpersonal interactions, including most therapies.

DOES MOTIVATIONAL INTERVIEWING WORK?

Numerous studies have shown support for the efficacy of MI for addictions; MI has compared favorably to no treatment, wait-list control, and as an additive to other treatments (Hettema et al., 2005). Specifically, support has been shown for the efficacy of MI in treating misuse of alcohol (e.g., Burke, Arkowitz, & Menchola, 2003; Vasilaki, Hosier, & Cox, 2006), tobacco (e.g., Soria, Legido, Escolano, Lopez Yeste, & Montoya, 2006), and use of street drugs (e.g., Hettema et al., 2005).

Although MI has received empirical support in numerous studies for its efficacy in treating addictions, the mechanisms by which it operates still are being explored. Global characteristics of the therapist, particularly empathy, are believed to play a role, as are elements of the client–therapist relationship. From a behavioral standpoint, the therapist's ability to encourage the client to speak about change, that is, to evoke change talk, holds promise as a driving force in MI. Further research likely will illuminate the mechanisms behind the MI approach.

Although MI has demonstrated efficacy for changing addictions, it is just one of many tools available to addictions-treatment providers and should not be viewed as a panacea.

TRAINING AND EVALUATING MOTIVATIONAL INTERVIEWING

Several randomized controlled studies have been conducted to investigate strategies for teaching MI. In general, these studies find that workshop training produces significant gains in MI skills among participants (Baer et al., 2007; Martino, Ball, Nich, Frankforter, & Carroll, 2008; Miller, Yahne, Moyers, Martinez, & Pirritano, 2004; Moyers et al., 2008) and that these skill gains are lost rapidly without additional training enrichments. Both personalized feedback after direct observation of MI sessions and telephone consultation have been used to successfully augment workshop training in these studies. In addition, Moyers et al. (2008) found that the baseline skill level of counselors was predictive of MI skill acquisition during training. Counselors with poor basic counseling skills, particularly in reflective listening, showed fewer gains than those with higher levels of these skills prior to MI training. In general, these studies indicate that acquiring clinical competence in delivering MI is unlikely to be achieved with one-shot workshop training. Observation, supervision, and feedback are likely to be needed in order to ensure that trainees are able to deliver the treatment in a manner shown to be effective from previous clinical studies.

CONCLUSIONS

Motivational interviewing can help change the conversation about addictive behaviors. In helping clients recognize their own reasons and capacities for change, it can be the catalyst that facilitates self-change, without further professional intervention. It can also enhance the benefit that clients receive from traditional treatment, when that is their choice. Although MI is not appropriate for every counselor, client, or scenario, it is an approach to addictions treatment with strong empirical support across a variety of target behaviors and settings—particularly among clients who are viewed as hostile. Ideally, the use of MI will help counselors avoid resistance, evoke change talk, and gently guide clients toward lasting behavioral change.

Case Study 1: Susana

Susana is a 19-year-old Mexican-American woman in her second semester of college. She was referred to the campus counseling center after her RA found bottles of beer and a small bag of marijuana in her dormitory room during an unannounced walk-through. Because it was her first write-up, the RA allowed her to see a counselor in lieu of disciplinary action.

Susana reports that she drank alcohol a few times in high school but disliked feeling sick afterward. She no longer drinks alcohol, but instead smokes marijuana with friends as a way to relax after a long school week.

Because of the circumstances surrounding the write-up, the relatively recent onset of Susana's substance use, and the prevalence of drug use in the college environment, resistance is likely if the therapist jumps ahead of Susana's readiness. The goal of treatment might be harm reduction, rather than complete abstinence, and the counselor's role will be to convey that any choice to change will have to be

Susana's. Showing empathy toward the client will also be important in developing trust and building rapport, and using reflections and open questions might also encourage change talk.

Counselor: It's nice to meet you, Susana. Tell me why you're here today.

Susana: My roommate and I had a few friends over for a party the other night. I guess we didn't clean up very well, because the next day while I was at class my RA found alcohol and pot in my room. I came back and found out that we got busted and my roommate had blamed me for all of it. The beer wasn't even mine! Now they're making me go to counseling or I'll be on probation and could even lose my scholarship.

Counselor: It must've been really hard for you to come here today, knowing that your friends got away and you're stuck here.

Susana: It's not fair at all. No offense, but I'd rather be doing something else with my afternoon.

Counselor: Well, I appreciate that you showed up anyway. I'd like to help you sort through your thoughts, but I'm not here to tell you what to do—you're an adult, and deciding whether you need to make any changes is up to you. Let's start by talking a little about your drinking and pot use.

Susana: Actually, I don't even drink—like I said, the beer was my roommate's. I got drunk a few times in high school but I didn't really like how I felt afterward so I stopped doing it.

Counselor: Drinking's never really been your thing.

Susana: No, not at all. I haven't even had a drink for, like, a year. All I do now is pot.

Counselor: Oh, okay—sorry for misunderstanding that. Tell me how pot fits into your life.

Susana: It actually fits in just fine now. I only smoke a couple of times a week, and usually just on the weekends after I'm done studying. The first time I tried pot was during my senior year—a friend of mine smoked me out at a party and I liked it way better than alcohol. I didn't smoke much while I was still living at home, but once I moved to the dorms it was easy to get and people here are cool with it.

Counselor: You don't have to worry about your parents now that you're in college.

Susana: No, if my family knew that I put my scholarship at risk they'd freak out.

Counselor: It would be devastating for you.

Susana: Yes, and that's why I'm here—because I don't want them to know.

Counselor: It's important to you to be a good student and a good daughter.

Susana: Yeah. I study hard to keep my grades up because I want to get into law school—that will make my family really proud. But that's a long time from now and I don't want to miss out on the college experience in the meantime.

Counselor: On one hand, you're not seeing anything wrong with smoking pot once in a while to relax and have a good time, and on the other hand, you're wondering how it might affect keeping your scholarship and finishing your education.

Susana: Hmmm . . . I hadn't really thought about it that way, but I guess so.

Counselor: Looking out in 3 more years, how do you envision your life if you continue to smoke pot as you do right now?

Case Study 2: Matt

Matt is a 45-year-old European-American man who works as a truck driver making local deliveries. He recently failed a urinalysis at his work, testing positive for methamphetamine. As a condition for keeping his job, his employer recommended that Matt seek help through the company's employee-assistance plan.

Matt believes that quitting methamphetamine entirely is extremely important: He needs to keep his job to support his family, using drugs is inconsistent with his view of himself as a father, and his partner is fed up with his use and its consequences. However, he has tried to quit before but has not succeeded, fueling his lack of confidence to make a change. The therapist's goal will be to support Matt's efforts to quit methamphetamine while helping to build his confidence.

Therapist: You mentioned that your job, your kids, and your partner are all good reasons to quit methamphetamine completely and that you really want to make this change.

Matt: I don't know what I'd do without them. There's too much at stake not to do this, but I'm afraid that I'm going to fail again—fail myself and fail them.

Therapist: You're still looking for a way out that will work for you.

Matt: Yes. I've made it a couple of days, but then something just won't let me kick this thing.

Therapist: Despite how difficult it's been, you've managed to have some successes. That takes a lot of strength.

Matt: I've tried so hard to stick it out.

Therapist: When you've been able to go a day or two without using, how have you done it—what's helped you to be successful?

Matt: Probably not working the late shift and staying away from my buddies who use.

Therapist: Organizing your life so it's inconsistent with using.

Matt: Exactly.

Therapist: Okay, so remembering back to the times that you quit for a day or two, what eventually got in the way?

Matt: If I decided to pick up some overtime when I'm already tired, if a friend shows up with some crystal after work on a Friday, or if the kids are visiting their aunt and uncle—then I go use, I show up a day later looking like hell, and everyone is so disappointed.

Therapist: It's embarrassing for you and you feel like you've let them all down.
Matt: Isn't that the truth.
Therapist: If it's okay with you, I'd like to share with you about some ways that other people have gotten around similar obstacles and have been able to quit for good. . . .

Case Study 3: Louise

Louise is a 63-year-old African-American woman who recently retired from her career as a teacher. Last week she had a physical exam with her primary-care physician, who gave her a clean bill of health but recommended that she quit smoking. Although Louise is unsure whether quitting smoking will make a difference for her at this point, she is concerned about the effects of second-hand smoke upon her grandchildren. She self-referred for treatment, and today she is meeting with the hospital's tobacco-cessation specialist.

Because Louise is just entering the "contemplation" stage of change she is still very ambivalent about quitting smoking. The nurse's goal will be to increase the importance of making a change, which he will try to do by educating Louise about the risks of smoking (after receiving permission), querying about importance, and asking about the benefits of quitting, while taking care to roll with resistance.

Nurse: What made you decide to come in today, Louise?
Louise: At my physical last week, the doctor told me that I looked to be in great shape, but that I should think about quitting smoking. Now, I've smoked for almost 40 years and I figure that it won't do me much good to quit at this point, but I started wondering about what my smoking might be doing to my grandkids when they come over.
Nurse: Even though you haven't noticed any effects of your smoking on yourself, you're concerned that it might be harming them.
Louise: Yes. They only stay with me a few days a year, but I don't know if that's long enough to cause any problems. Can you tell me anything more?
Nurse: I'll be glad to tell you everything that I know about the effects of second-hand smoke, but first I'd like to ask what you already know.
Louise: Well, I've heard that children are more susceptible to smoke than adults.
Nurse: Yes, that's true. Their lungs are still growing, so it can affect them more. Also, kids exposed to smoke at home tend to get sick more often and to have more trouble with asthma. It's hard to know exactly what their risk is after a few days a year, but probably it's a bit higher than if you didn't smoke.

Louise: I'd hate to think that by visiting me my grandkids would be more likely to get sick, even if it's a pretty small chance.

Nurse: That seems scary to you.

Louise: Yes, it is. Maybe I should think about only smoking outside when they're here.

Nurse: That's a really good strategy for cutting down their risk, and I can give you a pamphlet with a list of other ideas to take home if you're interested. Also, you mentioned earlier that you didn't think that quitting smoking would do anything positive for you now, and I wanted to see if you were aware of some possible benefits to you of quitting smoking. May I share some other information with you?

Louise: Of course.

Nurse: Thanks. Actually, it's looking like quitting at any age can help you live longer and avoid many smoking-related diseases, even if you've smoked for years.

Louise: Oh, you really think it would help? It seems like any damage that I've done is already there.

Nurse: Well, many people have found that their bodies heal surprisingly well after quitting, but cutting down or quitting smoking would be a decision that only you could make.

Louise: Yes, you're right about that.

Nurse: I'd like to ask you to give me a rating of how important it is to you right now to quit smoking. Let's use a scale from 0 to 10, with "0" being "not at all important" and a "10" being "extremely important".

Louise: Oh, I'd say about a "6".

Nurse: A "6"—so, you're kind of in the middle but it's more important than not. What made you choose a "6" and not a "0"?

Louise: Well, I want my grandkids to be healthy. Plus, it would be nice to stay healthy myself when I start getting older.

Nurse: You have some good reasons why you think it might be important to quit. So, looking forward a few years, what might be some of the benefits that you think you might get if you gave up smoking?

Louise: I think I'd be able to breathe more easily and maybe keep up with my grandkids better.

Nurse: Those are good thoughts, too, and yes, I think you're right. Now I'd like to ask you about your confidence about making a change if you decided that you wanted to. . . .

MOTIVATIONAL INTERVIEWING RESOURCES

Online resources

- Motivational Interviewing Web site: http://www.motivationalinterview.org/
- University of New Mexico Center on Alcoholism, Substance Abuse, and Addictions (UNM CASAA) Web site: http://casaa.unm.edu/

- Substance Abuse and Mental Health Services Administration (SAMHSA), TIP 35: Enhancing Motivation for Change in Substance Abuse Treatment: http://www.ncbi.nlm.nih.gov/books/bv.fcgi?rid=hstat5.chapter.61302

- Clinical Trials Network (CTN), Motivational Interviewing Assessment Supervisory Tools for Enhancing Proficiency (MIA-STEP): http://ctndisseminationlibrary.org/PDF/146.pdf

FURTHER READING

Miller, W. R. (2000). Motivational interviewing. IV. Some parallels with horse whispering. *Behavioural and Cognitive Psychotherapy*, *28*, 285–292.

Miller, W. R. (Ed.) (2004). Combined Behavioral Intervention Manual: A clinical research guide for therapists treating people with alcohol abuse and dependence. *COMBINE Monograph Series, Volume 1.* (DHHS Publication No. NIH 04–5288). Bethesda, MD: National Institute on Alcohol Abuse and Alcoholism.

Miller, W. R., & Moyers, T. B. (2007). Eight stages in learning motivational interviewing. *Journal of Teaching in the Addictions*, *5*, 3–17.

Miller, W. R., & Rollnick, S. (2002). *Motivational interviewing: Preparing people for change* (2nd ed.). New York: Guilford Press.

Miller, W. R., Zweben, A., DiClemente, C. C., & Rychtarik, R. G. (1994). Motivational enhancement therapy manual: A clinical research guide for therapists treating individuals with alcohol abuse and dependence. *Project MATCH Monograph Series, Volume 2* (DHHS Publication No. 94-3723). Rockville, MD: National Institute on Alcohol Abuse and Alcoholism.

Moyers, T. B., Martin, T., Manuel, J. K., Hendrickson, S. M., & Miller, W. R. (2005). Assessing competence in the use of motivational interviewing. *Journal of Substance Abuse Treatment*, *28*, 19–26.

Rollnick, S., Mason, P., & Butler, C. (1999). *Health behavior change: A guide for practitioners*. New York: Churchill Livingstone.

Rollnick, S., & Miller, W. R. (1995). What is motivational interviewing?. *Behavioural and Cognitive Psychotherapy*, *23*, 325–334.

REFERENCES

Amrhein, P. C., Miller, W. R., Yahne, C. E., Palmer, M., & Fulcher, L. (2003). Client commitment language during motivational interviewing predicts drug use outcomes. *Journal of Consulting and Clinical Psychology*, *71*, 862–878.

Baer, J. S., Ball, S. A., Campbell, B. K., Miele, G. M., Schoener, E. P., & Tracy, K. (2007). Training and fidelity monitoring of behavioral interventions in multisite addictions research. *Drug and Alcohol Dependence*, *87*, 107–118.

Burke, B. L., Arkowitz, H., & Menchola, M. (2003). The efficacy of motivational interviewing: A meta-analysis of controlled clinical trials. *Journal of Consulting and Clinical Psychology*, *71*, 843–861.

Carroll, K. M., Ball, S. A., Nich, C., Martino, S., Frankforter, T. L., Farentinos, C., et al. (2006). Motivational interviewing to improve treatment engagement and outcome in individuals seeking treatment for substance abuse: A multisite effectiveness study. *Drug Alcohol Dependence*, *81*(3), 301–312.

Hettema, J., Steele, J., & Miller, W. R. (2005). Motivational interviewing. *Annual Review of Clinical Psychology*, *1*, 91–111.

Martino, S., Ball, S. A., Nich, C., Frankforter, T. L., & Carroll, K. M. (2008). Community program therapist adherence and competence in motivational enhancement therapy. *Drug and Alcohol Dependence*, *96*, 37–48.

Miller, W. R., Benefield, R., & Tonigan, J. S. (1993). Enhancing motivation for change in problem drinking: A controlled comparison of two therapist styles. *Journal of Consulting and Clinical Psychology*, *61*, 455–461.

Miller, W. R., & Rollnick, S. (2002). *Motivational interviewing: Preparing people for change* (2nd ed.). New York: Guilford Press.

Miller, W. R., Yahne, C. E., Moyers, T. B., Martinez, J., & Pirritano, M. (2004). A randomized trial of methods to help clinicians learn motivational interviewing. *Journal of Consulting and Clinical Psychology*, *72*, 1050–1062.

Moyers, T. B., Manuel, J. K., Wilson, P. G., Hendrickson, S. M., Talcott, W., & Durand, P. (2008). A randomized trial investigating training in motivational interviewing for behavioral health providers. *Behavioural and Cognitive Psychotherapy*, *36*, 149–162.

Moyers, T. B., & Martin, T. (2006). Therapist influence on client language during motivational interviewing sessions. *Journal of Substance Abuse Treatment*, *30*, 245–251.

Moyers, T. B., Martin, T., Christopher, P. J., Houck, J. M., Tonigan, J. S., & Amrhein, P. C. (2007). Client language as a mediator of motivational interviewing efficacy: Where is the evidence? *Alcoholism: Clinical and Experimental Research*, *31*, 40S–47S.

Moyers, T. B., Miller, W. R., & Hendrickson, S. M. (2005). How does motivational interviewing work? Therapist interpersonal skill predicts client involvement within motivational interviewing sessions. *Journal of Consulting and Clinical Psychology*, *73*, 590–598.

Patterson, G. R., & Forgatch, M. S. (1985). Therapist behavior as a determinant for client noncompliance: A paradox for the behavior modifier. *Journal of Consulting and Clinical Psychology*, *53*, 846–851.

Prochaska, J. O., DiClemente, C. C., & Norcross, J. C. (1992). In search of how people change: Applications to addictive behaviors. *American Psychologist*, *47*, 1102–1114.

Soria, R., Legido, A., Escolano, C., Lopez Yeste, A., & Montoya, J. (2006). A randomised controlled trial of motivational interviewing for smoking cessation. *British Journal of General Practice*, *56*, 768–774.

Vasilaki, E. I., Hosier, S. G., & Cox, W. M. (2006). The efficacy of motivational interviewing as a brief intervention for excessive drinking: A meta-analytic review. *Alcohol and Alcoholism*, *41*, 328–335.

Chapter | ten

Brief Intervention

Eileen Kaner,
Institute of Health & Society, Newcastle University, The Medical School, Newcastle upon Tyne, UK

Dorothy Newbury-Birch, and
Institute of Health and Society, Newcastle University, Newcastle upon Tyne, UK

Nick Heather
Division of Psychology Northumbria University, Newcastle upon Tyne, UK

SUMMARY POINTS

- At a population level, most alcohol-related problems are attributable to hazardous and harmful drinkers rather than to people with alcohol dependence. Most hazardous and harmful drinkers are unaware of their alcohol-related risk or harm.
- Secondary preventive work involves identifying alcohol-related risk or harm at an early stage via screening and then intervention to help reduce alcohol consumption.
- In community settings, where most preventive work occurs, brief intervention is the most feasible approach. Brief intervention can take a range of forms, from simple structured advice to motivationally enhanced lifestyle counseling.
- There is a long-standing and strong evidence base supporting the effectiveness of brief intervention at reducing alcohol consumption in people who are not actively seeking treatment for alcohol problems.
- The evidence base supporting brief alcohol intervention is strongest in primary care where most research has taken place. However, there

Evidence-Based Addiction Treatment

is a growing body of research on brief interventions in other health and social care settings with some promising early findings.
- There are several short and accurate screening tools and clinical protocols to guide brief alcohol intervention in practice.
- Recent research in this field has focused on identifying effective and efficient strategies to encourage the uptake and use of brief interventions in practice so as to reduce alcohol-related problems across the population.

INTRODUCTION

This chapter provides a description and discussion of the theory and practice of brief alcohol intervention together with scientific evidence to support its inclusion as an "evidence-based" treatment. This chapter focuses on brief intervention in primary care settings, as this is where the bulk of the research evidence has been collected. However, there is also a short assessment of the evidence on brief intervention in other settings. Finally, there is a consideration of methods to encourage the uptake and implementation of brief interventions by health and social care professionals.

BACKGROUND

Epidemiological data have shown that the majority of alcohol-related problems that occur in a population are not due to the most problematic drinkers, generally individuals with alcohol dependence, but to a much larger group of hazardous and harmful drinkers. For instance, in the United Kingdom, hazardous and harmful drinkers outnumber dependent drinkers by a ratio of 7:1 (Drummond et al., 2004). The former collectively contribute to a very large number of chronic health problems due to frequent heavy drinking and acute health problems due to intoxication and social disorder; these can have adverse consequences for both the drinkers themselves and for other people affected by their drinking. Thus it has been suggested that the greatest impact in reducing alcohol-related problems at a population level can be made by reducing alcohol consumption in hazardous and harmful drinkers rather than by focusing on the most extreme or heaviest drinkers; this is sometimes known as the preventive paradox (Kreitman, 1986). Recent research has provided empirical support for the preventive paradox, although it appears to be most pronounced in populations where heavy episodic drinking or intoxication is a common part of the drinking pattern (Poikolainen, Paljarvi, & Makela, 2007; Rossow & Romelsjo, 2006). Thus there is a clear rationale for interventions that help reduce alcohol consumption in hazardous and harmful drinkers. Such work fits within a secondary preventive approach in terms of a public health agenda, which aims to detect health problems at an early stage, when they are likely to be most amenable to change, and then intervene to promote positive adjustments in lifestyle behavior (Winett, 1995).

Brief alcohol intervention is a specific example of secondary preventive work, which aims at reducing excessive drinking and alcohol-related problems in a large section of the population. This chapter focuses on brief alcohol intervention within the aforementioned public health context and its focus on preventive health and social care. Thus we are concerned primarily with individuals who are not formally seeking help for alcohol problems but who attend generalist (primary care) health and social care settings for reasons linked to their drinking behavior. However, it should be noted that, slightly confusingly, the term brief intervention has also sometimes been used to describe shorter forms of therapy within a specialist care context; this is best referred to as less intensive treatment (Raistrick, Heather, & Godfrey, 2006) and will be dealt with elsewhere.

ORIGINS AND THEORY BASE

The early development of brief interventions occurred in the alcohol field in the late 1970s and early 1980s as a result of several influences. Research by Edwards et al. (1977) into abstinence-oriented treatment and by Miller and colleagues (Miller & Taylor, 1980; Miller, Taylor, & West, 1980) into moderation-oriented treatment had suggested that less intensive treatment was often as effective as more intensive treatment. While these studies were confined to the specialist context, work by Shaw, Sprately, Cartwright, and Harwin (1978) in London encouraged the move toward a community-based response to alcohol problems involving general medical practitioners and other frontline professionals. At about the same time, the fierce controversy over "controlled drinking" as a solution to an alcohol problem (Heather & Robertson, 1983) raised the possibility that moderation was an appropriate goal for problem drinkers without signs of alcohol dependence or, at least, with low levels of dependence (Sobell & Sobell, 1995). While there is no reason in principle why brief interventions should not be aimed at total abstinence, in practice, almost all brief interventions are aimed at cutting down drinking to less risky levels.

A model for brief alcohol intervention in primary health care was derived from Russell, Wilson, Taylor, and Baker (1979) who worked in the smoking cessation field in the United Kingdom. This research had shown that patients given advice by a general practitioner (GP) to stop smoking, plus a leaflet to assist them to do so, had a quit rate of 5.1% 1 year later. While this may not seem a high rate of success, Russell and colleagues were able to show that if this simple intervention were applied consistently by GPs to all smokers they encountered, this would result in over half a million ex-smokers per year. This figure could not be matched by increasing the number of specialist withdrawal clinics in the country from 50 to 10,000. The question then arose whether the same public health logic could be applied to excessive alcohol consumption.

Another influential study from the alcohol field itself was that of Kristenson, Ohlin, Hulten-Nosslin, Trell, and Hood (1983) in Scandinavia. These researchers invited all male residents of Malmö, Sweden, between 45 and 50 years of age to a health screening interview and selected those who were in the top decile of the distribution of γ-glutamyl transferase (GGT) readings on two successive occasions. (GGT is a biochemical indicator of increased liver enzyme levels, which are often due to elevated alcohol consumption.) These individuals were then assigned randomly to (i) an intervention that included a detailed physical examination and interview regarding drinking history, alcohol-related problems and symptoms of dependence, an offer of an appointment with the same physician every 3 months, and monthly visits to a nurse who gave feedback on GGT results or (ii) controls who were informed by letter that they showed evidence of impaired liver function and were advised to cut down drinking. At follow-ups 2 and 4 years after initial screening, the control group showed a significantly greater number of sick days per individual, more days of hospitalization in the follow-up period, and a strikingly greater number of days in hospitals for alcohol-related conditions. At a later 10–16-year follow-up of this cohort, the intervention group continued to show reduced mortality. Although it is doubtful whether this intervention would qualify as "brief" in current terms (see later), research from the Malmö group provided a considerable impetus to research on brief interventions in the alcohol field.

Regarding its theory base, brief intervention is grounded in social cognitive theory from the psychological tradition of understanding, predicting, and changing human behavior. Social cognitive theory is drawn from the concept of social learning, which was influenced heavily by Albert Bandura (1986) who posited that behavior occurs as a result of a dynamic and reciprocal interaction among individual, behavioral, and environmental factors, the latter including both physical (structural) and social aspects. Thus each individual has personal, cognitive (thinking), and affective (feeling) attributes that affect how they respond to the external world. Individuals also differ in how they construe and are reinforced by a particular behavior, such as drinking alcohol. In addition, individuals also have the capacity to observe and learn from the behavior of other people around them. Thus behavior change interventions based on social cognitive theory focus on both personal and contextual factors. Important components include individual's beliefs and attitudes about a behavior, their self-efficacy or the sense of personal confidence about changing behavior, and a view about how an individual's behavior sits in relation to the way that other people behave (normative comparison). All these factors influence an individual's motivation for and ability to change their behavior. Consequently, brief intervention addresses, in a structured format, individual's knowledge, attitudes, and skills in relation to drinking so as to encourage behavior change for subsequent health benefits.

In terms of therapeutic application, brief interventions in pioneering research (Heather, Whitton, & Robertson, 1986) were based on principles of cognitive behavioral therapy (CBT). This tradition was continued in the Drink-Less pack (McAvoy, Kaner, Haighton, Heather, & Gilvarry, 1997), a brief intervention developed for the WHO Collaborative Project, *The Identification and Management of Alcohol-Related Problems in Primary Care* (Heather, 2007). This is based on a six-step plan consisting of (i) examining reasons for drinking, (ii) selecting and endorsing good reasons for cutting down, (iii) identifying personal high-risk situations for excessive drinking, (iv) choosing and practicing coping skills in preparation for the high-risk situations, (v) eliciting social support for a change in drinking, and (vi) planning for relapse prevention. These elements represent a condensed version of the treatment modality known as *behavioral self-control training* (Hester, 1995).

More recently in research and practice on brief interventions there has been a move away from condensed CBT and toward adaptations of motivational interviewing (MI) (Miller & Rollnick, 2002). Although it is not possible in the time available for brief interventions to carry out MI in generalist health and social care settings, the spirit, style, and some of the techniques of MI can be adapted for this purpose (Rollnick, Mason, & Butler, 1999). This adapted and condensed version of MI is often called Behavior Change Counseling.

THE EVIDENCE BASE

There is now a very strong evidence base supporting the effectiveness of brief alcohol intervention at reducing alcohol-related problems in non-treatment-seeking adults. Numerous systematic reviews and meta-analyses have reported beneficial outcomes of brief intervention, compared to control conditions, in terms of reductions in hazardous and harmful drinking (Agosti, 1995; Ballesteros, Duffy, Querejeta, Arino, &

Gonzalez-Pinto, 2004; Bertholet, Daeppen, Wietlisbach, Fleming, & Burnand, 2005; Bien, Miller, & Tonigan, 1993; Freemantle et al., 1993; Kaner et al., 2007; Moyer, Finney, Swearingen, & Vergun, 2002; Poikolainen, 1999; Whitlock, Polen, Green, Orleans, & Klein, 2004; Wilk, Jensen, & Havinghurst, 1997). Most of this research evidence has focused on primary care and reported consistent beneficial effects of brief alcohol intervention in terms of reduced alcohol consumption and alcohol-related problems.

Primary care settings

The most recent review of brief interventions in primary care settings was a Cochrane Collaboration review of 29 randomized controlled trials of brief alcohol intervention in primary care. This work covered both general practice-based primary care and accident and emergency departments. The review reported a significant reduction in weekly drinking at 1-year follow-up compared to a range of control conditions (such as assessment only, treatment as usual, and written information) (Kaner et al., 2007). The magnitude of this effect was an average reduction of four to five standard drinks per week. In addition, the review found no significant benefit of increased treatment exposure during brief interventions. Thus, although spending extra time and/or delivering extra sessions did produce some additional reduction in alcohol consumption, this addition was not statistically superior to shorter single-session input. Moreover, there was no significant benefit of extended psychological intervention compared to brief intervention on weekly drinking outcomes (Kaner et al., 2007). Thus, in primary care contexts, short focused input appears to be the most effective approach to alcohol risk reduction work.

Over recent years, there have been two key challenges to the extensive evidence base of brief interventions in terms of its relevance to routine primary care and its relevance to different types of drinkers. Both issues were addressed specifically in the Cochrane review (Kaner et al., 2007). First, the review formally assessed the extent to which trials were "ideal world" efficacy trials or pragmatic, effectiveness trials. It has been reported that much of the published evidence on brief alcohol intervention consisted of efficacy trials (Babor et al., 2006) conducted in tightly controlled research conditions designed to optimize internal validity (Flay, 1986). Efficacy studies are important in "proof-of-concept" contexts where new or early stage treatments are considered. However, if clinicians are to deliver interventions in routine practice, it is necessary to establish that they are effective in clinically relevant contexts. Box 10.1 summarizes the eight assessment criteria used in the

Box 10.1 Assessment criteria—Trial design features of relevance to routine primary care

1. Were participants genuine patients with a full range of presenting conditions?
2. Did practices deliver the full range of medical services to patients?
3. Did practitioners routinely work in the health service?
4. Could the intervention be delivered in standard consultation times?
5. Was there therapeutic flexibility in the delivery of the intervention?
6. Could training occur in regular continuing professional development schemes?
7. Did intervention monitoring intrude on the consultation?
8. Were support procedures (e.g., case flagging) typically available in practice?

Cochrane review, which concluded that most of the trials had design features that were clearly relevant to routine primary care and thus that the evidence was pertinent to routine practice.

Second, the Cochrane review considered both the countries that brief intervention trials were based in and the characteristics of patients in these trials (Kaner et al., 2007). It was clear that the majority of this work had been conducted in the United States and other English-speaking countries, although there was a growing body of work emerging in the Mediterranean countries of Europe and in Scandinavia. However, there was no published research from developing or transitional countries. In addition, the majority of participants in the brief alcohol intervention trials were middle-aged males and there was insufficient work in women, young people, and individuals from black and minority ethnic backgrounds. Thus there is a need for more research in the developing world and in different types of drinkers.

Settings other than primary care

Although more work is needed in brief interventions in non-primary care settings, growing evidence shows that they have promise in a variety of health and social care contexts.

In general hospital wards, both patients and staff have more time available for alcohol screening and brief intervention than in primary care. Evidence shows that hospital wards contain high numbers of both hazardous and harmful drinkers, especially among males, as well as alcohol-dependent patients. Prevalence estimates for alcohol misuse have ranged up to 40% in male patients (Royal College of Physicians, 1987). Although individual studies in general hospital settings have reported that alcohol-related harm can be reduced after a brief intervention (Chick, Lloyd, & Crombie, 1985; Heather, 1996; Longabaugh et al., 2001; Monti et al., 1999; Richmond, Kehoe, Heather, Wodak, & Webster, 1996), a meta-analysis of eight studies (Emmen, Schippers, Bleijenberg, & Wollersheim, 2004) found that the evidence was equivocal due to methodological weaknesses in the research. Indeed only one study showed a significantly large reduction in alcohol consumption in the intervention group (Maheswaran, Beevers, & Beevers, 1992). Hence this review concluded that the evidence on brief interventions in general hospital settings was inconclusive. However, a recent three-armed cluster randomized controlled trial (face-to-face self-efficacy enhancement; a self-help booklet or usual care) among general hospital patients found a significant reduction in alcohol consumption because of brief intervention compared to the usual care controls (Holloway et al., 2007). Nevertheless, there was no evidence that self-efficacy enhancement had better results than the self-help booklet (Holloway et al., 2007).

Studies in the United States (Baer, Kivlahan, Blume, McKnight, & Marlatt, 2001; Baer et al., 1992; Borsari & Carey, 2000; Marlatt et al., 1998) have shown positive effects of brief interventions in university and college students. In a United Kingdom trial of students in 10 further education colleges, the effects of a single 1-hour, individual session of motivational interviewing on students' (aged 16–20 years) drug use, including alcohol, cigarettes, and cannabis, were evaluated (McCambridge & Strang, 2005). The control group received their usual education. Results showed a significant reduction in alcohol use in the intervention group at 3 months but this improvement was not found at the 12-month follow-up (McCambridge & Strang, 2005).

It should be possible to implement brief interventions within the criminal justice system—in prisons, probation settings, and even police stations. A recent trial has been carried out in magistrates' court in Cardiff with people who had been sentenced for a violent offense committed while intoxicated with alcohol (Watt, Shepherd, & Newcombe, 2008). Here outcome measures included reoffending, injury rates, and subjects' alcohol-related risk and harm status. Male participants were followed up at 3 and 12 months postsentence. Although there was a reduction in alcohol use, the authors found no significant reduction in any of the alcohol consumption measures at the 3 month follow-up (Watt et al., 2008). However, there was a significantly lower rate of injury in offenders who received the intervention compared to those who had not (Watt et al., 2008).

The United Kingdom government is presently funding two research projects that will evaluate brief interventions in criminal justice settings. First, a pilot of "arrest referral" alcohol screening and brief interventions in the custody suite of police stations is being carried out in Ealing, Manchester, Liverpool, and Cheshire (http://press.homeoffice.gov.uk/press-releases/action-alcohol-behaviour). Second, the SIPS (Screening and Intervention Programme for Sensible Drinking) research trial is underway across the northeast, London, and southeast of England, which will consider the effectiveness and cost-effectiveness of different models of screening and brief intervention in probation settings (www.sips.iop.kcl.ac.uk).

Other settings where research studies have shown some positive effects of brief intervention include somatic outpatient clinics (Persson & Magnusson, 1989), general population health screening work (Kristenson et al., 1983; Nilssen, 1991), and workplace or occupational settings (Higgins-Biddle & Babor, 1996; Richmond, Heather, Holt, & Hu, 1990). However, more research is needed before we could conclude that brief intervention in these settings was robustly evidence based. A final context where there appears to be no published evidence is that of social work. Again, there is a need for more evaluative work in this context.

DELIVERING SCREENING AND BRIEF INTERVENTION IN PRIMARY CARE SETTINGS

In terms of strength of evidence and relevance to practice, the most obvious setting for the early identification of alcohol-related risk and brief intervention to reduce excessive drinking is primary health care. This setting represents most peoples' first point of contact with health services in the majority of countries worldwide (Fry, 1980). Primary care generally refers to general-practice based health care with a relatively large distribution of health centers or doctors surgeries across a wide geographical area. However, primary care can be defined as all immediately accessible, general health care facilities that treat a broad range of possible presenting problems and that can be accessed by a wide range of patients on demand and not as the result of a referral for specialist care. Thus, emergency care (Accident and Emergency Departments) can also be considered to be part of primary care.

Although primary care clinicians have contact with the majority of the population, this high-volume clinical work typically occurs via relatively short treatment episodes. As a result of the time-limited nature of primary care consultations, alcohol intervention in this context needs to be short, simple, and easy to deliver by generalist health professionals. A further challenge is that most individuals who are drinking at hazardous and harmful levels in primary care will be unaware of their increased risk or early-stage harm. Thus, there is a requirement for simple screening approaches to identify excessive drinking in patients so that clinicians know to whom they should be giving brief interventions.

Screening in primary care

Screening is a systematic process of identifying patients whose alcohol consumption places them at increased risk of physical, psychological, or social complications and who might benefit from brief intervention. There are a number of laboratory indicators of excessive alcohol consumption, such as mean corpuscular volume, GGT, and carbohydrate-deficient transferrin. However, in medical practice, standardized questionnaires have been found to have a greater sensitivity and specificity than laboratory indicators; they are also far less intrusive and more acceptable to patients. In addition, questionnaire-based screening is less costly than laboratory analysis. Thus, use of a short validated questionnaire is the recommended screening method for primary care (Wallace, 2001).

The *Alcohol Use Disorders Identification Test* (AUDIT) was the first screening tool designed specifically to detect hazardous and harmful drinking in primary care and across a range of different countries and drinking cultures (Saunders, Aasland, Babor, De La Fuente, & Grant, 1993). The AUDIT is a 10-item questionnaire that includes items on drinking frequency and intensity (binge drinking), together with experience of alcohol-related problems and dependence (see Figure 10.1). At a score of 8 or more out of a possible 40, AUDIT detects 92% of genuine excessive drinkers (sensitivity) and excludes 93% of false cases (specificity). Thus the AUDIT is a highly accurate tool that has been validated in a large number of countries with consistently strong psychometric performance. It is now regarded as the "gold standard" screening tool to detect hazardous and harmful drinking in primary care patients. When the AUDIT has been applied in routine primary care, approximately one in five patients screen positive for hazardous or harmful alcohol consumption (Kaner, Heather, Brodie, Lock, & McAvoy, 2001).

Nevertheless, even with just 10 items, the full AUDIT has been considered too lengthy for use in routine practice because of the limited amount of time available to clinicians. Moreover, since four out of every five patients tend to screen negative for hazardous and harmful drinking, clinicians need an efficient detection method of identifying relevant patients needing alcohol intervention. For this reason, several shorter versions of the AUDIT have been developed, including the following.

- AUDIT-C—the first three (consumption) items of the full AUDIT. A score of 5+ indicates hazardous or harmful drinking (Bush, Kivlahan, McDonell, Fihn, & Bradley, 1998).

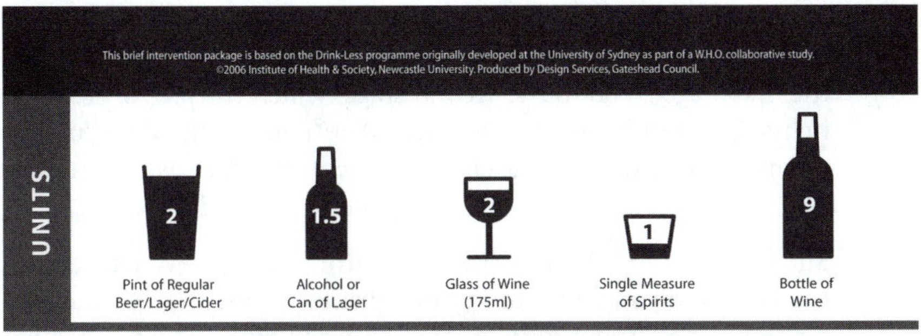
This brief intervention package is based on the Drink-Less programme originally developed at the University of Sydney as part of a W.H.O. collaborative study.
©2006 Institute of Health & Society, Newcastle University. Produced by Design Services, Gateshead Council.
UNITS
2
Pint of Regular Beer/Lager/Cider
1.5
Alcohol or Can of Lager
2
Glass of Wine (175ml)
1
Single Measure of Spirits
9
Bottle of Wine

Alcohol Users Disorders Identification Test (AUDIT)

Questions	Scoring System 0	1	2	3	4	Your Score
How often do you have a drink that contains alcohol?	Never	Monthly or less	2 - 4 times per month	2 - 3 times per week	4+ times per week	
How many standard alcoholic drinks do you have on a typical day when you are drinking?	1 – 2	3 – 4	5 – 6	7 – 8	10+	
How often do you have 6 or more standard drinks on one occasion?	Never	Less than monthly	Monthly	Weekly	Daily or almost daily	
How often in the last year have you found you were not able to stop drinking once you had started?	Never	Less than monthly	Monthly	Weekly	Daily or almost daily	
How often in the last year have you failed to do what was expected of you because of drinking?	Never	Less than monthly	Monthly	Weekly	Daily or almost daily	
How often in the last year have you needed an alcoholic drink in the morning to get you going?	Never	Less than monthly	Monthly	Weekly	Daily or almost daily	
How often in the last year have you had a feeling of guilt or regret after drinking?	Never	Less than monthly	Monthly	Weekly	Daily or almost daily	
How often in the last year have you not been able to remember what happened when drinking the night before?	Never	Less than monthly	Monthly	Weekly	Daily or almost daily	
Have you or someone else been injured as a result of your drinking?	No		Yes, but not in the last year		Yes, during the last year	
Has a relative/friend/doctor/health worker been concerned about your drinking or advised you to cut down?	No		Yes, but not in the last year		Yes, during the last year	

Scoring: 0-7 = sensible drinking, 8-15 = hazardous drinking, 16-19 = harmful drinking and 20+ = possible dependence

How much is too much? Screening Tools

FIGURE 10.1 *The AUDIT questionnaire.*

- AUDIT-PC—the first two (consumption) questions of the full AUDIT plus items 4, 5, and 10, which focus on alcohol-related problems and possible dependence. A score of 5+indicates hazardous or harmful drinking (Piccinelli et al., 1997).
- Fast Alcohol Screening Test (FAST)—a two-stage screening procedure based on four of the original AUDIT items. Item 3

is asked first and classifies over half of the respondents as either non-hazardous or hazardous drinkers. Only those not classified at the first stage go on to the second stage, which consists of AUDIT items 5, 8, and 10 (see Figure 10.1). A response other than "never" to any of these three items classifies the respondent as a hazardous drinker (Hodgson, Alwyn, John, Thom, & Smith, 2002).

- Single Alcohol Screening Questionnaire (SASQ)—"When was the last time you had more than *x* drinks in one day" (where *x* = 5 for men and 4 for women—United States values). Possible responses are never; over 12 months; 3–12 months; and within 3 months. The last response suggests hazardous or harmful drinking (Canagasaby & Vinson, 2005).

These short instruments take less time to administer than the full AUDIT but they are generally less accurate than the longer tool. In addition, they do not clearly differentiate among hazardous, harmful, and dependent drinking. Nevertheless, a recent review of AUDIT and its shorter variants reported that the shorter tools have relatively good psychometric properties and that AUDIT-C in particular was nearly as accurate as the full AUDIT (Reinert & Allen, 2007). Thus, a pragmatic approach for primary care clinicians may be to use AUDIT-C as a prescreening tool to filter out negative cases quickly and then administer the remaining seven AUDIT questions to the smaller pool of positive cases to provide an accurate and differential assessment of alcohol-related risk or harm.

There is current debate about the relative merits of two different approaches to screening: *universal screening*, aimed at all patients attending a medical facility, or *targeted screening*, aimed at predefined groups of patients with an increased likelihood of being hazardous and harmful drinkers. Research has shown that targeted screening is preferred by both practitioners and patients (Hutchings et al., 2006). Possible contexts that have been suggested are in new patient registration in general practice-based primary care, where patients expect to be asked about lifestyle issues, or in patients with a pre-existing condition that alcohol might have contributed to (e.g., hypertension). Targeted screening in new patient registrations minimizes the chances of embarrassment due to the sensitivity that surrounds alcohol-related problems, whereas a focus on specific conditions presents an efficient option for clinicians as it maximizes the chances that patient will be a hazardous or harmful drinker. However, evidence shows that clinicians may use stereotypical notions of heavy drinkers to determine if they will ask about or intervene for alcohol problems (Kaner et al., 2001; Lock & Kaner, 2004). Thus, universal screening, if practicable, would reduce the likelihood of systematic biases in the detection of hazardous and harmful drinking in primary care. The relative effectiveness, cost-effectiveness, and acceptability of universal versus targeted screening in routine practice are the focus of ongoing research in the United Kingdom (SIPS).

Brief intervention in primary care

In practical terms, brief intervention refers to a spectrum of clinical activity focused on the use of a talk-based therapeutic approach to reducing excessive drinking and its associated problems. Across a wide range of published studies (Kaner et al., 2007), brief interventions have included elements of simple structured advice, written information, and motivational counseling, and these components can either occur alone or in combination with each other (Babor & Higgins-Biddle, 2000). They have also been delivered either in a single session or in a series of linked appointments. Most last between 5 and 60 minutes and consist of no more than one to five sessions (Kaner et al., 2007). Given this variability, it is important to be clear about the key delivery principles, that it needs to be short and deliverable by health professionals without specialist training and who are working in busy health care settings. It is also important to be clear that brief intervention is not merely traditional (psychiatric or psychological) treatment done in a shortened time frame (Babor, 1994; Miller & Rollnick, 1991); it has an essential structure, which is summarized by the acronym FRAMES (Miller & Sanchez, 1993).

- Feedback—provides feedback on the client's risk for alcohol problems
- Responsibility—the individual is responsible for change
- Advice—advises reduction or gives explicit direction to change
- Menu—provides a variety of options for change
- Empathy—emphasizes a warm, reflective, and understanding approach
- Self-efficacy—encourages optimism about changing behavior

In order to facilitate the use of these principles in practice, two brief intervention protocols have been developed for the "How Much is Too Much" program to provide clinicians with clear guidance on how to deliver simple brief intervention (Figure 10.2) and behavior change counseling (Figure 10.3). Because the recent Cochrane review of brief interventions found that longer sessions and extended intervention did not provide significant additional benefit over more focused brief intervention, we recommended that clinicians follow up screening with simple structured advice on alcohol risk reduction. If patients are interested in receiving further input, this can then take the form of longer behavior change counseling.

Are you at risk from drinking alcohol?

Risk	AUDIT Score	Men	Women	Common Effects
SENSIBLE	0 – 7	21 units or fewer per week or up to 4 units per day	14 units or fewer per week or up to 3 units per day	• **Increased relaxation** • **Reduced risk of heart disease** • **Sociability**
HAZARDOUS (risky drinking)	8 – 15	22 – 49 units per week or regular drinking of more than 4 units per day	15 – 35 units per week or regular drinking of more than 3 units per day	• **Less energy** • **Depression/Stress** • **Insomnia** • **Impotence** • **Risk of injury** • **High blood pressure** • **Relationship problems** • **Increased risk interring with medication**
HARMFUL (very risky drinking)	16 – 19	50 + units per week	36 + units per week	• **All of the above and...** • **Memory loss** • **Increased risk of liver disease** • **Increased risk of cancer** • **Possible alcohol dependence**

- Binge drinking is considered to be drinking twice the daily limit in one sitting (8+ units for men, 6+ units for women).
- There are times when you will be at risk even after two or three drinks. For example, when exercising, operating heavy machinery, driving or if you are on certain medication.
- If you are pregnant it is recommended that you completely abstain from drinking alcohol.
- As well as keeping to weekly and daily limits it is recommended that 2 days of the week should be alcohol-free.

Your screening outcome is ______ How do you feel?

FIGURE 10.2 *Simple structured advice.*

IMPLEMENTATION ISSUES

Given the strong evidence-base on brief alcohol interventions in primary care, we will focus on implementation in this setting. It is hoped that lessons learned from primary care may be extended to other contexts as and when more evidence on effectiveness becomes available.

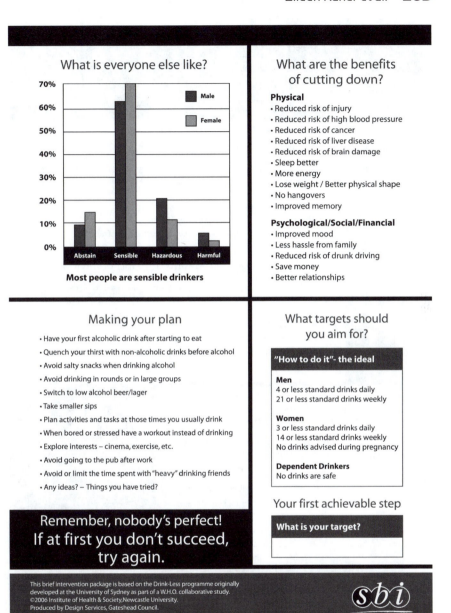

What is everyone else like?

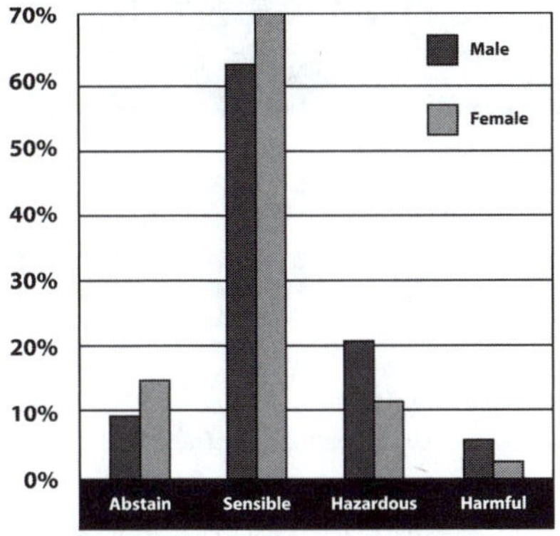

Most people are sensible drinkers

What are the benefits of cutting down?

Physical

- Reduced risk of injury
- Reduced risk of high blood pressure
- Reduced risk of cancer
- Reduced risk of liver disease
- Reduced risk of brain damage
- Sleep better
- More energy
- Lose weight / Better physical shape
- No hangovers
- Improved memory

Psychological/Social/Financial

- Improved mood
- Less hassle from family
- Reduced risk of drunk driving
- Save money
- Better relationships

Making your plan

- Have your first alcoholic drink after starting to eat
- Quench your thirst with non-alcoholic drinks before alcohol
- Avoid salty snacks when drinking alcohol
- Avoid drinking in rounds or in large groups
- Switch to low alcohol beer/lager
- Take smaller sips
- Plan activities and tasks at those times you usually drink
- When bored or stressed have a workout instead of drinking
- Explore interests – cinema, exercise, etc.
- Avoid going to the pub after work
- Avoid or limit the time spent with "heavy" drinking friends
- Any ideas? – Things you have tried?

Remember, nobody's perfect! If at first you don't succeed, try again.

What targets should you aim for?

"How to do it"- the ideal

Men
4 or less standard drinks daily
21 or less standard drinks weekly

Women
3 or less standard drinks daily
14 or less standard drinks weekly
No drinks advised during pregnancy

Dependent Drinkers
No drinks are safe

Your first achievable step

What is your target?

This brief intervention package is based on the Drink-Less programme originally developed at the University of Sydney as part of a W.H.O. collaborative study.
©2006 Institute of Health & Society, Newcastle University.
Produced by Design Services, Gateshead Council.

FIGURE 10.2 *Continued.*

There are many opportunities for identifying excessive drinking in primary care as patients are routinely asked about alcohol consumption during new patient registrations, general health checks, specific disease clinics (e.g., hypertension, diabetes), and other health screening procedures. However, despite considerable efforts over the years to persuade clinicians to use brief interventions in practice, most health professionals have yet

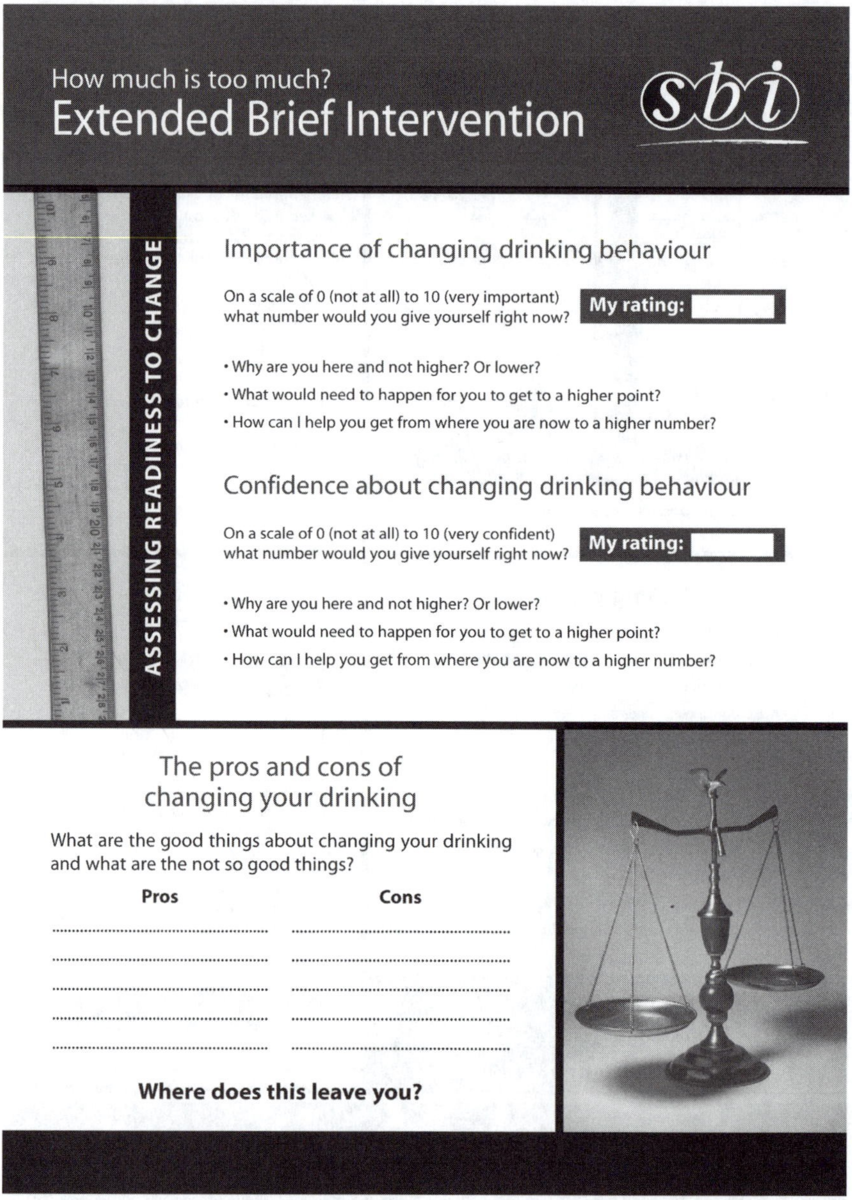
How much is too much?

Extended Brief Intervention

sbi

ASSESSING READINESS TO CHANGE

Importance of changing drinking behaviour

On a scale of 0 (not at all) to 10 (very important) what number would you give yourself right now? **My rating:**

- Why are you here and not higher? Or lower?
- What would need to happen for you to get to a higher point?
- How can I help you get from where you are now to a higher number?

Confidence about changing drinking behaviour

On a scale of 0 (not at all) to 10 (very confident) what number would you give yourself right now? **My rating:**

- Why are you here and not higher? Or lower?
- What would need to happen for you to get to a higher point?
- How can I help you get from where you are now to a higher number?

The pros and cons of changing your drinking

What are the good things about changing your drinking and what are the not so good things?

Pros	**Cons**
....	....
....	....
....	....
....	....
....	....

Where does this leave you?

FIGURE 10.3 *Behavior change counseling.*

to do so. There is large international literature on obstacles and incentives that affect the implementation of screening and brief alcohol intervention (Aalto, Pekuri, & Seppa, 2003; Babor & Higgins-Biddle, 2000; Heather, 1996; Roche & Freeman, 2004; Roche, Hotham, & Richmond, 2002).

In 1999, a United Kingdom survey found that most GPs did not make routine inquiries about alcohol, with 67% inquiring only "some

A six-step plan for changing your drinking habits

Identify good reasons for changing: Can you think of 2–3 good reasons?

Reason 1 ....

Reason 2 ....

Reason 3 ....

Set yourself a goal to achieve change: Is this achievable?

What? ....

Where? ....

When? ....

Recognise difficult times or situations: When might be the hardest times?

Time 1 ....

Time 2 ....

Time 3 ....

Prepare for difficult times/situations: Think of a ways of dealing with hard times?

Time 1 ....

Time 2 ....

Time 3 ....

Find someone to support you: Is there a family member/friend who might help?

Who? ....

Remember, nobody's perfect!

If at first you don't succeed, try again.

This brief intervention package is based on the Drink-Less programme originally developed at the University of Sydney as part of a W.H.O. collaborative study.

Produced by Design Services, Gateshead Council.

sbi

FIGURE 10.3 *Continued.*

of the time" (Kaner, Heather, McAvoy, Lock, & Gilvarry, 1999a). In addition, two-thirds of GPs had managed only one to six patients for excessive drinking in the previous year. Given figures on GPs' average list size in the United Kingdom, this suggested that the majority of GPs were missing as many as 98% of the hazardous and harmful drinkers presenting to their practices. In addition, around this time a household survey in England (Malbon, Bridgewood, Lader, & Matheson, 1996) found that, of current and former drinkers who had spoken to a health professional in the last year, only 7% (12% men and 5% women) reported having discussed alcohol consumption with their GP at the doctor's office. A similar lack of attention to excessive drinkers applies to other health professionals, including general hospital doctors (Barrison et al., 1982; Lloyd, Chick, Crombie, & Anderson, 1986), psychiatrists (Farrell & David, 1988), emergency care doctors (Huntley, Blain, Hood, & Touquet, 2001), and primary care nurses (Lock, Kaner, Lamont, & Bond, 2002) and to other settings in which brief intervention might be delivered, such as occupational and specialized health care settings (Kaariainen, Sillanaukee, Poutanen, & Seppa, 2001).

The following barriers to screening and brief intervention work have been reported by U.K. GPs (Kaner et al., 1999a) and reiterated more recently by GPs in Scandinavian countries (Aira, Kauhanen, Larivaara, & Rautio, 2003).

- Lack of time among busy health care professionals
- Lack of appropriate training to carry out screening and brief interventions
- Little support from government health policies
- A belief that patients will not take advice to change drinking behavior
- Lack of suitable screening and intervention materials
- Lack of reimbursement from government health schemes
- Health professionals may fear offending patients by raising the topic of drinking and find it difficult to do so
- Negative attitudes to patients with drinking problems derived from their experience of those with more severe problems

Some of these obstacles are simple to address. Screening and brief intervention materials are available and should be disseminated; appropriate training could be provided; and evidence that brief interventions are effective could be transmitted to clinicians. Some of the negative attitudes to this work could be changed by emphasizing the difference between the targets for brief intervention and the management of severely dependent individuals with serious problems, and by facilitating arrangements for referring the latter to specialist treatment. Fear of offending patients could be partly assuaged by evidence that most patients expect GPs and nurses to enquire about their drinking in appropriate circumstances and see this as a legitimate part of medical practice (Hutchings et al., 2006; Richmond et al., 1996; Rush, Urbanoski, & Allen, 2003; Wallace & Haines, 1984). Probably the most difficult obstacles are those to do with lack of time and of reimbursement for this work. Thus there is a need for such work to be prioritized and reimbursed in general medical services contracts by those in charge of health systems.

Nevertheless, specific promotional interventions can be used to disseminate and facilitate the implementation of screening and brief alcohol intervention. Telemarketing has been found to be a cost-effective means of disseminating brief intervention programs in primary health care (Lock, Kaner, Heather, McAvoy, & Gilvarry, 1999). In addition, trained and supported GPs have implemented screening and brief intervention on a wide-scale both nationally (Kaner, Lock, McAvoy, Heather, & Gilvarry, 1999b) and internationally (Funk et al., 2005), although this work was time limited. Indeed, Anderson and colleagues (2003, 2004a) have reported that when GPs and nurses are adequately trained and supported, screening and brief intervention activity increases. Moreover, clinicians who express higher role security and greater therapeutic commitment to working with alcohol issues are more likely to manage patients with alcohol-related problems than clinicians who do not hold these views (Anderson et al., 2003, 2004a). However, training and support did not improve attitudes toward working with drinkers and could worsen the attitudes of those who were already insecure and uncommitted (Anderson et al., 2004a). This suggests that training and support for screening and brief intervention work should be geared to the needs and attitudes of health professionals to avoid being counterproductive.

Anderson, Laurant, Kaner, Wensing, and Grol (2004) carried out a meta-analysis of studies testing the effectiveness of different strategies for increasing GPs' screening and advice-giving rates for hazardous and harmful alcohol consumption. The most effective programs were found to be those with a specific focus on alcohol (rather than general prevention programs) and those that were multicomponent in nature (Anderson et al., 2004b).

Recent work in the United States has investigated implementation in managed care contexts and found that it is influenced by a complex array of provider and organization factors (Babor, Higgins-Biddle, Dauser, Higgins, & Burleson, 2005). The ability of primary care clinics to conduct screening and brief intervention was influenced by prior experience of providers, stability of the managed care organization, and the number of clinicians trained. In addition, lack of time, staff turnover, and competing priorities could impede screening and brief intervention work. However, later evaluation has shown that licensed practitioners and/or nurses can implement screening and brief intervention on a wide scale in busy primary care practices and produce modest but statistically significant reductions in patients drinking (Babor et al., 2006). Thus the focus of future research in this field should be on evaluating different promotional approaches, including policy-level interventions, which will encourage wider scale adoption of screening and brief intervention approaches by primary care practitioners in their day-to-day practice.

CONCLUSION

Alcohol-related problems are widespread in the population and most result from hazardous or harmful drinking rather than alcohol dependence. As many hazardous and harmful drinkers are not consciously aware that their health or social well-being is affected by their drinking, there is a tremendous scope for preventive work in this area. There is a very strong evidence base supporting screening and brief alcohol intervention in primary care setting as a means of reducing hazardous and harmful drinking and its associated problems. Indeed a growing body of research is focused on brief interventions in a range of other health and social care settings, with early promising findings. Thus the imperative for researchers, clinicians, and social care professionals is to identify efficient ways of incorporating brief interventions into practice so as to help reduce excessive drinking across the population.

REFERENCES

Aalto, M., Pekuri, P., & Seppa, K. (2003). Obstacles to carrying out brief intervention for heavy drinkers in primary health care: a focus group study. *Drug and Alcohol Review*, *22*, 169–173.

Agosti, V. (1995). The efficacy of treatments in reducing alcohol consumption: A meta-analysis. *International Journal of the Addictions*, *30*(8), 1067–1077.

Aira, M., Kauhanen, J., Larivaara, P., & Rautio, P. (2003). Factors influencing inquiry about patients' alcohol consumption by primary health care physicians: Qualitative semi-structured interview study. *Family Practice*, *20*(3), 270–275.

Anderson, P., Kaner, E., Wutzke, S., Funk, M., Heather, N., Wensing, M., et al. (2004a). Attitudes and managing alcohol problems in general practice: An interaction analysis based on findings from a WHO collaborative study. *Alcohol & Alcoholism*, *39*, 351–359.

Anderson, P., Kaner, E., Wutzke, S., Wensing, M., Grol, R., Heather, N., et al. (2003). Attitudes and management of alcohol problems in general practice: Descriptive analysis based on findings of a World Health Organisation international collaborative survey. *Alcohol & Alcoholism*, *38*(6), 597–601.

Anderson, P., Laurant, M., Kaner, E., Wensing, M., & Grol, R. (2004b). Engaging general practitioners in the management of alcohol problems: Results of a meta-analysis. *Journal of Studies on Alcohol*, *65*(2), 191–199.

Babor, T. E., Higgins-Biddle, J., Dauser, D., Higgins, P., & Burleson, J. A. (2005). Alcohol screening and brief intervention in primary care settings: Implementation models and predictors. *Journal of Studies on Alcohol*, *66*(3), 361–368.

Babor, T. F. (1994). Avoiding the horrid and beastly sin of drunkenness: Does dissuasion make a difference? *Journal of Consulting and Clinical Psychology, 62*(6), 1127–1140.

Babor, T. F., & Higgins-Biddle, J. (2000). Alcohol screening and brief intervention: Dissemination strategies for medical practice and public health. *Addiction, 95*(5), 677–686.

Babor, T. F., Higgins-Biddle, J. C., Dauser, D., Burleson, J. A., Zarkin, G. A., & Bray, J. (2006). Brief interventions for at-risk drinking: Patient outcomes and cost-effectiveness in managed care organizations. *Alcohol & Alcoholism, 41*(6), 624–631.

Baer, J., Kivlahan, D. R., Blume, A., McKnight, P., & Marlatt, G. (2001). Brief Intervention for heavy-drinking college students: 4-year follow-up and natural history. *American Journal of Public Health, 91*(8), 1310–1315.

Baer, J. S., Marlatt, G. A., Kivlahan, D. R., Fromme, K., Larimer, M. E., & Williams, E. (1992). An experimental test of three methods of alcohol risk reduction with young adults. *Journal of Consulting and Clinical Psychology, 60*(6), 974–979.

Ballesteros, J. A., Duffy, J. C., Querejeta, I., Arino, J., & Gonzalez-Pinto, A. (2004). Efficacy of brief interventions for hazardous drinkers in primary care: Systematic review and meta-analysis. *Alcoholism, Clinical & Experimental Research, 28*(4), 608–618.

Bandura, A. (1986). *Social foundations of thought and action: A social cognitive theory*. Englewood Cliffs, NJ: Prentice Hall.

Barrison, I. G., Viola, L., Mumford, J., Murray, R. M., Gordon, M., & Murray-Lyon, I. M. (1982). Detecting excessive drinking among admissions to a general hospital. *Health Trends, 14*, 80–83.

Bertholet, N., Daeppen, J.-B., Wietlisbach, V., Fleming, M., & Burnand, B. (2005). Brief alcohol intervention in primary care: Systematic review and meta-analysis. *Archives of Internal Medicine, 165*, 986–995.

Bien, T. H., Miller, W. R., & Tonigan, J. S. (1993). Brief interventions for alcohol problems: A review. *Addiction, 88*(3), 315–335.

Borsari, B., & Carey, K. B. (2000). Effects of a brief motivational intervention with college student drinkers. *Journal of Consulting and Clinical Psychology, 68*(4), 728–733.

Bush, K., Kivlahan, D. R., McDonell, M. B., Fihn, S. D., & Bradley, K. A. (1998). The AUDIT alcohol consumption questions (AUDIT-C): An effective brief screening test for problem drinking. *Archive of Internal Medicine, 158*, 1789–1795.

Canagasaby, A., & Vinson, D. C. (2005). Screening for hazardous or harmful drinking using one or two quantity-frequency questions. *Alcohol & Alcoholism, 40*(3), 208–213.

Chick, J., Lloyd, G., & Crombie, E. (1985). Counselling problem drinkers in medical wards: A controlled study. *BMJ, 290*, 965–967.

Drummond, C., Oyefeso, A., Phillips, T., Cheeta, S., Deluca, P., Perryman, K., et al. (2004). *Alcohol needs assessment research project (ANARP): The 2004 national needs assessment for England*. Department of Health, London.

Edwards, G., Orford, J., Egert, S., Guthrie, S., Hawker, A., Hensman, C., et al. (1977). Alcoholism: A controlled trial of treatment and advice. *Journal of Studies on Alcohol, 38*(5), 1004–1031.

Emmen, M. J., Schippers, G. M., Bleijenberg, G., & Wollersheim, H. (2004). Effectiveness of opportunistic brief interventions for problem drinking in a general hospital setting: Systematic review. *BMJ, 328*, 318–320.

Farrell, M., & David, A. (1988). Do psychiatric registrars take a proper drinking history? *British Journal of Addiction*, *296*, 395–396.

Flay, B. R. (1986). Efficacy and effectiveness trials (and other phases of research) in the development of health promotion programs. *Preventive Medicine*, *15*, 451–474.

Freemantle, N., Gill, P., Godfrey, C., Long, A., Richards, C., Sheldon, T., et al. (1993). Brief interventions and alcohol use. *Effective Health Care Bulletin*, *7*, 1–13.

Fry, F. (1980). *Primary care*. London: Heineman Medical Books Limited.

Funk, M., Wutzke, S., Kaner, E., Anderson, P., Pas, L., McCormick, R., et al. (2005). A multicountry controlled trial of strategies to promote dissemination and implementation of brief alcohol intervention in primary health care: Findings of a World Health Organization collaborative study. *Journal of Studies on Alcohol*, *66*(3), 379–388.

Heather, N. (1996). The public health and brief interventions for excessive alcohol consumption: The British experience. *Addictive Behaviors*, *21*(6), 857–868.

Heather, N. (2007). A long-standing WHO collaborative Project on early identification and brief alcohol intervention in primary care comes to an end (editorial). *Addiction*, *38*, 1004–1031.

Heather, N., & Robertson, I. (1983). *Controlled drinking*. London: Methuen.

Heather, N., Whitton, B., & Robertson, I. (1986). Evaluation of a self-help manual for media recruited problem drinkers: Six month follow-up results. *British Journal of Clinical Psychology*, *25*, 19–34.

Hester, R. (1995). Behavioural self-control training. In R. Hester & W. Miller (Eds.), *Handbook of alcoholism treatment approaches: Effective alternatives* (2nd ed., pp. 148–159) Massachusetts: Needham Heights.

Higgins-Biddle, J. C., & Babor, T. F. (1996). *Reducing risky drinking*. Connecticut: University of Connecticut.

Hodgson, R., Alwyn, T., John, B., Thom, B., & Smith, A. (2002). The FAST alcohol screening test. *Alcohol & Alcoholism*, *37*(1), 61–66.

Holloway, A. S., Watson, H. E., Arthur, A. J., Starr, G., McFadyen, A. K., & McIntosh, J. (2007). The effect of brief interventions of alcohol consumption among heavy drinkers in a general hospital setting. *Addiction*, *102*, 1762–1770.

Huntley, D., Blain, C., Hood, S., & Touquet, R. (2001). Improving detection of alcohol misuse in patients presenting to accident and emergency departments. *Emergency Medicine Journal*, *18*, 99–104.

Hutchings, D., Cassidy, P., Dallolio, E., Pearson, P., Heather, N., & Kaner, E. (2006). Implementing screening and brief alcohol interventions in primary care: Views from both sides of the consultation. *Primary Care Research and Development*, *7*, 221–229.

Kaariainen, J., Sillanaukee, P., Poutanen, P., & Seppa, K. (2001). Opinions on alcohol-related issues among professionals in primary, occupational and specialized health care. *Alcohol & Alcoholism*, *36*(2), 141–146.

Kaner, E., Beyer, F., Dickinson, H., Pienaar, E., Campbell, F., Schlesinger, C., et al. (2007). Effectiveness of brief alcohol interventions in primary care populations Art. No.: CD004148.DOI:004110.001002/14651858.CD14654148.pub14651853. *Cochrane Database of Systematic Reviews, Issue 2*.

Kaner, E., Heather, N., Brodie, J., Lock, C., & McAvoy, B. (2001). Patient and practitioner characteristics predict brief alcohol intervention in primary care. *British Journal of General Practice*, *51*, 822–827.

Kaner, E. F. S., Heather, N., McAvoy, B. R., Lock, C. A., & Gilvarry, E. (1999a). Intervention for excessive alcohol consumption in primary health care: Attitudes and practices of English general practitioners. *Alcohol and Alcoholism*, *34*(4), 559–566.

Kaner, E. F. S., Lock, C. A., McAvoy, B. R., Heather, N., & Gilvarry, E. (1999b). A RCT of three training and support strategies to encourage implementation of screening and brief alcohol intervention by general practitioners. *British Journal of General Practice*, *49*, 699–703.

Kreitman, N. (1986). Alcohol consumption and the preventive paradox. *British Journal of Addictions*, *81*, 353–363.

Kristenson, H., Ohlin, H., Hulten-Nosslin, M., Trell, E., & Hood, B. (1983). Identification and intervention of heavy drinking in middle-aged men: Results and follow-up of 24–60 months of long-term study with randomized controls. *Alcohol Clinical and Experimental Research*, *7*, 203–210.

Lloyd, G., Chick, J., Crombie, E., & Anderson, S. (1986). Problem drinkers in medical wards: Consumption patterns and disabilities in newly identified male cases. *British Journal of Addiction*, *81*, 789–795.

Lock, C., Kaner, E., Lamont, S., & Bond, S. (2002). A qualitative study of nurses' attitudes and practices regarding brief alcohol intervention in primary health care. *Journal of Advanced Nursing*, *39*(4), 333–342.

Lock, C. A., & Kaner, E. F. S. (2004). Implementation of brief alcohol interventions by nurses in primary care: Do non-clinical factors influence practice? *Family Practice*, *21*(3), 270–275.

Lock, C. A., Kaner, E. F. S., Heather, N., McAvoy, B. R., & Gilvarry, E. (1999). A randomised trial of three marketing strategies to disseminate a screening and brief alcohol intervention programme to general practitioners. *British Journal of General Practice*, *49*, 695–698.

Longabaugh, R., Woolard, R. F., Nirenberg, T. D., Minugh, A. P., Becker, B., Clifford, P. R., et al. (2001). Evaluating the effects of a brief motivational intervention for injured drinkers in the emergency department. *Journal of Studies on Alcohol*, *62*, 806–816.

Maheswaran, R., Beevers, M., & Beevers, D. G. (1992). Effectiveness of advice to reduce alcohol consumption in hypertensive patients. *Hypertension*, *19*(1), 79–84.

Malbon, G., Bridgewood, A., Lader, D., & Matheson, J. (1996). *Health in England 1995: What people know, what people think, what people do*. London, UK: Office for Population and Census Surveys.

Marlatt, G. A., Baer, J. S., Kivlahan, D. R., Dimeff, L. A., Larimer, M. E., Quigley, L. A., et al. (1998). Screening and brief intervention for high-risk college student drinkers: Results from a 2-year follow-up assessment. *Journal of Consulting and Clinical Psychology*, *66*(4), 604–615.

McAvoy, B., Kaner, E., Haighton, K., Heather, N., & Gilvarry, E. (1997). "Drinkless"—Marketing a brief intervention package in UK general practice. *Family Practice*, *14*(5), 427–428.

McCambridge, J., & Strang, J. (2005). Deterioration over time in effect of motivational interviewing in reducing drug consumption and related risk among young people. *Addiction*, *100*(4), 470–478.

Miller, W., & Rollnick, S. (1991). *Motivational interviewing; preparing people to change addictive behavior*. New York: Guildford Press.

Miller, W., & Rollnick, S. (2002). *Motivational interviewing: Preparing people for change*. New York: Guilford.

Miller, W., & Sanchez, V. (1993). *Motivating young adults for treatment and lifestyle change*. Notre Dame, IN: University of Notre Dame Press.

Miller, W., Taylor, C. A., & West, J. (1980). Focused versus broad spectrum behaviour therapy for problem drinkers. *Journal of Consulting and Clinical Psychology, 48*, 590–601.

Miller, W. R., & Taylor, C. A. (1980). Relative effectiveness of bibliotherapy, individual and group self-control training in the treatment of problem drinkers. *Addictive Behaviours, 5*, 13–24.

Monti, P. M., Spirito, A., Myers, M., Colby, S. M., Barnett, N. P., Rohsenow, D. J., et al. (1999). Brief intervention for harm reduction with alcohol-positive older adolescents in a hospital emergency department. *Journal of Consulting and Clinical Psychology, 67*(6), 989–994.

Moyer, A., Finney, J. W., Swearingen, C. E., & Vergun, P. (2002). Brief interventions for alcohol problems: A meta-analytic review of controlled investigations in treatment-seeking and non-treatment-seeking populations. *Addiction, 97*(3), 279–292.

Nilssen, O. (1991). The Tromso Study: Identification of and a controlled intervention on a population of early-stage risk drinkers. *Preventive Medicine, 20*, 518–528.

Persson, J., & Magnusson, P. H. (1989). Early intervention in patients with excessive consumption of alcohol: A controlled study. *Alcohol, 6*(5), 403–408.

Piccinelli, M., Tessari, E., Bortolomasi, M., Piasere, O., Semenzin, M., Garzotto, N., et al. (1997). Efficacy of the alcohol use disorders identification test as a screening tool for hazardous alcohol intake and related disorders in primary care: A validity study. *British Medical Journal, 314*, 420–424.

Poikolainen, K. (1999). Effectiveness of brief interventions to reduce alcohol intake in primary health care populations: A meta-analysis. *Preventive Medicine, 28*, 503–509.

Poikolainen, K., Paljarvi, T., & Makela, P. (2007). Alcohol and the preventive paradox: Serious harms and drinking patterns. *Addiction, 102*(4), 571–578.

Raistrick, D., Heather, N., & Godfrey, C. (2006). Review of the effectiveness of treatment for alcohol problems. *National Treatment Agency for Substance Misuse, NHS, UK.*

Reinert, D., & Allen, J. (2007). The alcohol use disorders identification test: An update of research findings. *Alcoholism: Clinical and Experimental Research, 31*(2), 185–199.

Richmond, R., Heather, N., Holt, P., & Hu, W. (1990). *Workplace policies and programmes for tobacco, alcohol and other drugs in Australia*. Canberra: Australian Government Printing Service.

Richmond, R., Kehoe, L., Heather, N., Wodak, A., & Webster, I. (1996). General practitioners' promotion of healthy life styles: What patients think. *Australian and New Zealand Journal of Public Health, 20*(2), 195–200.

Roche, A., Hotham, E., & Richmond, R. (2002). The general practitioner's role in AOD issues: Overcoming individual, professional and systemic barriers. *Drug and Alcohol Review, 21*, 223–230.

Roche, A. M., & Freeman, T. (2004). Brief interventions: Good in theory but weak in practice. *Drug and Alcohol Review, 23*, 11–18.

Rollnick, S., Mason, P., & Butler, C. (1999). *Health behaviour change: A guide for practitioners*. Edinburgh: Churchill Livingstone.

Rossow, I., & Romelsjo, A. (2006). The extent of the "prevention paradox" in alcohol problems as a function of population drinking patterns. *Addiction, 101*(1), 84–90.

Royal College of Physicians. (1987). *A great and growing evil: The medical consequences of alcohol abuse*. London/New York: Tavistock.

Rush, B. R., Urbanoski, K. A., & Allen, B. A. (2003). Physicians' enquiries into their patients' alcohol use: Public views and recalled experiences. *Addiction*, *98*, 895–900.

Russell, M. A. H., Wilson, C., Taylor, C., & Baker, C. (1979). Effect of general practitioners' advice against smoking. *British Medical Journal*, *283*, 231–234.

Saunders, J. B., Aasland, O. G., Babor, T. F., De La Fuente, J. R., & Grant, M. (1993). Development of the Alcohol Use Disorders Identification Test (AUDIT): WHO collaborative project on early detection of persons with harmful alcohol consumption. II. *Addiction*, *88*(6), 791–804.

Shaw, S., Sprately, T., Cartwright, A., & Harwin, J. (1978). *Responding to drinking problems*. London: Croom Helm.

Sobell, M. B., & Sobell, L. L. (1995). Controlled drinking after 25 years: How important was the great debate? *Addiction*, *90*, 1149–1153.

Wallace, P. (2001). Patients with alcohol problems: Simple questioning is the key to effective identification and management. *British Journal of General Practice*, *51*, 172–173.

Wallace, P. G., & Haines, A. P. (1984). General practitioner and health promotion: What patients think. *British Medical Journal*, *289*, 534–536.

Watt, K., Shepherd, J., & Newcombe, R. (2008). Drunk and dangerous: A randomised controlled trial of alcohol brief intervention for violent offenders. *Journal of Experimental Criminology*, *4*, 1–19.

Whitlock, E. P., Polen, M. R., Green, C. A., Orleans, T., & Klein, J. (2004). Behavioral counseling interventions in primary care to reduce risky/harmful alcohol use by adults: A summary of the evidence for the US Preventive Services Task Force. *Annals of Internal Medicine*, *140*, 557–568.

Wilk, A. I., Jensen, N. M., & Havinghurst, T. C. (1997). Meta-analysis of randomized control trials addressing brief interventions in heavy alcohol drinkers. *Journal of General Internal Medicine*, *12*, 274–283.

Winett, R. A. (1995). A framework for health promotion and disease prevention programs. *American Psychologist*, *50*(5), 341–350.

Chapter | eleven

Relapse Prevention: Evidence Base and Future Directions

G. Alan Marlatt and Sarah W. Bowen
Addictive Behaviors Research Center, University of Washington

Katie Witkiewitz
Alcohol and Drug Abuse Institute, University of Washington

SUMMARY POINTS

- Lapses are the most common outcome following addiction treatment, and oftentimes a lapse can lead to a complete return to problematic substance use.
- Several factors have been identified that are often significant predictors of lapses, including negative effect, self-efficacy, coping, psychological functioning, and social support.
- A key challenge for addictive behaviors researchers and clinicians is to identify those factors that are most predictive for a particular client and then use that information to inform intervention.
- Relapse prevention techniques have been developed to forestall lapses and prevent lapses from turning into a relapse.
- Relapse prevention and other cognitive behavioral aftercare approaches are effective at reducing total relapse rates.
- Mindfulness-based relapse prevention, a treatment shown to be effective in reducing substance use following treatment, has great promise as an intervention strategy for reducing lapse and relapse.

Evidence-Based Addiction Treatment

BACKGROUND OF RELAPSE PREVENTION

In 1985 Marlatt and Gordon published the seminal text on relapse prevention (RP), which was designed to help explain the contexts in which lapses occur and how a lapse can lead to a relapse. In this book and for this chapter a lapse is defined as the initial use of a substance following a period of abstention or reduced use, whereas a relapse is defined as the return to problematic substance use following the initial transgression. Regardless of how one defines "relapse," it is the case that using substances at some point following treatment is the most common outcome of nearly all substance use treatment programs. The first 3 months following treatment appear to be the most critical for lapsing and thus implementing a program to prevent relapse during this time can be very helpful in improving overall treatment outcomes (Witkiewitz, 2008). Throughout this chapter we will be focusing primarily on relapse to substance use; however, it is important to keep in mind that relapse prevention has been applied successfully to several other addictive and nonaddictive behaviors, including problem gambling, eating disorders, depression, schizophrenia, and bipolar disorder.

The development of relapse prevention originated from a "failed" drinking treatment study in which Marlatt (1980) took careful notes on the factors that commonly triggered relapse in his sample of treated alcoholics. Marlatt (1980, see also Marlatt [1996]) organized these risk factors into a taxonomy of high-risk situations for relapse. The taxonomy consists of three hierarchical levels of categories used in the classification of relapse episodes. The first level of the hierarchy distinguishes between intrapersonal and interpersonal precipitants for relapse. The second level consists of eight subdivisions within the two Level 1 categories, including five within the intrapersonal category—coping with negative emotional states, coping with negative physical-psychological states, enhancement of positive-emotional states, testing personal control, and giving in to temptations and urges—and three within the interpersonal category—coping with interpersonal conflict, social pressure, and enhancement of positive emotional states. The third level of the taxonomy provides a more detailed inspection of five of the eight Level 2 subdivisions (e.g., coping with negative emotional states is segregated into coping with frustration and/or anger and coping with other negative emotional states). Drawing from this taxonomy, Marlatt proposed the first cognitive behavioral model of relapse (Marlatt & Gordon, 1985), which is shown in Figure 11.1.

As seen in Figure 11.1, the risk of relapse is heightened via a sequence of cognitions and behaviors that either precipitate lapses (e.g., negative effect) or increase the risk of a lapse turning into a relapse (e.g., the abstinence violation effect). In addition, the model highlights protective factors (e.g., coping responses) that will help forestall a lapse. Following from this model, Marlatt and colleagues developed an intervention that targeted many aspects of the model and was intended as an aftercare treatment for substance abuse disorders. Since the original publication in 1985, relapse prevention has been adapted to be used in a variety of treatment settings and has also been used as a stand-alone treatment.

The core component of relapse prevention interventions is the assessment of high-risk situations for relapse and the client's ability to cope with high-risk situations. If coping deficits are recognized then the therapist incorporates coping skills training and addresses the issue of client self-efficacy. Self-efficacy is a client's belief in his/her ability to maintain abstinence or some other goal (e.g., moderate drinking), and low self-efficacy has been shown to be a consistent predictor of relapse. The collaboration between client and therapist can play a critical role in increasing self-efficacy. Relapse prevention practitioners attempt to engage the client in the therapeutic process, thereby increasing the client's sense of ownership of a successful therapy outcome. Providing positive feedback to the client regarding successful completion of homework and related tasks during therapy can help increase a sense of self-efficacy overall, which can further motivate clients to believe in their ability to maintain treatment gains.

The assessment of high-risk situations should encompass the assessment of interpersonal, intrapersonal, environmental, and physiological risk factors. Once potential relapse triggers are identified, cognitive and behavioral techniques are implemented that incorporate specific strategies for reducing risks associated with relapse, as well as global strategies to increase lifestyle balance and prevent future occasions of high-risk situations. For example,

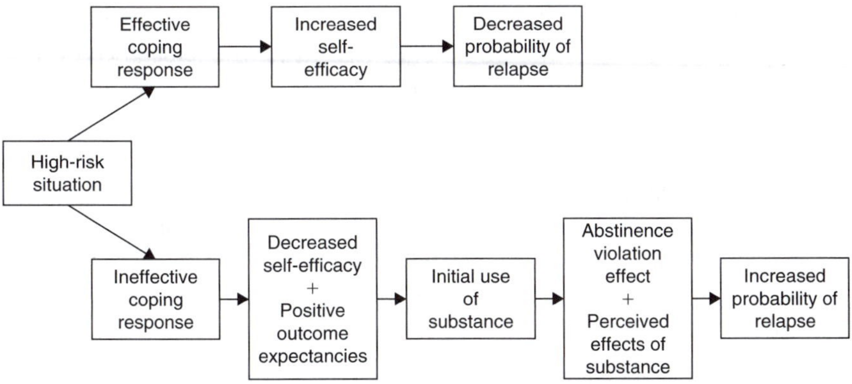

FIGURE 11.1 *The first cognitive behavioral model of relapse.*

if an individual describes a particular street corner (where he or she previously purchased crack cocaine) as an environmental risk factor, then the therapist works with the client to examine ways to avoid that street corner. When a high-risk situation is unavoidable (e.g., interactions with a family member), then coping skills training and cognitive restructuring techniques can be used to help the client cope with or restructure their experience during an interaction with a family member.

Relapse prevention also includes topic-focused psychoeducational and cognitive components, problem-solving skills, and opportunities to engage social support. Identifying the client's thoughts surrounding addictive behavior is a critical aspect of relapse prevention. One technique that is commonly used is the decisional balance tool, which provides the client with the opportunity to discuss the pros and cons of using a substance, as well as the pros and cons of not using a substance. This activity can help the practitioner identify discrepancies among a client's thoughts, feelings, and actions. If necessary, the practitioner can discuss the issue of maladaptive thoughts and how to challenge cognitive distortions (e.g., "I am worthless and never will be able to quit"). The final component of relapse prevention is addressing lifestyle balance and encouraging clients to identify healthy alternative activities that do not involve the addictive behavior. As described in the last section of this chapter, mindfulness meditation can serve as a rewarding, healthy, and helpful alternative to substance use.

THEORETICAL MODELS BEHIND RELAPSE PREVENTION

The cognitive behavioral model of relapse provides the backbone for relapse prevention. Shown in Figure 11.1, the relationships among situations, thoughts, and feelings are all considered in tandem in order to understand lapse events. The lack of an effective coping response leads to decreased self-efficacy (Bandura, 1977) in conjunction with increased positive expectancies for the initial effects of using the substance (Jones, Corbin, & Fromme, 2001). If these cognitive and behavioral processes, in combination with other determinants of relapse, lead to the first use of the substance, then the individual may be vulnerable to experience an "abstinence violation effect." This effect involves the loss of perceived control that an individual experiences after the defiance of self-imposed rules (Curry, Marlatt, & Gordon, 1987).

The cognitive behavioral model of relapse addresses several key questions:

1. Are there specific situational events that serve as triggers for lapses?

2. Are the determinants of the first lapse the same as those that cause a complete relapse to occur; if not, how can they be distinguished from one another?

3. How does an individual react to and conceptualize the events preceding and following a lapse and how do these reactions affect the person's subsequent behavior regarding the probability of a full-blown relapse?

4. Is it possible for an individual to covertly plan a relapse by setting up a situation in which it is virtually impossible to resist temptation?

5. At which points in the relapse process is it possible to intervene and alter the course of events so as to prevent a return to the addictive habit pattern?

6. Is it possible to prepare individuals during treatment to anticipate the likelihood of relapse and to teach them coping behaviors that might reduce the likelihood of lapses and the probability of subsequent relapse?

These six questions, in combination with a series of studies that questioned the validity of the original relapse taxonomy (see Lowman, Allen, Stout, & Relapse Research Group, 1996), led to the development of a revised cognitive behavioral conceptualization of the relapse process, which incorporated both dynamic and static risk factors (Witkiewitz & Marlatt, 2004). The "dynamic model of relapse," shown in Figure 11.2, provides a more complex view of the factors leading up to a lapse and potentially subsequent relapse and adds to the model an emphasis on the timing and interrelatedness of events. An individual's response in a high-risk situation is influenced by the underlying tonic and phasic processes, where tonic processes include the stable and enduring risk factors and phasic processes include more immediate precipitants of the high-risk situation.

The dynamic model of relapse was designed to emphasize the complexity of the relapse process and the multiple pathways to substance use. Recent empirical studies have provided support for the dynamic role of physical withdrawal in predicting smoking behavior (Piasecki et al., 2000) and the complex relationship between self-efficacy and post-treatment alcohol use (Witkiewitz, van der Maas, Hufford, & Marlatt, 2007). These studies provide initial support for the utility of the dynamic model being incorporated into relapse prevention interventions. For example, based on the work of Piasecki and colleagues (2000) it is important for smoking cessation counselors to provide an ongoing assessment of withdrawal symptoms and not assume (or, even worse, tell their clients) that withdrawal symptoms tend to decrease over time.

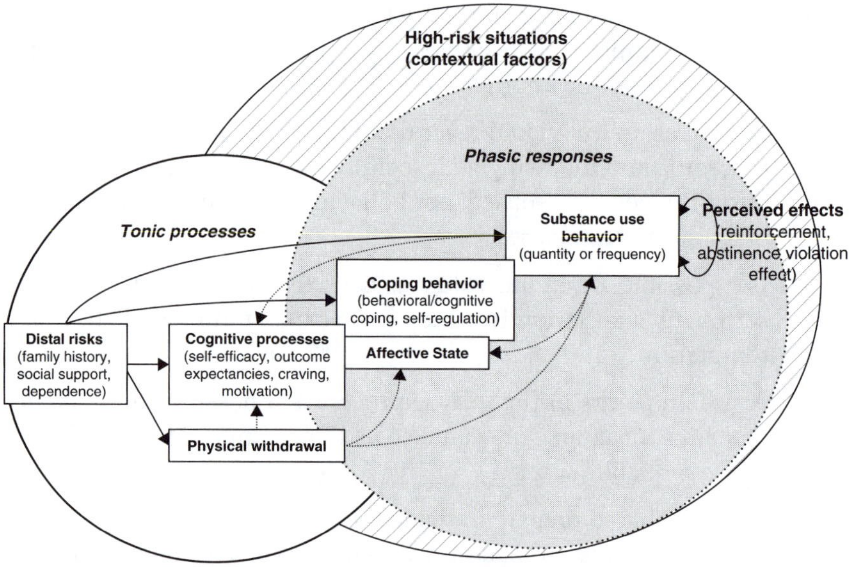

FIGURE 11.2 *The "dynamic model of relapse."*

EMPIRICAL EVIDENCE SUPPORTING RELAPSE PREVENTION

Three reviews, two meta-analyses (Dutra et al., 2008; Irvin, Bowers, Dunn, & Wang, 1999), and one qualitative review (Carroll, 1996) have concluded that relapse prevention is as effective as any other active treatment for substance use disorders and significantly more effective than no treatment. Carroll reviewed 24 randomized controlled trials of relapse prevention for smoking, alcohol, marijuana, and cocaine addiction. Based on her review, Carroll introduced the idea that relapse prevention, in comparison to other treatments, may provide continued improvement over a longer period of time (indicating a "delayed emergence effect"). Irvin and colleagues (1999) conducted a meta-analysis of 26 alcohol, tobacco, cocaine, and polysubstance use studies. Overall, the treatment effects suggested that relapse prevention successfully reduced substance use and led to improvements in psychosocial functioning. Importantly, relapse prevention was most effective in the treatment of alcohol dependence as compared to relapse prevention for other substance use. This finding is not surprising considering that relapse prevention was developed for alcohol dependence initially.

The most recent meta-analysis of relapse prevention for substance use disorders (Dutra et al., 2008) included five studies that were described specifically as using relapse prevention treatment and 10 additional studies that were defined as "other cognitive behavior therapy." Relapse prevention evidenced low/moderate effects sizes ($d = 0.32$), but was the second most effective treatment evaluated (combined cognitive behavioral therapy with contingency management and contingency management alone were the most effective treatments [$d = 1.02$ and $d = 0.58$, respectively]). Importantly, none of the five relapse prevention studies targeted alcohol dependence. Two of the studies examined relapse prevention as a treatment for cocaine use (Carroll, Rounsaville, Nich, & Gordon, 1994; Schmitz et al., 2002), one targeted opiate use (McAuliffe, 1990), and two of the studies evaluated relapse prevention for marijuana use (Roffman & George, 1988; Stephens, Roffman, & Curtin, 2000). Effect sizes were strongest for relapse prevention for marijuana use ($d = 0.31$ to $d = 0.73$) and were smallest for cocaine use disorders ($d = 0.03$ to $d = 0.05$).

In addition to standard "relapse prevention" programs, several other treatments that have incorporated components of relapse prevention have been developed. For example, the matrix model (Rawson et al., 2004) is a manualized outpatient treatment program for treating stimulant disorders, which combines cognitive behavioral techniques with 12-step program participation, and has been shown to be effective in the treatment of methamphetamine and cocaine dependence. Relapse prevention has also been combined with other approaches for the treatment of substance abuse in conjunction with other comorbid disorders. "Seeking safety" (Najavits, 2002) is an evidence-based treatment that combines aspects of relapse prevention with interpersonal therapy and case management for individuals with comorbid substance use disorders and post-traumatic stress disorder. "Focus on families" (Catalano & Hawkins, 1996) provides a combination of relapse prevention for parents in methadone maintenance programs with a multifaceted program to help increase protective factors against drug abuse among children of methadone-treated parents. Pharmacotherapy in the treatment of substance use disorders is commonly referred to as "relapse prevention" (for a review, see Spanagel & Kiefer, 2008); however, a complete description of the pharmacotherapy treatment literature is beyond the scope of this chapter. The interested reader is referred to the chapter on adjunctive pharmacotherapy in this volume.

THERAPEUTIC COMPONENTS OF RELAPSE PREVENTION INTERVENTIONS

Relapse prevention is designed to teach clients to anticipate and cope with the possibility of relapse. In the beginning of relapse prevention training, clients are taught to recognize and cope with high-risk situations that may precipitate a lapse and to modify cognitions and other reactions to prevent a single lapse from developing into a full-blown relapse. Because these procedures are focused on the immediate precipitants of the relapse process, they are referred to collectively as "specific intervention strategies." As clients master these techniques, clinical practice extends beyond a microanalysis of the relapse process and the initial lapse and involves strategies designed to modify the client's lifestyle and to identify and cope with covert determinants of relapse (early warning signals, cognitive distortions, and relapse setups). As a group, these procedures are called "global intervention strategies."

SPECIFIC INTERVENTION STRATEGIES

Assessment of motivation and commitment

Prochaska and DiClemente (1983) have described relapse within a transtheoretical model of six stages of change: precontemplation, contemplation, preparation, action, maintenance, and relapse. These stages of change have been applied successfully to understanding the motivation of patients receiving treatment for substance use disorders (DiClemente & Hughes, 1990). Motivation for change has been found to be highly correlated with treatment outcomes and relapse. Relapse prevention and lapse management strategies are necessary at the action, maintenance, and relapse stages in order for habit change to be successful over time.

The decision matrix is one tool that can be used to evaluate the client's motivations to change. The primary assumption in using this technique is that people will not decide to change their behavior or to continue an ongoing behavior unless they expect their gains to exceed their losses. To complete the decision matrix, the client is presented a four-way table with the following factors represented: the pros and cons of the decision to remain abstinent and the pros and cons of the decision to resume using alcohol or drugs. Further, the practitioner can review both the immediate and the delayed positive and negative effects of either alternative.

Relapse history and relapse susceptibility

One of the first homework assignments is for clients to write an autobiography describing the history and development of their addictive behavior problem. The clients are asked to focus on their subjective image of themselves as they progressed through the stages of habit acquisition from first experimentation to abuse of or dependence on alcohol or drugs. The purpose of this technique is to identify high-risk situations and to get a baseline assessment of the client's self-image while engaging in the addictive habit.

Most clients in treatment will have tried, either on their own or in previous treatment, to abstain from alcohol and drugs. Asking clients to describe past relapses may provide important clues to future high-risk situations for relapse. The therapist and the client can classify the descriptions of past relapses into the situational or personal factors that had the greatest impact. The idea that things can be different this time is a good topic to explore and challenges the client to "make it so."

When clients who are still drinking alcohol or using drugs enter therapy, they are asked to self-monitor their use on a daily basis by keeping track of the behavior and the situational context in which it occurs, as well as the immediate consequences of the behavior. In most cases, relapse prevention programs are initiated after abstinence or some reductions in use have been achieved by some means. In this situation, self-monitoring of exposure to high-risk situations is a useful technique. Clients are asked to keep track of exposure to situations or personal factors that cause them to have urges or craving to resume drinking or take drugs.

Coping skills training

Once high-risk situations have been identified, the client can then be taught to respond to these situational cues as discriminative stimuli (highway signs provide a good analogy) for behavior change. Taken collectively, the assessment of high-risk situations and coping skills deficits can be used to target areas that require special training or attention during the coping skills training components of the relapse prevention program. Effective coping skills training focuses on those high-risk situations identified in the client's assessment as creating the greatest potential for increasing the probability of relapse. As stated earlier, in some cases, it might be best to simply avoid risky situations, if possible. In most cases, however, the high-risk situations or psychological states cannot be avoided easily, and the client must rely on coping skills or alternative strategies to "get through" the situation without engaging in substance use.

Coping skills training methods incorporate components of direct instruction, modeling, behavioral rehearsal, therapist coaching, and feedback from the therapist. Therapists can help clients identify their style of approaching problems either by eliciting examples from them or by giving them a problem and asking them to outline how they would go about solving it. Generating alternatives is perhaps the most important step to effective problem solving. Once a list of alternative solutions has been generated a particular solution can be selected by evaluating the "pros" and "cons" of each solution and selecting what promises to be the best available option.

In addition to teaching clients to respond effectively when confronted with specific high-risk situations, there are a number of additional relaxation training and stress management procedures the therapist can draw upon to increase the client's overall capacity to deal with stress. Relaxation training may provide the client with a global increased perception of control, thereby reducing the stress that any given situation may pose for the individual. Such procedures as progressive muscle relaxation training, meditation, exercise, and various stress management techniques are extremely useful in aiding the client to cope more effectively with the hassles and demands of daily life.

Increasing self-efficacy

In many cases, a particular coping response may fail to be executed despite high levels of motivation if the individual has low self-efficacy concerning his or her capacity to engage in the behavior. The converse is equally true, of course; an individual may fail to engage in a specific behavior despite high levels of self-efficacy if the motivation for performance is low or absent ("I knew what to do, but I just didn't feel like doing it").

The probability of relapse in a given high-risk situation decreases considerably when the individual harbors a high level of self-efficacy for performing a coping response. If a coping response is performed successfully, the individual's judgment of efficacy will be strengthened for coping with similar situations as they arise on subsequent occasions. Repeated experiences of successful coping strengthen self-efficacy and reduce the risk that occasional slips will precipitate relapse in the future. Guided imagery techniques may also be used to help clients imagine coping successfully with a high-risk situation. Efficacy-enhancing imagery is used to augment coping skills training and to assess the client's current level of self-efficacy and coping skills mastery.

Coping with lapses

An individual is most vulnerable to return to problematic substance use during the time immediately following an initial lapse. The follow list contains a variety of recommended strategies to employ whenever a lapse occurs. Clients can be told to think of this list as a set of emergency procedures to be used in case a lapse occurs. The strategies are listed in order of temporal priority, with the most important immediate steps listed first. The main points of this information can be presented to clients in summary form by use of a reminder card that should be kept handy in the event that a lapse occurs. Because specific coping strategies will vary from client to client, therapists may wish to help a particular client prepare an individualized reminder card that fits that person's unique set of vulnerabilities and resources.

1. *Stop, look, and listen.* The first thing to do when a lapse occurs is to *stop* the ongoing flow of events and to *look* and *listen* to

what is happening. The lapse is a warning signal indicating that the client is in danger.

2. *Keep calm*. Just because the client slipped once does not indicate failure. One slip does not have to make a total relapse. Look upon the slip as a single, independent event, something that can be avoided in the future. A slip is a mistake, an opportunity for learning, not a sign of total failure.

3. *Renew commitment*. After a lapse, the most difficult problem to deal with is motivation. The client may feel like giving up and may need reminding of the long-range benefits to be gained from this change. Clients should be encouraged to reflect optimistically on their past successes in being able to quit the old habit instead of focusing on current setbacks.

4. *Review the situation leading up to the lapse*. Look at the slip as a specific unique event. The following questions may help clarify the lapse episode: What events led up to the slip? Were there any early warning signals that preceded the lapse? What was the nature of the high-risk situation that triggered the slip? Each of these questions may yield valuable information concerning high-risk situations for the client.

5. *Make an immediate plan for recovery*. After a slip, renewed commitments should be turned into a plan of action to be carried out immediately. Therapists can help clients identify *emergency action plans*, which may include a crisis hotline telephone number, an alternative activity, or a trustworthy friend.

6. *Dealing with the abstinence violation effect*. It is important to teach clients not to view the cause of the lapse as a personal failure or as a lack of willpower, but instead ask them to pay attention to the environmental and psychological factors in the high-risk situation, to review what coping skills they had available but didn't implement, and to note how they felt when they couldn't deal with the situation adequately.

7. *Dealing with guilt and shame*. Clients often need help recovering from the inevitable feelings of guilt and shame and the cognitive dissonance that usually accompanies a lapse. Guilt and shame reactions are particularly dangerous because the emotions they produce are likely to motivate further substance use or other addictive behaviors as a means of coping with these unpleasant reactions to the slip.

8. *Learning from the lapse*. After the lapse has occurred, the relapse prevention therapist reacts to the client with compassion and understanding. It is important to approach the situation with the encouragement to learn everything possible about how to cope with similar situations in the future by a thorough debriefing of the lapse. Clinicians must help clients identify any of the cognitive distortions they may have succumb to in exposing themselves to the high-risk situation, limiting their ability to engage in an effective coping response, and, finally, making the decision to resume substance use.

GLOBAL INTERVENTION STRATEGIES

Providing clients with behavioral skills training and cognitive strategies to cope effectively with high-risk situations and lapses is vital to the success of any relapse prevention program. These techniques are likely to be the exclusive focus of efforts to abstain and to remain abstinent from the addictive habit in the early part of the maintenance stage of therapy. However, simply teaching clients to cope with one high-risk situation after another is not enough for long-term success in addictive or criminal behavior habit change. This is true because it is impossible for the therapist and client to identify all possible high-risk situations that the client may encounter.

Lifestyle balance

Oftentimes the degree of balance or imbalance in a person's daily life has a significant impact on the desire for indulgence and immediate gratification. Lifestyle balance refers to the amount of stress in a person's daily life compared with stress-reducing activities, such as social support, exercise, mediation, or other stress-buffering or -relieving activities. Lifestyle balance is also related to diet, social relationships, and spiritual endeavors. Whatever the cause of lifestyle imbalance, this factor is likely to be the first in a chain of covert antecedents that become relapse setups by creating exposure to high-risk situations that may precipitate a lapse or evolve into a full-blown relapse.

Lifestyle modification procedures are designed to identify the covert antecedents of relapse that set up exposure to high-risk situations and to promote lifelong habit change to create greater mental, emotional, physical, and spiritual well-being. The specific lifestyle modifications recommended in the relapse prevention approach depend on the client's unique needs and abilities. A program of exercise such as jogging, hiking, or walking; meditation, yoga, or reading; enhanced social activities with new friends; or weekly massage to reduce muscle tension are among the many possibilities.

Because lifestyle imbalance is likely to create a desire for indulgence, one effective strategy is to search for activities that might be substitute indulgences that are not harmful or addictive, but that over time with repeated practice can become adaptive wants that provide some of the same pleasure and enjoyment that addictive behaviors have provided without the delayed costs. In this regard, Glasser (1976) has described behaviors such as excessive drinking and drug abuse as negative addictions that initially feel good, but produce long-term harm. Conversely, Glasser describes positive addictions (e.g., running, meditation, hiking, hobbies) as producing short-term discomfort or even pain while creating long-term benefits to physical health and to psychological well-being.

Extending relapse prevention to include a focus on mindfulness

Marlatt and colleagues have integrated mindfulness meditation practices and standard relapse prevention techniques into a new program called Mindfulness-Based Relapse Prevention (MBRP; Marlatt, Bowen, Chawla, & Witkiewitz, 2004; Marlatt et al., 2008; Witkiewitz, Marlatt, & Walker, 2005). MBRP is designed to enhance both specific and global intervention strategies of relapse prevention, providing further techniques that enable clients to increase awareness and practice effective coping strategies. MBRP shares the RP goals of decreasing contact with high-risk situations, increasing coping in high-risk situations, keeping lapses from becoming full-blown relapses, and developing lifestyle balance.

The techniques used in MBRP originate from the Buddhist practice of Vipassana (or "insight") meditation. These practices were assessed for use with treatment of substance use in a small study demonstrating the effectiveness of Vipassana in reducing substance use rates among an incarcerated population (Bowen et al., 2006). Traditional mindfulness meditation practice involves sitting, walking, and lying down meditations, with a focus on the observation of one's experience in a nonjudgmental and accepting manner. Meditators focus on physical sensations, as well as on any thoughts or emotions that might arise. They practice observing the mind as it becomes involved in thoughts or stories, repeatedly bringing their focus back to the present moment.

A central component of MBRP is recognizing the tendency to behave on "automatic pilot," which can often lead to reactive, habitual, and unhealthy behaviors. The mindfulness practices help clients step out of this automatic mode by increasing attentional control, allowing improved ability to maintain focus on the present moment, and developing a metacognitive awareness of the behavior of the mind. For example, meditators practice observation of the mind's "automatic" tendency to make attributions and assumptions about neutral or ambiguous stimuli. The processes that are strengthened through mindfulness practice foster awareness of how "triggers" can lead to subsequent proliferations of thoughts, emotions, and behavior. Clients learn to differentiate between what is actually happening in the moment and what the mind "says" is happening, cultivating the awareness and flexibility needed to make healthier choices.

Mindfulness-Based Relapse Prevention combines meditation practices with standard relapse prevention strategies throughout eight 2-hour weekly sessions. Clients are asked to continue meditation practice throughout the week with the aid of audio-recorded instructions. Additionally, they are assigned meditation exercises to implement throughout their day, such as eating a meal mindfully or practicing walking meditation. After 3 weeks of basic practice, clients begin engaging in practices designed to increase awareness and coping in high-risk situations. Worksheets designed to help clients identify their own high-risk situations, as well as healthy and unhealthy coping strategies for managing high-risk situations, are employed throughout the course.

A core component of RP is addressing and coping with the abstinence violation effect, in which individuals experience thoughts and emotions following an initial lapse that can increase the probability of escalation into full relapse. For example, in standard RP, clients are to stop, look, and listen as first steps following an initial lapse. MBRP practices promote skills that increase the awareness of problematic signs both prior to and following a lapse (stop) and increase the observational skills (look and listen) to enable a client to monitor his or her own experience and reactions. A client might notice thoughts such as "I blew it so I might as well just keep drinking. I'm a failure." Practicing observation of thoughts and recognition that they are not always an objective reflection of the truth helps clients view these as merely "automatic" thoughts, allowing them to simply observe the thoughts without engaging in or "buying into" them, thus preventing a chain of reactive or "automatic" thoughts and behaviors that might have led previously to continued use.

In addition to teaching observational skills, standard RP teaches clients to "keep calm" after an initial lapse. MBRP includes meditations designed to increase clients' willingness and ability to endure emotionally or physically uncomfortable states with a calm and nonjudgmental attitude. This can prevent further exacerbation of the distress by cultivating calmness rather than "feeding" the anxiety or discomfort. RP encourages clients to learn from their lapse and suggests that therapists respond to their clients' lapses with compassion and understanding. MBRP further encourages clients to adopt an encouraging and compassionate stance toward their own experience and, as best as they can, to refocus their attitude from one of shame and discouragement to one of compassion and encouragement. MBRP practices adopt an underlying attitude of compassion toward experience, with the understanding that this is the nature of mind and of addiction; it is not their *fault*. MBRP purports that initial reactions, urges, cravings, and emotions are often conditioned and thus are not under volitional control. What can be fostered, however, is the ability to mindfully choose how to respond.

The specific practices of coping in high-risk situations are a fundamental part of both RP and MBRP. Both therapies also recognize the importance of the broader aspects of lifestyle balance in maintaining recovery. MBRP includes exercises and practices assessing daily activities and relationships and whether they are beneficial or detrimental to overall health and recovery. Additionally, MBRP clients practice interact with "depleting" or aversive experiences that might be inevitable in daily life in a way that decreases the aversive nature, thus reducing the stress or negative effect that may increase a vulnerability to relapse.

Case Study

In "relapse prevention over time" (American Psychological Association, 2007), Dr. Marlatt demonstrates his approach to helping clients with substance use disorders prevent or cope with relapses during efforts to change addictive behavior. In this series of six monthly sessions, he works with a man, Kevin, in his 30s who is striving to overcome a crack cocaine addiction. Although he is a successful African-American businessman, Kevin experiences a number of problems in his personal life, having recently separated from his wife and his young daughter over problems associated with his drug use. When the treatment sessions began, Kevin was living in a recovery center following his prior inpatient treatment for cocaine addiction. Although he was successful in abstaining from drug use for weeks at a time, he also experienced several setbacks or lapses during the 6 months of relapse prevention. During these six sessions, Dr. Marlatt helped the client determine high-risk situations and potential triggers for relapse and taught skills for getting through these situations. One common high-risk situation for Kevin was his tendency to become excessively self-critical and depressed about his life situation. When feeling down, Kevin had thoughts of using cocaine as a means of self-medicating his low moods. His temptation to buy crack was particularly difficult to resist whenever he had cash on hand (e.g., paydays). He would then tell himself that he needed to buy a pack of cigarettes and would go to a store near where one of his dealers would be selling drugs (this is an example of what is known as a "seemingly unimportant decision" to buy cigarettes in an area where he would run into his dealer). Under the influence of this drug, he felt powerful and confident about his life, but this was usually followed by another period of self-criticism and guilt over the fact that he violated his commitment to abstinence (abstinence violation effect). Together they worked to restructure the guilt and shame that arise after lapses in abstinence. This compassionate intervention effectively reframes relapse as a mistake to learn from—and avoid—as the client moves toward recovery.

SUMMARY AND CONCLUSIONS

Relapse prevention has accumulated a strong evidence base over the past 23 years, particularly for the treatment of alcohol use disorders (Irvin et al., 1999). RP is a versatile and straightforward cognitive behavioral therapy-based treatment that is well liked by clients and implemented easily in a variety of settings. Although it can be used as a stand–alone treatment, RP is often incorporated into other behaviorally oriented treatments for addiction (e.g., coping skills therapy and mindfulness-based therapy). For more information on the implementation of RP, the interested reader is referred to Marlatt and Donovan (2005) and Witkiewitz and Marlatt (2007).

REFERENCES

American Psychological Association. (2007). *Relapse prevention over time with G. Alan Marlatt, Ph.D.* APA Psychotherapy Video Series. Washington, DC: American Psychological Association.

Bandura, A. (1977). Self-efficacy: Toward a unifying theory of behavioral change. *Psychological Review*, *84*, 191–215.

Bowen, S., Witkiewitz, K., Dillworth, T., Chawla, N., Simpson, T., Ostafin, B., et al. (2006). Mindfulness meditation and substance use in an incarcerated population. *Psychology of Addictive Behaviors*, *20*, 343–347.

Carroll, K. M. (1996). Relapse prevention as a psychosocial treatment: A review of controlled clinical trials. *Experimental and Clinical Psychopharmacology*, *4*, 46–54.

Carroll, K. M., Rounsaville, B. J., Nich, C., & Gordon, L. T. (1994). One-year follow-up of psychotherapy and pharmacotherapy for cocaine dependence: Delayed emergence of psychotherapy effects. *Archives of General Psychiatry*, *51*, 989–997.

Catalano, R. F., & Hawkins, J. D. (1996). The social development model: A theory of antisocial behavior. In J. D. Hawkins (Ed.), *Delinquency and crime: Current theories*. New York: Cambridge University Press.

Curry, S., Marlatt, G. A., & Gordon, J. R. (1987). Abstinence violation effect: Validation of an attributional construct with smoking cessation. *Journal of Consulting and Clinical Psychology*, *55*, 145–149.

DiClemente, C. C., & Hughes, S. O. (1990). Stages of change profiles in outpatient alcoholism treatment. *Journal of Substance Abuse*, *2*, 217–235.

Dutra, L., Stathopoulou, G., Basden, S. L., Leyro, T. M., Powers, M. B., & Otto, M. W. (2008). A meta-analytic review of psychosocial interventions for substance use disorders. *American Journal of Psychiatry*, *165*, 179–187.

Glasser, W. (1976). *Positive addiction*. New York: Harper and Row.

Irvin, J. E., Bowers, C. A., Dunn, M. E., & Wang, M. C. (1999). Efficacy of relapse prevention: A meta-analytic review. *Journal of Consulting and Clinical Psychology*, *67*, 563–570.

Jones, B. T., Corbin, W., & Fromme, K. (2001). A review of expectancy theory and alcohol consumption. *Addiction*, *96*, 57–72.

Lowman, C., Allen, J., Stout, R. L., & Relapse Research Group. (1996). Replication and extension of Marlatt's taxonomy of relapse precipitants: Overview of procedures and results. *Addiction*, *91*(Suppl.), S51–S71.

Marlatt, G. (1980). A cognitive behavioral model of the relapse process. In N. A. Krasnegor (Ed.), *Behavioral analysis and treatment of substance abuse*. Rockville, MD: National Institute on Drug Abuse.

Marlatt, G. A. (1996). Section I. Theoretical perspectives on relapse: Taxonomy of high-risk situations for alcohol relapse: Evolution and development of a cognitive behavioral model. *Addiction*, *91*(Suppl.), S37–S49.

Marlatt, G. A., Bowen, S., Chawla, N., & Witkiewitz, K. (2008). Mindfulness-based relapse prevention for substance abusers: Therapist training and therapeutic relationships. In S. Hick & T. Bien (Eds.), *Mindfulness and the therapeutic relationship*. New York: Guilford Press.

Marlatt, G. A., & Gordon, J. R. (Eds.) (1985). *Relapse prevention: Maintenance strategies in the treatment of addictive behaviors*. New York: The Guilford Press.

Marlatt, G. A., Witkiewitz, K., Dillworth, T. M., Bowen, S., Parks, G. A., MacPherson, L. M., et al. (2004). Vipassana meditation as a treatment for alcohol and drug use disorders. In S. C. Hayes, M. M. Linehan, & V. M. Follette (Eds.), *Mindfulness and acceptance: In the new cognitive behavior therapies*. New York: Guildford Press.

McAuliffe, W. E. (1990). A randomized controlled trial of recovery training and self-help for opioid addicts in New England and Hong Kong. *Journal of Psychoactive Drugs*, *22*, 197–209.

Piasecki, T. M., Niaura, R., Shadel, W. G., Abrams, D., Goldstein, M., Fiore, M. C., & Baker, T. B. (2000). Smoking withdrawal dynamics in unaided quitters. *Journal of Abnormal Psychology*, *109*, 74–86.

Prochaska, J. O., & DiClemente, C. C. (1983). Stages and processes of self-change of smoking: Toward an integrative model of change. *Journal of Consulting and Clinical Psychology*, *51*, 390–395.

Rawson, R. A., Marinelli-Casey, P., Anglin, M. D., Dickow, A., Frazier, Y., Gallagher, C., et al. (2004). A multi-site comparison of psychosocial approaches for the treatment of methamphetamine dependence. *Addiction*, *99*, 708–717.

Roffman, R. A., & George, W. H. (1988). Assessment of cannabis abuse. In D. M. Donovan & G. A. Marlatt (Eds.), *Assessment of addictive behaviors*. New York: Guilford.

Schmitz, J. M., Averill, P., Sayre, S., McCleary, P., Moeller, F., & Swann, A. (2002). Cognitive behavioral treatment of bipolar disorder and substance abuse: A preliminary randomized study. *Addictive Disorders Treatment*, *1*, 17–24.

Spanagel, R., & Kiefer, F. (2008). Drugs for relapse prevention of alcoholism: Ten years of progress. *Trends in Pharmacological Sciences*, *29*, 109–115.

Stephens, R. S., Roffman, R. A., & Curtin, L. (2000). Comparison of extended versus brief treatments for marijuana use. *Journal of Consulting and Clinical Psychology*, *68*, 898–908.

Witkiewitz, K. (2008). Lapses following alcohol treatment: Modeling the falls from the wagon. *Journal of Studies on Alcohol and Drugs*, *69*, 594–604.

Witkiewitz, K., & Marlatt, G. A. (2004). Relapse prevention for alcohol and drug problems: That was Zen, this is Tao. *American Psychologist*, *59*, 224–235.

Witkiewitz, K., Marlatt, G. A., & Walker, D. D. (2005). Mindfulness-based relapse prevention for alcohol use disorders. *Journal of Cognitive Psychotherapy*, *19*, 211–228.

Witkiewitz, K., van der Maas, H. J., Hufford, M. R., & Marlatt, G. A. (2007). Non-normality and divergence in post-treatment alcohol use: Re-examining the Project MATCH data "Another Way." *Journal of Abnormal Psychology*, *116*, 378–394.

Chapter | twelve

Behavioral Couples Therapy in the Treatment of Alcohol Problems

Adrian B. Kelly
The Centre for Youth Substance Abuse Research, University of Queensland

SUMMARY POINTS

- Alcohol behavioral couples therapy (ABCT) has the strongest empirical support of available couple-based approaches in the treatment of couples with alcohol and relationship problems, and evidence shows that it performs better than individual therapies for these couples.
- ABCT is based heavily on skills-deficits models of couple relationship quality.
- The skills-deficit model may be limited because it contains insufficient focus on intense negative feelings underlying the use/nonuse of communication skills.
- Other couple therapy approaches place greater emphasis on the reexperiencing of intense negative feelings and the reframing of these as existential distress. Emotion-focused therapy is one such approach to couple relationship distress.
- Given the likely importance of forgiveness in couples with alcohol problems, ABCT may benefit from moderation of the skills-deficit model to a more flexible and modularized therapy, where there is a heavier emphasis on intense negative feelings and forgiveness of the partner.

Evidence-Based Addiction Treatment

Links between relationship problems and heavy drinking/alcohol dependence are undoubtedly complex and reciprocal. Alcohol dependence and heavy drinking can be a source of relationship distress and conflict, which in turn can create a context in which further drinking episodes are initiated. Alcohol problems are common in people with couple relationship problems, couples with alcohol problems report particularly low confidence about resolving marital disagreements with their partner (Kelly, Halford, & Young, 2001), there are high rates of physical aggression in couples with alcohol problems (O'Farrell, Murphy, Stephan, Fals-Stewart, & Murphy, 2004), and marital conflict is a common cue to relapse (Kelly et al., 2001). Heavy drinking may affect the spouse's emotional health because of the drinker's reduced capacity to fulfill roles inside and outside the home, the common legal/financial consequences of heavy drinking, and the impact of heavy drinking on sexual functioning (e.g., Kelly et al., 2001). The reciprocity of effects between alcohol and relationship problems has long been a basis for behaviorally oriented therapies that address the two problems together.

This chapter focuses on behavioral couple therapy approaches to alcohol problems (alcohol-focused behavioral couples therapy [ABCT]) because this form of therapy is the most extensively evaluated, and ABCT now has extensive support for its efficacy. The aim of this chapter is not to provide a comprehensive "how-to-do-it" manual for the treatment of couples with alcohol and relationship problems, but rather to overview the basic components, processes, and strategies of established ABCT programs. A key focus of the chapter is the discussion of possibilities for further developing the content and processes of ABCT to better meet the dominant issues reported by these couples and improve the flexibility of ABCT to better suit individual couples.

INTRODUCTION TO ALCOHOL BEHAVIORAL COUPLES THERAPY

Alcohol behavioral couples therapy typically has four goals: (i) to engage both partners in therapy, (ii) to achieve abstinence, (iii) to improve relationship satisfaction, and (iv) to maintain therapy gains.

Engaging the partner

Spouses of male problem drinkers frequently present to treatment agencies seeking assistance with the stress imposed by their partner's behavior, and a common first goal of ABCT is to engage the partner in the program. This can be an elusive goal. In our research we used several strategies to engage the male partner (Halford, Price, Kelly, Bouma, & Young, 2001). During the first session with the spouse we discussed the idea of involving the partner in an assessment session and possible therapy. If the spouse was willing to give it a try, the therapist and spouse arrived at an agreement of who would approach the male partner (spouse or both the spouse and the therapist) and how and when they would approach the partner. The spouse rehearsed how to raise and frame the issue, using nonblaming language that communicated concern. If the partner was not inclined to participate, therapy focused on ways of increasing pressures on the partner to address his/her drinking (Barber & Crisp, 1995). For example, the spouse might more strongly state the implications of not seeking help for the long-term stability of the relationship and/or explore the options for ending the relationship if change seems very unlikely. Although these options may not always be ideal and may warrant ongoing individual support, such strategies may empower the presenting spouse to take greater control of his/her life situation.

Promoting reduced drinking

A goal of couple therapy is that both partners will agree to a contract that rebuilds trust and safety between the partners on alcohol-related issues. For the identified drinker, a commitment to an alcohol-related goal is made. The initial alcohol-related goal is initially framed as a daily commitment of intention not to drink—an achievable goal that can build the nondrinking partner's optimism. For some couples, time may need to be spent on engaging the partner in the idea of change and firming up the commitment to change. The motivational interviewing processes of Miller and Rollnick (1996) may be useful in building a commitment to reduce or stop drinking.

Alcohol behavioral couples therapy typically has a major focus on the negotiation of a recovery contract. In O'Farrell and Fals-Stewart's (2006) ABCT paradigm, the recovery contract centers around a *trust discussion*, in which each day the identified drinker states his/her intentions not to drink for that day, the spouse expresses support for this commitment, and the identified drinker thanks his/her partner for this support. The contract is renewed on a daily basis, and a high degree of structure is brought into the exercise. Couples rehearse the interaction in therapy with modeling and guidance from the therapist, couples choose a mutually agreeable time to conduct the trust discussion, and results of the discussion are recorded for review in therapy. As with monitoring regimes in other behavioral therapies, there are sometimes difficulties with compliance in tasks of this sort. Noncompliance can signal corrosive factors such as punishing references to past failures. The therapist can help each partner articulate trust statements with positivity and without qualifiers that detract from the authentic and unconditional nature of the contract.

Spouse-focused interventions

During ABCT, the therapist often works with each partner in the presence of the other to maximize the likelihood of abstinence and to improve the coping and stress experienced by the partner. Given the importance of maintaining abstinence and sustaining any improvements in relationship functioning that may result, early strategies focus on the person with alcohol problems. Strategies include identifying feelings and situations where urges to drink are experienced, building self-efficacy through reinforcement of alcohol-related successes, working to reduce exposure to alcohol cues, addressing stressful events, developing drinking-incompatible pleasurable events, decreasing spouse behaviors that may cue drinking, and developing a plan for dealing with lapses. Having the partner present is useful in several respects. For example, understanding when and how urges to drink are experienced helps the partner understand the normality of these occurrences for the recovering drinker and is a first step in understanding how and when to support the partner through high-risk periods. By focusing on coping strategies that worked when urges occur, the spouse hears about successful strategies, which in turn contribute to a sense of optimism about change.

Stressful events, such as occupational, medical, financial, or family problems, can increase the likelihood of relapse. Helping the couple find solutions to these problems is likely to reduce a key source of risk. The partner may have a very important supporting role in this process (Cohan & Bradbury, 1997). The couple session can be used to evaluate the nature of the problems and some likely sources of assistance. The therapist may prioritize where relatively quick movement toward a solution can be obtained, leaving other more complex problems until abstinence has become more entrenched.

For many reasons, partners may interact or react to their spouse in such a way that the likelihood of drinking is increased. Examples of these interactions include drinking in the presence of the spouse, dredging up past arguments or embarrassing drinking-related events, and canceling social events because of the spouse's drinking behavior. ABCT strategies commonly involve changing the partner's behavior so that minimizing the negative effects of heavy drinking occurs less frequently. These sorts of strategies are also common in spouse-focused interventions, where the partner does not engage in therapy directly (e.g., Halford et al., 2001). We suspect that the effectiveness of such strategies on alcohol consumption depends on whether the partner with alcohol problems is engaged in conjoint therapy. In our randomized control of a spouse-focused intervention consisting of many of these strategies, we found no impact on the partner's alcohol consumption (Halford et al., 2001).

However, it seems likely that spouse-focused interventions may reduce the stress of the nondrinking partner. We found that when these strategies were combined with the scheduling of pleasurable activities independent of the drinker, there was a reduction of stress of female partners of male drinkers (Halford et al., 2001). The partner may find it liberating to give up the battle to cover up or stop the drinking and to get on with enjoying his/her life.

Most alcohol-related interventions have an emphasis on relapse prevention, and ABCT is no different in this regard. The therapist should help couples work through an early intervention strategy for dealing with an imminent lapse, or an actual lapse, should it occur. The central aim of the strategy should be to prevent a lapse if possible or to prevent a lapse from becoming a relapse. Effective strategies may include contacting the partner and telling them about the situation, talking with the partner about ways of coping, reiterating support for the drinker, enlisting the support of the partner in doing something that is drinking incompatible, or contacting the therapist. Any plan should emphasize the importance of acting quickly. A prompt post hoc analysis of lapses/relapses is important for understanding how/why the relapse happened and to modify the relapse plan to deal with similar future events. The abstinence violation effect is important for both partners to consider. It is often enlightening for the partner to understand the negative self-talk that precedes a relapse and the potential value of managing high anger and criticality at these crucial times (however understandable these responses might be).

Behavioral couple interventions (BCT)

Once abstinence is attained, the third challenge is to focus on the enhancement of relationship functioning. Traditional BCT interventions form the basis for the enhancement of relationship functioning. BCT aims to increase the rewarding experience of couple relationships by adopting a largely skills training approach (Kelly, Fincham, & Beach, 2003). Couples learn how to improve communication skills (e.g., effective problem-solving processes and conflict management), as well as increase the frequency of caring and otherwise positive behaviors. BCT is an extensively tested form of therapy with good evidence of its efficacy. Jacobson and Addis (1993) report that two-thirds of distressed couples report improvements following BCT, and one-third of couples who show improvements in BCT by the end of treatment have relapsed 1 to 2 years after therapy. In all, we can expect that around 50% of distressed couples will show significant medium- to long-term change.

Unhappy couple relationships frequently show a dearth of positive couple activities and, if they occur, tend to be overlooked. BCT approaches seek an early focus on injecting positive events into the lives of couples, and helping partners detect these events when they do occur. As with the recovery contract, this is typically done in a structured way, but of course there is variation in how the intervention is implemented. For couples in which a reasonable number of positive interactions are occurring, therapists may request each partner to look out for, record, and acknowledge any positive relationship behavior the partner does over a given time period (e.g., offer to pick the children up from school). For couples where there is a real poverty of positive events, the therapist may ask each partner to generate a list of simple pleasurable or positive events. These lists are then swapped, and each partner makes a commitment to both enact one of the behaviors each day and look out for any of the behaviors recorded on the list. Where possible, each spouse acknowledges with thanks the partner's caring behavior. Pleasurable (alcohol-incompatible) couple activities are also likely to need a boost in frequency. The therapist may help each partner generate a list of realistic and practical activities (e.g., going out to a movie or for coffee) and assist the couple in scheduling the event(s) for the coming week. On the return visit, the therapist reviews each partner's records and explores the reactions of the positive behavior/event. The hope with this continued strategy is that caring behaviors/positive events are experienced as reinforcing and that couples continue to enact these behaviors.

A focus on improving communication skills in ABCT is based on many research findings that distressed and nondistressed couples differ in how they interact, and that distressed couples often communicate with criticality, defensiveness, and contempt (Kelly et al., 2003). By restructuring the way couples communicate (verbally and nonverbally), it is possible to maximize the likelihood that communicating will be more rewarding and that problem issues can be dealt with effectively early in their development. For couples in which one partner has alcohol problems, the art of communicating without the involvement of alcohol may be an unfamiliar and awkward skill. Furthermore, couples may have difficulties keeping to the issue at hand, with discussions drifting to alcohol-related issues that engender anger and reduce the likelihood of problem resolution. Consequently, couples may need a high degree of structure to repair (or develop) these processes.

Communication skills training commonly involves a rationale for the importance of effective communication, with demonstrations of the skills involved, followed by systematic attempts and support/reinforcement by the therapist. The therapist begins by outlining and illustrating the differences between speaker and listener skills and between verbal and nonverbal behavior. The therapist may choose to begin with each partner talking the ups and downs of their day to each other, with the therapist managing the interaction to ensure that partners are able to take turns, that they allow each other to finish, that key aspects are reflected accurately (with few negative "add ons"), and that checks are made that messages have been received correctly (i.e., that they match the spouse's intended message). As interchanges are experienced positively (perhaps for the first time in a long while), couples often soften their nonverbal behavior (e.g., they move from anger to tears). The therapist might set the couple up with a couple of nonalcohol-related issues to practice with over the week and encourage the couple to audiotape the discussion for review in the following session. In this instance, the therapist may help the couple pinpoint the time, place, and materials needed to achieve this.

Among couples with alcohol problems, criticism can sometimes have a highly contemptuous edge. In our clinical experience, contemptuous behaviors are often a sharp-edged reaction to existential crises for each partner, such as feeling alone or not feeling valued. These are important feelings to let out in the presence of the partner. However, the therapist may use Rogerian-style counseling to elicit the underlying themes of the anger/contempt. This may help the partner understand why their partner reacts so strongly and offer the opportunity to model effective listening and support. Later in this chapter, adaptations to traditional BCT approaches are discussed that focus on eliciting vulnerable themes underlying intense anger and contempt.

For couples with a recent history of crisis, there are likely to be problems that are beyond the scope of simple resolutions and requests for change. For example, there may be difficulties with parenting, meeting financial obligations, worries about work performance, and unresolved legal issues (e.g., charges for offenses involving alcohol). The therapist may need to work with the couple to define the problems in terms that are solvable, generate possible solutions, weigh up the positives and negatives, arrive at an agreement, and develop some concrete ways of knowing there has been movement on a problem. As part of the solution generation, the therapist may recommend consultations with other professionals (e.g., seeing a financial consultant or a lawyer). In some ABCT approaches, a more structured educational approach to problem solving is taken. For example, couples receive education on the conventional steps to problem solving (defining the problem, generating ideas, examining the "fors and againsts" of each potential solution, making a plan to enact the solution, and following up on progress). Whether or not the therapist engages in a more generic education of couples in problem solving may depend on their existing skills. A good way of assessing their existing problem-solving skills is to explore previous problems (in and outside the relationship) and examine how these problems were addressed.

As couples negotiate a new life without alcohol problems, intense conflict is likely to surface. Old hurts and fears may result in couples losing the capacity to engage in effective communication and problem solving. The therapist may work with the couple to pinpoint risky times for talking about problems, early signs that strong anger is building, particularly sensitive topics that may need careful rescheduling, possibly to therapy sessions. For couples with alcohol problems, a drinking incident is inevitably a critical risk situation. In this case, discussions may need termination and prioritization given to the lapse/relapse plan (see earlier discussion). It is crucial that the female spouse has an action plan for potentially violent or violent situations should there be a history of this sort of behavior in the relationship. As part of the routine assessment of violence risk, the female partner may need specific advice and planning on how to detect early warning signals and establish an escape plan (e.g., having a safe place to go to).

HOW WELL DOES ABCT WORK?

Recent narrative reviews (e.g., O'Farrell & Fals-Stewart, 2003) and meta-analytic reviews (e.g., Powers, Vedel, & Emmelkamp, 2008) conclude that ABCT has better outcomes than individual-based treatment for alcoholism, and indeed other drug use problems. Based on 12 randomized controlled trials of BCT (8 relating to alcohol and 4 relating to other substance abuse), Powers et al. (2008) found that ABCT outperformed controlled conditions when all follow-up time points were combined. When results were assessed for specific post-therapy time points, results were somewhat different. Specifically, ABCT produced improvements in relationship satisfaction at post-treatment, but did not result in improvements in the frequency or consequences of alcohol/substance use relative to control conditions. At follow-up, ABCT retained its superiority in terms of elevated relationship satisfaction, but also showed better outcomes on alcohol/substance use measures at later follow-ups. As noted earlier, ABCT programs contain some variability in therapeutic factors that may differentially account for positive findings. For example, three studies reviewed by Powers et al. (2008) included naltrexone or disulfiram in the couple conditions and not others. However, Powers and colleagues found that the effect sizes for BCT with and without these medication regimes were comparable. These authors conclude that the improvements in relationship satisfaction evident at the end of therapy may provide a context for improved substance-related gains in the longer term.

In general, ABCT has been used with couples in which only one partner (typically the male) is the identified drinker and the alcohol problems are moderate to severe. It is less clear how well ABCT works for couples where both partners have substance abuse problems and how well ABCT works for problem drinkers (as opposed to alcohol-dependent people). O'Farrell and Fals-Stewart (2006) recommend that a couples approach is contraindicated when both partners have substance abuse problems. Preliminary research suggests that ABCT may not be any more efficacious than alcohol-focused spouse involvement for people with mild to moderate alcohol problems. Walitzer and Dermen (2004) compared BCT (group format) to alcohol-focused spouse involvement and treatment for problem drinkers only. For those whose partners participated, identified drinkers reported fewer heavy drinking days and more abstinence/light drinking days in the year following treatment relative to treatment for problem drinkers only. However, the combination of alcohol-focused spouse involvement and BCT yielded no better outcomes than alcohol-focused spouse involvement alone. More research is needed on the utility of ABCT for problem drinkers. It is possible that couples with less severe alcohol problems may also have less severe couple relationship problems, so ABCT-related improvements may not be as marked. It is also possible that these couples may have more circumscribed problems than those with severe alcohol problems and that a tailored ABCT program to meet circumscribed relationship issues might yet prove effective. It would be surprising if such couples approaches were not helpful to couples with less severe alcohol problems, but this remains an empirical question yet to be tested.

SOME CRITICISMS OF THE ABCT APPROACH

Traditional BCT approaches have been criticized because the model is based heavily on the assumptions that couple relationship distress is the result of an absence in certain interactional skills, and that if couples acquire these skills, relationship satisfaction will increase. There are some potential caveats/challenges to these assumptions. The first caveat is that some people in distressed relationships may have excellent communication skills, but for various reasons are unmotivated or unable to use them with their partner when needed. For example, Burleson and Denton (1997) found that maritally distressed males had good skills in predicting how their messages would affect their partners, and these authors suggested that such skills may be used to cause pain or distress. Consistent with the possibility that communication behaviors may have functional or strategic value, conversational withdrawal is common among maritally distressed males and may be a way of maintaining a relationship power structure that they have a low investment in changing (Heavey, Christensen, & Malamuth, 1995).

Providing extensive communication skills training to such couples may be demotivating, and, for some couples, this may actually serve to sharpen the communication-based weapons available to fight the partner if the underlying themes driving the conflict are not addressed. As a consequence of its focus on the skills-deficit model, ABCT is arguably at risk of deemphasizing powerful emotional states (e.g., hurt, shame, guilt, anger) that override the use of communication skills. This is not to say that the structure and processes of communication skills training are not useful—we often conceptualize the structure and processes of communication skills training as a set of useful tools for uncovering and addressing underlying negative emotions rather than an end in itself. As it stands presently, ABCT may benefit from a more in-depth assessment of skills availability versus intent, and a greater modulation of communication skills training in response to this assessment. A more clinically flexible model is recommended, where strategies such as communication skills training are viewed as modules rather than core components of therapy.

A second concern relates to the skills we try to impart to couples receiving ABCT. Communication skills training has typically been based on active listening and problem-solving skill models (see Kelly et al., 2003). For example, ABCT targets marital communication by training couples in the use of "I statements," turn taking, reflecting and clarifying the partner's requests, and expressing problems noncritically. Problem-solving training includes behavioral operationalization of the problem, generating alternative solutions, agreeing on a solution, and implementing the solution. It seems that these skills are not especially common among happy couples (Kelly, Halford, & Young, 2002) and that improvements in key behaviors such as self-disclosure are unrelated to improvements in relationship satisfaction (Johnson & Talitman, 1997). Arguably, there is something potentially odd about training unhappy couples in skills that their satisfied counterparts use rather infrequently. Of course, just because most happy couples may not use these sorts of communication skills does not mean that this sort of communication skills training may not be helpful. While real couples do not seem to fit our communication models particularly well, such interventions may ensure the maximization of positive reinforcement and the minimized likelihood of punishment.

Physical violence is common in couples where one partner is drinking heavily, and there is much debate about the appropriateness of couples' interventions for couples where violence is evident. There is a strong association between male-perpetrated intimate partner violence and alcohol problems, with about 50–60% violence prevalence in the year before alcohol treatment (O'Farrell et al., 2004). The debate about the appropriateness of couples therapy where violence is evident centers on the potential disempowerment of the victim (usually the female partner). A couples approach can implicitly diffuse responsibility for violence away from the offending partner, muffle the victim because of fear or intimidation, and potentially cue violent behavior after therapy sessions (Galvani, 2007).

Other theorists/researchers argue that there is variation in couple dynamics around the occurrence of violence within couples and that ABCT may be appropriate for some dynamics and not others. O'Farrell and Fals-Stewart (2006) argue that most violence in couples with alcohol problems results from escalations in conflict that result in mild-to-moderate mutual physical aggression; these couples do not show significant patterns of intimidation, fear, and self-defense. ABCT may be appropriate and helpful for these couples in reducing violence, as well as for alcohol and relationship problems. O'Farrell and Fals-Stewart have data to support this assertion (O'Farrell et al., 2004; Birchler & Fals-Stewart, 2003). In the years after receiving ABCT, violence decreased significantly from initial prevalence rates (60%) to 24%, and ABCT combined with individual counseling was found to reduce violence more than individual counseling alone (Birchler & Fals-Stewart, 2003). In contrast, a minority of couples (around 2%) evidence "patriarchal terrorism," which is characterized by severe male-to-female aggression (punching, using weapons), domination and control behaviors on the part of the male, fear and intimidation on the part of the female partner, with female-to-male violence occurring primarily as a form of self-defense (O'Farrell & Fals-Stewart, 2006). ABCT is contraindicated for these couples, and referral to individual therapy/legal advice is warranted.

Galvani (2007) argues that ABCT inclusion criteria with respect to violence are too liberal. It is argued on ethical/safety grounds that a more conservative inclusion criterion should be used (e.g., infrequent low-level physical aggression with minimal risk of physical harm). In any case, ABCT (including O'Farrell and Fals-Stewart's model) takes a strong explicit stance against violent behavior. Couples at risk of mild to moderate physical aggression should understand and commit to a contract of nonviolence, reviews of nonviolence agreements should occur at each session, and strategies to protect the partner from injury should be discussed and enacted.

EXPANDING ABCT TO FIT INNOVATIONS IN EFT

A theme of this chapter relates to the challenges of dealing with powerful emotional distress underlying difficulties with communicating, managing conflict, and resolving problems. Previous references have been made to the emotional distress of the partner of the problem drinker, but it is also well established that anger and resentment are at far higher levels in people with alcohol and other substance use problems than the general population (Reilly et al., 1994) and that these states are potent triggers of relapse (Marlatt & Gordon, 1985). Theorists in and outside the addiction area propose that intense negative feelings between partners arise from existentially oriented crises of trust and security and that forgiveness can be an important step in improving relationship quality and communication (Fincham, Beach, & Davila, 2007; Lin et al., 2004; Makinen & Johnson, 2006). For example, longitudinal studies on couple relationships show that for women, forgiveness of male partner transgressions is associated with later improvements in conflict resolution, after accounting for initial levels of conflict resolution (Fincham et al., 2007). These findings seem likely to apply to alcohol-related transgressions. Fincham and colleagues suggest that forgiveness may be one way of "short circuiting" ineffective conflict management.

A number of forgiveness-oriented approaches have been developed in recent years. One such approach, emotion-focused therapy (EFT; Johnson & Greenberg, 1985b), is a brief psychodynamically oriented approach to couples therapy that emphasizes the acknowledgement and expression of intense and uncomfortable emotional themes, and the breaking down of rigid and constricted negative cycles of interaction. The themes are typically around existential vulnerability, such as aloneness, rejection, fear, and are unearthed and experienced in the safety of a Rogerian-style counseling format with the partner present (Greenberg, Ford, Alden, & Johnson, 1993; Johnson & Greenberg, 1985a,b). Makinen and Johnson (2006) integrate forgiveness processes into EFT by providing a context in which the offending partner witnesses the expression of this vulnerability, understands its significance, acknowledges responsibility for his/her role in the pain, and expresses empathy and remorse. The hurt partner then asks for the support and caring that were previously unavailable, and the offending partner tries to do this. The process is designed to reexperience a secure bond and to initiate a rebuilding of trust—two goals crucial to forgiveness.

The potential value of forgiveness-oriented interventions for couples with alcohol and relationship problems is rather obvious at a clinical level; empirically, good data support its inclusion in ABCT interventions. First, EFT has received considerable empirical attention and has been found to be at least as effective in treating relationship distress as BCT (Johnson, Hunsley, Greenberg, & Schindler, 1999; Denton, Burleson, Clark, Rodriguez, & Hobbs, 2000). Second, communication skills training has been found to be more effective when delivered following a program of EFT (James, 1991). Third, forgiveness predicts improved conflict management; by enabling forgiveness in couples with alcohol problems, communication problems may be resolved or at least be improved substantially. Perhaps the current focus on skills-deficit models of communication training may be usefully reformulated to better address forgiveness needs in couples with alcohol problems. Such a reformulation may also have the additional benefit of improving the face validity of communication-oriented components of ABCT as experienced by couples.

CONCLUSIONS

Alcohol behavioral couples therapy remains the most systematically evaluated and validated couples-based therapy for the treatment of couples where one partner has alcohol problems, with evidence that it has significant long-term benefits for couples over individual interventions. Couples approaches are difficult to implement, in part because identified drinkers are often resistant to participation. Nevertheless, ABCT, by virtue of its various delivery modes (i.e., the various levels in which each partner may be involved), can be adapted readily to the presenting problems of couples affected by alcohol problems and usually complements standard treatment programs well. ABCT has typically been a highly structured approach that draws on traditional behavioral couple interventions. There is debate about the need for ABCT to update its emphasis on skills-deficit models of communication to better address underlying and intense negative emotions that drive conflict and override potentially preexisting skills. EFT is a couples approach that lends itself well to couples where there has been intense hurt and ongoing anger and has proven itself as efficacious as traditional BCT. ABCT may fit better with what we know about happy couple relationships and the realities of couples affected by alcohol if EFT-based, forgiveness-oriented approaches are incorporated. This is an area for further research.

ACKNOWLEDGMENT

This study was funded in part by a Career Development Award from the National Health and Medical Research Council.

REFERENCES

Barber, J. G., & Crisp, B. R. (1995). The "pressures to change" approach to working with the partners of heavy drinkers. *Addiction*, *90*, 269–276.

Birchler, G. R., & Fals-Stewart, W. (2003). Does reduced conflict during treatment mediate the effect of BCT on partner violence after treatment among male alcoholics? *In a symposium conducted at the annual meeting of the Association for the Advancement of Behavior Therapy.* Boston.

Burleson, B. R., & Denton, W. H. (1997). The relationship between communication skill and marital satisfaction: Some moderating effects. *Journal of Marriage and the Family*, *59*, 884–902.

Cohan, C. L., & Bradbury, T. N. (1997). Negative life events, marital interaction, and the longitudinal course of newlywed marriage. *Journal of Personality and Social Psychology*, *73*, 114–128.

Denton, W. H., Burleson, B. R., Clark, T. E., Rodriguez, C. P., & Hobbs, B. V. (2000). A randomized trial of emotion-focused therapy for couples in a training clinic. *Journal of Marital and Family Therapy*, *26*, 65–78.

Fincham, F. D., Beach, S. R. H., & Davila, J. (2007). Longitudinal relations between forgiveness and conflict resolution in marriage. *Journal of Family Psychology*, *21*(3), 542–545.

Galvani, S. A. (2007). Safety in numbers? Tackling domestic abuse in couples and network therapies. *Drug and Alcohol Review*, *26*, 175–181.

Greenberg, L. S., Ford, C. L., Alden, L. S., & Johnson, S. M. (1993). In-session change in emotionally focused therapy. *Journal of Consulting and Clinical Psychology*, *61*(1), 78–84.

Halford, W. K., Price, J., Kelly, A. B., Bouma, R., & Young, R. McD. (2001). Helping the wives of men who abuse alcohol: A comparison of the effects of three treatments. *Addiction*, *96*, 1497–1508.

Heavey, C. L., Christensen, A., & Malamuth, N. M. (1995). The longitudinal impact of demand and withdrawal during marital conflict. *Journal of Consulting and Clinical Psychology*, *63*, 797–801.

Jacobson, N. S., & Addis, A. (1993). Research on couples and couple therapy. What do we know? Where are we going? *Journal of Consulting and Clinical Psychology*, *61*, 85–93.

James, P. S. (1991). Effects of a communication training component added to an emotionally focused couples therapy. *Journal of Marital and Family Therapy*, *17*, 263–275.

Johnson, S., & Greenberg, L. (1985a). Emotionally focused couples therapy: An outcome study. *Journal of Marital & Family Therapy*, *11*, 313–317.

Johnson, S., & Greenberg, L. (1985b). The differential effectiveness of experiential and problem solving interventions in resolving marital conflict. *Journal of Consulting & Clinical Psychology*, *53*, 175–184.

Johnson, S. M., Hunsley, J., Greenberg, L., & Schindler, D. (1999). Emotionally focused couples therapy: Status and challenges. *Clinical Psychology: Science and Practice*, *6*(1), 67–79.

Johnson, S. M. V., & Talitman, E. (1997). Predictors of success in emotionally focused marital therapy. *Journal of Marital and Family Therapy*, *23*, 135–152.

Kelly, A. B., Fincham, F. D., & Beach, S. R. H. (2003). Communication skills in couples: A review and discussion of emerging perspectives. In J. O. Greene & B. R. Burleson (Eds.), *The handbook of communication and social interaction skills* (pp. 723–752). Mahwah, NJ: Lawrence Erlbaum.

Kelly, A. B., Halford, W. K., & Young, R. McD. (2002). Couple communication and problem drinking: A behavioral observation study. *Psychology of Addictive Behaviors*, *16*, 269–271.

Lin, W., Mack, D., Enright, R. D., Krahn, D., & Baskin, T. W. (2004). Effects of forgiveness therapy on anger, mood, and vulnerability to substance use among inpatient substance-dependent clients. *Journal of Consulting and Clinical Psychology*, *72*(6), 1114–1121.

Makinen, J. A., & Johnson, S. M. (2006). Resolving attachment injuries in couples using emotionally focused therapy: Steps toward forgiveness and reconciliation. *Journal of Consulting and Clinical Psychology*, *74*(6), 1055–1064.

Marlatt, G. A., & Gordon, J. R. (1985). *Relapse prevention: Maintenance strategies in the treatment of addictive behaviors*. New York: Guilford Press.

Miller, W. R., & Rollnick, S. (1996). *Motivational interviewing: Preparing people to change addictive behavior*. New York: Guilford Press.

O'Farrell, T. J., & Fals-Stewart, W. (2003). Alcohol abuse. *Journal of Marital and Family Therapy*, *29*, 121–126.

O'Farrell, T. J., & Fals-Stewart, W. (2006). *Behavioral couples therapy for alcoholism and drug abuse*. New York: Guilford Press.

O'Farrell, T., Murphy, C. M., Stephan, S. H., Fals-Stewart, W., & Murphy, M. (2004). Partner violence before and after couples-based alcoholism treatment for male alcoholic patients: The role of treatment involvement and abstinence. *Journal of Consulting and Clinical Psychology*, *72*, 202–217.

Powers, M. B., Vedel, E., & Emmelkamp, P. M. G. (2008). Behavioral couples therapy (BCT) for alcohol and drug use disorders: A meta-analysis. *Clinical Psychology Review*, *28*, 952–962.

Reilly, P. M., Clark, H. W., Shopshire, M. S., Lewis, E. W., & Sorenson, D. J. (1994). Anger management and temper control: Critical components of post-traumatic stress disorder and substance abuse. *Journal of Psychoactive Drugs*, *26*, 401–407.

Walitzer, K. S., & Derman, K. H. (2004). Alcohol-focused spouse involvement and behavioral couples therapy: Evaluation of enhancements to drinking reduction treatment for male problem drinkers. *Journal of Consulting and Clinical Psychology*, *72*, 944–955.

Chapter | thirteen

Contingency Management and the Community Reinforcement Approach

Stephen T. Higgins and Randall E. Rogers
Departments of Psychiatry and Psychology, University of Vermont

SUMMARY POINTS

- A fundamentally important discovery made in the 1960s was that drugs that humans abuse function as positive reinforcers in laboratory animals just as do food, water, and sex. This discovery situated drug use within the domain of learning and conditioning theory and was an important starting point for a scientific analysis of substance use disorders.
- Laboratory and clinical research on substance use disorders within that theoretical framework provides compelling evidence for the notion that drug use should be considered a normal, learned behavior. Within this framework, all humans are assumed to have the potential to develop substance use disorders (SUDs), although certain individual and family histories can increase risk significantly.
- The community reinforcement approach (CRA)+ vouchers intervention is based on this learning and conditioning conceptual framework, with special emphasis on operant conditioning.

Evidence-Based Addiction Treatment

- Treatments developed within this framework are designed to systematically increase the availability and frequency of alternative reinforcing activities either through naturalistic sources of reinforcement as in the CRA or relatively contrived sources of reinforcement as in contingency management (CM) interventions.
- Following demonstrations of the efficacy of the CRA+ vouchers treatment for cocaine dependence, there was a substantial increase in research demonstrating the efficacy of CM for treatment of a wide range of different SUDs.
- CM interventions have been shown to be effective with a variety of different types of substance use disorders, including cocaine, opiates, marijuana, nicotine, and alcohol, and in special populations, including pregnant women, adolescents, and persons with other serious mental illness.

INTRODUCTION

Community reinforcement approach (CRA) therapy and contingency management (CM) interventions for substance use disorders (SUDs) are based in learning and conditioning theory. Operant conditioning is especially fundamental to these treatment approaches, which is the study of how systematically applied environmental consequences alter the frequency and patterning of voluntary behavior (Mazur, 2002).

The study of SUDs within an operant conditioning framework began in earnest in the 1960s and early 1970s (Schuster & Thompson, 1969). Evidence from studies conducted with laboratory animals, humans residing in controlled research settings, and humans seeking treatment for SUDs converged in supporting the operant nature of drug use. In studies with laboratory animals, subjects fitted with intravenous catheters readily learned arbitrary behavioral responses such as pressing a lever or pulling a chain when the consequence for doing so was the delivery of an injection of a commonly abused drug (e.g., morphine or cocaine). Injections of drugs that humans rarely abuse (e.g., chlorpromazine) or saline failed to generate or maintain responding. Residential studies provided strong evidence that drug use was sensitive to environmental consequences even among individuals with severe SUDs (Bigelow, Griffiths, & Liebson, 1975). Initial studies with treatment seekers typically involved demonstrations that systematically applied environmental consequences for achieving therapeutic targets improved treatment outcome (Miller, Hersen, & Eisler, 1974). These studies illustrated the clinical implications of the emerging body of evidence supporting the operant nature of SUDs.

Overall, this body of studies provided the empirical foundation for a conceptual model wherein drug use is considered a normal, learned behavior that falls along a continuum ranging from little use and few problems to excessive use and many untoward effects (Higgins, Heil, & Lussier, 2004a). The same principles of learning and conditioning are assumed to operate across this continuum. Within this framework, all humans are assumed to have the potential to develop SUDs. Particular genetic vulnerabilities, family histories, or other psychiatric problems affect the probability of developing SUDs, but are not considered to be necessary characteristics for SUDs to emerge.

CONCEPTUALIZING TREATMENT

Treatments developed within an operant framework are designed to reorganize the user's environment to systematically (a) increase the rate of reinforcement obtained while abstinent from drug use and (b) reduce or eliminate the rate of reinforcement obtained through drug use and associated activities. Primary emphasis is placed on decreasing drug use by systematically increasing the availability and frequency of alternative reinforcing activities either through naturalistic sources of reinforcement as in CRA therapy or relatively contrived sources of reinforcement as in CM interventions (Higgins, 1996).

Some treatments, such the CRA+ vouchers treatment for cocaine dependence (Budney & Higgins, 1998; Higgins et al., 1991), are designed to deliver contrived consequences during the initial treatment period, with a transition to more naturalistic sources later in treatment. The rationale for that sequence is that the contrived sources of alternative reinforcement delivered through CM are designed to promote initial abstinence, thereby allowing time for therapist and patient to work toward reestablishing more naturalistic alternatives (e.g., job, stable family life, participation in self-help and other social groups that reinforce abstinence) that will contribute to longer term abstinence.

For whatever reason, some patients may have behavioral repertoires that are too limited to recruit sufficient sources of naturalistic reinforcement to compete effectively with drug use; as such, these patients will need some form of maintenance treatment involving contrived reinforcement contingencies in order to sustain long-term abstinence. Certainly that is widely recognized with opioid-dependent individuals who often need a maintenance pharmacotherapy in order to sustain long-term abstinence from illicit drug use. Similarly, others may need lifelong participation in self-help programs (e.g., Alcoholics or Narcotics Anonymous) or similar support groups in order to succeed (Higgins, 1996).

COMMUNITY REINFORCEMENT APPROACH

The specific content of CRA will vary depending on the population being treated. However, the overarching goal of systematically changing the patient's environment to reinforce abstinence from substance use remains a constant.

The CRA component of the CRA+ vouchers treatment developed to treat cocaine dependence in outpatient settings has seven components that are outlined briefly here (for more details, see Budney & Higgins, 1998). First, patients are taught to recognize antecedents and consequences of their cocaine use, that is, how to functionally analyze the conditions under which their cocaine use occurs. Associated with this, patients are counseled in how to restructure their daily activities in order to minimize contact with known antecedents of cocaine use, to find alternatives to the positive consequences of cocaine use, and to make the negative consequences of cocaine use explicit.

Second, patients are counseled in how to develop a new social network that will support a healthier lifestyle and getting involved with recreational activities that are enjoyable and do not involve cocaine or other drug use. Systematically developing and maintaining contacts with "safe" social networks and participation in "safe" recreational activities remains a high priority throughout treatment for the vast majority of patients. For those patients who are willing to participate, self-help groups can be an effective way to develop a new network of associates who will support a sober lifestyle.

Third, various other forms of individualized skills training are provided, usually to address some specific skill deficit that may influence a patient's risk for cocaine use directly or indirectly (e.g., time management, problem solving, assertiveness training, social skills training, and mood management).

Fourth, unemployed patients are offered Job Club, which is an efficacious method for assisting chronically unemployed individuals obtain employment (see the Job Club manual; Azrin & Besalel, 1980). For others, help is given in pursuing educational goals or new career paths.

Fifth, patients with romantic partners who are not drug abusers are offered behavioral couples therapy, which is designed to teach couples how to negotiate reciprocal contracts for desired changes in each other's behavior (O'Farrel & Fals-Stewart, 2002).

Sixth, HIV/AIDS education is provided to all patients (Heil, Sigmon, Mongeon, & Higgins, 2005). We address the potential for acquiring HIV/AIDS from sharing injection equipment and through sexual activity. Patients are given information about testing for HIV and hepatitis B and C and are encouraged to get tested. Those interested in being tested are assisted in scheduling an appointment to do so.

Seventh, all who meet diagnostic criteria for alcohol dependence or report that alcohol use is involved in their use of cocaine are offered disulfiram therapy. Disulfiram therapy is an integral part of the CRA treatment for alcoholism (Smith & Meyers, 1995) and decreases alcohol and cocaine use in clients dependent on both substances (Carroll, Nich, Ball, McCance, & Rounsavile, 1998). Patients generally ingest a 250-mg daily dose under clinic staff observation on urinalysis test days and, when possible, under the observation of a significant other on the other days. Disulfiram therapy is only effective when implemented with procedures to monitor compliance with the recommended dosing regimen.

Use of substances other than tobacco and caffeine is discouraged as well via CRA therapy. Anyone who meets criteria for physical dependence on opiates is referred to an adjoining service located within our clinic for methadone or other opioid-replacement therapy. We recommend marijuana abstinence because of the problems associated with its abuse. Importantly, though, we never dismiss or refuse to treat a patient due to other drug use.

Upon completion of the 24 weeks of treatment, patients are encouraged to participate in 6 months of aftercare in our clinic, which involves at least once-monthly brief therapy sessions and urine toxicology screening. More frequent clinic contact is recommended if the therapist or patients deem it necessary.

CONTINGENCY MANAGEMENT

The efficacy of CM interventions depends on how they are structured and implemented. In the CM component of the CRA+ vouchers treatment, vouchers exchangeable for retail items are earned contingent on cocaine-negative results in thrice-weekly urine toxicology testing. The program is 12 weeks in duration (Monday, Wednesday, and Friday). The first cocaine-negative specimen earns a voucher worth \$2.50. The value of each subsequent consecutive cocaine-negative specimen increases by \$1.25. The equivalent of a \$10 bonus is provided for each three consecutive cocaine-negative specimens. The intent of the escalating magnitude of reinforcement and bonuses is to reinforce continuous cocaine abstinence. A cocaine-positive specimen or failure to submit a scheduled specimen resets the value of vouchers back to the initial \$2.50 value. This reset feature is designed to punish relapse to cocaine use following a period of sustained abstinence. In order to provide patients with a reason to continue abstaining from drug use following a reset, a submission of five consecutive cocaine-negative specimens following a cocaine-positive specimen returns the value of points to where they were prior to the reset. Points cannot be lost once earned. No cash is ever given to patients and all purchases are made by clinic staff. If someone were continuously abstinent throughout the 12-week intervention, total earnings would be approximately $997.50. However, because most patients are unable to sustain abstinence throughout the intervention, the average earning is usually about half that maximal amount.

EMPIRICAL SUPPORT

Studies on the community reinforcement approach

The CRA was developed and researched most extensively in the treatment of alcohol-dependent adults. Subsequently, CRA was extended to the treatment of cocaine- and opioid-dependent adults, adolescents with SUDs, and families of treatment-resistant patients with SUDs.

INITIAL STUDY

The seminal CRA study was conducted with severe alcoholics admitted to a rural state hospital for the treatment of alcoholism (Hunt & Azrin, 1973). These men were divided into matched pairs, with one member of each pair being assigned randomly to receive CRA+ standard hospital care or standard care alone. Standard hospital care consisted of 25 one-hour didactic sessions involving lectures on Alcoholics Anonymous, alcoholism, and related medical problems. CRA was designed to rearrange and improve the quality of the reinforcers obtained by patients through their vocational, family, social, and recreational activities. The goal was for these reinforcers to be available and of high quality when the patient was sober and to be unavailable when drinking resumed. Plans for rearranging these reinforcers were individualized to conform to each patient's unique situation.

During the 6-month period following hospital discharge, time spent drinking was 14% for participants in CRA versus 79% for those in standard treatment, with those treated with CRA also experiencing superior outcomes on percentage time unemployed, away from home, and institutionalized (Figure 13.1).

The CRA was subsequently expanded to include disulfiram therapy, with patient significant others monitoring medication compliance; a buddy system was also added (Azrin, 1976). Outcomes achieved with this expanded form of CRA were superior to standard care in a study that followed hospitalized alcoholics for 6 months following discharge, including percentage time spent drinking (2% vs 55%), time unemployed (20% vs 56%), time away from family (7% vs 67%), and time institutionalized (0% vs 45%). The CRA group spent 90% or more time abstinent during a 2-year follow-up period; comparable data were not reported for the standard treatment group.

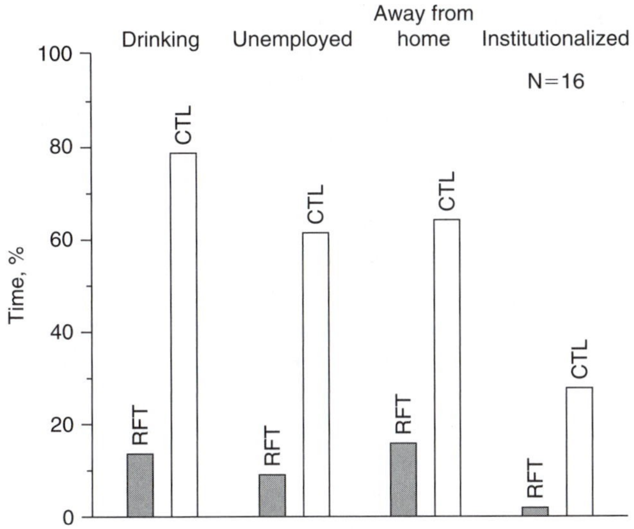

FIGURE 13.1 *Comparison of CRA and control groups on key dependent measures during the 6-months of follow-up following hospital discharge: mean percentage of time spent drinking, unemployed, away from home, and institutionalized. From Hunt and Azrin (1973), reprinted with permission.*

Azrin, Sisson, Meyers, and Godley (1982) dissociated the effects of monitored disulfiram therapy from the other aspects of CRA in the first full report on the efficacy of CRA with less-impaired outpatients. Male and female alcoholic outpatients were randomized to receive usual care plus disulfiram therapy without compliance support, usual care plus disulfiram therapy involving significant others to support compliance, or CRA in combination with disulfiram therapy and significant-other support. CRA in combination with disulfiram and compliance procedures produced the greatest reductions in drinking, disulfiram in combination with compliance procedures but without CRA produced intermediate results, and the usual care plus disulfiram therapy without compliance support produced the poorest outcome. Married patients did equally well with the full CRA treatment or disulfiram plus compliance procedures alone. Only unmarried subjects appeared to need CRA treatment plus monitored disulfiram to achieve abstinence. With these less impaired individuals, treatment group differences were noted on measures of drinking only.

EXTENDING CRA TO TREATMENT OF PATIENTS WITH COCAINE AND OPIOID USE DISORDERS

Studies on the use of CRA to treat cocaine use disorders as part of the CRA+ vouchers treatment represented, to our knowledge, the first reports on the use of CRA from investigators who were not part of the original investigative team of Azrin and colleagues. The initial two trials involved comparisons of this combined treatment to standard outpatient drug abuse counseling (Higgins et al., 1991, 1993). The first trial was 12 weeks in duration, and 28 cocaine-dependent outpatients were assigned as consecutive admissions to their respective treatment conditions. The second trial was 24 weeks in duration, and 38 cocaine-dependent patients were assigned randomly to the same two treatment conditions. Outcomes in both trials were significantly better among those treated with the CRA+ vouchers treatment than standard drug abuse counseling. In the randomized trial (Higgins et al., 1993), for example, 58% of patients assigned to CRA+ vouchers completed the recommended 24 weeks of treatment compared to 11% of those assigned to drug abuse counseling. Regarding cocaine use, 68% of those assigned to CRA+ vouchers were verified objectively to have achieved 8 or more weeks of continuous cocaine abstinence compared to only 11% of those treated with drug abuse counseling.

A randomized clinical trial examined the contributions of CRA to the combined effects of the CRA+ vouchers intervention (Higgins et al., 2003). Cocaine-dependent outpatients were assigned randomly to receive the CRA+ vouchers treatment or the vouchers component only. Vouchers were in place for 12 weeks, CRA for 24 weeks, and patients were assessed at least every 3 months for 2 years after treatment entry. Patients treated with CRA+ vouchers were retained better in treatment, used cocaine at a lower frequency during treatment but not follow-up, and reported a lower frequency of drinking to intoxication during treatment and follow-up compared with patients treated with vouchers only. Patients treated with CRA+ vouchers also reported a higher frequency of days of paid employment during treatment and 6 months of post-treatment follow-up, decreased depressive symptoms during treatment only, and fewer hospitalizations and legal problems during follow-up.

FURTHER EXTENSIONS

There has been an impressive array of other extensions of CRA therapy. In at least two trials, CRA improved treatment outcomes with opioid-dependent patients receiving opioid pharmacotherapy (Abbott, Moore, Weller, & Delaney, 1998; Bickel, Amass, Higgins, Badger, & Esch, 1997). CRA also has been extended successfully to at least two special subpopulations—adolescents (Azrin et al., 1996; Dennis et al., 2004) and the homeless (Smith, Meyers, & Delaney, 1998), including street-living adolescents (Slesnick, Prestopnik, Meyers, & Glassman, 2007).

As part of the original series of studies on CRA, Azrin and colleagues demonstrated that CRA could be adapted to effectively assist significant others in encouraging treatment-resistant alcoholics to enter treatment (Sisson & Azrin, 1986). A series of subsequent controlled trials have consistently supported the efficacy of CRA in assisting concerned significant others to get unmotivated individuals with SUDs to enter treatment (Kirby, Marlowe, Festinger, Garvey, & La Monaca, 1999; Meyers, Miller, Smith, & Tonigan, 2002).

Studies on contingency management interventions

INITIAL CM STUDIES

An impressive early CM study on SUDs was a randomized controlled trial conducted with 20 chronic public drunkenness offenders (Miller, 1975). Subjects randomized to the CM group earned housing, employment, medical care, and meals based on sobriety (measured by direct staff observation or blood alcohol level <0.01%), whereas those in the control group received the same goods and services independent of sobriety status. The intervention produced a fivefold decrease in arrests for subjects in the CM group and no or minimal change for the control group.

Another early approach to treating alcohol use disorders with CM involved reinforcing disulfiram treatment compliance (Bickel et al., 1989; Liebson, Tommasello, & Bigelow, 1978). For example, in a well-controlled study, alcoholic methadone patients whose daily methadone doses were contingent upon compliance with disulfiram spent 2% of study days drinking, as compared to 21% for the noncontingent control group (Liebson et al., 1978).

Despite these impressive results, the use of CM to treat primary alcohol use disorders has largely failed to gain a toehold within the alcohol research or clinical communities. A major obstacle is the absence of a biological marker of recent alcohol use that can be detected beyond just a few hours, which makes it difficult to systematically confirm alcohol abstinence and administer planned consequences.

DEVELOPING CM AS A TREATMENT FOR ILLICIT-DRUG USE DISORDERS

Unlike with alcohol use disorders, a concerted body of work emerged during the 1970s and 1980s on the use of CM to treat illicit-drug use disorders. That initial work was conducted almost exclusively with patients enrolled in methadone treatment for opioid use disorders. While methadone and related substitution therapies are effective at eliminating the use of illicit opioids, a subset of patients continues abusing other nonopioid drugs. A commonly used reinforcer in this area of CM research is the medication take-home privilege, where an extra daily dose of opioid medication is dispensed to the patient for ingestion at home on the following day, thereby granting the patient a break from the grind of having to travel daily to the clinic to ingest the medication under staff supervision (Milby et al., 1978; Stitzer, Iguchi, & Felch, 1992). For example, the use of take-home incentives was examined with newly admitted methadone maintenance patients in what was probably the most rigorous evaluation of the use of contingent medication take-home privileges (Stitzer et al., 1992). Half the group received take-home privileges contingent on abstinence from illicit drug use, whereas the other half received take-home doses noncontingently. Overall, 32% of the contingent patients achieved sustained periods of abstinence during the intervention (mean, 9.4 weeks; range, 5 to 15 weeks) compared with approximately 10% in the control group.

An introduction of voucher-based CM in the 1990s was associated with a substantial increase in research on the use of CM to treat SUDs (Higgins et al., 2004b). A major reason why this intervention garnered significant interest was its efficacy with cocaine use disorders. At a time when most clinical trials investigating treatments for cocaine use disorders were consistently producing negative outcomes, a series of controlled trials examining voucher-based CM produced reliably positive outcomes (Higgins et al., 1991, 1993, 1994, 2000, 2007).

The seminal voucher-based procedure was described earlier. The initial two trials involving this intervention combined voucher-based CM with CRA using research designs that did not permit a dissociation of the separate effects of the two interventions (Higgins et al., 1991, 1993). The first randomized trial designed to isolate the contribution of voucher-based CM to outcome was conducted with 40 cocaine-dependent outpatients assigned to receive CRA with or without vouchers (Higgins et al., 1994). Seventy-five percent of patients in the group with vouchers completed 24 weeks of treatment compared to 40% in the group without vouchers. The average duration of continuous cocaine abstinence in the two groups was 11.7 ± 2.0 weeks in the vouchers group versus 6.0 ± 1.5 in the no-vouchers group (Figure 13.2). In more recent randomized trials further examining the efficacy of contingent vouchers when combined with CRA, positive effects on cocaine abstinence remained discernible through post-treatment follow-up periods extending out approximately 2 years following discontinuation of the voucher program (Higgins et al., 2000, 2007).

The series of studies by Higgins and colleagues were all conducted in a clinic located in relatively rural Vermont. The seminal study demonstrating the generality of this approach to abusers residing in a large urban area examined the efficacy of the voucher program with cocaine-abusing methadone maintenance patients (Silverman et al., 1996). During a 12-week study, subjects in the experimental group ($N = 19$) received vouchers exchangeable for retail items contingent on cocaine-negative urinalysis tests. A matched control group ($N = 18$) received the vouchers independent of urinalysis results. Both groups received a standard form of outpatient drug abuse counseling. Cocaine use was reduced substantially in the experimental group, but remained relatively unchanged in the control group (Figure 13.3). The use of opiates decreased during the voucher period in contingent compared to noncontingent conditions even though the contingency was exclusively on cocaine use. Subsequent randomized trials from this same group (Silverman et al., 1998, 1999) and others (Kirby, Marlowe, Festinger, Lamb, & Platt, 1998) further demonstrated the efficacy of this approach in decreasing cocaine use among inner-city drug abusers.

Subsequent studies supported the efficacy of vouchers in promoting abstinence from cocaine and heroin use along with participation in vocational training among pregnant and recently postpartum cocaine- and opioid-dependent women (Silverman et al., 2002). Forty women who continued abusing cocaine and heroin despite receiving methadone and intensive psychosocial treatment participated. Half were randomized to a therapeutic workplace (TW) intervention, whereas the other half served as controls. Women in the TW condition earned vouchers for cocaine and heroin abstinence and for participating in vocational training. Across a 3-year period, women assigned to the therapeutic workplace sustained cocaine abstinence greater than controls (54% vs 28% negative) and opiate abstinence greater than controls (60% vs 37% negative).

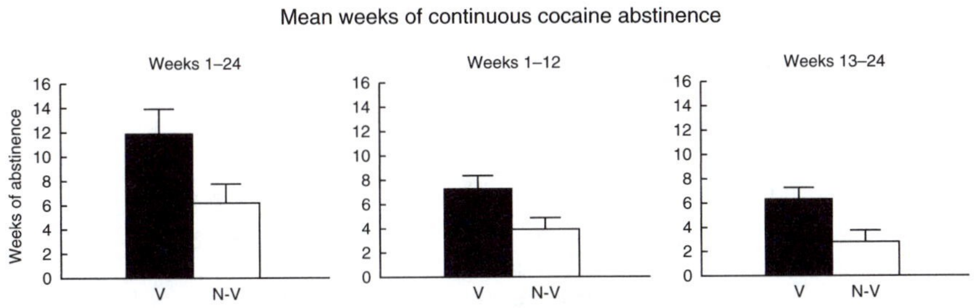

FIGURE 13.2 *Mean durations of continuous cocaine abstinence documented via urinalysis testing in each treatment group during weeks 1–24, 1–12, and 13–24 of treatment. Solid and shaded bars indicate voucher and no-voucher groups, respectively. Error bars represent ± SEM. From Higgins et al. (1994), reprinted with permission.*

FURTHER EXTENSIONS

Numerous other innovative approaches have involved CM in the treatment of SUDs (Higgins, Silverman, & Heil, 2008). In the area of illicit drug abuse, Milby and colleagues, for example, successfully combined day-treatment with access to work therapy and housing contingent on drug abstinence (Milby, Schumacher, Wallace, Freedman, & Vuchinich, 2005; Milby et al., 1996). Voucher-based CM were extended to the treatment of marijuana use disorders, including use among patients with serious mental illness (Budney, Higgins, Radonovich, & Novy, 2000; Budney, Moore, Higgins, & Rocha, 2006; Sigmon & Higgins, 2006; Sigmon, Steingard, Badger, Anthony, & Higgins, 2000).

With regard to licit substances, voucher-based CM has been extended successfully to promoting smoking cessation among pregnant women (Donatelle, Prows, Champeau, & Hudson, 2000; Heil et al., 2008; Higgins et al., 2004b). In two of those trials, for example, women received a relatively intense schedule of abstinence monitoring and voucher-based contingent reinforcement during pregnancy and 3 months postpartum (Heil et al., 2008; Higgins et al., 2004b). In both studies, approximately 40% of women assigned to receive abstinence-contingent

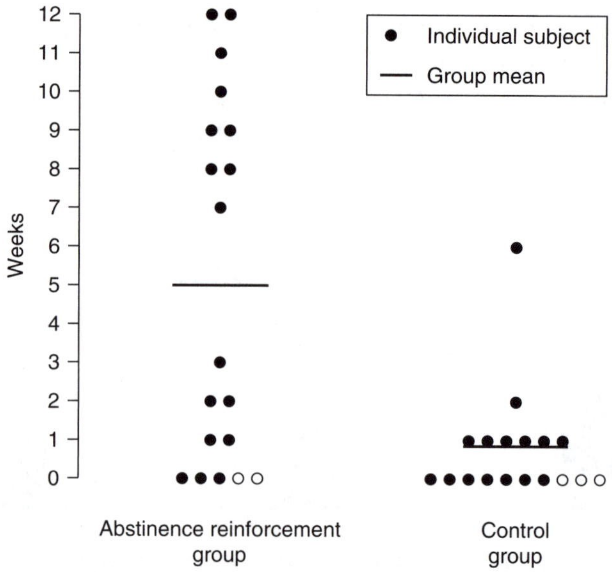

FIGURE 13.3 *Longest duration of sustained cocaine abstinence achieved during the 12-week voucher condition. Each data point indicates data from an individual subject, and lines represent group means. Subjects in the reinforcement and control conditions are displayed in the left and right columns, respectively. Open circles represent early studydrop outs. From Silverman et al. (1996), reprinted with permission.*

vouchers were abstinent at an end-of-pregnancy assessment compared to approximately 10% who received vouchers independent of smoking status (i.e., noncontingently) (Figure 13.4). Estimated fetal growth also was significantly greater in the contingent compared to the noncontingent conditions in the most recent voucher trial (Figure 13.5).

In other extensions involving licit substances, CM was extended successfully to several special populations of cigarette smokers, including adolescents (Krishnan-Sarin et al., 2006), smokers with serious mental illness (Roll, Higgins, Steingard, & McGinley, 1998; Tidey, O'Neill, & Higgins, 2002), and opioid-dependent cigarette smokers (Dunn, Sigmon, Thomas, Heil, & Higgins, 2008; Shoptaw et al., 2002). In the study that combined CM with psychosocial treatment for adolescent smokers in a school setting, for example, participants who received a 4-week CM plus cognitive behavioral therapy (CBT) intervention had more biochemically verified abstinence in weeks 1 and 4 compared to those in CBT only (Krishnan-Sarin et al., 2006). Another study examined CM for smoking in 23 adolescent smokers and found that reinforcing smoking reductions contingently for several days prior to an abstinence-based CM trial enhanced CM effects (Tevyaw et al., 2007).

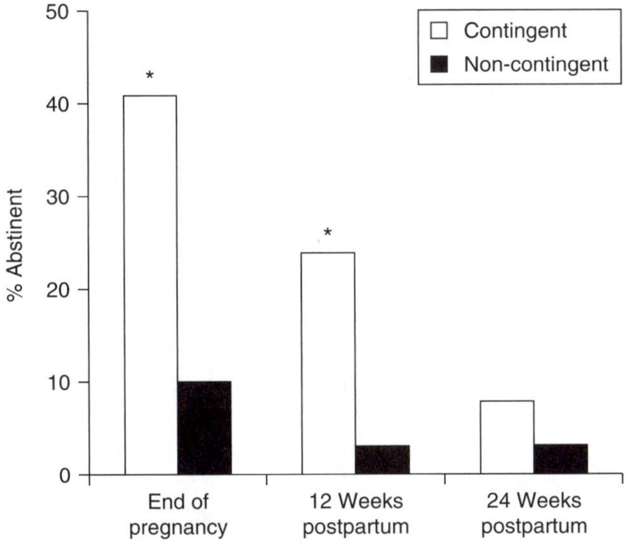

FIGURE 13.4 *Point prevalence abstinence at end of pregnancy and 12 and 24 weeks postpartum. Women in the contingent conditions (n = 37) were treated with voucher-based reinforcement contingent upon biochemically verified abstinence, whereas those in the noncontingent condition (n = 40) received vouchers independent of smoking status. An asterisk indicates significant differences between treatment conditions at p < .05. From Heil et al. (2008).*

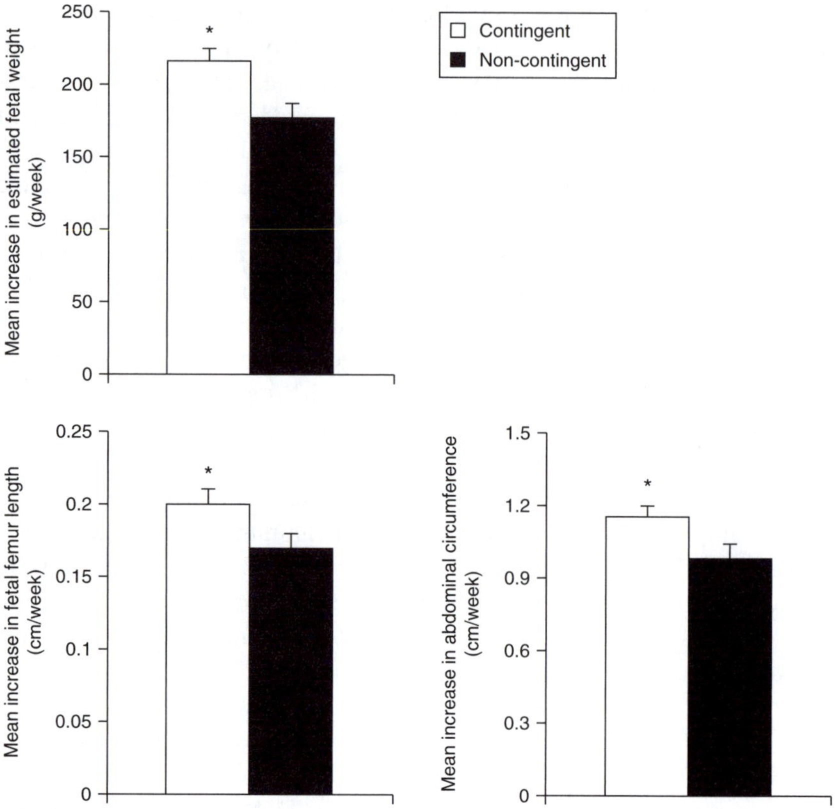

FIGURE 13.5 *Measures of fetal growth during the third trimester. Mean (± standard error) rates of growth in estimated fetal weight (top), fetal femur length (bottom left), and fetal abdominal circumference (bottom right) between ultrasound assessments conducted during the third trimester. See the legend for Figure 13.3 for a description of treatment conditions. An asterisk indicates significant differences between treatment conditions at p<.05. From Heil et al. (2008).*

CONCLUSIONS

This chapter reviewed how drug use within an operant framework is conceptualized as learned behavior that falls along a continuum ranging from light use with no problems to heavy use with many untoward effects. The same basic learning principles are assumed to operate across the drug-use continuum. The overarching goal of treatments based in this framework is to decrease the rate of reinforcement obtained through drug use and related activities by enhancing the material and social reinforcement obtained through an alternative, nondrug source of reinforcement, especially from participation in activities deemed to be incompatible with a drug-abusing lifestyle. CRA and CM procedures are based on this general strategy and offer empirically based and effective strategies for treating SUDs.

ACKNOWLEDGMENT

Preparation of this chapter was supported by Research Grants DA09378, DA08076, and DA14028 and by Training Grant DA07242 from the National Institute on Drug Abuse.

REFERENCES

Abbott, P. J., Moore, B. A., Weller, S. B., & Delaney, H. D. (1998). AIDS risk behavior in opioid dependent patients treated with community reinforcement approach and relationships with psychiatric disorders. *Journal of Addictive Diseases*, *17*, 33–48.

Azrin, N. H. (1976). Improvements in the community-reinforcement approach to alcoholism. *Behaviour Research and Therapy*, *14*, 339–348.

Azrin, N. H., Acierno, R., Kogan, E. S., Donohue, B., Besalel, V. A., & McMahon, P. T. (1996). Follow-up results of supportive versus behavioral therapy for illicit drug use. *Behaviour Research and Therapy*, *34*, 41–46.

Azrin, N. H., & Besalel, V. A. (1980). *Job club counselor's manual*. Baltimore, MD: University Park Press.

Azrin, N. H., Sisson, R. W., Meyers, R., & Godley, M. (1982). Alcoholism treatment by disulfiram and community reinforcement therapy. *Journal of Behavior Therapy and Experimental Psychiatry*, *13*, 105–112.

Bickel, W. K., Amass, L., Higgins, S. T., Badger, G. J., & Esch, R. A. (1997). Effects of adding behavioral treatment to opioid detoxification with buprenorphine. *Journal of Consulting and Clinical Psychology*, *65*, 803–810.

Bickel, W. K., Rizzuto, P., Zielony, R. D., Klobas, J., Pangiosonlis, P., Mernit, R., et al. (1989). Combined behavioral and pharmacological treatment of alcoholic methadone patients. *Journal of Substance Abuse*, *1*, 161–171.

Bigelow, G. E., Griffiths, R., & Liebson, I. (1975). Experimental models for the modification of human drug self-administration: Methodological developments in the study of ethanol self-administration by alcoholics. *Federation Proceedings*, *34*, 1785–1792.

Budney, A. J., Moore, B. A., Higgins, S., & Rocha, H. L. (2006). Clinical trial of abstinence-based vouchers and cognitive behavioral therapy for cannabis dependence. *Journal of Consulting and Clinical Psychology*, *74*, 307–316.

Budney, A. J., & Higgins, S. T. (1998). *The community reinforcement plus vouchers approach: Manual 2. National Institute on Drug Abuse therapy manuals for drug addiction.* NIH publication # 98-4308. Rockville, MD: National Institute on Drug Abuse.

Budney, A. J., Higgins, S. T., Radonovich, K. J., & Novy, P. L. (2000). Adding voucher-based incentives to coping skills and motivational enhancement improves outcomes during treatment for marijuana dependence. *Journal of Consulting and Clinical Psychology*, *68*, 1051–1061.

Carroll, K. M., Nich, C., Ball, S. A., McCance, E., & Rounsavile, B. J. (1998). Treatment of cocaine and alcohol dependence with psychotherapy and disulfiram. *Addiction*, *93*, 713–728.

Dennis, M., Godley, S. H., Diamond, G., Tims, F. M., Babor, T., Donaldson, J., et al. (2004). The cannabis youth treatment (CYT) study: Main findings from two randomized trials. *Journal of Substance Abuse Treatment*, *27*, 197–213.

Donatelle, R. J., Prows, S. L., Champeau, D., & Hudson, D. (2000). Randomised controlled trial using social support and financial incentives for high risk pregnant smokers: Significant other supporter (SOS) program. *Tobacco Control*, *9*(Suppl. 3), III67–III69.

Dunn, K. E., Sigmon, S. C., Thomas, C. S., Heil, S. H., & Higgins, S. T. (2008). Voucher-based contingent reinforcement of smoking abstinence among methadone-maintained patients: A pilot study. *Journal of Applied Behavior Analysis*, *41*, 527–538.

Heil, S. H., Higgins, S. T., Bernstein, I. M., Solomon, L. J., Rogers, R. E., Thomas, C. S., et al. (2008). Effects of voucher-based incentives on abstinence from cigarette smoking and fetal growth among pregnant women. *Addiction*, *103*, 1009–1018.

Heil, S. H., Sigmon, S., Mongeon, J. A., & Higgins, S. T. (2005). Characterizing and improving HIV/AIDS knowledge among cocaine-dependent outpatients. *Experimental and Clinical Psychopharmacology*, *13*, 238–243.

Higgins, S. T. (1996). Some potential contributions of reinforcement and consumer-demand theory to reducing cocaine use. *Addictive Behaviors*, *21*, 803–816.

Higgins, S. T., Budney, A. J., Bickel, W. K., Foerg, F. E., Donham, R., & Badger, G. J. (1994). Incentives improve treatment retention and cocaine abstinence in ambulatory cocaine-dependent patients. *Archives of General Psychiatry*, *51*, 568–576.

Higgins, S. T., Budney, A. J., Bickel, W. K., Hughes, J. R., Foerg, F., & Badger, G. (1993). Achieving cocaine abstinence with a behavioral approach. *American Journal of Psychiatry*, *150*, 763–769.

Higgins, S. T., Delaney, D. D., Budney, A. J., Hughes, J. R., Foerg, F., & Fenwick, J. W. (1991). A behavioral approach to achieving initial cocaine abstinence. *American Journal of Psychiatry*, *148*, 1218–1224.

Higgins, S. T., Heil, S. H., Dantona, R. L., Donham, R., Matthews, M., & Badger, G. J. (2007). Effects of varying the monetary value of voucher-based incentives on abstinence achieved during and following treatment among cocaine-dependent outpatients. *Addiction*, *102*, 271–281.

Higgins, S. T., Heil, S. H., & Lussier, J. P. (2004a). Clinical implications of reinforcement as a determinant of substance use disorders. *Annual Review of Psychology*, *55*, 431–461.

Higgins, S. T., Heil, S. H., Solomon, L. J., Bernstein, I. M., Lussier, J. P., Abel, R. L., et al. (2004b). A pilot study on voucher-based incentives to promote abstinence from cigarette smoking during pregnancy and postpartum. *Nicotine & Tobacco Research*, *6*, 1015–1020.

Higgins, S. T., Sigmon, S. C., Wong, C. J., Heil, S. H., Badger, G. J., Donham, R., et al. (2003). Community reinforcement therapy for cocaine-dependent outpatients. *Archives of General Psychiatry*, *60*, 1043–1052.

Higgins, S. T., Silverman, K., & Heil, S. H. (Eds.). (2008). *Contingency management in substance abuse treatment*. New York: Guilford Press.

Higgins, S. T., Wong, C. J., Badger, G. J., Haug Ogden, D. E., & Dantona, R. L. (2000). Contingent reinforcement increases cocaine abstinence during outpatient treatment and 1-year of follow-up. *Journal of Consulting and Clinical Psychology*, *68*, 64–72.

Hunt, G. M., & Azrin, N. H. (1973). A community-reinforcement approach to alcoholism. *Behaviour Research and Therapy*, *11*, 91–104.

Kirby, K. C., Marlowe, D. B., Festinger, D. S., Garvey, K. A., & La Monaca, V. (1999). Community reinforcement training for family and significant others of drug abusers: A unilateral intervention to increase treatment entry of drug users. *Drug and Alcohol Dependence*, *56*, 85–96.

Kirby, K. C., Marlowe, D. B., Festinger, D. S., Lamb, R. J., & Platt, J. J. (1998). Schedule of voucher delivery influences initiation of cocaine abstinence. *Journal of Consulting and Clinical Psychology*, *66*, 761–767.

Krishnan-Sarin, S., Duhig, A. M., McKee, S. A., McMahon, T. J., Liss, T., McFetridge, A., et al. (2006). Contingency management for smoking cessation in adolescent smokers. *Experimental and Clinical Psychopharmacology*, *14*, 306–310.

Liebson, I. A., Tommasello, A., & Bigelow, G. E. (1978). A behavioral treatment of alcoholic methadone patients. *Annals of Internal Medicine*, *89*, 342–344.

Lussier, J. P., Heil, S. H., Mongeon, J. A., Badger, G. J., & Higgins, S. T. (2006). A meta-analysis of voucher-based reinforcement therapy for substance use disorders. *Addiction*, *101*, 192–203.

Mazur, J. E. (2002). *Learning and behavior* (5th ed). Englewood Cliffs, NJ: Prentice-Hall.

Meyers, R. J., Miller, W. R., Smith, J. E., & Tonigan, J. S. (2002). A randomized trial of two methods for engaging treatment-refusing drug users through concerned significant others. *Journal of Consulting and Clinical Psychology*, *70*, 1182–1185.

Meyers, R. J., & Smith, J. E. (1995). *Clinical guide to alcohol treatment: The community reinforcement approach*. New York: Guilford Press.

Milby, J. B., Garrett, C., English, C., Fritschi, O., & Clarke, C. (1978). Take-home methadone: Contingency effects on drug-seeking and productivity of narcotic addicts. *Addictive Behaviors*, *3*, 215–220.

Milby, J. B., Schumacher, J. E., Raczynski, J. M., Caldwell, E., Engle, M., Michael, M., et al. (1996). Sufficient conditions for effective treatment of substance abusing homeless persons. *Drug and Alcohol Dependence*, *43*, 39–47.

Milby, J. B., Schumacher, J. E., Wallace, D., Freedman, M. J., & Vuchinich, R. E. (2005). To house or not to house: The effects of providing housing to homeless substance abusers in treatment. *American Journal of Public Health*, *95*, 1259–1265.

Miller, P. M. (1975). A behavioral intervention program for chronic public drunkenness offenders. *Archives of General Psychiatry*, *32*, 915–918.

Miller, P. M., Hersen, M., & Eisler, R. M. (1974). Relative effectiveness of instructions, agreements, and reinforcement in behavioral contracts with alcoholics. *Journal of Abnormal Psychology*, *83*, 548–553.

O'Farrel, T. J., & Fals-Stewart, W. (2002). Alcohol abuse. In D. H. Sprenkle (Ed.), *Effectiveness research in marriage and family therapy* (pp. 123–161). Alexandria, VA: American Association for Marriage and Family Therapy.

Roll, J. M., Higgins, S. T., Steingard, S., & McGinley, M. (1998). Investigating the use of monetary reinforcement to reduce the cigarette smoking of schizophrenics: A feasibility study. *Experimental and Clinical Psychopharmacology*, *6*, 157–161.

Schuster, C. R., & Thompson, T. (1969). Self-administration of and behavioral dependence on drugs. *Annual Review of Pharmacology*, *9*, 483–502.

Shoptaw, S., Rotheram-Fuller, E., Yang, X., Frosch, D., Nahom, D., Jarvik, M. E., et al. (2002). Smoking cessation in methadone maintenance. *Addiction*, *97*(10), 1317–1328.

Sigmon, S. C., & Higgins, S. T. (2006). Voucher-based contingent reinforcement of marijuana abstinence among individuals with serious mental illness. *Substance Abuse Treatment*, *30*, 291–295.

Sigmon, S. C., Steingard, S., Badger, G. J., Anthony, S. L., & Higgins, S. T. (2000). Contingent reinforcement of marijuana abstinence among individuals with serious mental illness: A feasibility study. *Experimental and Clinical Psychopharmacology*, *8*, 509–517.

Silverman, K., Chutuape, M. A., Bigelow, G. E., & Stitzer, M. L. (1999). Voucher-based reinforcement of cocaine abstinence in treatment-resistant methadone patients: Effects of reinforcer magnitude. *Psychopharmacology*, *146*, 128–138.

Silverman, K., Higgins, S. T., Brooner, R. K., Montoya, I. D., Cone, E. J., Schuster, C. R., et al. (1996). Sustained cocaine abstinence in methadone maintenance patients through voucher-based reinforcement therapy. *Archives of General Psychiatry*, *53*, 409–415.

Silverman, K., Svikis, D., Wong, C. J., Hampton, J., Stitzer, M. L., & Bigelow, G. E. (2002). A reinforcement-based therapeutic workplace for the treatment of drug abuse: Three-year abstinence outcomes. *Experimental and Clinical Psychopharmacology*, *10*, 228–240.

Silverman, K., Wong, C. J., Umbricht-Schneiter, A., Montoya, I. D., Schuster, C. R., & Preston, K. L. (1998). Broad beneficial effects of reinforcement for cocaine abstinence in methadone patients. *Journal of Consulting and Clinical Psychology*, *66*, 811–824.

Sisson, R. W., & Azrin, A. H. (1986). Family-member involvement to initiate and promote treatment of problem drinkers. *Journal of Behaviour Research and Therapy*, *7*, 15–21.

Slesnick, N., Prestopnik, J. L., Meyers, R. J., & Glassman, M. (2007). Treatment outcome for street-living, homeless youth. *Addictive Behaviors*, *32*, 1237–1251.

Smith, J. E., & Meyers, R. J. (1995). The community reinforcement approach. In R. Hester & W. Miller's (Eds.), *Handbook of alcoholism treatment approaches: Effective alternatives* (2nd ed). New York: Allyn & Bacon.

Smith, J. E., Meyers, R. J., & Delaney, H. D. (1998). The community reinforcement approach with homeless alcohol-dependent individuals. *Journal of Consulting and Clinical Psychology*, *66*, 541–548.

Stitzer, M. L., Iguchi, M. Y., & Felch, L. J. (1992). Contingent take-home incentive: Effects on drug use of methadone maintenance patients. *Journal of Consulting and Clinical Psychology*, *60*, 927–934.

Tevyaw, T., Gwaltney, C., Tidey, J. W., Colby, S. M., Kahler, C. W., Miranda, R., et al. (2007). Contingency management for adolescent smokers: An exploratory study. *Journal of Child & Adolescent Substance Abuse*, *16*, 23–44.

Tidey, J. W., O'Neill, S. C., & Higgins, S. T. (2002). Contingent monetary reinforcement of smoking reductions, with and without transdermal nicotine, in outpatients with schizophrenia. *Experimental and Clinical Psychopharmacology*, *10*, 241–247.

Chapter | fourteen

How Much Treatment Does a Person Need? Self-Change and the Treatment System

Harald Klingemann

Unit of Substance Use Disorders, University Clinic, University of Zürich, Switzerland

Justyna Klingemann

Department of Alcohol and Drug Dependence, Institute of Psychiatry and Neurology, Warsaw, Poland

SUMMARY POINTS

- Treatment programs usually reach only a small fraction of their potential target groups. The assumption that change from addictive behaviors occurs within a wider framework than just professional treatment has received broad support. An analysis of the interface between professional and lay referral systems highlights the need to learn more about the large group of people who refused to accept professional help to solve their addiction problem.
- The traditional concept that resolution of addiction problems can be achieved only by abstinence is no longer tenable given the research findings on self-change and from large longitudinal surveys. The pursuit of low-risk drinking behavior has been shown to be the most frequent self-change strategy.
- The majority of addiction self-change studies indicate a better chance of natural recovery among less severe cases even though survey results show a 25% self-change rate (abstinence or low-risk drinking) also among DSM-IV-dependent cases. Cognitive appraisal and

decisional balancing processes have turned out to be "the motor of self-change" mediated by societal conditions. Maintenance of self-change is much more likely with social support from friends and family combined with a change of lifestyle in which risky behaviors lose their appeal.

- From a sociological point of view, the likelihood of self-change depends, among other factors, on the social stigmatization of addictive behaviors, media portrayals of the nature of addiction, population attitudes about the changeability of misuse and dependency, the availability of drugs, and the makeup of the treatment system.
- Clinicians are still needed and can assist self-change by minimal interventions and/or by facilitating individual appraisal processes. More specifically, therapists may assist self-change by helping set realistic objectives of change. Self-change research also informs treatment providers about the reasons why their programs are not accepted and helps them adopt a more consumer-oriented perspective.
- From a policy point of view, the frequent occurrence of self-change, coupled with the general public's lack of awareness of such recoveries, suggests that disseminating knowledge about the prevalence of self-change could be a type of intervention itself. Individuals who have achieved self-recoveries could make public declarations in order to encourage others to try the self-change process.
- Future research direction perspectives include the use of detailed case analysis to determine if lay strategies may be used in professional settings. This strategy would require an ongoing dialogue between researchers and treatment providers. Prospective longitudinal studies, including control group designs, are needed. Finally, qualitative and quantitative research strategies must be combined in a meaningful way.

PROFESSIONAL HELP AND LAY HELP—TREATMENT SYSTEMS IN CRISIS

In the recent past, addiction treatment systems have come under increasing pressure to legitimize their function and to prove their efficacy and efficiency. Treatment programs usually reach only a small fraction of their potential target groups. The assumption that change from addictive behaviors occurs within a wider framework than just professional treatment has received broad support, most recently from studies based on data from the National Epidemiologic Survey on Alcohol and Related Conditions (NESARC) (Cohen, Feinn, Arias, & Kranzler, 2007; Dawson et al., 2005; Dawson, Goldstein, & Grant, 2007; Dawson, Grant, Stinson, & Chou, 2006).

The NESARC sample consisted of 4422 individuals with prior-to-past year onset of DSM-IV alcohol dependence of which only one-quarter reported ever having sought help for alcohol problems. Approximately half of all recoveries were achieved via low-risk drinking rather than abstinence, thus questioning the traditional focus of treatment on chronic, severely dependent cases with abstinence as the only treatment goal. A return to low-risk drinking was far more common among those who recovered without treatment. Finally, in the year of the study, 28% of treated individuals compared to 24% of those who were "never treated" were still dependent (Dawson et al., 2005). However, conclusions based on these findings must be interpreted cautiously, as only prospective studies controlling for background characteristics of the study group would allow definitive conclusions about treatment effectiveness. The NESARC study leads to the notion that various degrees of use, misuse, and addiction must be linked to a treatment continuum ranging from unassisted individual change to residential specialized addiction clinics. At the same time, a range of outcome goals including abstinence as only one among various pathways out of addiction should be taken into consideration. Prominent examples of flexible treatment goals include adoption of the harm reduction approach—initially applied to illicit drug consumption only—in the area of licit drugs (see Klingemann, 2006) and the growing acceptance of controlled drinking programs (see Klingemann & Rosenberg 2009; Koerkel, 2006; Rosenberg & Melville, 2005), as well as moderation management approaches in some countries.

Faced with empirical evidence showing the efficiency of short-term, minimal interventions, inpatient programs in particular have come under increasing pressure. From an international perspective, the expansion of welfare-oriented provision of treatment has come to a halt in the 1980s and has been replaced by an increased emphasis on efficiency, cost control, and evidence-based treatments (Trinder & Reynolds, 2003). This change was accompanied by an increasing acceleration in the treatment system (Klingemann, 2000). However, the attempt to legitimize and promote addiction treatment by emphasizing its scientific basis has not led to a better outreach and acceptance of treatment. The programmatic challenge of evidence-based action has not been adopted in the daily business of addiction treatment. Furthermore, the inherent logic of empirical science implies that more findings often lead to more ambivalence and insecurity. Continuous criticism of available research findings is the driving force of science, although it increases ambivalence in professional practice (Beck, 1999; Cottorell, 1999; Klingemann & Bergmark, 2006).

Currently, treatment systems are challenged by a dwindling trust in expert knowledge, together with an increasing belief in an individual's ability to cope with problems using lay knowledge (Blendon & Benson, 2001; Brooks & Cheng, 2001). The broad acceptance of complementary and alternative medicine in the health care system illustrates this point (Easthope, Tranter, & Gill, 2000; Eisenberg et al., 1993; Furnam & Lovett, 2001). Back in the 1960s the medical sociologist Freidson (1960, 1961) pointed out that professional problem solutions compete with everyday theories and lay wisdom when people are trying to solve their problems or want to bring about change. Lay theories are often highly complex and not necessarily less useful than knowledge produced by science (see, for example, Ogborne and Smart, 2001, on the perception of moderate drinking or Furnham and Lowick, 1984, on lay theories on "alcoholism").

Keeping these societal changes in mind, the current crisis in addiction treatment systems appears to be caused by an insufficient adaptation of clinical treatment options to potential customers' needs. Expressed differently, treatment programs might not be customized to what the potential patient wants, leading to low levels of acceptance by potential consumers of the services.

An analysis of the interface between professional and lay referral systems highlights the need to learn more about the large group of people who refuse to accept professional help to solve their addiction problem. The focus of treatment research on easy-to-reach clinical populations is one of the reasons that has kept us from progressing in this area, as Orford has argued in his review entitled "Asking the right questions the right way: The need for a shift in research on psychological treatments for addiction." Increased attention to change processes as a dynamic interaction between treatment provider and patient in both clinical and nonclinical populations is at the heart of a reorientation of research in this area (Orford, 2008).

Among the key issues to be addressed are the following.

- What are the barriers keeping individuals from treatment seeking? Are we able to replicate and adopt lay strategies of quitting in professional settings?
- Which strategies of change are chosen when people with addiction problems do not rely on expert help?
- How do substance users incorporate offers of minimal intervention by professionals into their individual change process?
- What can professional treatment providers learn from laypeople changing on their own?

SELF-ORGANIZED QUITTING, SELF-CHANGE FROM ADDICTIVE BEHAVIORS

What is self-change?

The use of the term "self-change" or "spontaneous remission" is by no means restricted to addictions. Clinically, "spontaneous remission" occurs when an improvement in the state of the patient in the absence of effective treatment can be observed (Roizen, Cahalan, & Shanks, 1978). Working definitions in psychology emphasize cognitive elements of a self-initiated recovery or change in behavior (Biernacki, 1986). The sociological perspective conceptualizes self-change as quitting or interrupting a deviant pattern without formal interventions (Stall, 1983) and/or the mobilization of external resources or social capital ("self-organized quitting"). Working definitions for research typically define self-change by referring to a change in consumption behavior—or not meeting diagnostic criteria for dependence such as DSM-IV any longer—which has been accomplished without professional help or self-help groups within various time frames (e.g., John, 1982). A period of 5 years of remission is considered a relatively stable change (Bischof, Rumpf, Meyer, Hapke, & John, 2007).

Self-change research and the disease concept

The idea that the majority of problem alcohol or drug users give up their problem consumption without massive professional support usually meets with skepticism among both treatment professionals and the general population. This does not mean that professional and self-help treatment options and a differentiated treatment network are no longer needed. However, the self-change approach challenges the concept of addiction as a disease that inevitably progresses in the absence of treatment (Bergmark & Oscarsson, 1987; Burman, 1994). The controversy on abstinence versus the possibility of a return to controlled consumption illustrated the pessimistic view on an individual's chances to change without professional therapy. Commonalities between the change processes involved in individual drug and alcohol careers and "privately organized quitting processes" from nicotine dependency and eating disorders (Biernacki, 1986) usually have been ignored altogether. Therefore, for many years, questions about the possibility and frequency of "natural recoveries" and the change processes underlying them were not raised in mainstream treatment research.

However, research efforts in the area of self-change have gained momentum during the last decades. Peele (1989), a critic of the abstinence dogma and the "the diseasing of America," favors a "strength-based" or empowerment perspective. Furthermore, the increasing acceptance of the harm reduction concept in both the alcohol and drug policy (at least outside the United States) and the recognition of a wide range of outcome parameters, including quality of life and moderation, have contributed to a shift of research perspectives. The improvement of general conditions of life of target groups, for example, work and housing combined with limited low-threshold interventions, are considered as possible strategies to strengthen the individual's potential to modify addictive behavior.

Self-change studies in practice

RECRUITMENT OF SELF-CHANGERS

Reaching and studying clinical populations are relatively straightforward matters. Studying individuals who have changed on their own and who often do not feel comfortable in sharing this with others (i.e., hidden populations) represents quite a different challenge. Strategies to study natural recovery include cross-sectional or longitudinal population surveys, the analysis of official registers (e.g., police records) over time, snowball sampling techniques, the study of dropouts from waiting lists, and, used most frequently, media recruitment. Survey methods using large population samples are appropriate particularly when the central aim is to obtain rates and outcomes (e.g., abstinence, controlled drinking) of self-change. However, such methods provide little insight into the processes of change. Questions about stages of change, what triggers such processes, and what strategies self-changers use are typically addressed by qualitative studies using media recruitment and snowball sampling. In this regard, however, all methods have drawbacks. Survey methods, especially cross-sectional retrospective designs, require very large samples and lead to a rather superficial analysis of self-change. Snowball sampling mirrors social networks or subcultures and excludes subjects who have weak or no communication ties. This bias is avoided by media recruitment that reaches a wide range of community populations. Then again, media-recruited subjects tend to include more severe cases of individuals who change late in their addiction career and are most likely to choose abstinence as their goal for problem resolution (Rumpf, Bischof, Hapke, Meyer, & John, 2000).

STUDY DESIGN—VALIDITY

Ideal study designs would include the use of control groups, prospective analysis of change processes over long time intervals, and measures to ensure the validity of data. Can we believe retrospective reports of self-changers if they claim a return to controlled drinking? To tackle these issues, some studies have used collateral reports to validate data obtained from study participants and a combination of screening and extensive life history interviews to check the consistency of self-reports. Other studies, using the timeline follow-back method, have demonstrated the validity of self-reports (Sobell & Sobell, 1992; Sobell et al., 2003).

Figure 14.1 shows an example of the typical stages of research fieldwork in finding and selecting self-changers.

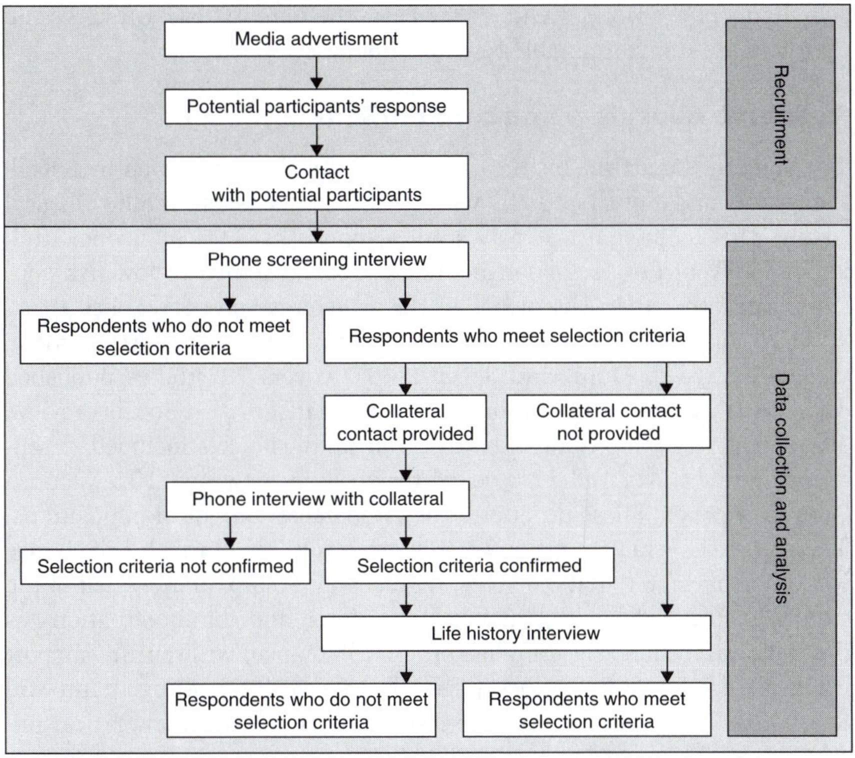

FIGURE 14.1 *Self-change studies: Typical stages of fieldwork and the selection process.*

DEFINITIONAL ISSUES

The meaning of "change in the absence of treatment" requires a working definition of what constitutes treatment (Blomqvist, 1998). In practice, some studies include individuals in the self-change category even when the respondent reports (1) minimal therapeutic intervention at any point in their life, (2) infrequent attendance at self-help groups, or (3) nonspecific interventions (hospital stay without counseling and detox, advice by a general practitioner to quit or cut down). Humphreys, Moos, and Finney (1995) argue that self-help organizations should not be considered as treatment—(1) they can be viewed as a natural community resource and way of life rather than treatment and (2) they do not require public funds or licensure. In addition to the definition of "nontreated," the severity of the addiction prior to self-change must be defined. Researchers in this area have been using various criteria; some studies have focused only on dependence, others also on abuse or harmful use of substances according to ICD-10 or DSM-IV criteria, and some on the perception of severity by study participants. A close look at definitions used is important, as critics of self-change research claim that self-changers are not dependent (at best, they are at-risk drinkers) and therefore are not comparable to clinical populations.

Research overview and core findings

The state of the art in this area of research has been reviewed by Sobell, Ellingstad, and Sobell (2000), with a special focus on methodological issues. This meta-analysis of 39 studies shows that 79% of alcohol studies and 46% of drug self-change studies report a return to low-risk consumption rather than abstinence in the self-change process (Sobell et al., 2000). A follow-up review by Carballo, Secades-Villa, Fernández-Hermida, García-Rodríguez, Dum, and Sobell (2007) covers 22 studies published between 1999 and 2005 and provides a comparison with Sobell's review. The average duration of the addiction careers of subjects included in self-change studies averaged 12.8 years in Sobell's review and 10.9 years in Carballo's paper. These durations are comparable to clinical populations. The reported average duration of problem resolution through self-change was, on average, 8.0 and 6.3 years, respectively. Approximately half of the studies mentioned health, financial situations, and family situations as the most important triggering factors in self-change, with family support being pivotal for maintenance (Carballo et al., 2007). Klingemann and Sobell (2007) provide the most up-to-date collection of review articles on self-change. This text looks at the field from an international perspective and applies the self-change approach beyond the classic addiction field to nonsubstance-related addictions such as gambling, the desistance from crime, and natural recovery from eating disorders and speech impairments.

Based on these works, the major core findings and research themes include the following.

- The traditional concept that the resolution of addiction problems can be achieved only by abstinence is no longer tenable given the research findings on self-change and recent findings from the NESARC studies mentioned earlier. The pursuit of low-risk drinking behavior has been shown to be the most frequent self-change strategy.
- The majority of addiction self-change studies indicate a better chance of natural recovery among less severe cases (e.g., Cunningham, Blomqvist, Koski-Jännes, & Cordingley, 2005), even though NESARC results show a 25% self-change rate (abstinence or low-risk drinking) among DSM-IV-dependent cases (Dawson et al., 2005).
- Cognitive appraisal and decisional balancing processes, including affective pros and cons for a behavior change, have turned out to be "the motor of self-change" mediated by societal conditions

(e.g., stigma) that facilitate or impede change (Klingemann & Sobell, 2007).

- Maintenance of self-change is much more likely with social support from friends and family (Cloud & Granfield, 2004) combined with a change of lifestyle in which risky behaviors lose their appeal.
- Clinicians are still needed and can assist self-change by minimal interventions and/or by facilitating individual appraisal processes (e.g., Tubman,Wagner, Gil, & Pate, 2002; see overview by Heather and Stockwell, 2004). More specifically, Polivy (2001) notes that therapists may assist self-change by helping set realistic objectives of change, thus avoiding the "false hope syndrome." Self-change research also informs treatment providers about the reasons why their programs are not accepted and helps them adopt a more consumer-oriented perspective.

Figure 14.2 provides an overview of the various parameters guiding self-change processes.

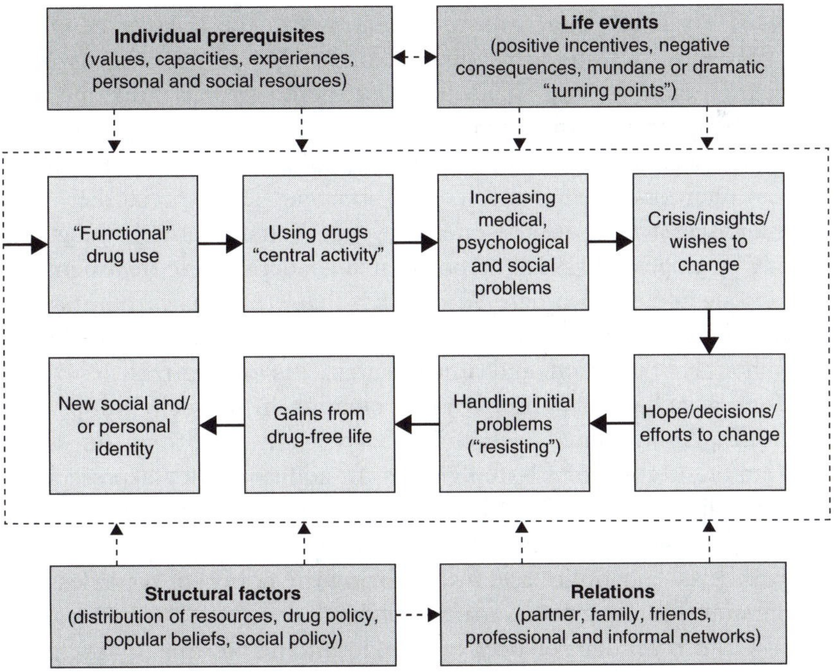

FIGURE 14.2 *Entry into and exit from drug addiction. "Inner logic" and main driving forces (Blomqvist, 2005, p. 159).*

Selected issues

BARRIERS TO TREATMENT

Researchers studying natural recovery have identified various barriers to treatment seeking by addicted individuals. Tucker and Vuchinich (1994) list the following reasons for avoiding treatment even among individuals who are willing to change: potential embarrassment (66%), concerns about stigma or being labeled as an alcoholic (63%), not wanting to share personal problems (58%), negative attitudes toward treatment or hospitals in general (53%), and cost of treatment (13%). Surprisingly, local availability of programs was considered of no importance. Luoma et al. (2007; Luoma, Kohlenberg, Hayes, Bunting, & Rye, 2008) found high levels of stigma, both self-imposed and imposed by the treatment system, among patients in 15 U.S. substance abuse treatment centers. Furthermore, the authors note that "experiences with stigma-related rejection continued to be related to number of previous episodes of treatment even after controlling for other explanatory variables" (Luoma et al., 2007). This study among patients in treatment mirrors the negative view of self-changers toward professional treatment. While information about treatment options is easily available and not usually a deterrent to treatment seeking (Copeland, 1997,1998; Klingemann, 1991), questions about the quality of treatment services and the ability of treatment providers to be sensitive to special needs are more prominent barriers to the acceptance of professional help. In a study by Klingemann (1991), respondents typically anticipate moral pressure, inadequate treatment methods, and emotional strain when entering treatment ("therapy robs you of everything...my personality would not have been worth anything anymore"). In addition, subjects mentioned self-change coping strategies (e.g., special diet; spiritual exercises), which are not offered by traditional treatment programs. A study by Copeland (1998) demonstrated gender-specific treatment barriers among addicted women. Women felt that programs with a majority of male clients were not sensitive to their problems, including child care needs, hours of operation, and time requirements for treatment.

When asked about barriers to participation in self-help groups (e.g., Alcoholics Anonymous), self-changers typically mention the strong religious orientation of 12-step groups. In addition, they express a dislike for reliving their alcoholic past instead of focusing on positive, life-changing skills. Respondents also expressed resistance to labeling themselves as "alcoholic" and internalizing the notion of powerlessness and of being a lifelong "recovering alcoholic" (Burman, 1997; Copeland, 1998). From a gender perspective, the dominance of male participants in self-help groups appears to serve as an obstacle to participation by women (Copeland, 1998).

LAY STRATEGIES OF RECOVERY

Self-changers rely on everyday behavioral concepts such as thinking about the negative effects of drugs, developing adequate substitutes for drugs, and distancing oneself physically and cognitively from drugs. More specifically, strategies mentioned in the literature include avoiding drug use environments (change of job or apartment or choosing alternative routes from work to home), eliminating consumption-related stimuli (bottles, ashtrays, syringes), leaving drug subcultures or user networks, and scheduling alternative, pleasurable activities and hobbies. In a qualitative study of self-change strategies in young adults, Finfgeld and Lewis (2002) found that self-changers tried "to seek solid ground" by engaging in school or volunteer activities, child care, writing, painting, and music, as well as abandoning drinking friends. Comparing samples of treated versus natural recovered individuals in Canada, Collins (2006) found low levels of religiousness and spirituality among current alcohol-dependent subjects, as well as among spontaneous remitters. However, a quarter of the natural recovered subjects considered spirituality important for maintenance. Pursuing a spiritual path to problem solving appears to be a more typical characteristic of 12-step programs. Self-changers typically pursue strategies of retreat (self-imposed, physical withdrawal from temptations). Some self-changers use a public pledge and commitment to change as a strategy, whereas others change without such public commitment because of frequent failure in the past and anticipatory regret at having to admit to another failure. Some self-changers report that they keep written diaries during their change, whereas others use images of the negative aspects of their previous addiction experiences.

> "This is where I put my fist through the door when I was drunk... We re-did the entire kitchen, but I left the damaged door as it was." (Burman, 1997)

Finally, "multiple resolutions" are reported by self-changers. Successful techniques of self-change in one problem area (e.g., alcohol) are often applied to other undesirable behaviors (e.g., smoking) (Burman, 1997; Klingemann, 1992; Sobell, Sobell, & Agrawal, 2002).

In summary, qualitative studies on self-change show how impressive and varied the "tool box" of self-changers is.

Trends and recent studies

The self-change concept has been applied to other problem areas, such as gambling (Toneatto et al., 2008), smoking (also cannabis) (Doran, Valenti, Robinson, Britt, & Mattick, 2006; Ellingstad, Sobell, Sobell, Eickleberry, & Golden, 2006), mental illness (Bischof, Rumpf, Meyer, Hapke, & John,

2005b), eating disorders, and criminality (Takala, 2007; overview: Klingemann & Sobell, 2007). In addition, an international perspective in self-change research is gaining ground. Outside of North America, studies have been conducted in Finland (Hänninen & Koski-Jännes, 1999, 2004), Sweden (Blomqvist, 2004), Switzerland (Klingemann, 1991; Klingemann & Aeberhard, 2004), Italy (Scarscelli, 2006), and Spain (Carballo Crespo, Secades Villa, Sobell, Fernández Hermida, & García-Rodríguez, 2004; Carballo et al., 2008).

Because of successful media recruitment strategies that attract more severe cases, self-change studies have begun to focus on addictive problems of long-term duration. Studies have also highlighted self-change processes in early stages of addiction. Vik, Cellucci, and Ivers (2003) reported that 22% of student binge drinkers managed to reduce their alcohol consumption without professional counseling. Misch (2007) suggests that researchers "… observe the natural recovery from excessive alcohol consumption among college students and then identify and extract the active ingredients of that transformation whether they be … processes involving the academic enterprise, the social structure or other variables of college life." From a more general perspective, self-resolution processes in young adulthood can be characterized as a maturing-out process and a transition to independence and adult roles (O'Malley, 2004).

Recent studies have focused increasingly on a better understanding of the process characteristics and course of natural recoveries; more specifically on cultural and group factors and dynamics.

Research on ethnic groups has stressed both commonalities and culture-specific notions related to self-change. A prominent element in the heuristic model of natural recovery among Alaskan natives (the People Awakening study) is a reference to the responsibility to the extended kinship structure (family and community) and disavowal of the notion of alcoholism as an incurable disease (Mohatt et al., 2008).

Bendek, Cory, Spicer, and Team (2004) use anthropological analysis of content to analyze reasons for reducing alcohol consumption among members of American-Indian communities. Results reflect the salient themes in the natural recovery literature, with only partial transformation of self-change processes in the specific cultural context. This study, in addition to Grant's research on "rural women's stories of recovery from addiction," illustrates strategies in the recovery process in areas with little access to treatment. From a methodological point of view, Tucker (2008) comments on the potential merits of such qualitative cultural studies: "By studying natural resolutions, the cultural and other contextual elements that motivate and sustain positive change begin to emerge with clarity not possible in studies of problem drinkers who seek help."

The heterogeneity of nontreated populations has not only been researched from an anthropological perspective in terms of cultural diversity, but also with respect to a number of background variables as predictors of problem resolution. Bischof, Rumpf, Hapke, Meyer, and John (2003) claim "...data suggest strongly that a lack of identifying specific variables of natural recovery in previous research might be due to heterogeneous subgroups of natural remitters.... both resources and stressors play an important role for processes of remission without formal help." In subsequent research they stress the importance of interaction among gender, problem severity, and social capital/social support (Bischof, Rumpf, Meyer, Hapke, & John, 2005a; Bischof et al., 2003, 2007). Cunningham and colleagues (2005) highlight group-specific aspects of the recovery process by analyzing the interaction between addiction severity and reported reasons for recovery. Based on a general population sample, they show that consequence-driven reasons (e.g., particular life events) for recovery compared to drifting-out reasons (e.g., role changes, growing older) occur significantly more frequently among lifetime alcohol-dependent cases than among less severe cases. A third recovery process characterized by "reflective maturational reasons" (e.g., not getting anywhere in life) was not sensitive to problem severity.

Group heterogeneity may also influence the course of change processes over time. Bischof and colleagues (2007) investigated in a 2-year follow-up a self-change population in Germany with an average remission from DSM-IV alcohol dependence at a baseline of 6.7 years. The majority of natural remitters remained in full remission. However, differences were apparent based on subgroups as characterized by different combinations of problems, social support, and addiction severity at baseline. The "low problem–low support" group was the most unstable, with 12.7% utilization of formal help and 6.3% with dependence symptoms compared with the "high problem–medium support" and "low problem–high support" groups, with unstable natural remissions at follow-up of 3 and 4%, respectively (Bischof et al., 2007). The authors comment that "... social support also plays an important role in individuals who remitted from less severe alcohol problems and that these individuals might be in more need to turn to formal help, when critical events take place" (Bischof et al., 2007). The stability of natural recovery from problem alcohol use among natural remitters is also shown by a 4/14-year qualitative follow-up study conducted in Switzerland (Klingemann, 1991, 1992; Klingemann & Aeberhard, 2004). Of 17 alcohol remitters interviewed in 1988, 1992, and 2002, only 4 reported relapse in 1992 but improved their consumption status again by the time of the follow-up interview in 2002 (return to controlled drinking). Of the remaining cases, only 1 respondent received treatment that was not considered helpful (Klingemann & Aeberhard, 2004). Group heterogeneity is also highlighted in this study by media-recruited subjects who considered themselves as "subjective spontaneous remitters" and who managed their alcohol problems despite the fact that they evaluated treatment exposure negatively. Along the same lines, individuals who engaged in a help-seeking process but did not receive help represent a specific subgroup that cannot be compared with remitters who never sought treatment (e.g., Moos & Moos, 2006). To conclude, the issue of group heterogeneity has methodological implications: Qualitative studies highlight the various meanings that patients attribute to treatment episodes, as well as the interaction between self-management techniques and professional help (see also Orford, 2008). This information is essential in identifying and describing change processes and mechanisms. As DiClemente (2007) states: "Treatment and any type of intervention to modify drinking behaviors enter a flowing stream of process activity and do not encounter a completely stationary object.... It is a collaborative enterprise that when successful interacts with ... the change process ... than being a mediator or mechanism which completely accounts for a change."

Finally, the field of self-change research has been dominated by an individual, psychological approach. A more recent research trend favors an interdisciplinary approach. The sociological perspective opens a view to societal, structural antecedents of individual self-change processes and asks "what are the characteristics of a self-change-friendly society?"

The likelihood of self-change depends, among other factors, on the social stigmatization of addictive behaviors, media portrayals of the nature of addiction, population attitudes about the changeability of misuse and dependency, the availability of drugs jeopardizing maintenance, and the makeup of the treatment system (consumer versus expert perspective). Recent surveys in various countries show that the disease concept of addiction is still predominant in the general population, which results in skepticism about the chances for untreated recovery or moderation (e.g., Cunningham et al., 2007; Klingemann & Klingemann, 2007).

Future research directions perspectives include the use of detailed case analysis to determine if lay strategies may be used in professional settings. This strategy would require an ongoing dialogue between researchers and treatment providers. Prospective longitudinal studies including control group designs are needed. Finally, qualitative and quantitative research strategies must be combined in a meaningful way. The use of life curve drawings, combined with narrative interviews and computer-assisted content analysis, is an excellent example of this combined approach (see Sobell et al., 2001).

CREATING A SOCIETAL CLIMATE FRIENDLY TO INDIVIDUAL CHANGE: ADVICE FOR POLICY MAKERS

Many individuals with alcohol, drug, tobacco, and gambling problems overcome their addictions without treatment. Unfortunately, awareness of this phenomenon is limited (Cunningham, Sobell, & Sobell, 1998). In this regard, efforts are needed to increase awareness among the general public that many people with addictive behaviors can change on their own. Increased awareness may also encourage friends and relatives to support self-change attempts.

The frequent occurrence of self-change, coupled with the general public's lack of awareness of such recoveries, suggests that disseminating knowledge about the prevalence of self-change could be a type of intervention itself. Individuals who have achieved self-recoveries could make public declarations in order to encourage others to try the self-change process. Efforts could also be made to inform substance abusers about the possibility that others can aid in their recovery by being supportive. Self-help manuals could be widely available and could inform addicted individuals that they may be able to recover without professional treatment. More specifically, natural contact points could be identified for disseminating information on behavior change/health information and "teachable moments" (e.g., medical-visit waiting time, pharmacists as credible reference persons). In addition, Internet health advice and expert systems should be made accessible to large segments of the population. Such policy interventions, in turn, are likely to trigger and facilitate change at the grass roots level (e.g., Mothers against Drunk Driving; Moderation Management, a self-help group for problem drinkers who did not feel comfortable with traditional self-help groups such as Alcoholics Anonymous).

Public health campaigns can be an effective means for raising public awareness. For example, community interventions, rather than targeting individuals for change efforts, could target opinion leaders, medical practitioners, and public health officials. Community-oriented interventions should be developed, including both information campaigns and treatment-umbrella or resource-umbrella organizations that assist individuals in addressing specific problems.

Drug, alcohol, and smoking campaigns are currently conducted to sensitize the public and to influence attitudes and behavior patterns of risk groups. Similar to the question "how does the amount of advertising influence consumption," we may also ask "how is the motivation for and likelihood of self-change affected by national sensitization campaigns?" Unfortunately, the conclusions presented by Wilde (1993)—from a decade ago—demonstrate that mass communication prevention programs for health are hardly ever evaluated systematically, a criticism that is still valid today.

Attempts to provide information about self-change to policy makers may evoke opposition from a number of fronts. For example, pharmaceutical companies marketing smoking-cessation products, groups seeking more recognition and treatment for recently recognized addictive problems (e.g., gambling), and advocates of traditional substance abuse treatment may be opposed. Strategies will be needed to (a) overcome resistance, (b) build coalitions, and (c) support policies derived from self-change research.

Stereotypes of alcohol (and drug) addiction in the general population can be considered major stumbling blocks to people who try to recover on their own: Stigma will reduce social support. In addition, societal beliefs about the nature and cause of social problems will shape individual and collective responses to individual self-change. How visible are these problems? How confident are we that people may eventually change their eating disorders, heroin or alcohol use, or pathological gambling on their own?

The answers to these questions will depend on the overall attitudes toward the addiction paradigms that prevail in societies. Are addictive behaviors seen as medical problems, social problems, or criminal/moral issues?

REFERENCES

Beck, U. (1999). *World risk society*. Cambridge: Polity Press.

Bendek, M., Cory, C., Spicer, P., & Team, A.-S. (2004). Documenting natural recovery in American-Indian drinking behavior: A coding scheme. *Journal of Studies on Alcohol, 65*, 428–433.

Bergmark, A., & Oscarsson, L. (1987). The concept of control and alcoholism. *British Journal of Addiction, 82*, 1203–1212.

Biernacki, P. (1986). *Pathways from heroin addiction: Recovery without treatment*. Philadelphia: Temple University Press.

Bischof, G., Rumpf, H.-J., Meyer, C., Hapke, U., & John, U. (2007). Stability of subtypes of natural recovery from alcohol dependence after two years. *Addiction (Abingdon, England), 102*, 904–908.

Bischof, G., Rumpf, H. J., Hapke, U., Meyer, C., & John, U. (2003). Types of natural recovery from alcohol dependence: A cluster analytic approach. *Addiction (Abingdon, England), 98*, 1737–1746.

Bischof, G., Rumpf, H. J., Meyer, C., Hapke, U., & John, U. (2005a). Gender differences in temptation to drink, self-efficacy to abstain and coping behavior in treated alcohol-dependent individuals: Controlling for severity of dependence. *Addiction Research & Theory, 13*, 129–136.

Bischof, G., Rumpf, H. J., Meyer, C., Hapke, U., & John, U. (2005b). Influence of psychiatric comorbidity in alcohol-dependent subjects in a representative population survey on treatment utilization and natural recovery. *Addiction, 100*, 405–413.

Blendon, R. J., & Benson, J. M. (2001). Americans' view on health policy: A fifty-year historical perspective. *Health Affairs, 20*, 33–46.

Blomqvist, J. (1998). *Beyond treatment? Widening the approach to alcohol problems and solutions*. Stockholm: Department of Social Work, Stockholm University.

Blomqvist, J. (2004). Sweden's "War on Drugs" in the light of addicts' experiences. In P. Rosenqvist, J. Blomqvist, A. Koski-Jännes, & L. Öjesjö (Eds.), *Addiction and life course* (Vol. *44*, pp. 139–172). Helsinki: NAD.

Brooks, C., & Cheng, S. (2001). Declining government confidence and policy preferences in the US: Devolution, regime effects, or symbolic change? *Social Forces*, *79*, 1343–1375.

Burman, S. (1994). The disease concept of alcoholism: Its impact on women's treatment. *Journal of Substance Abuse Treatment*, *11*, 121–126.

Burman, S. (1997). The challenge of sobriety: Natural recovery without treatment and self-help groups. *Journal of Substance Abuse*, *9*, 41–61.

Carballo, J. L., Fernández-Hermida, J. R., Sobell, L. C., Dum, M., Secades-Villa, R., García-Rodríguez, O., et al. (2008). Differences among substance abusers in Spain who recovered with treatment or on their own. *Addictive Behaviors*, *33*, 94–105.

Carballo, J. L., Fernández-Hermida, J. R., Secades-Villa, R., Sobell, L. C., Dum, M., & García-Rodríguez, O. (2007). Natural recovery from alcohol and drug problems: A methodological review of the literature from 1999 through 2005. In H. Klingemann & L. C. Sobell (Eds.), *Promoting self-change from addictive behaviours: Practical implications for policy, prevention, and treatment*. New York: Kluwer, pp. 87–101.

Carballo Crespo, J. L., Secades Villa, R., Sobell, L. C., Fernández Hermida, J. R., & García-Rodríguez, O. (2004). Reupercacion de los problemas de juego patologico con y sin tratamiento. *Salud y Drogas*, *4*, 61–78.

Cloud, W., & Granfield, R. (2004). A life course perspective on exiting addiction: The relevance of recovery capital in treatment. In P. Rosenqvist, J. Blomqvist, A. Koski-Jännes, & L. Öjesjö (Eds.), *Addiction and life course:* (*Vol. 44*, pp. 185–202). Helsinki: NAD.

Cohen, E., Feinn, R., Arias, A., & Kranzler, H. R. (2007). Alcohol treatment utilization: Findings from the National Epidemiologic Survey on Alcohol and Related Conditions. *Drug & Alcohol Dependence*, *86*, 214–221.

Collins, M. A. (2006). Religiousness and spirituality as possible recovery variables in treated and natural recoveries: A qualitative study. *Alcoholism Treatment Quarterly*, *24*, 119–135.

Copeland, J. (1997). A qualitative study of barriers to formal treatment among women who self-managed change. *Journal of Substance Abuse Treatment*, *14*, 183–190.

Copeland, J. (1998). A qualitative study of self-managed change in substance dependence among women. *Contemporary Drug Problems*, *25*, 327–347.

Cottorell, R. (1999). Transparency, mass media, ideology and community. *Cultural Values*, *3*, 414–426.

Cunningham, J. A., Blomqvist, J., & Cordingley, J. (2007). Beliefs about drinking problems: Results from a general population telephone survey. *Addictive Behaviors*, *32*, 166–169.

Cunningham, J. A., Blomqvist, J., Koski-Jännes, A., & Cordingley, J. (2005). Maturing out of drinking problems: Perceptions of natural history as a function of severity. *Addiction Research & Theory*, *13*, 79–84.

Cunningham, J. A., Sobell, L. C., & Sobell, M. B. (1998). Awareness of self-change as a pathway to recovery for alcohol abusers: Results from five different groups. *Addictive Behaviors*, *23*, 399–404.

Dawson, D. A., Goldstein, R. B., & Grant, B. F. (2007). Rates and correlates of relapse among individuals in remission from DSM-IV alcohol dependence: A 3-year follow-up. *Alcoholism, Clinical and Experimental Research, 31*, 2036–2045.

Dawson, D. A., Grant, B. F., Stinson, F. S., & Chou, P. S. (2006). Estimating the effect of help-seeking on achieving recovery from alcohol dependence. *Addiction, 101*, 824–834.

Dawson, D. A., Grant, B. F., Stinson, F. S., Chou, P. S., Huang, B., & Ruan, W. J. (2005). Recovery from DSM-IV alcohol dependence: United States, 2001–2002. *Addiction, 100*, 281–292.

DiClemente, C. C. (2007). Mechanisms, determinants and processes of change in the modification of drinking behavior. *Alcoholism: Clinical & Experimental Research, 31*, 13s–20s.

Doran, C. M., Valenti, L., Robinson, M., Britt, H., & Mattick, R. P. (2006). Smoking status of Australian general practice patients and their attempts to quit. *Addictive Behaviors, 31*, 758–766.

Easthope, G., Tranter, B., & Gill, G. (2000). General practitioners' attitudes toward complementary therapies. *Social Science and Medicine, 51*, 1555–1561.

Eisenberg, D. M., Kessler, R. C., Foster, C., Norlock, F. E., Calkins, D., & Delbanco, T. L. (1993). Unconventional medicine in the United States: Prevalence, costs, and patterns of use. *New England Journal of Medicine, 328*, 246–252.

Ellingstad, T. P., Sobell, L. C., Sobell, M. B., Eickleberry, L., & Golden, C. J. (2006). Self-change: A pathway to cannabis abuse resolution. *Addictive Behaviors, 31*, 519–530.

Finfgeld, D. L., & Lewis, L. M. (2002). Self-resolution of alcohol problems in young adulthood: A process of securing solid ground. *Qualitative Health Research, 12*, 581.

Freidson, E. (1960). Client control and medical practice. *American Journal of Sociology, 65*, 374–382.

Freidson, E. (1961). *Patients' view on medical practice*. New York: Russel, Sage.

Furnam, A., & Lovett, J. (2001). The perceived efficacy and risks of complementary and alternative medicine and conventional medicine: A vignette study. *Journal of Applied Biobehavioral Research, 6*, 39–63.

Furnham, A., & Lowick, V. (1984). Lay theories of the causes of alcoholism. *The British Journal of Medical Psychology, 57*(Pt 4), 319–332.

Hänninen, V., & Koski-Jännes, A. (1999). Narratives of recovery from addictive behaviours. *Addiction, 94*, 1837–1848.

Hänninen, V., & Koski-Jännes, A. (2004). Stories of attempts to recover from addiction. In P. Rosenqvist, J. Blomqvist, A. Koski-Jännes, & L. Öjesjö (Eds.), *Addiction and life course* (Vol. 44, pp. 231–246). Helsinki: NAD.

Heather, N., & Stockwell, T. (Eds.). (2004). *The essential handbook of treatment and prevention of alcohol problems*. England: Wiley.

Humphreys, K., Moos, R. H., & Finney, J. W. (1995). Two pathways out of drinking problems without professional treatment. *Addictive Behaviors, 20*, 427–441.

John, U. (1982). Zur verbreitung des alkoholismus: Das problem unbehandelter alkoholiker. *Öffentliches Gesundheitswesen, 44*, 774–780.

Klingemann, H. (2000). "To every thing there is a season"—social time and clock time in addiction treatment. *Social Science & Medicine, 51*, 1231–1240.

Klingemann, H. (2006). Internationaler Vergleich: Staatliche Interventionen im Suchtbereich-Hindernisse auf dem Weg zu einem Integrationsmodell. *Abhängigkeiten, 06*, 55–63.

Klingemann, H., & Aeberhard, M. (2004). Biographie und Suchtkarrieren 1988–2002: Longitudinale Fallanalysen von Alkohol- und Heroinselbst-Heilerinnen und- heilern. Abhängigkeiten. *Sonderdruck forel klinik*, 52–63.

Klingemann, H., & Bergmark, A. (2006). The legitimacy of addiction treatment in a world of smart people. *Addiction*, *101*, 1230–1237.

Klingemann, H., & Klingemann, J. (2007). Hostile and favorable societal climates for self-change: Some lessons for policymakers. In H. Klingemann & L. C. Sobell (Eds.), *Promoting self-change from addictive behaviours: Practical implications for policy, prevention and treatment* (pp. 187–212). New York: Kluwer.

Klingemann & Rosenberg (2009). Acceptance and therapeutic practice of controlled drinking as an outcome goal by swiss alcohol treatment programmes.

Klingemann, H., & Sobell, L. C. (Eds.). (2007). *Promoting self-change from addictive behaviours: Practical implications for policy, prevention and treatment*. New York: Kluwer.

Klingemann, H. K. (1992). Coping and maintenance strategies of spontaneous remitters from problem use of alcohol and heroin in Switzerland. *International Journal of the Addictions*, *27*, 1359–1388.

Klingemann, H. K. H. (1991). The motivation for change from problem alcohol and heroin use. *British Journal of Addiction*, *86*, 727–744.

Koerkel, J. (2006). Behavioural self-management with problem drinkers: One year follow-up of a controlled drinking group treatment approach. *Addiction Research and Theory*, *4*, 35–49.

Luoma, J. B., Kohlenberg, B. S., Hayes, S. C., Bunting, K., & Rye, A. K. (2008). Reducing self-stigma in substance abuse through acceptance and commitment therapy: Model, manual development, and pilot outcomes. *Addiction Research & Theory*, *16*, 149–165.

Luoma, J. B., Twohig, M. P., Waltz, T., Hayes, S. C., Roget, N., Padilla, M., et al. (2007). An investigation of stigma in individuals receiving treatment for substance abuse. *Addictive Behaviors*, *32*, 1331–1346.

Misch, D. A. (2007). "Natural recovery" from alcohol abuse among college students. *Journal of American College Health*, *55*, 215–218.

Mohatt, G. V., Rasmus, S. M., Thomas, L., Allen, J., Hazel, K., & Marlatt, G. A. (2008). Risk, resilience, and natural recovery: A model of recovery from alcohol abuse for Alaska Natives. *Addiction*, *103*, 205–215.

Moos, R. H., & Moos, B. S. (2006). Rates and predictors of relapse after natural and treated remission from alcohol use disorders. *Addiction*, *101*, 212–222.

O'Malley, P. M. (2004). Maturing out of problematic alcohol use. *Alcohol Research & Health*, *28*, 202–204.

Ogborne, A. C., & Smart, R. G. (2001). Public opinion on the health benefits of moderate drinking: Results from a Canadian National Population Health Survey. *Addiction*, *96*, 641–649.

Orford, J. (2008). Asking the right questions the right way: The need for a shift in research on psychological treatments for addiction. *Addiction*, *103*, 875–885.

Peele, S. (1989). *Diseasing of America: Addiction treatment out of control*. Lexington, MA: Lexington Books.

Polivy, J. (2001). The false hope syndrome: Unrealistic expectations of self-change. *International Journal of Obesity & Related Metabolic Disorders*, *25*, S80.

Roizen, R., Cahalan, D., & Shanks, P. (1978). Spontaneous remission among untreated problem drinkers. In D. B. Kandel (Ed.), *Longitudinal research on drug use: Empirical findings and methodological issues* (pp. 197–221). Washington, DC.

Rosenberg, H., & Melville, J. (2005). Controlled drinking and controlled drug use as outcome goals in British treatment services. *Addiction Research & Theory, 13*, 85–92.

Rumpf, H. J., Bischof, G., Hapke, U., Meyer, C., & John, U. (2000). Studies on natural recovery from alcohol dependence: Sample selection bias by media solicitation? *Addiction, 95*, 765–775.

Scarscelli, D. (2006). Drug addiction between deviance and normality: A study of spontaneous and assisted remission. *Contemporary Drug Problems, 33*, 237–274.

Sobell, L., Klingemann, H., Toneatto, T., Sobell, M., Agrawal, S., & Leo, G. (2001). Alcohol and drug abusers' perceived reasons for self-change in Canada and Switzerland: Computer-assisted content analysis. *Substance Use & Misuse, 36*, 1467.

Sobell, L. C., Agrawal, S., Sobell, M. B., Leo, G. I., Johnson Young, L., Cunningham, J. A., et al. (2003). Comparison of a quick drinking screen with the timeline followback for individuals with alcohol problems. *Journal of Studies on Alcohol, 64*, 858–861.

Sobell, L. C., Ellingstad, T. P., & Sobell, M. B. (2000). Natural recovery from alcohol and drug problems: Methodological review of the research with suggestions for future directions. *Addiction, 95*, 749–764.

Sobell, L. C., & Sobell, M. B. (1992). Time-line follow-back: A technique for assessing self-reported alcohol consumption. In R. Z. Litten & A. J. Towota (Eds.), *Measuring alcohol consumption: Psychosocial and biological methods* (pp. 41–72). Totowa, NJ: Humana Press.

Sobell, L. C., Sobell, M. B., & Agrawal, S. (2002). Self-change and dual recoveries among individuals with alcohol and tobacco problems: Current knowledge and future directions. *Alcoholism, Clinical and Experimental Research, 26*, 1936–1938.

Stall, R. (1983). An examination of spontaneous remission from problem drinking in the bluegrass region of Kentucky. *Journal of Drug Issues, 13*, 191–206.

Takala, J.-P. (2007). Spontaneous desistance from crime. In H. Klingemann & L. C. Sobell (Eds.), *Promoting self-change from addictive behaviours: Practical implications for policy, prevention and treatment* (pp. 127–138). New York: Kluwer.

Toneatto, T., Cunningham, J., Hodgins, D., Adams, M., Turner, N., & Koski-Jännes, A. (2008). Recovery from problem gambling without formal treatment. *Addiction Research & Theory, 16*, 111–120.

Trinder, L., & Reynolds, S. (2003). *Evidence-based practice: A critical appraisal.* Oxford.

Tubman, J., Wagner, E. F., Gil, A. G., & Pate, K. N. (2002). Brief motivational intervention for substance-abusing delinquent adolescents: Guided self-change as a social work practice innovation. *Health/Social Work, 27*, 208–212.

Tucker, J. A. (2008). Different pathways to knowledge about different pathways to recovery: A comment on the people awakening study. *Addiction (Abingdon, England), 103*, 216–217.

Tucker, J. A., & Vuchinich, R. E. (1994). Environmental events surrounding natural recovery from alcohol-related problems. *Journal of Studies on Alcohol, 55*, 401.

Vik, P. W., Cellucci, T., & Ivers, H. (2003). Natural reduction of binge drinking among college students. *Addictive Behaviors, 28*, 643.

Wilde, G. J. S. (1993). Effects of mass media communications on health and safety habits: An overview of issues and evidence. *Addiction, 88*, 983–996.

Chapter | fifteen

Adjunctive Pharmacotherapy in the Treatment of Alcohol and Drug Dependence

Robert Swift
Providence VA Medical Center

Lorenzo Leggio
Brown University Medical School

INTRODUCTION

Current thinking about addictive disorders posits that addiction is a chronic, relapsing condition with a multifactorial etiology that includes genetic, neurobiological, psychological, and environmental components (Addolorato, Leggio, Abenavoli, Gasbarrini, & Alcoholism Treatment Study Group, 2005; Koob, 2006a). In this regard, addictive disorders are similar to other "medical" illnesses, including asthma, hyperlipidemia, and type 2 diabetes, in which there are both genetic/biological and psychosocial causes and for which the optimal treatment combines both biological (usually pharmacological) and psychosocial treatments (McLellan, Lewis, O'Brien, & Kleber, 2000). Despite the importance of the biological component of addictive disorders, clinicians and patients have been slow to adopt biologically based treatments. Historically, the mainstay of addiction treatment in the United States has been psychosocial treatment. Some of the reasons for the reluctance to use evidence-based pharmacotherapies as adjunctive treatments include clinicians' lack of knowledge about the neurobiology of addiction, the lack of knowledge about the mechanisms of action of medications,

Evidence-Based Addiction Treatment

the increased cost of adding medications to treatment, and a paucity of prescribers. Moreover, some clinicians and patients are uncomfortable in treating a drug problem with another drug. However, evidence for the effectiveness of adjunctive pharmacotherapy in addiction treatment along with the increased number of agents available is gradually increasing the use of adjunctive medications by clinicians and their patients.

The clinical course of patients with addictive disorders is characterized by phases of repeated intoxication, withdrawal, and abstinence. Each of these states is associated with characteristic neurobiological changes in the brain that are amenable to modification by pharmacological agents. Advances in understanding the neurobiology of addiction have identified specific brain neurotransmitter systems that are associated with these phases of addiction; medications that target these neurotransmitter systems have the potential to be effective treatments. Accordingly, using medications to lessen withdrawal, alter the effects of drug and alcohol intoxication, and maintain abstinence or at least reduce substance use can reduce the impact of substance use and improve the quality of life for patients and their families. Consistent with this need, research on the development of pharmacotherapies for addiction is undergoing a period of rapid growth. In the last 2–3 decades, both the number of medications found to be effective in treating addictive disorders and the rate of approval of new medications for specific addictive disorders have been increasing. At this time, effective medications are approved by the Food and Drug Administration (FDA) for alcohol, opiates, and nicotine. While there are no approved medications for stimulants (amphetamines and cocaine), there are some promising candidates. Table 15.1 presents several adjunctive medications used in the treatment of specific drug dependences.

This chapter briefly reviews the neurobiology of addiction that represents the basis for applying evidence-based pharmacotherapies for addictive disorders. Then, the most important medications for the treatment of addictions are discussed, focusing on those that are FDA approved. Finally, the chapter discusses practical aspects of using pharmacotherapies in treatment, including strategies for choosing the optimal medication for particular patients, common side effects, and optimal methods for combining psychosocial and pharmacological treatment. The case of the Combined Pharmacological and Behavioral Interventions (COMBINE) trial is also discussed as an example of a method to incorporate medications into psychosocial treatment processes.

THE NEUROBIOLOGY OF ADDICTIONS

Drugs and alcohol share common neurochemical substrates that produce acute rewarding effects and long-term neuroadaptations that ultimately lead to addiction (Heidbreder & Hagan, 2005). Although it is unclear precisely how these neural systems lead to dependence, it is thought

Table 15.1 Medications used as antirelapse pharmacotherapies in the treatment of addictions

Substance	FDA-approved medications	Non-FDA-approved medications
Alcohol	Acamprosate (Campral) Naltrexone, oral (Revia and generics) Naltrexone, sustained release (Vivitrol) Disulfiram (Antabuse)	Topiramate (Topamax) Baclofen (Liorasil) Ondansetron (Zofran) Olanzepine (Zyprexa) Quetiapine (Seroquel)
Heroin/opiates	Methadone levo-alpha-acetylmethadol (LAAM) Buprenorphine (Subutex) Buprenorphine/naloxone (Suboxone) Naltrexone	
Cocaine/stimulants		Disulfiram (Antabuse) Topiramate (Topamax) Modafinil (Provigil) Baclofen (Liorasil) Vigabatrin (Sabril) Tiagabine (Gabitril)
Nicotine	Nicotine replacement (gum, patch, nasal spray, inhaler) Bupropion (Zyban) Varenicline (Chantix)	Rimonabant (Accomplia)

that drugs of abuse and alcohol initially enhance reward mechanisms (Robinson & Berridge, 1993; Wise & Bozarth, 1987). Over time, continued use engenders a state of withdrawal, dysphoria, and distress, called allostasis (Koob, 2006a,b), that is relieved only by continued drug and alcohol use. Individuals vary in their drug reward and susceptibility to allostasis; both environmental factors and genetic factors account for this variance, as well as gene by environment interactions (Koob, 2006b).

Drug and alcohol rewards are, in part, mediated through activation of the mesolimbic dopamine pathway by drugs and alcohol (Figure 15.1). The mesolimbic pathway and related limbic circuits, including the amygdala, hippocampus, and medial prefrontal cortex, are part of the motivational system that regulates responses to natural reinforcers, such as food and beverages, sex, and social interaction, as well as the acute reinforcing properties of most drugs of abuse (Heidbreder & Hagan, 2005). Activation of the mesolimbic pathway increases the activity of dopamine neurons in the ventral tegmental area of the midbrain and increases the release of dopamine into the nucleus accumbens (also called the ventral striatum) and other areas of the limbic forebrain, such as the amygdala and prefrontal cortex. Some

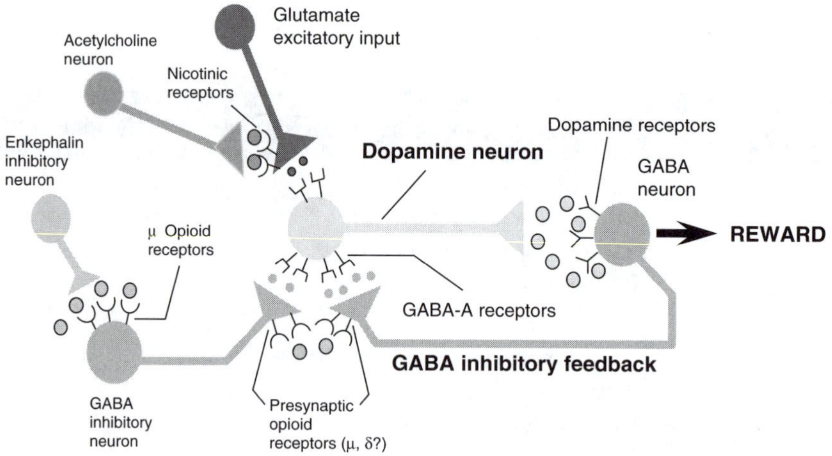

FIGURE 15.1 *Brain circuitry for drug and alcohol reward. Drugs and alcohol activate the mesolimbic dopamine pathway either directly by affecting dopamine or indirectly by affecting other neurotransmitters, resulting in reward and sensitization.*
Source: Copyright by the Alcohol Scholar's Programs, used with permission.

drugs, such as cocaine and stimulants, activate the mesolimbic pathway directly. Other drugs, such as nicotine and alcohol, activate the pathway indirectly. Alcohol and morphine enhance endogenous opioid pathways that innervate the ventral tegmental area and the nucleus accumbens, producing a net effect of increasing dopamine release. It is thought that repeated activation of this motivation-reward system by drugs and alcohol sensitizes the system, resulting in increased motivation to use addictive substances and the development of craving in response to stimuli associated with substance use (Nestler, 2001).

Most drug and alcohol dependence is associated with an unpleasant and distressing withdrawal syndrome that appears upon cessation of drug use; avoidance of withdrawal is an important factor in maintaining drug use. Withdrawal occurs because of adaptive changes in the nervous system in response to chronic drug or alcohol use. Typically, withdrawal symptoms are behaviorally opposite to the drug effects. Thus, sedative drugs such as alcohol or benzodiazepines produce a withdrawal characterized by excitation; stimulant drugs such as cocaine or amphetamines produce a withdrawal characterized by lethargy. γ-Aminobutyric acid (GABA) and glutamate are the major inhibitory and excitatory neurotransmitters, respectively, in the nervous system. Acutely, alcohol facilitates the inhibitory GABA and inhibits the excitatory glutamate. With repeated and chronic alcohol administration, the brain adapts to downregulate the inhibitory GABA receptors and upregulate the excitatory glutamate receptors, producing an excitatory state to balance the sedative effects of alcohol. However, if the alcohol-dependent person stops drinking abruptly, the sedative effects of alcohol are not present to balance the excitatory state and the person experiences a state of generalized central nervous system excitation, typically anxiety, tremors, insomnia, and, in severe cases, seizures and hallucinations (delirium tremens) (Swift, 1999). It has been suggested that withdrawal symptoms intensify as withdrawal episodes grow in number, a phenomenon called "kindling" (Leggio, Kenna, & Swift, 2008).

Chronic alcohol and drug use also activates the stress response system, resulting in abnormalities in corticotrophin-releasing factor, neuropeptide Y, and other neurotransmitters involved in the stress response (Lappalainen et al., 2002; Schroeder, Overstreet, & Hodge, 2005). Long after acute withdrawal symptoms have abated, abstinent drug- and alcohol-dependent individuals continue to experience a protracted, distressing state known as allostasis, characterized by increased anxiety, dysphoria, and difficulty coping with stress and just not feeling okay. Because this allostasis can be relieved by the alcohol or drugs, it is a powerful inducer of relapse.

A growing understanding of the neurobiology of addictions has led to the development of pharmacologic agents that can complement psychosocial treatment approaches.

PHARMACOTHERAPY OF ADDICTIONS

Alcohol

Currently, three medications are approved by the FDA for the treatment of alcohol dependence; disulfiram, naltrexone (oral and intramuscular formulations), and acamprosate. Several other medications are not FDA approved, but have shown efficacy in controlled studies and are used for adjunctive treatment off-label (off-label refers to prescribing a drug for a purpose outside the scope of the drug's approved label). The National Institute on Alcohol Abuse and Alcoholism (NIAAA) recommends consideration of pharmacotherapies in the treatment of all patients (NIAAA, 2007) (Figure 15.2).

DISULFIRAM

Disulfiram is an aversion-based therapy that produces sensitivity to alcohol, resulting in a highly unpleasant reaction even when small amounts of alcohol are consumed. Disulfiram alters the normal metabolism of alcohol by inhibiting the enzyme aldehyde dehydrogenase and increases the levels of the toxic alcohol metabolite acetaldehyde. Clinical manifestations include flushing, tachycardia, hypotension, nausea, vomiting, diarrhea, and headache (Swift, 2007). These effects provide a strong deterrent for alcohol use.

NIAAA Recommended Guidelines on
Pharmacotherapies for Alcoholism

"All approved drugs have been shown to be effective adjuncts to the treatment of alcohol dependence. Thus, consider adding medication whenever you are treating someone with active alcohol dependence or someone who has stopped drinking in the past few months but is experiencing problems such as craving or slips."

NIAAA NIH Government Publications. *Helping Patients Who Drink Too Much: A Clinician's Guide.*2005, 2007 Edition.
Available at http://www.niaaa.nih.gov/publications/Practitioner/guide.pdf.

FIGURE 15.2 *NIAAA recommended clinician guidelines on pharmacotherapies for alcoholism.*

Although disulfiram has been available since the late 1950s, there have been few well-controlled studies on the effectiveness of disulfiram treatment. The largest treatment study compared 1 year of 250 mg daily disulfiram, 1 mg disulfiram (placebo), and a multivitamin in 605 male alcohol-dependent subjects (Fuller et al., 1986). Results showed no differences in abstinence rates or time to first drink among the groups. More recent studies have suggested that disulfiram may be efficacious for some alcohol-dependent patients. A 6-month, double-blind study in 126 British patients found that those who received 200 mg disulfiram daily had more total days abstinent, reduced weekly drinking, and lower levels of γ-glutamyltransferase (a blood protein used commonly as a biomarker for heavy alcohol use) compared with those who received a vitamin placebo (Chick et al., 1992). In a 12-week treatment study of 122 patients with combined cocaine and alcohol dependence receiving psychotherapy and either disulfiram or no medication, those receiving disulfiram were found to have better treatment retention, as well as a longer duration of abstinence for both cocaine and alcohol use. Importantly, the treatment benefits were retained at the 1-year follow-up (Carroll et al., 2000).

Direct supervision of disulfiram ingestion and involvement in psychosocial treatment have been shown to increase its effectiveness. O'Farrell studied couples receiving behavioral marital therapy with and without a contract for spousal supervision of disulfiram compliance and found that the disulfiram contract reduced drinking compared to therapy alone (O'Farrell, Allen, & Litten, 1995).

Although the evidence for efficacy of disulfiram therapy is limited, disulfiram is still used, especially when a patient needs "external" control to maintain long-term abstinence. Enhancing medication adherence with direct supervision and involvement in psychosocial therapies that support medication use improve the effectiveness of disulfiram greatly

(Suh, Pettinati, Kampman, & O'Brien, 2006). Patients receiving disulfiram must receive education about the consequences of drinking alcohol while taking the drug and must be committed to complete abstinence.

Disulfiram is available in 250-mg tablets. The usual oral dose is 250 mg once daily, although doses range from 125 to 500 mg, depending on side effects and patient response. Some researchers recommend higher doses, as a significant proportion of patients may not experience a disulfiram-alcohol reaction at the usual 250-mg daily dose (Brewer, 1993). However, side effects are increased at doses greater than 250 mg.

NALTREXONE

Naltrexone is an antagonist of opioid receptors and blocks the effects of both natural endorphins and opiate medications. Evidence suggests that naltrexone reduces alcohol consumption in two ways: blocking the positive reinforcing effects of alcohol and suppressing craving. Naltrexone-treated alcoholics who drank during treatment reported less "high" from alcohol (Volpicelli, Watson, King, Sherman, & O'Brien, 1995). Nonalcoholic, social drinkers receiving naltrexone and alcohol reported less positive effects and more sedative effects of alcohol (Swift, Whelihan, Kuznetsov, Buongiorno, & Hsuing, 1994). Naltrexone attenuates craving in both alcoholics (Monti et al., 1999) and social drinkers (Davidson, Swift, & Fitz, 1996); the reduction in craving may help patients to abstain from drinking.

The oral formulation of naltrexone, in conjunction with psychosocial support, has shown demonstrated efficacy in clinical trials for alcohol dependence. In a 12-week, randomized controlled trial in 70 alcohol-dependent patients following alcohol detoxification, treatment with naltrexone resulted in a significantly reduced alcohol craving and alcohol consumption, with an approximately 50% lower incidence of relapse to heavy drinking (Volpicelli, Alterman, Hayashida, & O'Brien, 1992). In another 12-week, randomized controlled trial in 97 alcohol-dependent individuals, naltrexone significantly increased abstinence, decreased the number of drinking days, decreased relapse to heavy drinking, and reduced the severity of alcohol-related problems (O'Malley et al., 1992). Based on these two pivotal clinical trials, the Food and Drug Administration (FDA) approved naltrexone for the treatment of alcoholism in 1994.

Subsequent clinical studies with oral naltrexone have shown both positive and negative results, although there are more positive studies. Several meta-analyses that compare naltrexone effects statistically across several studies have supported the efficacy of naltrexone, particularly in reducing heavy drinking, with small effect sizes (Bouza, Angeles, Muñoz, & Amate, 2004; Srisurapanont & Jarusuraisin, 2005). The U.S. multisite COMBINE study, involving 1380 alcohol-dependent patients, found naltrexone, compared to placebo, to produce small but significant reductions in relapse to heavy drinking in patients receiving a medical-oriented behavioral intervention (Anton et al., 2006).

Studies show that several patient characteristics are associated with a positive response to naltrexone. Medication adherence is extremely important for naltrexone effectiveness. In three different clinical trials, naltrexone had a positive effect on drinking outcomes only in patients showing high medication adherence (Chick et al., 2000; Monti et al., 2001; Volpicelli et al., 1997). Other predictors of a positive response to naltrexone include a high level of craving, a positive family history of alcoholism, and possessing a specific genetic polymorphism (Asn40Asp) in the μ opioid receptor gene (Oslin et al., 2003).

SUSTAINED-RELEASE NALTREXONE

In order to improve adherence, long-acting forms of naltrexone that are administered by a once-monthly injection have been developed. One of these sustained-released naltrexone preparations, known as Vivitrol, was FDA approved for the treatment of alcohol dependence in 2004. In a 3-month, multicenter, randomized, placebo-controlled trial, long-acting, injectable naltrexone administered with motivational enhancement therapy was associated with an increased number of days abstinent and a longer median time to first drinking day (Kranzler, Wesson, & Billot, 2004). A 6-month, multicenter, randomized controlled trial of placebo and two doses of sustained-release naltrexone in 627 actively drinking alcohol-dependent adults showed a significant dose-dependent decrease in the rate of heavy drinking (26% at the highest dose) compared with placebo (Garbutt et al., 2005). In this study, naltrexone was not effective in reducing the number of heavy drinking days in women. Subjects who received naltrexone attended more sessions of psychosocial therapy than subjects who received placebo. In general, the injections were well tolerated. The most common adverse events associated with extended-release naltrexone are injection site tenderness, nausea (which affected 33%), headache, and fatigue. In addition to improved adherence, sustained release naltrexone may produce less hepatotoxicity than oral naltrexone, as the injected, sustained-release drug does not undergo first-pass metabolism in the liver.

ACAMPROSATE

Acamprosate is a compound with a chemical structure similar to that of the neurotransmitter GABA and the neuromodulator taurine. Its mechanism of action is not completely understood but most likely involves a functional antagonism or modulation of the glutamate NMDA receptor, which is upregulated in chronic alcoholism.

In double-blind, placebo-controlled trials, mostly conducted in Europe, acamprosate effectively maintained complete abstinence in detoxified alcohol-dependent patients (Swift, 2007). When used as an adjunct to psychosocial interventions, acamprosate improves drinking outcomes such as the length and rate of abstinence. Three European multicenter, randomized, double-blind studies of acamprosate as an adjunct to psychosocial treatment supported the FDA approval of acamprosate as an effective agent in the maintenance of abstinence from alcohol (Paille et al., 1995; Pelc et al., 1997; Sass, Soyka, Mann, & Zieglgansberger, 1996). Meta-analyses that compare acamprosate statistically across several studies have supported the efficacy of acamprosate in improving the rates of abstinence and increasing the time to first drink, with small effect sizes (Bouza et al., 2004; Mann, Lehert, & Morgan, 2004).

Interestingly, the efficacy of acamprosate seems most strong only in those trials conducted in Europe; two U.S. trials, a 6-month multisite study (Mason, Goodman, Chabac, & Lehert, 2006) and the COMBINE study (Anton et al., 2006), failed to find similar efficacy. Reasons for the differences in the effectiveness of acamprosate between European and U.S. studies are unclear. Differences in terms of severity of alcoholism, typologies of patients, and use of inpatient detoxification in Europe have been suggested.

OTHER POTENTIAL PHARMACOTHERAPIES FOR ALCOHOLISM

The antiepileptic medication topiramate represents a promising medication for the treatment of alcohol dependence, although it is not approved by the FDA. In a 12-week, randomized controlled trial in 150 patients with alcohol dependence receiving medication-adherence therapy, topiramate treatment significantly decreased the numbers of drinks per day, drinks per drinking day, and drinking days and increased the number of days of abstinence compared to placebo (Johnson et al., 2003). A successive U.S. multisite trial (Johnson et al., 2007) showed its efficacy in reducing heavy drinking. Topiramate causes a number of dose-dependent neurological side effects, and further studies are required to determine optimal dosing.

Baclofen, a GABA-B receptor agonist that is used to treat spasticity, has shown efficacy in a small trial (Addolorato et al., 2002) and in a subsequent larger trial (Addolorato et al., 2007). In the latter trial, baclofen showed its efficacy and safety in a subset of alcohol dependence with advanced liver cirrhosis. Finally, some interesting results suggest the efficacy of ondansetron in alcohol-dependent subjects with an early onset of alcoholism (Johnson et al., 2000).

Given the importance of dopamine neurobiology of alcohol dependence, there is interest in dopaminergic medications for the adjunctive treatment of alcohol dependence. The atypical neuroleptic olanzapine, compared to placebo, reduced alcohol craving and alcohol consumption in a 12-week trial of patients with alcohol dependence without a comorbid psychiatric disorder (Hutchison et al., 2006). Another atypical neuroleptic, quetiapine, was found to reduce heavy drinking in a 12-week placebo-controlled trial with heavy drinking alcoholics (Kampman et al., 2007).

COMBINING PHARMACOTHERAPIES

The rationale for combining medications is that medications with different mechanisms of action have the potential to yield additive or synergistic treatment effects. The most frequent combination has been the use of naltrexone and acamprosate together. Kiefer and colleagues (2003) tested this combination in a double-blind, German single-center study randomizing abstinent, alcohol-dependent patients followed up to 3 months. All patients received cognitive behavioral group therapy and were randomized to receive placebo, naltrexone, acamprosate, or naltrexone+acamprosate. Results showed that acamprosate, naltrexone, and their combination all outperformed placebo in delaying the time to relapse. Combination pharmacotherapy also fared better than acamprosate alone, although not naltrexone alone (Kiefer et al., 2003). In an Australian single-center study, Feeney, Connor, Young, Tucker, and McPherson (2006) enrolled alcohol-dependent patients treated by naltrexone or acamprosate or their combination; all received cognitive behavioral therapy (CBT). Results of this cohort study suggested that the combination of naltrexone and acamprosate had a trend in improving treatment outcomes as measured by attendance and total abstinence rates.

THE COMBINE STUDY

The COMBINE study evaluated the combinations naltrexone, acamprosate, and the combination and two psychosocial treatments differing in intensity (medical management alone versus medical management plus moderate-intensity specialty alcohol dependence therapy). Eight treatment groups received medical management; these patients received naltrexone, acamprosate, both naltrexone and acamprosate, or placebo pills. Half of these patients also received specialized alcohol counseling, the Combine Behavioral Intervention (CBI), that combined elements of motivational enhancement therapy, cognitive behavioral therapy and twelve step facilitation therapy. A ninth group received the Combine Behavioral Intervention (CBI) alone without medical management or pills. COMBINE results showed that percentage days abstinent from baseline to study end point increased from 25 to 73%. The only interaction that significantly improved the percentage of the number of days of abstinence was naltrexone in the absence of the Combine Behavioral Intervention (CBI) (Anton et al., 2006). Within the context of medical management, CBI was as effective as naltrexone in reducing heavy drinking; however, combining CBI and naltrexone had no added benefit (Anton et al., 2006). Acamprosate did not show efficacy either alone or in combination with naltrexone or CBI for any drinking outcome (Anton et al., 2006). Treatment groups that showed improvement during the 16 weeks of treatment also showed improvement 1 year post-treatment (Donovan et al., 2008). Although the results have been criticized as not being representative of clinical treatment settings, the COMBINE study confirmed previous findings for the effectiveness of naltrexone and the interaction between pharmacotherapy and behavioral treatment. The COMBINE study also confirmed the findings that carriers of a specific single nucleotide polymorphism (Asn40Asp) in the μ opioid receptor gene were more likely to respond positively to naltrexone (Anton et al., 2008).

Opiates

Opiate drugs produce euphoria, decreases in stress and anxiety, and analgesia because they bind to neuronal opioid receptors, and mimic the action of the endogenous opioid peptide neurotransmitters enkephalin, endorphin, and dynorphin. Over time, regular opiate users develop tolerance and dependence due to neuronal adaptations; then, cessation of opiate use results in an unpleasant withdrawal syndrome, characterized by anxiety, dysphoria, nausea/vomiting, tremors, sweats, abdominal cramps, diarrhea, and an intense craving for opiates.

OPIATE SUBSTITUTION TREATMENTS

The concept of opioid substitution is to provide patients with a medically monitored opiate substitute to maintain opioid dependence, thereby preventing withdrawal and increasing tolerance to diminish the effects of illicit opiates. Three medications are FDA approved for substitution: methadone, levo-alpha-acetylmethadol (LAAM), and buprenorphine.

METHADONE MAINTENANCE

Methadone is a synthetic opiate, which is orally active, possesses a long duration of action, produces minimal sedation or "high," and has few side effects at therapeutic doses. Methadone was first shown to be an effective pharmacological adjunct to psychosocial treatment in an open-label study of 22 patients in New York City (Dole & Nyswander, 1965) and is now used worldwide. Since the late 1960s, studies consistently have shown methadone maintenance to be effective in the treatment of addicts who are dependent on heroin and other opiates (O'Brien, 2005; Senay, 1985). A meta-analysis of studies comparing methadone maintenance to placebo or drug-free treatment found methadone maintenance to be significantly better than nonpharmacological therapy in reducing heroin use and improving program retention (Mattick, Breen, Kimber, & Davoli, 2003). In addition, methadone maintenance has been shown to reduce opiate-related mortality and morbidity, reduce HIV transmission, decrease criminal activity, and increase employment (Vocci, Acri, & Elkashef, 2005). A longitudinal study that compared more than 100 representative methadone maintenance programs found that the most effective programs provided intensive psychosocial and medical services, flexibility in methadone dosing, and allowed higher doses of methadone in excess of 80 mg per day (D'Aunno & Pollack, 2002).

Methadone treatment is integrated with a comprehensive psychosocial treatment program. Long-standing program participants are allowed to "take home" some doses of methadone under a contingency contract that permits take-home doses as long as treatment compliance is maintained. Counseling sessions are held weekly with a counselor trained and certified in addiction treatment. Medical care, employment counseling, and other rehabilitative services are provided on a regular basis. Urine toxicological screening is performed randomly and periodically to assess compliance with treatment.

In 1993 the FDA approved levo-alpha-acetylmethadol acetate, the α-acetyl congener of methadone. However, subsequently the FDA issued a "black box" warning for LAAM, as the appearance of cardiac arrhythmias occurred during the postmarketing surveillance. Today, LAAM is rarely used (Vocci et al., 2005).

In 2002, the FDA approved sublingual buprenorphine tablets (Subutex) and buprenorphine/naloxone tablets (Suboxone) for the management of opiate dependence (Ling, Rawson, & Compton, 1994; Vocci et al., 2005). Buprenorphine is a partial μ- and κ-agonist opiate that was used medically as an analgesic. Importantly, the agonist properties of the drug predominate at lower doses and antagonist properties predominate at higher doses. These properties have led to its increasing use as an adjunctive substitution/maintenance treatment for opioid dependence. A randomized trial comparing buprenorphine maintenance to methadone maintenance for 16 weeks in 164 newly treated opiate users showed similar reductions in illicit drug use and a similar retention in treatment (Strain, Stitzer, Liebson & Bigelow, 1994). A 6-month study comparing methadone maintenance with a stepped care approach to buprenorphine found identical rates of treatment retention (Kakko et al., 1997). Possible advantages of buprenorphine compared to methadone include a less intense withdrawal upon discontinuation and less potential for abuse, as agonist effects diminish at higher doses.

Federal law now permits individual physicians who are certified in buprenorphine to possess a special license from the Drug Enforcement Administration to prescribe buprenorphine and buprenorphine/naloxone to up to 100 opioid-dependent patients who are also receiving psychosocial treatment. In the setting of a structured treatment program, daily buprenorphine dosing has been shown to be an effective maintenance treatment. Medication doses usually range from 4 to 16 mg per day, administered sublingually, since the medication is not effective orally.

Despite the demonstrated evidence of effectiveness of maintenance treatment with methadone, LAAM, and buprenorphine, the concept of opioid substitution therapy remains extremely controversial. Indeed, opioid substitution therapies are among the most highly regulated treatments and must follow strict guidelines described in the code of Federal Regulations (Code of Federal Regulations (CFR) 42, section 8). Certification of Opioid Treatment Programs.

NALTREXONE

Another pharmacological adjunctive treatment for the treatment of opioid dependence is antagonist therapy with naltrexone. Naltrexone is an opioid antagonist at μ-, κ-, and δ-opioid receptors. When taken regularly, an oral daily dose of 50 mg naltrexone completely blocks the euphoric, analgesic, and sedative properties of opiates (Resnick, Schuyten-Resnick, & Washton, 1980). Patients receiving naltrexone first must be completely detoxified from opiates or risk experiencing opioid withdrawal. Despite its potential, studies with oral naltrexone as an adjunctive treatment have shown high treatment dropout and poor medication compliance, particularly in poorly motivated individuals with poor social supports (Capone et al., 1986). Naltrexone was most effective in highly motivated individuals, such as impaired professionals and parolees (Kosten & Kleber, 1984).

To address poor medication adherence with oral naltrexone, several sustained-release, injectable forms of naltrexone have been developed. Sixty detoxified opioid-dependent patients receiving once-monthly injections of a sustained release naltrexone preparation in conjunction with twice-weekly counseling showed dose-dependent reductions in illicit drug use and improvements in treatment retention (Comer et al., 2006). A sustained release naltrexone preparation (Vivitrol) is marketed for the treatment of alcohol dependence; however, it is not FDA approved for opioid dependence treatment, although studies are in progress.

Cocaine

Cocaine is a potent stimulant of the central nervous system, potentiating the action of central catecholamine neurotransmitters, norepinephrine, and dopamine. Its effects include increased arousal, euphoria, a sense of creativity, expansiveness, excitement, and motor activation. This may progress to agitation, irritability, apprehension, and paranoia at high doses. Chronic users experience dysphoria, depression, and drug craving with abstinence. Relapses are common. The inclusion of individual and group counseling, group therapy, and cognitive behavioral therapy and contingency contracting has been shown to be effective in maintaining abstinence (Higgins, 1996; Rounsaville, Gawin, & Kleber, 1985).

So far, there are no FDA-approved medications for the adjunctive treatment of cocaine dependence. However, several compounds have shown evidence of efficacy in preliminary studies (Vocci et al., 2005). Disulfiram, used for treating alcohol dependence, may also have efficacy in cocaine treatment by altering brain dopamine activity through an inhibitory effect on the enzyme dopamine-β-hydroxylase. A clinical trial in 121 cocaine-dependent patients randomized to placebo or disulfiram, also receiving one of two types of behavioral therapy, showed a significant reduction in cocaine use in the disulfiram group (Carroll, 1994). Preliminary evidence suggests the utility of GABAergic medications such as baclofen, vigabatrin, and tiagabine for the treatment of cocaine dependence (O'Brien, 2005). A clinical trial comparing the GABA B-agonist baclofen to placebo in 70 cocaine-dependent outpatients found reduced cocaine use in baclofen-treated patients, particularly heavy users (Shoptaw et al., 2003). Interestingly, a pilot trial testing topiramate in cocaine dependence showed that topiramate-treated subjects were more likely to be abstinent from cocaine compared to placebo-treated subjects (Kampman et al., 2004). However, perhaps the most promising compound is represented by modafinil (O'Brien, 2005; Vocci et al., 2005). Modafinil is a stimulant that increases daytime alertness in narcoleptic patients. While its mechanism of action is unknown, modafinil, like cocaine, binds to norepinephrine and dopamine transporters. A clinical trial comparing placebo to 400 mg modafinil in 62 cocaine-dependent subjects, also receiving twice-weekly CBT, found significant decreases in cocaine use (Dackis et al., 2003). Modafinil appears to reduce craving, anergia, and anhedonia associated with cocaine withdrawal.

Nicotine

Nicotine is an alkaloid drug present in the leaves of the tobacco plant *Nicotiana tabacum*. Native Americans used the plant for centuries in ceremonies, in rituals, and as a medicinal herb. Since its discovery by Europeans, tobacco use has spread worldwide, and today nicotine is the most prevalent psychoactive drug in use. Approximately 42 million persons in the United States (about 25% of the population) are daily users of cigarettes, with another 10 million using another form of tobacco. Nicotine appears to activate the mesolimbic dopamine system through the activation of cholinergic systems in the ventral tegmental area (Corrigall et al., 1994) (Figure 15.1).

The morbidity and mortality resulting from the use of nicotine are extensive and include cardiovascular and respiratory disease and cancers, particularly of the lung and oropharynx. Many deleterious effects of tobacco are not due to nicotine, but are due to other toxic and carcinogenic compounds present in tobacco extract or smoke.

The successful treatment of nicotine dependence occurs with interventions that combine pharmacological and behavioral therapies (Hughes, Goldstein, Hurt, & Shiffman, 1999). According to the clinical practice guidelines review (Fiore et al., 2008), all nicotine-dependent patients should be offered some form of pharmacotherapy unless medical conditions contraindicate it.

Three types of pharmacotherapies have demonstrated their efficacy for smoking cessation: nicotine replacement therapy (NRT), bupropion, and varenicline. The goal of NRT is to reduce withdrawal symptoms associated with smoking cessation, thus helping resist the urge to smoke cigarettes (Silagy, Lancaster, Stead, Mant, & Fowler, 2004). NRT is the most widely recommended approach, with cessation rates for NRT plus counseling ranging between 20 and 30% at 1 year follow-up. Several forms of NRT are available commercially, for example, gum, transdermal patch, nasal spray, inhaler, and sublingual tablets/lozenges. Bupropion is an antidepressant with a dopaminergic–noradrenergic profile and may also bind to nicotinic receptors (Le Foll & George, 2007). A 7-week, double-blind controlled trial of sustained-release bupropion enrolling 615 smokers showed that the drug was effective for smoking cessation (Hurt et al., 1997). A successive study enrolled healthy community volunteers motivated to quit smoking. After an open-label treatment with sustained-release bupropion, subjects (n = 784) were randomized to receive sustained-release bupropion or placebo for 45 weeks. Results showed that sustained-release bupropion for 12 months delayed smoking relapse (Hays et al., 2001). Interestingly, a double-blind controlled trial also showed that treatment with sustained-release bupropion alone or in combination with a nicotine patch resulted in significantly higher long-term rates of smoking cessation than either nicotine patch alone or placebo (Jorenby et al., 1999). Varenicline is a nicotinic receptor partial agonist. It represents a novel medication available for the treatment of tobacco dependence. For example, a large multicenter randomized study showed its tolerability and effectiveness in the treatment of tobacco dependence (Nides et al., 2006; Oncken et al., 2006). Interestingly, a recent meta-analysis has also suggested that varenicline is more efficacious than bupropion (Eisenberg et al., 2008). A main side effect is nausea. In addition, the FDA has released an advisory letter that varenicline use may be associated with changes in behavior, including agitation, depressed mood, suicidal ideation, and suicide.

Among possible therapies currently under investigation, the most promising is rimonabant, a specific antagonist at cannabinoid CB-1 receptors. A recent meta-analysis of three placebo-controlled studies showed that 20 mg rimonabant, combined with behavioral treatment, increased the odds of smoking cessation and prevented weight gain (Cahill & Ussher, 2007); however, there are concerns that the medication may increase depression and suicidality and it is not available in the United States.

PHARMACOTHERAPY AS AN "ADJUNCTIVE" THERAPY

While the first part of this chapter briefly reviewed the neurobiological basis of addiction, mentioning the most important pharmacotherapies, including FDA-approved medications and promising compounds (Table 15.1), this second part is devoted to analyzing the concept of pharmacotherapy as an "adjunctive" therapy in the treatment of addiction. In particular, alcohol dependence is used as an example with which to discuss both advantages and limits of treating patients with a pharmacotherapy adjunctive to psychotherapy or counseling.

Adjunctive pharmacotherapy

Although many evidence-based psychotherapeutic and behavioral techniques have been developed to treat addictive disorders, even the best behavioral treatments have a high rate of relapse (O'Brien, 2005). As discussed in the first part of this chapter, the combination of psychosocial therapy and medication therapy can play a crucial role in improving addiction treatment, as both components are necessary to address the biological and psychosocial aspects of addiction. Moreover, when appropriate psychosocial therapies are used, the effects of pharmacotherapy are enhanced because the use of psychosocial therapy can increase patient retention, enhance medication compliance, and foster the acquisition of new skills that reinforce the effects of the medication (O'Malley & Carroll, 1996; Weiss & Kueppenbender, 2006).

Despite this evidence for efficacy, medications are rarely used for alcoholism treatment in community-based addiction treatment centers (Thomas, Wallack, Lee, McCarty, & Swift, 2003). Barriers to the use of medications include lack of knowledge about alcoholism medications by clinicians, concerns about medication effectiveness, insufficient education, and a belief system that is antithetical to the use of medications (Thomas & Miller, 2007).

It is important to understand the optimal ways to combine psychosocial and psychopharmacological treatment. In particular, it is important to know whether a psychosocial intervention enhances the efficacy of specific pharmacotherapies and vice versa. The most appropriate psychotherapy to use may depend on characteristics of the patient, the medication, the setting, and the experiences of the provider. For example, evidence suggests that supervision of disulfiram administration is necessary for efficacy (Weiss & Kueppenbender, 2006). In regard to naltrexone, efficacy may depend on the specific psychosocial treatment. O'Malley and colleagues (1992) found that supportive therapy plus naltrexone was associated with a significantly higher abstinence rate (68%) compared with coping skills/relapse prevention therapy and naltrexone (43%). In contrast, those treated with coping skills/relapse prevention therapy were more likely to reduce heavy drinking. A multisite VA trial that tested naltrexone in conjunction with Twelve-Step Facilitation therapy (Krystal et al., 2001) did not find any differences in outcome among the treatment groups. In a primary care-based study, naltrexone-treated patients were randomized to receive either primary care management or primary care management plus weekly CBT. No difference was found in heavy drinking, but there was greater abstinence among those patients receiving CBT (O'Malley et al., 2003). In regard to acamprosate, this drug may be used equally effectively with a variety of psychosocial treatments (de Wildt et al., 2002; Pelc et al., 2002; Soyka, Preuss, & Schuetz, 2002). However, definitive conclusions on the interaction between acamprosate and psychosocial therapies are difficult to make because of the frequent use of nonstandard psychosocial treatments (Weiss & Kueppenbender, 2006).

Integrating psychosocial and pharmacological approaches

In order to optimally deliver combined pharmacological and psychosocial treatments, medication-prescribing clinicians delivering psychosocial treatment and patients should work together to develop a treatment plan that provides education, information, and actions. Because of potential differences in theoretical orientation, training, and experience among clinicians that prescribe medication are those that deliver psychosocial therapy, it is important to keep open communication among all members of the treatment team and to provide information and education about medications to those who require it. Several step-by-step treatment procedures have been developed to integrate psychosocial therapies with pharmacotherapies for alcoholism and drug abuse (O'Malley & Carroll, 1996;

Pettinati, Volpicelli, Pierce, & O'Brien, 2000). These procedures utilize patient education, feedback, emotional support, medication monitoring, and, in the context of a brief intervention and motivational enhancement model, support for medication adherence.

CONCLUSIONS

This chapter summarized both FDA-approved and new promising pharmacotherapies in the treatment of drug addiction. Considerable evidence exists that adding adjunctive pharmacological treatment to traditional psychosocial treatments can improve therapeutic success significantly. Effective, FDA-approved pharmacotherapies currently exist for alcohol, opiate, and nicotine dependence. In the future, new pharmacotherapies will be developed that are even more therapeutically effective, cost-effective, matched to treatment based on patient characteristics, and used easily outside of specialty settings (e.g., in primary care). However, pharmacotherapies will only be effective to the extent they are accepted by clinicians and patients.

REFERENCES

Addolorato, G., Caputo, F., Capristo, E., Domenicali, M., Bernardi, M., Janiri, L., et al. (2002). Baclofen efficacy in reducing alcohol craving and intake: A preliminary double-blind randomized controlled study. *Alcohol and Alcoholism*, *37*, 504–508.

Addolorato, G., Leggio, L., Abenavoli, L., Gasbarrini, G., & Alcoholism Treatment Study Group. (2005). Neurobiochemical and clinical aspects of craving in alcohol addiction: A review. *Addictive Behaviors*, *30*, 1209–1224.

Addolorato, G., Leggio, L., Ferrulli, A., Cardone, S., Vonghia, L., Mirijello, A., et al. (2007). Effectiveness and safety of baclofen for maintenance of alcohol abstinence in alcohol-dependent patients with liver cirrhosis: Randomised, double-blind controlled study. *Lancet*, *370*, 1915–1922.

Anton, R. F., O'Malley, S. S., Ciraulo, D. A., Cisler, R. A., Couper, D., Donovan, D. M., et al. (2006). Combined pharmacotherapies and behavioral interventions for alcohol dependence: The COMBINE study: A randomized controlled trial. *JAMA*, *295*, 2003–2017.

Anton, R. F., Oroszi, G., O'Malley, S., Couper, D., Swift, R., Pettinati, H., et al. (2008). An evaluation of mu-opioid receptor (OPRM1) as a predictor of naltrexone response in the treatment of alcohol dependence: Results from the Combined Pharmacotherapies and Behavioral Interventions for Alcohol Dependence (COMBINE) study. *Archives of General Psychiatry*, *65*, 135–144.

Bouza, C., Angeles, M., Muñoz, A., & Amate, J. M. (2004). Efficacy and safety of naltrexone and acamprosate in the treatment of alcohol dependence: A systematic review. *Addiction*, *99*, 811–828.

Brewer, C. (1993). Recent developments in disulfiram treatment. *Alcohol and Alcoholism*, *28*, 383–395.

Cahill, K., & Ussher, M. (2007). Cannabinoid type 1 receptor antagonists (rimonabant) for smoking cessation. *Cochrane Database of Systematic Reviews*, Issue 4. Art. No.: CD005353.

Capone, T., Brahen, L., Condren, R., Kordal, N., Melchionda, R., & Peterson, M. (1986). Retention and outcome in a narcotic antagonist treatment program. *Journal of Clinical Psychology*, *42*, 825–833.

Carroll, K. M., Nich, C., Ball, S. A., McCance, E., Frankforter, T. L., & Rounsaville, B. J. (2000). One-year follow-up of disulfiram and psychotherapy for cocaine-alcohol users: Sustained effects of treatment. *Addiction*, *95*, 1335–1349.

Chick, J., Anton, R., Checinski, K., Croop, R., Drummond, D. C., Farmer, R., et al. (2000). A multicentre, randomized, double-blind, placebo-controlled trial of naltrexone in the treatment of alcohol dependence or abuse. *Alcohol and Alcoholism*, *35*, 587–593.

Chick, J., Gough, K., Falkowski, W., Kershaw, P., Hore, B., Mehta, B., et al. (1992). Disulfiram treatment of alcoholism. *British Journal of Psychiatry*, *161*, 84–89.

Code of Federal Regulations (42 CFR, Part 8). Certification of Opioid Treatment Programs.

Comer, S. D., Sullivan, M. A., Yu, E., Rothenberg, J. L., Kleber, H. D., Kampman, K., et al. (2006). Injectable, sustained-release naltrexone for the treatment of opioid dependence: A randomized, placebo-controlled trial. *Archives of General Psychiatry*, *63*, 210–218.

Dackis, C. A., Lynch, K. G., Yu, E., Samaha, F. F., Kampman, K. M., Cornish, J. W., et al. (2003). Modafinil and cocaine: A double-blind, placebo-controlled drug interaction study. *Drug and Alcohol Dependence*, *70*, 29–37.

D'Aunno, T., & Pollack, H. A. (2002). Changes in methadone treatment practices: Results from a national panel study, 1988–2000. *JAMA*, *288*, 850–856.

Davidson, D., Swift, R. M., & Fitz, E. (1996). Naltrexone increases the latency to drink alcohol in social drinkers. *Alcoholism: Clinical and Experimental Research*, *20*, 732–739.

de Wildt, W. A., Schippers, G. M., Van Den Brink, W., Potgieter, A. S., Deckers, F., & Bets, D. (2002). Does psychosocial treatment enhance the efficacy of acamprosate in patients with alcohol problems? *Alcohol and Alcoholism*, *37*, 375–382.

Dole, V. P., & Nyswander, M. (1965). A medical treatment for diacetylmorphine (heroin) addiction: Clinical trial with methadone hydrochloride. *JAMA*, *193*, 646–650.

Donovan, D. M., Anton, R. F., Miller, W. R., Longabaugh, R., Hosking, J. D., Youngblood, M., et al. (2008). Combined pharmacotherapies and behavioral interventions for alcohol dependence (The COMBINE study): Examination of posttreatment drinking outcomes. *Journal of Studies on Alcohol and Drugs*, *69*, 5–13.

Eisenberg, M. J., Filion, K. B., Yavin, D., Bélisle, P., Mottillo, S., Joseph, L., et al. (2008). Pharmacotherapies for smoking cessation: A meta-analysis of randomized controlled trials. *Canadian Medical Association Journal*, *179*, 135–144.

Feeney, G. F., Connor, J. P., Young, R. M., Tucker, J., & McPherson, A. (2006). Combined acamprosate and naltrexone, with cognitive behavioural therapy is superior to either medication alone for alcohol abstinence: A single centres' experience with pharmacotherapy. *Alcohol and Alcoholism*, *41*, 321–327.

Fiore, M. C., Jaén, C. R., Baker, T. B., et al. (May 2008). *Treating tobacco use and dependence:* 2008 update. *Clinical practice guideline*. Rockville, MD: U.S. Department of Health and Human Services. Public Health Service.

Fuller, R. K., Branchley, L., Brightwell, D. R., Derman, R. M., Emrick, C. D., Iber, F. L., et al. (1986). Disulfiram treatment of alcoholism: A Veterans Administration cooperative study. *JAMA, 256*, 1449–1455.

Garbutt, J. C., Kranzler, H. R., O'Malley, S. S., Gastfriend, D. R., Pettinati, H. M., Silverman, B. L., et al. (2005). Efficacy and tolerability of long-acting injectable naltrexone for alcohol dependence: a randomized controlled trial. *JAMA, 293*, 1617–1625.

Hays, J. T., Hurt, R. D., Rigotti, N. A., Niaura, R., Gonzales, D., Durcan, M. J., et al. (2001). Sustained-release bupropion for pharmacologic relapse prevention after smoking cessation: A randomized, controlled trial. *Annals of Internal Medicine, 135*, 423–433.

Heidbreder, C. A., & Hagan, J. J. (2005). Novel pharmacotherapeutic approaches for the treatment of drug addiction and craving. *Current Opinion in Pharmacology, 5*, 107–118.

Higgins, S. T. (1996). Some potential contributions of reinforcement and consumer-demand theory to reducing cocaine use. *Addictive Behavior, 21*, 803–816.

Hughes, J. R., Goldstein, M. G., Hurt, R. D., & Shiffman, S. (1999). Recent advances in the pharmacotherapy of smoking. *JAMA, 281*, 72–76.

Hurt, R. D., Sachs, D. P., Glover, E. D., Offord, K. P., Johnston, J. A., Dale, L. C., et al. (1997). A comparison of sustained-release bupropion and placebo for smoking cessation. *New England Journal of Medicine, 337*, 1195–1202.

Hutchison, K. E., Ray, L., Sandman, E., Rutter, M. C., Peters, A., Davidson, D., et al. (2006). The effect of olanzapine on craving and alcohol consumption. *Neuropsychopharmacology, 31*, 1310–1317.

Johnson, B. A., Ait-Daoud, N., Bowden, C. L., DiClemente, C. C., Roache, J. D., Lawson, K., et al. (2003). Oral topiramate for treatment of alcohol dependence: A randomised controlled trial. *Lancet, 361*, 1677–1685.

Johnson, B. A., Roache, J. D., Javors, M. A., DiClemente, C. C., Cloninger, C. R., Prihoda, T. J., et al. (2000). Ondansetron for reduction of drinking among biologically predisposed alcoholic patients: A randomized controlled trial. *JAMA, 284*, 963–971.

Johnson, B. A., Rosenthal, N., Capece, J. A., Wiegand, F., Mao, L., Beyers, K., et al. (2007). Topiramate for treating alcohol dependence: A randomized controlled trial. *JAMA, 298*, 1641–1651.

Jorenby, D. E., Leischow, S. J., Nides, M. A., Rennard, S. I., Johnston, J. A., Hughes, A. R., et al. (1999). A controlled trial of sustained-release bupropion, a nicotine patch, or both for smoking cessation. *New England Journal of Medicine, 340*, 685–691.

Kakko, J., Grönbladh, L., Svanborg, K. D., von Wachenfeldt, J., Rück, C., Rawlings, B., Nilsson, L. H., & Heilig, M. (2007). A stepped care strategy using buprenorphine and methadone versus conventional methadone maintenance in heroin dependence: A randomized controlled trial. *American Journal of Psychiatry, 164*(5): 797–803.

Kampman, K. M., Pettinati, H., Lynch, K. G., Dackis, C., Sparkman, T., Weigley, C., & O'Brien, C. P. (2004). A pilot trial of topiramate for the treatment of cocaine dependence. *Drug and Alcohol Dependence, 75*, 233–240.

Kampman, K. M., Pettinati, H. M., Lynch, K. G., Whittingham, T., Macfadden, W., Dackis, C., et al. (2007). A double-blind, placebo-controlled pilot trial of quetiapine for the treatment of type A and type B alcoholism. *Journal of Clinical Psychopharmacology*, *27*, 344–351.

Kiefer, F., Jahn, H., Tarnaske, T., Helwig, H., Briken, P., Holzbach, R., et al. (2003). Comparing and combining naltrexone and acamprosate in relapse prevention of alcoholism: A double-blind, placebo-controlled study. *Archives of General Psychiatry*, *60*, 92–99.

Koob, G. F. (2006a). The neurobiology of addiction: A neuroadaptational view relevant for diagnosis. *Addiction*, *101*(Suppl 1), 23–30.

Koob, G. F. (2006b). Alcoholism: Allostasis and beyond. *Alcoholism: Clinical and Experimental Research*, *27*, 232–243.

Kosten, T. R., & Kleber, H. D. (1984). Strategies to improve compliance with narcotic antagonists. *American Journal of Drug and Alcohol Abuse*, *10*, 249–266.

Kranzler, H. R., Wesson, D. R., & Billot, L. (2004). Naltrexone depot for treatment of alcohol dependence: A multicenter, randomized, placebo-controlled clinical trial. *Alcoholism: Clinical and Experimental Research*, *28*, 1051–1059.

Krystal, J. H., Cramer, J. A., Krol, W. F., Kirk, G. F., Rosenheck, R. A., & Veterans Affairs Naltrexone Cooperative Study 425 Group. (2001). Naltrexone in the treatment of alcohol dependence. *New England Journal of Medicine*, *345*, 1734–1739.

Lappalainen, J., Kranzler, H. R., Malison, R., Price, L. H., Van Dyck, C., Rosenheck, R. A., et al. (2002). A functional neuropeptide Y Leu7Pro polymorphism associated with alcohol dependence in a large population sample from the United States. *Archives of General Psychiatry*, *59*, 825–831.

Le Foll, B., & George, T. P. (2007). Treatment of tobacco dependence: Integrating recent progress into practice. *Canadian Medical Association Journal*, *177*, 1373–1380.

Leggio, L., Kenna, G. A., & Swift, R. M. (2008). New developments for the pharmacological treatment of alcohol withdrawal syndrome: A focus on non-benzodiazepine GABAergic medications. *Progress in Neuropsychopharmacology and Biological Psychiatry*, *32*, 1106–1117.

Ling, W., Rawson, R. A., & Compton, P. A. (1994). Substitution pharmacotherapies for opioid addiction: From methadone to LAAM and buprenorphine. *Journal of Psychoactive Drugs*, *26*, 119–128.

Mann, K., Lehert, P., & Morgan, M. Y. (2004). The efficacy of acamprosate in the maintenance of abstinence in alcohol-dependent individuals: Results of a meta-analysis. *Alcoholism: Clinical and Experimental Research*, *28*, 51–63.

Mason, B. J., Goodman, A. M., Chabac, S., & Lehert, P. (2006). Effect of oral acamprosate on abstinence in patients with alcohol dependence in a double-blind, placebo-controlled trial: The role of patient motivation. *Journal of Psychiatric Research*, *40*, 383–393.

Mattick, R. P., Breen, C., Kimber, J., & Davoli, M. (2003). Methadone maintenance therapy versus no opiate replacement therapy for opiate dependence. *Cochrane Database of Systematic Reviews 2003*, CD002209.

McLellan, A. T., Lewis, D. C., O'Brien, C. P., & Kleber, H. D. (2000). Drug dependence, a chronic medical illness, implications for treatment, insurance, and outcomes evaluation. *JAMA*, *284*, 1689–1695.

Monti, P., Rohsenow, D., Hutchison, K., Swift, R. M., Mueller, T. I., Colby, S. M., et al. (1999). Naltrexone's effect on cue-elicited craving among alcoholics in treatment. *Alcoholism: Clinical and Experimental Research*, *23*, 1386–1394.

Monti, P. M., Rohsenow, D. J., Swift, R., Gulliver, S. B., Colby, S. M., Mueller, T. I., et al. (2001). Naltrexone and cue-exposure with coping and communications skills training for alcoholics: Treatment process and one-year outcomes. *Alcoholism: Clinical and Experimental Research*, *25*, 1634–1647.

Nestler, E. J. (2001). Molecular basis of long-term plasticity underlying addiction. *Nat Rev Neurosci*, *2*, 119–128.

NIAAA (2007). *Helping patients who drink too much: A clinician's guide*. NIAAA NIH Government Publications 2007 Edition. Available at http://www.niaaa.nih.gov/publications/Practitioner/guide.pdf.

Nides, M., Oncken, C., Gonzales, D., Rennard, S., Watsky, E. J., Anziano, R., et al. (2006). Smoking cessation with varenicline, a selective alpha4beta2 nicotinic receptor partial agonist: Results from a 7-week, randomized, placebo- and bupropion-controlled trial with 1-year follow-up. *Archives of Internal Medicine*, *166*, 1561–1568.

O'Brien, C. P. (2005). Anticraving medications for relapse prevention: A possible new class of psychoactive medications. *American Journal of Psychiatry*, *162*, 1423–1431.

O'Farrell, T. J., Allen, J. P., & Litten, R. Z. (1995). Disulfiram (antabuse) contracts in treatment of alcoholism. *NIDA Research Monograph*, *150*, 65–91.

O'Malley, S. S., & Carroll, K. M. (1996). Psychotherapeutic considerations in pharmacological trials. *Alcoholism: Clinical and Experimental Research*, *20*(7 Suppl), 17A–22A.

O'Malley, S. S., Jaffe, A. J., Chang, G., Schottenfeld, R. S., Meyer, R. E., & Rounsaville, B. (1992). Naltrexone and coping skills therapy for alcohol dependence: A controlled study. *Archives of General Psychiatry*, *49*, 881–887.

O'Malley, S. S., Rounsaville, B. J., Farren, C., Namkoong, K., Wu, R., Robinson, J., et al. (2003). Initial and maintenance naltrexone treatment for alcohol dependence using primary care vs specialty care: A nested sequence of 3 randomized trials. *Archives of Internal Medicine*, *163*, 1695–1704.

Oncken, C., Gonzales, D., Nides, M., Rennard, S., Watsky, E., Billing, C. B., et al. (2006). Efficacy and safety of the novel selective nicotinic acetylcholine receptor partial agonist, varenicline, for smoking cessation. *Archives of Internal Medicine*, *166*, 1571–1577.

Oslin, D. W., Berrettini, W., Kranzler, H. R., Pettinati, H., Gelernter, J., Volpicelli, J. R., et al. (2003). A functional polymorphism of the mu-opioid receptor gene is associated with naltrexone response in alcohol-dependent patients. *Neuropsychopharmacology*, *28*(8), 1546–1552.

Paille, F. M., Guelfi, J. D., Perkins, A. C., Royer, R. J., Steru, L., & Parot, P. (1995). Double-blind randomized multicentre trial of acamprosate in maintaining abstinence from alcohol. *Alcohol and Alcoholism*, *30*, 239–247.

Pelc, I., Ansoms, C., Lehert, P., Fischer, F., Fuchs, W. J., Landron, F., et al. (2002). The European NEAT program: An integrated approach using acamprosate and psychosocial support for the prevention of relapse in alcohol-dependent patients with a statistical modeling of therapy success prediction. *Alcoholism, Clinical and Experimental Research*, *26*, 1529–1538.

Pelc, I., Verbanck, P., LeBon, O., Gavrilovic, M., Lion, K., & Lehert, P. (1997). Efficacy and safety of acamprosate in the treatment of detoxified alcohol-dependent patients: A 90-day placebo-controlled dose finding study. *British Journal of Psychiatry*, *171*, 73–77.

Pettinati, H. M., Volpicelli, J. R., Pierce, J. D., & O'Brien, C. P. (2000). Improving naltrexone response: An intervention for medical practitioners to enhance medication compliance in alcohol dependent patients. *Journal of Addictive Diseases, 19*(1), 71–83.

Resnick, R. B., Schuyten-Resnick, E., & Washton, A. M. (1980). Assessment of narcotic antagonists in the treatment of opioid dependence. *Annual Review of Pharmacology and Toxicology, 20*, 463–474.

Robinson, T. E., & Berridge, K. C. (1993). The neural basis of drug craving: An incentive-sensitization theory of addiction. *Brain Research Reviews, 18*, 247–291.

Rounsaville, B. J., Gawin, F. H., & Kleber, H. D. (1985). Interpersonal psychotherapy adapted for ambulatory cocaine users. *American Journal of Drug and Alcohol Abuse, 11*, 171.

Sass, H., Soyka, M., Mann, K., & Zieglgansberger, W. (1996). Relapse prevention by acamprosate: Results from a placebo controlled study on alcohol dependence. *Archives of General Psychiatry, 53*, 673–680.

Schroeder, J. P., Overstreet, D. H., & Hodge, C. W. (2005). The neuropeptide-Y Y5 receptor antagonist L-152,804 decreases alcohol self-administration in inbred alcohol-preferring (iP) rats. *Alcohol, 36*, 179–186.

Senay, E. C. (1985). Methadone maintenance treatment. *International Journal of the Addictions, 20*, 803–821.

Shoptaw, S., Yang, X., Rotheram-Fuller, E. J., Hsieh, Y.-C., Kintaudie, P. C., Charuvastra, V. C., et al. (2003). Randomized placebo-controlled trial of baclofen for cocaine dependence: Preliminary effects for individuals with chronic patterns of cocaine use. *Journal of Clinical Psychiatry, 64*, 1440–1448.

Silagy, C., Lancaster, T., Stead, L., Mant, D., & Fowler, G. (2004). Nicotine replacement therapy for smoking cessation. *Cochrane Database of Systematic Reviews 2004*, CD000146(3).

Soyka, M., Preuss, U., & Schuetz, C. (2002). Use of acamprosate and different kinds of psychosocial support in relapse prevention of alcoholism: Results from a non-blind, multicentre study. *Drugs R&D, 3*, 1–12.

Srisurapanont, M., & Jarusuraisin, N. (2005). Naltrexone for the treatment of alcoholism: A meta-analysis of randomized controlled trials. *International Journal of Neuropsychopharmacology, 8*, 267–280.

Strain, E. C., Stitzer, M. L., Liebson, I. A., & Bigelow, G. E. (1994). Comparison of buprenorphine and methadone in the treatment of opioid dependence. *American Journal of Psychiatry, 151*, 1025–1030.

Suh, J. J., Pettinati, H. M., Kampman, K. M., & O'Brien, C. P. (2006). The status of disulfiram: A half of a century later. *Journal of Clinical Psychopharmacology, 26*, 290–302.

Swift, R. (2007). Emerging approaches to managing alcohol dependence. *American Journal of Health-System Pharmacy, 64*(5 Suppl 3), S12–S22.

Swift, R. M. (1999). Drug therapy for alcohol dependence. *New England Journal of Medicine, 340*, 1482–1490.

Swift, R. M., Whelihan, W., Kuznetsov, O., Buongiorno, G., & Hsuing, H. (1994). Naltrexone-induced alterations in human ethanol intoxication. *American Journal of Psychiatry, 151*, 1463–1467.

Thomas, C. P., Wallack, S. S., Lee, S., McCarty, D., & Swift, R. (2003). Research to practice: Adoption of naltrexone in alcoholism treatment. *Journal of Substance Abuse Treatment, 24*, 1–11.

Thomas, S. E., & Miller, P. M. (2007). Knowledge and attitudes about pharmacotherapy for alcoholism: A survey of counselors and administrators in community-based addiction treatment centres. *Alcohol and Alcoholism*, *42*, 113–118.

Vocci, F. J., Acri, J., & Elkashef, A. (2005). Medication development for addictive disorders: The state of the science. *American Journal of Psychiatry*, *162*, 1432–1440.

Volpicelli, J. R., Alterman, A. I., Hayashida, M., & O'Brien, C. P. (1992). Naltrexone in the treatment of alcohol dependence. *Archives of General Psychiatry*, *49*, 876–880.

Volpicelli, J. R., Rhines, K. C., Rhines, J. S., Volpicelli, L. A., Alterman, A. I., & O'Brien, C. P. (1997). Naltrexone and alcohol dependence: Role of subject compliance. *Archives of General Psychiatry*, *54*, 737–742.

Volpicelli, J. R., Watson, N. T., King, A. C., Sherman, C., & O'Brien, C. P. (1995). Effect of naltrexone on alcohol "high" in alcoholics. *American Journal of Psychiatry*, *152*, 613–615.

Weiss, R. D., & Kueppenbender, K. D. (2006). Combining psychosocial treatment with pharmacotherapy for alcohol dependence. *Journal of Clinical Psychopharmacology*, *26*(Suppl 1), S37–S42.

Wise, R. A., & Bozarth, M. A. (1987). A psychomotor stimulant theory of addiction. *Psychological Reviews*, *94*(4), 469–492.

PART | FOUR

Special Populations and Applications

Chapter | sixteen

Addiction Treatment Disparities: Ethnic and Sexual Minority Populations

Arthur W. Blume, Michelle R. Resor, and Anthony V. Kantin
University of North Carolina Charlotte

SUMMARY POINTS

- Some minority groups are at high risk for substance-related health consequences.
- Health disparities exist that prevent some minority groups from accessing treatment.
- Little is known about whether empirically supported therapies (those shown by research to have efficacy to treat addictive behaviors) work well for specific minority groups.
- Cultural mismatch, prejudice, and therapist insensitivity can contribute to poorer treatment outcomes.
- Many minority communities are partnering with researchers and service providers to re-create empirically supported therapy that is culturally relevant for their communities.

Some segments of American society do not benefit from treatment services in the same way as the majority population. When minority groups do not experience the same benefits from treatment as the

Evidence-Based Addiction Treatment

majority population, it is referred to as a treatment disparity (Institute of Medicine, 2003). Disparities can exist for any portion of the population that is in the minority and subject to disempowerment in the greater society. Health care disparities represent a major public health problem that contributes to poorer health, decreased quality of life, and lower life expectancy (Centers for Disease Control and Prevention, 2004).

Many ethnic minority groups have been identified as having unique challenges with regard to substance use problems. For example, African-American men tend to have higher alcohol abuse rates than European-American men (Galvan & Caetano, 2003). African Americans tend to be greatly overrepresented in jails and prisons across the United States, many convicted of crimes that are the direct or indirect result of substance abuse (Bureau of Prisons, 2008; U.S. Department of Justice, 2007). In 2005, homicides, often linked to substance abuse, were the sixth leading cause of death for all African Americans, whereas liver diseases that often are attributable to alcohol abuse were a leading cause of death for African Americans ages 45–64 (National Center for Injury Prevention and Control [NCIPC], 2008).

Some American-Indian and Alaska Native communities have high rates of substance abuse or dependence, although there is a great deal of variation between nations and communities. American Indians and Alaska Natives have been identified as having higher rates of substance abuse and dependence than the general population (Substance Abuse and Mental Health Services Administration [SAMHSA], 2003), but many communities also have higher abstinence rates than European Americans. The sixth leading cause of death in 2005 for American Indians and Alaska Natives was liver disease, often secondary to alcohol abuse. In fact, the eight leading causes of death for Native people in 2005 were heart disease, cancer, unintentional injury, diabetes, strokes, liver diseases, chronic lower respiratory disease, and suicide (NCIPC, 2008); all have been linked directly or indirectly to substance abuse.

Asian and Pacific Island American communities have been identified as generally experiencing lower substance abuse rates than the general population in the United States (e.g., Grant et al., 2004), although liver diseases are a leading cause of death for those aged 25–64 (NCIPC, 2008). However, there is a wide variation in substance use experiences between Asian and Pacific Islander subgroups (SAMHSA, 2008). For example, Pacific Islander groups, including Native Hawaiians, often have substance abuse rates that match or exceed those in the general population (e.g., Wong, Klingle, & Price, 2004). Furthermore, evidence exists that substance dependence may be on the rise among this population group (Grant et al., 2004).

Hispanic and Latino populations vary widely as well. Vast generalizations about substance abuse are difficult and often misleading, as there are major differences between subgroups. However, studies have found portions of Hispanic and Latino populations to be at risk for substance abuse and its associated negative health outcomes. Mexican and Puerto-Rican Americans have been identified as being at risk for substance dependence, with males especially at risk (SAMHSA, 2008). Liver disease is the sixth leading cause of death for Hispanics and Latinos of all ages, and like Native Americans, the eight leading causes of death for Hispanic and Latino Americans have been linked directly and indirectly to addictions (heart disease, cancers, unintentional injuries, heart disease, diabetes, liver disease, homicide, and chronic lower respiratory disease; NCIPC, 2008).

Sexual minorities, namely lesbian, gay, bisexual, and transgender (LGBT) people, also have unique concerns with regard to substance abuse. Very little is known about the prevalence of substance abuse and dependence among LGBT Americans. Data from the National Household Survey on Drug Abuse indicate that participants who reported same sex or both sex partners experienced a greater number of substance dependence symptoms than participants who reported opposite sex partners only (Cochran, Sullivan, & Mays, 2003). Additionally, lesbians may abstain less often and experience more substance use-related consequences than heterosexual women (Skinner, 1994). In another study conducted in Washington State, LBGT treatment clients reported significantly less alcohol abuse than heterosexual clients; bisexual, gay, or transgender men were more likely to report stimulant abuse than heterosexual men; and lesbian, bisexual, and transgender women were more likely to report heroin abuse than heterosexual women (Cochran & Cauce, 2006). Sexual minorities may decrease their alcohol and drug use at a slower rate than other groups as they age (Labouvie, 1996; McKirnan & Peterson, 1989), but the general trend has been toward lower overall rates of substance use among older gays and lesbians (Hughes & Eliason, 2002).

ADDICTION TREATMENT DISPARITIES

Addiction treatment disparities can be conceptualized broadly as indicating poorer clinical outcomes among minority groups than for the majority population with regard to substance abuse treatment or therapy. Addiction treatment disparities can be generally linked to two sources: poorer utilization of treatment by the minority group or poorer outcomes after completion of treatment when compared to the majority.

African Americans tend to be overrepresented in treatment centers (SAMHSA, 2002) and may do better than European Americans with regard to treatment outcomes. However, evidence also shows that African-Americans may be more dissatisfied with the delivery of treatment than European Americans despite positive outcomes (Tonigan, 2003). Communicating dissatisfaction with treatment to others in the African American community could potentially dissuade others from seeking treatment. African Americans also report being dissuaded from seeking treatment because of lengthy waiting lists to enter treatment (Grant, 1997).

However, many other minority groups are highly underrepresented in treatment. Although it is difficult to know with certainty, it is likely that American Indians and Alaska Natives are underserved when it comes to the treatment needs, especially with regard to treating people with co-occurring psychiatric disorders (U. S. Department of Health and Human Services, 2001). Very little is known about treatment outcomes among American Indians and Alaska Natives. One small study that examined American Indians in California found that those who completed treatment had comparable outcomes to all others but that the American-Indian participants were significantly less likely to complete treatment or receive as many individual counseling sessions (Evans, Spear, Huang, & Hser, 2006). Asian and Pacific Islander Americans with substance dependence are significantly less likely to admit the need for or seek treatment than Caucasians with substance dependence (Sakai, Ho, Shore, Risk, & Price, 2005) and, like African Americans, those who do seek treatment tend to be more dissatisfied about it than other population groups (Niv, Wong, & Hser, 2007). Hispanics and Latinos also have been found to be highly underrepresented in treatment except for court-mandated drinking and driving programs (National Institute on Alcohol Abuse and Alcoholism, 1997).

CONDITIONS THAT CREATE DISPARITIES

Poverty is one of the leading contributors to disparities (Krieger, Chen, Waterman, Rehkopf, & Subramanian, 2005). The working poor often are un- or underinsured, and those who live in impoverished neighborhoods tend to have limited access to state-of-the-art treatment providing empirically supported therapies and other needed services (Stockdale, Tang, Zhang, Belin, & Wells, 2007; Wu, Gilbert, Piff, & Sanders, 2004). Lack of insurance is a major factor preventing access to health care services, and ethnic minorities often bear the brunt of being uninsured in the United States. For example, an estimated one-third of all Hispanic and Latinos are uninsured, including 40% of Mexican Americans in the United States without insurance (Healthy People 2010, 2000). Being uninsured can be a double-bind, given that uninsured workers are also at greater risk for substance abuse than those workers who have insurance (Galvin, Miller, Spicer, & Waehrer, 2007).

ASSESSMENT ISSUES

Biased mental health assessment has contributed to the misdiagnosis and mistreatment of some ethnic minority clients (e.g., Snowden, 2003). Regarding substance use, evidence shows that ethnic minority clients may respond differently than European-American clients on substance use measures in ways that can lead to diagnostic misinterpretation (Choca, Shanley, Peterson, & Van Denburg, 1990; Volk, Cantor, Steinbauer, & Cass, 1997; Zager & Megargee, 1981). There are multiple problems with assessing addictive behaviors across cultures. Translating addictive behavior measures into other languages can cause the content and meaning of questions to change when English words do not have equivalents in other languages (e.g., Leung & Arthur, 2000; Mason, 1995). Because many assessments have not been normed on a specific ethnic minority population, normal or abnormal substance use behavior cannot be defined well for that population. What may be normative for majority society may not be normative for its subgroups. Measurement constructs that may be applicable in one culture may not be applicable in another. In other words, psychopathology as defined in one culture may be completely acceptable behavior in another, and important constructs in U.S. majority society such as individualism, autonomy, or self may not be important for other cultures, therefore rendering measures that assume individualism, autonomy, or self meaningless (Blume, Morera, & García de la Cruz, 2005).

TREATMENT ISSUES

Delivering treatment across cultures also can be fraught with problems. This is especially true for first-generation Americans or others who continue to live in small communities where English is seldom spoken. Under these conditions, having bilingual staff improves the utilization of treatment services (Snowden, Masland, Ma, & Ciemens, 2006). Cultural stigma associated with professional treatment is another factor that may prevent individuals from seeking treatment. Seeking substance abuse treatment may run counter to prevailing cultural beliefs concerning self-control of personal behavior. Admitting to drinking or drug use problems may bring shame upon families (Fong & Tsuang, 2007; Grandbois, 2005; Ja & Aoki, 1993). Another serious roadblock involves the possibility of a cultural mismatch between treatment staff and their treatment model and a client's cultural beliefs and values.

DIFFERENCE IN CULTURAL VALUES MAY IMPACT TREATMENT OUTCOMES

A clash of values between minority clients and the prevailing models of therapy can cause problems with treatment accessibility, adherence, persistence, and completion. Important ethnic minority cultural values that may clash with prevailing treatment models include the esteemed place of family and community over the roles of individuals, cultural understandings of respect and shame, process and style of social interactions, pace of life, gender roles, and spiritual practices (e.g., Marin, 1990; Sue & Sue, 2003a). As an example concerning the role of family, treatment accessibility for Hispanic and Latino clients may be impacted negatively because individuals have concerns being separated from their families (Kline, 1996).

Most addiction treatment is focused on treating individuals but many minority groups are collectivistic in outlook and insist on full extended family participation in treatment. Family life and relationships are highly valued and tend to heavily influence the behaviors of its members. Effective treatment requires working with the extended families rather than focusing on individual progress and autonomy (Gaines et al., 1997; Sue & Sue, 2003a). In addition, treatment professionals may not be aware that gender roles may be quite different in a minority culture. Professionals may not be sensitive to the fact that birth order often defines specific roles in families and communities (Gushue & Sciarra, 1995; Sue & Sue, 2003b,c). The cultural expectations of these roles can represent barriers to seeking and completing treatment. These barriers are more pronounced for clients who are not highly acculturated (i.e., those who do not feel competent in negotiating the prevailing beliefs, values, and traditions of the majority society).

PREJUDICE, RACISM, AND HOMOPHOBIA

Minority groups often encounter stereotypes and prejudice in their daily lives. Ethnic minorities may face racism, whereas sexual minorities may experience homophobia and heterosexism. Research has found that exposure to these adverse events can be quite harmful to individual physical and mental health (Gee, Spencer, Chen, Yip, & Takeuchi, 2007; Harrell, Hall, & Taliaferro, 2003). Stigmatization can serve as a trigger for increased substance abuse in members of historically oppressed groups (e.g., Cochran, Peavy, & Cauce, 2007).

For example, being a victim of racism has been associated with poor mental health, including substance abuse (Carter, 1994; Wingo, 2001). Prejudice and racism have been associated with being financially disadvantaged, a factor that has been linked to poor treatment outcomes

(Brewer, Catalano, Haggerty, Gainey, & Fleming, 1998; Ellis & McClure, 1992). Typically, therapists do not address the experience of prejudice and racism in therapy even though it may be a critically relevant factor in whether the client does well or not (Rhodes & Johnson, 1997). Furthermore, little research has been conducted to examine how prejudice and racism may be addressed in therapy.

Lesbian, gay, and bisexual youths may be at risk for unique stressors as they develop their sexual identities and cope with homophobic reactions from peers and adults (Savin-Williams, 1994). Depression can lead individuals to hesitate to disclose their sexual orientation (Ullrich, Lutgendorf, & Stapleton, 2003); in some cases, substance use can be a reaction to stress and depression related to these processes. In addition, LGBT individuals from ethnic minorities are at risk for exposure to multiple stereotypes (Cochran, Mays, Ortega, Alegria, & Takeuchi, 2007; Siegel & Epstein, 1996). Stigmatization based on sexual orientation is often widespread, including in treatment situations (Cochran, Peavy, & Cauce, 2007; Page, 2005; Travers & Schneider, 1996). Treatment professionals often will overlook issues of sexual orientation and may be poorly trained to work with LGBT clients, potentially jeopardizing treatment outcomes (Eliason, 2000; Eubanks-Carter, Burckell, & Goldfried, 2005; Hellman, Stanton, Lee, Tytun, & Vachon, 1989; Safren, 2005). Ideally, therapy for substance use disorders in sexual minorities will specifically address psychological factors associated with sexual identities (Barbara, 2002).

EMPIRICALLY BASED TREATMENT AND MINORITY CLIENTS

Treatment providers often assume that empirically supported therapy, tested in the majority culture, will be equally as effective with minority populations. In reality, there has been very little research testing whether therapy that has been tested scientifically and found to be effective for majority society actually is effective among minority clients (Voss Horrell, 2008). For example, McCrady (2000) reviewed evidence-based therapies for alcohol use disorders, but none of the studies reviewed targeted ethnic or sexual minorities exclusively and many of the studies had poor representation of one or many of the groups discussed in this chapter. The Project MATCH study, which tested three well-known therapies empirically—cognitive behavioral therapy (CBT), motivational enhancement therapy (MET), and 12-step facilitation therapy (TSF)—found that Hispanic and Latino clients with alcohol dependence did slightly better in CBT and MET than TSF (Arroyo, Miller, & Tonigan, 2003) and that American-Indian and Alaska Native clients did better in MET than CBT or TSF (Villanueva, Tonigan, & Miller, 2007). However, the samples for the minority participants were rather small.

Fortunately, there have been several recent efforts to transport empirically supported substance use interventions into ethnic minority communities, and many of the efforts involve cultural relevancy, usually by the addition of culturally relevant practices and traditions and the use of the native language in intervention materials (e.g., Hernandez et al., 2006; Marlatt et al., 2003). An ideal model for culturally relevancy is to include community stakeholders in the development, implementation, and evaluation of the treatment programs; a process often referred to as the community-based participatory model.

Similarly, treatment outcomes for sexual minorities in any types of psychotherapy are extremely limited (Cochran, Sullivan, & Mays, 2003). One randomized controlled trial examined the effectiveness of four types of treatment for gay and bisexual men who were dependent on methamphetamine (Shoptaw et al., 2005). Treatment modalities included combinations of CBT and contingency management. Results demonstrated overall reductions in methamphetamine use over time that did not significantly differ between treatment conditions at follow-ups.

SUMMARY

Ethnic minority and sexual minority individuals face unique challenges in accessing treatment services. Once treatment is accessed, additional problems are faced by minority clients. Frequently, the prevailing treatment models do not account for minority cultural values and traditional practices, and therapists often are insensitive to cultural differences inherent in their minority clients. Addressing specific issues of relevance to positive outcomes for minority clients is often overlooked or avoided. A long history of minority clients being underserved and understudied has contributed to a general lack of understanding about how to effectively help them therapeutically. However, researchers and treatment professionals are now partnering with key stakeholders to improve treatment in ethnic minority communities. Much needs to be accomplished to reduce treatment disparities in the United States, but the new model of community-based participation in the development, implementation, and evaluation of treatment programs holds great promise in improving services to people who have been traditionally disempowered and poorly served in society.

REFERENCES

Arroyo, J. A., Miller, W. R., & Tonigan, J. S. (2003). The influence of Hispanic ethnicity on long-term outcome in three alcohol-treatment modalities. *Journal of Studies on Alcohol*, *64*, 98–104.

Barbara, A. M. (2002). Substance abuse treatment with lesbian, gay and bisexual people: A qualitative study of service providers. *Journal of Gay and Lesbian Social Services*, *14*, 1–17.

Blume, A. W., Morera, O. F., & García de la Cruz, B. (2005). Assessment of addictive behaviors in ethnic-minority populations. In D. M. Donovan & G. A. Marlatt (Eds.), *Assessment of addictive behaviors* (2nd ed., pp. 49–70). New York: Guilford Press.

Brewer, D. D., Catalano, R. F., Haggerty, K., Gainey, R. R., & Fleming, C. B. (1998). A meta-analysis of predictors of continued drug use during and after treatment for opiate addiction. *Addiction*, *93*, 73–92.

Bureau of Prisons. (2008). Quick facts about the Bureau of Prisons. Retrieved April 25, 2008, from http://www.bop.gov/news/quick.jsp.

Carter, J. H. (1994). Racism's impact on mental health. *JAMA*, *86*, 543–547.

Centers for Disease Control and Prevention. (2004). Health disparities experienced by racial/ethnic minority populations. *Morbidity and Mortality Weekly Report*, *53*, 755.

Choca, J. P., Shanley, L. A., Peterson, C. A., & Van Denburg, E. (1990). Racial bias and the MCMI. *Journal of Personality Assessment*, *54*, 479–490.

Cochran, B. N., & Cauce, A. M. (2006). Characteristics of lesbian, gay, bisexual, and transgender individuals entering substance abuse treatment. *Journal of Substance Abuse Treatment*, *30*, 135–146.

Cochran, B. N., Peavy, K. M., & Cauce, A. M. (2007). Substance abuse treatment providers' explicit and implicit attitudes regarding sexual minorities. *Journal of Homosexuality*, *53*, 181–207.

Cochran, S. D., Sullivan, J. G., & Mays, V. M. (2003). Prevalence of mental disorders, psychological distress, and mental health services use among lesbian, gay, and bisexual adults in the United States. *Journal of Consulting & Clinical Psychology*, *71*, 53–61.

Cochran, S. D., Mays, V. M., Ortega, A. N., Alegria, M., & Takeuchi, D. (2007). Mental health and substance use disorders among Latino and Asian American lesbian, gay, and bisexual adults. *Journal of Consulting & Clinical Psychology*, *75*, 785–794.

Eliason, M. J. (2000). Substance abuse counselors' attitudes regarding lesbian, gay, bisexual, and transgendered clients. *Journal of Substance Abuse*, *12*, 311–328.

Ellis, D., & McClure, J. (1992). In-patient treatment of alcohol problems: Predicting and preventing relapse. *Alcohol and Alcoholism*, *27*, 449–456.

Eubanks-Carter, C., Burckell, L. A., & Goldfried, M. R. (2005). Enhancing therapeutic effectiveness with lesbian, gay, and bisexual clients. *Clinical Psychology: Science and Practice*, *12*, 1–18.

Evans, E., Spear, S. E., Huang, Y.-C., & Hser, Y.-I. (2006). Outcomes of drug and alcohol treatment programs among American Indians in California. *American Journal of Public Health*, *96*, 889–896.

Fong, T., & Tsuang, J. (2007). Asian-Americans, addictions, and barriers to treatment. *Psychiatry*, *4*, 51–58.

Gaines, S. O., Jr., Marelich, W. D., Bledsoe, K. L., Steers, W. N., Henderson, M. C., Granrose, C. S., Barajas, L., et al. (1997). Links between race/ethnicity and cultural values as mediated by racial/ethnic identity and moderated by gender. *Journal of Personality and Social Psychology*, *72*, 1460–1476.

Galvan, F. H., & Caetano, R. (2003). Alcohol use and related problems among ethnic minorities in the United States. *Alcohol Research & Health*, *27*, 87–94.

Galvin, D., Miller, T., Spicer, R., & Waehrer, G. (2007). Substance abuse and the uninsured worker in the United States. *Journal of Public Health Policy*, *28*, 102–117.

Gee, G., Spencer, M., Chen, J., Yip, T., & Takeuchi, D. (2007). The association between self-reported racial discrimination and 12-month DSM-IV mental disorders among Asian Americans nationwide. *Social Science & Medicine*, *64*, 1984–1996.

Grandbois, D. (2005). Stigma of mental illness among American Indian and Alaska Native nations: Historical and contemporary perspectives. *Issues in Mental Health Nursing*, *26*, 1001–1024.

Grant, B. F. (1997). Barriers to alcoholism treatment: Reasons for not seeking treatment in a general population sample. *Journal of Studies on Alcohol*, *58*, 365–371.

Grant, B., Dawson, D., Stinson, F., Chou, S., Dufour, M., & Pickering, R. (2004). The 12-month prevalence and trends in DSM-IV alcohol abuse and dependence: United States, 1991–1992 and 2001–2002. *Drug and Alcohol Dependence*, *74*, 223–234.

Gushue, G. V., & Sciarra, D. T. (1995). Culture and families: A multidimensional approach. In J. G. Ponterotto, J. M. Casas, L. A. Suzuki, & C. M. Alexander (Eds.), *Handbook of multicultural counseling* (pp. 586–606). Thousand Oaks, CA: Sage.

Harrell, J., Hall, S., & Taliaferro, J. (2003). Physiological responses to racism and discrimination: An assessment of the evidence. *American Journal of Public Health*, *93*, 242–248.

Healthy People 2010. (2000). Access to quality health services. Retrieved April 25, 2008, from http://www.healthypeople.gov/Document/HTML/Volume1/01Access.htm.

Hellman, R. E., Stanton, M., Lee, J., Tytun, A., & Vachon, R. (1989). Treatment of homosexual alcoholics in government-funded agencies: Provider training and attitudes. *Hospital and Community Psychiatry*, *40*, 1163–1168.

Hernandez, D. V., Skewes, M. C., Resor, M. R., Villanueva, M. R., Hanson, B. S., & Blume, A. W. (2006). A pilot test of an alcohol skills training programme for Mexican-American college students. *International Journal of Drug Policy*, *17*, 320–328.

Hughes, T. L., & Eliason, M. (2002). Substance use and abuse in lesbian, gay, bisexual and transgender populations. *Journal of Primary Prevention*, *22*, 263–298.

Hughes, T. L., & Wilsnack, S. C. (2002). Use of alcohol among lesbians: Research and clinical implications. *American Journal of Orthopsychiatry*, *67*, 20–36.

Institute of Medicine. (2003). *Unequal treatment: Confronting racial and ethnic disparities in health care*. Washington, DC: Author.

Ja, D., & Aoki, B. (1993). Substance abuse treatment: Cultural barriers in the Asian-American community. *Journal of Psychoactive Drugs*, *25*, 61–71.

Kline, A. (1996). Pathways into drug user treatment: The influence of gender and racial/ethnic identity. *Substance Use and Misuse*, *31*, 323–342.

Krieger, N., Chen, J., Waterman, P., Rehkopf, D., & Subramanian, S. (2005). Painting a truer picture of US socioeconomic and racial/ethnic health inequalities: The public health disparities geocoding project. *American Journal of Public Health*, *95*, 312–323.

Labouvie, E. (1996). Maturing out of substance use: Selection and self correction. *Journal of Drug Issues*, *26*, 457–477.

Leung, S. F., & Arthur, D. (2000). The alcohol use disorders identification test (AUDIT): Validation of an instrument for enhancing nursing practice in Hong Kong. *International Journal of Nursing Studies*, *37*, 57–64.

Marin, B. V. (1990). Hispanic drug abuse: Culturally appropriate prevention and treatment. In R. R. Watson (Ed.), *Drug and alcohol abuse prevention* (pp. 151–165). Clifton, NJ: Humana Press.

Marlatt, G. A., Larimer, M. E., Mail, P. D., Hawkins, E. H., Cummins, L. H., Blume, A. W., et al. (2003). Journeys of the circle: A culturally congruent life skills intervention for adolescent Indian drinking. *Alcoholism: Clinical and Experimental Research*, *27*, 1327–1329.

Mason, M. J. (1995). A preliminary language validity analysis of the Problem Oriented Screening Instrument for Teenagers (POSIT). *Journal of Child and Adolescent Substance Abuse*, *4*, 61–68.

McCrady, B. S. (2000). Alcohol use disorders and the Division 12 task force of the American Psychological Association. *Psychology of Addictive Behaviors*, *14*, 267–276.

McKirnan, D. J., & Peterson, P. L. (1989). Alcohol and drug use among homosexual men and women: Epidemiology and population characteristics. *Addictive Behaviors*, *14*, 545–553.

National Center for Injury Prevention and Control. (2008). WISQARS leading causes of death reports, 1999–2005. Retrieved April 12, 2008, from http://webappa.cdc.gov/sasweb/ncipc/leadcaus10.html.

National Institute on Alcohol Abuse and Alcoholism. (1997). *Ninth special report to the U.S. congress on alcohol and health*. Bethesda, MD: Author.

Niv, N., Wong, U. C., & Hser, Y. I. (2007). Asian Americans in community-based substance abuse treatment: Service needs, utilization, and outcomes. *Journal of Substance Abuse Treatment*, *33*, 313–319.

Page, E. H. (2005). Mental health services experiences of bisexual women and bisexual men: An empirical study. *Journal of Bisexuality*, *4*, 137–160.

Rhodes, R., & Johnson, A. (1997). A feminist approach to treating alcohol and drug addicted African-American women. *Women and Therapy*, *20*, 23–37.

Safren, S. A. (2005). Affirmative, evidence-based, and ethically sound psychotherapy with lesbian, gay, and bisexual clients. *Clinical Psychology: Science and Practice*, *12*, 29–32.

Sakai, J. T., Ho, P. M., Shore, J. H., Risk, N. K., & Price, R. K. (2005). Asians in the United States: Substance dependence and use of substance-dependence treatment. *Journal of Substance Abuse Treatment*, *29*, 75–84.

Savin-Williams, R. C. (1994). Verbal and physical abuse as stressors in the lives of lesbian, gay male, and bisexual youths: Associations with school problems, running away, substance abuse, prostitution, and suicide. *Journal of Consulting & Clinical Psychology*, *62*, 261–269.

Shoptaw, S., Reback, C. J., Peck, J. A., Yang, X., Rotheram-Fuller, E., Larkins, S., et al. (2005). Behavioral treatment approaches for methamphetamine dependence and HIV-related sexual risk behaviors among urban gay and bisexual men. *Drug and Alcohol Dependence*, *78*, 125–134.

Siegel, K., & Epstein, J. A. (1996). Ethnic-racial differences in psychological stress related to gay lifestyle among HIV-positive men. *Psychological Reports*, *79*, 303–312.

Skinner, W. F. (1994). The prevalence and demographic predictors of illicit and licit drug use among lesbians and gay men. *American Journal of Public Health*, *84*, 1307–1310.

Snowden, L., Masland, M., Ma, Y., & Ciemens, E. (2006). Strategies to improve minority access to public mental health services in California: Description and preliminary evaluation. *Journal of Community Psychology*, *34*, 225–235.

Snowden, L. R. (2003). Bias in mental health assessment and intervention: Theory and evidence. *American Journal of Public Health*, *93*, 239–243.

Stockdale, S., Tang, L., Zhang, L., Belin, T., & Wells, K. (2007). The effects of health sector market factors and vulnerable group membership on access to alcohol, drug, and mental health care. *Health Services Research*, *42*, 1020–1041.

Substance Abuse and Mental Health Services Administration. (2002). *The DASIS Report: Black admissions to substance abuse treatment 1999*. Rockville, MD: Author.

Substance Abuse and Mental Health Services Administration. (2003). *The DASIS Report: Substance use among American Indians or Alaska Natives*. Rockville, MD: Author.

Substance Abuse and Mental Health Services Administration. (2008). *Prevalence of substance use among racial & ethnic subgroups in the U.S.* Rockville, MD: Author. Author. Retrieved March 24, 2008, from http://www.oas.samhsa.gov/NHSDA/Ethnic.ethn1006.htm.

Sue, D. W., & Sue, D. (Eds.) (2003a). Barriers to effective multicultural counseling/therapy. *Counseling the culturally diverse: Theory and practice* (pp. 95–121). New York: Wiley.

Sue, D. W., & Sue, D. (Eds.) (2003b). Counseling and therapy with racial/ethnic-minority populations. *Counseling the culturally diverse: Theory and practice* (pp. 291–376). New York: Wiley.

Sue, D. W., & Sue, D. (Eds.) (2003c). Multicultural family counseling and therapy. *Counseling the culturally diverse: Theory and practice* (pp. 151–176). New York: Wiley.

Tonigan, J. S. (2003). Project match treatment participation and outcome by self-reported ethnicity. *Alcoholism: Clinical and Experimental Research*, *27*, 1340–1344.

Travers, R., & Schneider, M. (1996). Barriers to accessibility for lesbian and gay youth needing addictions services. *Youth and Society*, *27*, 356–378.

Ullrich, P. M., Lutgendorf, S. K., & Stapleton, J. T. (2003). Concealment of homosexual identity, social support and CD4 cell count among HIV-seropositive gay men. *Journal of Psychosomatic Research*, *54*, 205–212.

U.S. Department of Health and Human Services. (2001). *Mental health: Culture, race, and ethnicity. A supplement to Mental Health: A report of the surgeon general*. Rockville, MD: Author.

U.S. Department of Justice. (2007). Prison and jail inmates at midyear 2006. Retrieved April 25, 2008, from http://www.ojp.usdoj.gov/bjs/pub/pdf/pjim06.pdf.

Villanueva, M., Tonigan, J. S., & Miller, W. R. (2007). Response of Native American clients to three treatment methods for alcohol dependence. *Journal of Ethnicity in Substance Abuse*, *6*, 41–48.

Volk, R. J., Cantor, S. B., Steinbauer, J. R., & Cass, A. R. (1997). Item bias in the CAGE screening test for alcohol use disorders. *Journal of General Internal Medicine*, *12*, 763–769.

Voss Horrell, S. (2008). Effectiveness of cognitive behavioral therapy with adult ethnic minority clients: A review. *Professional Psychology: Research & Practice*, *39*, 160–168.

Wingo, L. K. (2001). Substance abuse in African American women. *Journal of Cultural Diversity*, *20*, 23–37.

Wong, M. M., Klingle, R. S., & Price, R. K. (2004). Alcohol, tobacco, and other drug use among Asian American and Pacific Islander adolescents in California and Hawaii. *Addictive Behaviors*, *29*, 127–141.

Wu, E., Gilbert, L., Piff, J., & Sanders, G. (2004). Sociodemographic disparities in supplemental service utilization among male methadone patients. *Journal of Substance Abuse Treatment*, *26*, 197–202.

Zager, L. D., & Megargee, E. I. (1981). Seven MMPI alcohol and drug abuse scales: An empirical investigation of their interrelationships, convergent and discriminant validity, and degree of racial bias. *Journal of Personality and Social Psychology*, *40*, 532–544.

Chapter | seventeen

Treating the Patient with Comorbidity

Morten Hesse

University of Aarhus, Centre for Alcohol and Drug Research, Denmark Mats Fridell, Lund University, Department of Psychology, Sweden

SUMMARY POINTS

- Anxiety, depression, and personality disorders all co-occur with substance use disorders at a rate that exceeds chance.
- These co-occurring disorders can and should be considered illnesses in their own right.
- Treating depression and treating personality disorders have been shown to improve substance use outcomes over treating substance use alone. Therefore, integrating treatment of these disorders into treatment for substance use disorders may be considered evidence based.
- For depression, both pharmacotherapy and psychotherapy have been evaluated, although the total number of patients and trials for psychotherapy are both low.
- For comorbid anxiety disorders, there is little evidence for the effectiveness of pharmacotherapy, and trials on psychotherapy have yielded mixed findings.
- For comorbid personality disorders, only psychotherapies have been tested.

Evidence-Based Addiction Treatment

EMPIRICALLY SUPPORTED TREATMENT AND COMORBIDITY

Cases presenting for substance abuse treatment vary in terms of their comorbidity. Some patients have relatively few problems aside from their addiction, but most patients have several adjunctive concerns, such as psychiatric comorbidities, relationship problems, and problems with support, housing, and employment.

If patients present for treatment with comorbid psychiatric conditions, and treatments have been evaluated only on their efficacy for substance use disorders, then what is the impact of comorbid psychiatric conditions on treatment outcome and compliance? What is the course of symptoms of comorbid conditions?

IS PSYCHIATRIC COMORBIDITY AN INDICATOR OF POOR PROGNOSIS?

Depression and anxiety

Approximately 25% of people in the community with alcohol dependence and 50% of those with drug dependence have comorbid depression (Grant et al., 2004b). Depression increases the likelihood that a patient with a substance use disorder will seek treatment for their addiction (Grant et al., 2004b). Persons with substance use disorders who stop using drugs often cite reasons such as "I hit rock bottom" or refer to traumatic events to explain why they changed their behavior (Matzger, Kaskutas, & Weisner, 2005). Perhaps feelings of depression give emotional salience to experiences of "hitting rock bottom." It may also be that anxious or depressed patients are more likely to seek treatment for their substance use disorders because they want help with their depression, but are more aware of treatment options for substance use disorders than for depression.

However, symptoms of depression may interfere with compliance to and retention in treatment (e.g., Elbogen, Swanson, Swartz, & Van Dorn, 2005), impact substance use prognosis (e.g., Hesse, 2006; Matzger et al., 2005), or directly affect quality of life (e.g., Lubman, Allen, Rogers, Cementon, & Bonomo, 2007; Saatcioglu, Yapici, & Cakmak, 2008).

But how do symptoms of depression influence outcome of substance abuse treatment as well as participation and retention in treatment? Some studies have shown that symptoms of depression lower the risk of continued drug use during or after treatment (Charney, Paraherakis, Negrete, & Gill, 1998; Rao, Broome, & Simpson, 2004), whereas other studies have shown that depressive symptoms increase the risk of relapse (Compton, Cottler, Jacobs, Ben-Abdallah, & Spitznagel, 2003; Curran, Flynn, Kirchner, & Booth, 2000; Curran, Kirchner, Worley, Rookey, & Booth,

2002; Driessen et al., 2001; Hesse, 2006; Matzger et al., 2005; McCusker, Goldstein, Bigelow, & Zorn, 1995; Rounsaville, Kosten, Weissman, & Kleber, 1986; Subramaniam, Lewis, Stitzer, & Fishman, 2004).

Still other studies have shown a matching effect. In more structured treatment settings, clients with depression fare better than other patients, but in less structured settings, depressed patients fare worse and less depressed patients fare better (Carroll et al., 1994; Gonzalez, Feingold, Oliveto, Gonsai, & Kosten, 2003; Thornton et al., 2003). In structured treatment settings, the clinician is typically more directive, that is, suggesting goals, describing details of the treatment approach, and proceeding through predefined stages of treatment. Examples of structured treatment approaches include cognitive behavioral therapy or manual-driven drug counseling. Examples of less structured treatment include existential, client centered, and gestalt therapies (Thornton et al., 2003).

To say that depression is a complication of a substance use disorder appears to be a misleading simplification. In some types of treatment, depression may be a hindrance to a positive therapeutic response. In other types of treatment, depression may facilitate a good response to treatment.

Anxiety disorders can be diagnosed in approximately 25% of alcohol-dependent individuals and 43% of those who are drug dependent (Grant et al., 2005c). Studies of anxiety in clinical addiction settings are few, although some research has indicated that anxiety has little negative impact on substance use outcomes (Mann, Hintz, & Jung, 2004; Marquenie et al., 2006; Schade et al., 2005).

Although more research is needed, current evidence suggests that treatment structure makes a large difference in terms of patient outcome, especially with comorbid depression.

Personality disorders

Among the most common comorbidities in substance-dependent patients, personality disorders are diagnosed in about half of all alcohol-dependent patients and in 7 in 10 drug-dependent patients (Grant et al., 2004a). The most commonly co-occurring personality disorder among substance-dependent patients is antisocial personality disorder, found in about 20% of alcohol-dependent patients and 40% of drug-dependent patients (Grant et al., 2004a).

Antisocial personality disorder is generally considered a negative prognostic factor, but in circumstances where there is much to be gained from remaining in treatment, for example, under legal supervision, antisocial patients can actually be more stable in treatment than other patients, even though they are much less stable when they seek treatment voluntarily (Daughters et al., 2007). Also, patients with antisocial personality disorder show a similar rate of improvement as other patients, although they experience a greater number of life problems than other patients (Fridell, Hesse, Jaeger, & Kuhlhorn, 2008; McKay, Alterman, Cacciola, Mulvaney, & O'Brien, 2000).

In summary, the relationship among comorbidity, treatment participation, and outcome is complex. There is little evidence that comorbidities indicate that a patient will not benefit from treatment. However, with comorbid conditions, treatment outcome appears related to what the individual clinician does, and how the clinic operates, depending on the specific type of comorbidity in question.

WHAT HAPPENS OVER TIME WITH COMORBID SYMPTOMS?

Feeling depressed or anxious is associated with a lowered quality of life (Lubman et al., 2007; Saatcioglu et al., 2008). The clinician who is responsible for treating a patient should therefore pay attention to such symptoms, regardless of whether they appear to be substance induced or not.

In some studies it appears that depression in drug users remits regardless of treatment or abstinence status (Dennis, Foss, & Scott, 2007; Nunes & Levin, 2004; Verthein, Degkwitz, Haasen, & Krausz, 2005) or with abstinence (Driessen et al., 2001; Riehman, Iguchi, & Anglin, 2002), but some reports indicate that depression is also quite resistant to change in a significant minority of patients (Subramaniam et al., 2004). In the very early phases of treatment, several studies have shown that depressive symptoms improve dramatically (Brown, Evans, Miller, Burgess, & Mueller, 1995; Strain, Stitzer, & Bigelow, 1991). A possible explanation for this finding is that patients come to treatment at a time when their problems are most severe, including symptoms of anxiety and depression. As noted earlier, patients who discontinue drug or alcohol use on their own or who seek treatment for addictive behaviors often refer to reasons such as "I hit rock bottom" (Matzger et al., 2005). However, despite the positive initial effects of substance abuse treatment on comorbid conditions, patients may still experience clinically significant comorbid symptoms during and after treatment.

Treatment of comorbid illness

For any clinician who is responsible for the treatment of a patient with a number of different serious problems, the task will always be to prioritize various concerns and construct a meaningful treatment plan. Problems can exacerbate each other or point toward conflicting solutions.

TREATMENT OF COMORBID MENTAL ILLNESS AND SUBSTANCE ABUSE

It is well established that psychiatric disorders are highly prevalent among patients with substance abuse (Grant et al., 2005a,b).

Should comorbid mental illness be treated simultaneously with substance abuse in order to facilitate treatment retention or clinical outcome? In other words, is there an indirect effect of treating comorbid conditions on substance use outcomes? Such an indirect effect would occur if the comorbid mental illness either is a direct cause of substance use or is an important hindrance for recovery from substance use disorders.

Treatments for comorbid depression

One important option for the treatment of depression is the use of antidepressant medications, including serotonin-specific reuptake inhibitors (SSRI), such as fluoxetine or sertraline, or tricyclic antidepressants, such as desipramine or imipramine.

Nunes and Levin (2004) conducted a meta-analysis of antidepressants for comorbid depression in substance abusers in which they combined findings from 14 studies with a total of 848 patients assigned randomly to medication or placebo. They found clear effects on depressive symptoms. Effects were larger when patients were abstinent from alcohol and drugs for at least 1 week prior to the initiation of medication, and apparently effects were repressed in some studies by large pre–post changes in the control groups. If large pre–post changes occur in the control group, it is difficult for even a potentially helpful medication to "outperform" the changes in the control group.

Their review and another review by Hesse indicate that there is an indirect effect of treating depression on substance use (Hesse, 2004; Nunes & Levin, 2004).

No meta-analytic reviews have been published concerning the treatment of comorbid disorders with psychosocial interventions. Table 17.1 shows published studies of integrated treatment for mood disorders and substance use disorders that have provided manual-guided treatment to an experimental group, included a control group, or compared several different treatment models. These studies included patients with substance use disorders and some comorbidity who were also offered substance abuse-focused intervention in both control and experimental groups.

Four studies have provided manual-guided treatment for comorbid depression and substance use disorders, comparing treatment with a control group (Bowman, Ward, Bowman, & Scogin, 1996; Brown et al.,

Table 17.1 Studies of integrated treatment of comorbid depression and substance use disorders[a]

Reference	*N* and type of subjects (experimental/control)	Intervention	Control	Outcome	Results
Depression					
Bowman et al. (1996)	11/11	Self-examination therapy	Current events comparison group	SCL-90-R global severity and depression	Better outcomes in experimental group
Brown et al. (1997)	19/16	Cognitive therapy	Relaxation training	Depression (HRSD, POMS, BDI), alcohol (% days abstinent)	Better outcomes in experimental group in all outcomes
Brown et al. (2006)	47/42	Integrated cognitive therapy and alcoholism treatment	Twelve Steps Facilitating Therapy (12FT)	HRSD, % days abstinent	No significant differences. Better outcomes for TSF at 3 months, better for experimental condition at 6 months
Daughters et al. (2008)	22/22	Brief behavioral treatment for comorbid depression and substance abuse	Treatment as usual, including groups, AA meetings, functional analysis	Depression (HRSD, BDI, BAI), treatment satisfaction, retention	Better retention in experimental group (18 vs 14), better improvement in HRSD

[a] *HRSD, Hamilton Rating Scale for Depression; BDI, Beck Depression Inventory; POMS, Profile of Moods Scale; SCL-90-R, Symptoms Rating Scale-90-Revised; ASI, Addiction Severity Index.*

1997, 2006; Daughters et al., 2008). The studies are small, with only 190 patients randomized in total.

Three of the four studies using a control group all reported statistically significant effects on depressive symptoms. Bowman and colleagues compared self-examination therapy with an attention placebo treatment for comorbid depression in patients with substance use disorders and comorbid depressive symptoms during inpatient treatment. In self-examination therapy, "people are given a booklet which uses a flow chart format and encourages them to: (a) determine what matters to them, (b) think less negatively about things that do not matter to them, (c) invest their energy in things that are important to them, and (d) accept situations they cannot change" (Bowman et al., 1996, p. 130). Symptom reductions were larger in the self-examination therapy group than in the attention control group (Bowman et al., 1996). Brown and colleagues compared cognitive therapy for depression with relaxation training as part of a partial hospitalization program for alcohol dependence. The cognitive therapy condition, called the "coping with depression course," incorporated training in depression-relevant skills such as mood monitoring, pleasant activities, constructive thinking, and social skills. Compared with standard treatment and relaxation training, the coping with depression course resulted in higher reductions in Hamilton Rating Scale for Depression (HRSD) scores during treatment and lower relapse rates to alcohol use at 6 months follow-up (Brown et al., 1997).

Brown and colleagues compared integrated cognitive therapy for depression and substance dependence with Twelve Step Facilitating (TSF) therapy. The study found no differences in outcome, but the authors mention a trend toward deterioration in outcomes for the TSF therapy, but stable outcomes in both depression and substance use in the integrated condition (Brown et al., 2006). The study excluded early dropouts, and dropout was nonsignificantly higher in TSF than in the integrated treatment (15% vs 12%).

Daughters and colleagues (2008) provided a brief behavioral activation therapy for patients with comorbid depression and illicit drug use. The program was called Life Enhancement Treatment for Substance Use (LETS Act). The treatment ran over six sessions, plus optional maintenance sessions, and involved defining life goals, identifying relevant activities, self-monitoring, and progressive muscle relaxation. LETS Act led to significantly lower HRSD scores in the experimental group than in the control group, post-treatment, and significantly lower Beck Depression Inventory (BDI) scores at a 2-week follow-up.

In summary, evidence shows that treating comorbid depression with antidepressants can have an impact on depressive symptoms, and potentially such treatment can also have an impact on substance use.

Psychotherapies that address depression in substance abusers are promising, but given the small number of patients treated in the trials so far and the short follow-up times of most trials, further research on this topic is needed.

Treatments for comorbid anxiety and substance use disorders

There are few studies of pharmacotherapy for comorbid anxiety and substance use disorders. The studies reported have yielded mixed findings (Goldstein, Diamantouros, Schaffer, & Naranjo, 2006). A single study has shown that treating anxiety with an SSRI, paroxetine, led to significant changes in anxiety symptoms, but that improvements in drinking problems were unrelated to improvement in anxiety, and paroxetine was not different than placebo in changing quantity and frequency of drinking (Thomas, Randall, Book, & Randall, 2008).

Four trials have been published of the treatment of comorbid anxiety and substance dependence, three targeting alcohol dependence (Bowen, D'Arcy, Keegan, & Senthilselvan, 2000; Randall, Thomas, & Thevos, 2001; Schade et al., 2005) and one targeting a mixed population of drug and alcohol abusers (Fals-Stewart & Schafer, 1992)(Table 17.2).

Bowen and colleagues (2000) assigned patients randomly to either alcoholism treatment alone or alcoholism treatment plus cognitive behavioral therapy (CBT) for comorbid anxiety. The treatment group received 12 h of CBT for panic disorder in addition to the regular alcoholism treatment program; the control group received a 4-week regular program. The group treated for both alcohol and social anxiety problems had worse outcomes on alcohol use indices, and no treatment group effects were observed on social anxiety indices. The authors noted that the therapy program faced resistance on the treatment unit; because of this, the CBT sessions were appended to the end of the day, which may have been an inconvenience for subjects.

Fals-Stewart and Schafer (1992) assigned patients in a therapeutic community with obsessive-compulsive disorder (OCD) to a control group, progressive muscle relaxation, or individual behavior therapy for OCD. Patients assigned to individual behavior therapy had lower National Institute of Mental Health obsessive-compulsive scale scores at post-treatment and 12 months follow-up than patients in the other groups, and a higher proportion of these patients remained abstinent (11 of 19 vs 11 of 38).

Randall and colleagues (2001) assigned patients randomly to alcoholism treatment alone or to alcoholism treatment plus CBT for social anxiety disorder. Findings indicated that anxiety outcomes were similar,

Table 17.2 Studies of integrated treatment of comorbid anxiety and substance use disorders[a]

Reference	*N* and type of subjects (experimental/control)	Intervention	Control	Outcome	Results
Bowen et al. (2000)	146/85	Usual treatment plus group-based panic management	Usual treatment	MM-FNEQ, BDI, AA attendance, drinking outcomes	Nonsignificant differences favoring CBT in drinking outcomes and higher drop out from treatment in experimental group
Fals-Stewart and Schafer (1992)	19/38	Behavioral therapy for obsessive-compulsive disorder in a therapeutic community	Therapeutic community alone or therapeutic community plus progressive muscle relaxation	Retention, NIMH Obsessive-Compulsive Scale, drug relapse, retention	Better outcomes in all areas
Randall et al. (2001)	49/44	Cognitive behavioral therapy for social anxiety disorder and alcoholism	Alcoholism treatment only	BDI, drinking outcomes, SPAI, LSAS	No difference on anxiety outcomes, better drinking outcomes with control
Schade et al. (2005)	47/49	Integrated cognitive therapy for substance abuse and social anxiety plus optional pharmacotherapy	Intensive psychosocial relapse-prevention program alone	SCL-90, FQ, ADS, relapse to drinking	Better anxiety outcomes with treatment. No differences in drinking outcomes

[a] *BDI, Beck Depression Inventory; SCL-90, Symptoms Rating Scale; MM-FNEQ, Mark-Matthews Fear of Negative Evaluation Questionnaire; SPAI, Social Phobia and Anxiety Inventory; LSAS, Liebowitz Social Anxiety Scale; FQ, Fear Questionnaire; ADS, Anxiety Discomfort Scale.*

but alcoholism treatment alone was superior in terms of drinking outcomes. The treatment sessions were longer for the integrated treatment (90 min versus 60 min).

Schadé and colleagues (2005) assigned patients randomly to either treatment for alcoholism alone or treatment for anxiety plus alcoholism in weekly 60-min therapy sessions. No significant differences were found for drinking outcomes, but anxiety reductions were significantly higher for the integrated treatment group.

These mixed findings might indicate that integrated treatments for anxiety disorders and substance use disorders are of limited value at best. However, another explanation is that a higher degree of treatment contact may be detrimental for patients with social phobia in particular. In both trials for social phobia plus alcohol dependence, no beneficial effects of treatment were found (Bowen et al., 2000; Randall et al., 2001). In both trials, patients assigned to the experimental group received a higher dose of treatment. There is indication from another study that a high dose of treatment is detrimental for patients with social anxiety (Avants, Margolin, Kosten, Rounsaville, & Schottenfeld, 1998).

In summary, there is little evidence for additional therapy for social phobia along with treatment for alcohol problems, particularly if additional therapy means adding extra treatment time to what is already being offered to the patient. There is, however, limited evidence (from a single small trial) for additional treatment for obsessive-compulsive disorder, and some evidence (from a single, somewhat bigger trial) for integrated treatment for anxiety disorder and alcoholism when the treatment is not added to, but integrated with, the ongoing treatment.

Treating comorbid personality disorders and substance use disorders

Six studies have compared substance abuse treatments tailored to specific personality types with control treatments (Table 17.3). In total, 496 patients have been included in these studies. Ball developed Dual Focused Schema Therapy (DFST). DFST is a 24-week manualized treatment based on Schema Focused Therapy that integrates substance abuse relapse prevention with targeted interventions for early maladaptive schemas. Early maladaptive schemas are enduring negative beliefs about oneself, others, and events that are closely related to personality disorders. In early sessions, the therapist helps the patient explore relevant schemas and triggers for drug use, and patients are given psychoeducation about personality problems and schemas. In later sessions, treatment goals are formulated to modify maladaptive coping styles and develop alternative schemas.

Table 17.3 Studies of integrated treatment of specific comorbidities and substance use disorders (continued—personality traits and personality disorders)[a]

Reference	*N* and type of subjects (experimental/control)	Intervention	Control	Outcome	Results
Ball (2007)	52 opioid substitution patients with PD	Dual Focus Schema Therapy (DFST)	Twelve Step Facilitation Therapy (12FT)	Drug use, psychopathology, alliance, retention	DFST better for drug use, 12FT better for symptoms
Ball et al. (2005)	30 homeless patients with SUD and PD	DFST	Group substance abuse counseling	Retention	Better retention in dual focus schema therapy
Conrod et al. (2000)	94/97 + 52 community recruited women with SUD	Motivation-matched brief intervention for SUD	Motivation-mismatched brief intervention or motivational film ($n = 52$)	Drinking, substance use	Better outcomes in experimental group
Gregory et al. (2008)	15/15 patients from various clinical settings with borderline PD and alcohol use disorders	Dynamic deconstructive psychotherapy (DDP)	Treatment as usual	Drinking, symptoms of borderline personality disorder, depression	Better outcomes in experimental group
Linehan et al. (2002)	11/12 opioid substitution patients with borderline PD	Dialectical Behavior Therapy	Validation Therapy with 12FT	Urine tests, symptoms, retention	Better retention in experimental group, less positive urine specimens in DBT
Nielsen et al. (2007)	47/61 patients in residential alcoholism treatment	Personality-Guided Treatment for Alcohol Dependence	Group relapse prevention	Retention, alcohol drinking	Higher PDA for experimental, nonsignificantly better retention

[a]*SUD, substance use disorders; PD, personality disorder.*

Ball compared DFST with TSF therapy for patients with comorbid personality disorder and opioid dependence in a methadone clinic. Retention did not differ, but substance use outcomes favored DFST, and outcomes in self-reported depressive symptoms favored TSF therapy (Ball, 2007). Ball, Cobb-Richardson, Connolly, Bujosa, and O'Neall (2005) compared DFST with group substance abuse counseling in a drop-in center for homeless patients and reported superior retention in DFST.

Conrod and colleagues (2000) compared different brief interventions for community-recruited women with substance use disorders. Their study compared a single session developed specifically to target the women's personality profile (one of the following: impulsive, hopeless, sensation seekers, anxiety sensitive). Interventions consisted of one session and focused on ways of dealing with impulsivity and sensation seeking, dealing with hopelessness based on a CBT treatment for depression, or dealing with anxiety based on a CBT model for anxiety. Women were assigned randomly to receive (1) a treatment that matched their profile, (2) a treatment that did not match their profile, for example, a woman could get the treatment for impulsivity, even though she matched the anxious profile, or (3) a motivational film designed to enhance motivation for change and a discussion of the film with a therapist. The researchers found higher postintervention treatment seeking and lower substance use in the personality-matched group than either the unmatched group or the attention control group (Conrod et al., 2000).

Gregory and colleagues (2008) developed a manualized psychodynamic treatment for comorbid borderline personality disorder and substance dependence dynamic deconstructive psychotherapy (DDP). In a randomized trial, DDP participants showed a statistically significant improvement in parasuicide behavior, alcohol misuse, institutional care, depression (as measured by the BDI), and core symptoms of borderline personality disorder. Treatment retention was better in the DPP group than in treatment as usual (Gregory et al., 2008).

Dialectical Behavior Therapy (DBT) is a cognitive behavioral treatment program developed to treat suicidal clients meeting criteria for borderline personality disorder. It directly targets (1) suicidal behavior, (2) behaviors that interfere with treatment delivery, and (3) other dangerous, severe, or destabilizing behaviors. Standard DBT addresses the following five functions: (1) increasing behavioral capabilities, (2) improving motivation for skillful behavior, (3) assuring generalization of gains to the natural environment, (4) structuring the treatment environment so that it reinforces functional rather than dysfunctional behaviors, and (5) enhancing therapist capabilities and motivation to treat patients effectively. These functions are divided among four modes of service: (1) weekly individual psychotherapy, (2) group skills training, (3) telephone consultation, and (4) weekly therapist consultation team meetings.

Linehan and colleagues (2002) compared DBT with validation therapy and TSF therapy for comorbid borderline personality disorder and substance use disorders. The sample was small (N = 23). Toward the end of follow-up, patients in DBT had more urine tests free from opiates than control patients.

Based on DFST and Millon Clinical Multiaxial Inventory-guided treatment, Nielsen developed a manual-guided model for integrating a focus on personality disorder with treatment for alcohol dependence in an inpatient alcohol dependence treatment setting that provided personality-guided alcoholism treatment. The treatment involved individual psychoeducation, group skills training, and regular therapist consultation team meetings. Nielsen, Røjskjær, and Hesse (2007) compared personality-guided alcoholism treatment with cognitive behavioral relapse prevention in a residential treatment unit. Findings indicated that retention was improved with personality-guided treatment and higher percent days abstinent in the experimental group at 6 months follow-up (Nielsen et al., 2007).

In summary, there is some evidence that taking personality disorders into consideration when treating patients with comorbid personality disorder and substance use disorders is likely to improve substance use outcomes.

REFERENCES

Avants, S. K., Margolin, A., Kosten, T. R., Rounsaville, B. J., & Schottenfeld, R. S. (1998). When is less treatment better? The role of social anxiety in matching methadone patients to psychosocial treatments. *Journal of Consulting and Clinical Psychology*, *66*, 924–931.

Ball, S. A. (2007). Comparing individual therapies for personality disordered opioid dependent patients. *Journal of Personality Disorder*, *21*, 305–321.

Ball, S. A., Cobb-Richardson, P., Connolly, A. J., Bujosa, C. T., & O'Neall T. W. (2005). Substance abuse and personality disorders in homeless drop-in center clients: Symptom severity and psychotherapy retention in a randomized clinical trial. *Comprehensive Psychiatry*, *46*, 371–379.

Bowen, R. C., D'Arcy, C., Keegan, D., & Senthilselvan, A. (2000). A controlled trial of cognitive behavioral treatment of panic in alcoholic inpatients with comorbid panic disorder. *Addictive Behaviors*, *25*, 593–597.

Bowman, V., Ward, L. C., Bowman, D., & Scogin, F. (1996). Self-examination therapy as an adjunct treatment for depressive symptoms in substance abusing patients. *Addictive Behaviors*, *21*, 129–133.

Brown, R. A., Evans, D. M., Miller, I. W., Burgess, E. S., & Mueller, T. I. (1997). Cognitive behavioral treatment for depression in alcoholism. *Journal of Consulting and Clinical Psychology*, *65*, 715–726.

Brown, S. A., Glasner-Edwards, S. V., Tate, S. R., McQuaid, J. R., Chalekian, J., & Granholm, E. (2006). Integrated cognitive behavioral therapy versus twelve-step facilitation therapy for substance-dependent adults with depressive disorders. *Journal of Psychoactive Drugs*, *38*, 449–460.

Brown, S. A., Inaba, R. K., Gillin, J. C., Schuckit, M. A., Stewart, M. A., & Irwin, M. R. (1995). Alcoholism and affective disorder: Clinical course of depressive symptoms. *American Journal of Psychiatry*, *152*, 45–52.

Carroll, K. M., Rounsaville, B. J., Gordon, L. T., Nich, C., Jatlow, P., Bisighini, R. M., et al. (1994). Psychotherapy and pharmacotherapy for ambulatory cocaine abusers. *Archives of General Psychiatry*, *51*, 177–187.

Charney, D. A., Paraherakis, A. M., Negrete, J. C., & Gill, K. J. (1998). The impact of depression on the outcome of addictions treatment. *Journal of Substance Abuse Treatment*, *15*, 123–130.

Compton, W. M., 3rd, Cottler, L. B., Jacobs, J. L., Ben-Abdallah, A., & Spitznagel, E. L. (2003). The role of psychiatric disorders in predicting drug dependence treatment outcomes. *American Journal of Psychiatry*, *160*, 890–895.

Conrod, P. J., Stewart, S. H., Pihl, R. O., Cote, S., Fontaine, V., & Dongier, M. (2000). Efficacy of brief coping skills interventions that match different personality profiles of female substance abusers. *Psychology of Addictive Behaviors*, *14*, 231–242.

Curran, G. M., Flynn, H. A., Kirchner, J., & Booth, B. M. (2000). Depression after alcohol treatment as a risk factor for relapse among male veterans. *Journal of Substance Abuse Treatment*, *19*, 259–265.

Curran, G. M., Kirchner, J. E., Worley, M., Rookey, C., & Booth, B. M. (2002). Depressive symptomatology and early attrition from intensive outpatient substance use treatment. *Journal of Behavioral Health Services Research*, *29*, 138–143.

Daughters, S. B., Braun, A. R., Sargeant, M. N., Reynolds, E. K., Hopko, D. R., Blanco, C., et al. (2008). Effectiveness of a brief behavioral treatment for inner-city illicit drug users with elevated depressive symptoms: The Life Enhancement Treatment for Substance Use (LETS Act!). *Journal of Clinical Psychiatry*, e1–e8.

Daughters, S. B., Stipelman, B. A., Sargeant, M. N., Schuster, R., Bornolova, M. A., & Lejuez, C. W. (2007). The interactive effects of antisocial personality disorder and court-mandated status on substance abuse treatment dropout. *Journal of Substance Abuse Treatment*, *34*, 157–164.

Dennis, M. L., Foss, M. A., & Scott, C. K. (2007). An eight-year perspective on the relationship between the duration of abstinence and other aspects of recovery. *Evaluation Review*, *31*, 585–612.

Driessen, M., Meier, S., Hill, A., Wetterling, T., Lange, W., & Junghanns, K. (2001). The course of anxiety, depression and drinking behaviours after completed detoxification in alcoholics with and without comorbid anxiety and depressive disorders. *Alcohol and Alcoholism*, *36*, 249–255.

Elbogen, E. B., Swanson, J. W., Swartz, M. S., & Van Dorn, R. (2005). Medication nonadherence and substance abuse in psychotic disorders: Impact of depressive symptoms and social stability. *Journal of Nervous and Mental Disease*, *193*, 673–679.

Fals-Stewart, W., & Schafer, J. (1992). The treatment of substance abusers diagnosed with obsessive-compulsive disorder: An outcome study. *Journal of Substance Abuse Treatment*, *9*, 365–370.

Fridell, M., Hesse, M., Jaeger, M. M., & Kuhlhorn, E. (2008). Antisocial personality disorder as a predictor of criminal behaviour in a longitudinal study of a cohort of abusers of several classes of drugs: Relation to type of substance and type of crime. *Addictive Behaviors*, *33*, 799–811.

Goldstein, B. I., Diamantouros, A., Schaffer, A., & Naranjo, C. A. (2006). Pharmacotherapy of alcoholism in patients with co-morbid psychiatric disorders. *Drugs*, *66*, 1229–1237.

Gonzalez, G., Feingold, A., Oliveto, A., Gonsai, K., & Kosten, T. R. (2003). Comorbid major depressive disorder as a prognostic factor in cocaine-abusing buprenorphine-maintained patients treated with desipramine and contingency management. *American Journal of Drug and Alcohol Abuse*, *29*, 497–514.

Grant, B. F., Hasin, D. S., Stinson, F. S., Dawson, D. A., June Ruan, W., Goldstein, R. B., et al. (2005a). Prevalence, correlates, co-morbidity, and comparative disability of DSM-IV generalized anxiety disorder in the USA: Results from the national epidemiologic survey on alcohol and related conditions. *Psychological Medicine*, *35*, 1747–1759.

Grant, B. F., Hasin, D. S., Stinson, F. S., Dawson, D. A., Patricia Chou, S., June Ruan, W., et al. (2005b). Co-occurrence of 12-month mood and anxiety disorders and personality disorders in the US: Results from the national epidemiologic survey on alcohol and related conditions. *Journal of Psychiatric Research*, *39*, 1–9.

Grant, B. F., Hasin, D. S., Stinson, F. S., Dawson, D. A., Patricia Chou, S., June Ruan, W., et al. (2005c). Co-occurrence of 12-month mood and anxiety disorders and personality disorders in the US: Results from the national epidemiologic survey on alcohol and related conditions. *Journal of Psychiatric Research*, *39*, 1–9.

Grant, B. F., Stinson, F. S., Dawson, D. A., Chou, P. S., June Ruan, W., & Pickering, R. (2004a). Co-occurrence of 12-month alcohol and drug use disorders and personality disorders in the United States: Results from the national epidemiologic survey of alcohol and related conditions. *Archives of General Psychiatry*, *61*, 361–368.

Grant, B. F., Stinson, F. S., Dawson, D. A., Chou, S. P., Dufour, M. C., Compton, W., et al. (2004b). Prevalence and co-occurrence of substance use disorders and independent mood and anxiety disorders: Results from the national epidemiologic survey on alcohol and related conditions. *Archives of General Psychiatry*, *61*, 807–816.

Gregory, R. J., Chlebowski, S., Kang, D., Remen, A. L., Soderberg, M. G., Stepkovich, J., et al. (2008). A controlled trial of psychodynamic psychotherapy for co-occurring borderline personality disorder and alcohol use disorder. *Psychotherapy: Theory, Research, Practice, Training*, *41*, 28–41.

Hesse, M. (2004). Achieving abstinence by treating depression in the presence of substance-use disorders. *Addictive Behaviors*, *29*, 1137–1141.

Hesse, M. (2006). The Beck Depression Inventory in patients undergoing opiate agonist maintenance treatment. *British Journal of Clinical Psychology*, *45*, 417–425.

Linehan, M. M., Dimeff, L. A., Reynolds, S. K., Comtois, K. A., Welch, S. S., Heagerty, P., et al. (2002). Dialectical behavior therapy versus comprehensive validation therapy plus 12-step for the treatment of opioid dependent women meeting criteria for borderline personality disorder. *Drug and Alcohol Dependence*, *67*, 13–26.

Lubman, D. I., Allen, N. B., Rogers, N., Cementon, E., & Bonomo, Y. (2007). The impact of co-occurring mood and anxiety disorders among substance-abusing youth. *Journal of Affective Disorders*, *103*, 105–112.

Mann, K., Hintz, T., & Jung, M. (2004). Does psychiatric comorbidity in alcohol-dependent patients affect treatment outcome? *European Archives of Psychiatry and Clinical Neuroscience*, *254*, 172–181.

Marquenie, L. A., Schade, A., Van Balkom, A. J., Koeter, M., Frenken, S., van den Brink, W., et al. (2006). Comorbid phobic disorders do not influence outcome of alcohol dependence treatment: Results of a naturalistic follow-up study. *Alcohol and Alcoholism*, *41*, 168–173.

Matzger, H., Kaskutas, L. A., & Weisner, C. (2005). Reasons for drinking less and their relationship to sustained remission from problem drinking. *Addiction*, *100*, 1637–1646.

McCusker, J., Goldstein, R., Bigelow, C., & Zorn, M. (1995). Psychiatric status and HIV risk reduction among residential drug abuse treatment clients. *Addiction*, *90*, 1377–1387.

McKay, J. R., Alterman, A. I., Cacciola, J. S., Mulvaney, F. D., & O'Brien, C. P. (2000). Prognostic significance of antisocial personality disorder cocaine-dependent patients entering continuing care. *Journal of Nervous and Mental Disease*, *188*, 287–296.

Nielsen, P., Røjskjær, S., & Hesse, M. (2007). Personality-guided treatment for alcohol dependence: A quasi-randomized experiment. *American Journal on Addictions*, *16*, 357–364.

Nunes, E. V., & Levin, F. R. (2004). Treatment of depression in patients with alcohol or other drug dependence: A meta-analysis. *Journal of the American Medical Association*, *291*, 1887–1896.

Randall, C. L., Thomas, S., & Thevos, A. K. (2001). Concurrent alcoholism and social anxiety disorder: A first step toward developing effective treatments. *Alcoholism: Clinical and Experimental Research*, *25*, 210–220.

Rao, S. R., Broome, K. M., & Simpson, D. D. (2004). Depression and hostility as predictors of long-term outcomes among opiate users. *Addiction*, *99*, 579–589.

Riehman, K. S., Iguchi, M. Y., & Anglin, M. D. (2002). Depressive symptoms among amphetamine and cocaine users before and after substance abuse treatment. *Psychology of Addictive Behaviors*, *16*, 333–337.

Rounsaville, B. J., Kosten, T. R., Weissman, M. M., & Kleber, H. D. (1986). Prognostic significance of psychopathology in treated opiate addicts: A 2.5-year follow-up study. *Archives of General Psychiatry*, *43*, 739–745.

Saatcioglu, O., Yapici, A., & Cakmak, D. (2008). Quality of life, depression and anxiety in alcohol dependence. *Drug and Alcohol Review*, *27*, 83–90.

Schadé, A., Marquenie, L. A., van Balkom, A. J., Koeter, M. W., de Beurs, E., van den Brink, W., et al. (2005). The effectiveness of anxiety treatment on alcohol-dependent patients with a comorbid phobic disorder: A randomized controlled trial. *Alcoholism: Clinical and Experimental Research*, *29*, 794–800.

Strain, E. C., Stitzer, M. L., & Bigelow, G. E. (1991). Early treatment time course of depressive symptoms in opiate addicts. *Journal of Nervous and Mental Disease*, *179*, 215–221.

Subramaniam, G. A., Lewis, L. L., Stitzer, M. L., & Fishman, M. J. (2004). Depressive symptoms in adolescents during residential treatment for substance use disorders. *American Journal on Addictions*, *13*, 256–267.

Thomas, S. E., Randall, P. K., Book, S. W., & Randall, C. L. (2008). A complex relationship between co-occurring social anxiety and alcohol use disorders: What effect does treating social anxiety have on drinking? *Alcoholism: Clinical and Experimental Research*, *32*, 77–84.

Thornton, C. C., Patkar, A. A., Murray, H. W., Mannelli, P., Gottheil, E., Vergare, M. J., et al. (2003). High- and low-structure treatments for substance dependence: Role of learned helplessness. *American Journal of Drug and Alcohol Abuse*, *29*, 567–584.

Verthein, U., Degkwitz, P., Haasen, C., & Krausz, M. (2005). Significance of comorbidity for the long-term course of opiate dependence. *European Addiction Research*, *11*, 15–21.

Chapter | eighteen

Evidence-Based Interventions for Adolescent Substance Users

Josephine M. Hawke and Yifrah Kaminer
Department of Psychiatry, University of Connecticut Health Center

SUMMARY POINTS

- Systematic reviews and meta-analysis indicate that the most effective evidence-based interventions have small-to-moderate effect sizes.
- Only a handful of interventions are considered evidence based. They include family therapies (i.e., mutidimensional family therapy, functional family therapy, multisystemic therapy, brief strategic family therapy, and family behavior therapy), as well as cognitive behavioral, pharmacotherapies, and recent advances in continuing care.
- Evidence-based family therapies share several characteristics: they are structured, manualized, research-based interventions that target risks and protective factors and address motivational and engagement issues as specific phases or stages of treatment.
- Cognitive behavioral therapy (CBT) teaches new skills that address cognitions, emotional responses, and interpersonal dynamics related to substance use, coping, and relapse. The strongest evidence in support of CBT comes from studies of group-based CBT interventions with manuals that share similar content and structure.

Evidence-Based Addiction Treatment

- Active aftercare or continuing care that is flexible and addresses motivational issues reduces the chances that adolescents will relapse.
- More information is needed about mechanism of change and systems issues to effectively implement evidence-based treatments in real-world settings and address the shortage in effective, developmentally appropriate treatment services for adolescents.

INTRODUCTION

Alcohol and other drug use among adolescents continues to be a critical public health concern in the United States. According to the Youth Risk Behavior Surveillance Survey, 75% of teenagers have had at least one drink of alcohol in their lives and nearly 45% have had at least one drink in the last 30 days (U.S. Department of Health and Human Services, 2008). Nearly half (47%) will have tried an illicit drug before they finish high school (U.S. Department of Health and Human Services, 2007).

Adverse consequences of adolescent alcohol and drug use can be severe and far-reaching, including fatal and nonfatal injuries from alcohol- and drug-related motor vehicle accidents, victimization and violence, delinquency and legal problems, psychiatric disorders, risk behaviors, and neurological impairments. Substance use can derail normative patterns of development, jeopardize youths' abilities to negotiate critically important developmental tasks and make successful transitions into adulthood, and increase the risks of alcohol and drug abuse and dependence in adulthood (Brown et al., 2008; Maggs, Patrick, & Feinstein, 2008).

Three decades of research on the effectiveness of treatment interventions for adolescent substance users demonstrate that treatment works (Orford, 2008; Williams & Chang, 2000). The purpose of this chapter is to summarize the current wisdom in the field about evidence-based interventions for substance-using adolescents. It is organized into three parts. First, we discuss the criteria for determining evidence-based treatments. Second, we describe treatments that have been consistently identified as empirically supported. Third, we discuss future research directions.

SYSTEMATIC REVIEWS AND META-ANALYSES

Systematic reviews and meta-analyses compare findings across studies. Compared to reviews that rely heavily on descriptors across studies or the authors' expertise in the interpretation of the literature, methods used for systematic reviews and meta-analyses are more rigorous. They start with fairly extensive literature searches to identify published articles and clearly articulated inclusion criteria. They often supplement the published studies with unpublished ones obtained from investigators to reduce "publication bias"—the tendency for published literature to report predominately positive findings. They calculate effect sizes and provide additional quantitative analyses of pooled data in order to draw conclusions about the therapeutic effectiveness of treatment interventions. Finally, they use criteria to evaluate the robustness of the study's methods (e.g., Nathan & Gorman, 2002) and categorize the interventions according to empirical evidence demonstrating their effectiveness (e.g., Chambless & Hollon,1998). Thus, evidence from systematic reviews and meta-analyses is the best source of information about which interventions for adolescent substance use have the greatest empirical support.

There have been several published systematic reviews of evidence-based interventions to treat adolescent substance abuse that summarize the evidence base for treatments for adolescent substance use in general (e.g., Deas, 2008; Deas & Thomas, 2001; Jenson, Howard, & Vaughn, 2004; Slesnick, Kaminer, & Kelly, 2008; Williams & Chang, 2000), in outpatient modalities (Waldron & Turner, 2008), for family therapies (Austin, Macgowan, & Wagner, 2005; Ozechowski & Liddle, 2000), and psychopharmacology (Waxmonsky & Wilens, 2005), as well as reviews that address relevant subpopulations, such as ethnic minorities (e.g., Huey & Polo, 2008) and patients with co-occurring disorders (Bender, Springer, & Kim, 2006).

Treatment effectiveness

Studies typically report the statistical significance of the findings. However, statistical significance does not tell you how large the effect is. An effect size refers to the strength of the relationship between two variables. Statistical measures of the effect size do. The best known measure of effect size is Cohen's (1988) d. Cohen's d measures the overlap in two distributions. Cohen's thresholds for small, moderate, and large are 0.20, 0.50, and 0.80. Recent meta-analyses report effect sizes that range from small to moderate for interventions to treat adolescent substance abuse. Huey and Polo's (2008) meta-analysis of 22 controlled trials of treatments for children and adolescents seeking treatment for mental health disorders reported that psychotherapy was associated with small to medium average effect sizes across all the studies (Cohen's $d = 0.44$ for the entire sample and Cohen's $d = 0.57$ for studies comparing active treatments to no treatment or placebo conditions). These findings suggest that slightly more than two-thirds of youths who receive treatment for mental health problems (including but not limited to substance use treatments) are better off than the average child receiving no treatment. In a meta-analysis of clinical trials of outpatient substance abuse treatments for adolescents, Waldron and Turner (2008) also found small-to-moderate average effect sizes for active treatments (Cohen's d = 0.45). They concluded that evidence across clinical trials suggests that a number of distinct treatment approaches are effective.

In general, reviews of treatment effectiveness have demonstrated that treatment is effective in treating adolescent substance abuse. However, it is still premature to make definitive conclusions about the superiority of one intervention over another. A handful of interventions are considered evidence based. Family therapies and cognitive behavioral therapies (CBTs) were recognized most consistently as well supported compared to other approaches. There are also treatments such as the Assertive Community Reinforcement Approach and pharmacotherapies for which the empirical literature with adolescents is beginning to emerge. The following contains short descriptions of the interventions that were evaluated as meeting the most stringent criteria for being evidence based.

INTERVENTIONS

Family-based approaches

Family therapies are by far the most often cited as being validated empirically. Evidence-based family therapies have several characteristics in common. These methods are manualized, research-based therapies that view adolescent substance use and other problem behaviors as being symptomatic of the dysfunctional family environment. Treatment begins with a comprehensive, multidimensional assessment of the youth and family to identify intra- and extrafamilial patterns of interaction that contribute to problematic behaviors. Family-based approaches are individualized to the specific needs of the family and use multiple empirically validated intervention strategies borrowed from other approaches to target risks and protective factors. Motivational and engagement issues are addressed as specific phases or stages of treatment.

Mutidimensional family therapy (MDFT) is an outpatient family-based treatment for adolescent substance abuse and related problems (Liddle, 2002). It is a developmentally and ecologically oriented treatment that takes into account the interlocking environmental and individual systems, such as schools, juvenile justice, and peer and social support networks. MDFT focuses on four domains: (1) the adolescent, (2) the parent and other family members, (3) family interaction patterns, and (4) extrafamilial systems of influence (Liddle, Rowe, & Dakof, 2007). Treatment techniques include parental reconnection, engaging the family and youth in self-help groups and drug counseling, enhancing parenting skills (e.g., monitoring and discipline), developing support networks, and fostering improved communication and interaction skills, as well as case management. Treatment objectives for the adolescent include transformation of a drug-using lifestyle into a developmentally normative lifestyle and improved functioning in several developmental domains, including positive peer relations, healthy identity formation, bonding to school and other pro-social institutions, and autonomy within the parent–adolescent relationship. For the parent(s), objectives include enhancing parental commitment and preventing parental abdication; improving parent–child relationships and communication patterns; and fostering better parenting practices (e.g., limit setting, monitoring, and appropriate autonomy granting). Effect sizes with MDFT are also moderate to large depending on the study (Austin, Macgowan, & Wagner, 2005; Waldron & Turner, 2008).

Functional family therapy (FFT) is an empirically grounded, family-based intervention program for acting-out youths (Alexander, Pugh, Parsons, & Sexton, 2000; Sexton & Alexander, 2000). The FFT intervention focuses on the treatment system, family and individual functioning, and the therapist as major components. Treatment consists of 8 to 30 sessions of direct service depending on the severity of need. The model includes three phases: (1) engagement and motivation, (2) behavioral change, and (3) generalization. Each phase utilizes assessment and specific empirically validated intervention strategies to accomplish therapeutic goals. FFT incorporates a strong cognitive component, which is integrated into systematic skill training in family communication, parenting skills, and conflict management skills.

Vaughn and Howard (2004) found strong evidence for the effectiveness of FFT alone and combined with other interventions (e.g., CBT). Meta-analyses (Austin, Macgowan, & Wagner, 2005; Waldron & Turner, 2008) report large effect sizes related to reductions in alcohol and drug use for FFT in clinical trials with relatively rigorous research. Research by Waldron and colleagues (Waldron, Slesnick, Brody, Turner, & Peterson, 2001; Waldron, Turner, & Ozechowski, 2005) showed significant reductions in substance use at post-treatment and at follow-up. Waldron and colleagues compared FFT alone and in combination with CBT and skills-based group therapy. Findings showed statistically significant declines in the days of alcohol and marijuana use and improvements in the proportion of the youths who remained abstinent at follow-up.

Multisystemic therapy (MST) is an intensive, home-based intervention that views adolescent substance use as a product of the family environment. Treatment consists of an average of 60 h of contact over a 4-month period. MST is based on a social ecological model that views problem behaviors as multidetermined from the reciprocal interplay of individual, family, peer, school, and community factors. Services are delivered in the natural environment (e.g., home, school, community) and treatment is family driven; families determine treatment goals and therapists help families accomplish them. Treatment often focuses on strengthening natural support systems and removing barriers that keep them from accessing services (e.g., parental substance abuse, high stress, poor relationships between partners). Therapists have small caseloads and meet with the family two to three times per week and are available 24 h a day, 7 days a week to respond to the family crises. Specific intervention strategies include empirically validated treatment techniques from cognitive behavioral, behavioral, and the pragmatic family therapies.

Multisystemic therapy is effective in treating various problem behaviors, including delinquency, violence, and substance use (Waldron & Turner, 2008). Substance-related outcomes were reported in two of the early randomized trials of MST with violent and chronic juvenile offenders (Borduin et al., 1995; Henggeler, Melton, & Smith, 1992). Substance use outcomes were published in one report (Henggeler et al., 1991), and effect sizes were reported in a meta-analysis of seven outcome studies of MST by Curtis, Ronan, and Borduin (2004). Although MST was associated with moderate-to-large effect sizes across multiple outcomes, effect sizes for substance use outcomes were moderate ($d = 0.64$, $sd = 0.33$) in one study and weak ($d = 0.25$, $sd = 0.08$) in the other.

Brief strategic family therapy (BSFT) seeks to change dysfunctional family interactions and cultural/contextual factors that influence adolescent problem behaviors. The drug-using adolescent is viewed as a family member who displays symptoms, including drug use and related co-occurring problem behaviors that are indicative of problems in the family system (Szapocznik & Kurtines, 1989). Treatment consists of 8 to 12 weekly meetings organized into four phases: (1) team and therapeutic alliance building (joining), (2) diagnosing the family's strengths and problem relations (diagnosis), (3) developing a change strategy (restructuring), and (4) implementing the change strategy and reinforcing new levels of family competence. Therapists target repetitive patterns of family interaction (i.e., negativity and blaming behaviors) and use practical therapeutic strategies tailored to a family's situation to bring about change in the patterns of interactions that influence the youth's psychosocial adjustment and antisocial behaviors most directly. Problems are addressed sequentially and strategically.

Results from meta-analyses regarding the effectiveness of BSFT are somewhat mixed. Clinical trials have documented pre–postreductions in substance use and higher rates of post-treatment abstinence among youths who received BSFT compared to youths in other treatment conditions (e.g., Coatsworth, Santisteban, McBride, & Szapocznik, 2001; Joanning, Thomas, Quinn, & Mullen, 1992; Robbins, Szapocznik,

Dillon, Turner, Mitrani, & Feaster, 2008; Santisteban Coatsworth, Perez-Vidal, & Kurtines, 2003; Szapocznik, Kurtines, Foote, Perez-Vidal, & Hervis, 1983, 1986). Reported effect sizes ranged from small to moderate for pre–postsubstance use changes and at follow-up. However, Austin, Macgowan, and Wagner (2005) report that their meta-analysis revealed no clinically significant effect sizes associated with BSFT for either alcohol or drug use and effect sizes were small. This suggests a need for further evaluation of BSFT for adolescent substance users.

Family behavior therapy (FBT) is an outpatient behavioral treatment for substance use and related problem behaviors such as depression, family conflicts, school and work attendance, and conduct problems in youth. Based on the Community Reinforcement Approach, FBT incorporates validated methods to enhance engagement and attendance (Donohue & Azrin, 2001). Adolescents attend therapy sessions with at least one family member, typically a parent. Other interventions include behavioral contracting to reinforce positive abstinence behaviors and skill-building techniques to improve relapse prevention, assist in dealing with urges, improve communication, and enhance skills associated with getting a job and/or attending school.

Studies have shown that FBT is associated with reductions in alcohol and illicit drug use compared to supportive and cognitive behavioral therapies (e.g., Azrin et al., 1994). Austin, Macgowan, and Wagner (2005) reported small-to-large effect sizes for FBT associated with pre–postchanges in alcohol use ($d = 0.30$) and illicit drug use ($d = 0.84$). Bender, Springer, and Kim (2006) suggested that FBT was one of the better choices for dually diagnosed youths because it produced consistently large effect sizes for internalizing and externalizing symptoms among youths with comorbid disorders. Thus, there is support for FBT as an evidence-based treatment, but clearly more research is warranted.

Cognitive behavioral therapy

Cognitive behavioral therapy is typically used in outpatient settings and can be administered in either individual or group formats. The underlying principles of CBT emerged from behaviorism and social learning theories. Substance use is seen as a learned behavior that is influenced by cognitive processes and the environmental contexts in which it occurs. CBT creates behavioral change by teaching new skills for modifying cognitions, emotional responses, and interpersonal dynamics to help youths problem solve without reverting to drugs, cope with intense emotions, communicate more effectively, refuse opportunities to use drugs, and manage drug-related thoughts and cravings (Myers & Brown, 1990). The goal is to diminish interpersonal and intrapersonal determinants that contribute to drug involvement and promote factors that protect against relapse (Kaminer, Burleson, & Goldberger, 2002). Therapists help youths identify contextual factors (e.g., situations, triggers, the influence of drug-using peers) and alternatives to substance use. They also teach problem-solving skills and positive coping strategies through the use of modeling, behavioral rehearsal, feedback, and homework assignments.

There is some variability across CBT interventions. CBT has been used alone (e.g., Kaminer et al., 2002) and in combination with other interventions (e.g., Dennis et al., 2004; Latimer, Winters, D'Zurilla, & Nichols, 2003), as well as in group (e.g., Kaminer et al., 2002) and individual (e.g., Waldron et al., 2005) modalities. Waldron and Turner (2008) subdivided CBT by modality for their meta-analysis. They found more variability in the content of interventions among individual CBTs than group interventions. Of the seven studies that examined individual CBT, four tested CBT in combination with other interventions. However, group versions of CBT, especially those with 12 or more sessions, generally used therapy manuals that were very similar. CBT in both modalities was associated with reductions in substance use at discharge from treatment and post-treatment follow-up assessments. Effect sizes varied across studies, and outcome studies of individual CBT tended to produce smaller effect sizes than for group CBT.

Pharmacotherapies

There is relatively little scientific evidence to guide the choice of pharmacological interventions with youth. Most controlled studies of the effects of medications for alcohol and substance use disorders (SUDs) accrue from the adult literature. Although several medications show promise in treating symptoms associated with alcohol and substance use disorders among adults, there have been concerns about the safety of using psychotropic medications with adolescents (Dawes & Johnson, 2004). Specifically, there have been concerns that pharmacological treatments would exacerbate substance use and promote dependency and that interactions between pharmacological agents and substances of abuse may cause problems (Bukstein, 2005). However, in a systematic review of 16 published studies of pharmacological interventions for adolescents with alcohol and substance use disorders, Waxmonsky and Wilens (2005) concluded that most medications were well tolerated by adolescents and that fears about their abuse liability were not supported by the existing studies.

Several studies have investigated the use of psychotropic medications as adjuncts to psychotherapy for adolescents with comorbid psychiatric disorders. Selective serotonin reuptake inhibitors are often chosen for treating pediatric psychiatric disorders and are recommended for treating substance-using adolescents (Connor & Meltzer, 2006), although much of the evidence regarding their effectiveness with adolescents to date is based primarily on small, open trials rather than controlled studies. Prior to initiating antidepressant treatment, it is critical to provide both the adolescent and the family with information about depression and all risks, especially the risk of suicide. Given the small, but statistically significant, association between antidepressants and suicidal ideation and, to a lesser extent, suicidal attempts, it is recommended that all patients receiving these medications be monitored carefully for suicidal thoughts and behavior, as well as other side effects thought to be possibly associated with increased suicidality, such as akathisia (a syndrome characterized by unpleasant sensations of "inner" restlessness that manifests itself in an inability to sit still or remain motionless), irritability, withdrawal effects, sleep disruption, increased agitation, and induction of mania or a mixed state, particularly during the first weeks of treatment. Monitoring is important for all patients, but patients at an increased risk for suicide (e.g., those with current or prior suicidality, impulsivity, substance abuse, history of sexual abuse, family history of suicide) should be scrutinized particularly closely. Those with a family history of bipolar disorder should be monitored carefully for an onset of mania or mixed state. The Food and Drug Administration recommends that depressed youth should be seen every week for the first 4 weeks and biweekly thereafter. For adolescents with comorbid SUDs, this initial heightened level of monitoring seems reasonable. Evidence suggests that youths with bipolar disorder appear to have the best responses to medications for the treatment of active substance use disorders (Donovan et al., 1997; Geller et al., 1998), supporting the simultaneous treatment of mood and substance use disorders. Findings are mixed regarding the simultaneous treatment of other co-occurring psychiatric disorders and substance use (Waxmonsky & Wilens, 2005). Although data are limited and more research is still needed, some evidence suggests that pharmacological agents can be used to reduce cravings and substance use (Kaminer, 1992, 1994; Lifrak, Alterman, O'Brien, & Volpicelli, 1997; Niederhofer & Staffen, 2003; Upadhyaya & Deas, 2008).

Continuing care

Relapse is common among adolescent substance users who receive treatment (Brown, Vik, & Creamer, 1989). The emerging consensus that a SUD is a chronic, relapsing and remitting disorder similar to other chronic diseases (McLellan, Lewis, O'Brien, & Kleber, 2005) has led to the initiation of studies addressing models of continuing care known also as aftercare for adolescents. The growing consensus is that active interventions alone are not sufficient to end substance use and related problems for adolescents (McKay, 2005; McLellan, McKay, Forman, Cacciola, & Kemp, 2005; Scott, Foss, & Dennis, 2005). Continuing care refers to the flexible provision of aftercare that is tailored to the youth's needs and motivation for change (American Society of Medicine, 2001). Components of effective continuing care interventions include (a) proactively tracking patients and providing regular checkups, (b) screening patients for early evidence of problems, (c) motivating patients to maintain or make changes including returning to treatment, (d) assisting with gaining access to additional formal care, and (e) directing reintervention when problems do arise (Dennis, Scott, & Funk, 2003).

Kaminer, Burleson, and Burke (2008) found that active aftercare was associated with lower frequencies of both any alcohol use and heavy alcohol use from the start to the end of aftercare. Godley, Godley, Dennis, Funk, and Passetti (2007) found that adolescents who received assertive continuing care (ACC) services after discharge from residential treatment were significantly more likely to attend treatment sessions, remain abstinent from marijuana, and reduce alcohol use in the 3 months following discharge compared to adolescents who received services as usual. ACC provided case management, home visits, and community reinforcement approach as contrasted to usual continuing care, including outpatient services and encouragement to attend self-help groups. The investigators also found that motivated adolescents were more likely to remain abstinent during aftercare and to show improved engagement (Godley, Dennis, Godley, & Funk, 2004). The effectiveness of different models of continuing care and recovery management strategies is in need of further investigation.

WHERE DO WE GO FROM HERE

Although there is growing consensus about which interventions for adolescent substance users have the strongest empirical support, evidence-based interventions represent only a fraction of the treatments provided in real-world settings. Relatively few adolescents in need of services receive treatment approaches and interventions that have been validated empirically as effective in reducing and eliminating substance use and the risks of relapse. There is a national public health crisis involving the capacity, availability, and accessibility of developmentally appropriate evidence-based practice in adolescent substance abuse treatment programs and services. Of an estimated 2.1 million youths who need treatment for substance abuse and dependence (U.S. Department of

Health and Human Services, 2007), less than 10% receive any treatment. There is a critical need to make evidence-based treatment available in settings that will broaden accessibility, including primary care settings, emergency rooms, and schools. Additionally, we need to better understand the impact of involvement in multiple systems of care (e.g., juvenile justice and child welfare systems) on outcomes and how to adapt and implement evidence-based practices within these systems to serve these populations.

An understanding of mechanisms of change is also essential to the successful implementation of evidence-based interventions in real-world settings. Despite the enormous progress in research on interventions to treat adolescent substance users, there is little understanding of how or why the most well-studied interventions produce change (Kazdin, 2007). In order to implement evidence-based interventions in real-world settings, it is necessary to understand what key components must remain undiluted for evidence-based treatments to work. Several potential mechanisms of change that have been posited include motivation to change (e.g., Battjes et al., 2004), therapeutic alliance or involvement, self-efficacy and coping skills (Burleson & Kaminer, 2005), family functioning (Henggeler et al., 1992; Liddle et al., 2004), or parenting skills for family therapies (e.g., Liddle et al., 2004). However, we know very little about the mechanisms of change for specific treatments or psychotherapy in general because few studies have been designed to test mechanisms that affect outcomes. Future research should build on theories of how change occurs in general and in particular the relationship to different interventions at various critical stages of treatment (e.g., during continuing care)(Kaminer, 2001). Research designs should incorporate tests of potential multiple mediators of change that are assessed during treatment to demonstrate causal ordering and, when possible, potential mediators that are manipulated experimentally.

More attention should be devoted to potential moderators of treatment effects. In particular, the developmental stage of adolescents undergoing treatment for substance use problems may be an important predictor of response to treatment. However, few studies include developmentally sensitive measurement strategies and analyses, although most clinicians and researchers recognize the need for developmentally appropriate treatment. Developmental variables must be included in studies of treatment effectiveness (Wagner, 2008).

Finally, we must turn our attention to factors and processes that affect the implementation of evidence-based interventions in the field. Currently, there is very little science to guide the implementation of evidence-based treatments and some uncertainty about their effectiveness in real-world settings. Clinical trials are typically conducted in university-based settings, under conditions that are difficult to replicate in nonresearch settings. They often have well-trained clinical staff that provide services with a high degree of fidelity. They also use intensive strategies to recruit, engage, and maintain clients in the study. On the streets, the general lack of age-appropriate treatment services, workforce shortages, and funding shortfalls hamper efforts to provide effective, developmentally appropriate services for adolescents (McLellan & Meyers, 2004). Routine treatment practices and model adherence may go unmonitored. Factors such as organizational climates, referral sources, or policy can pose significant challenges to the implementation of evidence-based treatments. Implementation of evidence-based models cannot occur without well-trained staff supported by informed, competent supervisors, coaches, and program managers. Knowledge of "what works" in program implementation is as important as understanding "what works" in treatment intervention. To achieve state-of-the-art treatment for adolescents, we must continue to expand our knowledge of evidence-based treatments by testing effective, innovative approaches; utilizing integrative models across various treatment settings; and strengthening the science that guides implementation.

REFERENCES

Alexander, J. F., Pugh, C., Parsons, B. V., & Sexton, T. L. (2000). Functional family therapy. In D. S. Elliott (Ed.), *Blueprints for violence prevention (Book 3)* (2nd ed.). Boulder, CO: Center for the Study and Prevention of Violence, Institute of Behavioral Science, University of Colorado.

Austin, A. M., Macgowan, M. J., & Wagner, E. F. (2005). Effective family-based interventions for adolescents with substance use problems: A systematic review. *Research on Social Work Practice*, *15*(2), 67–83.

Azrin, N. H., McMahon, P. T., Donohue, B., Besalel, V. A., Lapinski, K. J., Kogan, E. S., et al. (1994). Behavior therapy for drug abuse: A controlled treatment outcome study. *Behaviour Research and Therapy*, *32*, 857–866.

Battjes, R. J., Gordon, M. S., O'Grady, K. E., Kinlock, T. W., Katz, E. C., & Sears, E. A. (2004). Evaluation of a group based substance abuse treatment program for adolescents. *Journal of Substance Abuse Treatment*, *27*(2), 123–134.

Bender, K., Springer, D. W., & Kim, J. S. (2006). Treatment effectiveness with dually diagnosed adolescents: A systematic review. *Brief Treatment and Crisis Intervention*, *6*(3), 177–205.

Borduin, C. M., Henggeler, S. W., & Manley, C. M. (1995). Conduct and oppositional disorders. In V. B. Van Hasselt & M. Hersen (Eds.), *Handbook of adolescent psychopathology: A guide to diagnosis and treatment* (pp. 349–383). Lexington, MA: Lexington Books.

Brown, S. A., McGue, M., Maggs, J., Schulenberg, J., Hingson, R., Swartzwelder, S., et al. (2008). A developmental perspective on alcohol and youths 16 to 20 years of age. *Pediatrics*, *121*(S4), 290–310.

Brown, S. A., Vik, P. W., & Creamer, V. A. (1989). Characteristics of relapse following adolescent substance treatment. *Addictive Behaviors*, *14*, 291–300.

Bukstein, O. (2005). AACAP Work Group on Quality Issues: AACAP official action: Practice parameters for assessment and treatment of children and adolescents with substance use disorders. *Journal of the American Academy of Child and Adolescent Psychiatry*, *44*(6), 609–621.

Chambless, D. L., & Hollon, S. D. (1998). Defining empirically supported therapies. *Journal of Consulting and Clinical Psychology*, *66*(1), 7–18.

Coatsworth, J. D., Santisteban, D. A., McBride, C. K., & Szapocznik, J. (2001). Brief strategic family therapy versus community control: Engagement, retention and an exploration of the moderating role of adolescent symptom severity. *Family Process*, *40*, 313–332.

Cohen, J. (1988). *Statistical power analysis for the behavioral sciences* (2nd ed.). Hillsdale, NJ: Lawrence Earlbaum Associates.

Connor, D. F., & Meltzer, B. M. (2006). *Pediatric psychopharmacology: Fast facts*. New York: W. W. Norton and Company.

Curtis, N. M., Ronan, R. R., & Borduin, C. M. (2004). Multisystemic treatment: A meta-analysis of outcome studies. *Journal of Family Psychology*, *18*, 411–419.

Dawes, M. A., & Johnson, B. A. (2004). Pharmacotherapeutic trials in adolescent alcohol use disorders: Opportunities and challenges. *Alcohol and Alcoholism*, *39*(3), 166–177.

Deas, D. (2008). Evidence-based treatments for alcohol use disorders in adolescents. *Pediatrics*, *121*(4), S348–S354.

Dennis, M., Godley, S. H., Diamond, G., Tims, F. M., Babor, T., Donaldson, J., et al. (2004). The Cannabis Youth Treatment (CYT) study: Main findings from two randomized trials. *Journal of Substance Abuse Treatment*, *27*(3), 197–213.

Dennis, M., Scott, C. K., & Funk, R. (2003). An experimental evaluation of recovery management checkups (RMC) for people with chronic substance use disorders. *Evaluation and Programing Planning*, *26*, 339–352.

Donohue, B., & Azrin, N. H. (2001). Family behavior therapy. In E. Wagner & H. Waldron (Eds.), *Innovations in adolescent substance abuse interventions*. Tarrytown, NY: Pergamon.

Donovan, S., Susser, E., Nunes, E., Stewart, J., Quitkin, F., & Klein, D. (1997). Divalproex treatment of disruptive adolescents: A report of 10 cases. *Journal of Clinical Psychiatry*, *58*(1), 12–15.

Geller, B., Cooper, T., Sun, K., Zimerman, B., Frazier, J., Williams, M., et al. (1998). Double-blind and placebo controlled study of lithium for adolescent bipolar disorders with secondary substance use dependency. *Journal of the American Academy of Child and Adolescent Psychiatry*, *37*(2), 171–178.

Godley, M. D., Godley, S. H., Dennis, M. L., Funk, R. R., & Passetti, L. L. (2007). The effectiveness of assertive continuing care on continuing care linkage, adherence, and abstinence following residential treatment. *Addiction*, *102*, 81–93.

Godley, S. H., Dennis, M. L., Godley, M. D., & Funk, R. R. (2004). Thirty-month relapse trajectory cluster groups among adolescents discharged from outpatient treatment. *Addiction*, *99*(S2), 129–139.

Henggeler, S. W., Melton, G. B., & Smith, L. A. (1992). Family preservation using multisystemic therapy: An effective alternative to incarcerating serious juvenile offenders. *Journal of Consulting and Clinical Psychology*, *60*, 953–961.

Henggeler, S. W., Borduin, C. M., Melton, G. B., Mann, B. J., Smith, L., Hall, J. A., Cone, L., & Fucci, B. R. (1991). Effects of multisystemic therapy on drug use and abuse in serious juvenile offenders: A progress report from two outcome studies. *Family Dynamics of Addiction Quarterly*, *1*, 40–51.

Huey, S. J., & Polo, A. J. (2008). Evidence-based psychosocial treatments for ethnic minority youth. *Journal of Clinical Child and Adolescent Psychology*, *37*(1), 262–301.

Jensen, J. M., Howard, M. O., & Vaughn, M. G. (2004). Assessing social work's contribution to controlled studies of adolescent substance abuse treatment. *Journal of Social Work Practice in the Addictions*, *4*(4), 51–65.

Joanning, H., Quinn, W., Thomas, F., & Mullen, R. (1992). Treating adolescent drug abuse: A comparison of family systems therapy, group therapy, and family drug education. *Journal of Marital and Family Therapy*, *18*, 345–356.

Kaminer, Y. (1992). Case study: Desipramine facilitation of cocaine abstinence in an adolescent. *Journal of Child and Adolescent Psychopharmacology*, *31*(2), 312–317.

Kaminer, Y. (2001). Adolescent substance abuse treatment: Where do we go from here?. *Psychiatric Services*, *52*(2), 147–149.

Kaminer, Y., Burleson, J. A., & Burke, R. (2008). Efficacy of outpatient aftercare for adolescents with alcohol use disorders: A randomized controlled study. *Journal of the American Academy Child and Adolescent Psychiatry*, *47*, 1405–1412.

Kaminer, Y., Burleson, J. A., & Goldberger, R. (2002). Psychotherapies for adolescent substance abusers: Short-and long-term outcomes. *Journal of Nervous and Mental Disease*, *190*, 737–745.

Kazdin, A. E. (2007). Mediators and mechanisms of change in psychotherapy research. *Annual Review of Clinical Psychology*, *3*, 1–27.

Latimer, W. W., Winters, K. C., D'Zurilla, T., & Nichols, M. (2003). Integrated family and cognitive behavioral therapy for adolescent substance abusers: A stage I efficacy study. *Drug and Alcohol Dependence*, *71*, 303–317.

Liddle, H. A. (2002). *Multidimensional family therapy treatment (MDFT) for adolescent cannabis users* (*Volume 5 of the Cannabis Youth Treatment (CYT) manual series*). Rockville, MD: Center for Substance Abuse Treatment, Substance Abuse and Mental Health Services Administration.

Liddle, H. A., Rowe, C. L., & Dakof, G. A. (2007). Clinical and empirical foundations of effective family based treatment for adolescent drug abuse. In E. Gilvarry (Ed.), *Clinics in developmental medicine: Substance misuse in young people* (pp. 185–196). Boston, MA: Cambridge University Press.

Liddle, H. A., Rowe, C. L., Dakof, G. A., Ungaro, R. A., & Henderson, C. E. (2004). Early intervention for adolescent substance abuse: Pretreatment to posttreatment outcomes of a randomized clinical trial comparing multidimensional family therapy and peer group treatment. *Journal of Psychoactive Drugs*, *36*(1), 49–63.

Lifrak, P., Alterman, A., O'Brien, C., & Volpicelli, J. (1997). Naltrexone for alcoholic adolescents: Letter to the editor. *American Journal of Psychiatry*, *154*(3), 439–440.

Maggs, J. L., Patrick, M. E., & Feinstein, L. (2008). Childhood and adolescent predictors of alcohol use and problems in adolescence and adulthood in the National Child Development Study. *Addiction*, *103*(Suppl. 1), 7–22.

McKay, J. R. (2005). Is there a case for extended interventions for alcohol and drug use disorders? *Addiction*, *100*, 1594–1610.

McLellan, A. T., McKay, J. R., Forman, R., Cacciola, J., & Kemp, J. (2005). Reconsidering of the evaluation of addiction treatment: From retrospective follow-up to concurrent recovery monitoring. *Addiction*, *100*, 447–458.

McLellan, A. T., & Meyers, K. (2004). Contemporary addiction treatment: A review of systems problems for adults and adolescents. *Society of Biological Psychiatry*, *56*, 764–770.

Myers, M. G., & Brown, S. A. (1990). Coping responses and relapse among adolescent substance abusers. *Journal of Substance Abuse*, *2*(2), 177–189.

Nathan, P. E., & Gorman, J. M. (2002). *A guide to treatments that work* (2nd ed.). New York: Oxford University Press.

Niederhofer, H., & Staffen, W. (2003). Comparison of disulfiram and placebo in treatment of alcohol dependence of adolescents. *Drug and Alcohol Review*, *22*(3), 295–297.

Orford, J. (2008). Asking the right questions in the right way: The need for a shift in research on psychological treatments for addiction. *Addiction*, *103*(6), 875–885.

Ozechowski, T. J., & Liddle, H. A. (2000). Family-based therapy for adolescent drug abuse: Knowns and unknowns. *Clinical Child and Family Psychology Review*, *3*(4), 269–298.

Robbins, M. S., Szapocznik, J., Dillon, F. R., Turner, C. W., Mitrani, V. B., & Feaster, D. J. (2008). The efficacy of structural ecosystems therapy with drug-abusing/dependent African American and Hispanic American adolescents. *Journal of Family Psychology*, *22*(1), 51–61.

Santisteban, D. A., Coatsworth, J. D., Perez-Vidal, A., Kurtines, W. M., Schwartz, S. J., LaPerriere, A., et al. (2003). The efficacy of brief strategic family therapy in modifying Hispanic adolescent behavior problems and substance use. *Journal of Family Psychology*, *17*(1), 121–13.

Scott, C. K., Foss, M. A., & Dennis, M. L. (2005). Utilizing recovery management checkups to shorten the cycle of relapse, treatment reentry, and recovery. *Drug and Alcohol Dependence*, *78*, 325–338.

Sexton, T. L., & Alexander, J. F. (2000). *Functional family therapy.* Juvenile Justice Bulletin, 1–7. U.S. Department of Justice, Office of Juvenile Justice and Delinquency Prevention.

Slesnick, N., Kaminer, Y., & Kelly, J. (2008). Most common psychosocial interventions for adolescent substance use disorders. In Y. Kaminer & O. G. Bukstein (Eds.), *Adolescent substance abuse: Psychiatric comorbidity and high-risk behaviors*. New York: Routledge, Taylor, and Francis Group.

Szapocznik, J., & Kurtines, W. M. (1989). *Breakthroughs in family therapy with drug-abusing and problem youth*. New York: Springer.

Szapocznik, J., Kurtines, W. M., Foote, F., Perez-Vidal, A., & Hervis, O. E. (1983). Conjoint versus one person family therapy: Some evidence for effectiveness of conducting family therapy through one person. *Journal of Consulting and Clinical Psychology*, *51*, 889–899.

Szapocznik, J., Kurtines, W. M., Foote, F., Perez-Vidal, A., & Hervis, O. E. (1986). Conjoint versus one person family therapy: Further evidence for the effectiveness of conducting family therapy through one person. *Journal of Consulting and Clinical Psychology*, *54*, 395–397.

Upadhyaya, H., & Deas, D. (2008). *Pharmacological interventions. Adolescent substance abuse: Psychiatric comorbidity and high-risk behaviors*. New York: Routledge, Taylor, and Francis Group.

U.S. Department of Health and Human Services. (2007). *Substance Abuse and Mental Health Services Administration. Results from the 2006 National Survey on Drug Use and Health*. Rockville, MD: Office of Applied Studies.

U.S. Department of Health and Human Services. (2008). Centers for Disease Control and Prevention. Youth Risk Behavior Surveillance—United States, 2007. *Morbidity and Mortality Weekly Report*, *57*, SS–S4.

Vaughn, M. G., & Howard, M. O. (2004). Adolescent substance abuse treatment: A synthesis of controlled evaluations. *Research on Social Work Practice*, *14*, 325–335.

Wagner, E. F. (2008). Developmentally informed research on effectiveness of clinical trails: A primer for assessing how developmental issues may influence treatment response among adolescents with alcohol use problems. *Pediatrics*, *121*(4), S337–S347.

Waldron, H. B., Slesnick, N., Brody, J. L., Turner, C. W., & Peterson, T. R. (2001). Treatment outcomes for adolescent substance abuse at 4- and 7-month assessments. *Journal of Consulting and Clinical Psychology*, *5*(2), 802–813.

Waldron, H. B., & Turner, C. W. (2008). Evidence-based psychosocial treatments for adolescent substance abuse. *Journal of Clinical Child and Adolescent Psychology*, *37*(1), 238–261.

Waldron, H. B., Turner, C. W., & Ozechowski, T. J. (2005). Profiles of drug use behavior change in adolescents in treatments. *Addictive Behaviors*, *30*(9), 1775–1796.

Waxmonsky, J. G., & Wilens, T. E. (2005). Pharmacotherapy of adolescent substance use disorders: A review of the literature. *Journal of Child and Adolescent Psychopharmacology*, *15*(5), 810–825.

Williams, R. J., & Chang, S. Y. (2000). A comprehensive and comparative review of adolescent abuse treatment outcome. Clinical Psychology, 7(2), 138–166.

Chapter | nineteen

College Student Applications

Clayton Neighbors, Eric R. Pedersen, and Mary E. Larimer
University of Washington

SUMMARY POINTS

- Substance use and risk-related behaviors are more common among college students than the general population.
- Heavy substance use in college students is usually a time-limited phenomenon.
- Heavy drinking is the most common and most problematic addictive behavior among college students.
- Most evidence-based addiction approaches in college students are best classified as indicated prevention.
- Delivery methods for college student interventions include in-person, group, computer/Internet, and mail.
- Common intervention components include a review of personal behavior and consequences, social norms, expectancies, and protective behaviors. These are commonly presented in a nonjudgmental, nonconfrontational manner.
- Harm reduction may often be a more appropriate strategy in comparison to requiring abstinence in the college student population.

Evidence-Based Addiction Treatment

During your time in college, you may have witnessed an occasion where friends or peers had too much to drink. They may have become sick or vomited, acted aggressively or loudly, or made a poor decision such as driving while intoxicated. Although you may have witnessed what seemed like a one-time incident, heavy drinking among college students is a national concern that negatively impacts the lives of many college students each year. It is estimated that approximately 1700 U.S. college students between ages 18 and 24 die each year from alcohol-related incidents, while nearly 500,000 are unintentionally injured while drinking, 600,000 are assaulted by another student who has been drinking, and more than 97,000 students experience alcohol-related sexual assault or date rape (Hingson, Heeren, Winter, & Wechsler, 2005). Although heavy drinking does not always lead to death, injury, or assault, there is an increased potential for heavy drinkers to experience a multitude of additional consequences, such as academic problems, hangovers, damaged property, fighting, and legal trouble (Wechsler et al., 2002; Wechsler, Moeykens, Davenport, Castillo, & Hansen, 1995).

Alcohol consumption is the most prevalent risky behavior among students, with approximately 85% consuming alcohol at least occasionally and about 44% recently consuming at least four drinks (for women) or five drinks (for men) during one sitting (Johnston, O'Malley, Bachman, & Schulenberg, 2007; Wechsler et al., 2002). However, drinking is not the only risky behavior present among students. Other drug use, particularly marijuana use, can also lead to negative consequences and has been a targeted focus of researchers and college student personnel in the last several years. Data from 2006 indicate an annual college student prevalence rate of 30% for marijuana use, with 17% of students reporting past 30-day use and 4% reporting daily use (Johnston et al., 2007). Consequences from marijuana use range from accidents and injuries to decreased academic performance (Bachman, Wadsworth, O'Malley, & Johnston, 1997; Gledhill-Hoyt, Lee, Strote, & Wechsler, 2000). Beyond marijuana, approximately 18.1% of college students report using other illicit drugs within the past year, including amphetamines, narcotics, cocaine, and hallucinogens, with 8.2% reporting monthly use (Johnston et al., 2007). Cigarette use is also fairly common among students. A large-scale survey study found that approximately 19% of students reported smoking during the past month (Johnston et al., 2007). Fortunately, these data suggest a decreasing trend in use over the past year of about 5%. Approximately 9% of college students report smoking every day. Other behaviors that are often classified among the "addictions" and are germane to college students include problematic gambling and disordered eating. For both of these behaviors, prevalence rates are lower than for alcohol, marijuana, or cigarette use but higher among college students than in the general population.

Approximately 5% of college students can be classified as probable pathological gamblers and approximately 10% more have experienced at least some problems related to gambling (Shaffer, Hall, & Vanderbilt, 1999). Similarly, between 2 and 4% of college women meet diagnosable criteria for an eating disorder (Fairburn & Beglin, 1990; Striegel-Moore et al., 2003), but concerns related to body image and weight control are reported by a majority of college women and by a smaller but substantial portion of college men (e.g., Bergstrom & Neighbors, 2006; Braun, Sunday, Huang, & Halmi, 1999; Olivardia, Pope, Borowiecki, & Cohane, 2004).

Research suggests that heavy drinking and drug experimentation by college students represents a temporary increase in use that tends to decrease postgraduation (Schulenberg et al., 2001; White, Labouvie, & Papadaratsakis, 2005). However, there is considerable potential for some students to drink heavily and use drugs in a reckless manner and thus harm themselves during this period of risk. Students are also at increased risk for diagnosable alcohol use disorders. The annual prevalence of alcohol abuse using DSM-IV criteria has been estimated at 31% in college samples (Knight et al., 2003), with about 6% of college students meeting criteria for the more severe diagnosis of alcohol dependence. Regarding marijuana use, approximately 7.4% of 18 to 25 year olds met past-year dependence criteria (Chen, Kandel, & Davies, 1997). This greatly exceeds the percentage of the general population that is projected to receive these diagnoses. In the general U.S. population, 3.1% of people can be diagnosed with alcohol abuse and 1.3% with alcohol dependence. For substance abuse and dependence not including alcohol, general population prevalence rates are 1.4 and 0.4%, respectively (Kessler, Chiu, Demler, & Walters, 2005). Although for the majority of students problems with alcohol and drugs do not persist after college (Schulenberg et al., 2001; White et al., 2005), for some young adults this pattern of heavy alcohol or drug use does continue into adulthood. Despite this, the vast majority of students with alcohol use disorders never seek treatment nor do they perceive their drinking to be a problem (Wu, Pilowsky, Schlenger, & Hasin, 2007). Therefore, the primary focus of intervention with this population has been in prevention and brief intervention formats. Intervening or treating students while in college may help prevent the continuation of heavy drinking patterns and problematic drug use into further adulthood, as well as reduce the serious consequences associated with heavy alcohol and drug use during college.

PREVENTION/BRIEF INTERVENTION FOCUS VERSUS TREATMENT

Given the high prevalence of use and consequences associated with alcohol and other substances in the college environment, it should come as no surprise that substantial efforts are expended by many people in attempting to address these issues. The bulk of these efforts in practice is associated with the establishment and enforcement of substance use policies by college administrators. All college campuses in the United States have policies related to the use of alcohol and other substances. Although there is considerable variation in policies across campuses, most campuses have established contingencies for violating substance use policies that may include suspension, fines, and/or probation. Very often students who violate substance use policies are mandated to attend some form of educational program, brief intervention, or brief treatment. In the ideal case, requiring brief treatment in this context exposes students to methods for reducing substance-related problems. However, what mandated students receive varies widely from campus to campus and many students receive commercially distributed programs with little or no objective documentation of empirical support.

Independent from whether efforts to address substance use among college students are effective, they can be classified as falling on a continuum from prevention to treatment. The Institute of Medicine suggests that prevention efforts be classified into one of three categories (*universal*, *selective*, or *indicated approaches*) according to the level of specificity of the population these efforts are intended to reach (Mrazek & Haggerty, 1994). Universal prevention strategies are appropriate for and/or intended to reach all members of a given population. Examples of universal strategies include public service announcements, policies regarding substance use (e.g., no alcohol allowed in the dorms), and social marketing campaigns (e.g., posters with prevention messages). Selective prevention strategies are intended to reach those who are considered at risk on the basis of group membership or have characteristics associated with risk. Examples of selective prevention approaches include alcohol education programs tailored for and presented to fraternity members. Another example might include substance use information for students suffering from depression. Finally, indicated prevention approaches are intended to reach individuals who have already begun to experience some problems related to substance use but presumably do not yet meet criteria for a substance use disorder. Many indicated prevention approaches consist of brief interventions (see Chapter 3) and can be considered brief treatment. In practice, the boundary between prevention and treatment for college student substance use is fuzzy, and indicated prevention approaches often fall in the gray area. Moreover, the majority of empirically supported treatment approaches specific to the population of college students falls in this category (Larimer & Cronce, 2002, 2007; National Institute on Alcohol Abuse and Alcoholism, 2002).

DELIVERY METHODS OF INTERVENTION

Individual in-person

ALCOHOL

College counseling centers utilize a variety of techniques to treat students with alcohol use disorders, including cognitive therapy, supportive-expressive therapy, behavioral therapy, and abstinence approaches (Chambless et al., 1998; DeRubeis & Crits-Christoph, 1998). However, little research has been conducted specifically evaluating these approaches with students. Additionally, many students seen for alcohol-related services in counseling centers may be mandated for treatment due to a violation of some campus alcohol policy or are presenting for other disturbances in their lives (e.g., adjustment disorders or depression)(Benton, Robertson, Tseng, Newton, & Benton, 2003; Birky, 2005). Therefore, important issues to address when treating this population include resistance to treatment or lack of motivation to change behavior.

BASICS

Although college campuses use a multitude of in-person approaches to intervene with college student drinkers (Larimer & Cronce, 2007), the majority of successful interventions are based on the components included in the Brief Alcohol Screening and Intervention for College Students (BASICS; Dimeff, Baer, Kivlahan, & Marlatt, 1999). BASICS is a two-session brief intervention (one session assessment and one session feedback) originally designed for students who abuse alcohol (Marlatt et al., 1998). The intervention is based on the harm-reduction approach (Marlatt, 1998) and utilizes the skills and techniques of Motivational Interviewing (Miller & Rollnick, 2002) in combination with cognitive behavioral skills training. The underlying assumption behind BASICS is that students may not see their alcohol use as harmful and thus lack motivation to decrease their use. As drinking or experimenting with drugs during college is often viewed as common, acceptable, and/or nonproblematic, strict abstinence or information-only approaches may not be as effective within the population of students. Therefore, in a harm-reduction approach, any reduction in use, consequences, or movement toward considering change is seen as a significant improvement.

The initial BASICS session consists of a 50-min assessment interview. A BASICS facilitator meets with an individual student and builds rapport through a nonjudgmental, nonconfrontational approach while assessing a student's typical alcohol use behavior. During the assessment, the facilitator assesses typical drinking behaviors, occasions of heavier drinking, alcohol dependence criteria, and family history risk for substance use disorders (Dimeff et al., 1999). Students may also be asked to complete measures of alcohol expectancies, perceived normative behavior of students on campus, reasons for consuming alcohol, and protective strategies used to avoid drinking in excess. Although the majority of the alcohol information presented occurs during the second session, the facilitator reviews the definition of "standard drinks" (one drink that contains ½ oz. of ethyl alcohol) with students. This review seeks to inform students of the approximate alcohol content in various types of drinks, as well as to standardize responses to the assessment questions (12 oz. of beer, 4 oz. of wine, 1.25 oz. shot of liquor, 8 oz. of malt liquor). At the end of this first session, participants are encouraged to monitor their drinking behavior during the time between the initial session and the follow-up session using monitoring cards provided by the facilitator (Dimeff et al., 1999).

The components of the second 50-min BASICS session include general alcohol information, social norms feedback, didactic alcohol expectancy challenge, and personalized blood alcohol concentration (BAC) discussion (Dimeff et al., 1999). Alcohol information reviewed includes gender differences in alcohol metabolism, factors and rates of alcohol processing, tolerance, and negative consequences of alcohol (e.g., sleep disturbance, academic problems). Students are also provided with a BAC card tailored toward their gender and weight. These pocket-sized cards help students estimate their level of intoxication based on the number of drinks consumed over specific time periods. Family history risk and substance use dependence issues are also reviewed.

Social norms feedback is provided to show students the discrepancies between how they think other students on campus drink and how students on campus actually drink. This is based on social norms theory (see Berkowitz, 2004; Perkins, 2003), which suggests that students tend to have skewed perceptions of peers' alcohol and other drug use. These misperceptions can actually influence one's own behavior. For example, if a student believes the majority of students at her school consume more than five drinks during a typical night out, she may drink to match and fit in with a misperceived norm. Students have been shown to consistently overestimate the degree to which students in general, proximal peer groups (e.g., members of one's athletic team, fraternity brothers), and close friends drink alcohol (Baer, Stacy, & Larimer, 1991; Borsari & Carey, 2003; Neighbors, Dillard, Lewis, Bergstrom, & Neil, 2006; Perkins, 2007; Perkins & Berkowitz, 1986). Thus, providing students with accurate normative data to correct these misperceptions is an essential component of BASICS and many other brief in-person, group, mailed, and computer-based interventions with college students (Larimer & Cronce, 2007; Walters & Neighbors,

2005). In BASICS, students are generally presented with graphs of typical student drinking behavior and informed of how much they drink compared to their peers.

Another important component of the second session is the challenge of alcohol expectancies, or beliefs and ideas about the positive and negative effects of alcohol. Positive expectancies that alcohol will increase sociability, enhance sexual opportunity, reduce stress and tension, and increase courage or creativity have all been associated with heavier drinking (e.g., Fromme, Stroot, & Kaplan, 1993; Goldman, Brown, & Christiansen, 1987; Jones, Corbin, & Fromme, 2001; Read, Wood, Lejuez, & Palfai, 2004). Thus, the BASICS protocol includes the provision of evidence for alcohol expectancy effects. For example, students can be informed of the many alcohol expectancy studies run in the University of Washington Behavioral Alcohol Research Laboratory (BarLab) where participants consumed nonalcoholic drinks under the guise of "real drinks." Participants in multiple studies acted as if they had actually consumed alcohol (Marlatt & Rosenhow, 1980). Beyond those described in BASICS, studies of in vivo expectancy challenge generally involve distribution of either alcohol or nonalcoholic placebo to students and assigning group-based tasks. After the tasks, students are asked to guess who was given real alcohol and who received placebo. The long-term effects of these interventions are not well understood, and studies provide disparate findings regarding the short-term effects of challenging alcohol expectancies on changes in drinking, problems, and expectancies (e.g., Darkes & Goldman, 1993; Dunn, Lau, & Cruz, 2000; Musher-Eizenman & Kulick, 2003; Wood, Capone, LaForge, Erickson, & Brand, 2007).

There is evidence strongly supporting the BASICS protocol in its original format (e.g., Baer, Kivlahan, Blume, McKnight, & Marlatt, 2001; Borsari & Carey, 2000; Marlatt et al., 1998). However, as individual interventions can be time-consuming and tax limited campus resources, many of the BASICS components have been adapted to be used in both multiple and single component brief interventions during both individual and group delivery. Utilization of the BASICS components during brief motivational enhancement interventions has been effective in preventing heavy drinking and in intervening with established drinkers among at-risk populations (e.g., first year students, athletes), voluntary samples, and mandated samples (see review by Larimer & Cronce, 2007).

BEHAVIORS AND SUBSTANCES OTHER THAN ALCOHOL

As alcohol is the primary drug of choice among college students, research on risky behavior among students generally focuses on drinking interventions. Therefore, limited empirical evidence exists to support treatments and interventions for other behaviors with this population. However, some work has evaluated the use of individual motivational enhancement interventions in reducing cigarette, marijuana, and other drug use in university students. Compared to an educational "treatment as usual" session, volunteer students who received a one-session, 60-min brief motivational enhancement intervention targeted toward increasing motivation to change behavior reduced cigarette and marijuana use over 3 months of follow-up (McCambridge & Strang, 2004). White and colleagues (2006) found similar reductions in cigarette and marijuana use over 3 months among mandated students in both a motivational enhancement plus feedback intervention and a written motivational feedback condition alone (with no in-person component). Thus, there is not ample evidence to support the superiority of brief motivational enhancement interventions for drug use in college students as compared to the effects of feedback alone. Providing feedback regarding personal use, monitoring behavior, or increasing knowledge of the short- and long-term effects of substance use may assist in reduction or cessation. Interestingly, in the studies reviewed here, the use of drugs other than cigarettes and marijuana did not decrease postintervention in any condition. Although the base rates of other drug use were low, these findings and the limited research on other drugs besides alcohol suggest that more research in the area of treatment and brief intervention with marijuana, cigarettes, and other drugs specifically within college student populations is needed.

Just as BASICS and similar brief interventions have been adapted and evaluated with other substances, they have also been adapted and preliminarily evaluated for behavioral addictions, including problem gambling (Takushi et al., 2004) and binge eating (Dunn, Neighbors, & Larimer, 2006). In both cases, some support has been reported.

Social norms interventions

As noted, one of the components of BASICS is the provision of social norms information. Previous research has found this to be one of the more effective components of the BASICS intervention (Borsari & Carey, 2000; Carey, Scott-Sheldon, Carey, & DeMartini, 2007). Thus it may not be surprising that approaches have since been developed that rely entirely on the provision of social norms. To date, these more specific interventions have been implemented in at least three ways: personalized normative feedback, social norms marketing, and brief live interactive group feedback.

Personalized normative feedback (PNF) has most often been implemented via computer and as an *indicated prevention* approach provided to heavy drinking students. Personalized normative feedback is preceded by a brief survey or assessment of a student's drinking and his or her perceptions of peer drinking. Students are then provided with feedback, usually via computer, which consists of three key pieces of information: (A) the student's own drinking, (B) the student's perception of other students' drinking, and (C) the actual norms for other students' drinking (e.g., see Figure 19.1). This simple approach has been shown to reduce students' misperceptions regarding the prevalence of drinking among their peers and, more importantly, to result in reductions of their own drinking in multiple studies (Lewis & Neighbors, 2007; Lewis, Neighbors, Oster-Aaland, Kirkeby, & Larimer, 2007; Neighbors, Lewis, & Larimer, 2004; Neighbors, Lewis, Bergstrom, & Larimer, 2006).

A related and much more common approach typically employed as a *universal prevention* approach is social norms marketing. This approach is not personalized but rather consists of providing the accurate norms for a given campus or a subpopulation of a given campus, usually in the form of posters, flyers, campus newspaper ads, radio ads, and many other creative media (e.g., fortune cookies, frisbees, t-shirts, pencils, coffee cups). The efficacy of this approach has been hotly debated with staunch supporters and vehement critics. This approach has been implemented in some form on a majority of U.S. campuses (Wechsler et al., 2003). Whereas some studies have documented clear and strong support for the approach (e.g., Perkins & Craig, 2003) and others have found no support, the most likely conclusion is that the approach is provisionally effective. Example provisions include extensive and extended campaigns, the absence of conflicting messages (DeJong et al., 2006), and the requirement that the campaign effectively changes perceptions (Mattern & Neighbors, 2004).

Finally, among the most recently developed empirically validated brief intervention approaches is brief live interactive norms feedback for groups (e.g., LaBrie, Hummer, Neighbors, & Pedersen, 2008). This novel approach utilizes hand-held "clickers," which have become common in college classrooms. The initial evaluation of this approach, best categorized as a selective prevention study, involved a controlled study of over 1000 students who were members of fraternities, sororities, or service organizations. Groups were assigned randomly to receive the intervention or assessment-only control. In the intervention groups, students were asked to record responses assessing their own attitudes and behaviors related to drinking as well as their estimates of their fellow group members' attitudes and behaviors related to drinking. Immediately afterward, the responses to both sets of questions were displayed in summary to the group. For all groups, the summary revealed students' estimates of their fellow group members' attitudes

SNAP

Social Norms and Alcohol Prevention (SNAP)
University of Washington
Dept. of Psychiatry and Behavioral Sciences Box 356560
Seattle, WA 98195-6560
Phone: 206-221-5344 / Fax: 206-543-9520
snap@u.washington.edu

Personalized Feedback

According to the information you provided us during the computer assessment, the number of occasions you drank (frequency) was **3** times a week. The average amount you drank on each occasion (quantity) was **6** drinks.

You completed questions asking you what you believed the average frequency and quantity of alcohol consumed by other college students to be. You told us that you believed that the average student drank **4** times a week and during each occasion, s/he consumed **12** drinks.

The actual drinking norm for students at the University of Washington is **1.5** times a week drinking about **3.3** drinks on each drinking occasion.*

Your percentile rank (comparing you to other college students) is **93%**, which suggests that you drink more than **93%** of other college students.

*Note: This information comes from a random sample of 2,548 UW students.

Please print this page and keep it for your records.

Frequency of Alcohol Consumption (days per week)

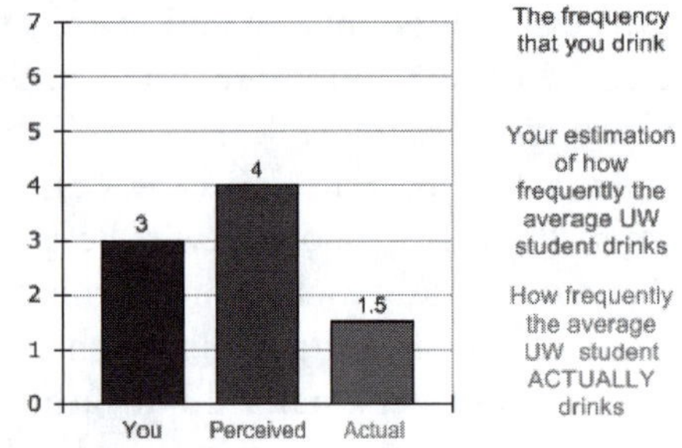

Quantity of Alcohol Consumption (drinks per week)

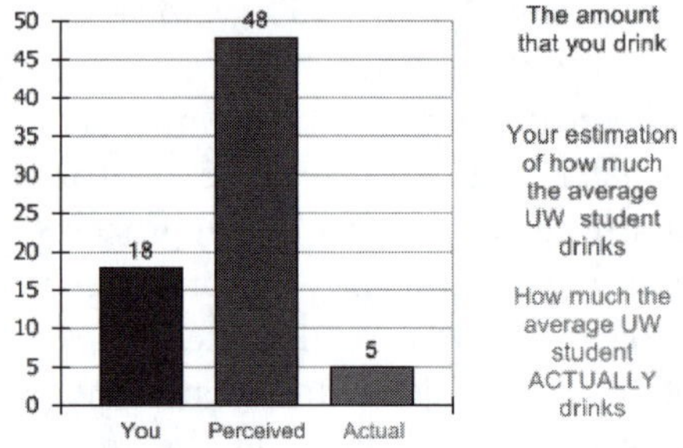

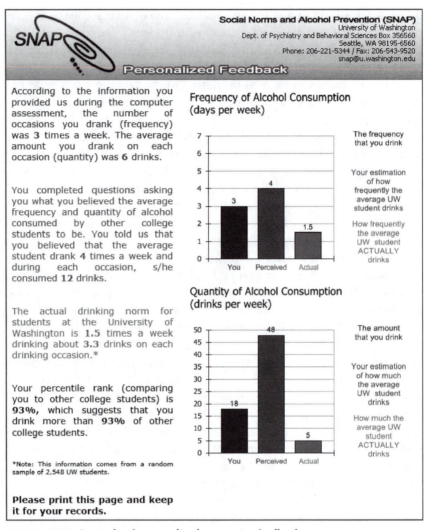

FIGURE 19.1 *Example of personalized normative feedback.*

and drinking behaviors were overestimates with respect to approval of heavy drinking and actual drinking behavior based on students' reports. Moreover, when assessed 1 and 2 months later, participants in the intervention groups reported more accurate perceptions of group norms and reduced drinking in comparison to control participants.

Group-based interventions

ALCOHOL SKILLS TRAINING PROGRAM

A predecessor of the BASICS intervention is the alcohol skills training program. Developed at the University of Washington, this program includes much of the same content provided in BASICS but in the context of group discussion. Formats including eight sessions (Kivlahan, Marlatt, Fromme, Coppel, & Williams, 1990), six sessions (Baer et al., 1992), and two sessions (Miller, Kilmer, Kim, Weingardt, & Marlatt, 2001) have been found to be effective in reducing alcohol use among students at risk for alcohol problems.

Internet-based approaches

Whether it is a personal laptop computer in a dorm room or a desktop computer in one of the multiple campus computer laboratories, students generally have considerably easy access to a computer during college. Thus, intervening with students via the Internet can be an advantageous method to provide information to and intervene with a large number of students (Zisserson, Palfai, & Saitz, 2007). Benefits of Internet-based approaches include ease and expanded time of access (e.g., students can view an intervention when it is convenient for them even if it is 1 a.m.), standardized intervention formats, potential for individual tailored feedback presentations, reduced cost and less burden on campus resources, and ability to reach a broader population of students (e.g., the entire student population of a school via an email Web link).

Computer-based approaches have utilized many of the BASICS components using on-screen assessments and interventions in controlled on-site settings (e.g., in a computer laboratory) or personal settings (e.g., student's home computer). On-site interventions have shown promise with college students. Kyrpi and colleagues (2004) found short-term reductions in drinking for students receiving PNF and alcohol information via a computer. Likewise, using a PNF-only intervention, Neighbors and colleagues (2004) found an intervention group to have greater reductions in drinking behavior than a control group at 3- and 6-month follow-up assessments. The intervention also assisted in correcting misperceptions of campus-specific norms at the 3-month follow-up, which influenced reductions in drinking found at the 6-month follow-up. Regarding comparisons of Web-based intervention and printed postal mail intervention, to date there appears to be little difference in the effectiveness of these two approaches over brief follow-ups (Moore, Soderquist, & Werch, 2005).

Multiple alcohol-based Internet Web sites exist to provide students with information regarding the consequences of heavy alcohol use. A limited number of these Web pages have been tested empirically for efficacy (e.g., Walters, Hester, Chiauzzi, & Miller, 2005). My Student Body is a Web site with information, individually tailored motivational and social norms feedback, substance use disorders assessment, and multiple resources related to alcohol, tobacco, and other drug use. The electronic Check Up and Go (e-Chug) for alcohol and the electronic THC Online Knowledge Experience (e-Toke) for marijuana provide students with an assessment followed by a detailed feedback presentation of drinking or marijuana use. Individualized feedback covers a wide range of topics similar to those within the BASICS protocol. Topics include the following: comparisons of use to national- and school-specific norms; information related to BAC and drug interaction effects; risk factors, protective strategies; an alcohol information quiz; and personalized information related to one's own expectancies, typical and peak BAC; money spent on alcohol; dependence risk, family history risk; and caloric content of beverages consumed. For example, the e-Chug Web site calculates the number of cheeseburger equivalents for the calories consumed in a typical month's alcohol consumption. Note that there are approximately 140 calories in a typical standard drink and 350 calories in a typical cheeseburger. Thus, approximately every 2.5 drinks is equivalent calorically to a cheeseburger.

These three sites use aggregate data from campus-specific users to provide accurate and updated normative feedback. My Student Body appears to contribute to drinking reductions in women, heavier drinkers, and students less motivated to change their drinking prior to viewing the Web page (Chiauzzi, Green, Lord, Thum, & Goldstein, 2005). Likewise, e-Chug appears to aid in the prevention of heavy drinking among first-year students (Dumas, 2007), accelerate drinking reductions in heavier drinkers (Walters, Vader, & Harris, 2007), and enhance effects of a group workshop (Walters et al., 2005).

While computer and Internet-based approaches appear promising, more research is needed to determine the long-term effectiveness of these interventions. Calls for more thorough investigations of what specific components of these interventions are most necessary to include, as well as how novel technologies can enhance these interventions (e.g., text/instant messaging), are needed.

Mail approaches

In addition to in-person and computer-delivered interventions, another empirically supported approach utilizes mail (e.g., Agostinelli, Brown, & Miller, 1995; Collins, Carey, & Sliwinski, 2002; Larimer et al., 2007). For the most part, studies that have found empirical support have used the same kinds of feedback as described earlier (e.g., norms feedback; feedback regarding personal use, consequences, and risks; moderation tips; reference information; contact information for where to get help). As with other empirically supported approaches for intervention strategies in the college population, most research related to mailed interventions to date has focused on alcohol. For example, Collins and colleagues (2002) studied 100 students who reported two or more heavy drinking episodes in the previous month at screening. Based on an initial assessment, pamphlets were created for a random half of students and included a review of the student's personal alcohol use and consequences; comparisons between the students' personal drinking behavior and U.S.- and university-specific norms; and information regarding BAC and tolerance. At the 6-week follow-up, students in the mailed feedback condition drank significantly fewer drinks during their heaviest drinking week and reported fewer heavy drinking episodes in comparison to the control group. However, differences between the groups were no longer evident at the 6-month follow-up.

In another example, using a similar methodology, Larimer and colleagues (2007) studied a random sample of 1488 students, including abstaining, light drinking, and heavy drinking students. A random half of students received mailed feedback, which included a review of personal use and consequences; comparison of personal use to campus norms; personalized BAC information regarding typical and peak drinking; personalized information regarding expected effects of alcohol; and strategies students could use to reduce their risks of experiencing negative alcohol related consequences (i.e., protective behaviors). Students were also sent weekly nonpersonalized postcards including alcohol information (e.g., campus norms, gender differences, protective strategies, and costs). Results revealed students in the mailed feedback condition consumed less alcohol a year later in comparison to students in the control group. In addition, students who were nondrinkers at baseline were twice as likely to remain nondrinkers if they were in the mailed feedback condition. Moreover, results suggested that the feedback was effective at least in part because it increased students' use of protective behaviors.

CONCLUSIONS

In sum, a number of empirically supported treatment approaches for addictive behaviors are available for college students. Many of these treatment approaches are brief in focus and fall in the gray area between prevention and treatment. Empirically supported approaches for college students have focused most often on alcohol, but other substances, including cigarettes and marijuana, have been targeted using similar approaches. Primary themes of most approaches include addressing potential resistance to change and social factors that have considerable influence on addictive behaviors in this population.

REFERENCES

Agostinelli, G., Brown, J. M., & Miller, W. R. (1995). Effects of normative feedback on consumption among heavy drinking college students. *Journal of Drug Education*, *25*, 31–40.

Bachman, J. G., Wadsworth, K. N., O'Malley, P. M., & Johnston, L. D. (1997). *Smoking, drinking, and drug use in young adulthood: The impacts of new freedoms and new responsibilities*. Hillsdale, NJ: Lawrence Erlbaum Associates.

Baer, J. S., Kivlahan, D. R., Blume, A. W., McKnight, P., & Marlatt, G. A. (2001). Brief intervention for heavy drinking college students: 4-year follow-up and natural history. *American Journal of Public Health*, *91*, 1310–1316.

Baer, J. S., Marlatt, G. A., Kivlahan, D. R., Fromme, K., Larimer, M., & Williams, E. (1992). An experimental test of three methods of alcohol risk reduction with young adults. *Journal of Consulting and Clinical Psychology*, *60*, 974–979.

Baer, J. S., Stacy, A., & Larimer, M. (1991). Biases in the perception of drinking norms among college students. *Journal of Studies of Alcohol*, *52*, 580–586.

Benton, S. A., Robertson, J. M., Tseng, W., Newton, F. B., & Benton, S. L. (2003). Changes in counseling center client problems across 13 years. *Professional Psychology: Research and Practice*, *34*, 66–72.

Bergstrom, R. L., & Neighbors, C. (2006). Body image disturbance and the social norms approach: An integrative review of the literature. *Journal of Social and Clinical Psychology*, *25*, 975–1000.

Berkowitz, A. D. (2004). *The social norms approach: Theory, research, and annotated bibliography*. Available at http://www.edc.org/hec/socialnorms/theory.html.

Birky, I. T. (2005). Evidence-based and empirically supported college counseling center treatment of alcohol related issues. *Journal of College Student Psychotherapy*, *20*, 7–21.

Borsari, B., & Carey, K. B. (2000). Effects of a brief motivational intervention with college student drinkers. *Journal of Consulting and Clinical Psychology*, *68*, 728–733.

Borsari, B., & Carey, K. B. (2003). Descriptive and injunctive norms in college drinking: A meta-analytic integration. *Journal of Studies on Alcohol*, *64*, 331–341.

Braun, D. L., Sunday, S. R., Huang, A., & Halmi, K. A. (1999). More males seek treatment for eating disorders. *International Journal of Eating Disorders*, *25*, 415–424.

Carey, K. B., Scott-Sheldon, L. A. J., Carey, M. P., & DeMartini, K. S. (2007). Individual-level interventions to reduce college student drinking: A meta-analytic review. *Addictive Behaviors*, *32*, 2469–2494.

Chambless, D. L., Baker, M. J., Baucom, D. H., Beutler, L. E., Calhoun, K. S., Crits-Christoph, P., et al. (1998). Update on empirically supported therapies. II. *The Clinical Psychologist*, *51*, 3–16.

Chen, K., Kandel, D. B., & Davies, M. (1997). Relationships between frequency and quantity of marijuana use and last year proxy dependence among adolescents and adults in the United States. *Drug and Alcohol Dependence*, *46*, 53–67.

Chiauzzi, E., Green, T. C., Lord, S., Thum, C., & Goldstein, M. (2005). My Student Body: A high-risk drinking prevention web site for college students. *Journal of American College Health*, *53*, 263–275.

Collins, S. E., Carey, K. B., & Sliwinski, M. J. (2002). Mailed personalized normative feedback as a brief intervention for at-risk college drinkers. *Journal of Studies on Alcohol, 63*, 559–567.

Darkes, J., & Goldman, M. S. (1993). Expectancy challenge and drinking reduction: Experimental evidence for a mediational process. *Journal of Consulting and Clinical Psychology, 61*, 344–353.

DeJong, W., Schneider, S. K., Towvim, L. G., Murphy, M. J., Doerr, E. E., Simonsen, N. R., et al. (2006). A multisite randomized trial of social norms marketing campaigns to reduce college student drinking. *Journal of Studies on Alcohol, 67*, 868–879.

DeRubeis, R. J., & Crits-Christoph, P. (1998). Empirically supported individual and group psychological treatments for adult mental disorders. *Journal of Consulting and Clinical Psychology, 66*, 37–52.

Dimeff, L. A., Baer, J. S., Kivlahan, D. R., & Marlatt, G. A. (1999). *Brief Alcohol Screening and Intervention for College Students (BASICS): A harm reduction approach*. New York: Guilford Press.

Dumas, D. (2007). Decreasing heavy drinking and smoking in college freshman: Evaluation of e-chug administered during freshman seminar. *Report prepared for health, wellness, and counseling services and advising and academic enhancement*. Boise, ID: Institute for the Study of Addiction, Boise State University.

Dunn, E. C., Neighbors, C., & Larimer, M. E. (2006). Motivational interviewing and self-help treatment for binge eaters. *Psychology of Addictive Behaviors, 20*, 44–52.

Dunn, M. E., Lau, H. C., & Cruz, I. Y. (2000). Changes in activation of alcohol expectancies in memory in relation to changes in alcohol use after participation in an expectancy challenge program. *Experimental and Clinical Psychopharmacology, 8*, 566–575.

Fairburn, C. G., & Beglin, S. J. (1990). Studies of the epidemiology of bulimia nervosa. *American Journal of Psychiatry, 147*, 401–408.

Fromme, K., Stroot, E., & Kaplan, D. (1993). The comprehensive effects of alcohol: Development and psychometric assessment of a new expectancy questionnaire. *Psychological Assessment, 5*, 19–26.

Gledhill-Hoyt, J., Lee, H., Strote, J., & Wechsler, H. (2000). Increased use of marijuana and other illicit drugs at US colleges in the 1990s: Results of three national surveys. *Addiction, 95*, 1655–1667.

Goldman, M. S., Brown, S. A., & Christiansen, B. A. (1987). Expectancy theory: Thinking about drinking. In H. T. Blane & K. E. Leonard (Eds.), *Psychological theories of drinking and alcoholism* (pp. 181–226). New York: Guilford Press.

Hingson, R., Heeren, T., Winter, M., & Wechsler, H. (2005). Magnitude of alcohol-related mortality and morbidity among U.S. college students ages 18–24: Changes from 1998 to 2001. *Annual Review of Public Health, 26*, 259–279.

Johnston, L. D., O'Malley, P. M., Bachman, J. G., & Schulenberg, J. E. (2007). *Monitoring the Future national survey results on drug use, 1975–2006: Volume II, College students and adults ages 19–45* (NIH Publication No. 07-6206). Bethesda, MD: National Institute on Drug Abuse.

Jones, B. T., Corbin, W., & Fromme, K. (2001). A review of expectancy theory and alcohol consumption. *Addiction, 96*, 57–72.

Kessler, R. C., Chiu, W. T., Demler, O., & Walters, E. E. (2005). Prevalence, severity, and comorbidity of 12-month DSM-IV disorders in the National Comorbidity Survey Replication. *Archives of General Psychiatry, 62*, 617–627.

Kivlahan, D. R., Marlatt, G. A., Fromme, K., Coppel, D. B., & Williams, E. (1990). Secondary prevention with college drinkers: Evaluation of an alcohol skills training program. *Journal of Consulting and Clinical Psychology, 58*, 805–810.

Knight, J. R., Wechsler, H., Kuo, M., Seibring, M., Weitzman, E. R., & Schuckit, M. A. (2003). Alcohol abuse and dependence among U.S. college students. *Journal of Studies on Alcohol, 63*, 263–270.

Kyrpi, K., Saunders, J. B., Williams, S. M., McGee, R. O., Langley, J. D., Cashell-Smith, M. L., et al. (2004). Web-based screening and brief intervention for hazardous drinking: A double-blind randomized controlled trial. *Addiction, 99*, 1410–1417.

LaBrie, J. W., Hummer, J. F., Neighbors, C., & Pedersen, E. R. (2008). Live interactive group-specific normative feedback reduces misperceptions and drinking in college students: A randomized trial. *Psychology of Addictive Behaviors, 22*, 141–148.

Larimer, M. E., & Cronce, J. M. (2002). Identification, prevention and treatment: A review of individual-focused strategies to reduce problematic alcohol consumption by college students. *Journal of Studies on Alcohol, 14*(Suppl.), 148–163.

Larimer, M. E., & Cronce, J. M. (2007). Identification, prevention, and treatment revisited: Individual-focused college drinking prevention strategies: 1999–2006. *Addictive Behaviors, 32*, 2439–2468.

Larimer, M. E., Lee, C. M., Kilmer, J. R., Fabiano, P. M., Stark, C. B., & Geisner, I. M. (2007). Personalized mailed feedback for college drinking prevention: A randomized clinical trial. *Journal of Clinical and Consulting Psychology, 75*, 285–293.

Lewis, M. A., & Neighbors, C. (2007). Optimizing personalized normative feedback: The use of gender-specific referents. *Journal of Studies on Alcohol and Drugs, 68*, 228–237.

Lewis, M. A., Neighbors, C., Oster-Aaland, L., Kirkeby, B., & Larimer, M. E. (2007). Indicated prevention for incoming college freshmen: Personalized feedback and high risk drinking. *Addictive Behaviors, 32*, 2495–2508.

Marlatt, G. A. (Ed.). (1998). *Harm reduction: Pragmatic strategies for managing high-risk behaviors*. New York: Guilford Press.

Marlatt, G. A., Baer, J. S., Kivlahan, D. R., Dimeff, L. A., Larimer, M. E., Quigley, L. A., et al. (1998). Screening and brief intervention for high-risk college student drinkers: Results from a two-year follow-up assessment. *Journal of Consulting and Clinical Psychology, 66*, 604–615.

Marlatt, G. A., & Rosenhow, D. J. (1980). Cognitive processes in alcohol use: Expectancy and the balanced placebo design. In N. K. Mello (Ed.), *Advances in substance use: Behavioral and biological research* (pp. 159–199). Greenwich, CT: JAI Press.

Mattern, J., & Neighbors, C. (2004). Social norms campaigns: Examining changes in perceived norms and changes in drinking levels. *Journal of Studies on Alcohol, 65*, 489–493.

McCambridge, J., & Strang, J. (2004). The efficacy of single-session motivational interviewing in reducing drug consumption and perceptions of drug-related risk and harm among young people: Results from a multi-site cluster randomized trial. *Addiction, 99*, 39–52.

Miller, E. T., Kilmer, J. R., Kim, E. L., Weingardt, K. R., & Marlatt, G. A. (2001). Alcohol skills training for college students. In P. M. Monti, S. M. Colby, &

T. A. O'Leary (Eds.), *Adolescents, alcohol and substance abuse: Reaching teens through brief intervention* (pp. 183–215). New York: Guilford Press.

Miller, W. R., & Rollnick, S. (2002). *Motivational interviewing: Preparing people for change* (2nd ed.). New York: Guilford Press.

Moore, M. J., Soderquist, J., & Werch, C. (2005). Feasibility and efficacy of a binge drinking prevention intervention for college students delivered via internet versus postal mail. *Journal of American College Health*, *54*, 38–44.

Mrazek, P. J., & Haggerty, R. J. (1994). *Reducing risks for mental disorders: Frontiers for preventive intervention research*. Washington, DC: National Academy Press.

Musher-Eizenman, D. R., & Kulick, A. D. (2003). An alcohol expectancy-challenge prevention program for at risk college women. *Psychology of Addictive Behaviors*, *17*, 163–166.

National Institute on Alcohol Abuse and Alcoholism. (2002). *A call to action: Changing the culture of drinking at U.S. colleges* (NIH Publication No. 02-5010). Rockville, MD: Author.

Neighbors, C., Dillard, A. J., Lewis, M. A., Bergstrom, R. L., & Neil, T. A. (2006). Normative misperceptions and temporal precedence of perceived norms and drinking. *Journal of Studies on Alcohol*, *67*, 290–299.

Neighbors, C., Larimer, M. E., & Lewis, M. A. (2004). Targeting misperceptions of descriptive drinking norms: Efficacy of a computer-delivered personalized normative feedback intervention. *Journal of Consulting and Clinical Psychology*, *72*, 434–447.

Neighbors, C., Lewis, M. A., Bergstrom, R. L., & Larimer, M. E. (2006). Being controlled by normative influences: Self-determination as a moderator of a normative feedback alcohol intervention. *Health Psychology*, *25*, 571–579.

Olivardia, R., Pope, H. G., Borowiecki, J. J., & Cohane, G. H. (2004). Biceps and body image: The relationship between muscularity and self-esteem, depression, and eating disorder symptoms. *Psychology of Men and Masculinity*, *5*, 112–120.

Perkins, H. W. (Ed.). (2003). *The social norms approach to preventing school and college age substance abuse: A handbook for educators, counselors, and clinicians*. San Francisco: Jossey-Bass.

Perkins, H. W. (2007). Misperceptions of peer drinking norms in Canada: Another look at the 'reign of error' and its consequences among college students. *Addictive Behaviors*, *32*, 2645–2656.

Perkins, H. W., & Berkowitz, A. D. (1986). Perceiving the community norms of alcohol use among students: Some research implications for campus alcohol education programming. *International Journal of the Addictions*, *21*, 961–976.

Perkins, H. W., & Craig, D. A. (2003). *A multi-faceted social norms approach to reduce high-risk drinking: Lessons from Hobart and William Smith Colleges*. Newton, MA: The Higher Education Center for Alcohol and Other Drug Prevention.

Read, J. P., Wood, M. D., Lejuez, C. W., & Palfai, T. P. (2004). Gender, alcohol consumption, and differing alcohol expectancy dimensions in college drinkers. *Experimental and Clinical Psychopharmacology*, *12*, 298–308.

Schulenberg, J., Maggs, J. L., Long, S. W., Sher, K. J., Gotham, H. J., Baer, J. S., et al. (2001). The problem of college drinking: Insights from a developmental perspective. *Alcoholism: Clinical and Experimental Research*, *25*, 473–477.

Shaffer, H. J., Hall, M. N., & Vander Bilt, J. (1999). Estimating the prevalence of disordered gambling behavior in the United States and Canada: A research synthesis. *American Journal of Public Health*, *89*, 1369–1376.

Striegel-Moore, R. H., Dohm, F. A., Kraemer, H. C., Taylor, C. B., Daniels, S., Crawford, P. B., et al. (2003). Eating disorders in white and black women. *American Journal of Psychiatry*, *160*, 1326–1331.

Takushi, R., Neighbors, C., Larimer, M., Lostutter, T., Cronce, J., & Marlatt, G. A. (2004). Indicated prevention of problem gambling among college students. *Journal of Gambling Studies*, *20*, 83–93.

Walters, S. T., Hester, R. K., Chiauzzi, E., & Miller, E. (2005). Demon rum: High-tech solutions to an age-old problem. *Alcoholism: Clinical and Experimental Research*, *29*, 270–277.

Walters, S. T., & Neighbors, C. (2005). Feedback interventions for college alcohol misuse: What, why and for whom? *Addictive Behaviors*, *30*, 1168–1182.

Walters, S. T., Vader, A. M., & Harris, T. R. (2007). A controlled trial of web-based feedback for heavy drinking college students. *Prevention Science*, *8*, 83–88.

Wechsler, H., Lee, J. E., Kuo, M., Seibring, M., Nelson, T. F., & Lee, H. P. (2002). Trends in college binge drinking during a period of increased prevention efforts: Findings from four Harvard School of Public Health study surveys, 1993–2001. *Journal of American College Health*, *50*, 203–217.

Wechsler, H., Moeykens, B., Davenport, A., Castillo, S., & Hansen, J. (1995). The adverse impact of heavy episodic drinkers on other college students. *Journal of Studies on Alcohol*, *56*, 628–634.

Wechsler, H., Nelson, T. F., Lee, J. E., Seibring, M., Lewis, C., & Keeling, R. P. (2003). Perception and reality: A national evaluation of social norms marketing interventions to reduce college students' heavy alcohol use. *Journal of Studies on Alcohol*, *64*, 484–494.

White, H., Labouvie, E., & Papadaratsakis, V. (2005). Changes in substance use during the transition to adulthood: A comparison of college students and their noncollege age peers. *Journal of Drug Issues*, *35*, 281–305.

White, H. R., Morgan, T. J., Pugh, L. A., Celinska, K., Labouvie, E., & Pandina, R. J. (2006). Evaluating two brief substance-use interventions for mandated college students. *Journal of Studies on Alcohol*, *67*, 309–317.

Wood, M. D., Capone, C., Laforge, R., Erickson, D., & Brand, N. (2007). Brief motivational interview and alcohol expectancy challenge with heavy drinking college students: A randomized factorial study. *Addictive Behaviors*, *32*, 2509–2528.

Wu, L., Pilowsky, D. J., Schlenger, W. E., & Hasin, D. (2007). Alcohol use disorders and the use of treatment services among college-age young adults. *Psychiatric Services*, *58*, 192–200.

Zisserson, R. N., Palfai, T. P., & Saitz, R. (2007). "No contact" interventions for unhealthy college drinking: Efficacy of alternatives to person-delivered intervention approaches. *Substance Abuse*, *28*, 119–132.

Chapter | twenty

Internet Evidence-Based Treatments

John A. Cunningham

Centre for Addiction and Mental Health, Toronto, Ontario, Canada

SUMMARY POINTS

- This chapter provides an overview of Internet-based interventions (IBIs) for addictive behaviors.
- Section one discusses the components commonly found in IBIs, explains the rationale for their use, and identifies variations that occur in these components.
- Section two reviews the types of research evidence that exists for IBIs and highlights areas where evidence of efficacy is lacking.
- Section three concludes the chapter with a brief discussion of future directions for IBIs.

Section One

- This section focuses on four of the key components found in IBIs: screeners, registration pages, diaries of different addictive behaviors, and social support groups/social networks.

- *Screeners* provide the participant with a summary of their addiction concern, usually contain a research-evaluated questionnaire of addiction severity, and are often brief.
- A *registration page* allows the IBI to keep a record of participants' ongoing use of the IBI tools and allows the IBI administrator to implement Web site rules and regulations.
- *Diaries*, a tool from cognitive behavioral therapy, allow participants to record information relating to their substance use and their change attempts.
- *Social support groups/social networks* provide a community of active users in which participants can support each other (keep in mind that some groups are moderated whereas others are not).
- The two main opinions about how IBIs should be structured are (1) participants should be guided through a set of exercises in a specific order or (2) participants should be able to choose when and in what order they use different exercises in an IBI.

Section Two

- This section focuses on the types of research that support IBIs effectiveness and highlights areas where evidence of efficacy is lacking.
- *Descriptive studies* usually contain a summary of the content of an IBI, the characteristics of participants who use the Web site, and often follow-up data that describe how participants of the IBI have reduced their addictive behavior over time. However, descriptive studies cannot be taken as evidence that the IBI caused any reductions due to a lack of randomly assigned control groups.
- *Randomized controlled trials* are the gold standard for evaluating the efficacy of any intervention, but keep in mind that this does not necessarily mean that the IBI will work in the setting you are interested in.
- Other research contributions include investigating the process by which participants use an IBI, analyses of social support groups/social networks postings, and how the use of IBIs grows over time.
- *Review papers* play a key role in summarizing research conducted to date and evaluating the quality of existing IBIs.

Section Three

- This section discusses the future of IBIs and the two main factors of development: *new technology* and *conduct of research* demonstrating what works (or does not) in IBIs.
- Developing an evidence base for IBIs is an important goal regardless of the speed in which technology changes.

Internet-based interventions (IBIs) are a promising avenue to help those with alcohol, tobacco, and other substance abuse concerns. The number of IBIs continues to multiply and, in recent years, tools have become available on the Internet for illicit drug use as well as tobacco and alcohol. This increase seems to be driven by several factors: (1) the improved capabilities and availability of the Internet, (2) the cost-effectiveness of IBIs once they have been set up, and (3) a growing recognition that many people with addictions will never seek face-to-face treatment (e.g., Cunningham & Breslin, 2004). This last issue, combined with the fact that many people appear interested in alternate forms of treatment services (Cunningham, 2005, 2008; Koski-Jännes & Cunningham, 2001), has led to the development of an array of treatment options. One of these new treatment options, Internet-based interventions, is the topic of this chapter. The first section describes the typical content of IBIs. The second section provides a discussion of the research conducted to evaluate IBIs. The chapter concludes with speculation on where IBIs may go in the future.

WHAT DO INTERNET-BASED INTERVENTIONS LOOK LIKE?

There are a large number of IBIs already developed and more appear every year. This section describes some of their typical components. Examples of IBIs are described that have some research-based evidence of effectiveness (and, of which, the author helped to develop). The intent of this section is to familiarize the reader with IBI elements that already have research evidence. The figures depicting different types of IBI tools are derived from currently available versions of IBIs. It is to be expected that these IBIs may be modified over time to incorporate improvements in content, technology, or design philosophy. Thus, future versions might look slightly or significantly different.

Personalized feedback screeners

Internet-based interventions commonly contain screeners that allow participants to evaluate their substance use. Ideally, these screeners contain a validated scale, allowing participants to assess the severity of their substance use. As examples, the Check Your Cannabis screener (see www.CheckYourCannabis.net) employs the Alcohol, Smoking and Substance Involvement Test, a brief screener developed by the World Health Organization (for an example, see Figure 20.1; Group, 2002), or the Check Your Drinking screener (see www.CheckYourDrinking.net) (Cunningham, Humphreys, Kypri, & van Mierlo, 2006a) incorporates the Alcohol Use Disorders Identification Test (Saunders, Aasland,

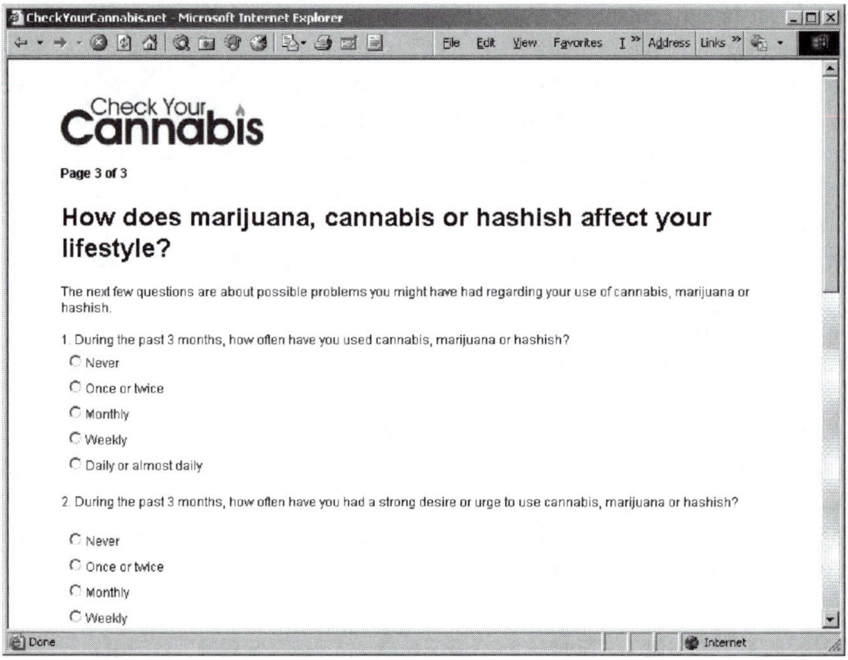

FIGURE 20.1 *Example screener page from www.CheckYourCannabis.net.*

Babor, De La Fuente, & Grant, 1993). Common to both of these instruments is their brevity, their extensive research base, and the fact that they can be used free of charge. Brevity may be an important element in the Web pages that participants first contact, as there is a tendency for people to visit new Web sites only for a brief time before losing interest and moving on to another Web site (Danaher, McKay, & Seeley, 2005).

Personalized feedback screeners often include an assessment of the quantity and frequency of substance use. This information is summarized for the participant in a personalized feedback report. Some of these reports incorporate normative feedback, providing a comparison of the individual's level of use to that of the general population. Figure 20.2 provides a sample feedback chart from a screener for problem gambling (see www.CheckYourGambling.net). Incorporating normative feedback transforms screeners from introductory IBI portals to interventions in their own right. Evidence shows that even the briefest of screeners that incorporate normative feedback can motivate reductions in alcohol use (Neighbors, Larimer, & Lewis, 2004) and that personalized feedback interventions can have a significant impact on drinking when delivered over the Internet (Cunningham, Humphreys, Wild, Cordingley, & van Mierlo, manuscript under review). It is unclear, as of yet, whether normative feedback will motivate change in other addictive behaviors.

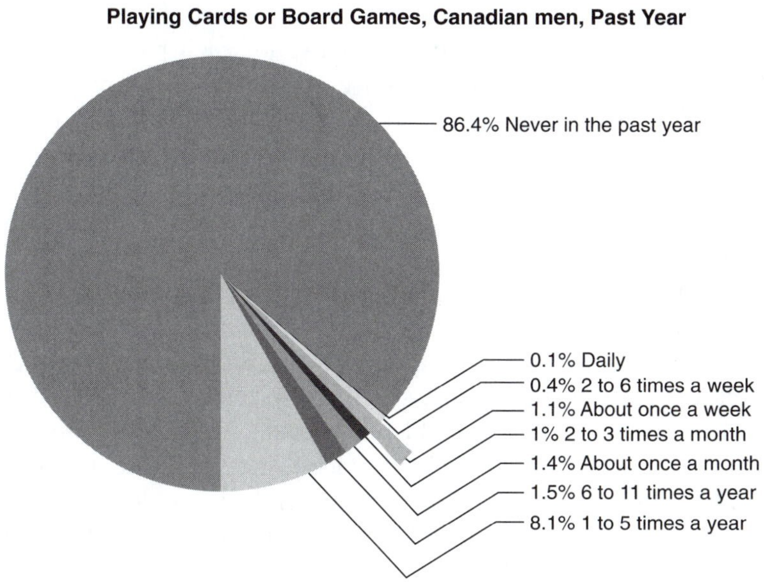

FIGURE 20.2 *Example normative feedback from a personalized feedback screener for problem gambling (www.CheckYourGambling.net).*

Registration pages for larger Web sites

Many IBIs require potential participants to register before entering the main content areas of the Web site. Often the personalized feedback screener is situated outside of the main content of the IBI so that prospective participants can screen themselves before deciding if they want to commit to viewing more content. The primary purpose of registration is usually to allow the IBI to set up an account for the participant. This account allows a history of the participant's past use of the Web site to be saved. This history can then be employed by intervention tools that benefit from the longitudinal recording of data (e.g., diaries). A registration process also allows the IBI owner to have the potential participant read and endorse a user agreement that covers the Web site rules. As an example, if the IBI contains a social support group, the user agreement will probably list the rules of conduct for posting on the support group, such as being courteous to other participants, avoiding the recommendation or endorsement of medications or courses of therapy, staying on topic, and being aware of the consequences for breaking the rules. Finally, the registration process also allows some IBI Web sites to only allow a subset of participants to access the Web site (e.g., a Web site that requires a password to use so that only members of a particular health care plan can use the IBI) or that require payment from the potential participant before allowing access.

Having a registration process has costs as well as benefits. The primary benefit is to allow a history of use for each participant. The potential cost is that registration raises concerns about privacy and confidentiality. IBIs can include instructions on how to minimize privacy risks by, for example, suggesting that the participant use a nickname and anonymous email address in the sign-up process. However, it is possible that any type of registration process might make some potential participants hesitant to sign up if concerns about privacy are of importance to them. The issue of privacy is not unique to IBIs, as this is a common barrier to seeking help in face-to-face treatment as well (Cunningham, Sobell, Sobell, Agrawal, & Toneatto, 1993). In fact, many participants in IBIs report specifically seeking out a Web-based solution to their addiction problems because they were concerned about privacy issues inherent with face-to-face treatment (Cooper, 2004; Humphreys & Klaw, 2001). In the end, many decide that the benefits of using a quality online IBI outweigh any perceived concerns about privacy. Interestingly, there is also evidence that use of an IBI might allow some individuals to overcome their concerns about face-to-face treatment and to seek this type of help as well (Cooper, 2004).

There are other elements to a good IBI and its registration process that can help identify it as a quality tool. First, quality Web sites often provide information on the developers and content experts. This information can then be used to identify whether the Web site has been evaluated and if research has been published demonstrating its efficacy. Second, a Web site may provide the potential participant with a bibliography that outlines the source of the content. Finally, a quality Web site will most likely, and is often legally required to, outline any use to which the participants' data will be made (i.e., will the participant's responses be used for research purposes in addition to helping the participant directly).

Diaries

Tools from cognitive behavioral therapy that translate well into IBIs are diaries of different addictive behaviors (e.g., drinking diary). These tools allow the participant to log on and record the quantity and frequency of their use of a particular substance. The IBI program then generates a summary of the participant's use (see Figure 20.3 for an example from the Stop Smoking Center; www.StopSmokingCenter.net). Some diaries also allow the participant to record other information relevant to his or her change attempt (e.g., experience of urges, other precipitating events, use of medications, general environmental factors, feelings, and emotions) (Figure 20.3).

Other cognitive behavioral tools

Any cognitive behavioral tool that can be put on paper appears to translate well into an Internet-based format. Some exercises are fairly static (e.g., set a goal; create a list of techniques you will use if you feel urges to smoke or drink). Others take advantage of the ability of programs to personalize feedback and summarize changes over time. An example is a downloadable quit meter from the Stop Smoking Center displayed in Figure 20.4. The quit meter sits on the participant's desktop and acts as a motivator to continue with a quit attempt by providing the smoker

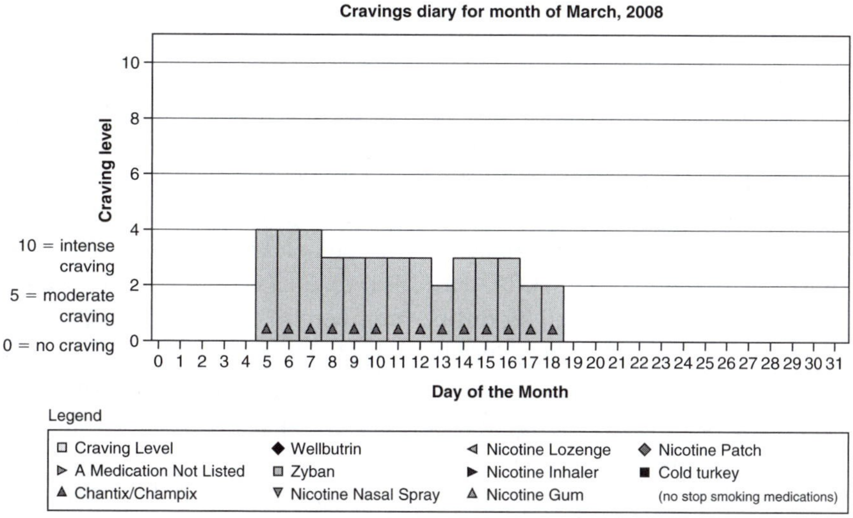

FIGURE 20.3 *Example craving diary summary generated by the Stop Smoking Center (www.StopSmokingCenter.net).*

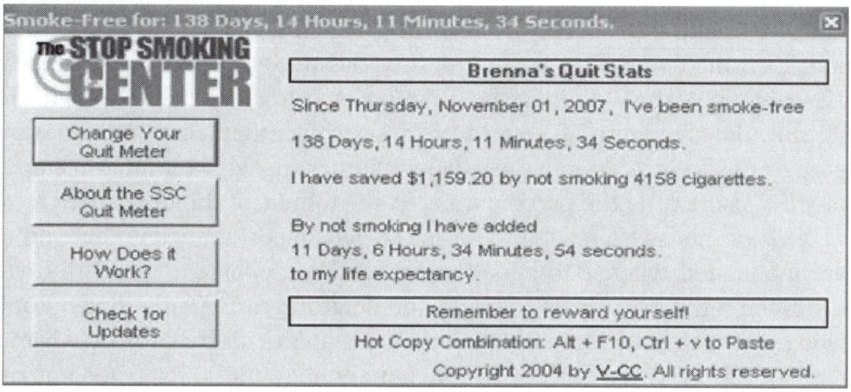

FIGURE 20.4 *Example of a quit meter from the Stop Smoking Center (www.StopSmokingCenter.net).*

with a reminder of his or her continual progress and quit statistics (and the advantages to staying off cigarettes).

Social support groups

One of the real advantages of well-established IBIs that have a large community of active users is the ability to create a medium within which participants can support each other in their change attempt. Imagine a situation where someone trying to quit drinking or stop smoking experiences a strong urge to use. Some individuals may have someone that they could contact to help them with a craving any time of the day or night. However, many others have to try to deal with these urges by themselves, either because they have no one in their social network that can provide this type of support (or cannot provide support in the middle of the night) or because the individual is unwilling to risk the stigma of sharing the addiction problem with someone who knows them. Online social support groups (also referred to as online social networks) have the advantage of anonymity so that participants feel able to discuss their concerns with less fear of personal reprisal (Burri, Baujar, & Etter, 2006; Humphreys & Klaw, 2001). The content of messages provided by online members to each other is also frequently of high quality (Burri et al., 2006; Cunningham, van Mierlo, & Fournier, 2008). Figure 20.5 displays an example screenshot of some support group postings from the Alcohol Help Center to illustrate the content of some posts.

Beyond the content of the messages, a key element to the usefulness of online support groups is the speed with which participants can receive a reply. In an analysis of the patterns of use of the Stop Smoking Center online support group, Selby, van Mierlo, Parent, and Cunningham (manuscript under review) found that the average length of time between participants making their first post on the group and getting their first reply was 29 min. Twenty-five percent of the posts received a response within 12 min, and three-quarters of first posts were responded to within 90 min, day or night. The speed of these replies may allow online support groups to provide much needed aid in dealing with temptations and distress at the time the participant is in the middle of their experience.

One of the issues related to online social support groups is that some are moderated whereas others are not. Although there is no definitive research on the advantages of having moderators, particularly moderators who are health professionals, there is some speculation as to the advantages of this type of service (Cunningham et al., 2008). First, moderators have the ability to purge messages that are inappropriate or off-topic, leading to a support group that is potentially more helpful for its participants.

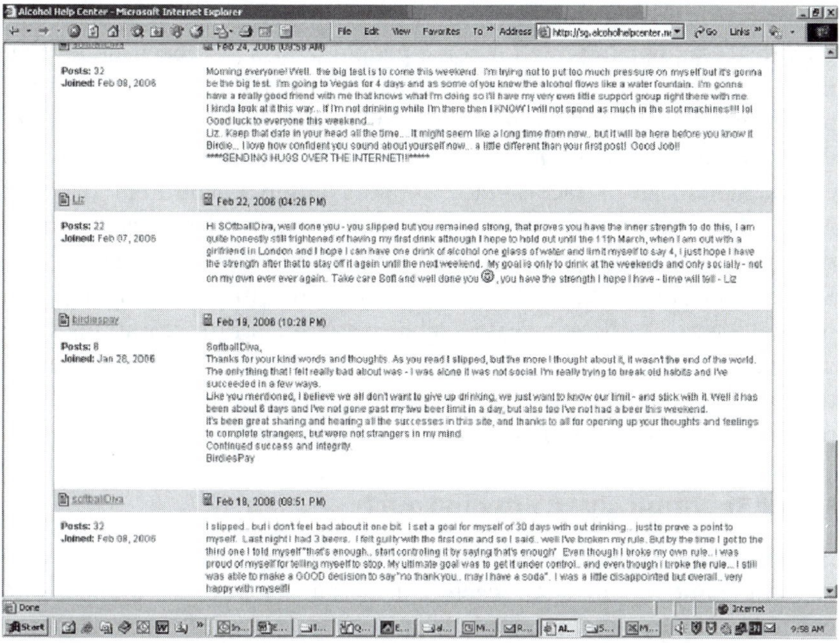

FIGURE 20.5 *Screenshot of support group postings made on the Alcohol Help Center (www.AlcoholHelpCenter.net).*

Second, moderators appear particularly useful in support groups where there is not yet a critical mass of active participants. In such cases, posting on an unmoderated support group runs the risk of not receiving a response to one's request for help. When few people are using a moderated Web site, the moderator can reply to participants and provide them with support (albeit often not as quickly as the responses that are received on large active support groups). In addition, moderators can stimulate discussion (or direct it to certain topics) by "seeding" the Web site with posts on relevant topics to which participants can respond. An important factor to consider when deciding to recommend a specific support group is to determine whether there is a user agreement. As mentioned earlier, user agreements will often explicitly state appropriate behavior and remedies for inappropriate behavior. Then, if a participant continues to act in an inappropriate manner, he or she can be excluded from the group. This is a useful power for moderators to have, although it appears to rarely be used (Fournier, Czukar, Selby, van Mierlo, & Pereira, 2006, October).

There are two final issues to consider with social support groups. The first is that posts are read most often many more times by "lurkers" than by active participants engaging in the discussions (Cunningham et al., 2008). "Lurkers" are generally defined as participants who read the posts but who do not make posts themselves. It is possible that just reading the posts (i.e., "lurking") on support groups provides a supporting role for some people. It has also been noted that there appears to be a pattern of support group use in which potential participants start off just reading posts before building up the confidence required to participate actively and make their own posts and even graduating to face-to-face support group encounters (Cooper, 2004). The second issue is that some support group participants prefer the option of having private conversations with other members. Some IBIs provide an instant messaging option in which participants can mutually agree to have private exchanges while still maintaining their anonymity (i.e., they do not need to give out any personal information to allow this contact since it is provided through the IBI). Figure 20.6 provides an example of this feature from the Stop Smoking Center.

Using technology to stay in touch

Beyond cognitive behavioral tools and support groups, some IBIs also contain components that reach out to participants as a means to bolster motivation to maintain change. As examples, both the Stop Smoking Center and the Alcohol Help Center have options in which participants can sign up to have topical emails and text messages sent to them. These messages contain content that is intended to help participants continue in their quit or reduction attempt. Other programs have employed interactive voice response technology in order to ask participants, at the end of each day, if they succeeded in abstaining from smoking (and provided tailored responses depending on participants' answers; Brendryen & Kraft, 2008; Helzer et al., 2008). As technological capabilities develop, it is likely that more tools of this type will be incorporated into IBIs.

How is the IBI structured?

There is variability in how IBIs are structured. In developing IBIs, there appear to be two main opinions on what might work best for participants. The first view is that participants should be guided through a set of exercises in a specific order such that participants have to finish one set of exercises before they are allowed access to the next. The other camp holds that participants may benefit more from allowing choice as to what order exercises be completed. Of course, there can be hybrid designs that incorporate components from each of these design philosophies (Danaher et al., 2005). As of yet, there is no clear evidence that one style of Web site necessarily works better than others, and the functionality of IBIs may continue to evolve. It is up to participants to decide which version they personally prefer.

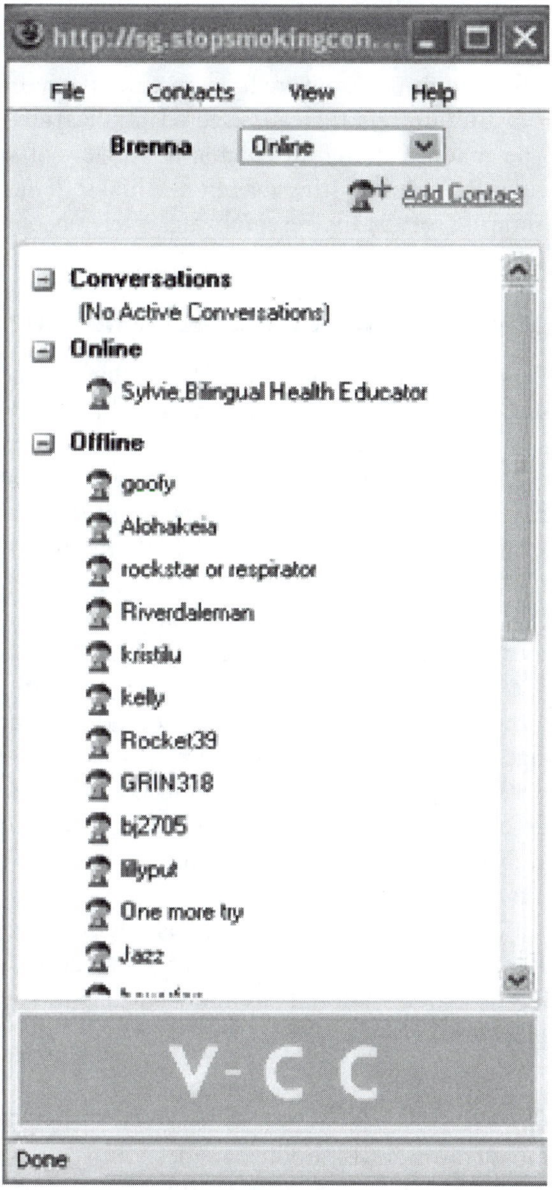

FIGURE 20.6 *Example of an instant messenger portal for private exchangers between members of the Stop Smoking Center (www.StopSmokingCenter.net).*

CONSIDERATIONS FOR CREATING AN EVIDENCE BASE

Stating that an IBI is evidence based implies that there is a body of research that supports its effectiveness. There are varying levels of evidence base that need to be interpreted in order to make a judgment as to whether an IBI might help participants. These issues are described in detail elsewhere (Cunningham & van Mierlo, 2009), but are summarized here. This chapter does not include an exhaustive list of research trials conducted to date but instead selected publications to illustrate the points to be made. Having an exhaustive review of studies would not be particularly useful to the reader as this is a fast developing field and summaries of extant research are often obsolete soon after they are published.

Is there evidence of efficacy in another format?

At the most basic level is the question of whether the content of the Web site is derived from an intervention that has been found to be effective in a different format (i.e., in a face-to-face intervention; over the telephone; as a self-help book). It should be noted that the need to evaluate the research base of an intervention is not restricted to IBIs, as many of the interventions used in face-to-face treatment settings rely on content that has little or no research support (Miller & Wilbourne, 2002). In addition, having a good research base in another format does not necessarily indicate that the intervention will translate into an IBI format. As an example, an intervention that has a lengthy assessment or multistage intervention may not be utilized because people tend to move from page to page on the Internet fairly quickly (Danaher et al., 2005). Another example is that an intervention that relies heavily on therapist interaction may not work as well on the Internet (or might require a great deal of translation and evaluation before it becomes useful for the participant). However, having some type of evidence for the effectiveness in another format is a good base upon which to evaluate the quality of an intervention. Some Web sites also contain a bibliography of the source of their materials to allow participants to identify the theoretical underpinnings of the IBI.

Descriptive studies of IBIs

Perhaps the most common IBI studies are descriptive ones. That is, the authors are describing the content of an IBI and the characteristics of participants who have used the Web site. Also common in these reports are the results of surveys that IBI participants complete regarding their impressions of the Web site (e.g., did they like it?; was it useful?) and, also, follow-up data based on participant outcomes (for an example of this type of study see, Cunningham et al., 2006a). These studies provide a useful background to illustrate the process of developing an IBI. It is also reassuring to determine if people are drinking less (or smoking less) several months after they participated in the IBI. However, this type of study cannot be taken as evidence that the IBI caused any reduction observed because they have no randomly assigned control groups not using the IBI. As such, we cannot know if the reductions in drinking or other addictive behavior were the result of using the IBI or due to other factors (e.g., the participants who used the IBI were especially motivated to change, or received help from another source, and would have reduced their drinking even if they had not used the IBI).

Randomized controlled trials

In some ways, randomized controlled trials (RCT) are the gold standard for evaluating the efficacy of any intervention, IBIs included. Having random assignment of participants to an intervention and a control group allows confidence that any differences observed are caused by the intervention. However, along with this strength comes a number of limitations. Are the participants enrolled in the research trial similar enough to those people who sign up to use the IBI in real life so that a finding that the IBI helped participants in the research trial indicates that the intervention will also be effective for regular participants? How have the participants in the RCT been selected (i.e., who was excluded from the trial)? What kind of assessments were used (there is growing recognition that assessments have an impact in their own right; Kypri, Langley, Saunders, & Cashell-Smith, 2007; McCambridge & Day, 2008)? In addition, is the setting of the RCT similar to the way in which the IBI will be used in real life? As an example, if an IBI is evaluated in a setting where participants are invited to come to a research facility to access the IBI, can we assume that the program will work in the same way if the participant is using the IBI at home? Sometimes the intervention may actually be designed to be implemented in a face-to-face setting (e.g., Kypri, Langley, Saunders, Cashell-Smith, & Herbison, 2008). In other studies, an intervention designed for use in the home has been evaluated in a face-to-face research setting (Hester, Squires, & Delaney, 2005). Finally, what is being evaluated in the RCT? Some trials compare the effects of the IBI to a no intervention control group (Cunningham, Humphreys, Wild, Cordingley, & van Mierlo, manuscript, under review), an information-only Web site (Riper, Kramer, Smit, Conijn, Schippers, & Cuijpers, 2008), or a self-help booklet (Brendryen & Kraft, 2008). Other trials compare different levels of personalization of an IBI (Strecher et al., 2008) or brief versus extended IBIs (Saitz et al., 2007). Still other evaluations compare regular care (e.g., a face-to-face treatment) to regular care plus access to an IBI (Doumas & Hannah, 2008; Japuntich et al., 2006) or to the evaluation of IBIs focused on multiple health behaviors (Kypri

& McAnally, 2005; Oenema, Brug, Dijkstra, de Weerdt, & de Vries, 2008). As with any research evaluation, it is the accumulation of multiple studies, using a variety of different research methods, that leads to the most confidence that an IBI is effective.

Other research contributions

Several other types of research protocols are used to evaluate IBIs. The first of these includes studies in which the researcher is investigating the process by which participants use a Web site. Understandably, this type of research is important, not only to provide suggestions for ways to improve an existing IBI, but also to provide insight into the mechanisms by which these interventions may help participants. One example would be a study in which the patterns of use of an IBI are examined. Linke, Murray, Butler, and Wallace (2007) reported on the use of the original version of the Down Your Drink IBI. This intervention required that participants go through each step of the IBI in consecutive order, with incorporated time locks, so that the participant was only able to access one module each week. The authors noted that most people did not complete all the modules. An offshoot of this study was a decision to allow participants to access the modules in an order of their choosing and to remove the time locks.

Another type of process research design has been used to investigate social support groups. A study mentioned earlier in this chapter outlined the speed with which posts on active support groups receive replies (Selby, van Meirlo, Parent, & Cunningham, manuscript under review). Other research has reported on content analyses of the types of posts and responses (Burri et al., 2006; Cunningham et al., 2008). This research is useful in developing an impression of the quality of support provided by other participants in relation to guidelines that summarize recommended evidence-based support. Other research has noted the self-correcting nature of online support postings (Esquivel, Meric-Bernstam, & Bernstam, 2006). That is, it has been noted that incorrect postings on support groups with a large active membership are often corrected by other members of the group, thus providing evidence of the therapeutic usefulness of these online groups.

Also of interest in studying evidence-based IBIs for substance abuse is the investigation of who uses these interventions and how the population of participants grows over time. These questions can be addressed in several different ways. First, general population survey data can be used to examine whether a population (e.g., problem drinkers or smokers) has access to the Internet (a relatively obvious precondition for the use of IBIs: Cunningham, Selby, Kypri, & Humphreys,

2006b). Other studies of this type also report on the extent to which those with addictions report that they would be interested in using an IBI (Cunningham, 2008; Cunningham et al., 2008). It should be stressed that while information on the proportion of people who say they would be interested in using an IBI has some merit, it cannot be taken as a measure of the true level of usage as many would be unlikely to act on this interest. Finally, there are studies that focus on factors that might be important in promoting the dissemination of an IBI so that its use will become more widespread in the general population (or by relevant health practitioners with their clients; Brouwer et al., 2008; Crutzen et al., 2008).

The final research products relevant to the evaluation of an evidence base for IBIs are review papers summarizing research conducted to date or evaluating the quality of existing IBIs. The latter usually consists of an article that summarizes a search for all existing IBIs in a particular area (Bock et al., 2004; Copeland & Martin, 2004; Toll et al., 2003) and then applies a set of criteria to judge their quality (not unlike criteria used to describe the different components of IBIs discussed in this chapter). There have been a number of reviews of research conducted to date in the area of smoking (probably reflecting the fact that IBIs for tobacco cessation are further along in their development; Etter, 2006; Walters, Wright, & Shegog, 2006). There have also been a few on IBIs for problem drinkers, some focusing on special populations (e.g., college students) and others on more general population groups (Bewick et al., 2008; Walters, Miller, & Chiauzzi, 2005). While these reviews can be a good introduction to the existing evidence base for IBIs, because this is a fast developing field, there are often several relevant studies in press or published after the review itself has been published.

LOOKING TO THE FUTURE

Two factors will most likely drive future developments of evidence-based IBIs for substance abuse—the development or increased availability of new technology and the conduct of research demonstrating what works (or does not work). As far as technology is concerned, increases in the abilities of communication tools (e.g., personal digital assistants) will most likely result in IBIs that have easier access and improved personalization capabilities (e.g., IBI components available for access over cell phones; personalized text messages). In addition, it is likely that online support groups will incorporate more features of Web sites with member-generated content, such as Web logs (or "blogs"), YouTube, Facebook, and MySpace. In reality, it is difficult to envision what IBIs will look like several years from now because there are so many new technologies that are being developed that could profitably be applied in this area.

The primary challenge for research will be to keep pace with IBIs that incorporate new technological features. Already, research reports of outcome evaluations are in some ways obsolete by the time they are published, as the IBIs under study have already been modified. However, developing an evidence base for IBIs is still an important goal. First, there is an insufficient body of evidence to firmly establish the effectiveness of IBIs as a useful tool for alcohol, tobacco, and other addictions. Second, research has already (and will continue to) helped identify types of intervention tools that appear to be most useful in an Internet-based context. Research also helps identify the ways in which people use IBIs—information that is useful in planning further development. It is clear that, given the work already accomplished in this area and the promise for more developments in the near future, IBIs are likely to play an increasing role in attempts to modify addictive behaviors.

REFERENCES

Bewick, B. M., Trusler, K., Barkham, M., Hill, A. J., Cahill, J., & Mulhern, B. (2008). The effectiveness of web-based interventions designed to decrease alcohol consumption: A systematic review. *Preventative Medicine*, *47*, 17–26.

Bock, B., Graham, A., Sciamanna, C., Krishnamoorthy, J., Whiteley, J., Carmona-Barros, R., et al. (2004). Smoking cessation treatment on the Internet: Content, quality, and usability. *Nicotine & Tobacco Research*, *6*, 207–219.

Brendryen, H., & Kraft, P. (2008). Happy ending: A randomized controlled trial of a digital multi-media smoking cessation intervention. *Addiction*, *103*, 478–484.

Brouwer, W., Oenema, A., Crutzen, R., de Nooijer, J., de Vries, N. K., & Brug, J. (2008). An exploration of factors related to dissemination of and exposure to internet-delivered behavior change interventions aimed at adults: A Delphi study approach. *Journal of Medical Internet Research*, *10*, e10.

Burri, M., Baujar, V., & Etter, J. F. (2006). A qualitative analysis of an Internet discussion forum for recent ex-smokers. *Nicotine & Tobacco Research*, *8*, S13–S19.

Cooper, G. (2004). Exploring and understanding online assistance for problem gamblers: The pathways disclosure model. *eCommunity: International Journal of Mental Health and Addiction*, *1*, 32–38.

Copeland, J., & Martin, G. (2004). Web-based interventions for substance use disorders: A qualitative review. *Journal of Substance Abuse Treatment*, *26*, 109–116.

Crutzen, R., de Nooijer, J., Brouwer, W., Oenema, A., Brug, J., & de Vries, N. K. (2008). Internet-delivered interventions aimed at adolescents: A Delphi study on dissemination and exposure. *Health Education Research*, *23*, 427–439.

Cunningham, J. (2005). Is level of interest among cannabis users in self-help materials and other services aimed at reducing problem use? *Addiction*, *100*, 561–562.

Cunningham, J. A. (2008). Access and interest: Two important issues in considering the feasibility of Web-assisted tobacco interventions. *Journal of Medical Internet Research, 10*, e37.

Cunningham, J. A., & Breslin, F. C. (2004). Only one in three people with alcohol abuse or dependence ever seek treatment. *Addictive Behaviors, 29*, 221–223.

Cunningham, J. A., Hodgins, D. C., & Toneatto, T. (2008). Interest in different types of self-help services for problem gamblers. *Psychiatric Services, 59*, 695–696.

Cunningham, J. A., Humphreys, K., Kypri, K., & van Mierlo, T. (2006a). Formative evaluation and three-month follow-up of an online personalized assessment feedback intervention for problem drinkers. *Journal of Medical Internet Research, 8*, e5.

Cunningham, J. A., Selby, P. L., Kypri, K., & Humphreys, K. N. (2006b). Access to the Internet among drinkers, smokers and illicit drug users: Is it a barrier to the provision of interventions on the World Wide Web?. *Medical Informatics and the Internet in Medicine, 31*, 53–58.

Cunningham, J. A., Sobell, L. C., Sobell, M. B., Agrawal, S., & Toneatto, T. (1993). Barriers to treatment: Why alcohol and drug abusers delay or never seek treatment. *Addictive Behaviors, 18*, 347–353.

Cunningham, J. A., & Van Mierlo, T. (2009). Methodological issues in the evaluation of Internet-based interventions for problem drinking. *Drug and Alcohol Review, 28*, 12–17.

Cunningham, J. A., van Mierlo, T., & Fournier, R. (2008). An online support group for problem drinkers: AlcoholHelpCenter.net.. *Patient Education and Counseling, 70*, 193–198.

Danaher, B. G., McKay, H. G., & Seeley, J. R. (2005). The information architecture of behavior change websites. *Journal of Medical Internet Research, 7*, e12.

Doumas, D. M., & Hannah, E. (2008). Preventing high-risk drinking in youth in the workplace: A web-based normative feedback program. *Journal of Substance Abuse Treatment, 34*, 263–271.

Esquivel, A., Meric-Bernstam, F., & Bernstam, E. V. (2006). Accuracy and self correction of information received from an internet breast cancer list: Content analysis. *British Medical Journal, 332*, 939–942.

Etter, J. F. (2006). Internet-based smoking cessation programs. *International Journal of Medical Informatics, 75*, 110–116.

Fournier, R., Czukar, D., Selby, P., Van Mierlo, T., & Pereira, M. (2006, October). Helping quitters when and where they need it most? Challenges and learnings in building and growing the Canadian Cancer Society's web-assisted tobacco intervention "Smokers' Helpline Online" support group. Presented at "Mednet," Toronto.

Group, W. A. W. (2002). The Alcohol, Smoking and Substance Involvement Screening Test (ASSIST): Development, reliability and feasibility. *Addiction, 97*, 1183–1194.

Helzer, J. E., Rose, G. L., Badger, G. J., Searles, J. S., Thomas, C. S., Lindberg, S. A., et al. (2008). Using interactive voice response to enhance brief alcohol intervention in primary care settings. *Journal of Studies on Alcohol and Drugs, 69*, 251–258.

Hester, R. K., Squires, D. D., & Delaney, H. D. (2005). The drinker's check-up: 12-month outcomes of a controlled clinical trial of a stand-alone software program for problem drinkers. *Journal of Substance Abuse Treatment*, *28*, 159–169.

Humphreys, K., & Klaw, E. (2001). Can targeting nondependent problem drinkers and providing internet-based services expand access to assistance for alcohol problems? A study of the moderation management self-help/mutual aid organization. *Journal of Studies on Alcohol*, *62*, 528–532.

Japuntich, S. J., Zehner, M. E., Smith, S. S., Jorenby, D. E., Valdez, J. A., Fiore, M. C., et al. (2006). Smoking cessation via the internet: A randomized clinical trial of an internet intervention as adjuvant treatment in a smoking cessation intervention. *Nicotine & Tobacco Research*, *8*(Suppl. 1), S59–S67.

Koski-Jännes, A., & Cunningham, J. A. (2001). Interest in different forms of self-help in a general population sample of drinkers. *Addictive Behaviors*, *26*, 91–99.

Kypri, K., Langley, J. D., Saunders, J. B., & Cashell-Smith, M. L. (2007). Assessment may conceal therapeutic benefit: Findings from a randomized controlled trial for hazardous drinking. *Addiction*, *102*, 62–70.

Kypri, K., Langley, J. D., Saunders, J. B., Cashell-Smith, M. L., & Herbison, P. (2008). Randomized controlled trial of web-based alcohol screening and brief intervention in primary care. *Archives of Internal Medicine*, *168*, 530–536.

Kypri, K., & McAnally, H. M. (2005). Randomized controlled trial of a web-based primary care intervention for multiple health risk behaviors. *Preventive Medicine*, *41*, 761–766.

Linke, S., Murray, E., Butler, C., & Wallace, P. (2007). Internet-based interactive health intervention for the promotion of sensible drinking: Patterns of use and potential impact on members of the general public. *Journal of Medical Internet Research*, *9*, e10.

McCambridge, J., & Day, M. (2008). Randomized controlled trial of the effects of completing the Alcohol Use Disorders Identification Test questionnaire on self-reported hazardous drinking. *Addiction*, *103*, 241–248.

Miller, W. R., & Wilbourne, P. L. (2002). Mesa Grande: A methodological analysis of clinical trials of treatments for alcohol use disorders. *Addiction*, *97*, 265–277.

Neighbors, C., Larimer, M. E., & Lewis, M. A. (2004). Targeting misperceptions of descriptive drinking norms: Efficacy of a computer-delivered personalized normative feedback intervention. *Journal of Consulting and Clinical Psychology*, *72*, 434–447.

Oenema, A., Brug, J., Dijkstra, A., de Weerdt, I., & de Vries, H. (2008). Efficacy and use of an Internet-delivered computer-tailored lifestyle intervention, targeting saturated fat intake, physical activity and smoking cessation: A randomized controlled trial. *Annals of Behavioral Medicine*, *35*, 125–135.

Riper, H., Kramer, J., Smit, F., Conijn, B., Schippers, G., & Cuijpers, P. (2008). Web-based self-help for problem drinkers: A pragmatic randomized trial. *Addiction*, *103*, 218–227.

Saitz, R., Palfai, T. P., Freedner, N., Winter, M. R., Macdonald, A., Lu, J., et al. (2007). Screening and brief intervention online for college students: The ihealth study. *Alcohol and Alcoholism*, *42*, 28–36.

Saunders, J. B., Aasland, O. G., Babor, T. F., De La Fuente, J. R., & Grant, M. (1993). Development of the Alcohol Use Disorders Identification Test (AUDIT): WHO collaborative project on early detection of persons with harmful alcohol consumption. II. *Addiction*, *88*, 791–804.

Strecher, V. J., McClure, J. B., Alexander, G. L., Chakraborty, B., Nair, V. N., Konkel, J. M., et al. (2008). Web-based smoking-cessation programs results of a randomized trial. *American Journal of Preventative Medicine*, *34*, 373–381.

Toll, B. A., Sobell, L. C., D'Arienzo, J., Sobell, M. B., Eickleberry-Goldsmith, L., & Toll, H. J. (2003). What do Internet-based alcohol treatment websites offer?. *Cyberpsychology & Behavior*, *6*, 581–584.

Walters, S. T., Miller, E., & Chiauzzi, E. (2005). Wired for wellness: e-Interventions for addressing college drinking. *Journal of Substance Abuse Treatment*, *29*, 139–145.

Walters, S. T., Wright, J. A., & Shegog, R. (2006). A review of computer and Internet-based interventions for smoking behavior. *Addictive Behaviors*, *31*, 264–277.

PART | FIVE

Evidence-Based Treatment in Action

Chapter | twenty-one

Evidence-Based Treatment Planning for Substance Abuse Therapy

Nora E. Noel
University of North Carolina Wilmington

SUMMARY POINTS

- Matching specific treatments to specific types of clients is the ideal for evidence-based treatment planning. Unfortunately, despite extensive research, that ideal has yet to be achieved.
- Nonetheless, guidelines for effective treatment planning can still be formulated based on post hoc evidence and sound behavioral principles. The most fundamental principle is that clients will benefit most from individually tailored treatment programs. Therapists should be open to a variety of evidence-based treatment modalities.
- The first step in treatment planning is an assessment and formulation of the client's long-term goals for therapy. These goals form the basis of the client's treatment program.
- The therapist assists the client in formulating goals that are positive, realistic, and measurable. In addition, the therapist assists in prioritizing those goals.
- The client and therapist together then develop a plan that addresses each goal through describing intermediate, achievable steps and some methods for accomplishing each.

- When implemented, such a treatment plan becomes the central organizing factor in therapy. The plan should be addressed in each session and modified as needed to meet the client's changing circumstances.
- Thus, continuous planning and monitoring (assessment) become two sides of ongoing evidence-based treatment and determine the criteria for successful termination.
- Careful documentation allows each client/therapist dyad to contribute to the development of more precise client–treatment matching principles in addiction.

Treatment planning: art or science? The challenge in writing a chapter on using evidence-based substance abuse treatment planning is the overwhelming consensus that there is very little scientific evidence to direct differential treatment planning. Several evidence-based treatments for substance abuse are described in this book, but evidence-based treatment *planning* requires research on client–treatment matching; that is, what works best, most importantly, *for whom*? To meet the standards for evidence-based treatment planning, research would have to show that a specific set of defined client characteristics consistently predicted better outcomes with one specific "matched" treatment versus another "mismatched" treatment. Such research would be able to answer, when a specific client enters treatment, how does a therapist choose the most effective set of strategies for this particular person's problems? Selecting and planning treatment for a specific client should be guided by several factors related to the client as an individual and to the client's current circumstances. Which key factors direct the use of one strategy versus another? Unfortunately, the field of client–treatment matching research, still in its infancy, offers few answers.

However, client–treatment matching is not a neglected infant. While it is beyond the scope and purpose of this chapter to conduct an extensive review and evaluation of the literature, it is important to note that several large, well-funded, visible studies have been undertaken with the aim of developing theory-based algorithms for matching treatments and clients in the substance abuse field. An example in the alcohol area is the National Institute of Alcohol Abuse and Alcoholism-Sponsored Project MATCH, a multisite, randomized, controlled trial (Project MATCH Research Group, 1999). Several matching hypotheses guided the choice of the three treatment strategies assessed in Project MATCH (motivational enhancement, cognitive behavioral, and 12-step facilitation) (Del Boca, Mattson, & Fuller, 2003). Briefly, rather than using a research design in which one treatment is pitted against either another treatment or a control treatment with a heterogeneous population, a "matching hypothesis" posits that clients with a particular set of individual characteristics will experience more success in a treatment program "matched" to their needs versus another, or "mismatched" program (i.e., "matching" hypotheses predict interactions of treatment type with client type).

Following years of gathering data on treatment and follow-up of thousands of clients, the Project MATCH Research Group reported that, unfortunately, none of the a priori matching hypotheses were supported, although a large percentage of the clients enrolled in the study successfully decreased their abusive drinking. All three treatments seemed to produce good results, but predictions about certain types of clients benefiting from treatments matched to their characteristics were not fulfilled (Project MATCH Research Group, 1997). While the results of Project MATCH delivered the encouraging message that many clients appear to benefit from each of the three alcohol treatments, little evidence supported the hypothesis that matching specific treatments to specific types of clients could *increase* these benefits (Cooney, Babor, DiClemente, & Del Boca, 2003).

An earlier multiyear matching study investigated the question of when relationship enhancement therapy might be differentially beneficial versus therapy administered to the client as an individual (Longabaugh, Beattie, Noel, Stout, & Malloy, 1993). By the 18-month follow-up (Longabaugh, Wirtz, Beattie, Noel, & Stout, 1995), some evidence emerged suggesting that the addition of extended relationship enhancement therapy (e.g., couples or family therapy), compared to a broad spectrum treatment, benefited clients who entered treatment with either a social network that was unsupportive of alcohol health or a low investment in their social network. In addition, clients who entered treatment with both (i.e., low investment in a social network that was unsupportive of alcohol health) had greater success with broad spectrum treatment. Unfortunately, at 18 months, the reanalysis plan included some confounds that led to somewhat post hoc interpretations. Nevertheless, social investment is discussed further later.

A large seven-site study of alcohol treatment in the United Kingdom (Heather & UKATT Research Team, 2008) has reported findings consistent with those of Project MATCH. None of the UKATT treatment matching hypotheses was supported, leading the authors to conclude that matching approaches to specific client characteristics did not look promising as a method of improving treatment outcome. Widening the scope to substance abuse, Finney (1999) noted the similarity of the Project MATCH results to those of a large multisite matching study of substance abuse treatment sponsored by the Veterans' Administration and concluded that "matching individual patients to treatment remains more of a clinical art than a science."

Despite these large-scale matching studies, we still do not have a strong scientific basis for clinical decisions in individual cases. Further, a note of caution about the clinical stakes involved was sounded by a recent post hoc analysis of Project MATCH data (Karno & Longabaugh, 2007). Researchers concluded that *mis*matches were associated with detrimental effects, even though matches showed no added benefit to clients. Further research will be necessary to test this finding, but it highlights the need to avoid *poor* treatment planning.

The ultimate purpose of client–treatment matching research is to uncover unifying principles that will inform the clinician in making clinical decisions. In other words, the clinician should be able to say, "For this client, with these characteristics, the best treatment is...." Researchers have also used post hoc analyses of existing treatment outcome data to assess the strength of association between treatment outcomes and certain client characteristics. Obviously, these studies lack the rigor of a priori matching hypotheses including consistent, valid, and reliable measures across studies and the ability to avoid confounding variables through random assignment, but post hoc analyses of carefully collected client data may provide guidance for treatment decisions and for future research in treatment matching. A few of these variables are addressed in the "Advances" section later in the chapter. In this regard, therapists can contribute to post hoc research by keeping comprehensive, accurate, and thorough records on clients. Such records benefit the client, but may also benefit future clients in the larger sense of providing a good database for testing post hoc hypotheses.

So, the bottom-line question that substance abuse therapists confront is: "How can I tailor a unique, individual treatment plan in the relative absence of scientific evidence for differential selection of treatment types and modalities?" Fortunately, some guidelines exist.

Probably the most fundamental implicit assumption of treatment planning is that "individualized" treatment will benefit the client more than a uniform ("one size fits all") program (Sobell & Sobell, 2000). Although this principle seems self-evident, Miller and Hester (2003) pointed out that until the recent past, most alcohol and drug treatment programs advocated treatment from "the one true light" perspective and treatment planning centered on making the client more amenable to the monolithic program offered by the particular clinic. Substance abuse treatment planning began to change in the 1970s with the introduction of more individualized treatment goals (e.g., Marlatt & Gordon, 1985; Sobell & Sobell, 1978) and the radical idea that alcoholics might select their own individualized treatment from several offered by inpatient rehabilitation programs (Ewing, 1977). In a 1982 chapter describing several outpatient cases (Noel, Sobell, Cellucci, Nirenberg, & Sobell, 1982), Sobell briefly outlined an individualized treatment planning template developed for working with alcoholics that can still be recognized as the basis for the guidelines described later in this chapter. Alcohol treatment was particularly affected by these significant changes in treatment planning, but the rest of the substance abuse field experienced parallel, although somewhat separate, development (Alexander, Nahra, Lemack, Pollack, & Campbell, 2008).

Thus, the primary purpose of this chapter (paraphrasing McCrady, 2001) is to present a state-of-the-art method for learning not "how-to-do" but "how-to-think-about" planning treatment for substance abusing clients. The following is a detailed set of flexible guidelines for clinicians to adapt for each client. While using these guidelines, the therapist should be mindful of three central assumptions of "informed eclecticism" (Miller & Hester, 2003). To paraphrase, first, there is no scientific support for the belief that one approach is superior to others for all individuals. Therapists should be open to all empirically supported possibilities. Second, programs should strive to provide the greatest variety they can in a menu of effective options, including different modalities and philosophies underlying treatment. Third, because people will respond to different treatments differentially, the therapist's central question should be "Which set of these options will maximize this particular client's success?"

OVERVIEW OF TREATMENT PLANNING

Treatment planning is a process in which the therapist tailors, to the greatest extent possible, the application of available treatment resources to each client's individual goals and needs. A thorough multidimensional assessment is essential to individualized treatment planning (see earlier chapters on assessment). In addition, a carefully kept accurate record of each client's assessment, ongoing treatment, and outcome evaluation is necessary for planning and fine-tuning each client's program. Finally, these carefully collected data can be aggregated to provide program evaluation, leading to eventual improvement in client–treatment matching knowledge.

The guidelines for treatment planning presented here can be adapted for use at any level of treatment, but probably are most flexible at the outpatient level. Level of care refers to the frequency and intensity of the treatment that the client initially enters and, in many treatment settings, is usually determined on the basis of criteria outlined by the American Society of Addiction Medicine (ASAM) for patient placement (Mee-Lee, Shulman, Fishman, Gastfriend, & Griffith, 2001). The most restrictive level of care, for example, is for clients who are in immediate danger (e.g., suicidal, in medical crisis). Most substance abuse clients are treated at ASAM level 1 (outpatient), which is the least restrictive placement.

In their discussion of fundamental principles of health care, Sobell and Sobell (2000) described the ideal of treating each client in the "least restrictive" treatment environment most suited to that client. Their concept of restriction is somewhat broader than the ASAM criteria and includes consideration of personal and financial costs to the client as well as physical restrictions. As an example, a mother who has difficulty finding competent, affordable child care may not benefit from treatment requiring frequent attendance as part of an intensive outpatient program. More effective alternatives for her may include a plan of well-timed home visits by the therapist or a treatment program that addresses her issues through child care at a clinic or temporary vouchers for a nearby day-care center while she is in treatment.

A second fundamental principle of health care discussed by Sobell and Sobell (2000) is the obligation of a therapist to stay current with knowledge in the treatment field. To the extent that therapists can apply scientifically based findings to treatment, they should. To stay abreast of developments in the field, therapists should review the scientific literature on a regular basis, attend workshops and conferences, participate in peer networks, and contribute to knowledge on any level they can (e.g., take advantage of opportunities to participate in clinical trials). Further, therapists should be well acquainted with the roles and abilities of other treatment and service personnel related to the clients' needs (e.g., social workers, psychologists, rehabilitation specialists, criminal justice personnel, and medical professionals) and actively inform themselves about local community resources available for their clients including, but not limited to, local self-help groups for substance abusers and programs offered by social services and other community agencies. Finally, supervision by an experienced, qualified clinical supervisor is essential to treatment planning, especially because there are so few scientific guidelines for a therapist to follow. Even an experienced therapist becomes a better treatment planner when a supervisor or clinical supervision team is involved and the clinic holds frequent interdisciplinary case staffing meetings.

The third principle of health care described by Sobell and Sobell (2000) was discussed previously. Treatment plans should be individualized based on the specific client's needs and resources. A review of client–treatment matching research (Andreasson & Ojehagen, 2003) concluded that even though support for large-scale matching hypotheses is weak, outcome studies suggest that specific treatment, tailored to each unique individual, yields more success than standard treatment. The next section of this chapter provides guidelines for individualizing tailored treatment plans.

STEPS IN THE INDIVIDUAL TREATMENT PLANNING PROCESS

Treatment planning should be integrated in the client's therapeutic process from the first meeting. Setting goals and specifying methods of achieving those goals provide a blueprint for treatment and a therapeutic structure for the client. Substance abuse clients often feel overwhelmed by their problems and not in control of the most important aspects of their lives. The world feels like a chaotic place. Providing the structure of a set of goals and procedures can help relieve anxiety and enhance the client's self-efficacy.

Step 1: Assist the client in determining his/her long term goals

Treatment goals should be the client's goals. At the lowest level of intervention, the therapist may even be described as the client's guide for self-change (Sobell & Sobell, 1996). The therapist's role in initial treatment is to assist the client in naming, defining, quantifying, and prioritizing meaningful goals, including those directly related to substance abuse or indirectly related, such as family issues or vocational and financial concerns.

FORMULATE INDIVIDUALIZED LONG-TERM GOALS

Ask the client what he/she would like to be doing in 6 months or a year. Some clients have a well-planned agenda, especially if they have had previous treatment or have been referred, including self-referred, for a specific problem. Alternately, clients' goals may be quite limited (e.g., "I just want to be able to walk down the street without the cops looking at me all the time") or perhaps somewhat grandiose ("I want to have a million dollars"), but even these are goals a therapist can help shape into something reasonable by working with the client to discover what he or she really desires to achieve. For example, the former might be reframed as "Staying 'clean' and on the right side of the law for at least a year" and the latter goal as "Having a stable source of adequate income."

Six to 12 months probably exceeds the limits of most insurance coverage, but using this time frame acknowledges that formal treatment is part of a vast array of events in a client's life that facilitate and support reaching ultimate goals and that the client's life changes will continue long after formal therapy has provided the initial impetus, tools, and organizational structure for change (for a more in-depth discussion, see Orford & UKATT Research Team, 2006). Clients can focus on "the big picture" and take on some meaningful responsibility for their own future.

Determining goals is a collaborative process with both therapist and client suggesting and discussing ideas, but therapists should be wary of assuming and imposing their own values as part of the agenda. For example, the concept of "spirituality" has been a flashpoint in the substance abuse field. Until recently, therapists less oriented to traditional 12-step approaches tended to ignore or even actively discourage clients from dealing with their spiritual or religious concerns in therapy. Spirituality issues are now more mainstream, but at times the pendulum seems to have swung too far, with some therapists insisting that clients must address spirituality, even if the client is reluctant. Similar differences of opinion between client and therapist may arise in views on furthering the client's education or vocational training, women's roles, sexual issues, and so on.

Negotiating long-term goals for drinking and drug use is especially critical. Assuming, without discussion, that a client is committed to lifelong abstinence may lead to misunderstanding and may even sabotage treatment. Connors, Donovan, and DiClemente (2001) offer the example of a client who enters treatment in the contemplation stage, not at all persuaded that he has a substance abuse problem. His most important long-term goal may be a full assessment of the pros and cons of his continued substance use to inform a decision about whether he needs treatment beyond that.

To whatever extent possible, goals should be expressed in positive terms, giving the client something to work toward. What is a logical and achievable end point for this client? For example, "regular involvement in social activities with some sober friends" would be better than "avoid all alcoholic or drug using friends." Other examples of long-term goals may include "client substance use is reduced to abstinence" (or "limited to [quantity] per day"), "client returns to college," "client resolves major relationship issue," and "client's daily feelings of happiness are increased."

The client should have reasonable control over the goal. For example, "client moves back in with spouse" is achievable only if the spouse agrees. If both parties are in family or couples therapy, perhaps they can agree on this as a long-term goal, but, if not, "resolving major relationship issues" may make the goal more realistic for the individual client and provide some flexibility. As another example, a client cannot control the hiring process, but she can increase her prospects for employment through several methods so "increased employability" may be a reasonable long-term goal.

PRIORITIZE LONG-TERM GOALS

For most people, three to four long-term goals are the maximum. Working on too many goals simultaneously may exacerbate the client's perception of being overwhelmed. The therapist can review the list of goals and ask, "Which of these are the most important to you for this year? What do you hope to accomplish in 6 months or a year?" Again, the therapist follows the client's lead on priorities, assisting in clarification and specification of what is achievable. For example, returning to college might be accomplished in a year, but graduating from college usually takes 4 years. What can the client do this year to work toward eventual graduation? Perhaps "finish my freshman year in good academic standing" is feasible. If the client endorses many high-priority goals, the therapist can help establish the key goals for now and suggest that the rest get "moved to the back burner" with a plan to revisit them on a certain date in a year (and set the date on a calendar). Generally, if the client is seeking treatment for substance abuse, especially if the legal system motivated the referral, the highest priority goal will relate to reducing or eliminating substance use.

QUANTIFY EACH LONG-TERM GOAL

Long-term goals are often idealized constructs, but knowing when and if a goal is achieved requires a specific, objective end point. Specifying a measurable behavior or score on an assessment instrument can help quantify a goal. For example, "a significantly lowered level of depression" is quantifiable with the addition of "as measured by a 10-point decrease in the Beck Depression Inventory score." When the score has been lowered, the goal has been achieved. "Regular involvement in social activities with some sober friends" could include "as demonstrated by at least three social activities each week with friends who are sober." Table 21.1 illustrates more examples of reasonable quantified long-term goals.

Step 2: Develop short-term goals and methods based on long-term goals

With established individual long-term goals providing the overarching organization, the client and therapist then move on to specify the variety of small but significant changes in behavior required to achieve those goals. Short-term goals can be described and defined semi-independently from the client's long-term goals. However, in keeping with the ideal that a treatment plan brings some organization into a chaotic life, many clients benefit from conceptualizing each short-term achievement as progress toward the eventual goal. Short-term goals, then, are the steps leading to the long-term goals. Time frames for short-term goals could range from a few days to several months. Short-term goals can be sequential or occur in a parallel process.

As a case example, suppose "Claudia's" husband has forced her to leave their home because of her drug use so she has been living haphazardly with drug-using friends. Resolving her marital issues is a long-term goal for her. Short-term goals leading to the long-term goal of resolution may include (a) finding stable, safe housing, (b) meeting with

Table 21.1 Examples of quantified long-term goals

Long-term goal	How measured?
Heroin use reduced to abstinence	Client self-report of abstinence for at least 6 months
	Random urine screens "clean" for at least 6 months
Resolve major marital issue (spouse "threw out" client)	Client/spouse report of specific plan to separate or reunite
	Clarified legal status (through binding written agreement, with help from attorney)
	Increase in average relationship satisfaction self-rating (actual quantity specified)
Effective communication skills	Role plays in social skills therapy group demonstrate better communication
	Client self-report of increased satisfying communication
Daily stress reduced to nonproblem level	Daily self-report of anxiety level reduced to (actual quantity specified)
Good level of physical health	Normal blood pressure
	Passes complete physical examination at physician's office
	Scores in normal range for age group on physical fitness test

an attorney to clarify her legal and financial status, (c) contacting her husband to renew communication with him, (d) exploring the possibility of marital therapy to increase emotional support and promote communication, and, of course, (e) reducing or eliminating her drug use.

Developing effective short-term goals and plans to achieve them really is a clinical art that is often best learned with an experienced clinical supervisor. With a set of short-term goals specifying steps toward each long-term goal, treatment becomes a process of shaping new behavior. Accomplishing the first goal is reinforcing, and each progressive success in moving toward the long-term goal is reinforcing. To "prime the pump," initial goals should be kept relatively simple and easy, albeit meaningful, for the client. By starting with an easy goal, the therapist improves the client's chances for initial success, thereby reinforcing his/her commitment to change and ability to continue to more difficult, complex short-term goals. Defining "easy" for an individual client requires awareness of the client's limitations, but, more importantly, awareness of the client's strengths as well. Strengths may include client characteristics (e.g., organized, assertive, intelligent, affable), the client's current state of functioning (e.g., very motivated to change, physically healthy), the client's accomplishments (e.g., raised a family, finished a master's degree, or even managed a week of abstinence), and environmental supports and resources (e.g., has supportive relatives and friends, can access many neighborhood services, lives on a pension that provides a reasonable income). These strengths help guide the therapist in determining what the client can do, with an accent on the positive.

The therapist and the client (and spouse, family members, or friends, if present in therapy) collaborate to draw up a list of the client's strengths and then use those strengths to ask what the client can do to get started on his or her long-term goals. The resulting list will constitute the client's initial short-term goals. The therapist, with continually updated knowledge of evidence-based treatments, clinic programs, and available community resources, can help prescribe and implement one or more methods to reach the goals. Each goal should be considered an accomplishment. In contrast, the way to arrive there is through a method. For example, "demonstrate ability to refuse a drink assertively" is a short-term goal. "Group therapy" to learn that skill is a method. "Find sober people to befriend" is a goal; "by attending Alcoholics Anonymous meetings" is a method. "Five weeks of clean urines" is a goal; "daily methadone dosing" is a method. The point is that methods are specified separately from goals so that if one method fails to accomplish the goal, then another may be implemented to reach the same goal.

As with long-term goals, short-term goals should be specific, quantifiable, and worded in a positive manner. To avoid vague phrasing, the therapist again can think in terms of specific behaviors. For example, instead of "client socialization," the goal may be "client will attend (some number of) social activities with family and friends." "Practice better personal hygiene" becomes "shower and brush teeth at least once daily." "Client will be less dependent on his mother" becomes "client will pay own bills on time." "Client will purchase and use own alarm clock to awake on time for work"; and eventually, "client will rent and maintain own apartment." Additionally, each short-term goal should include a specific date for completion or reevaluation.

It is not necessary at any one time to describe in detail the entire array of short-term goals leading to each long-term goal. Sometimes the goals will reflect the fact that a therapist and client will have only a short time to interact, such as in a short inpatient stay. Sometimes it is difficult to project all the necessary steps to the goal in the initial part of treatment. Given that the long-term goal remains the target, new short-term goals will present themselves as others are accomplished.

To return to the client, Claudia, as an example, each ideal short-term goal (a) is specific (e.g., Claudia and her husband will set conditions for her "reentry" into their home); (b) has a specific time frame (e.g., by the conclusion of next week's session with the therapist); (c) can be measured (e.g., did Claudia and her husband actually write the list of conditions?); (d) specifies at least one or more methods (e.g., Claudia and her husband will meet in a treatment session with a therapist present to write the list or Claudia and her husband will each write a separate list and meet to agree on the conditions); and (e) can be modified if not achieved by the specified time frame (e.g., her husband keeps refusing to meet with Claudia to make the list so after 2 weeks she moves to a new goal: Claudia contacts a lawyer to clarify marital, child custody, and financial arrangements for the future).

Finally, a therapist and client formulating an individualized treatment plan should spell out the steps necessary to accomplish each short-term goal and help the client rehearse those behaviors before each goal is set and the methods are described. Sometimes, barriers to accomplishing goals are uncovered and limitations can be dealt with before they impede treatment. For example, one therapist almost sent an elderly male client home with instructions to access extensive information from Web sites. Fortunately, the therapist discovered, before he departed, that the client was too proud to admit he had no idea how to access or use the Internet. Learning how to access the information became the client's first short-term goal. Alternately, another therapist missed an opportunity to give her client some useful Web sites because she assumed that homeless substance abusers have little access to the Internet.

If the client needs a physical examination, does he know who to call, how to set up the appointment time, and how to find affordable safe transportation to arrive and leave on time? If a client's plans include attending a self-help meeting, does she know how to locate meetings and what she will encounter when she attends a meeting? Does she know that these groups vary widely and that she may choose to attend another that "fits" better for her?

Step 3: Write the treatment plan

A treatment plan should be flexible because major events (e.g., a job loss, a need for detoxification, a death in the family) can cause necessary changes, but both client and therapist benefit from access to a detailed written document. A narrative in the client's record with details should be available for review and adaptation, but clients and therapists can use a shorthand format in treatment sessions and as a take-home document for a client to review. Sometimes a clinic has developed a standard treatment plan form, but if the therapist is able to choose his/her own form, an example of an organized treatment plan ("Claudia's" initial plan) appears in Table 21.2 and could be used as a template.

Table 21.2 Sample initial treatment plan for "Claudia"

Long-term goals	Time frame	Short-term goals	Methods	Time frame	Measure
Heroin abstinence (100% clean urine for 4 months)	1 year	Prevention of withdrawal symptoms	Enroll in methadone program	1 month	Daily methadone pick-up
		Understands environmental cues	Complete functional analysis	2 weeks	Functional analysis forms completed
		Understands internal cues for use	"Mindfulness" meditation exercises with group	6 weeks	Client self-monitoring in diary
Resolve marital issue (living with family or legal separation)	6 months	Conditions for reentry established with spouse	Meet with spouse in therapist's office to negotiate list	2 weeks	List drawn up
		Emotional support from spouse	Marital therapy	4 months	Client and spouse score change on marital adjustment measure
Social network of nonuser friends	1 year	Two social activities per week with NA	Attend regular NA meetings	2 weeks	Chips brought to therapy
		Close relationship with female nonuser	Get a sponsor	4 weeks	Client/sponsor report
Safe, stable living environment	6 months	"Clean" residence	Contact Social Services	1 week	Client address change
			Moves back with family	3 months	Client address change

Step 4: Implement and modify the treatment plan as needed

Since the treatment plan organizes treatment, it should be reviewed as part of every treatment session. Therapists should address each of the short-term goals and methods to assess clients' progress toward achievement. Additionally, the therapist can assess impediments, barriers, and any setbacks or potential problems. Progress notes should be integrated with and reflect the treatment plan. For example, a therapist might write, "Client attended group and spoke only once." While descriptive, this note does not specifically address the client's goals. A more helpful note might read, "Client spoke only once during group session, but he did report a full week without drinking. In addition, while he did not attend any social functions this week without alcohol, he has one planned for next week."

Modification of the plan depends on continued multidimensional assessment throughout treatment. Assessment and the treatment plan should interface and inform each other, in a give-and-take fashion, with assessment reflecting progress toward goals, and the plan determining the essential variables to be assessed. Additionally, modification may be warranted when major changes in the client's life require attention (e.g., "I just discovered I am pregnant").

Finally, as noted previously, each short-term goal has a *date* for review. The therapist should use these dates for special review of the plan to determine whether goals have been accomplished or if modifications are necessary. Meeting a goal can be reinforcing for a client and can lead to increased self-efficacy. Each goal accomplished should be noticed, even "celebrated" as a milestone. However, difficulties, intercepted early through assessment, can increase the probability of "on target" behavior. For example, Sobell and Sobell (2000) outline a procedure for "stepped" care, similar to that used with physical illness, beginning with "the least intrusive" alternative suitable for each client, but with the therapist continually reviewing the plan and fine-tuning to a higher level of care if the client appears in danger of failing to meet a goal.

ADVANCES TOWARD THE GOAL OF EVIDENCE-BASED TREATMENT PLANNING

Although, to date, client–treatment matching research has failed to provide definitive evidence-based "prescriptions" for treatment based on a unified set of client characteristics and circumstances, available post hoc interpretations and experience suggest that certain therapy components could be effective differentially with certain clients. For example, early results of a client–treatment matching study with alcoholics suggested that adding a relationship enhancement component benefited clients between ages 30 and 50, when many people are invested in forming and raising families. After age 50, clients appeared to be more successful in a straightforward cognitive behavioral program (Rice, Longabaugh, Beattie, & Noel, 1993). Based on this research and studies described previously, Longabaugh (2003) concluded that researchers should give high priority to studying substance abusers' social networks and identifying the specific sets of conditions under which they would be involved most effectively in treatment. Given that social networks and a client's social investment seem promising predictors of differential treatment planning, gender and diverse cultural/ethnic background assume great importance, as they are often the initial determinants of an individual's social network. Currently, little empirical evidence exists to guide differential treatment recommendations for clients of color and especially for women. As further examples, more data are needed, not just on treatment outcome, but how treatment outcome relates to the use of different treatment components for a variety of people, including the elderly (see Gossop & Moos, 2008), people of diverse sexual orientations, and people of diverse social classes. Researchers have suggested other client variables likely to determine a differential choice of treatment are the client's stage of change or level of motivation (Connors et al., 2001); neuropsychological status, which affects the client's ability to process and retain information (Passetti, Clark, Mehta, Joyce, & King, 2008); psychological factors, such as dual diagnosis issues or personality characteristics (Hopwood, Baker, & Morey, 2008), which might affect, for example, drug of choice; and extreme life circumstances, such as homelessness (Milby, Schumacher, Vuchinich, Freedman, Kertez, & Wallace, 2008), poverty, and poor health. In addition, for financial, practical, and other reasons, certain treatment components may or may not be available to the therapeutic environment, including, for example, addiction medications (Horgan, Reif, Hodkin, Garenick, & Merrick, 2008) and intensive case management for women (Morgenstern et al., 2008), which may increase treatment engagement. All of these remain areas of interest, but little research has been conducted.

Providing these data requires diligence from all members of the substance abuse treatment community. Currently, individualized treatment planning using the guidelines provided in this chapter is determined on a case-by-case basis, but therapists and clients can contribute to developing more unified hypotheses about principles of effective evidence-based client treatment planning by keeping careful and detailed records of the treatment process as well as treatment outcome. Developing individual plans for each individual presenting for treatment is an important short-term goal. Documenting all aspects of treatment is an important short-term goal. Developing principles for practical and effective treatment "prescriptions" is the long-term goal for evidence-based treatment planning.

REFERENCES

Alexander, J., Nahra, T., Lemack, C., Pollack, H., & Campbell, C. (2008). Tailored treatment in the outpatient substance abuse treatment sector: 1995–2005. *Journal of Substance Abuse Treatment*, *34*, 282–292.

Andreasson, S., & Ojehagen, A. (2003). Psychosocial treatment for alcohol dependence. In M. Breglund, S. Thelander, & E. Jonsson (Eds.), *Treating alcohol and drug abuse: An evidence-based review*. Weinheim, Germany: Wiley-VCH.

Connors, G., Donovan, D., & DiClemente, C. (2001). *Substance abuse treatment and stages of change: Selecting and planning interventions*. New York: Guilford Press.

Cooney, N., Babor, T., DiClemente, C., & Del Boca, F. (2003). Clinical and scientific implications of Project MATCH. In T. Babor & F. Del Boca (Eds.), *Treatment matching in alcoholism*. New York: Cambridge University Press.

Del Boca, F., Mattson, M., & Fuller, R. (2003). Planning a multisite matching trial: Organizational structure and research design. In T. Babor & F. Del Boca (Eds.), *Treatment matching in alcoholism*. New York: Cambridge University Press.

Ewing, J. (1977). Matching therapy and patients: The cafeteria plan. *British Journal of Addictions*, *72*, 13–18.

Finney, J. (1999). Some treatment implications of Project MATCH. *Addiction*, *94*, 42–44.

Gossop, M., & Moos, R. (2008). Substance misuse among older adults: A neglected but treatable problem. *Addiction*, *103*, 347–348.

Heather, N., & UKATT Research Team (2008). UK alcohol treatment trial: Client-treatment matching effects. *Addiction*, *103*, 228–238.

Hopwood, C., Baker, K., & Morey, L. (2008). Personality and drugs of choice. *Personality and Individual Differences*, *44*, 1413–1421.

Horgan, C., Reif, S., Hodkin, D., Garenick, D., & Merrick, E. (2008). Availability of addiction medications in private health plans. *Journal of Substance Abuse Treatment*, *34*, 147–156.

Karno, M., & Longabaugh, R. (2007). Does matching matter? Examining matches and mismatches between patient attributes and therapy techniques in alcoholism treatment. *Addiction*, *102*, 587–596.

Longabaugh, R. (2003). Involvement of support networks in treatment. In M. Galanter (Ed.), *Recent developments in alcoholism* (Vol. 16, pp. 133–147). New York: Kluwer Academic/Plenum.

Longabaugh, R., Beattie, M., Noel, N., Stout, R., & Malloy, P. (1993). The effect of social investment on treatment outcome. *Journal of Studies on Alcohol*, *54*, 465–478.

Longabaugh, R., Wirtz, P., Beattie, M., Noel, N., & Stout, R. (1995). Matching treatment focus to patient social investment and support: 18 month follow up results. *Journal of Consulting and Clinical Psychology*, *63*, 296–307.

Marlatt, G. A., & Gordon, J. (Eds.) (1985). *Relapse prevention*. New York: Guilford Press.

McCrady, B. (2001). Foreword. In G. Connors, D. Donovan, & C. DiClemente (Eds.), *Substance abuse treatment and stages of change: Selecting and planning interventions*. New York: Guilford Press.

Mee-Lee, D., Shulman, G., Fishman, M., Gastfriend, D., & Griffith, J. (2001). *ASAM patient-placement criteria for the treatment of substance-related disorders* (2nd ed., Rev.). Chevy Chase, MD: American Society of Addiction Medicine.

Milby, J., Schumacher, J., Vuchinich, R., Freedman, M., Kertez, S., & Wallace, D. (2008). Towards cost-effective initial care for substance-abusing homeless. *Journal of Substance Abuse Treatment*, *34*, 180–191.

Miller, W., & Hester, R. (2003). Treating alcohol problems: Towards an informed eclecticism. In R. Hester & W. Miller (Eds.), *Handbook of alcoholism treatment approaches: Effective alternatives* (3rd ed.). Boston: Allyn and Bacon.

Morgenstern, J., Blanchard, K., Kahler, C., Barbosa, K., McCrady, B., & McVeigh, K. (2008). Testing mechanisms of action for intensive case management. *Addiction*, *103*, 469–477.

Noel, N., Sobell, L., Cellucci, T., Nirenberg, T., & Sobell, M. (1982). Behavioral treatment of outpatient problem drinkers: Five clinical case studies. In W. Hay & P. Nathan (Eds.), *Clinical case studies in the behavioral treatment of alcoholism*. New York: Plenum.

Orford, J., & UKATT Research Team (2006). The client's perspective on change during treatment for an alcohol problem: Qualitative analysis of follow-up interviews in the UK Alcohol Treatment Trial. *Addiction*, *101*, 60–68.

Passetti, F., Clark, L., Mehta, M., Joyce, E., & King, M. (2008). Neuropsychological predictors of clinical outcome in opiate addiction. *Drug and Alcohol Dependence*, *94*, 82–91.

Project MATCH Research Group. (1997). Matching alcoholism treatments to client heterogeneity: Project MATCH post treatment drinking outcomes. *Journal of Studies on Alcohol*, *58*, 7–29.

Project MATCH Research Group. (1999). Summary of Project MATCH. *Addiction*, *94*, 31–34.

Rice, C., Longabaugh, R., Beattie, M., & Noel, N. (1993). Age group differences in response to treatment for problematic alcohol use. *Addiction*, *88*, 1369–1375.

Sobell, M., & Sobell, L. (1978). *Behavioral treatment of alcohol problems: Individualized treatment and controlled drinking*. New York: Plenum.

Sobell, M., & Sobell, L. (1996). *Problem drinkers: Guided self-change treatment*. New York: Guilford Press.

Sobell, M., & Sobell, L. (2000). Stepped care as a heuristic approach to the treatment of alcohol problems. *Journal of Consulting and Clinical Psychology*, *68*, 573–579.

Chapter | twenty-two

Adoption and Implementation of Evidence-Based Treatment

Patrick M. Flynn and D. Dwayne Simpson
Institute of Behavioral Research, Texas Christian University

SUMMARY POINTS

- The National Registry of Evidence-Based Programs and Practices is a searchable database of research-tested interventions (http://www.nrepp.samhsa.gov/).
- Four key stages in transferring research-tested interventions into practice include (1) training, (2) adoption, (3) implementation, and (4) practice improvement.
- Good leadership and management are needed for practice improvement, which can be attained through adoption, implementation, and sustainability of evidence-based treatments.
- Training intensity should be commensurate with the complexity of innovations.
- Adoption is a decision to try a selected intervention for a limited period of time.
- Adoption involves a two-step activity, including decision-making and action taking.
- Implementation is the consistent use of an innovation with good fidelity while intending to incorporate it into routine practice.

- Technology transfer can include adoption and implementation of clinical practice innovations/interventions, as well as new business/operational strategies.
- Organizational functioning is a key ingredient in successful implementation of evidence-based treatment.
- For innovation adoption, organizations should be ready for change and organizational assessments can be used to help determine readiness.
- Mapping, a graphical representation tool, can be used to plan and implement organizational change.

BACKGROUND AND INTRODUCTION

In part, because physicians were providing different care for basically the same patients, "evidence-based medicine" became the health care exemplar ever since the "evidence-based" expression first entered mainstream medicine around 1990 (Eddy, 2005). This research-tested nomenclature has slowly infiltrated the addiction treatment field, which is another health services delivery system providing different types of care for essentially the same patients. Despite the broad types of clinical care (e.g., treatment modalities) and specific practices utilized in substance abuse treatment programs, there is general consensus that some basic components of current treatment are "best practices." Included among these are patient need assessments, linkage with and referral to comprehensive services (e.g., medical, mental health, and vocational services), and pharmacotherapies, as well as efforts to retain patients, sustain care, and use follow-up strategies (Institute of Medicine, 2005; Lamb, Greenlick, and McCarty, 1998; National Institute on Drug Abuse, 1999). Additionally, there are some research-based clinical interventions, ranging from brief protocols (i.e., several sessions) to intensive full-blown programs designated as evidence-based practices (EBPs) for substance-abusing patients (National Institute on Drug Abuse, 1999). The migration toward EBPs mirrors the movement in the medical field to improve treatments and services by incorporating only those protocols, manuals, procedures, strategies, and so forth that have been "proven effective" and have an adequate research base to support their use. Although there is sufficient evidence to support the implementation of EBPs, they are generally underused in substance abuse treatment programs throughout the United States (Institute of Medicine, 2005).

Even though effective innovations are readily available, barriers such as time, money, staff resources, and other organizational issues still need to be transcended before the innovations spread and become sustained in routine practice. Other obstacles include lack of knowledge about existing practices and their use to meet the needs of various patient profiles, lack of understanding of successful strategies for implementation, and inadequate mechanisms to determine patient benefits from these new and innovative approaches. When faced with a decision to change and adopt a new practice, staff may resist and rely on current traditions, be affected by myths about effective methods, or be influenced by personal ideology about what constitutes appropriate treatment (D'Aunno, 2006).

More than 30 years ago at the federal level, there was a concern that research was not being put into practice and thus initiatives were undertaken to increase technology transfer and utilization (Brown & Flynn, 2002). Since that time, progress has indeed been slow. It has been suggested that the federal government has an important role and a major responsibility to move technology and research-based practices into the substance abuse treatment arena (Brown & Flynn, 2002). In part, as a response to improve the quality of treatment services and to bridge the gap between research and practice, federal and state agencies have begun to encourage and, in some instances, require the adoption and utilization of EBPs (cf. Miller, Zweben, & Johnson, 2005). One federal agency, the Substance Abuse Mental Health Administration, has established the National Registry of Evidence-Based Programs and Practices and charged the national network of Addiction Technology Transfer Centers with advancing the movement of research into practice. Despite these efforts and those of numerous state agencies, there still is little consensus among researchers and treatment developers about how much research is needed to certify that an innovation or new treatment technology can carry the "evidence-based" warranty. Another difficulty is the lack of an agreed-upon set of standards for use in determining quality care in substance abuse treatment that can be used as a foundation for decisions about what to adopt and implement (Garnick et al., 2002; McCorry, Garnick, Bartlett, Cotter, & Chalk, 2000). Further confounding all of these difficulties is a deficient system for tracking service provision to determine just what patients receive when they are enrolled in treatment. In contrast to the medical field where there are established terms and codes for reporting medical procedures and services (e.g., Current Procedural Terminology), which are required for reimbursement, the substance abuse treatment field has only recently begun to move toward such a system (e.g., the Texas Behavioral Health Integrated Provider System—a computerized system to record service information provided to patients while in treatment). Despite these deficiencies and barriers to adoption and implementation of EBPs, there is some progress. Indeed, the substance abuse treatment field has benefited greatly from transfer efforts in other disciplines.

ADOPTION AND IMPLEMENTATION

Clear distinctions are presented in the business literature covering technology transfer and describing the processes of adoption and implementation. Adoption typically involves decisions and actions where a new and innovative technology is selected and tried out for a limited period of time. According to the NIH, "Implementation is the use of strategies to adopt and integrate evidence-based health interventions and change practice patterns within specific settings" (National Institutes of Health, 2007, p. 8). Klein and colleagues from the business world (Klein & Knight, 2005; Klein & Sorra, 1996) emphasize that *implementation* serves as the crucial stage that connects an *adoption* decision with routine *practice.* Although they are linked, the decision to adopt is not synonymous with routine practice. In the business world, much more attention has been given to the adoption of innovations than to implementation (Klein, Conn, & Sorra, 2001). Klein and Knight (2005) identified a number of key factors that shape implementation and contribute to its success, including (a) the quality and amount of training and technical assistance, rewards for usage, and user-friendliness; (b) a positive organizational climate for innovation implementation; (c) support from management; (d) time and money; (e) an organizational learning orientation; and (f) managerial patience. Fairly recently in the United Kingdom, a conceptual model for spreading and sustaining innovations in health service delivery organizations was developed. It clearly defines innovation as "a novel set of behaviors, routines, and ways of working that are directed at improving health outcomes, administrative efficiency, cost effectiveness, or users' experience" (Greenhalgh, Robert, MacFarlane, Bate, & Kyriakidou, 2004, p. 582).

LEADERSHIP

Leadership is a key ingredient in the transfer of new technology with the mainstream health care and business literature currently accounting for a majority of our knowledge regarding the role of leaders in this process. In recent years, there has been some interest in leadership functions in the addictions field. The role of leadership in transferring research into substance abuse treatment practice is now recognized as important (cf. Compton et al., 2005; Simpson & Flynn, 2007a), and connections between leadership and adoption of innovations are being demonstrated (Roman & Johnson, 2002). Overall, good leadership is viewed as an antecedent to and necessary component of implementation and sustainability (Aarons, 2006; Fixsen, Naoom, Blase, Friedman, & Wallace, 2005; Greenhalgh et al., 2004). Management support is also a precursor to innovation–implementation success (Klein & Knight, 2005; Klein et al., 2001; Simpson & Flynn, 2007a). Commitment, involvement, and accountability of leaders are needed for successful implementation (Gustafson et al., 2003), and better leadership is associated with more positive attitudes toward the adoption of innovations (Aarons, 2006). Leadership support is crucial for gaining and sustaining an innovation's visibility, resource allocations, performance feedback, and endurance (Klein et al., 2001; Sirkin, Keenan, & Jackson, 2005).

Despite conceptual differences between leadership and management, leaders and managers are often viewed as one and the same. Consequently, leaders are sometimes required to manage, and managers are sometimes required to lead. Many treatment programs can be characterized as small organizations where roles may be filled by a single individual and the lines between leadership and management can be blurred. Leaders/managers have important roles in the adoption and successful implementation of practices within substance abuse treatment programs. Because of the inseparable link between leadership and management, however, the terms "leaders" and "managers" are used interchangeably throughout this chapter.

Advances in other disciplines have also begun to affect change in the substance abuse treatment arena. Because there is an extensive research gap regarding effective implementation strategies that have practical application in community-based treatment programs for increasing the probability of adopting and implementing best practices, a program of research at Texas Christian University has evolved around a theme of implementation science. These efforts have included the development and testing of a conceptual model of stage-based program change focused on the treatment organization as the context in which technological innovations are adopted and implemented.

IMPLEMENTATION SCIENCE: A MODEL FOR PROGRAM CHANGE

There are at least two distinct but complementary approaches to changing practices in addiction service delivery systems that are currently being applied. The Network for the Improvement of Addiction Treatment (NIATx; see www.niatx.com) addresses barriers to treatment access and retention using a *business/operations approach* to change (Ford et al., 2007). This initiative "uses a Plan-Do-Study-Act cycle to identify the problems and generate solutions (Plan), implement new processes (Do), measure and assess the outcomes (Study), and institutionalize the change or make additional changes (Act)" (Gitlow, Gitlow, Oppenheim, & Oppenheim, 1989; McCarty et al., 2007, p. 139; Shewart, 1939). NIATx, funded by the Robert Wood Johnson Foundation and Federal agencies seeking to improve treatment, aims to reduce treatment admission wait time and no-shows, while increasing admissions and treatment retention. Strategies are based on successful business practices, such as using a "customer satisfaction perspective" to improve services. A second approach is directed toward *clinical processes* and changes to improve therapeutic effectiveness. Emphasis is on the clinical dynamics involved in disseminating new evidence-based practices and the use of patient assessment procedures coupled with innovative interventions. Evidence is growing for the value of this approach, which follows a deliberate and stage-based method to facilitate changes in service delivery systems (Simpson & Flynn, 2007b).

The *TCU Program Change Model* (adapted from Simpson & Flynn, 2007a), illustrated in Figure 22.1, incorporates additional focus on the role of leadership and converges closely with elements of the process described by Klein and colleagues (1996, 2001, 2005). The model conceptually decomposes explicit influences on the implementation process. Counselor perceptions related to innovations and organizational functioning within the program context are primary ingredients in planning for and changing practice. The central portion of Figure 22.1 portrays several crucial features of the process involved in the adoption

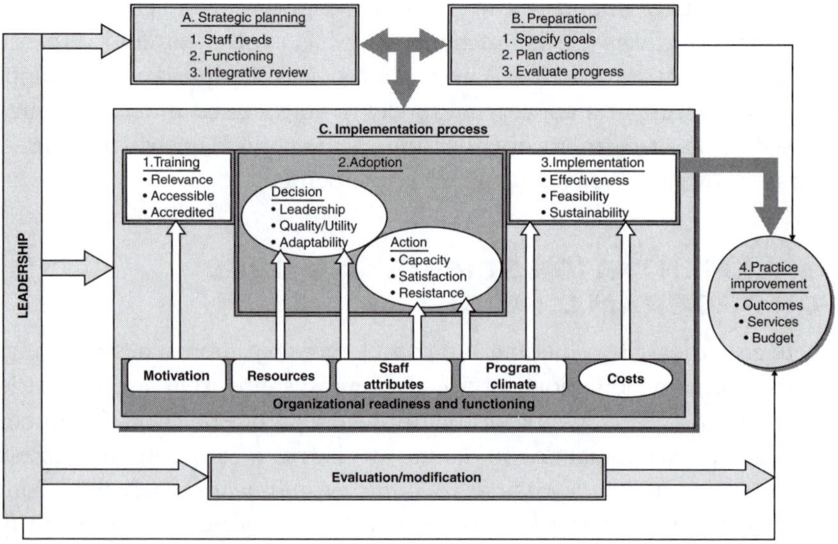

FIGURE 22.1 *TCU Program Change Model for planning and implementing innovations.*

of treatment innovations. Putting innovations into use and improving practice are the goals of successful implementation. In Figure 22.1, the key factors that represent individual-level staff reactions and support of an innovation implementation are listed as bullets under major stages of the change process, whereas program-level organizational readiness and functioning domains that influence the process are grouped across the bottom. Leadership plays a critical role in this process and sets the stage for successful change, thus the latest version emphasizes the role of leadership in changing program practices. Counselor perceptions about innovations and the contextual platform of organizational functioning interact and affect technology transfer and program change as depicted in general aspects of the conceptual model. Included are three important stages: (1) training, (2) adoption, and (3) implementation of innovations. Routine practice, the fourth phase, is the successful maintenance and sustainability of innovation adoption and program enhancements. Staff knowledge about an innovation and perceptions of organizational functioning influence progress through these stages (Simpson, 2009). The stages of change are not necessarily sequential, but rather dynamic steps that can be targeted for action. Motivation, organizational readiness, and resources definitely impact the early process, but they can also affect the change process at any point in its progression.

In this model, adoption is viewed as a two-step activity requiring *leadership* support and staff empowerment to implement change. The strength of management commitment and endorsement increases the likelihood of success. At the organizational level, staff capacity and a positive, supportive, organizational climate are necessary to the decision and action processes.

Adoption is followed by implementation and, if successful, a state of sustainable practice may be achieved, resulting in a positive change and improvements in patient care. It is important that program leadership be involved in ongoing monitoring and evaluation of effectiveness indicators such as patient engagement, progress, and outcomes while extending continued attention to organizational functioning. As this process unfolds, leadership attention may also be necessary to modify the plans and strategies.

The model is best thought of as a heuristic framework, still in progress. Continuous refinements are expected as research evolves and the measurement domains receive additional empirical support. It should be emphasized that the stages of change are not rigidly linear. Rather, they involve cyclical phases of progress with potential setbacks, and it is through these fluid and dynamic points of impact that change factors can be studied. Impact and change throughout the process are not necessarily singular events but can be cumulative in attaining practice improvement.

Training

The first stage of innovation adoption involves training. Format and the complexity of the innovation are important considerations. Highly complicated innovations require greater investments, more intensive instruction, and a greater quantity of role playing, practice rehearsal, monitoring, "booster" sessions, and ongoing technical assistance to ensure successful implementation. Decisions by staff on whether to attend training are influenced by (1) *relevance* to their needs, (2) *accessibility*—location, scheduling, and cost, and (3) *credentialing*—educational or certification benefits. The value of training is intertwined with the quality of innovation materials and training experience, which further affect adoption and implementation. Internal organizational and external funding pressures and needs for applying innovations can also influence attendance at workshops and training sessions.

Surprisingly, little empirical research has been published on key elements of training (Fixsen et al., 2005). However, there is general agreement that learning objectives include acquisition of *practical* knowledge. The training curriculum should target higher levels of learning outcomes, such as comprehension of therapeutic delivery mechanisms, application of techniques through practice, analysis of active therapeutic ingredients, and ability to evaluate and judge other available innovations. Manualized interventions are becoming the norm and serve as guides for fidelity monitoring. These materials should also include a concise presentation of the core components or ingredients necessary to apply the innovation as it was designed and tested to avoid drifting away from the original intent. Because counseling staff release time is needed for training and places a demand on limited resources, care should be given to designing training sessions that require the least amount of time and resources. Other important aspects include the need for realistic views of skill requirements and limitations, team building and peer support activities, and empirical evaluations of results.

Adoption

Although the term adoption is often used in a broad fashion to refer to the entire process of innovation adoption and implementation, it is more beneficial to parse these activities into separate tasks. In the current model (see Figure 22.1), adoption is a two-step activity involving decision-making and action taking. Based on the literature, several prerequisites are involved in the decision to adopt. First, *leadership* support must be available, at both formal and informal levels. This support is crucial for the efforts' visibility, allocation of resources, performance feedback, and endurance (Klein et al., 2001; Sirkin et al., 2005). Leaders and managers are often viewed as being synonymous. The lack of effective and committed personnel in these positions in the endorsement of adoption along with inadequate resources, both human and financial, increases the likelihood that innovations will be ineffectual, particularly when their complexity and intensity increase. Second, for practical applications in community-based, real-world settings, innovations should be perceived as having sufficient *quality* and *utility* to fit into routine practice within the organizational context. Acceptance by patients and an ability to meet their needs are also essential components (Gotham, 2004). Some language adjustments may be required for different populations and settings, but this should not imply that matters of fidelity can be compromised, such as a change in core components and ingredients. Third, frontline staff should be able to see the innovations as having some degree of *adaptability* for specific treatment applications and settings (McGovern, Fox, Xie, & Drake, 2004). These new evidence-based treatments (EBTs) and EBPs must be compatible with other materials and fit with existing values and cultures within treatment programs (Klein & Sorra, 1996; Rogers, 2003). For example, attitudes about abstinence versus reduced drug use and use of pharmacotherapies in treatment offer classic examples of values that influence utilization of EBTs and EBPs. Some innovations will fit in selected programs, but not all. Staff skill and ability levels must concur with the complexity of the innovations to implement new technologies successfully.

When the adoption decision is made, a next step is to develop an action plan, including a trial period. At least a few days or weeks are typically needed for a test run by potential adopters to allow them to form opinions about applications. At least four prominent considerations are essential to the process. First, the *capacity* and proficiency of the innovation must be consistent with initial expectations. It should appear to work well enough to induce further investments of time and energy. Second, those involved should experience a degree of *satisfaction* with results from the trial. Third, *resistance* and barriers to change must be manageable. Finally, staff capacity and a positive, supportive organizational climate are necessary in the decision and action steps during the adoption phase.

Implementation

The third stage in the transfer process is *implementation*. The brief trial phase described earlier regarding adoption provides a foundation for extending the application. It moves from a test phase to one of actually putting it in place with an expectation that it will be sustained as part of future routine practices. Following the trial phase, and during the implementation stage, the innovation must be seen by program staff and leadership as being *effective*, thereby adding value to clinical practice. Empirical evidence and feedback will provide a more convincing foundation. Beyond effectiveness, *feasibility* within a program's context is an essential component for success. Some interventions might have therapeutic value, but be applicable for only a few patients or be too complex or demanding for some staff. *Sustainability* is another important consideration. High rates of staff turnover in substance abuse treatment programs require ongoing resources such as training and supervision. Attention to innovation fidelity will be required, and additional resource outlays will be needed to support these efforts. Organizational level factors such as motivation, resources from program management, staff attributes, and climate affect long-range implementation and ultimate sustainability in routine clinical practice.

Innovations that proceed through the stages successfully tend to become routine clinical practices, which have good potential for program improvements. Effectiveness indicators are needed by program managers to evaluate and, if needed, modify practices. In general, the next step for the field is to begin to pay attention to adoption and implementation start-up and ongoing costs (e.g., cost of materials, training, supervision, loss of billable hours associated with training and supervision) and develop prices for EBTs and EBPs so that other programs intending to adopt and implement new innovations and change their practices will have important information for planning and guiding decisions and actions.

PRACTICAL APPLICATIONS: ASSESSING THE ORGANIZATION

In preparation for adoption and implementation of EBPs or EBTs (i.e., program change), assessments of organizational functioning are the first steps along the pathway to change. Similar to the patients they serve, treatment programs attempting to change their own behaviors and practices must have a sufficient amount of motivation to undergo and sustain the change process (Backer, 1995). Human and financial resource availability, leadership, staff skills and working relationships, and internal and external pressures are some of the factors affecting a substance abuse treatment organization's ability to change (Simpson & Brown, 2002). Leadership is also involved in the timing of innovation adoption, particularly regarding those who are first to embrace new ideas (i.e., "early adopters"; Rogers, 1995). Fertile organizational contexts for change are characterized by climates of vision, tolerance, and commitment. Too often, substance abuse treatment programs faced with changing their organizational behaviors exhibit some of the same deficits they see in their patients, such as insufficient motivation, poor cognitive focus (e.g., uncertain mission), and little discipline. If the organizational environment does not provide a healthy level of support, the change process may be impeded.

The national network of Addiction Treatment Technology Centers (2004) in their *Change Book* describes a comprehensive 10-step process for selecting, planning, implementing, and evaluating appropriate change strategies for drug treatment systems. This chapter provides a case study to demonstrate step 4, which is a preliminary assessment of a program's readiness to undertake significant change. The *TCU Organizational Readiness for Change* (ORC) (Lehman, Greener, & Simpson, 2002) survey, scoring guide, and other materials described herein are available free for download from the Institute of Behavioral Research Web site (www.ibr.tcu.edu). Following is an outline of the properties of the ORC and an explanation of how to use it to identify and improve weak areas of functioning in preparation for program change.

The ORC survey (Lehman et al., 2002) is a self-administered assessment of program functioning and readiness for change. During the past 5 years more than 4000 ORC surveys have been administered in over 650 organizations across the United States, Italy, and England (e.g., see Rampazzo, De Angeli, Serpelloni, Simpson, & Flynn, 2006).

The ORC includes scales covering four major domains assessing staff perceptions about the adequacy of resources, counselor attributes, work climate, and motivation or pressures for change. Each of its 18 scales consists of about six items scored on a five-point Likert scale ranging from strongly disagree to strongly agree. They include confirmed factor structures, adequate reliabilities, and predictive validities documented by relationships with selected indicators of patient and program functioning. Score profiles are organized around four key organizational domains: (a) needs—program and training needs and pressures for program changes, (b) resources—offices, equipment, staff, Internet, and training, (c) staff attributes—growth, efficacy, influence, and adaptability, and (d) organizational climate—mission, cohesion, autonomy, communication, stress, and change. This survey takes approximately 25 min to complete.

There are director and staff versions designed specifically for community treatment programs. Item responses to the Likert continuum of disagreement to agreement for each scale are averaged and then multiplied by 10, yielding score ranges from 10 to 50 with a midpoint of 30. A score of 30 falls in the neutral range because it reflects an uncertain response to items for all scales. Thus, scores of 50 would indicate that an individual agrees strongly with the item and those of 10 disagree strongly. Aggregate staff scale scores can be plotted graphically in a line chart to display a

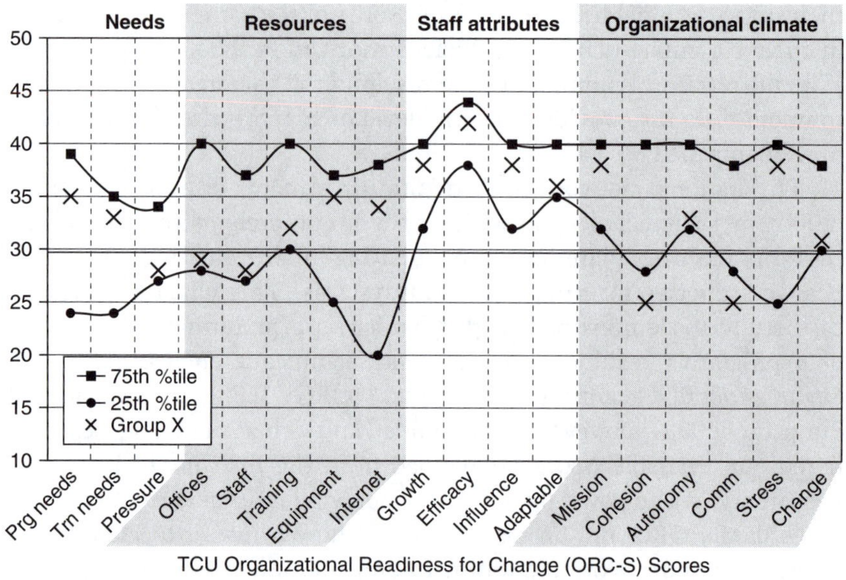

FIGURE 22.2 *Sample ORC profile scores with 25th–75th percentile norms (based on TCU files, N = 2031).*

program functioning profile (see Figure 22.2). ORC norms for the 25th and 75th percentiles are included in line charts to allow interpretations. Programs can determine where they stand in comparison to the neutral point (i.e., scale score 30), as well as how they compare to other substance abuse treatment agency staffs that have completed the ORC.

GUIDELINES FOR ADMINISTRATION

A data collection and management team, either internal or external to the organization, conducts the survey several months before initiating the innovation adoption process. Communicating the intent of the survey, establishing clear lines of authority, and stipulating procedures will help ensure staff cooperation and maximize response rates. The survey is self-administered anonymously and includes an optional two-page introductory section that covers background information. This information is valuable for comparing results across programs and interpreting score differences. Other practical field data collection procedures are outlined by Simpson and Dansereau (2007) and are beyond the scope of this chapter.

INTERPRETATION

Figure 22.2 shows the scores of an example program (plotted as a series of Xs) along with the 25th and 75th percentile norms. Upon initial inspection, this program can be seen as having low scores on two organizational climate scales, cohesion, and communication. The program mission can be characterized as well defined, but autonomy and openness to change are close to the 25th percentile and stress is close to the 75th percentile.

When initiating the innovation adoption process, attention should be given to these climate scores, as well as some potential barriers to change that appear in the needs and resources scales. In the needs domain, program staff are giving ratings close to the 75th percentile for program and training needs, and their below 30 rating of pressure to change suggests complacency. In the area of resources, offices and staff scores are below the neutral score of 30, and training is below the middle of the normal 25th–75th percentile range. There are adequate equipment and Internet resources based on the scale scores. Overall, the staff attributes are positive and represent staff strengths.

Essentially, the program profile represented in the example indicates a weak organizational climate, high needs, and low resources. Within the existing program milieu, the path to innovation implementation will likely be rough and difficult.

REFORMATIVE STRATEGIES

When using the ORC assessment results to move a program toward change, the first step is to present a summary to staff and encourage them to buy-in while asking for feedback and suggestions and beginning to lay the groundwork for future actions. Avoid technical and statistical presentations and use practical examples to help explain major points. Written and brief one- to three-page reports providing an overview emphasizing strengths and weaknesses will offer a concise and meaningful supplement that can serve as a reference for future activities.

A guidebook, *Mapping Organizational Change* (MOC), was developed as a supplement to the ORC assessment system. It includes graphic tools for planning and implementing changes (see Figure 22.3). The MOC, which is a heuristic display, includes a set of interrelated "fill-in-the-blank" charts that can be used as a discussion guide. This exploratory problem-solving technique has been shown to facilitate communication, group focus, and memory in education (Dansereau, 1995), business (Newbern & Dansereau, 1995), and counseling (Dansereau & Dees, 2002). The strategy used in organizational mapping is organized around three key areas: selecting goals, planning, and actions. The following is based on a case example using the ORC and MOC.

Upon review of the ORC assessment profile, a program director met with the clinical staff/team to review the results and develop an action

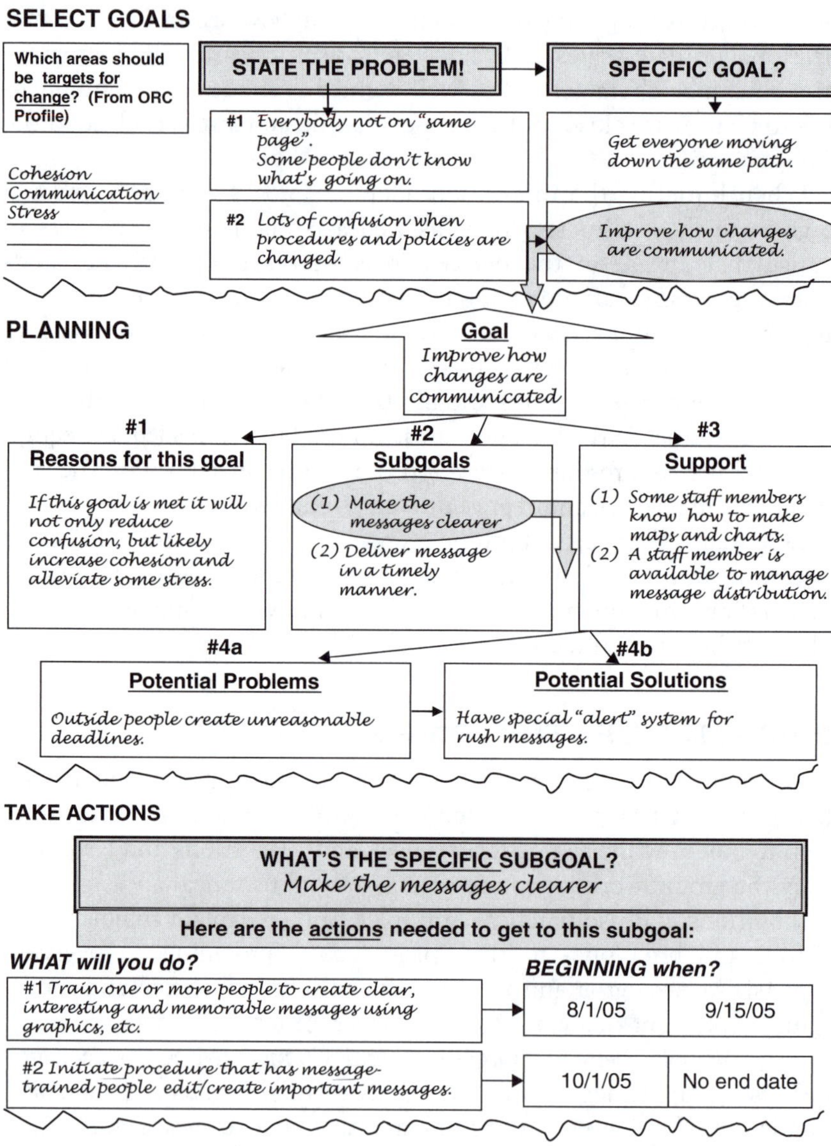
SELECT GOALS
Which areas should be targets for change? (From ORC Profile)
Cohesion
Communication
Stress
STATE THE PROBLEM!
SPECIFIC GOAL?
#1 Everybody not on "same page". Some people don't know what's going on.
Get everyone moving down the same path.
#2 Lots of confusion when procedures and policies are changed.
Improve how changes are communicated.
PLANNING
Goal
Improve how changes are communicated
#1
Reasons for this goal
If this goal is met it will not only reduce confusion, but likely increase cohesion and alleviate some stress.
#2
Subgoals
(1) Make the messages clearer
(2) Deliver message in a timely manner.
#3
Support
(1) Some staff members know how to make maps and charts.
(2) A staff member is available to manage message distribution.
#4a
Potential Problems
Outside people create unreasonable deadlines.
#4b
Potential Solutions
Have special "alert" system for rush messages.
TAKE ACTIONS
WHAT'S THE SPECIFIC SUBGOAL?
Make the messages clearer
Here are the actions needed to get to this subgoal:
WHAT will you do?
BEGINNING when?
#1 Train one or more people to create clear, interesting and memorable messages using graphics, etc.
8/1/05
9/15/05
#2 Initiate procedure that has message-trained people edit/create important messages.
10/1/05
No end date

FIGURE 22.3 *Case study illustration for mapping organizational change.*

plan using the MOC strategy. Three areas of concern (i.e., cohesion, communication, and stress) were identified as targets for change (see Figure 22.3). "Improve how changes are communicated" was selected as the key topic. As a starting point for subsequent actions, a subgoal, "Make the message clearer," was established and specific steps toward goal attainment were agreed upon. Over the next year, the clinical team followed the proposed actions, evaluated progress, and proceeded to

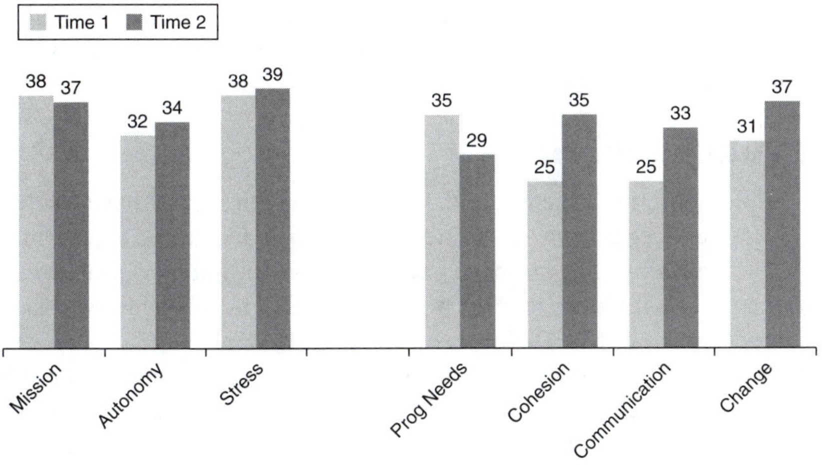

FIGURE 22.4 *Changes in ORC scale score means from Time 1 to Time 2.*

other subgoals to get ready to implement clinical changes. Two more ORC assessments were completed during the year's activities, and the MOC was reviewed to determine problem resolution and/or to set new interim goals. Throughout the process, experience was gained and confidence increased, receptivity to new ideas grew, and the team was able to undertake multiple goals simultaneously.

A year later, the team completed another ORC. When reviewing the results compared with those of their original ORC (see Figure 22.4), there was still agreement about a clearly defined mission, and the high levels of stress remained unchanged. The four measures in the right half of Figure 22.4 show considerable improvements in program needs (i.e., fewer needs), cohesion, communication, and openness to change. While staff perceptions of mission remained relatively stable over time, other areas of the organizational climate improved.

CONCLUSIONS AND IMPLICATIONS

Organizational functioning is a key ingredient in the successful implementation of EBPs and EBTs. Tools are available to assess the organization and begin to remedy identifiable weaknesses that may inhibit the process of innovation adoption. Similar to what occurs with treatment patients, organizations have varying levels of functioning and they manifest strengths and weaknesses that influence their ability to change. Technology transfer, which is often thought to mostly entail clinical practice, involves much more, and when moving research-tested therapies into practice an organization must be ready for and embrace change. Resistance to change at the patient level also is all too common; however, resistance at the organizational level is a likely occurrence that can be addressed through interventions, a process not unlike that which is used with patients.

FUTURE DIRECTIONS

As implementation science and organizational research have evolved over the years, we have discovered new needs and areas of organizational functioning that are pertinent to change and are associated with patient progress. Consequently, we developed a number of new scales for supplementing the ORC to assess an additional range of staff self-perceptions and their views of the day-to-day working environment. The survey form that includes the ORC and nine new scales is called the Survey of Organizational Functioning (available from www.ibr.tcu.edu). The new scales are conceptualized as representing two major domains (i.e., job attitudes and workplace practices). *Job Attitudes* includes three scales: (1) burnout—perceptions of exhaustion, cynicism, and ineffectiveness on the job, (2) satisfaction—value and positive feelings toward the work, and (3) director leadership—the use of "transformational" leadership strategies. *Workplace Practices* includes six scales: (1) peer collaboration—actively working together on tasks, (2) deprivatized practice—counselors observing and learning from one another's approach, (3) collective responsibility—shared sense of responsibility for operations and improvements, (4) focus on outcomes—focus on patient change and treatment outcomes, (5) reflective dialogue—regular staff conversations about counseling and behavior change, and (6) counselor socialization—efforts made to welcome and include new employees into the organization and employment setting.

These organizational assessments are being formatted into one-page scannable forms for automated data capture. These forms can be processed by Scantron scanners. Customized Microsoft Excel-based scoring and feedback templates are being developed for these forms to provide reports and charts for immediate feedback. Like the larger inventory of other TCU forms available from our Web site, these organizational survey forms will be available for download and use without cost in nonprofit applications for direct administration and hand scoring as well.

ACKNOWLEDGMENTS

This work was funded, in part, by the National Institute on Drug Abuse (Grants R37 DA013093 and R01 DA014468). The interpretations and conclusions are, however, entirely those of the authors and do not necessarily represent the position of the NIDA, NIH, or Department of

Health and Human Services. More information (including data collection instruments and intervention manuals that can be downloaded without charge) is available on the Internet at www.ibr.tcu.edu, and electronic mail can be sent to ibr@tcu.edu.

REFERENCES

Aarons, G. A. (2006). Transformational and transactional leadership: Association with attitudes toward evidence-based practice. *Psychiatric Services, 57*(8), 1162–1169.

Addiction Technology Transfer Centers (2004). *The change book: A blueprint for technology transfer*. Kansas City, MO: ATTC National Office.

Backer, T. E. (1995). Assessing and enhancing readiness for change: Implications for technology transfer (National Institute on Drug Abuse Research Monograph 155, NIH Publication No. 95-4035). In T. E. Backer, S. L. David, & G. Soucy (Eds.), *Reviewing the behavioral science knowledge base on technology transfer* (pp. 21–41). Rockville, MD: National Institute on Drug Abuse.

Brown, B. S., & Flynn, P. M. (2002). The federal role in drug abuse technology transfer: A history and perspective. *Journal of Substance Abuse Treatment, 22*(4), 245–257.

Compton, W. M., Stein, J. B., Robertson, E. B., Pintello, D., Pringle, B., & Volkow, N. D. (2005). Charting a course for health services research at the National Institute on Drug Abuse. *Journal of Substance Abuse Treatment, 29*, 167–172.

Dansereau, D. F. (1995). Derived structural schemas and the transfer of knowledge. In A. McKeough, J. Lupart, & A. Marini (Eds.), *Teaching for transfer: Fostering generalization in learning* (pp. 93–121). Hillsdale, NJ: Lawrence Erlbaum Associates.

Dansereau, D. F., & Dees, S. M. (2002). Mapping training: The transfer of a cognitive technology for improving counseling. *Journal of Substance Abuse Treatment, 22*(4), 219–230.

D'Aunno, T. (2006). The role of organization and management in substance abuse treatment: Review and roadmap. *Journal of Substance Abuse Treatment, 31*, 221–233.

Eddy, D. M. (2005). Evidence-based medicine: A unified approach. *Health Affairs, 24*(1), 9–17.

Fixsen, D. L., Naoom, S. F., Blase, K. A., Friedman, R. M., & Wallace, F. (2005). *Implementation research: A synthesis of the literature* (No. Louis de la Parte Florida Mental Health Publication #231). Tampa: University of South Florida.

Ford, J. H., Green, C. A., Hoffman, K. A., Wisdom, J. P., Riley, K. J., Bergmann, L., et al. (2007). Process improvement needs in substance abuse treatment: Admissions walk-through results. *Journal of Substance Abuse Treatment, 33*, 379–389.

Garnick, D. W., Lee, M. T., Chalk, M., Gastfriend, D., Horgan, C. M., McCorry, F., et al. (2002). Establishing the feasibility of performance measures for alcohol and other drugs. *Journal of Substance Abuse Treatment, 23*, 375–385.

Gitlow, H., Gitlow, S., Oppenheim, A., & Oppenheim, R. (1989). *Tools and methods for the improvement of quality*. Homewood, IL: Irwin.

Gotham, H. J. (2004). Diffusion of mental health and substance abuse treatments: Development, dissemination, and implementation. *Clinical Psychology: Science and Practice*, *11*, 160–176.

Greenhalgh, T., Robert, G., MacFarlane, F., Bate, P., & Kyriakidou, O. (2004). Diffusion of innovations in service organizations: Systematic review and recommendations. *The Milbank Quarterly*, *82*(4), 581–629.

Gustafson, D. H., Sainfort, F., Eichler, M., Adams, L., Bisognano, M., & Steudel, H. (2003). Developing and testing a model to predict outcomes of organizational change. *Health Services Research*, *38*(2), 751–776.

Institute of Medicine (2005). *Improving the quality of health care for mental and substance abuse conditions: Quality chasm series*. Washington, DC: The National Academy Press.

Klein, K. J., Conn, A. B., & Sorra, J. S. (2001). Implementing computerized technology: An organizational analysis. *Journal of Applied Psychology*, *86*, 811–824.

Klein, K. J., & Knight, A. P. (2005). Innovation implementation: Overcoming the challenge. *Current Directions in Psychological Science*, *14*(5), 243–246.

Klein, K. J., & Sorra, J. S. (1996). The challenge of innovation implementation. *Academy of Management Review*, *21*(4), 1055–1080.

Lamb, S., Greenlick, M. R., & McCarty, D. (1998). *Bridging the gap between practice and research*. Washington, DC: Institute of Medicine, National Academy Press.

Lehman, W. E. K., Greener, J. M., & Simpson, D. D. (2002). Assessing organizational readiness for change. *Journal of Substance Abuse Treatment*, *22*(4), 197–209.

McCarty, D., Gustafson, D. H., Wisdom, J. P., Ford, J., Choi, D., Molfenter, T., et al. (2007). The Network for the Improvement of Addiction Treatment (NIATx): Enhancing access and retention. *Drug and Alcohol Dependence*, *88*, 138–145.

McCorry, F., Garnick, D., Bartlett, J., Cotter, F., & Chalk, M. (2000). Developing performance measures for alcohol and other drug services in managed care plans. *Joint Commission Journal on Quality Improvement*, *26*, 633–643.

McGovern, M., Fox, T., Xie, H., & Drake, R. (2004). A survey of clinical practices and readiness to adopt evidence-based practices: Dissemination research in an addiction treatment system. *Journal of Substance Abuse Treatment*, *26*, 305–312.

Miller, W. R., Zweben, J., & Johnson, W. R. (2005). Evidence-based treatment: Why, what, where, when, and how? *Journal of Substance Abuse Treatment*, *29*(4), 267–276.

National Institute on Drug Abuse (1999). *Principles of drug abuse treatment: A research-based guide*. NIH Publication No. 00-4180. Rockville, MD: National Institute on Drug Abuse.

National Institutes of Health (2007). *Dissemination and implementation research in health (R01)*. Retrieved December 1, 2007, from http://grants.nih.gov/grants/guide/pa-files/PAR-07-086.html.

Newbern, D., & Dansereau, D. F. (1995). Knowledge maps for knowledge management. In K. Wiig (Ed.), *Knowledge management methods* (pp. 157–180). Arlington, TX: Schema Press.

Rampazzo, L., De Angeli, M., Serpelloni, G., Simpson, D. D., & Flynn, P. M. (2006). Italian survey of Organizational Functioning and Readiness for

Change: A cross-cultural transfer of treatment assessment strategies. *European Addiction Research*, *12*, 176–181.
Rogers, E. M. (1995). *Diffusion of innovations* (4th ed.). New York: The Free Press.
Rogers, E. M. (2003). *Diffusion of innovations* (5th ed.). New York: The Free Press.
Roman, P. M., & Johnson, J. A. (2002). Adoption and implementation of new technologies in substance abuse treatment. *Journal of Substance Abuse Treatment*, *22*(4), 211–218.
Shewart, W. A. (1939). *Statistical method from the viewpoint of quality control.* Lancaster, PA: Lancaster Press.
Simpson, D. D. (2009). Organizational readiness for stage-based dynamics of innovation implementation. *Research on Social Work Practice*.
Simpson, D. D., & Brown, B. S. (Guest Eds.). (2002). Special Issue: Transferring research to practice. *Journal of Substance Abuse Treatment, 22*(4), 169–257.
Simpson, D. D., & Dansereau, D. F. (2007). Assessing organizational functioning as a step toward innovation. *NIDA Science and Practice Perspectives*, *3*(2), 20–28.
Simpson, D. D., & Flynn, P. M. (2007a). Moving innovations into treatment: A stage-based approach to program change. *Journal of Substance Abuse Treatment*, *33*(2), 111–120.
Simpson, D. D., & Flynn, P. M. (Guest Eds.). (2007b). Organizational readiness for change. *Journal of Substance Abuse Treatment, 33*(2), 111–209.
Sirkin, H. L., Keenan, P., & Jackson, A. (2005). The hard side of change management. *Harvard Business Review October*, 109–118.

PART | SIX

A Look Toward the Future

Chapter | twenty-three

Challenges of an Evidence-Based Approach to Addiction Treatment

Peter M. Miller
Medical University of South Carolina

SUMMARY POINTS

- Closer collaborations between researchers and practitioners are needed for the development and refinement of evidence-based addiction treatments.
- Effectiveness clinical trials as well as efficacy trials are essential because they can show that treatments work in real-world clinical settings.
- It is important to determine what works (a particular technique) as well as why it works in evaluating new treatments.
- Outcome measures must include assessments of substance use as well as good clinical outcome.
- Treatments should be evaluated during their application and not just at longer term intervals after discharge from treatment.
- The opinions of both counselors and consumers should be considered when evaluating the practicality and "user-friendliness" of a treatment method.
- Adoption and routine use of evidence-based treatment methods will involve a restructuring of current community-based treatment programs.

Evidence-Based Addiction Treatment

As is clearly demonstrated in the preceding chapters, evidence-based addiction treatment represents state of the art in quality care for addicted individuals. However, evidence based does not imply that clinical experience and judgment should be discarded. In fact, closer collaboration between researchers and clinicians in developing and refining treatment methods is required, now, more than ever.

Historically, clinicians have viewed researchers with a jaundiced eye, considering them clinically naïve and out of touch with real clinical case management. However, researchers have viewed clinicians as being uninterested in data-driven research, uninformed about state-of-the-art treatments, and overly reliant on anecdotal experience to justify therapeutic methods. Obviously, neither stereotype is completely accurate, and those characterizations that are correct are understandable from a historical perspective. For example, addiction treatment grew from nonscientific, nonmedical roots when there was little interest in alcohol or substance dependence, and counselors were forced to rely on experience (mostly from 12-step programs), based on what seemed intuitively to be effective with individual clients. Evidence-based research on treatment effectiveness for addictions simply did not exist.

Unfortunately, both sides continue to exacerbate the problem by avoiding each other. Adding to the problem is that researchers and clinicians often speak a different language and use different jargon. Addiction scientists, especially, have had difficulty conveying their findings to clinicians in an understandable, straightforward manner, although recent publications have been more successful at "translating" addiction science in a meaningful way for nonresearchers (Erickson, 2007; Miller & Kavanagh, 2007). In addition, researchers publish their findings in scientific journals that are read by other researchers, not clinicians. A particularly noteworthy attempt to overcome this problem is the recent cooperative agreement between two journals, *Journal of Substance Abuse Treatment* (primarily a research journal) and *Counselor* (a magazine intended for practicing clinicians), by which scientific articles in the former journal will be modified and rewritten for publication in the latter (McLellan, 2006).

A notable attempt to narrow the researcher/clinician gap was reported by Thomas and colleagues (Thomas & Miller, 2007; Thomas, Miller, Randall, & Book, 2008) involving a unique collaborative project involving alcohol researchers (medical university faculty) working together with addiction counselors and administrators from community-based addiction treatment centers. The study was designed to develop and evaluate a prototype training module to teach nonmedical addiction counselors about the use of adjunctive pharmacotherapy (see Chapter 15) for the treatment of alcohol dependence. The assumption was that the counseling process could be aided by adjunctive pharmacotherapy (e.g., by reducing alcohol cravings and enabling clients to better focus on behavior change) and that counselors often are very influential in guiding clients to the use of new treatment options. Based on the extant evidence-based literature, an initial draft of an educational module (consisting of a PowerPoint presentation and written handout materials) was developed by four researchers. The researchers then met with addiction counselors and administrators for discussion, feedback, and recommendations about the clarity and relevance of the module. Examples of specific recommendations from treatment providers consisted of modifications to the language used (i.e., more everyday wording), the inclusion of more information on pricing (i.e., comparing the cost of alcoholism medications to the cost of beer, wine, and liquor), and the development of a simple but informative brochure for counselors to provide clients. The final module was then developed, further refined, and evaluated successfully. Researchers, counselors, and administrators in the project experienced a greater understanding of each other, leading to further collaborative educational and research efforts.

ONGOING ISSUES AND CHALLENGES

Even with collaborative efforts, the application of evidence-based methods to addiction treatment is not as straightforward as it may seem. Students and clinicians must be aware of the issues and challenges involved. In considering evidence-based therapies, Hoffman (2006) has cautioned that "we must be vigilant that those programs and services are at least as effective as the programs they might replace, and that the evidence in 'evidence based' supports real-world outcomes."

Some of the specific concerns that have been raised about the acceptance and implementation of evidence-based treatments include the (1) generalizability of clinical trials to clinical populations, (2) emphasis on technique over change processes, (3) question of the appropriateness of the chosen outcome measures, and (4) failure to take into account the practical utility and "user friendliness" of interventions.

Generalizability of evidence-based approaches

One of the most frequent criticisms of evidence-based treatment approaches is the fact that efficacy trials alone are most often used as the gold standard for their effectiveness. Efficacy trials are conducted by expert, highly trained practitioners in academic centers with patients who go through a highly selective screening process. In the alcohol field, for example, these trials often exclude alcohol-dependent patients who use or abuse other substances, those who show evidence of psychiatric comorbidities (e.g., depression, anxiety disorders), or those who are unable to keep regularly scheduled, and often lengthy, research appointments. Counselors in clinical settings are quick to point out that they never see alcoholics like this. Their typical clients not only are dependent on alcohol but are also on other substances such as cocaine and marijuana, are typically depressed or anxious or bipolar, and have few social or economic supports. The question, then, is whether the results of randomized controlled efficacy trials are truly generalizable to real-world addicts.

The answer lies in effectiveness trials. These studies compare clinically relevant treatments, include more heterogeneous study samples, are conducted in real-world practice settings with real-world providers, and evaluate a broad range of clinical outcomes. Thus, the ideal evidence-based treatment would have proved its worth first in efficacy trials and then in effectiveness trials. As described in Chapter 1 of this textbook, the National Institute on Drug Abuse has established the Clinical Trials Network whose goal is to evaluate treatment modalities in community-based addiction treatment centers. This project will potentially provide clinicians with more confidence in the feasibility and generalizability of evidence-based treatments that have been tested in this manner.

Emphasis on technique versus change processes

Orford (2008) has argued that instead of focusing on specific therapeutic techniques (e.g., cognitive behavior therapy) it would be more productive to explore change processes that are common to effective therapies in general. This thesis originates from the fact that since many different evidence-based treatments have similar outcomes, it is possible that there are more similarities in these treatments than differences. Thus, we should be studying these similar processes and formulating unified theories of addictive behavior change. In addition, he notes that current evidence-based treatments fail to take into account nonspecific and relationship factors (see Chapter 2) in the therapeutic process, as well as the undeniable fact that many people change on their own without the need for either professional or 12-step assistance (see Chapter 14). In a rebuttal to Orford, Michie (2008) emphasizes the importance of theory in designing and testing therapeutic interventions, which depends greatly on analyzing both technique *and* change process (i.e., theoretical mechanism). Basically, she warns against throwing the baby out with the bathwater and highlights the need to determine not only *if* treatments work but also *what* is it that works and what are the *causal mechanisms* that enable them to work.

Appropriateness of outcome measures

Some addiction specialists have questioned evidence-based research on the basis of what is being measured as an outcome and when it is measured. Outcomes for many studies include only very specific alcohol or drug use variables, such as time to first heavy drinking or drug use day, number of drinks or drug uses per drinking day, percent days abstinent, or heavy drinking or drug use days per month. While substance use is certainly of primary concern, other clinically relevant outcomes would provide clinicians with a more practical picture of the overall evidence-based treatments in their day-to-day practices. Two different evidence-based treatments may be equally effective in moderating or eliminating cocaine use but one may also help improve the client's social skills, marital relationship, and overall quality of life.

In evaluating a community reinforcement approach plus vouchers (see Chapter 13), Higgins and colleagues (2003) used a measure of retention in treatment in addition to assessments of substance use, demonstrating that clients receiving the treatment were more likely to remain in therapy. This finding is highly relevant to clinicians, as the retention of clients in treatment is a continual issue in the therapeutic process and appears to be a necessary prerequisite for a good therapeutic outcome (especially considering that addiction is a chronic, relapsing disease).

In addition to specific alcohol consumption measures, the recently reported COMBINE study (Anton et al., 2006) (see Chapter 15) included a more global composite secondary measure called "good clinical outcome." Good outcome was categorized as either abstinence or moderate drinking without problems. Moderate drinking was defined as a maximum of 11 (for women) or 14 (for men) drinks per week, with no more than 2 days on which more than 3 drinks (for women) or 4 drinks (for men) were consumed. Problems were defined as three or more physical, social, and/or psychological consequences of drinking as measured on a standardized questionnaire listing typical life problems resulting from heavy alcohol use. Routine reporting of good clinical outcomes in this manner would help ensure that research outcomes are more clinically significant and acceptable to nonresearch oriented clinicians.

Unfortunately, a related problem is that there is no standardized manner in which all treatment outcome researchers evaluate treatment outcomes. Each of several studies may use different primary and secondary outcomes as evidence for the efficacy of a particular treatment modality. This is why it is so difficult to compare one study to another, one treatment to another, or different treatments to each other. There is a great need to establish standards in this regard for measures of consumption, as well as assessments of other important clinical outcomes.

Finally, McLellan (2002) maintains that the problem is not only related to *what* we are measuring but *when* we are measuring it. He contends that since addiction is a chronic disease, we should be evaluating the effects of treatment *during* its application, not at intervals after it is no longer being conducted. He notes that in evaluating chronic medical diseases such as hypertension, it is assumed that, due to their chronic nature, treatment will be effective in controlling blood pressure as long as the treatment is being administered and that once medications or lifestyle changes are discontinued, high blood pressure will resume. Thus, the effectiveness of hypertension treatments is tested during their application, not (as in the case of addiction treatment) 6 or 12 months after treatment has been discontinued.

Although researchers and clinicians give lip service to the notion that addictions are chronic, relapsing disorders (much like hypertension), we expect treatments to result in a cure so that, for example, 6 months of behavioral counseling will result in long-term changes in substance use 12 months after discharge from treatment. This simply does not make sense even though this is exactly how most addiction treatments are evaluated. In fact, by using this approach, we are surely underestimating the true effects of addiction treatments.

Practical utility

Another issue related to evidence-based treatments is their practicality and feasibility in real-world clinical settings. That is, for each evidence-based treatment, the question must be asked, "Is this treatment user-friendly?" Will current practitioners be willing and able to adopt the treatment and use it regularly in clinical practice? In addition, if the treatment, as determined by both efficacy and effectiveness trials, requires 3 to 4 months of intensive, sophisticated individual counseling, will the counselor's caseload and the clinic's organizational structure allow for this time and effort? Indeed, most counseling in community-based treatment centers is conducted in groups and counselors are busy enough as it is. Surveys of current treatment programs indicate that they must dramatically improve the clinical skills and capabilities of their clinical personnel as well as enhance their information management systems in order to keep pace with the rapid development of new treatment methodologies (McLellan, Carise, & Kleber, 2003).

A related question that is seldom asked of new treatments is "Will they be acceptable to and requested by consumers?" It would seem self-evident that clients seeking treatment would want treatments that are the most effective or at least want an array of treatment options from which to choose. Clients or patients (depending on the setting in which an individual is being treated) have been left out of the loop and their opinions and demands should be proactively sought and seriously considered. Some treatments may be more acceptable to clients than others and, given two evidence-based methods that are equally effective, clients should be given a choice. Perhaps, just as pharmaceutical firms do in the United States, we should be going directly to the public to inform them of new methods of addiction treatment. Consumers, then, might help to pressure treatment providers to offer additional evidence-based options.

CONCLUSIONS

In order to develop new evidence-based treatment methods and improve upon the ones we have, researchers need to shadow clinicians in their clinical settings and learn more about the types of complex clinical cases they treat. In addition, scientists need to develop a better sense of the realities of substance abuse treatment centers in terms of organizational, financial, and caseload factors that may influence the adoption of evidence-based treatments. New treatments must be designed to take the current treatment infrastructure into account and develop ways to improve it.

Clinicians, however, need to become scientist–practitioners by carefully observing and recording specific aspects of the treatment process and its outcomes in order to assist researchers in developing workable and testable hypotheses about what works and what does not (see Chapter 21). In this regard, clinicians probably have a great deal of important things to say about their own theories of why their clients change. Unfortunately, no one is asking them for this "insider" information (Orford, 2008).

While there are certainly challenges in developing and implementing evidence-based addiction treatment, the emphasis on treatments that have proven their worth through controlled clinical trials is a welcome change in the substance abuse arena. It is essential that, despite the number of the challenges outlined earlier, evidence-based treatments are adopted and implemented routinely in clinical practice. This requires an overhaul of current graduate and undergraduate addictions courses as well as programs for licensure and certification of addictions counselors so that they include, as a minimum requirement, evidence-based assessment and treatment methods. Practitioners truly want to provide the best, most effective quality care to addicted individuals, and evidence-based treatments, especially if they are adapted and simplified for use in clinical settings, can help them in this worthwhile endeavor.

REFERENCES

Anton, R. F., O'Malley, S. S., Ciraulo, D. A., Cisler, R. A., Couper, D., Donovan, D. M., et al. (2006). Combined pharmacotherapies and behavioral interventions for alcohol dependence: The COMBINE study: A randomized controlled trial. *Journal of the American Medical Association*, *295*, 2003–2017.

Erickson, C. K. (2007). *The science of addiction*. New York: W.W. Norton & Company.

Higgins, S. T., Sigmon, S. C., Wong, C. J., Heil, S. H., Badger, G. J., Donham, R., et al. (2003). Community reinforcement therapy for cocaine-dependent outpatients. *Archives of General Psychiatry*, *60*, 1043–1052.

Hoffman, N. G. (2006, November). Evidence-based practices: Promotion or performance? *Addiction Professional*.

McLellan, A. T. (2002). Have we evaluated addiction treatment correctly? Implications from a chronic care perspective. *Addiction*, *97*, 249–252.

McLellan, A. T. (2006). Communicating across the "chasm": *Journal of Substance Abuse Treatment* and *Counselor* initiate cooperative agreement. *Journal of Substance Abuse Treatment*, *31*, 1.

McLellan, A. T., Carise, D., & Kleber, H. D. (2003). Can the national addiction treatment infrastructure support the public's demand for quality care? *Journal of Substance Abuse Treatment*, *25*, 117–121.

Michie, S. (2008). What works and how? Designing more effective interventions needs answers to both questions. *Addiction*, *103*, 886–887.

Miller, P. M., & Kavanagh, D. J. (Eds.). (2007). *Translation of addictions science into practice*. Amsterdam, The Netherlands: Elsevier.

Orford, J. (2008). Asking the right questions in the right way: The need for a shift in research on psychological treatment for addiction. *Addiction*, *103*, 875–885.

Thomas, S. E., Miller, P. M., Randall, P. K., & Book, S. W. (2008). Improving acceptance of naltrexone in community addiction treatment centers: A pilot study. *Journal of Substance Abuse Treatment*, *35*, 260–268.

Thomas, S. E., & Miller, P. M. (2007). Knowledge and attitudes about pharmacotherapy for alcoholism: A survey of counselors and administrators in community-based addiction treatment centres. *Alcohol and Alcoholism*, *42*, 113–118.

Index

A

B

L

M

N

S